This book belongs to

Judith A. Meyer

A GUIDE TO GRAPHIC PRINT PRODUCTION

SECOND EDITION

"But I, on the other hand, could perhaps measure the color as well: I might guess it had a wavelength of five hundred forty millionths of a millimeter; and then this green would apparently be captured and nailed to a specific point! But then it gets away from me again, because this ground color also has something material about it that can't be expressed in words of color at all, since it's different from the same green in silk or wool. And now we're back at the profound discovery that green grass is just grass green!"

ROBERT MUSIL IN THE MAN WITHOUT QUALITIES

Musil, Robert, Transl. Sophie Wilkins and Burton Pike. The Man Without Qualities, Volume II "From the Posthumous Papers" Part 1, Chapter 46, p. 1185. First Vintage International Edition, 1996, New York.

A Guide to Graphic Print Production, Second Edition

© Kaj Johansson, Peter Lundberg, Robert Ryberg and Bokförlaget Arena 2007
Published by John Wiley & Sons, Inc. Hoboken, New Jersey.

TEXT	Kaj Johansson Peter Lundberg Robert Ryberg
DESIGN	Urban Gyllström
ILLUSTRATIONS	Robert Ryberg
PHOTO	Gunnar Magnusson (cover) Albert Håkansson (food) Paul Brissman (food ingredients in chapter introductions) Tomas Ek and Johann Bergenholtz, Fälth & Hässler (technique) Robert Ryberg (technique and illustrating examples) Henrik Svensson (examples of object graphics with mesh function) Joanna Hornatowska, STFI (print in close-up) Johanna Löwenhamn (authors' portraits) Susanne Wrethstigh and John Nelander (screen shots)
TRANSLATIONS	Jennifer Bäverstam and Amy Oliver (glossary)
TEXTS ABOUT ENVIRONMENT	Eva Anderson, Eva Anderson Design (page 241 and page 376)
TYPEFACE	DIN Engschrift (chapter headings) Scala Sans (image captions) Minion (body text)
PAPER	Multiart Silk 130 g/m^2
PRINT	Fälth & Hässler, Värnamo, Sweden, www.foh.se
ISBN-10	0-471-76138-9
ISBN-13	978-0-471-76138-9

Printed in Sweden

foreword

TEN YEARS HAVE PASSED since we began our journey with *A Guide to Graphic Print Production*. Now, with slightly receding hairlines, slightly thicker waistlines, but equal fascination with the development of graphic production, we are presenting a completely revised edition. Just as with the first edition we thought this one would take a year to pro-

duce, and just as with the first edition it actually took two and a half years to complete.

Techniques have become simpler and responsibilities have shifted. Today everyone can do graphic production, the graphics industry has expanded and all boundaries as to who does what have been erased. Expensive equipment and special systems for producing printed products of the highest quality are no longer needed – only knowledge, interest and a pinch of passion.

This book has advanced from dealing mainly with how the graphics suppliers work, to how you yourself can produce image, layout and a print-ready files, and what the role of the customer involves.

We have also tried to practice what we preach as far as production of the book goes. We worked in both Windows and Mac environments, taking advantage of the simple, standard techniques that exist today to get as lean and secure a production as possible, going from idea, manuscript and automated layout to delivery of the print-ready PDF/X files [*read more in 1.6 How we made the book*].

Here's hoping you find reading the book as exciting as we found working on it.

Kaj, Peter och Robert

CONTENT

01. graphic print production

02. the computer

03. chromatics

04. digital images

05. image editing

06. layout

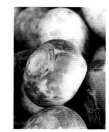

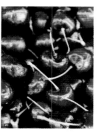

01.

graphic print production

Who actually does what in graphic print production today? What is prepress? How much of the printing cost is paper? What should you think about when getting a price quote? How do you avoid additional costs? What affects the price of a printed product? Who is responsible for what parts of the production?

GRAPHIC PRINT PRODUCTION IS a widely defined concept these days. It covers all the steps that are taken to produce a printed product. Of course it includes printing and finishing and binding, but is also includes all the steps that precede these, for example outline and execution of a design, photographing and editing images, producing text and layout, and prepress production such as creating PDF files for printing, printing adjustments, adjusting images for printing as well as proofs and printing plates.

In this chapter we will go over the graphic print production flow, giving an introduction to the different steps and providing examples of the typical roles of the participants who carry out the respective steps. Before we begin we should go through a number of basic questions. The answers to these determine to a large degree how you are going to set up your project.

Buying and planning graphic print production is more difficult than you think, since as a rule there are many people involved and you are dependent on a functioning partnership with everyone involved. It is not easy to predict costs either, and know what kind of information you will have to provide to get an accurate price and avoid additional costs, as are so common in the graphics industry.

We will therefore look at the underlying factors that influence cost when we purchase printed products, and there is a checklist of what should be included in the price quote. We will go over what you should think about when you evaluate and choose suppliers as well as how you will plan the graphic print production.

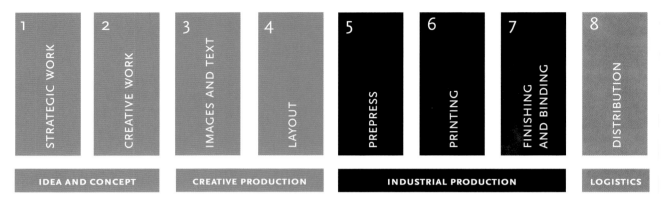

1	2	3	4	5	6	7	8
STRATEGIC WORK	CREATIVE WORK	IMAGES AND TEXT	LAYOUT	PREPRESS	PRINTING	FINISHING AND BINDING	DISTRIBUTION
IDEA AND CONCEPT		CREATIVE PRODUCTION		INDUSTRIAL PRODUCTION			LOGISTICS

THE EIGHT STEPS OF GRAPHIC PRINT PRODUCTION
Graphic print production can be divided into eight steps and four phases. The first phase deals with strategic and creative work, the final result consists of idea, concept and sketches of graphic design. The following phase could be labeled as creative production – here the product is still designed and changed. The third phase, which consists of prepress, printing and finishing and binding, is primarily industrial with a goal of carrying out what has been decided on and formed in the previous steps. The last step deals with distributing the finished printed product.

1.1 The Graphic Print Production Flow

The technology in graphic print production has become cheaper and today is accessible to everyone. This development has led to many specialized jobs disappearing during the last fifteen to twenty years. Today the same person can carry out work the previously required by a number of different specialists. For this reason the boundaries between the kinds of traditional graphic print production company have been loosened and the distribution of roles has been changed. The functions of companies overlap each other and it is no longer entirely clear who does what. There are advertising bureaus that edit images and printing houses that arrange layouts; there are prepress companies that do photography and purchasers of printed products who do a large part of the production themselves. Materials, production and information flows have also changed, which has led to a certain amount of ambiguity as to who is responsible for what.

One way to sort out the areas of responsibility is to break down the graphic print production flow into eight basic steps.

- *Strategic work*
- *Creative work*
- *Image and text*
- *Layout*
- *Prepress*
- *Printing*
- *Finishing and binding*
- *Distribution*

The first two deal with ideas, concept and outline work. Now is the time to consider the project as a whole and determine if a printed product is what is really needed. Ideas, sketch work and graphic design are a separate field, thus we will not go into these steps more than superficially. We will however go over the following two steps more in depth. They are comprised of the creative aspect of production (image, text and layout) and in these phases the product is still being formed and changed. The four last steps are mainly industrial and their aim is to carry out what has been decided and formulated during the previous steps. We will also take a closer look at these last steps, except for the very last one, logistics, which we will only touch on.

The same company can carry out many of these functions. Which one is actually not of interest if we are viewing graphic print production as a chain of functions. The important thing is that we know who is responsible for what and what demands on information and competence each function requires. Although the technology is more accessible today, it still demands special competence within many areas if you want to present a high quality printed product. Different productions set different demands, which means that roles and responsibilities as well as the production and information flows look different from project to project.

1.1.1 Strategic Work

In the first step you should ask questions that will help define the product you want to create more clearly. What are the goals of this project? For whom is this product intended? What will this product be used for? In this phase you also determine if a printed product is really needed. The typical participants in this phase are the marketing and information departments, but also advertising and design departments as well as media advisors participate.

1.1.2 Creative Work

The creative step is about developing the design, determining the message of the work and how best to communicate with the audience for whom the message is intended. More questions bring the project into focus. What type of printed product should be created? What should this product say? How should it say it? What should this product look like?

1.1.3 Images and Text

Digital images are created and edited today by just about everybody. With the aid of digital cameras, scanners, cell phones with cameras and widespread image editing programs in ordinary computers, large numbers of digital images are created. This has meant that traditional reproduction companies that previously did most of the image editing have almost disappeared.

Those who work with digital images are not always as experienced and knowledgeable at working with images as before, since they often have other work responsibilities. At the same time greater demands are being placed on image editing when the only existing original is digital, and you don't have any opportunity to go back to a negative or slide when the image is going to be reused.

The fact that an image is digital doesn't mean, unfortunately, that the image has enough quality, technically speaking, to be used in print. Therefore you

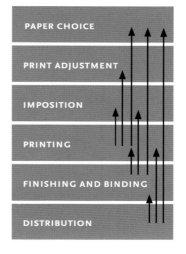

CHOICES ARE MADE IN REVERSE ORDER
What is common to all production phases is that you have to know what requirements the following steps place and adjust your work accordingly. Distribution can constitute a large part of a printed product's costs, and it is common to choose a paper with a lower weight to reduce costs. This can affect finishing and binding as well as printing. Finishing and binding can also govern the choice of paper at the same time as the information on the choice of paper an printing methods govern how the image will be prepared for printing and so on.

The graphic process consists of eight steps. In this book we focus on steps three to seven. We see the flow in these five phases on the far right. It is made up of the creative part of production (image, text and layout) and here is where the product is still formed and changed. The following three steps are mainly industrial with a goal of preparing for and physically multiplying what has been decided on in the previous steps (prepress, printing and finishing and binding.) After these steps distribution occurs. In the image on near right the flow is shown of a typical information printed product.

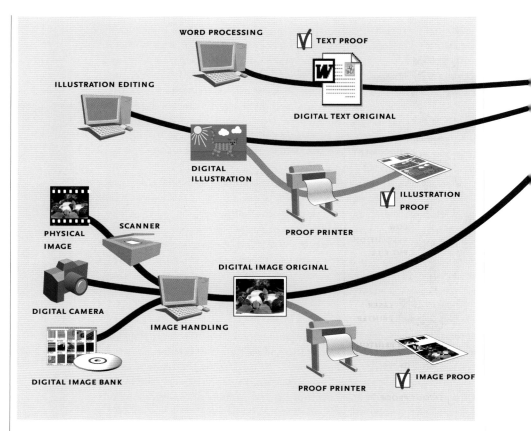

IMAGE AND TEXT

In this step the images are produced. They are scanned, digitally photographed, obtained from image banks or CDs. They are checked, adjusted and retouched. Usually you work in Adobe Photoshop. Illustrations are also drawn and checked with this program, but more typically in Adobe Illustrator. In addition texts are written, edited and checked in word processing programs, usually Microsoft Word.

CHECKING AND PROOFS

There are a number of checkpoints in the graphic process. It is important that these controls are made as early as possible so that resulting errors do not occur later on. Errors identified late cost more to correct and risk causing delays, sometimes even the entire delivery. On the right we see which controls have to be done and when, how they are done, who approves them and what should be checked.

Text proofing is done by the customer on a laser printout or directly in the word processing program. Language, spelling, content and facts are checked here as well as making sure the text's technical structure is correct, for example a heading being shown as a heading.

The customer also does an *illustration proof* by checking details, colors and texts in the illustrations. This is done on a high-resolution laser printer.

Colors, sharpness, touch ups and quality of *photographic images* is also checked by the customer on an image proof done on a high-resolution laser printer.

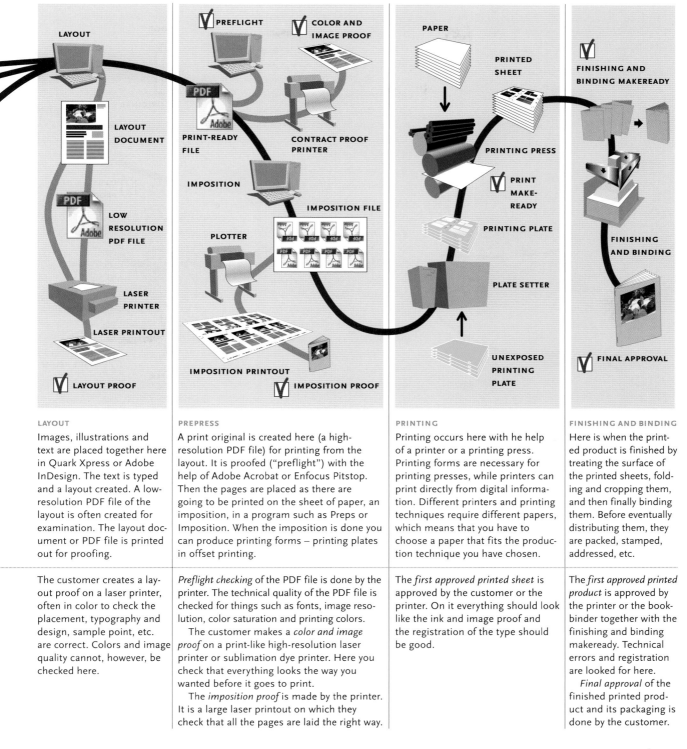

LAYOUT · LAYOUT DOCUMENT · LOW RESOLUTION PDF FILE · LASER PRINTER · LASER PRINTOUT · ☑ LAYOUT PROOF

☑ PREFLIGHT · ☑ COLOR AND IMAGE PROOF · PRINT-READY FILE · CONTRACT PROOF PRINTER · IMPOSITION · IMPOSITION FILE · PLOTTER · IMPOSITION PRINTOUT · ☑ IMPOSITION PROOF

PAPER · PRINTED SHEET · PRINTING PRESS · ☑ PRINT MAKE-READY · PRINTING PLATE · PLATE SETTER · UNEXPOSED PRINTING PLATE

☑ FINISHING AND BINDING MAKEREADY · FINISHING AND BINDING · ☑ FINAL APPROVAL

LAYOUT

Images, illustrations and text are placed together here in Quark Xpress or Adobe InDesign. The text is typed and a layout created. A low-resolution PDF file of the layout is often created for examination. The layout document or PDF file is printed out for proofing.

The customer creates a layout proof on a laser printer, often in color to check the placement, typography and design, sample point, etc. are correct. Colors and image quality cannot, however, be checked here.

PREPRESS

A print original is created here (a high-resolution PDF file) for printing from the layout. It is proofed ("preflight") with the help of Adobe Acrobat or Enfocus Pitstop. Then the pages are placed as there are going to be printed on the sheet of paper, an imposition, in a program such as Preps or Imposition. When the imposition is done you can produce printing forms – printing plates in offset printing.

Preflight checking of the PDF file is done by the printer. The technical quality of the PDF file is checked for things such as fonts, image resolution, color saturation and printing colors.

The customer makes a *color and image proof* on a print-like high-resolution laser printer or sublimation dye printer. Here you check that everything looks the way you wanted before it goes to print.

The *imposition proof* is made by the printer. It is a large laser printout on which they check that all the pages are laid the right way.

PRINTING

Printing occurs here with he help of a printer or a printing press. Printing forms are necessary for printing presses, while printers can print directly from digital information. Different printers and printing techniques require different papers, which means that you have to choose a paper that fits the production technique you have chosen.

The *first approved printed sheet* is approved by the customer or the printer. On it everything should look like the ink and image proof and the registration of the type should be good.

FINISHING AND BINDING

Here is when the printed product is finished by treating the surface of the printed sheets, folding and cropping them, and then finally binding them. Before eventually distributing them, they are packed, stamped, addressed, etc.

The *first approved printed product* is approved by the printer or the bookbinder together with the finishing and binding makeready. Technical errors and registration are looked for here.

Final approval of the finished printed product and its packaging is done by the customer.

always need to check and adjust digital images in general before they are printed, even images that originally come from a "professional" supplier.

In order to carry out these controls and adjustments in the right way you principally need knowledge, with good methods and a goal for your image editing as well. What are the elements of a digital image that make it of good quality? Here a technical image standard, that is specifications regarding the technical requirements placed on an image, can be of good use in order to effectively produce high quality color prints to send to the customer for approval.

Image editing does not only involve checking technical quality, but naturally involves achieving creative goals as well. There are few images published today that have not been retouched to a larger or smaller degree. One of the most common image editing steps is to select the image so that the subject gets a white or transparent background.

When we talk about digital images we usually divide them into pixel-based images and object graphics. Pixel-based images are photographic images while object graphics are illustrations, logotypes and graphics of different kinds. Pixel-based images are constructed of a number of small image elements in the computer called pixels, while object graphics are made up of mathematical curves and objects. Object graphics, in principle, can be enlarged endlessly, while pixel-based images, in principle, cannot be enlarged at all. The most typical program for editing pixel-based images is Adobe Photoshop, while Adobe Illustrator is usually used for object graphics.

It is important for pixel-based images to have enough resolution to be able to be reproduced in print with high quality. A simple rule of thumb is that pixel-based images should have a resolution of 300 pixels per inch. TIFF and EPS are typical image formats for printed production, but PDF and PSD are also becoming common image formats. Object graphics are generally saved in EPS or PDF format, but also the A1 format is beginning to be common.

The number of digital images these days has created the need to store images in different kinds of archives and image banks. To then be able to find the images demands that they be named in a standardized way, and that they be labeled with passwords, image descriptions and copyright information. This area has been developed much more recently, and now Adobe Photoshop has integrated support for labeling images according to the international IPTC standard. It has also appeared in several simple and inexpensive image bank programs such as Cumulus from Canto or Portfolio from Extensis.

At the same time as you produce images you usually compose text. The text fills a document that is generally produced in Microsoft Word. Even if it were possible to create some kind of layout in Word, you would be advised against it for use in printed materials. The program is not suitable for print production, but is excellent for producing and editing text.

1.1.4 Layout
Working with layouts involves putting together text and images to create finished original pages. Whoever prepares the layout document for printed products has to be conscious of the fact that creating an attractive layout isn't enough. It is at least important that the document works well both as a printout and for

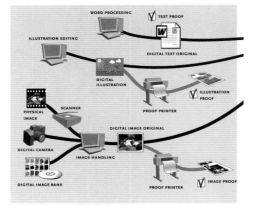

IMAGE AND TEXT
In this step the digital original images, illustrations and text that are going to be used in the printed product are produced. Those who work with producing the foundation of the printed product are everything from photographers, illustrators, journalists, authors, retouch specialists, prepress companies to printing houses. In this phase the customer approves it all in the forms of text, illustrations or image proofs.

preparing a printing plate that is suitable to be printed from. Documents that are not properly produced can cause cost increases and delayed production, or unintended final results. The most common program for professional layout work is Adobe InDesign or Quark Xpress.

Some important areas within layout work are typography, manuscript, image editing and logotypes, as well as the choice of colors and color combinations. In this book we will not deal with typography from the point of view of aesthetics, but instead, the handling of fonts as well as how they are made will be important to know about when creating a layout. When you create your layout you also need to know something about the printing process. Some common terms are overprint and bleeds [*see Layout 6.11.4 and 6.11.1*].

When you work with color you will come in contact with different color systems such as RGB, CMYK and Pantone. RGB (Red, Green, Blue) is the color system of computers and monitors, while CMYK (Cyan, Magenta, Yellow, Black) is that of printing. Pantone is a system for special printed colors that are used as complements to the four print colors, CMYK, since they are difficult to reproduce with the help of CMYK. Gold, silver, reflector blue or bright orange are examples of color that Pantone colors are used for.

When you work with layout you often handle a number of different files, especially images. It is important to organize your work and have a good basic structure for naming your small files and where they are saved so that it is easy to find the right file. Previously, low-resolution images were often used during layout work since software and computers were not powerful enough to handle high-resolution images, but this is seldom a problem today. If you want to have well-structured text document files it is possible to automate the layout work using templates or plug-ins for layout programs. This works when you are producing a printed product with a rather simple layout, for example novels or catalogues, and you can save a lot of time this way.

During layout work it is often necessary for several proofs to be sent to different interested parties for examination and approval before everything is ready. The PDF format has become a standard here for distributing proofs and the Acrobat program from Adobe also has a number of practical functions with whose help you can attach comments and instructions about changes you want carried out.

1.1.5 Prepress

Prepress is a rather clumsy collective name for all the work steps that you carry out before you begin the actual printing. Repro is an older term that has often been used for prepress. The boundaries between prepress, producing layout, and image editing are unclear and create a lot of problems and misunderstandings, practically speaking, as to who is responsible for what. There used to be prepress companies that dealt with prepress, layout production and image editing, something that leads to even greater confusion as to what prepress really is.

Today layout production is generally done by advertising bureaus and in-house departments or companies. Image editing has begun to be done by photographers or specialized image retouch companies. So what then is prepress? In this book we have chosen to define prepress as those work steps and techniques required to create print-adjusted digital files that can be the foundation for the

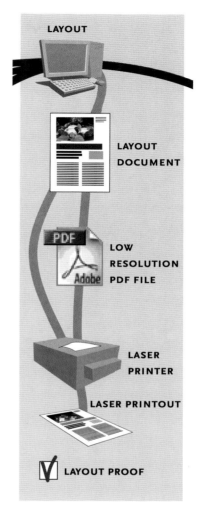

LAYOUT

Layout work deals with putting together text and images to make finished original pages. Some important areas within layout work are manuscript, typography, handling images and logotypes as well as choice of colors and color combinations.

Layout work is created in advertising bureaus, design studios, printing houses, marketing departments and companies. In this step the customer approves the finished layout.

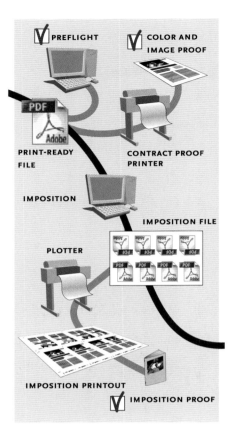

PREFLIGHT

COLOR AND
IMAGE PROOF

PDF
Adobe

PRINT-READY
FILE

CONTRACT PROOF
PRINTER

IMPOSITION

IMPOSITION FILE

PLOTTER

IMPOSITION PRINTOUT

IMPOSITION PROOF

PREPRESS

Prepress is a rather general catch-all name for all the work steps that are carried out before you begin with the actual printing. In actuality prepress is really the phases involving the creation of high-resolution PDF-files, making images and documents print-ready, controlling imposition and screen frequency, as well as technologies such as Postscript, PDF, JDF and different types of contract proofs. A large part of the prepress work is automated today and often done at the printer.

There are three proofing steps during the prepress stage:

- Checking the print-ready PDF files using preflight at the printing hose;
- Checking the printer's proof by the customer;
- Checking the imposition proof, something normally done at the printer's.

production of a printing form. In practice this includes work steps like creating high-resolution PDF files, print adjustment of images and documents, proofing, imposition and rasterizing, as well as technologies like PostScript, PDF, JDF and different kinds of printed proofs.

Most prepress steps are automated today and are sent out to printing houses to a large degree. All printing houses accept PDF files as the printed original and international standards have been developed for the production of PDF files for printing (PDF/X).

Adjusting images for printing is done with the aid of an ICC profile for different situations. For the most common printing techniques today there are also standardized ICC profiles.

Rasterizing occurs automatically when printing out printing plates. The raster dots are created here that determine the different colors and tones that are going to be created in print. There are several kinds of raster techniques with different advantages and disadvantages.

The printer's proof is a very important step in the prepress phase. It is a high-quality color printout that allows for the official approval of the customer before the actual print run begins. The printer's proof will simulate what the printed product will look like and show the printer what the customer expects as a final result. Without the printer's proof it would be very difficult to reject a printed result you weren't satisfied with. Since the border around prepress work is fluid, sometimes certain work steps are carried out by people working in layout production or image editing. The important thing is not actually what we call the different work steps, but rather that who is to do what has been defined and that you understand what work steps are required and what kind of competence is necessary in order to take responsibility for them.

1.1.6 **Printing**

The printing method you choose for a particular project is usually determined by the quality requirements, the edition size, the printing material and the format and type of printed product you are creating. We can create printed products with both printers and printing presses, and the boundaries between them are somewhat fluid. In this chapter, we will cover all the different printing methods and their characteristics.

The basic difference between printing press technique and printer technique is that the former always uses some sort of printing plates, or printing blocks for flexographic printing. Printing plates are static, which means that every printed product made from the same plates will look alike.

Printing press techniques generally lend themselves best to large print runs and the most common are offset printing, gravure printing, flexographic printing and screen printing. Printers don't use any printing plates which means that every printout can be unique and differ from the previous printout. Printer technology is better suited for editions from approximately 500 copies down to single examples, and the most common techniques are xerographic, inkjet and dye sublimation technique.

When we talk about digital printing we mean in general that the machine that is used is based on the technique of these printers, but that it has such high capacity that it can compete with a traditional printing press. The advantages with digital printing are that the contents can vary from sheet to sheet, as well as have low start-up costs since it does not require extensive makereadies and you don't have to develop film or printing plates. Traditional printing presses require printing plates and take a longer time to set up. They have higher start-up costs, but in general have a higher capacity, which means that they are more cost-effective with large editions. You can print on a number of different materials. Paper is the most usual, but you can also print on most other materials, such as plastic, paper or cloth.

1.1.7 Finishing and Binding

Though it is the final phase of the graphic print production process, finishing and binding has an impact on a project from the very beginning, and should be taken into account when the product is being designed. For example, some types of paper are more appropriate for different finishing and binding processes than others. The imposition of the pages (how they are arranged on the printed sheets) is also determined partly by the finishing and binding desired for the product. Therefore, it is important to decide early on in the planning stages what type of finishing and binding procedures your product will need. Finishing and binding can be divided into three areas: surface processing, off press processing, and binding.

Surface processing includes different stages that affect the surface of the printed product. There are many reasons why printed sheets have to be surface treated. It gives you the opportunity to created visual effects like foiling, create raised areas on the paper, emphasize a picture with partial varnishing or create metal effects with foiling. Often you surface treat a printed product to protect it against wear and tear, or laminate it to increase its folding endurance. It is also common today to varnish the printed sheets in order to be able to finish and bind them more quickly, without waiting for the printing ink to dry.

Cropping and trimming include the stages of book finishing when the paper is physically shaped. Cropping – the printed product is cut and trimmed to get the right format and even edges, die-cutting – the printed product is die-cut into another shape or is given perforations, punching – the printed product has holes punched in it to put it into binders, folding – used to form pages from the printed sheets, and creasing – the printed product is creased to mark a fold.

Binding is the joining of a number of individual printed sheets into a single entity, be it metal stitched brochures, spiral bound manuals, softcover books or hardcover books. The term stitching means how the insert is put together: metal stitching, spiral binding, Smyth-sewn stitching, thread stitching or glue binding. In metal stitching and spiral binding, the cover is attached during the actual binding process. In Smyth-sewn and thread sewing the spine of the insert is sewn together which is then attached to the cover. There are two ways of attaching, or casing, the cover. In the first version (for softcovers), the cover is glued to the spine of the bound material. In the second (for hardcovers), the first and last pages of the material, called the endpapers, are glued to the insides of the covers. In softcover books the cover is put on during stitching,

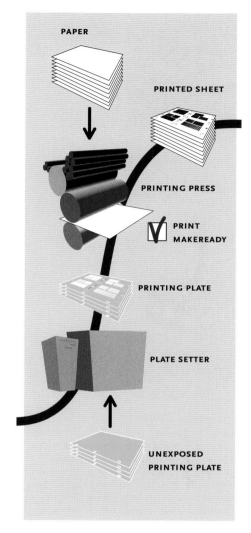

PAPER

PRINTED SHEET

PRINTING PRESS

PRINT MAKEREADY

PRINTING PLATE

PLATE SETTER

UNEXPOSED PRINTING PLATE

PRINTING

Today much printing is done with the help of digital printing technology or with printing technology. Printing requires you to create a printing form for each color in the print: clichés for flexographic printing, plates for offset printing, engraved printing cylinders for gravure printing and screens for screen printing. Digital printing technology requires no printing forms, but instead prints directly out from digital information.

In this phase you approve the final printing quality in conjunction with the makeready, before the print run begins. Approval can either be given by the customer or by someone at the printing house.

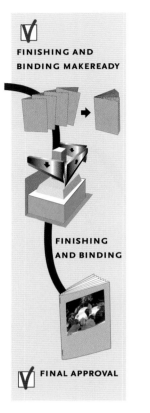

for example when glue binding softcover books. Hanging, or casing in, a cover is done separately from stitching.

The printed product's intended use affects which finishing and binding processes you choose. A manual that will be used in a garage has to be able to withstand oil and dirt, while a computer manual should be able to lie flat on a table. The choice is affected at the same time by economics and the number of copies printed. A newspaper doesn't have to last more than a day, which means that you would choose a cheap and simple finishing and binding process. With larger editions, you sometimes have to choose a cheaper binding to keep within an economic framework. If you print with web-fed offset printers or intaglio printing, as is usually done with larger runs, the finishing and binding processes are usually connected directly with the printing press: online-processing. This means you will have to select the finishing processes that are available with an on-line system.

Finishing and binding are done at printing houses and bookbinders. If you are working with a sheet-fed offset printer, you will often have to take the printed sheets to a separate bookbindery. Bookbinders often specialize in certain kinds of binding, so for different types of finishing and binding processes you will have to resort to different bookbinderies. It is even common for the sheet-fed printers themselves to offer some of the simpler off press services. Printing houses that do not have their own finishing equipment usually have close ties with a bookbinder.

1.1.8 Distribution

The printed product is now ready and is going to be distributed to the final user. The costs of distribution often surpass the printing costs. Distribution is often done by companies that specialize in it and in this book we will only take a general look at distribution.

1.2 Before Printed Production

There are a variety of questions to answer before you begin with the production of your printed product. Why you are making it, who it should reach, how they should be reached, what kind of printed product it should be, what the quality demands are, etc.?

1.2.1 Why do we make printed products?

To begin with you should ask yourself what the goal of the printed product is, who you want to reach and what it should communicate. Some typical answers can be:

- To inform
- To sell
- To entertain
- To package

FINISHING AND BINDING

Finishing and binding happens at the printer's or at a special finishing and binding company, and can be divided into three areas: surface processing (varnishing, laminating, embossing, etc.), cropping and trimming (cropping, stamping, creasing, etc.), as well as binding (stitching, covering and casing).

The approval that is given at this stage is for the final finishing and binding quality. It is given by someone responsible in the company carrying out the finishing and binding process, and is an approval of the fist correct copy before you produce the whole edition.

DISTRIBUTION

Distribution is often handled by the printer or, when it is on a large scale, by companies specializing in it. The costs of distribution often surpass the printing costs.

Normally the customer approves of the final quality of the printed product before it is distributed.

STRATEGIC PHASE	Design bureaus	LAYOUT	PREPRESS	FINISHING AND BINDING
• Marketing departments	IMAGES AND TEXT	• Advertising and design bureaus	• Prepress bureaus	• Printers
• Communications departments	• Photographers	• Production companies	• Copying companies	• Bookbinder
• Advertising agencies	• Photo labs	• Prepress companies	• Printers	DISTRIBUTION
• Media advisors	• Production companies	• Printers	• Production companies	• Printers
CREATIVE PHASE	• Prepress bureaus	• Inhouse bureaus	• Inhouse bureaus	• Bookbinders
• Marketing and communications departments	• Printers with own prepress		PRINTING	• Distributors
• Advertising and PR agencies	• Image bureaus		• Copying companies	
	• Writers		• Prepress companies	
	• Editors		• Printers	

The purpose of the printed product is especially important today when the printed product has received competition from many other media. The answer is often a combination of several different purposes. It affects what kind of printed product you are going to make, what form it will take, what material you will choose and how you will reach the user. Some examples can be:

- If you want to persuade someone to buy something you make an advertisement
- If you want to impart information you may choose to make a newsletter or folder
- If you want to entertain or educate you make a book
- If you want to package something you create packaging.

1.2.2 Who or what should be reached by a printed product?

Who is the target group, who is going to use the printed product? The target group affects what type of printed product you are going to make, how it is going to be formed and perhaps mainly what its contents will be. Today there are technical possibilities to adapt and aim the printed product toward the target group according to the customer information in your computer. Some typical examples of target groups are:

- Youth
- Retired people
- Median income earners
- Food lovers

1.2.3 How should the user be reached?

How should you reach the end user and what media/channels should be used so that the results will be the best possible? The choice of media can be decisive for how successful you are in reaching your target group. How should the printed product be distributed and by whom? Some examples can be:

- Large advertisements around town
- Advertisements in the daily press or weekly magazines
- Direct mailings

1.2.4 What type of product should be made?

What type of printed product should be made and what size edition should be printed? The type of printed product and size of the edition influences the price and determines what printing technique you have to print. Some examples of printed products and typical edition sizes:

- Flyer, 30,000 copies
- Catalogues, 100,000 copies
- Book, 5,000 copies
- Folders, 10,000 copies
- Packaging, 100,000 copies
- Advertisements, 200 copies
- Posters, 500 copies

1.2.5 How will the printed product be used?

How will the printed product be used? Will it be used for a long time and be durable? Some questions you can ask yourself are:

- Should it last a long time, be of archival quality?
- Will it be leafed through frequently?
- Is it going to be thrown away directly after reading?
- Will it fulfill a special function (for example packaging?)

The areas of use of the printed product and its durability determines how it will be printed, and finished and bound if applicable, and what material you will use. Some examples can be:

A catalogue that is going to be leafed through a lot should be finished and bound so that it can withstand this use. This may mean, for example, that you laminate the cover and use glue binding.

An outdoor poster that can withstand the elements during the time it is posted. It must always be printed with waterproof inks and on a durable paper.

A book that is to last should perhaps be hardbound with a surface finish that protects it, as well has have a high quality inner binding.

A daily newspaper that has a short life expectancy can be printed on cheap paper and be stapled.

The demands on quality affect the price and the delivery times. They also affect the choice of work partners for production. Is it important for it to be a high-quality product? Is it important to have top-quality images?

You can imagine that sharing graphic print production at three levels of quality: low, medium and high. Typical products with low quality can be made with product flyers, simpler folders, internal newsletters and such. Medium quality would be periodicals, folders, brochures, as well as higher quality annual reports, art books or exclusive packaging. Some examples of this are:

An art book should have the highest quality both with regard to image and print quality, paper quality and finishing and binding.

A direct mailing flyer advertising the pizzeria around the corner needs neither high-quality image printing nor high-quality paper. It is probably more important to keep the costs down.

1.3 **What affects the costs?**

When you request quotes from graphic print production companies it is important to include all the information. Both time and costs can easily add up. We will go through the main parameters that influence production costs and discuss things that are important to consider when you are planning your printed product and soliciting offers.

Pricing in graphic print production is far from standardized and can vary greatly from service provider to service provider. There are a number of different ways to be paid. Some service providers have standard prices and price lists while others can have differentiated pricing. It is important to talk about what you want to have included and not included in the prices you are being quoted. You should also consider if taxes will be added later on and under what conditions they would apply.

Another factor that affects the price is that you assign the right company to the right product. Different printing presses fit different types of production, which means that the printers are often limited in terms of equipment. This means that most printers are specialized for the type of production that is most appropriate for their printing equipment from an economic point of view. Therefore it is important to choose a service provider who normally works with the same type of production that you yourself are seeking. A printer that doesn't do this can often deliver what you are requesting, but probably you will have to pay an unnecessarily high price. If, for example, you want to print a catalogue you will most likely get the best price with a printer that specializes in such products. To get the right prices therefore you must choose the right printer.

When we talk about printed products sometimes we forget how the total cost picture of the printed product will look. Above and beyond the actual costs there are often costs for the advertising bureau that develops the idea and concept and writes the texts and designs to the printed product as well. In addition, there are overall costs for distribution of the printed product. If you work with a edition of a printed product the costs of the advertising bureau will make up the large portion of the total production costs. If you work instead with a large edition

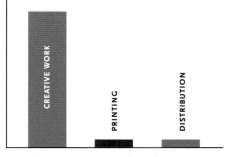

Costs for small editions and small volume.

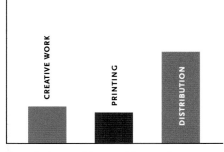

Costs for large editions and large volume.

THE COSTS OF A PRINTED PRODUCT
The relative costs when you produce a printed product are divided up differently depending on the size of the edition. With small editions the creative costs, for example images, text and design, have a great effect on the total cost, while with large editions and large volume the distributions costs dominate.

the advertising bureau costs will decrease proportionately and distribution will instead make up the largest part of the total cost.

Paper costs are usually calculated into the printing price and make up a very small part of the total cost when there are small editions (approximately 10,000 copies or fewer). With larger editions (approximately 100,000 copies or more), on the other hand, the paper cost can make up to 50% of the printing cost. If you work with a small edition the choice of paper is therefore in principle unimportant from an economic aspect, while it can be of the greatest importance when you have a large editon.

We will go through a number of different parameters that influence the actual printing costs.

1.3.1 Makeready and Start-up Costs

When you set a price for a printed product in general you start with a price per hour that stands in relation to what the printing press costs and how much time you expect to have it available on average during one year. Since printing presses are very expensive their price per hour is high and can lie anywhere between $300.00 and $900.00 per hour, depending on the press and the reserved time calculations.

The total printing price is affected by the start-up cost and the time it takes to make what is called a makereaady, as well as the cost of material such as printing plates and paper that are required for a makeready. The makeready serves to prepare the printing press and make the settings and adjustments that are required to get the first approved printed sheet. The costs of printing the run itself lie in direct relation to the number of sheets to be printed. The number of printed sheets is influenced by edition size, format and volume of the printed product.

1.3.2 Edition size, format and volume

The edition size is the number of copies you want to print, the format is the size of the actual printed product and the volume are the number of pages. These three parameters define the printed product and are also what mainly determines its costs.

The actual edition size affects of course the total printing cost. Because of start-up costs the printed product will be cheaper per copy when you print a larger edtion. Therefore it can sometimes be worthwhile to print a larger edition since it doesn't cost so much to print a few extra copies. If you want to know how large the price difference is to print more copies than planned you can ask the printer to supply this price on the quote, for example the cost of printing an additional 1,000 copies. The edition size is often a guideline for determining what type of printing technique is most suitable to use. Editions of less than 1,000 copies are usually digitally printed editions beyond this size are printed using sheet-fed offset printing. Web-fed offset printing is called for with editions of over 50,000 copies, while gravure printing is used with editions of 300,0000 copies and above. These edition guidelines can vary depending on format and volume of the printed product.

The format affects the costs of printing to a large degree since it determines how many pages you will get from one printed sheet. When you select the format is can be worthwhile to stay close to the A format to fully utilize the paper and the printing press as effectively as possible. If you halve the format you can count on diminishing the printing costs significantly since you only have to print half as many sheets. The cost is not halved however in terms of the start-up costs which will remain the same. With large runs you can almost halve the printing costs since the start-up cost comprises a very small amount of the total price in this case.

The volume is also an important factor that affects the printing cost. The more pages the printed product has, the more expensive the printing cost will be. Since sheet-fed offset printing in general is suited for several commonly used trim sizes, this means that you should plan your printed product with a number of pages that are evenly divisible by 4, 8 or 16. In practice there is a direct link between edition size, format and volume since all three factors affect how many printed sheets are necessary for a specific printed product.

1.3.3 Colors

Black and white printed products are cheaper to produce than printed products in four colors. If you want to add special colors, for example one or two Pantone colors, the printing cost is increased additionally. This is because you have to change ink and clean the printing press. The number of colors you can print with on a certain printing press has to do with how many ink ducts it has. Many of today's modern sheet-fed offset presses ha five or six ink ducts, which means that it isn't considerably more expensive to print with one or two extra colors. However, if you want to have three or more extra colors it can become a lot more expensive since then you have to change inks, clean the printing press, prepare a new makeready and do print runs with the extra colors separately.

With web-fed offset printing and digital printing you are often limited to printing in four colors since the printing presses that are based on this printing technique are seldom have more than four ink ducts. Flexographic printing presses often have more than four ink ducts, which means that, as in web-fed offset printing, you can print additional colors without any great extra cost.

1.3.4 Image Editing

Image editing deals basically with retouches, selections, proofing and different types of adjustments. Such work is often charged by the hour and the price generally varies between $65.00 per hour up to $300.00 per hour. The hourly price is influenced by the complexity and size of the task. Advanced retouches usually cost more than simpler image editing and it is not necessarily true that the same person or the same company should carry out both the simpler and the more advanced image editing. Printing houses are often good at simple image editing, while advanced retouches should perhaps be done by retouching specialists. It is not only a question of quality, but also of costs since an experienced retouch editor works considerably more quickly than one with less experience.

If you have greater volume you can demand a price per picture. The advantage with this is that it can be easier to judge the cost in advance when you are going to plan the economic side of your printed product. You may then need to describe selections or retouches so the service provider can appreciate the difficulties in advance and the time output. It takes, for example, considerably longer to select a pine tree than a ball. One simple way is to furnish the service provider with examples of previous image editing.

When you are going to scan or photograph images you often get a price per image. It is important to talk about desired size and resolution of the images even if these days it seldom affects the price. If there are many images in question you can often get a better price.

1.3.5 Layout Work

Layout work can include everything from simple template-based work to advanced design from a sketch or even just an idea. Simpler layout work may deal with proofs of an available document, typography of an existing document, fitting advertising to a format or fitting language into existing templates. More advance layout work can be making an original from a sketch, or starting completely from the beginning including design.

Layout work is most often billed per hour, but is sometimes billed per page on lager projects. Hourly and per page pricing varies depending on the complexity and size of the task. Advanced layout work usually costs more than simpler layout work and it is not necessarily the same person or company that should carry out both the simpler and the more advanced layout jobs.

If you have larger volumes you can demand a price per page. The advantage of this is that it can be easier to estimate the costs in advance when you are going to make a budget for production. You may then need to describe the layout work so the service provider can appreciate the difficulties and time outlay in advance. One easy way is to supply the service provider with an example of similar layout work. Sometimes you can even work with a price per page that includes scanning of images, image editing, creating a printed original and a proof print.

One important area that can affect time use and costs is handling proofs. For this reason it is important to define how the work with proofs will be carried out and what should be approved at what stages. It is easy to underestimate time outlay for proofing and it is therefore important to set aside time for checking proofs when planning your production. Sometimes people specify how many proofing rounds will be included in the price and charge extra for eventual additional proofing.

1.3.6 Prepress

Prepress work can include creating and/or checking PDF files or open documents such as, for example, Quark Xpress, Adobe Indesign or Adobe Illustrator files. It can even involve adjusting documents and images for printing as well as producing printing proofs. Finally, it can even include impositions and setting up printing forms. Sometimes it is appropriate to consider the costs of archiving digital material. Setting a price for prepress duties is not at all standardized since today this work is more or less automated and the prices can therefore vary enormously depending on whom you talk to.

Prepress work is billed in general per hour and varies between $65.00 per hour up to $250.00 per hour. The hourly rate is determined by the complexity and size of the task. Printer's proofs and printing forms are usually billed by the piece and usually cost somewhere between $40.00 and $150.00 per printer's proof and per printing form, respectively.

1.3.7 Finishing and Binding

Finishing and binding can mean surface treatment (varnishing, laminating, foiling, stamping), different kinds of handling the printed sheet of paper (cropping, hole-punching, perforating, or creasing), as well as bindings of different types (for example spiral, glue or thread sewing).

Varnishing adds no great cost in general since it is often done directly in the printing press. Laminating, foiling and stamping, on the other hand, can cost more since it is a more manual process. Different types of binding cost different amounts and generally you can say that a spiral binding and a thread-sewn binding is significantly more expensive than a simple stapled binding or a glue binding.

Setting prices for finishing and binding is based in general on the start-up costs of a makeready and the following makeready, and the cost per piece of the finishing and binding of the printed product. The number of pages and the imposition of the printed sheet affects the number of makereadies in the finishing and binding machine. The fewer pages the printed sheet has room for and the more pages there are in the printed product, the more makereadies. The size of the edition affects the price in its turn via price per piece.

1.3.8 Paper

When you choose paper you should also think about the cost aspect. A ground rule is that the larger the edition the greater the part of the production cost is made up of paper cost. With larger editions, for example 100,000 copies or more, a relatively small price difference between two different qualities of paper can still make a large difference in the total production cost. With small editions of a few thousand copies or fewer, the cost of paper makes up such a small amount of the total production cost that smaller price differences can be viewed as insignificant. The fact is that most ordinary qualities of paper do not differ more than +/-15% in price among themselves. Certain specialty papers can however differ significantly more.

If you choose another surface weight, gram per square meter, of a certain paper quality, the price is largely affected proportionately to the change in surface weight. This means that if the surface weight is halved the paper will cost approximately half as much. It is therefore usual that with large editions you choose paper with lower surface weight. The paper becomes cheaper but still feels as thick as a paper with a higher surface weight.

When we talk about print runs it is also important to think about the volume of the printed product, that is the number of pages. A book with many pages can require quite a lot of paper despite its being printed in a very small edition.

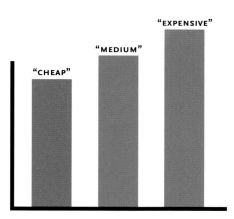

PRICE DIFFERENCE BETWEEN PAPER QUALITIES
Most ordinary qualities of paper do not differ more than +/-15% in price among themselves. Certain specialty papers can however differ significantly more.

PROJECT

- Project name and number
- Short description of the task
- Quality requirements
- Partners involved

TIMEFRAME

- Delivery of foundation
- Delivery of proofs
- Delivery of printer's proof
- Delivery of printed product

FOUNDATION

- Layout
- Images
- Text
- Sketches
- Open files or PDF files

EDITION, VOLUME AND FORMAT

- Edition
- Volume (body and cover)
- Format

COLORS

- Four-color on front and back covers
- Spot colors
- Varnish
- Image Editing
- Extractions
- Retouches
- Shadows
- Color correction

LAYOUT PRODUCTION

- Layout from sketch
- Layout from template
- Adapting or adjustments of existing original
- Software
- Proofs (PDF, printouts, etc.)

PREPRESS

- Screen frequency
- Raster type
- Contract proof

FINISHING AND BINDING

- Varnishing, laminating
- Foiling, embossing
- Cropping, stamping, perforating
- Folding, Creasing
- Type of stitching (metal, spiral, glue, thread, Smyth-sewn)

PAPER

- Coated or uncoated
- Matte or glossy
- Surface weight
- Quality
- Body and cover

PACKAGING AND DISTRIBUTION

- Delivery method (order, post, digitally)
- Delivery address
- Packaging
- Placing in envelopes
- Addressing
- Marking

OTHER

- Handling of reference copies
- Archiving of material

The format of the printed product is also important in conjunction with this. Certain odd formats make it difficult to optimally utilize the printed sheet, which means that a lot of the paper goes to waste. Small changes in the format can make big differences regarding the use of paper. The printer can help with advice on formatting.

You usually buy paper via the printer you rely on. Therefore it is important to remember that the price of paper is also affected by the agreement the printer has with various paper suppliers and by the quantity you buy of a certain paper. This entails that the price of the same paper can vary between different printers. If you want to know the price difference between different papers you can ask the printer to give you the figures for two or three different paper alternatives.

1.3.9 Packing and Distribution

Specify if delivery is included in the quote, otherwise you yourself will have to bear the costs of delivery. Most printing houses can help with jobs such as packing, placing in envelopes, addressing and distribution. With large editions the cost of distribution makes up a very large part of the total cost. In that case it is important to consider factors such as paper, format and volume to see if you can compromise somewhere to save on costs. It can be difficult to save on the distribution cost itself, but often you can get rates by weight from the post office or some other distributor. Then you pay for the postage of the shipment by volume and don't have to worry about exceeding specific postage limits.

1.3.10 Archiving

Some companies offer digital archiving of documents and image for future use. Remember that it isn't automatic that the service provider archives a job digitally even if many do. It is a service that many will offer for a fee and if you want to be sure that the material remains you have to stipulate it with the printer. Often it doesn't cost very much either. A common way to pay for archiving is to pay some kind of monthly fee in relation to the amount of archived material. Also, reusing the material usually costs something, often priced at how long it takes to retrieve the old material.

1.3.11 Environmental Concerns

To reduce the effects on the environment within graphic print production involves keeping yourself up-to-date on the environment and making active decisions regarding paper, material, ink and so on. Also being aware of the production processes, for example printing, finishing and binding, paper and material. This is an area that is continually developing, so it is important to keep yourself informed as to what alternatives are available.

You should also remember that environmental concerns are linked with the whole process, from the idea to the finished product: its life expectancy as well as how and where it will be used, all the way to the time it is disposed of and recycled. In practice this means using energy-saving processes, reducing and if possible eliminating use of materials, taking advantage of recycling opportunities and avoiding poisonous and non-recyclable material.

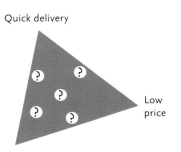

Quick delivery

Low price

High quality

PRIORITIZE IN PRODUCTION
Printers often have different strengths. Therefore it is hard to combine low price, quick delivery and the highest quality. You have to decide where in the triangle you want to place your printed product according to what you prioritize in the project.

SOME INTERESTING FACTORS WHEN CHOOSING A SERVICE PROVIDER:

- Quality and competence
- Delivery times and delivery guarantees
- Capacity and Resources
- Organization and working together
- Proximity and availability
- References and direction
- Routines and conditions
- Quality and environmental work
- Economy and future

Some typical questions to ask might be:

- How are the raw materials needed for paper and other materials produced and used?
- What type of printing inks are used and do they contain dangerous metals or are they from plants? Are the leftovers recycled?
- How much transport is required and what can one do to minimize it? Can we use recycled fiber-based paper and which chemicals have been used for bleaching?
- How are the development liquids and other chemicals handled in the process? In what way does the finishing and binding affect the possibility of recycling the printed product?
- Are the toner cartridges from the printers and digital printing presses recycled?
- Is the printing house environmentally certified?

1.4 **Choosing a Service provider**

To be successful with graphic print production you need to have a close and good working relationship with a number of service providers. It can therefore be wise to consider the choice of working partners carefully.

When you compare different service providers you should first and most importantly think through what kinds of demands you want to place on them. It is also important to think through what phases of the production you want to do yourself and which ones you will need help with. If you do large parts of the production yourself it can be cheaper but at the same time you take a larger responsibility for how the end result will be.

Remember that some types of production can be a good fit with one service provider while they may not be suited at all for others. This involves special printers that are often specialized for certain types of production. Below we will go through some different factors that can be of interest to consider when you choose service providers.

1.4.1 **Quality and Competence**
Competence and quality are often one of the most important factors when you are choosing a service provider. To begin with you have to create an understanding of what kind of missions and work tasks you will need help with, and what kind of competence is needed from the service provider to attain the quality you want.

The service provider's competence and level of quality are often difficult to judge before you have actually worked with them, but there are some things that can still give certain indications. One way is to ask the service provider if you can see some jobs they have done for other customers as reference.

You can even find out if the company has some specialty (kinds of services or products). A company that has image editing as a specialty should be reasonably proficient in this area, but probably expensive. If you don't have high demands on image quality you should maybe work with a service provider who doesn't have this as a specialty. Otherwise you will be paying a relatively large amount for your images despite the fact that the quality is not especially important.

You can also ask the service provider to describe how your working together will be carried out in practice, what factors and work steps they deem will be critical for good results, and in what way they can assure quality in the work flow.

1.4.2 Delivery Times and Delivery Guarantees

Delivery time and delivery guarantees are decisive factors when you are choosing a service provider. Even these areas can be hard to judge beforehand. In principle it is a question of how quickly the service provider can carry out certain tasks and how dependable the service provider is.

You can ask the service provider how the delivery time can be guaranteed. Guaranteed deliveries can in some cases be absolutely decisive, for example with the production and delivery of advertising. Sometimes it can be necessary to place some sort of delayed delivery clause in the agreement with the service provider. If you have high demands on quick delivery times it can also affect the price.

1.4.3 Capacity and Resources

If you are going to produce large volumes in a short time it is important to find out if the service provider is used to such demands and has the machinery and personnel capacity. Here it is also good to find out about what volumes, capacity and resources are needed for other customers the service provider is working with. Often these are connected with the size of the company, but it is also important that there be many people that can do the same things so that not all the work is on the shoulders of a few.

1.4.4 Organization and Working Together

Find out how the company's organization looks and how it works with customers. How important will you as a customer be to the service provider and will you receive the service you expect? Are there special contact personnel and will the contact person always be the same or will it vary depending on the type of task?

1.4.5 Proximity and Availability

It can often be an advantage to be geographically close to your service provider, especially if fast delivery times are important and you have high quality demands. If the delivery time is not of the greatest importance there may be economic reasons to turn to a service provider located outside the main city. Some of the drawbacks with this is that it can be hard to be on hand for the makereadies or make quick decisions if there is a problem.

Another important question can be the service level and availability outside of regular work hours. Find out what the hours of operation are and when and how the contact personnel are available. Printing houses and prepress companies often work in shifts or have some form of twenty-four hour system.

Companies that work with shifts can often produce more and offer shorter delivery times than companies that don't.

1.4.6 References and Direction

Ask to see samples of typical productions the company has done. Do they correspond to the productions you are asking about? Request names and contacts of others that have relied on the company and learn how their working together went.

Graphic print production to a large extent involves working together and communicating. Talk a lot to the service providers and make sure you get to know each other. Choosing work partners for graphic print production often means that you are beginning a relationship that will last for years. When you change service providers it often takes a long time to build up a well-functioning working relationship and in the beginning it can lead to unforeseen costs.

1.4.7 Routines and Conditions

Find out what routines and work agreements are to be upheld between you as a customer and the service provider. Most service providers use ALG2 that is a specific contract that has been worked out by representatives of both graphic print production customers and service providers. Find out your responsibilities as the customer placing the order and what area the service provider is responsible for. Sometimes there can also be other agreements or routines that are important to know about when you are going to work together with the company. Service provider conditions, quality guarantees and copyrights are areas where there might be routines that it can be especially important to know about. Even economic conditions for paying and accounting principles are important to be informed about.

1.4.8 Quality and Environmental Work

Sometimes you can have special requirements for quality and environmental work. In this case you should find out how the service provider works with environmental questions and if he or she is certified according to ISO 14001 [*see Printing 9.12*]. The same thing applies as to how the service provider works with quality issues. There are also standards here, ISO 9000, but it can be important to remember that these standards do not place requirements on the quality level. The standards are placed on the methods instead. Therefore it is important to find out what the service providers do to guarantee their quality and how they work on steadily improving in that area.

1.4.9 Economy and Future

The graphic print production industry is in constant flux and many graphic print production companies have a hard time staying in business. For this reason it is also important to gauge a company's economic stability and ownership. It can also be interesting to find out how the service provider's plans look for the future. It can have to do with future projects and direction as well as activities to guarantee the company's long-term survival.

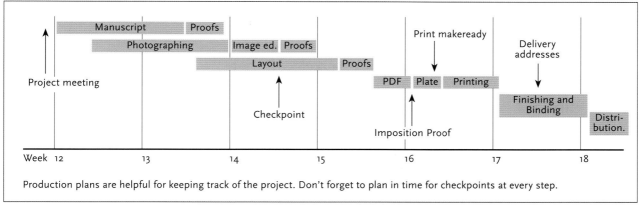

Production plans are helpful for keeping track of the project. Don't forget to plan in time for checkpoints at every step.

1.5 **Planning Graphic Print Production**

Once you have received offers and chosen service providers it is time to plan your production. Graphic print production is very difficult to plan since as a rule there are so many participants involved and you are dependent on a functioning working relationship with all parties. Unexpected incidents often pop up and there are few objective measures as to what is right or wrong. Much of the production is based on checking proofs until all parties are satisfied. Communication, feeling and working knowledge are decisive for a successful working partnership. It is to great advantage if the parties involved know each other and each other's demands and expectations well.

The fact that it is hard to plan graphic print production doesn't mean that you should just let things be. For this very reason the opposite is true and it is important to take the time to prepare and plan. There are a number of important subjects to take a position on when you are beginning to set up a project:

- Who is going to be in charge of the project? Do you have enough knowledge yourself or should someone else do it?
- Who is included in the project? Who is responsible for what?
- Who should check the proofs of texts, images, design, content and function?
- Who will give final approval of the project before it goes to print?
- What working partners are needed to carry out the project?
- How much and what should you do yourself and what do you need help with? What demands will you place on your work partners?
- Do you already have established contacts in all the areas or do you have to get these first?
- What people should be kept informed during the course of the project?
- How will you guarantee quality and time frames?

For spreading information and coordinating a project so that all works well, it is important to have a project leader. A project leader has to have a good overview and understanding of all the stages of the production flow. The different steps differ greatly from each other and it is important to plan each phase before carrying it out. Each step affects the conditions for how the next step can be carried out and failures in the flow of information lead directly to poorer quality and longer delivery times. Therefore the right material and the right information are prerequisites for everything in the final result being as expected from the beginning.

Production plans are of good help to keep control of the project. In general you begin planning backwards from when everything will be finished. Find out how long every phase in the production will take. Plan delivery times, part delivery, proofing eventualities, and possible reserve days. Remember to add a little time for safety margins; situations will often arise when you need it. Is the printed product going to be repeated, i.e. new versions, new editions, new numbers, etc.?

It is important to plan for everything properly with time allowed for checking everything. The later in production you discover errors the higher the cost of the errors will be. If you aren't careful enough with checkpoints during production it can be unnecessarily expensive.

1.6 How we made this book

Since work on the first edition of *A Guide to Graphic Print Production* began almost ten years ago a lot has happened in the graphic design industry. Techniques have been developed and other methods of working have become possible. When we first wrote the book we worked on a Macintosh, which completely dominated all graphic print production at the time. The programs we worked in were Microsoft Word, Adobe Illustrator and Adobe Photoshop. The layout was done in Quark Xpress and many images were low-resolution OPI images. When it was time for a total revision of *A Guide to Graphic Print Production*, we were curious to use the new and in many ways easier possibilities that were offered.

First of all we chose to do the layout in Adobe Indesign to try out many of the interesting capabilities that the program provides. In the production of the new book we have also worked in a combined computer environment with both Mac and PC, something that was made easier by Indesign and its support for Opentype fonts. We also chose to work with high-resolution images. In addition, we wanted to be a little more careful with handling the manuscript and revise texts in word processing programs as long as possible. In the old program a lot of text editing took place in the layout document and we wanted to avoid that this time.

1.6.1 Manuscript

When we worked on the old book Microsoft Word was the dominant word processing program just as it is today. The difference now is that the program has been greatly developed. At that time it wasn't so easy to keep track of what changes and corrections had been made in the text when it was passed around to each of the three authors. The same was true when it was proofread by our publisher.

This time we were able to take advantage of Word's functions to track changes. If we ever forgot to activate that function, we would instead use the function for comparing documents and got the same kind of help. We also used Word's comments function to exchange suggestions and thoughts about the manuscript. To keep the versions organized we named files by version numbers.

Really producing text in finally approved form before it was mounted in layout also made it possible for our publisher to send out translated manuscripts while production was underway – something that sped up the production of the foreign editions.

1.6.2 Graphic print production

For the third edition we thought it was time to change the appearance of the book. We met with the graphic designer, Urban Gyllström, and the chemistry was good right away. He had a tricky task since there already existed a functioning and established design that we didn't want to completely abandon. Not to mention that there were three authors with decided and not always unanimous opinions.

He had to strike a balance between what was to be changed and what was to be kept. A book with so many illustrations, table and marginal text like *A Guide to Graphic Print Production* tends to easily become messy. For this reason we wanted to clean it up and peel away everything that wasn't directly necessary for clarity. Where it was possible we tried to gather together illustrations and text that belong to the same subject within a common framework. Our goal has been to create a more easily read and airier book with mainly the same type of content as before.

1.6.3 Layout and Typography

We also had an idea for making layout more effective. For this reason we finalized a basic manuscript in Word where we defined paragraph and character formats, including headings, body text and image captions, which we later linked to Indesign. Since these paragraph formats followed Word's built-in headings levels, we could easily get an overview of the whole manuscript and rearrange things very simply using the outline mode and document overview functions.

It turned out that the glossary became twice as long compared with earlier editions. In addition, the book was going to be translated to a number of other languages this time. In order to be able to connect the glossary between the different languages, be had to collect them in a simple database to be able to sort and export to different formats. To do this in the easiest possible way we used Microsoft Excel. From Excel we exported the texts and converted them to XML format to be able to import them to Indesign and automatically typeset them.

TOOLS AND WORK METHODS 1998

- Mac
- Layout in Quark Xpress
- Word files for the basic manuscript
- Postscript Type 1 fonts for Mac
- OPI and low-resolution images
- Extractions with paths
- TIFF and EPS images in CMYK
- Open layout document to print
- Syquest disks to the printing house

TOOLS AND WORK METHODS 2006

- Windows and Mac
- Layout in Adobe Indesign
- Word manuscript with paragraph format connected to Indesign
- Our own digital photography in raw format
- Saved changes and comments in Word
- Clean macro in Word
- Opentype fonts
- Photographs in RGB
- Images in Illustrator and Photoshop format
- Extractions with transparency using layer mask
- Adobe Bridge for finding images
- Our own Preflight in Acrobat Professional
- PDF/X files adjusted for printing
- ICC profiles for print adjustment in Indesign
- FTP transfer of files to printing house

1.6.4 Layout Templates

Our designer Urban made basic sketches of the book's new design. When these were approved, we created production-ready Indesign templates. We created a macro in Word that cleaned out most of the common careless errors in the text, such as double spaces or spaces before a question mark.

When we then, after cleaning, imported Word manuscripts, all the text was automatically typeset with the correct paragraph and character formats since all the text in the manuscript followed corresponding formats.

1.6.5 Photographs and Illustrations

In the old book most of the photographs were saved in Tiff format except for images that were extracted with paths and which therefore were saved in EPS format. Extractions with paths sometimes results in edges that are too sharp and it is difficult to have a shadow behind an object in an image. For this reason we chose to select with transparency and save images in Photoshop format, which works well for mounting in Indesign. In addition, the format allows the possibility of using layers and adjustment layers.

Illustrations were created then, as now, in Adobe Illustrator and were often constructed with features such as layers, filters, etc. Since Quark Xpress did not have support for Illustrator format we had to resave all the illustrations in EPS format to be able to mount them in the layout. The drawback with EPS format is that it "flattens" the images and can therefore not handle the features that are used in Illustrator. Since Indesign handles Illustrator format we could now save and mount images in that format.

1.6.6 Image Adjustments

This time we wanted to be able to work in a more flexible way with image adjustments, extractions and illustration editing. Therefore we took advantage of the fact that Indesign handles both Photoshop and Illustrator format, with adjustment layers that we easily could change afterward without affecting image quality. Extractions were done with layer masks and transparency in Photoshop format. The illustrations were saved in Illustrator format with all the layers and filters intact so it was easy to open and adjust them. Some illustrations were also drawn directly in Indesign, which contains most of Illustrator's drawing tools.

1.6.7 Digital Photography

All the images were photographed with film for the previous book and then scanned with a drum scanner. In this edition all the new images were digitally photographed. In the old book we didn't take any photographs ourselves. Now we are complementing the images with some of our own photographs. We used a relatively simple digital camera that can take photos in raw format. It turned out to produce photographs of wholly adequate quality. See if you can guess which photographs in the book we took ourselves.

1.6.8 Images Linked to Text

The next step was the placement of images. We had a lot of trouble with this last time. When Kaj realized we needed to restructure the text in one chapter, it took several hours of manually moving the images so they would end up in the right place again.

We were very happy when we discovered there was a nifty function in Indesign that allows you to anchor an image in the place in the text where it belongs. This method of working made it easy for us to arrange text, images, tables and insets very conveniently. When we realized that we needed to reorganize a chapter and some text ended up on new pages, the mounted images were moved along with the text, and this worked even when the images had been placed out in the margins.

1.6.9 Mounting Images

To easily mount images we wanted to reuse from the old book, the Xpress document was converted to Indesign so we could simply cut and paste into the new document. In the old book we had a little over 800 images sorted in different folders in order to find the ones we were going to mount in the layout. Despite this and the fact that we tried to name the images clearly, it was difficult to find the right image. In addition, it was a lot of work if we had to move the folder with all the images and the links had to be updated, folder by folder. To facilitate mounting new illustrations, we used Adobe Bridge, which is included in Adobe Indesign, so that we could see how every image looked instead. Now we can easily have an overview of several hundred images in the same folder.

1.6.10 Images in RGB

When we made the old book, all the images had to be adjusted to CMYK for printing before they were placed in the layout. That meant that already at an early stage we had to decide on all the printing conditions. When we then wanted to reuse the images for other printing and in the digital overhead projection images that go along with the book, problems arose – we didn't have all the images left in RGB. Some had even been scanned to CMYK directly with the old scanners that were used then. This time we decided to let the photographs stay in RGB mode, even in the layout.

The actual basic layout was now ready according to our ground plan and we could deliver the Indesign document to our designer, Urban, who was going to polish up the final design. Urban didn't need to get any images from us since the preview images were already in the document.

1.6.11 Fonts

When we made the old book, it was practically impossible to move a layout document between Mac and Windows. Over the years it has become simpler, but fonts have still created a lot of problems when transferring documents between Mac and Windows. In order for Urban to work with the same document as us without problem, despite the fact that he worked in Mac and we in Windows, we chose to use fonts in Opentype format.

1.6.12 PDF

When Urban had fine-tuned our layout, we got the document back. We linked together the high-resolution images, and exported print-ready PDF/X files directly from Indesign. By using the printing house's ICC profile, all the RGB images were print adjusted together with the exported PDF.

1.6.13 Proofing

Finally, only doing a Preflight in Adobe Acrobat Professional remained in order to make sure that no fonts were missing or that no low-resolution images had slipped in. Then we sent the PDF files to the printing house via FTP. For the work on the old book we sent Syquest disks and external hard disks with all the material.

1.6.14 Reflections

Many of the new technical aids that have arrived since we produced the first edition of *A Guide to Graphic Print Production* have visibly simplified our own work. The new work methods have made possible a completely new flexibility in many regards: working together on a manuscript, image adjustments, mounting in layout, reorganization, working together with Urban who worked on another computer platform, having the photographs stay in RGB, being able to proof the material ourselves before printing. And last of all, but not least, production has gone faster and we have been able to devote more time to the creative work.

02.

the computer

Which screen is best for graphic production? Hard disk, tape or DVD – what works best for long-term storage? What is a utility software? Should you use USB or Firewire? How does Ethernet work? What affects the speed of the Internet? Should you send files via email or FTP? Can you connect to the Internet with a cell phone?

THE COMPUTER IS the foundation for all graphic production. It is used to create text, edit images and design a layout then merge all of these elements into a printable PDF file. Large amounts of material can be archived and stored on a computer. Computers also run printing presses, as well as other peripheral equipment essential to graphic production, like scanners and Raster Image Processors (RIPs). In this chapter, we will cover the basic components of the computer and its functions. For graphic production the graphic quality of the monitor and the need for storing and quickly transporting large files is of great importance. Therefore we will pay extra attention to monitors, different methods of storage and other types of networks. First we will look more closely at the computer.

Generally speaking, a computer consists of two main components, software and hardware. Hardware refers to the physical apparatus of the computer. Items such as the hard disk, the processor, random access memory, (or RAM, as it is commonly known), and the network interface card make up some of the basic elements of a computer's hardware. Additional hardware includes accessories like the monitor, keyboard, mouse, modem, printer, scanner, to name just a few. Software refers to the programs run by the computer. Basic computer software includes an operating system, utility software, drivers, applications and plug-ins.

THE COMPUTER
Essentially all production of graphic originals is done on this type of computer. The Macintosh computer is most commonly used by the graphic industry, but PCs are becoming more usual.

2.1 The Computer

Hardware refers to all the physical components of a computer – the things that you can touch. There are many different brands of computer hardware on the market today. In the graphic production industry however, Macintosh has long been the most commonly used. Now IBM PC-compatible computers with Windows as an operating system have become more and more common. The hardware for a PC is fundamentally the same, however. In addition, the most common programs are basically identical for the two operating systems and their hardware.

2.1.1 The Processor

The heart – or rather, the brain – of the computer is the central processing unit, or CPU. It performs all calculations - in other words, it does all the thinking – for the computer. The CPU executes all the functions requested by the operating system and other software, and controls the operations of the rest of the computer's hardware. Examples of central processing units are Motorola's Power PC-processor in Macintosh computers, or Intel's Pentium processor in Windows-compatible computers. The speed of processors is given with their clock frequencies in hertz, Hz. For example 4 GHz, or gigahertz, is 4 million clock cycles per second.

2.1.2 The Data Bus

The data bus handles the flow of information through the computer's hardware components. It transports data between different areas of the computer, like the random access memory, the video compatible care and the hard disk. The data bus is connected directly to the CPU, and the capacity, or "speed," of the data bus determines how fast information can be sent through the computer and at what speed it operates.

2.1.3 RAM – Random Access Memory

Random Access Memory is high-speed memory that is emptied each time you turn off your computer. Say, for example, you want to edit an image using Photoshop. The information necessary to execute this particular function – in this case, the actual Photoshop program, as well as the image – is transferred from the hard disk, via the data bus, into RAM so that you can use it efficiently. Remember to save your document on the hard disk because it will be lost once you turn off the computer. It is important for the computer to have enough internal memory so that the computer is not forced to use the considerably slower hard disk as memory. Photo retouch and video editing are examples of work requiring a lot of memory.

2.1.4 ROM – Read Only Memory

Some components of a computer's operating system are installed and stored in the ROM – Read Only Memory. They are the most fundamental elements of the operating system, including the information that the computer needs to start up, and to search for the rest of the operating system on the hard disk.

2.1.5 Integrated Circuits – IC

The CPU, RAM and ROM consist of so-called "integrated circuits", otherwise known as computer chips. These chips are mounted on a large circuit board called the "motherboard". All of the integrated circuits are connected to one another on the motherboard.

2.1.6 The Hard disk – Disk Memory

The hard disk is a storage medium where information, such as files or programs, is saved. When you open these saved items, they are retrieved from the hard disk. This type of information can also be stored and retrieved from external media such as a CD, DVD or other peripheral storage devices [see 2.6].

2.1.7 CD/DVD

Computers usually have a CD and DVD reader. Sometimes the equipment can write disks and has what is called a CD or DVD burner [see 2.6.4].

2.1.8 Video Card

A video card controls the display you see on your monitor. A good video card will allow for a wide range of colors, high resolution and high refresh rate, provided that you have monitor compatible with these capabilities. If you have several video cards or video cards with several outputs, you can connect several monitors to the same computer. Some video cards can even be connected to a TV.

2.1.9 Network Interface Card

To make communication between multiple computers and peripherals in a network possible, the computer is equipped with a network interface card. For example, the network interface card allows such functions as printing and sending and receiving mail within a network configuration [see 2.8.1]. The network interface card has built-in connectors so that a network cable can physically connect it to printers and/or other units in the same network. Alternatively, the network interface card is used in wireless networks that communicate via radio signals instead of cables. The network interface card can be built into the computer's motherboard.

2.2 Connections

2.2.1 Sound and Video Input Ports

Most computers have a connection for a microphone or other sound input devices, and one for sound output devices like speakers and headphones. The quality of the soundboard determines the quality of sound recording and play-back on your computer.

Some computers have a connection for receiving or playing video. It requires special hardware called a video card. Many computers now have a built-in video card. (However, digital video cameras are usually connected with Firewire.)

2.2.2 Serial and Parallel Ports

A serial port is used to connect the keyboard, mouse, basic printers, and other control devices to the computer. In modern computers these ports are being

BINARY NUMBERS

Most people know that computers speak a digital language comprised entirely of ones and zeros. But what does that actually mean? Simply put, every memory unit in the computer can only ave a one or a zero. So every piece of information you want to save must be translated into a series of ones and zeros.

For example, say you are trying to save a number on a computer. The computer cannot use the decimal system that we ordinarily use, in which every digit in a number can assume one of ten diffferent values, zero to nine. Instead, the computer works with a binary notation where every digit in a number must be expressed using 0 and 1. A binary digit is called a bit. Every new bit in a number has double the value of the previous bit, and is added to the number. The first bit in a number can assume the value $1\times2^0=2^0$ or $0\times2^0=0$, the next bit $1\times2^1=2$ or $0\times2^1=0$ and the next $1\times2^2=4$ or $0\times2^2=0$ and so on. This means a bit can only have $2^1=2$ values, 0 and 1. Three bits can represent $2\times2\times2^1=2=8$ values, 000–111, or the equivalent of 0–7 in the decimal system.

With the binary system, it is common to work in groups of eight bits, known as bytes. This system provides $2^8=256$ levels of value, 0000 0000–1111 1111, the equivalent of 0–255 in the decimal system. For example, the red, green and blue sources of light in the pixels have 256 distinct colors each in a computer running with eight bits.

In the table below, you find an example of how to calculate the decimal equivalent, 163, to the binary number 1010 0011.

Binary		Position Value		Decimal
1	×	2^7 (=128)	=	128
				+
0	×	2^6 (=64)	=	0
				+
1	×	2^5 (=32)	=	32
				+
0	×	2^4 (=16)	=	0
				+
0	×	2^3 (=8)	=	0
				+
0	×	2^2 (=4)	=	0
				+
1	×	2^1(=2)	=	2
				+
1	×	2^0 (=1)	=	1
				163

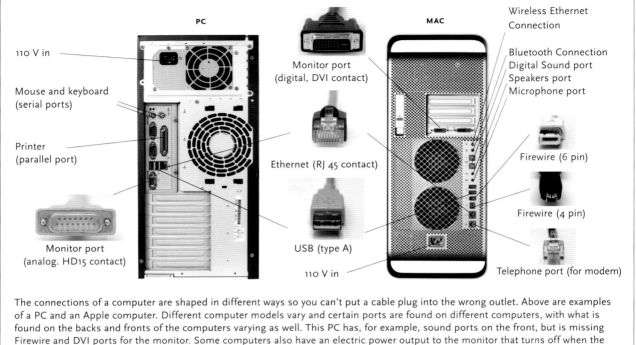

The connections of a computer are shaped in different ways so you can't put a cable plug into the wrong outlet. Above are examples of a PC and an Apple computer. Different computer models vary and certain ports are found on different computers, with what is found on the backs and fronts of the computers varying as well. This PC has, for example, sound ports on the front, but is missing Firewire and DVI ports for the monitor. Some computers also have an electric power output to the monitor that turns off when the computer is turned off.

replaced more and more by USB ports, and, for certain applications, by USB 2, Firewire and Bluetooth.

2.2.3 SCSI, USB and Firewire

SCSI, (pronounced "scuzzy") USB 1.1 and 2.0, along with Firewire are relatively high-speed interfaces. SCSI is an older type that is used mainly for hard disks, CD players, CD burners and scanners on Macintosh computers. USB 1.1 is used to connect mouses, keyboards, printers, monitors, digital cameras, handheld computers and many other kinds of equipment. USB 2.0 as well as Firewire transfers data at very high-speeds and works well with high-speed equipment such as hard disks, DVD burners and scanners [for more about SCSI, USB and Firewire see 2.7].

2.2.4 Bluetooth and IR

Bluetooth and infrared light (IR) are relatively slow wireless communication techniques suitable for connecting a wireless mouse or keyboard, cell telephones and handheld computers, etc., that don't require very large amounts of data. Bluetooth uses radio signals and IR uses invisible light [for more about Bluetooth and IR see 2.7.3 and 2.7.4].

2.2.5 Monitor Connections

Traditionally computers have an analog connection to the monitor. IBM-PC compatible computers and Macintosh computers uses different ports but the same type of monitors can be connected. Modern computers often have different kinds of digital connections for monitors, DVI, that come in several varieties [see 2.4].

2.2.6 Modem Ports

Most computers today come with built-in modems. There is a port where the telephone cable can be connected directly to the computer for modem communication.

2.2.7 Ethernet

A connection to network cabling via Ethernet is built into the mothercard on most computers. The port is the some regardless of what transmission speed is supported (10 Mbit, 100 Mbit or 1 Gbit). Most new computers also have built-in capabilities for wireless Internet [see 2.8].

2.2.8 Power Supply

Although it does not really contribute to the computer's functions, the power supply is the largest component in the computer. The power supply transforms the 110 or 220 volts of the outlet to line voltage, the voltage the computer is working wit, usually 12 and 5 volts.

Laptops usually have a small transformer on the power cord. It supplies the computer with the right power supply – usually between 12 and 20 volts.

2.3 What Makes a Computer Fast?

When you talk about how "fast" a computer is, what you are usually talking about is the "clock Speed" of its processor – i.e., something like 4 GHz. Clock speed is a measurement of how many calculations the processor can make per second. But there are other things that help determine the computer's speed. For example, the transmission speed of the data bus plays a major role. The faster it can send the information, the faster the computer becomes.

The computer also has something called a cache memory. Cache memory stores frequently accessed data for fast retrieval. The larger the cache, the more room for storing quickly accessible information.

2.3.1 Memory

The size of the internal memory, RAM, is also important, particularly if you work with large image files. The more RAM a computer has, the less information it needs to store on the considerably slower hard disk.

2.3.2 Video Card

Working with moving or large images also requires that the video card has a relatively large RAM, - also called video RAM or VRAM so that refreshing the screen won't slow down.

COMPUTERS AND THE ENVIRONMENT

DANGEROUS PARTS
A computer is made up of almost a thousand different parts, of which at least half are toxic to the environment. They contain everything from lead, mercury, arsenic, cadmium, chrome, PVC plastics to flame retardant material. A CRT screen can contain up to 2 kg of lead.

SHORTER LIFESPAN
The number of computers disposed of has increased with the decreased lifespan of computers. They used to last four or five years – now they last about two. If the number of monitors thrown out in the USA reaches 100 million, that means that 200,000 tons of lead is being disposed of.

RECYCLING
Since computers are environmentally unsafe as waste, it is important to recycle them. Companies exist that specialize in recycling computers and electronic equipment. They take apart the equipment and make sure the different components are properly taken care of. Gold, silver, copper, steel and aluminum are some of the materials salvaged from computers.

Displayed here are two types of screens. On top is a CRT screen and on the bottom an LCD screen.

2.3.3 Other Programs

If you have several programs running at once, or have installed many programs or extensions and these are being run in the background, it takes away power from the computer. Turn off any programs that are not being used and eliminate any extensions that drain power from the processor if the current program seems to be running slowly.

2.4 The Screen

Two kinds of screens are widely used today, Cathode Ray Tube (CRT) screens and Liquid Crystal Display (LCD) screens. CRT is the large, fixed screen that you usually see with desktop computers, and LCD is the flat-screen format used in laptop models, although LCD is becoming an increasingly popular option for desktops as well.

Regardless of the type of monitor, the images you see are the result of the illumination of thousands of tiny light sources. In color screens, the light sources are divided into three sections, one red, one green and one blue [*see Chromatics 3.3*]. If you look very closely at an active computer screen or television screen, preferably with a magnifying glass, you will see these three distinct colors of light arranged in tiny groups all across the screen. Each group is called a "pixel" – the word is derived from the phrase "picture element." Pixels are packed tightly in uniform rows across the screen.

Each light source in the pixel can vary in brightness. If you juxtapose the three colors (R, G and B) in different intensities, the brain will perceive a specific color. The exact color perceived depends on the relative intensities of the three colored light sources. Essentially, all colors can be created on the color screen [*see Chromatics 3.2*].

2.4.1 CRT Screens

The Cathode Ray Tube, or CRT, screen looks and functions like a television screen, with a higher resolution – i.e., the screen has more pixels and can there-

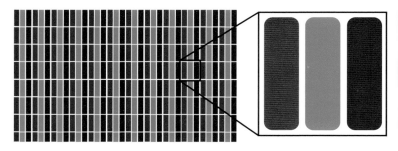

WHAT A SCREEN CONSISTS OF
A screen consists of many rows with small pixels. The pixels have light sources divided into three sections, one red, one green and one blue. Depending on the strength of the light, the three light sources can create all the colors that the monitor can display.

fore show more detailed images. The pixels are phosphorescent, and light up when bombarded with electrons. These electrons are generated by an electron gun. A cathode and a ray tube control the stream of electrons so that they hit the right pixels at exactly the right time, in order to produce the desired image. CRT monitors emit magnetic radiation, and their safety has been called into question as a result. This, along with the bulky size and weight of the CRT screen has encouraged a move towards the use of LCD screens with desktop computers.

2.4.2 LCD Screens

Liquid Crystal Display, (LCD) is a flat, low-power type of screen. This technology is based on polarized liquid crystals that are illuminated from behind. Because they are polarized, the liquid crystals can be "opened" or "closed" to the background light. It works exactly like two polarized lenses being rotated at 90 degrees to each other. At the start, no light is let through. By the time the 90-degree rotation has been achieved, all the light is let through. The LCD technique is used in black and white as well as color.

Besides the fact that LCD screens used to be more expensive than CRT screens, LCD screens have had problems with color calibrations since the colors and brightness varied widely depending on what angle the screen was viewed from. The screen had a different appearance depending on its position in relation to the viewer's head. Such problems have diminished, and today the more expensive flat screens are as good technically as high-quality CRT screens. There are also types of flat screens – for example plasma led and non-led screens – but they are not in use for graphic design at this time.

2.4.3 Refresh Rate

In LCD screens, the nature of the liquid crystals can restrict the image. When images change rapidly, the crystals cannot always open and close fast enough to control the luminous flux accordingly. As a result, LCD screens are not necessarily the best choices for displaying moving images. Sometimes moving images leave "tails," or the entire image is distorted.

The phosphorescent pixels in CRT screen only glow for a short while after being hit by an electron. In order to maintain an image on the screen, the pixels must constantly be re-lit. In the CRT screen, a beam of electrons sweeps across the screen surface, pixel by pixel, row by row, until all the pixels are illuminated. Then this process immediately starts over with the first pixel. The screen of a CRT screen stays constantly illuminated as long as the electron gun has time to hit all the pixels on the screen before the first pixel it hit goes dim. The speed of the beam of electrons moving across the monitor limits how fast the screen image can be changed. The faster the beam moves, the steadier the image. The speed at which all the pixels are re-lit is measured in Hertz (number of screen changes per second). To avoid a flickering image, the beam of electrons has to sweep across the screen at least 50 times per second, or 50 Hz. Today, monitors often have a speed of 70 Hz or more.

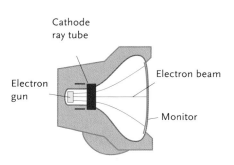

CRT – AT A GLANCE
The electron gun fires electrons controlled by the cathode ray tube. When the electrons hit the monitor they illuminate the phosphor in the pixels.

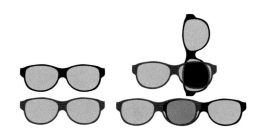

LCD – HOW IT WORKS
By rotating each crystal in the LCD screen 90 degrees, no light is let through. It works exactly like in the example of the Polaroid glasses above.

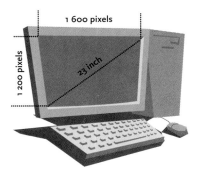

THE SCREEN SIZE
The screen size is measured diagonally across the screen and is stated in inches (for example 23 inches as above). Although not visible on the exterior of the monitor, the entire screen is measured. The screen resolution is stated in pixels, width × height (for example 1600 × 1200 as above).

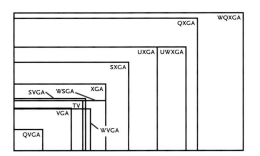

SCREEN RESOLUTIONS

QVGA	320 × 240 pixels
VGA	640 × 480 pixels
TV	768 × 576 pixels
SVGA	800 × 600 pixels
WVGA	854 × 480 pixels
WSGA	1 024 × 576 pixels
XGA	1 024 × 768 pixels
SXGA	1 280 × 1 024 pixels
UXGA	1 600 × 1 200 pixels
UWXGA	1 920 × 1 200 pixels
QXGA	2 048 × 1 536 pixels
WQXGA	2 560 × 1 600 pixels

2.4.4 Screen Size

Screen size is measured in two ways. The first measurement is the same as for televisions: the length of the diagonal of the screen, stated in inches. The second measurement is the number of pixels the screen holds, width by height. The smallest freestanding screens for computers are 15 inches and have 1024 × 768 pixels. Laptops can have smaller screens.

A typical screen size used in graphic production is 2 inches and has a maximum of 1600 × 1200 pixels. There are screens up to 30 inches in size for graphic production with a resolution of up to 2560 × 1600 pixels and there are extreme screens on the market with up to 3840 × 2400 pixels resolution. The density of the pixels determines the screen's resolution. The higher the resolution, the smaller the pixels and the greater the detail. The resolution is determined not only by the screen size, but also by the video card. A screen with a resolution of 2560 × 1600 pixels requires, for example, a two-channel digital connection to take advantage of its full resolution.

2.4.5 Screen Quality

There is a whole list of parameters that determine screen quality, technical possibilities and suitability for graphic production. Size, resolution, pixel size, sharpness, viewing angle, color range, contrast and brightness are basic factors.

In graphic production it is also important for the screen to have good color reproduction and that it can adjust colors in the correct way. In this context it is also important for the screen to be stable over time so that is doesn't vary a lot during the course of the working day, and that is doesn't suddenly change so that is has to be corrected very often.

The screen has to be even so that, for example, it doesn't show a darker picture in the corners, resulting in an image appearing different depending on where in the screen it is located.

The color range of the screen determines its suitability for color work as well as image handling. Even if the color range of the screen's RGB is in general much larger than printing's CMYK, there are just a few screen that show all the colors that can be reproduced in high quality four-color print reproduction. The RGB standard, Adobe RGB (1998) is created to cover the whole color range of printing, and only a few expensive monitors can reproduce Adobe RGB (1998).

For LCD screens the problem is that often the viewing angle is small, that is that the viewer has to be in exactly the right position to see a good screen image – the larger the viewing angle, the better. Another typical problem with LCD screens is that they are relatively slow in refreshing the screen image, which can cause problems with moving images.

For CRT screens the refresh rate is an important factor in avoiding a lot of flickering. CRT screens can also have a more or less flat screen face and give off reflections from their surroundings that disturb the screen appearance. The screens can also have built-in functions, like speakers, USB hubs, the capability of being turned vertically, capability of being connected to several computers simultaneously, and so on. The method of connecting them to the computer can also vary. Some monitors have an analog connection, while others have a more modern digital connection, which diminishes the risk of image disturbance from the computer.

In order to attain good color quality, sharpness and refresh rate, even greater demands are placed on the video card inside the computer, and the kind of connection. A fast video card with a lot of memory facilitates good image quality, and to get good image quality on screens with very high resolution a digital connection is necessary.

2.4.6 Screen Connections

Older computers, monitors and most computer projectors use an analog VGA connection with a HD15 connector. Some older Macintosh computers have instead a smaller connector with a mini-VGA.

Many flat screen monitors that are digital also have a connection following the DVI standard (Digital Visual Interface), which means the signal doesn't have to make a detour via analog. DVI was developed by a number of leading computer and monitor manufacturers and exists in an assortment of varieties: DVI-Analog (DVI-A), which only supports analog transfers and therefore works well with traditional CRT monitors. DVI-Digital (DVI-D), which only supports digital transfers. DVI-Integrated (DVI-I) which supports both digital and analog transfers and therefore works with both digital and traditional monitors.

DVI can also have one or two channels. One channel can send 165 million pixels per second with 24 bits per pixel to the monitor. With one channel, called Single Link, the computer can handle monitors up to UXGA resolution, (1600 × 1200) pixels, with a refresh rate of 60 Hz. With two channels, called Dual Link, you can use monitors with very high resolution, HDTV, (1920 × 1080 pixels), QXGA resolution, (2048 × 1536 pixels), or even higher.

The connectors on the DVI cable are constructed so that they can't be connected incorrectly, despite the fact that the connector for DVI exists in five variations, depending on whether it handles analog and/or digital transfer, and it the digital transfer occurs in one or two channels. Monitors and video cards that are exclusively digital cannot be connected to analog, for example. But they can be connected to equipment that handles both analog and digital signals.

The DVI standard also supports DCC (Display Data Channel) and EDID (Extended Display Identification Data) that enables the computer to communicate with the different extensions of the monitor, for example in order to show wide-screen images.

To connect a monitor or projector with a VGA connection to computers with DVI requires that the DVI signal be analog, as well as the use of a DVI-A to VGA adapter for connecting the signal.

Mini-DVI is a version of DVI that is used in some Apple laptops and, with the help of an adaptor, can be converted to DVI, VGA, S-video or composite video.

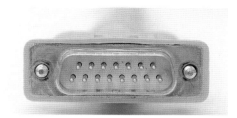

HD15 CONNECTOR FOR ANALOG MONITOR CONNECTIONS
HD15 is the traditional connector for analog connections of monitors and has 15 pins.

DVI CONNECTORS FOR DIGITAL MONITOR CONNECTIONS
DVI connectors exist in six varieties, depending on if they handle analog and/or digital transfers, and if the digital transfer occurs in one or two channels:

- **DVI-A** 12+5 pins (only analog)
- **DVI-D** single-link 18+1 pins (Digital 1 channel)
- **DVI-I** dual-link 24+1 pins (Digital 2 channels)
- **DVI-I** single-link 18+5 pins (Digital 1 channel + analog)
- **DVI-I** dual-link 24+5 pins (Digital 2 channels + analog)
- **Mini-DVI** is a version of DVI that is used some Apple laptops and which, using an adaptor can be converted to DVI, VGA, S-video or composite video.

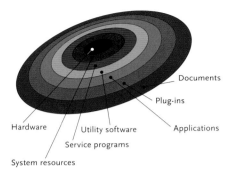

STRUCTURE OF A COMPUTER
The operating system (the red areas) functions as an interpreter between hardware and software.

Documents
Plug-ins
Hardware
Utility software
Applications
Service programs
System resources

2.5 **Software**

We will start by looking at computer software. In this section, we will cover the general definition of operating systems, utility software, drivers, applications and plug-ins, as well as some software specific to graphic production.

2.5.1 **Operating Systems**

The operating system is a computer's most fundamental software. Without it, the computer wouldn't even be able to start. The operating system runs all of the basic computer functions: displaying the user interface, receiving and translating signals from the computer keyboard, saving files to the hard disk, etc. It also facilitates communication between any additional programs you are using and the computer's hardware. Examples of operating systems include Mac, OS, Unix, Windows XP, LINUX and DOS.

2.5.2 **Utility Software**

Utility software works with the operating system to provide additional operating functions above and beyond the basic set-up. An example of utility software that is used in graphic production is one that improves the basic system's typeface or color management capabilities.

2.5.3 **Drivers**

Drivers are software that allows the computer to work with "peripheral" hardware, like printers and scanners. Peripheral devices almost always come packaged with their own driver software, which needs to be installed on the computer's hard disk in order for the device to work.

DIFFERENT KINDS OF SOFTWARE

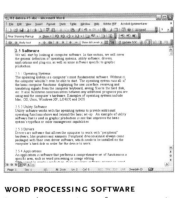

WORD PROCESSING SOFTWARE
In word processing software you write and edit texts.

IMAGE EDITING SOFTWARE
In image editing software pixel-based images are created and manipulated.

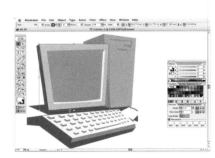

ILLUSTRATION SOFTWARE
In illustration software you create object-based graphics.

2.5.4 **Applications**

An application is software that performs a comprehensive set of functions in a specific area, such as word processing or image editing.

With regard to graphic production, there are many software categories: word processing, image editing, illustrations, page layout, preflight programs, imposition, and database software. In addition, there are many specialized software programs for particular graphic production needs. We will look more closely at the most important of these specialized applications in later chapters.

Word processing applications allow you to efficiently write and edit text in a simple format, prior to applying design elements. These applications are not meant to handle advanced design, typography, Postscript or four-color processes, and therefore are not used directly in the production of original artwork. Some commonly used word processing programs are Microsoft Word and Word Perfect from Corel.

Image editing applications are tools for graphically manipulating images intended for printing. One of the most popular image editing programs is Adobe Photoshop.

Illustration applications allow you to "draw" or create original images with the help of the computer. Commonly used programs are Adobe Illustrator and Macromedia Freehand. There are separate applications for "3D" illustration; 3D Studio and Strata Studio are two such programs.

Page layout software merges text and images into complete, laid-out pages. These applications allow you to output for professional graphic production.

Preflight programs are used to control that the original digital print is technically correct – for example, if the images have enough resolution and if the fonts are included. Examples of programs with preflight extensions are Adobe Acrobat Professional and Enfocus Pitstop.

ARCHIVE SOFTWARE

Archive software is a form of database software that is used to keep track of different documents and make them able to be located via metadata in their files.

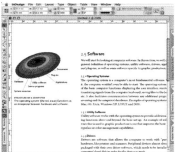

LAYOUT SOFTWARE

In layout software you put text and images together and create pages, as well as produce printed originals

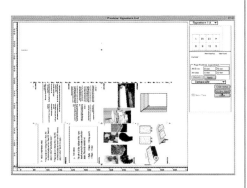

IMPOSITION SOFTWARE

In the imposition application, you "position" the pages into a digital imposition that can be output to a large film.

Imposition applications enable you to place several pages on the same film for a complete film assembly, rather than mounting several individual films (one for each page). Examples of imposition programs include Imposition from DK&A, Strip It from One Vision, PressWise from Scenicsoft and Impostrip from Ultimate [*see Prepress 7.6*].

Database applications are primarily used to archive and index production items, including text files, image files and page files, as well as film and sound files. Common programs are Fotostation from Fotoware, Portfolio from Extensis and Cumulus from Canto [*see Layout 6.15.6*].

Other common programs for graphic production needs include OPI software, trapping software, preflight software and software that controls RIPs, imagesetters and printing presses. In addition, administration software is also commonly used, to handle orders and invoicing, for example. We will look more closely at the most important of these specialized applications in later chapters.

2.5.5 Plug-Ins

Plug-ins are also called add-in programs or extensions. They are small programs that enhance existing applications software with additional functions. Sometimes plug-ins can cause problems when handing off documents from one computer to another. You may need the plug-in that was used to create a particular file on another computer in order to open it on yours.

2.6 Storage Media

Most people store the files they use frequently on their computer's hard disk. When you want to save files during production, make back-up copies, transport files, carry them in your pocket, or archive files different demands are placed on the storage media. When saving during production, storage media needs to be large and fast, but can require a lot of space and doesn't have to be so durable or cheap. In this case the hard disk is most appropriate. Short-term archiving, creating back-up files, and storing information for transportation and/or distribution all demand a secure and inexpensive storage medium. It doesn't matter if you can only write on a storage medium one time. For these reasons CDs and DVDs are well suited for this type of storage. For portable equipment the memory has to be small and durable, and so flash memories are used in digital cameras and music players, etc. For copying with security concerns, the storage medium must be able to record very large files and be inexpensive per gigabyte, but doesn't have to be very fast. Magnetic tapes are used under these circumstances, although hard disks and DVDs can also be used.

2.6.1 What Differentiates Storage Media?

The different devices for storage differ mainly in terms of price per gigabyte, storage capacity, read/write speed, access time, security, life span, standardization and availability. A medium's access time refers to how long it takes for your computer to find a file stored on that medium. Read/write speed is a measurement of the amount of data that can be read or written per second by

---

AREAS OF USE FOR DIFFERENT STORAGE MEDIA

- **Hard disks** – Production and transport. Very large storage capacity.
- **CD** – Archives and transport, music, small storage capacity.
- **DVD** – Archives and transport, film, medium-sized storage space.
- **Tape** – Secure copies of large amounts of data
- **Flash memory** – Portable equipment, small storage capacity.

PRICE DIFFERENCES

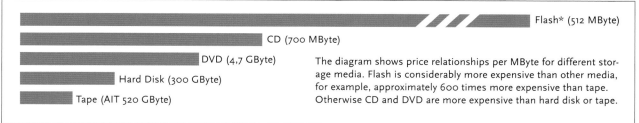

Flash* (512 MByte)
CD (700 MByte)
DVD (4,7 GByte)
Hard Disk (300 GByte)
Tape (AIT 520 GByte)

The diagram shows price relationships per MByte for different storage media. Flash is considerably more expensive than other media, for example, approximately 600 times more expensive than tape. Otherwise CD and DVD are more expensive than hard disk or tape.

a particular storage device. Security concerns how sensitive the medium is to damage from things like electromagnetic fields or physical shocks and jolts. The life span of a storage device is determined by how long information can be stored on it and still be read, and also by how physically durable the medium is. If a storage device is so commonly used that the industry has developed a standard version, made and sold by a variety of manufacturers and stores, the device is considered to be standardized and widely available.

2.6.2 Hard disks

Hard disks are the fastest storage medium when it comes to access time and read/write speed. They are generally used for storage during the course of a project, when speed is a priority. All computers have a built-in hard disk, called a local hard disk. If you need more hard disk space, you can add external hard disks to your computer via the SCSI, Firewire or USB port. External hard disks can also be used for the transportation of larger amounts of data. Hard disks are also built into powerful media players for music and video. These can often be used for file storage and transport just like an external hard disk.

A hard disk is made up of a number of disks stacked on top of each other. Each disk is coated with a magnetically sensitive layer. When you save information to the hard disk, these surfaces store information in magnetic "tracks" that the computer then reads and interprets as a series of ones and zeros. The hard disk's read/write head travels very close to the rotating disks when recording or reading information, making it sensitive to jolts while in operation. If the hard disk is jolted while in use, the read/write head may collide with the disks and damage the information on them. This is known as a "head crash."

ADVANTAGES AND DISADVANTAGES OF HARD DISKS
+ They are very fast
- They are relatively expensive
- They are sensitive to magnetic fields
- They are sensitive to jolts

HARD DISK

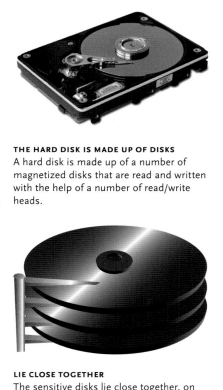

THE HARD DISK IS MADE UP OF DISKS
A hard disk is made up of a number of magnetized disks that are read and written with the help of a number of read/write heads.

LIE CLOSE TOGETHER
The sensitive disks lie close together, on above the other, and the information is stored on both sides.

THEORETICAL SPEEDS FOR DIFFERENT STORAGE MEDIA

Media	Read Speed	Write Speed	Access Time
CD	8 MByte/s	2,4 MByte/s	0.1 s
DVD	22 MByte/s	22 MByte/s	0.1 s
HD	150 MByte/s	150 MByte/s	0.009 s
Tape (DAT)	3 MByte/s	3 MByte/s	50 s
Flash	20 MByte/s	16 MByte/s	0.00000002 s

Note that the true speeds are lower but that the speed increases as new technology is developed.

SEQUENTIAL STORAGE
Tape stores information sequentially, that is all the data is stored in sequence along the length of the tape.

DAT WITH READING DEVICE
A DAT tape has space for up to 4 GBytes. When you want to read a file from a tape the reading device has to wind the tape until the sport where the file has been saved. This means that you don't have immediate access to files in the same way as magnetic or optical disks.

STORAGE SPACE ON TAPE
DAT tape – up to 72 GByte
AIT tape – up to 520 GByte
DLT tape – up to 80 GByte

ADVANTAGES AND DISADVANTAGES WITH TAPES
+ Tapes are cheap per MByte
- They take up large physical storage space
- They have a long access time (winding time)
- They are sensitive to magnetic fields
- They have poor standardization (different programs for the same type of tape)

CD AND DVD
A CD has space for 700 MBytes, a DVD 4.7 to 17 GBytes.

If the computer has two or more hard disks, you can link these together in such a way that they back up each other's contents for increased security. In this situation you would usually utilize a technique called Raid (Redundant Array of Independent Disks), which means that if one hard disk breaks, its contents are divided up between the remaining hard disks. If the broken hard disk is replaced by a new, the material from the broken one is automatically put onto the new one from the other hard disks.

2.6.3 **Tape**
Tape is also a magnetic medium. There are many different kinds, but the most common include DLT (Digital Linear Tape), DAT (Digital Audio Tape), AIT (Advanced Intelligent Tape) and Exabyte. Tape is a relatively slow medium, but its cost per megabyte is low and it can store large amounts of data. It is generally used as a backup medium, but it can also be effective for long-term archiving, especially when you have to store large amounts of data. All tapes require compatible read/write devices connected to the work station. Tape is not a particularly standardized medium; for example, there are often several different programs for a single type or tape. In order for a computer to read a tape, it often needs to have the exact program originally used to save the content of the tape. This makes the tape an inefficient means of distributing files.

Tapes store information sequentially, which means that in order to access the information you need, you have to locate the place on the tape where it was recorded. This means that you do no have immediate access to files like you do with magnetic disks and optical storage media. Tape access times can be several seconds, compared to access times of few milliseconds for magnetic or optical disks. On the other hand, tapes have relatively fact read/write speeds.

As with magnetic disks, the tape's surface is magnetized, making it sensitive to damage, from electromagnetic fields. Tape is also exposed to physical wear and tear when it is written to or read. Manufacturers estimate the life span of mast tapes at around 5–10 years.

2.6.4 **CD and DVD**
CD (Compact Disk) and DVD (Digital Versatile Disk) come in a number of different versions, and are best suited for archival storage and transport of large amounts of data. They are based on optical technology and do not have magnetized surfaces like those media we have just discussed. This means that they are insensitive to damage from electromagnetic fields and, therefore, safer for long-term storage. Optical disks are generally not rewriteable or erasable, which also makes team a very safe option for archiving. Though not as fast as magnetic disks, they have a life span of anywhere from 10–30 years, and are relatively inexpensive. There are two types of optical disks: CDs (Compact Disks), and DVDs (Digital Versatile Disks).

The CD us the most common type of optical storage medium and the most standardized of the optical media. Most computers have built-in CD drives, and are able to read CDs without any special programs. Because the CD is standardized, widely distributed, and cannot be erased, it makes an excellent medium for distribution and archiving. CDs do require careful handling, because the

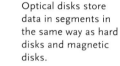

SEGMENTED STORAGE
Optical disks store data in segments in the same way as hard disks and magnetic disks.

READING A CD
Reading a CD is done with a low-grade laser that lights the track. The beam is reflected by "land". Going from groove to land is interpreted as one, while unchanged status is interpreted as zero.

disks can be scratched or damaged fairly easily. CDs generally have a storage capacity of 700 megabytes.

CDs produced in large volume are called CD ROMs (Compact Disk-Read Only Memory). CDs you produce with your own computer are called CD-R (Compact Disk Recordable). Another development of the CD-R technique is CD-RW (Compact Disk-Re-Writable). These rewriteable CDs allow you to delete or record over existing files. When a CD-ROM is produced, a master disk is created. Then a printing form of the master disk is made from which you print all the CDs needed for distribution. CD-ROMs are used for distribution of computer software, for example.

To produce your own CD-Rs or CD-RWs you need a special CD read/write drive and the accompanying software [see below].

The DVD (Digital Versatile Disk or Digital Video Disk) is a type of optical disk. The DVD is based on CD technology, but DVDs store information more densely, giving them the capacity to hold much more data than a CD.

Just like CDs, there are several types of DVDs. Video is stored on DVD-video, music on DVD-audio, and all other types of data on DVD-ROM. Writeable DVDs have two standards known as DVD-R or DVD+R, and there are three different kinds of rewriteable DVDs: DVD-RW, DVD-RAM and DVD+RW. The reason for the different variations on rewritable DVDs is that different manufacturers have launched or chosen to follow different technologies. In practice, DVD-R and DVD+R are pretty much alike and both can be read in most DVD readers. These are usually marked DVD-+R. Most DVD burners also handle both formats and are marked DVD-+RW.

There are different kinds of disks for DVDs that are supported by different standards. The disks can either be written on one side or on both sides, in

DVD STANDARDS

- DVD-ROM
- DVD+R/RW
- DVD-R/RW
- DVD-R DL
- DVD-RAM
- DVD+R DL

ABBREVIATIONS FOR CD AND DVD

ROM – Read Only (printed disk)
RAM – Random Access Rewritable
DL – Double Layer
R – Recordable once
RW – ReWritable

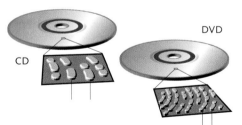

STORAGE TECHNIQE OF CD AND DVD
The CD is built of a continual spiral pattern with grooves and ridges. The tracks and ridges in a DVD are closer together than on a CD and therefore they can store more data.

CONSTRUCTION OF CDS AND DVDS
A CD physically consists of three layers: a foundation layer of polycarbonate, an information layer with a reflective aluminum coating, and a protective layer of varnish. Like an analog record album, information stored on the CD is laid out in a continuous spiral track. Along the spiral track are its and elevations that have been burned into the CD's surface by a powerful laser. A low-powered laser illuminates and "reads"

these variations, and the computer translates them into a series of ones and zeros. Transitions from pits to elevations are interpreted as ones, whereas no change in transition is interpreted as zeros. The difference between a DVD and a CD is that the tracks on a DVD are denser than those on a CD. A DVD can also build on several layers with the Dual Layer or Double Layer Technique, which gives it the possibility of double layers. A DVD can also be double-sided. A

double-sided DVD with double layers gives a four-layer capability, compared to a single-sided disk with one layer.

COMPACTFLASH

CompactFlash (CF) is based on the PC card standard. It is used in digital cameras, mp3 players and handheld computers, among other things. Note that the CF card can also be based on hard disk technology, and in that case is a much more sensitive memory.

SECURE DIGITAL

Secure Digital (SD) is a relatively small memory card and the most common and most inexpensive. It is used in cell telephones, digital cameras, handheld computers, etc. The name Secure Digital stems from the fact that the card is equipped with copying protection to protect against copyright infringement with music, etc. Secure Digital cards are less sensitive to static electricity than other memory cards.

MINI SD

This is based on the same standard as SD but 60 percent smaller. It can be used in SD readers with an adapter.

TRANSFLASH

Transflash ((TF) is a very small memory card based on the mini SD standard. It is used, for example, in cell phones.

MEMORY STICK

Memory Stick (MS) is a card developed by Sony and is used almost exclusively in Sony equipment, and is therefore one of the most expensive cards.

Memory Stick DUO is a variation of the same card. Memory Stick PRO is a further development of MS format that is not compatible with earlier MS cards.

MULTIMEDIA CARD

Multimedia card (MMC) is a relatively small and thin memory card. It is a less common type of card.

SMART MEDIA

Once smart media cards (SM) were quite common in digital cameras, etc.

XD, PICTURE CARD

A small and relatively expensive memory card that is used in Fuji and Olympus cameras.

one or two layers on each side. Single-sided disks with one layer can store 4.7 GB of data, while those with a double layer (or dual layer) can store up to 17 GB, that is between 7 and 28 times as much data as a CD. To handle double layers, special DVD readers/writers are needed. These can also handle disks with single layers. In graphic production DVDs are used for distribution and long-term archiving.

The equipment for writing CDs and DVDs is called a reader and a burner. The burners can also read the disks, and units for DVDs also handle CDs. Modern DVD equipment generally supports most DVD standards. To handle dual layers, however, special devices are necessary.

The speed of the burner is usually given according to how fast they can read written disks. The speed is given in how many times faster the unit can read the disk versus a normal music-CD or film-DVD, for example 52 times, normally indicated with 52×. A CD that can normally play up to 80 minutes of music (700MB) can be read in 80 minutes/52 = approximately 1.5 minutes.

2.6.5 Flash memory for Portable Equipment

Flash memory is used in equipment that requires small, durable memories where the information is stored even when the power is shut off. However, flash memories don't have to be as quick and inexpensive as other storage media. They are built into different equipment such as music players or digital cameras in the form of exchangeable memory cards. Flash memories are extra durable since they contain no moving parts, and information is stored in well-enclosed memory circuits.

There is an array of different kinds of memory cards that build on the flash technique, and that have been developed by different manufacturers. A few common ones are Compact Flash, Secure Digital and Smart Media. Overall they are the same practically speaking, but different equipment is built for different types of cards. A certain camera manufacturer may have chosen one type of card, while another may have chosen something else for the cameras they make. What differentiates cards, regardless of the kind, is the size of the memory as well as the speed of reading and writing.

The memory size varies from a few megabytes to a number of gigabytes. Reading and writing speeds are low compared to other storage media. The speed is usually given in the number of ×, where × means 150 KB per second. A card with a speed of 133 × can thus be read 133 × 150 KB = 19.5 MB/second.

Flash memory is expensive, several hundred times more expensive that other storage media per gigabyte. On the other hand, this type of memory is usually only used to store smaller, temporary files, for example pictures in a camera until they are moved to a server.

2.6.6 Older Types of Storage Media
Storage media must continually become faster and have increasing storage capacity. Older types of storage media are therefore continually being replaced by better ones.

Previously produced material can still be found stored on older types of storage media, and they must still be able to be read. We will go through some of these technologies.

2.6.7 Magnetic Disks
All removable magnetic disks required special disk drives which were connected or built into the computer. Everyone who was going to read the disk had to have the same disk drive. In general these were inexpensive, but the price of the magnetic disk per megabyte was high. In addition to floppy disks, disk drives and magnetic disks were often sold by the same company.

The removable magnetic disks were writeable, and were constructed and functioned the same way a hard disk functioned. They were covered by a protective plastic cover. Just like hard disks this medium was relatively sensitive to jolts and magnetic fields. Today these removable magnetic media have been replaced by optical media with larger storage capacity and security as well as a lower cost. Below we will look at the most common ones to have been discontinued.

FLOPPY DISK
A floppy disk has space for 1.3 Mbytes.

2.6.8 Floppy Disks
Despite their small storage space (maximum 1.3 megabytes), sensitivity and slowness, for a long time floppy disks were the most common removable storage medium. Floppy disks were used for transporting or distributing, for example, programs, text files, logo types and smaller image files.

2.6.9 Zip and Jaz
Other types of removable magnetic disks were Jaz and Zip. They were quick and held large amounts of data, usually 1 GB or 100 MB, respectively. They were used in general for transporting large files, for example layout and image files, between different users.

ZIP- DISK/DRIVE
A ZIP disk holds 100, 250 or 750 MBytes.

USB TYPE A
Connects normally
in the computer

USB TYPE B
Connects normally in
peripheral equipment
such as scanners and
hard disks

USB TYPE MINI B
Connects normally in
smaller equipment such
as camera or small hard
disks

FIREWIRE

FireWire

1394 9-PIN
Is used with 1934b
connections, also
called Firewire 800 by
Apple.

1394 6-PIN
Is used with Firewire
400.

1394 4-PIN
Is used with Firewire
400, normally in small-
er peripheral equip-
ment such as camera
or small hard disks.

2.6.10 Syquest

Syquest disks were for a long time the most wide-spread technology for storing files during graphic production. The disks held 44, 88 or 200 MB.

2.6.11 Magnetic Optical Disks

Magnetic Optical Disks (MO disks) were and middle stage between optical and magnetic media that combined the advantages of both. They were writeable, but at the same time very safe for long-term storage. An MO disk usually stores 1.3 GB of data, but there are types that store up to 99 GB.

2.7 Communication

Data has to be transmitted between computers and peripheral devices such as keyboards, scanners or external hard disks. This transmission of data can happen in a number of ways: by cable or wireless, depending on the need for speed. There are a number of different technologies for data transmission. Sometimes it is even necessary to connect computers to each other, or have them share the same equipment such as servers or printers. In this case we are talking about a network.

2.7.1 USB

USB, or Universal Serial Bus, is a kind of serial port. It is called a serial port because the signals (ones and zeros) are transmitted serially on the same circuit. Parallel ports are those where the signals are sent simultaneously on many parallel circuits.

USB version 1.0/1.1 makes it easy to connect accessories such as a mouse or keyboard to a computer since the computer itself knows which unit is being connected, and you can connect units with the computer turned on. USB 1.1 is so powerful (up to 12Mbits/sec) that it can serve as a connection for monitors, CD players, printer, simple scanners, etc. A USB can also provide a power supply for low-power equipment and up to 127 devices can be connected. USB version 2.0 has a transmission speed of 480 MB/sec – powerful enough for hard disks, video connections and other demanding transmissions. The USB version 2.0 is compatible with equipment based on USB version 1.1. Computers can supply units with power with the USB version 2.0 – up to 2.5 watts.

There are three types of contacts for USB – Type A that usually ends in the computer, as well as Type B and Type mini-B that ends in external equipment such as hard disks and cameras.

2.7.2 IEEE 1394 Firewire

A very powerful standard for data transfer is IEEE 1394, commonly known as Firewire or iLink as Sony calls the standard. The transmission speed of this device is as high as 400 MB/sec, which makes it appropriate for use with high-resolution video data, hard disks, etc. The maximum cable length is 4.5 meters. It's successor, Firewire 800, has a transmission speed of up to 800 MB/sec, and a maximum cable length of 100 meters and up to 63 computers and external units can be connected together to one Firewire port.

Firewire 800 follows the IEEE 1394b standard that allows a transmission speed of up to 3200 MB/sec and is at the same time compatible with older Firewire versions. Firewire can, in contrast with USB, be connected directly between different computers. Both Firewire and USB can be connected while computers and other units are running – so called "hot swap" – and the computer finds and recognizes connected units – "plug and play."

2.7.3 Bluetooth

Bluetooth is a technology for wireless computer communication via radio signals over a short distance – up to approximately 10 meters. The technology can be used for many things – for example connecting computers with cell phones or handheld computers, wireless mouses and keyboards, etc.

Bluetooth can replace transmission using IR (infrared light), and in many cases USB 1.1.

The technology has a transmission speed of up to 720 Kbit/sec, and up to 7 connections to different equipment can be done simultaneously. Bluetooth sends via 2.4 GHz – the same frequency as many wireless networks and the transfer can, if needed, be protected with encoding.

2.7.4 Infrared Light – IR

Many computers, cell phones, handheld computers, etc, have the technology built in to communicate wirelessly via invisible infrared light – IR [*see Chromatics 3.1*]. With the aid of infrared technique, you can, for example, connect a handheld computer with the Internet via your cell phone.

The units that are to communicate must be a few inches apart and have their IR ports facing each other. The infrared light can easily be disturbed by strong sunlight. The transmission speed with normal IR communication is maximum 4 MB/sec.

2.8 Network

Network and computer communication are areas the have a central role in graphic production today. With a network you are able to share units such as printers, servers and modems with other computers in your network. You can also make the information on your hard disk available to other computers in your network as well as share a common database with other computers in your network

Here we will discuss concepts like LAN and WAN, network components, and the basics of transmission technique and capability. We will also look at different types of networks, dial-up communications and the Internet. First we will define what a network is.

2.8.1 What is a network?

There is more to a network than just the physical cables or the base station for wireless Internet. A network can be defined by meeting the presence of network cables and special network interface cards in the computers and/or the presence of network protocol that manages network communication.

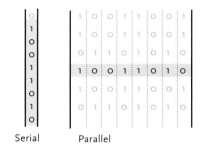

Bluetooth™

OLDER TYPES OF COMPUTER COMMUNICATION

SCSI

The SCSI device is an important feature of the Macintosh computer. SCSI (pronounced "skuzzy"), stands for Small Computer System Interface. It is a high-speed interface that connects directly to the data bus and can transport huge quantities of data. Using the SCSI interface, you can connect the computer to external hard disks, scanners, and other devices that handle large amounts of information. Even within the computer SCSI is used to send information between for example the hard disk, the CD and the internal memory.

Regular SCSI can transfer data with 24 MB/sec, which corresponds to 3 MB/sec. The successor, SCSI-2 or Fast SCSI, yields 80 MB/sec compared with 10 MB/sec. SCSI is used relatively seldom today.

SERIAL AND PARALLEL PORTS

On most older computers there are serial and parallel ports. A serial port is used to connect the keyboard and the mouse.

Parallel ports are usually used to connect the modem and printer, but also other peripheral equipment can be connected with these ports. On modern computers these ports have been complemented by or replaced with USB and Firewire ports.

Serial   Parallel

SERIAL AND PARALLEL

In a serial port all bits (ones and zeros) follow each other. In a parallel port all bits are transmitted in parallel in different paths.

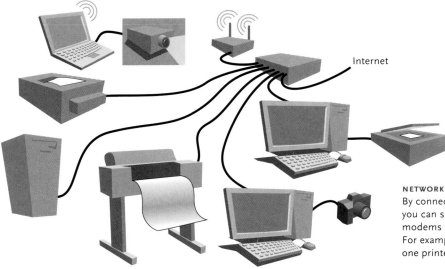

Internet

NETWORK
By connecting peripheral devices to a network, you can share units such as printers, servers, and modems with other computers in your network. For example, all computers in a network can share one printer.

DIFFERENT TYPES OF NETWORKS

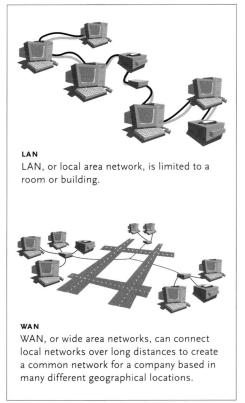

LAN
LAN, or local area network, is limited to a room or building.

WAN
WAN, or wide area networks, can connect local networks over long distances to create a common network for a company based in many different geographical locations.

Networks are sometimes defined by their geographical reach. A network limited to a room or a building is usually called a Local Area Network, or LAN. Networks that range over long distances, connected LANs, are called Wide Area Networks, or WANs. A company with offices in many different cities might use a WAN to connect all of its locations. You can use the Internet, or, for added security, you can use dedicated fiber-optic cables over long distances to connect several LANs to WAN. A network consists of a number of components, including cables or wireless base stations, network interface cards, network protocols and different network devices. The network interface facilitates communication between the computer and the cables. Network protocol contains the rules for how this communication should be conducted. Network servers and other network units such as repeaters, hubs, bridges, switches and routers are the physical components needed to build a network. We will now look more closely at the different elements of a network.

2.8.2 The Ethernet Network Standard
Ethernet is the most common type of standard for how a network should be constructed, and it specifies the how network's hardware, cables, contacts, base stations, network cards and network units should be set up. The standard that is actually called EEE 8023, also sets up certain traffic regulations for communication in the network. In an Ethernet network TCP/IP is usually used as protocol for communication.

2.8.3 Cable-connected Ethernet
Normally the Ethernet network is built on an number of users' computers and the servers are connected with a network unit, normally a switch. Several network units are connected with each other to build a larger network. The manner

of building up a network is usually called and star-shaped network, and gives a natural segmentation to the network so that the load within the star, or segment, doesn't unnecessarily affect the computers in another star [*see 2.8.17*].

Wire-connected Ethernet has been developed in different versions. Different generations of Ethernet build on similar technologies, which makes it easy to upgrade a network. You can use all kinds of cables and even combine different types of cables within the same network.

The most common today is Ethernet category 5, or Fast Ethernet, also called 100 base TX. It has a theoretical transmission speed of 100Mbit/sec, that is 12.5 Mbyte/sec, which is 10 times faster than the older Ethernet category 3, so-called 10 base T with a theoretical transmission speed of 10 megabits/sec.

The latest generation of Ethernet is 1000 base T, or so-called Gigabit Ethernet, and it is becoming more common. It has a theoretical transmission speed of 1000 megabits/sec, that is 1 gigabit/sec, which corresponds to 125 Megabytes/sec.

To be able to utilize a certain generation of Ethernet, it is necessary for the computers and the network unit at the other end of the cable to be able to support the same generation Ethernet. In the case where the other unit is not able to support it, the transmission is subject to the slower speed of the older generation. Ethernet can also be used directly between two computers. In this case a special, cross-connecting cable is used, an Ethernet cable.

2.8.4 Network Cables

The type of network cable used in creating your network is important because it determines the speed of the network, i.e., how long it takes to transfer data. The type of cable also determines how large a network can be (different types can carry data over different distances), as well as how secure those transmissions are. There are three main types of network cables: twisted-pair, coaxial and fiber-optic cable. Ethernet today uses either twisted-pair cable, with or without a shield to protect against the electric current, or fiber-optic cable.

Cable choice is generally a question of price versus capability. It is common to combine different types of cables in the same network. In some parts of the network, simple twisted-pair cable is sufficient, whereas areas carrying heavy data traffic over long distances might require capabilities only fiber-optic cable can offer.

2.8.5 Wireless Ethernet – WLAN

Beyond the traditional cable-connected networks there are wireless networks – called ELAN (Wireless Local Area Network). They have a number of advantages such as not having to pull on cables or being tied to one spot on the network. Their weakness is that they are much slower than the traditional networks.

Public wireless networks exist in many places such as hotels, cafés, airports, trains and airplanes. Their speed decreases if the distance increases or there are, for example, thick walls in the way, since these diminish the radio signal.

Most wireless networks build on a variation of an IEEE standard called 802.11. There are principally three varieties used: 802.11a, 802.11b and 802.11g. IEEE is a USA-based standardizing organization (Institute of Electrical and Electronics Engineers).

THREE TYPES OF NETWORK CABLES

From left:
A. Twisted-Pair Cable
B. Coaxial Cable
C. Fiber-optic Cable

A. TWISTED-PAIR CABLE
The twisted-pair cable is the most common and least expensive of the three main types. It consists of insulated copper wires twisted around each other, identical to a regular telephone line. Twisted-pair cables can carry a signal for about 100 meters. After that, electrical noise weakens the signal and the information may have to be retransmitted. This noise is caused by the electrical fields surrounding electrical cables and devices, etc. To provide protection against noise in twisted-pair wiring, shielded twisted-pair wiring has been developed. The shield consists of a protective foil sheath wrapped around the wires.

B. COAXIAL CABLE
The second type of cable, coaxial cable, consists of a copper wire shielded with plastic insulation. The insulation is wrapped in a protective copper insulation, which makes the cable insensitive to noise. A coaxial cable can carry a signal for up to 185 meters. Coaxial cable is very common, and although it is more expensive than twisted-pair cable, it is considerably less expensive than fiber-optic cable.

C. FIBER-OPTIC
Fiber-optic is the third type of network cable. Electronic signals are converted to light pulses in the network interface, which then travel through the glass fibers of the cable. This means that fiber-optic is completely insensitive to electronic noise. A fiber-optic cable can carry a signal for up to 20 kilometers, and allows higher transmission speeds than the two other types of cable. Transmissions via fiber-optic cables are secure because they can't be bugged. Fiber-optic cables are very costly and require expensive fiber-optic compatible hardware.

WiFi

IEEE 802.11B

IEEE 802.11b uses radio frequencies of around 2.4 GHz – approximately the same as Bluetooth, and communicates with a maximum transmission speed of 11 megabits per second, approximately the same rate as 10base Ethernet. This is the most common type of wireless network. It can have up to three base stations in the same place without them competing with each other.

Apple calls its IEEE 802.11b-compatible equipment Airport.

To obtain a higher transmission speed, some 802.11b-compatible networks allow you to use double channels so that the transmission speed can go up to 22 megabits per second.

IEEE 802.11A

The successor to IEEE 802.11b is called 802.11a. 802.11a has a maximum transmission speed of 54 megabits per second. That is half of the transmission speed of the most common type of cable-connected Ethernet and approximately on twentieth of the transmission speed of Gigabit Ethernet. IEEE 802.11b uses a frequency of 5 GHz, which generally covers a shorter range than a network that uses 2.4 GHz. In exchange, you can have several channels, which means that you can have up to 13 base stations in the same place.

IEEE 802.11G

IEEE 802.11g is a variation that communicates using 54 megabits per second on a 2.4 GHz-band, and is at the same time compatible with 802.11b, which makes this type popular. Its span extends farther than that of 802.11a. As with the 802.11b, you can have 3 base stations in the same place. Apple calls its IEEE 802.11g-compatible equipment Airport Extreme.

IEEE 802.11N

IEEE 802.11n is the future standard that is in the process of being developed with a planned transmission speed of 100 megabits per second or higher.

The variation that was first to spread widely was IEEE 802.11b, which sometimes is called WiFi. Today the concept WiFi has widened to include all equipment that supports one of the three standards named.

2.8.6 Base Stations for Wireless Networks

In order to build up wireless networks and connect wireless networks with wire-connected networks, base stations are necessary to receive signals form the computers and to pass on the communications to the wire-connected networks. Base stations are constructed to follow different standards for communications and they require network interface cards of corresponding standards for wireless communication in the computers [*see inset*].

2.8.7 Network Protocol

In order for all the units in a network to communicate with each other, they have to speak in the same language. This is where a network protocol comes in. A network protocol is a set of "rules" governing how computers and other units in a network communicate with each other – similar to the rules of grammar for a particular language. In other words, a network protocol defines how information is packaged when transmitted through a network.

When networks have a combination of MacOS, Windows and Unix computers, it is common to use TCP/IP. TCP/IP is also the protocol used when communicating via the Internet. TCP/IP is the most standardized network protocol and is compatible with most networks.

2.8.8 How TCP/IP Works

TCP/IP stands for Transmission Control Protocol and Internet Protocol. They are two different protocols that work together, each with its own task.

To send a file from one machine to another over the Internet or a local IP-based network, the IP protocol addresses a receiving unit. The sending unit provides an IP address, for example 195.47.247.68. Each unit, computer, printer, etc. in an IP-based network has a unique address. IP numbers are used, therefore, for Web and FTB servers as well.

If a computer in a local network sends a file of several megabytes to another computer, the entire communication is tracked the whole time. The file is therefore divided into several smaller packets, which are then placed together into the original file when all the packets have arrived. In an IP network, the packets cannot be larger than 1.5 MB. Each packet contains information about the sender's and the receiver's IP addresses.

TCP, Transmission Control Protocol, is the standard that monitors the transmission and divides up the files at the sending unit into pieces of data, or segments, that can be sent as IP packets. The IP address leads the packet to the right receiver. TCP makes sure that the packet arrives. When a packet is received, the sender is notified that the next packet can be sent. If no notification arrives the packet is sent again. The last packet of the file contains information that concludes the transfer. TCP contains mechanisms that control the speed of transmission so the network is not overloaded causing the packet to be lost and having to be sent again. TCP also makes sure that the packets are placed together in the right order at the receiver by giving each packet its number in sequence. This is important since some packets can go by different paths over the Internet and can arrive in the wrong order.

The transmission begins with the sending unit opening a connection to the receiver, and both units agreeing on a suitable size of the packets to be sent, as well as any special functions that both units can support, etc. Then the transmission of data occurs and all the packets are sent. When the sending computer has sent all the data, and the data's arrival has been confirmed, the sender sends a message to the receiver and the connection is terminated. Transmissions can cause delays that may be unwanted – for example when sending computer games or sound and video in real time, when you would use a protocol called UDP, User Data Protocol, that doesn't verify that the packet really reached the receiver.

2.8.9 Network Interface Cards
The network interface card is a circuit board, usually installed in a card slot on the computer. The card handles the communication between the computer and the network cables. Different network types require different network interface card. Network interface cards are also built into many printers, and also into some hard disks, projectors and web cameras.

2.8.10 Network Devices
In addition to the elements already discussed, a network also involves one or more servers and a variety of other connected units. The server is a computer in the network that handles the users' common tasks. Repeaters, hubs, bridges, switches and routers are examples of different network devices that are used to expand and/or divide a network into different zones or segments, or to connect different networks. What follows is a short discussion of the most common network devices.

2.8.11 Hubs
Hubs are units used to connect different parts of the network. Network units such as bridges and routers are connected via hubs. There are two types of hubs: active hubs and passive hubs. Active hubs function as repeaters and strengthen the signals that pass through them, while passive hubs only serve as connecting units between network devices.

2.8.12 Switches
Some hubs are built so that every unit that is connected to them always has a certain capacity of the network assigned to them. They are called switches. This means that the computers that are connected to the switches are not affected by other computers in the same network that are not connected to the switches. Switches are important in graphic design production networks with heavy traffic. It is common for most computers in these networks to be connected directly to a switch. Switches are the kind of network device that in the long run diminishes the different computers' influence on each others' performance in the network, since they prevent collisions of packets from occurring and each

THE CONTENT OF THE PACKET

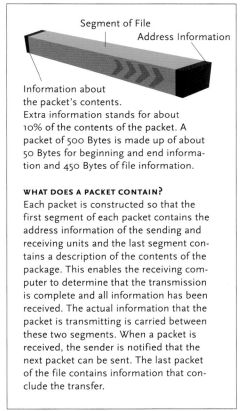

Segment of File

Address Information

Information about the packet's contents.
Extra information stands for about 10% of the contents of the packet. A packet of 500 Bytes is made up of about 50 Bytes for beginning and end information and 450 Bytes of file information.

WHAT DOES A PACKET CONTAIN?
Each packet is constructed so that the first segment of each packet contains the address information of the sending and receiving units and the last segment contains a description of the contents of the package. This enables the receiving computer to determine that the transmission is complete and all information has been received. The actual information that the packet is transmitting is carried between these two segments. When a packet is received, the sender is notified that the next packet can be sent. The last packet of the file contains information that conclude the transfer.

**EXAMPLES OF DIFFERENT
NETWORK DEVICES:**

- Servers
- Repeaters
- Network Hubs
- Bridges
- Routers
- Network

NETWORK UNITS
Network units are usually assembled in a rack like in the image above. Units like routers, hubs and switches look similar.

TASKS OF SERVERS
The most usual tasks are:

- Handling files
- Handling printouts
- Supervising the network
- Communication and email
- Security services
- Security copying/back up

computer can communicate when it wants to. Switches also give the benefit of allowing the computer to use what is called full duplex. This means that it can send and receive information simultaneously, which would otherwise be impossible.

2.8.13 Bridges and Routers

Bridges and routers are used to connect designated parts of a network called network zones or network segments. They only transfer information from one segment or zone to another. This helps minimize unnecessary traffic over the entire network and reduces the competition for network bandwidth.

2.8.14 Repeaters

Repeaters are used to extend the geographical reach of a network. As mentioned above in our discussion of cables, there are physical limitations to a network because a signal carried over a cable weakens as it travels further from its source. A repeater strengthens the signal and allows the network to extend beyond the limitations of cable alone. The repeater strengthens all signals in the cable regardless of origin or destination.

2.8.15 Servers

A server is a central computer that all the other computers in a network are connected to. It is usually a powerful computer that administers all the network devices. It can handle a number of different tasks.

The most common use for a server is storing files shared by many users. Certain applications can allow a server to administer printer or image setter outputs, also known as spooling. Software can also enable the server to provide information on network traffic and capacity, as well as identify which users are connected, and even track their network activity.

The server can also be connected to the Internet with a modem or IDSN. The users in the network can then dial up external computers (and vice versa) via the server. Using these telecommunications devices you can expand your LAN or WAN.

Email is often managed by a server. A network server can manage network security using password programs that allow for different levels of access to open files, but not to save or delete them. Only the user designated to save and delete files is enabled to do so. The risk that files will be modified or deleted by mistake is greatly diminished.

It is simple to administer and automate data backup via the server. Since servers handle frequently and commonly used functions, if you have a large network, you might consider dividing the workload among several servers to maintain optimal functionality and security of your system.

2.8.16 Transmission Technique and Capacity

When working with a network, transmission speed is an important consideration. Transmission speed is measured in bits per second, which refers to how much data can be transmitted over the network in a given amount of time.

Theoretically, the transmission speed of the network is primarily dependent upon what kind of network and cable you are using.

In reality, transmission speed also depends on which network protocol you are using, how the network is constructed and what the traffic volume is. Traffic volume is determined by how many users are connected to the network at any one time and the size of the files being utilized and transmitted. Because computers share the network capacity the transmission speed, the bandwidth, slows down when the traffic volume is high. The bandwidth is the maximum, theoretical transmission speed of a particular means of communication.

2.8.17 What Affects the Transmission Capability of the Network?

A typical network involves a number of users who might want to send information over the network at the same time. Ethernet only allows for transmission of one packet over the network at a time. A soon as a packet has been sent, the network is blocked until the packet has arrived at the correct address. Then it is available again and a new packet can be sent from another computer.

If two users send a packet at the same time, their transmissions will collide and neither packet will reach its destination. To prevent such collisions, a "random number" generator manages the transmission of the packets; this device nearly eliminates the risk for collisions. The more computers in the network, the more possibilities there are for collisions. The more packets transmitted, the more network bandwidth used.

Aside from traffic consisting of file transmissions and print jobs, there is also something called network control traffic. All connected machines have to constantly inform each other that they are available on the network. They do this by frequently sending small questions and answers to each other. The more machines you have in the network, the more network control traffic is generated.

2.8.18 Making the Best Use of Network Capacity

Control traffic diminishes the performance of the network to a certain degree. What has the worst effect on performance is when many computers are sending many large files in the same network. All the computers are dividing up the network's available capacity.

A common way of reducing network traffic is to divide your large network into a number of smaller independent networks called zones. The equivalent procedure in the Windows world is called segmentation. Each zone functions as its own self-contained network, which means, among other things, that no control traffic needs to be sent between machines in two different zones. In addition, the traffic load of one zone is not affected by the traffic load of another. If, for example, you put high traffic image editing computers in one zone, and less demanding page layout computers in a second zone, the users in the second zone would not notice any reduction in their network capacity. Zones make a big difference in network performance: an Ethernet that has not been divided into zones might only achieve half the efficiency of a network with well-designed zones.

NETWORK

PACKETS IN A NETWORK
If you have a file of 10 MBytes and break it into packets of 500 Bytes, the file is divided up into a total of 20,000 packets. Via a standard Ethernet category 5 you can theoretically send 100 Mbit per second, or 25,000 packets of 500 Bytes per second. A file of 10 Mbyte takes hardly a second to transmit.

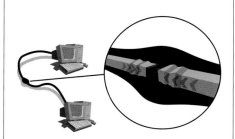

TRANSMISSION COLLISIONS
When two computers send data simultaneously, the two packets collide and neither of them is sent. The data is then resent and a random number generator makes sure the data is not sent simultaneously.

NETWORK CONTROL TRAFFIC
All connected machines have to constantly inform each other that they are available on the network. They do this by frequently sending small questions and answers to each other. The more machines you have in the network, the more network control traffic is generated.

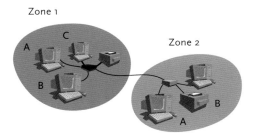

ZONE-DIVIDED NETWORKS
You can reduce network traffic by using routers or bridges to divide the traffic between the different zones. You don't need control traffic between the different zones, for example between machine A in zone 1 to machine A in zone 2. In addition, the traffic load of one zone does not affect the traffic load of another.

Another advantage of zone-divided networks is that they are not as sensitive to technical or mechanical failures. If a cable malfunctions in one zone, only that zone is affected; the rest of the network can continue to function without it. There is a lot to gain by giving careful thought to how your network is constructed.

2.9 The Internet

The "Internet" is the name for the global network that connects millions of LANs and WANs worldwide. TCP/IP is the network protocol for the Internet. The Internet can be reached from almost any computer, either via a dial-up connection or directly through a cable connection. There are many ways to connect a computer to the Internet, or a local network to the Internet. They offer different speeds and are either high-speed connections with constant access to the Internet, or dial-up connections that are made as needed. Common types of connections are dial-up via an analog modem using existing telephone lines, or digitally with ISDN or ADSI technique, via cell telephone, via a cable-TV net, or with a fiber-optic connection.

2.9.1 High Speed Connection

A high-speed connection means that you have a network cable with constant direct contact to the Internet connected to the local network or directly to a separate computer. With such a connection you are always connected to the Internet via an Internet service. Often you pay a set monthly fee for the connection regardless of how much is transmitted. Companies and larger businesses often have a permanent connection to the Internet via fiber-optic cable, with a very high transmission capacity. ADSL and cable modem are considered high-speed connections since they normally have constant contact with the Internet, but use the telephone lines or the cable-TV network for transmission.

2.9.2 ADSL and Cable Modem

There are many ways to connect to the Internet more quickly than with a traditional modem. These means are popularly called broadband connections. There are also different types of wireless connections.

ADSL stands for "Asymmetric Digital Subscriber Links" and is a method that builds on using the phone system's copper wires to transfer information digitally instead of as analog as is done with a traditional modem. The word "Assymetric" is used because the transmission speeds vary when uploading files versus downloading them via ADSL.

Theoretically regular ADSL can achieve downloading speeds of up to 6 Mbit per second, but normally the speed is under 1 Mbit per second. When you upload files, it goes considerably slower than with downloading.

The cable modem is based on the connection with the Internet via the cable-TV network. Normally downloading speeds are around 1 Mbit per second and here too uploading is slower.

In order to be able to connect to the Internet via ADSL or the cable-TV network, you need a special modem. In contrast to traditional modem connections, you often pay a set monthly fee and can stay continually connected without paying extra for use.

2.9.3 Analog Modems

Modems allow computers to communicate over regular telephone lines. With an analog modem, a computer can simply dial up another computer over a phone line. An analog modem converts digital information to analog tone signals that the telephone system can transmit. The receiving modem interprets the signals and converts them back to digital information. The name "Modem" comes from modulera demodulera, that is converting to and from analog signals.

The most common modem can transfer information at a maximum speed of 56,600 databits per second, which corresponds to 7.2 kilobytes per second. The receiving computer can use the modem connection to reach the Internet.

2.9.4 Connecting with a Cell Phone

You can also use a cell telephone to connect to the Internet, and depending on what technique that telephone and service support, different transmission speeds can be reached. You either use a cell phone or a PC card with the same technique. It is based on the GSM standard and can theoretically achieve a speed of 1.4 Kbits per second, GPRS ("2.5G") that reaches a maximum speed of 170 Kbits per second (in practice 30–70 bits per second), GPRS with Edge-technique 400 Kbits per second (in practice 100–200 Kbits per second). With additional help of 3G, transmission speeds of up to 1920 Kbits per second (in practice approximately 300 Kbits per second) be reached.

2.9.5 ISDN

ISDN (Integrated Services Digital Network) is a mode of telecommunication that was once popular within the graphic production industry. ISDN is based on the same premise as a regular modem, the dial-up connection. However, ISDN takes advantage of digital advancements in the regular analog telephone system.

With ISDN you can reach higher transmission speeds than with modems, which works well for text documents and low-resolution images, but it is still relatively slow when sending large amounts of information. ISDN transmission is done via one or more "channels," each with 64 Kbits per second, which corresponds to 7.5 Kbytes per second per channel.

2.9.6 Firewalls

Networks with an external connection, i.e., a modem or the Internet, should be protected from intrusion. This is often done by providing the computer that handles communications with something called a "firewall". A firewall is a specialized program that only allows authorized traffic to pass through the communication systems. There are many types of firewall applications on the market.

MODEM
An analog modem converts the computer's digital information to analog tone signals that the telephone system can transmit. The receiving modem interprets the signals and converts them back to digital information.

2.10 **Transferring Files**

Files are often transferred via the Internet in graphic production. They can contain anything from smaller files for manuscripts, for example, or low resolution touch-ups on high-memory image files, or print-ready PDF files. FTP, email attachments as well as downloads from a web site are the primary methods for transferring files via the Internet.

The speed at which you can send email, transfer files or view web pages on the Internet can vary tremendously. Generally, it is always slower to work on the Internet than on a local network. A dial-up connection combined with a standard modem at 56.6. kilobits per second only allows you to transfer compressed files at a rate of 6 kilobytes per second. Broadband speed can also vary greatly, but a common speed is 1 Megabit per second. This can be compared to a local network with theoretical speeds of 100 to 1000 megabits per second.

The Internet is based on a platform that transmits information to its destination over one of many different paths, which increases the probability of a successful transfer. The Internet first attempts to send information the fastest way possible, but if the transmission does not get through that way, it may take a different, slower path. As a result, it sometimes takes a little longer to receive email or view a web page.

To speed up transfer of files, it is recommended to compress them before sending them. With a compression program you can also combine several files into one. This makes transfer faster and more secure [*see Digital Images 4.9 and Layout 6.14.3*].

TRANSMISSION SPEEDS

Type of Connection	Speed (kbit/s)	Speed (kByte/s)	10 mByte
Modem	56.6	7,1	24 min
ISDN (one channel)	64	8	21 min
High-speed connection	1024	128	1.3 min

THEORETICAL TRANSMISSION SPEEDS
USING DIFFERENT TECHNIQUES
Here is a chart of theoretical transmission speeds for different types of networks and telecommunications. It also contains examples of file sizes and their transmission speeds.

Note that you can never reach these transmission speeds in reality – 60 to 70 % of the stated value is more realistic. Errors, superfluous information and high network traffic, etc. contribute to reducing the transmission speeds.

Type of Connection	Speed (mbit/s)	Speed (mByte/s)	100 mByte
High-speed connection	2	0.25	6 min 40 s
USB	12	1.5	1 min 6 s
SCSI	24	3	33 s
SCSI 2	80	10	10 s
Fast Ethernet	100	12,5	8 s
FDDI	100	12,5	8 s
IEEE 1394/Firewire	400	50	2 s
USB 2	480	60	1,7 s
IEEE 1394b/ Firewire 800	800	100	1 s
Gigabit Ethernet	1 000	125	0,8 s

2.10.1 Email Attachments

Email is electronic messages sent between two computers. The message is received in the recipients email server where the recipient can get his messages. A message can also be sent to more than one email address at a time. Email can carry attachments between computers. Any digitized file can be attached to an email text document and low-resolution images are frequently translated into email attachments. Some limitations can exist:

- The sizes of the attachments can be limited by the recipient's email server.
- The attachments cannot be handled by the recipient's operating system.
- Virus protection for the recipient's computer can block some types of files.

Email is a simple way to send files, and works best when a certain person is to receive the files and the files are relatively small.

2.10.2 FTP

FTP, or File Transfer Protocol, is a standard for transmitting files between two computers on the Internet. You can log on to another computer with FTP and put/get files your own. Both the sender and recipient must have FTP programs. There are many special FTP programs, but also newer web browsers handle FTP.

With FTP you can either leave the files with the recipient's server yourself, or let the recipient get the files from his or her own FTP server, or place the files with an FTP server for a third party.

FTP seldom has size limits for the files, but often only permits connection to the server with a user name and a password.

FTP is the fastest protocol for transmitting files via the Internet and works well with larger files, but can seem a little more difficult to use than Web transfers or email attachments.

2.10.3 Http/Web transfer

Transfer of web pages and displaying images on the Web happens using a protocol called "http" (hyper text transfer protocol). It can also be used for uploading files to a web server in the same manner files are loaded onto an FTP server. As a user, you then choose, via a web page, which files should be sent over. The only thing you need is a normal web browser. This makes the method easy to use, although a little slower than an FTP transfer.

FTP – FILE TRANSFER PROTOCOL
FTP, or File Transfer Protocol, is a standard for transmitting files between two computers on the Internet. You can log onto your computer with FTP and send/receive files from another. Both the sender and recipient must have FTP programs.

03.
chromatics

Why do images and colors look better on a monitor? Do you have to adjust the colors differently for different printings? Why can't you print in RGB mode? Why is a black t-shirt warmer than a white one? Why are logotypes usually defined in Pantone colors? Is there a connection between RGB and CIE? How is an ICC profile created? Which ICC profile should you use? Why do colors look different on the monitor, in printouts and when offset printed?

THE FIELD OF CHROMATICS is the basis of all graphic production and getting colors to be consistent is one of the most difficult areas, practically speaking. The reason for this is that the human eye can perceive considerably more colors than can be reproduced on paper. Therefore we have to compromise and try to attain a level of reproduction that is good enough. Chromatics deals to a large degree with light and how the human eye perceives colors, and how we describe and manage those colors on the monitor and in print.

In this chapter we will cover the basic terminology of chromatics, and look at how the human eye perceives color. We will review the most common color models and discuss color mixing. We will look at color reproduction, how to get the colors you want in your printed product, and what you should think about when working with color and light in graphic production. We will also deepen our knowledge of handling color and the ICC, which is the key to getting colors to balance in printing, copying and on display screens.

3.1 **What is Color?**

Color is really just a product of our minds. Our brain sees different colors when our eyes perceive light of different frequencies. Without light there would be no colors. Light is a type of electromagnetic radiation, just like radio waves, but with much higher frequencies and shorter wavelengths. The human eye is only

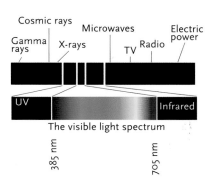

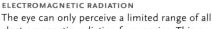

ELECTROMAGNETIC RADIATION
The eye can only perceive a limited range of all electromagnetic radiation frequencies. This portion is known as the visible light spectrum.

THE COLOR OF A SURFACE
Incoming light is filtered when it is reflected by a surface. The composition of the reflected light gives the surface its color.

ALL CATS ARE GRAY?
In the eye cones are used to register the intensity of light. At night, the light intensity is so weak that only the rods function and we perceive no colors in the twilight. Thus all cats are gray at night.

built to perceive a limited range of these frequencies, which is called the visible light spectrum. The visible light spectrum encompasses red hues at around 705 nanometers (nm) through blue/violet hues at around 385 nm, and all the colors in between. The wavelengths just outside of the red end of the spectrum are known as infrared waves, which we perceive as heat energy. Above the violet end of the visible light spectrum, we find what we call ultraviolet light, which has so much energy that it can tan our skin!

When light containing the same amount of each and every wavelength in the visible part of the spectrum hits our eyes, we perceive it as white light. Daylight, for example, contains all wavelengths and is perceived as "white."

When white light falls on a surface, some of the visible spectrum is absorbed by the surface and some is reflected. The color you see is the result of the reflected wavelengths of light. You could say that light is "filtered" by the surface on which it falls. For example, your lawn looks green in daylight because the surface of the grass reflects the green portion of the visible spectrum and absorbs the rest.

3.2 **The Eye and Color**

The retina of the eye is covered with light-sensitive receptors called rods and cones. Rods are sensitive to light, but not to color. We use the rods to see in low light – which is why everything appears almost black and white when it's dark. "At night all cats are gray."

There are three types of cones, each sensitive to a different part of the visible spectrum; one type sees red light, one green and one blue. This combination allows us to see all colors in the visible spectrum – almost ten million shades – many more than we can create in a four-color print.

Color perception varies from individual to individual. Some people have more difficulty perceiving colors than others. This is often referred to as color blindness, more commonly occurring in men than in women. There are different degrees of color blindness. People with color blindness may not be able to distinguish between shades of red and green, for instance.

A color photograph usually consists of thousands of different colors. When printing a color photograph, you cannot use thousands of different-colored inks to match these colors exactly, nor can you display such an image on a

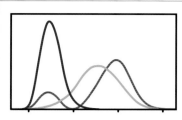

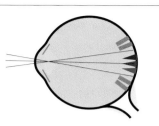

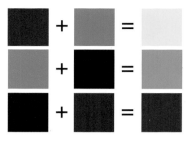

CONES' SENSITIVITY
There are three types of cone in the eye that are each sensitive for one third of the visible spectrum – one for red, one for green and one for blue colors. Above we see how the sensitivities of the three types of cone are divided across the spectrum.

RODS AND CONES
On the eye's retina are two types of sensory organs that register light: rods and cones. Rods are sensitive to differences in the light's intensity, but cannot perceive colors, while cones are sensitive to colors such as red, green and blue.

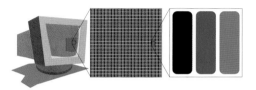

THE ADDITION TABLE
Here we can see how different light sources can be combined to generate the colors yellow, cyan and magenta.

THE PIXEL IN THE MONITOR
Monitors are constructed of a square pattern of pixels. Each pixel has a red, green and blue light source that can be altered in intensity. The somewhat grayish-blue color is created by a dimly lit red light source, mixing together with the green and blue light source.

monitor using thousands of different light sources. Instead, you need to try to approximate the thousands of colors in the photo by mixing together the three primary colors. The reason for the choice of primary colors is the eye's cones and their sensitivity to them. Red, green and blue (RGB) are therefore the basis for mixing colors.

3.3 RGB – Additive Color Mixing

Additive color mixing refers to the fact that you are adding some amount of red, green and blue (RGB) light to a mix in order to create new colors. If you mix together all three colored light sources at their full intensities, the eye will perceive the result as the color white. At a lower intensity, an equal mix of all three primary colors would appear to the eye as a neutral gray. If all the lights are turned off, the eye will see black.

If you mix two colors at their highest intensities, without the third, you will get the following results: red+green=yellow, blue+green=cyan, and red+blue=magenta. If we take a monitor as an example of use of the RGB system, it is made up of many groups of red, green and blue light sources, called pixels. By mixing two or more of the three primary colored light sources in different combinations at different intensities, your monitor is able to recreate the vast majority of colors that can be perceived by the human eye.

Additive color mixing is used in all devices that recreate colors using light, such as computer monitors, TV monitors, and video projectors, but it is also used in devices that capture light, such as digital cameras and scanners. A monitor screen consists of a number of pixels. Each pixel contains three small light sources, one each of red, green and blue. The mixing of the colors of these three light sources gives the pixel its color [see *The Computer 2.4*].

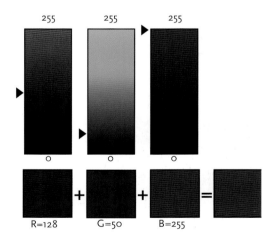

RGB COMBINATIONS
The RGB system creates colors by combining the light from three different light sources. In the computer they are assigned their respective values ranging from 0 to 255.

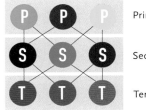

Primary colors

Secondary colors

Tertiary colors

PRIMARY, SECONDARY AND TERTIARY COLORS
Cyan, magenta and yellow are called primary colors in the subtractive color system. If you combine two primary colors you get secondary colors. In the image here are blue, green and red secondary colors. If you combine all three primary colors you get tertiary color. Since all tertiary colors are printed with the help of three printing inks, it is hard to keep colors stable in printing and they can easily vary throughout the edition.

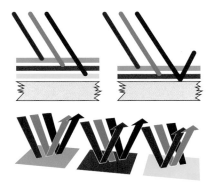

SUBTRACTIVE COLOR MIXING
Different surfaces filter (subtract) different wavelengths of light. The first surface filters out the red light component. Only the green and blue component are left, which, according to the table above, generated the color cyan. The other surfaces are perceived as magenta and yellow thanks to the wavelengths of light their surfaces filter.

RGB – Red, Green, Blue – is an additive color model used for digital images or for color monitor displays. Colors are clearly defined by values indicating the combination of the three primary colors. For example, a rich, warm, red is defined as R-255, G-0 and B-0. When all three primary colors have a value of 0, all three light sources are extinguished and it appears black to us. When all three primary colors have a value of 255 all three light sources are on at the maximum intensity, and it appears white to us. For equal values in between, such as R=100, G=100 and B=100, a gray tone is achieved. With the RGB-system you can normally create 256×256×256= approximately 16.7 million different color combinations.

However, this really says nothing about how the eye perceives the color. In addition, the actual perception of a certain color value is determined by the monitor or scanner that is being used. Thus a particular color value will not necessarily look the same on different machines. Color images that are to be printed have to be converted from the RGB system to the CMYK system. This is an advanced process that can be gone about in different ways. It strongly affects how the image's colors are reproduced in print [*see Prepress 7.4*].

3.4 **CMYK – Subtractive Color Mixing**

In printing, colors are created by mixing three primary-colored printing inks, cyan, magenta and yellow (CMY). This method is referred to as "subtractive color mixing" because the ink filters the white light that falls on its surface, "subtracting" or absorbing all the colors of the spectrum except for the tone it was mixed to reflect.

The color of the reflected light is determined by what wavelengths of white light are allowed in by the ink. Cyan, magenta and yellow each allow in two thirds of the spectrum of white light and filter out one third. These ink colors have been chosen because the third portion that is filtered out is composed of some of the three colors the different cones of the eye are sensitive to: red, green and blue. A magenta surface, for example, lets in the red and blue components of white light, while the green is absorbed. Red and blue light together become magenta and that is why the surface appears magenta to us. In the same manner yellow and cyan each filter out one third so that yellow lets in green and red, but filters out blue, and cyan lets in green and blue but filters out red. Since cyan,

ADDITIVE AND SUBTRACTIVE PRIMARY COLORS

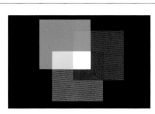

ADDITIVE PRIMARY COLORS
The additive color model's primary colors and their combinations.

SUBTRACTIVE PRIMARY COLORS
The subtractive color system's primary colors and their combinations.

magenta and yellow are each created by two of red, green and blue, CMY are called secondary colors to RGB.

In practice, black ink is used to complement the other three colors, from which comes the abbreviation CMYK and the concept of four-color printing. We will discuss this later in the chapter.

An unprinted surface reflects its own color – white, if the surface is a white piece of paper, for example. In theory, mixing an equal amount of cyan, magenta and yellow ink should create black – with the inks absorbing all visible wavelengths of light, and the light being transformed to heat. A practical example of the transformation of light to heat is when you wear a black t-shirt on a warm summer day. The sunlight hitting the t-shirt is transformed into heat, and you will want to quickly change to a white t-shirt to reflect most of the sunlight.

In the CMYK system the resultant colors are defined by the percentages of CMYK inks in the combination. For example, a warm red color might be C=0 %, M=100 %, Y=100 %, K=0 %. If you don't print with any color at all you will get white, or the color that the paper or the under layer you are printing on has. The amount of ink used can vary freely from 0 % (no ink) to 100 % (complete ink coverage) through large areas of the printed surface being covered with the aid of screen frequency percent values [see Prepress 7.7]. We don't recommend selecting colors based on what you see on your monitor, because it's too difficult to achieve color consistency between the monitor and the final print. Instead, use color guides with examples of printed surfaces in predefined colors. General color guides can be purchased on a variety of paper stocks, but printing houses sometimes supply their own color guides. Color guides define colors in CMYK values. If you are selecting a four-color hue you can use a general color guide, but because the printing conditions vary (paper, printing press, inks, etc.) the result may not always be an exact match. If you want to be absolutely certain about the color, you should try to work with a color guide specific to the printing house that is printing your product.

Although mixing an equal amount of cyan, magenta and yellow should theoretically produce black, the eye actually perceives a dark brownish color, especially on uncoated paper. This is because in practice exactly colored inks have not been produced, and inks do not adhere to each other perfectly. This is one of the reasons the three base colors C, M and Y, have been complemented with black in printing.

Another reason is that inks do not each perfectly filter their third of the color spectrum, and because of this a neutral gray tone is not the achieved when equal amounts C, M and Y are printed on top of each other. When 50 % of each color is used a reddish-brown shade is the result. To compensate for this, a lower value of magenta and yellow is chosen to get a neutral gray tone, i.e. C=50 %, M= 40 % and Y= 40 % [see Prepress 7.4.2].

One more reason to use black ink is because most printed products contain text that is to be printed in black. It is easier to print text with one color than to base it on a mixture of CMY, which would require exact controls of the printing stages to make sure the text was legible.

As with the RGB system, the CMYK system says nothing about how the eye perceives the colors. A specific CMYK combination can also have a varied

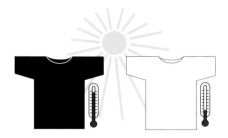

BLACK IS HOT
When you wear a black t-shirt on a hot summer day, the sunlight that strikes the shirt is absorbed and turned into heat. You will feel like quickly changing into a white t-shirt that reflects most of the sunlight instead.

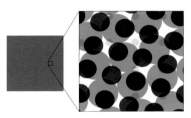

A PRINTED COLOR
Colors are created in print by combining halftone dots of cyan, magenta and yellow in different sizes.

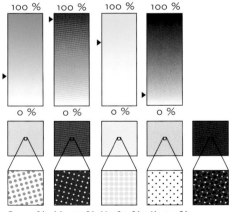

C=30 %   M=90 %   Y=60 %   K=10 %

CMYK COMBINATIONS
The CMYK system creates colors by combining halftone dots of different sizes and colors. How large a part of the surfaces is covered by the respective printing inks is indicated during the process.

THEORETICAL AND ACTUAL BLACK
Cyan, magenta and yellow printed on top of each other should theoretically make black, but actually become closer to a dark brownish gray. For this reason we also add some black printing ink. It is debatable whether the K in CMYK comes from Key color or from the K in blacK.

COLOR TERMINOLOGY

Color range – how saturated colors that can be made by a certain color model in a certain color system or by a certain device, for example a printer or monitor = the size of a certain color space.

Color system – for example, RGB, CMYK, CIELab, NCS, Pantone = different systems for creating or classifying colors.

Color standard – for example, Adobe RGB (1998), Eurostandard, Swop = standardized primary colors in a certain color system. In the case of RGB, also with specific gamma values defined.

Color space – a description of the volume that is created by the color range for a certain color system or a certain color standard.

Color correspondence – how well colors correspond, for example between an original and a print.

appearance, depending on the printing ink, paper stock, and printing press used. The CMYK color gamut is much smaller than the RGB color gamut, which requires great care in correctly converting from RGB to CMYK, using four-color separation for optimal color output.

The eye can also fool us. A particular color can be perceived in different ways depending on the color it is placed next to. A single color may be perceived as two totally different colors when placed next to different shades. This phenomenon is called contrast effect. There is also the situation in which two colors that look identical in a particular light become completely different in another light. For example, a surface perceived as red when lit by white light may be perceived as orange when lit up by yellow light.

For this reason it is important to standardize light relationships when you judge color in photographs, printouts and printed materials. The color of the light is usually given in a color temperature measured in Kelvin (K). Neutral lighting has the color temperature 5,000 Kelvin. This corresponds to a mean value that natural daylight usually has and is therefore used as a reference light for viewing images, printer's proofs and printed material. A higher color temperature yields a bluer light while a loser temperature yields a more yellowish light.

There are many solutions for creating neutral light for viewing transparent images, (slides and negatives), printed photos (copies on paper), printer's proofs and printed materials, for example light tables or desk lamps can provide light with the right color temperature.

3.5 **Pantone and HKS – Two Spot Color Systems**

If you want to print a certain color, but only use one ink for it you use a spot color. Spot colors are primarily used when you want to print certain colors that are hard to reproduce with regular four-color print or if for some other reason

COLOR TEMPERATURE

THE KELVIN SCALE
Kelvin is a measurement of temperature used to describe light sources. When using Kelvin to describe a light source you aren't referring to the actual temperature of the light source. Whet color temperature means is that the illumination of a particular light source is perceived in the same way as a completely black object heated to the corresponding temperature in Kelvin.

The temperature unit Kelvin begins at absolute zero, -273 degrees Celsius or -459.4 degrees Fahrenheit. Thus the Kelvin scale cannot go below zero.

This also means that a temperature stated in degrees Celsius is equal to the temperature stated in Kelvin (K) -273 degrees. For example, 5,000 K = 4,727 degrees Celsius. To calculate the temperature in Fahrenheit the following formula is used: F+9/5 (K-273)+32. Thus 5,000 K would equal 8,541.6 degrees Fahrenheit.

In the Celsius scale the steps of the temperature are called degrees. In the Kelvin scale the steps are only called Kelvin. In other words, no degrees.

	TEMPERATURE OF DIFFERENT LIGHT SOURCES
11 000 K	
10 000 K	• Light from blue sky 11,000 K
9 000 K	• Daylight (cloudy day) 5,500–7,000 K
8 000 K	• Viewing light 5,000 K
7 000 K	• Photo flood lights 3,200–3,400 K
6 000 K	• Light bulb 2,650 K
5 000 K	• Candle light 1,500 K
4 000 K	
3 000 K	
2 000 K	
1 000 K	

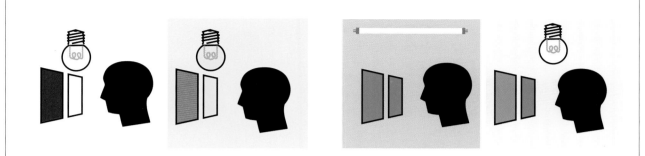

CORRECT VIEWING LIGHT
Because the color of a surface depends on the light falling on is, the same surface can appear as different colors under different lights.

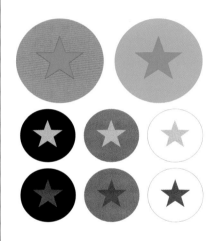

COLOR AND LIGHT PHENOMENON
The eye can play tricks when it comes to colors. A hue is perceived in a particular way because of its surroundings. It can appear to be two completely different hues if it is laid between two different colors. This is the color contrast effect. Another phenomenon occurs when two colors that look completely alike in one different light look different in another. This phenomenon is usually called metamerism and depends on the composition of the light and the printing ink's way of filtering the light.

DIFFERENT LIGHT SOURCES AT THE SAME TIME
Light from different light sources has different color temperatures. In the above images you can see that the light from a window and the artificial light in the room have different temperatures.

you want to avoid screen percent value combinations with four-color print. Pantone and HKS are two systems for spot color. Pantone Matching System, PMS, is a useful but somewhat inaccurate way of describing colors. Pantone colors often appear in a company's profile and logotype, and are very common when printing packaging.

The model is based on the combination of nine different colors that were selected the basis of their usability and hue. Every shade in the system is composed of a defined combination of the nine basic colors. The colors have been divided up according to a number system that makes it easy to select a shade, and the Pantone system incorporates a total of 114 different colors. However you can't see the color by its number. Therefore Pantone sells printed color guides on different papers and other materials so you can choose the color you want, or see how a certain Pantone color will look.

VIEWING BOX
It is important to view original artwork, proofs and prints in the correct light.

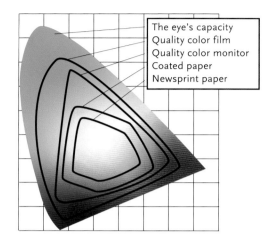

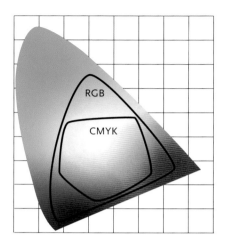

COLOR RANGE

The color range is dependent upon the medium it is reproduced on. The diagram shows what size color range you can obtain with various media. Transparant film has the widest color range whereas newsprint paper has a very narrow color range. As a result, transparant film can display a larger number of colors as well as more saturated colors.

RGB HAS A WIDER RANGE THAN CMYK

The RGB model has a wider color range than the CMYK model. This diagram as a whole represents the sensitive fields of the eye. The three corners represent the eye's cone cells, which are sensitive to red, green and blue.

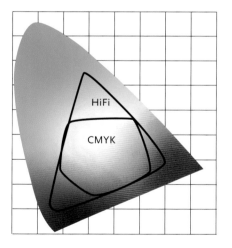

HIFI-COLOR

There are color models that are related to CMYK but generate more saturated colors. They are based on six to eight printing inks and are called HiFi colors because they are very faithful to the original.

The most common usage is six-color separations, adding a green and orange color to CMYK. By adding these colors you get a wider color range and, as a result of that, a better color reproduction in images. In practice, HiFi colors are not commonly used because they are more expensive to print and you need special programs for this type of advanced color separation. In addition, the higher quality rarely makes up for the increased costs.

NOTE

These illustrations are only schematic because they are printed in four colors and cannot reproduce the entire spectrum.

A color model like the Pantone model, which uses unique pigment combinations for each different color, has a greater ability to depict saturated colors. For example, a light yellow color in a Pantone model actually is a light yellow pigment – you don't have to fool the eye with screen percent values as with the CMYK model. When converting from Pantone to CMYK, be aware that you cannot recreate all the colors from the Pantone model.

A typical example is when you print an advertisement in a newspaper. Newspaper printers as a rule can only print in four-color, even if these colors are normally defined in Pantone colors. To predict how a Pantone color will look when it is printed in four-color, Pantone has produced special Pantone to CMYK guides. These contain Pantone colors printed with Pantone inks with their corresponding four-color example so you can see the differences clearly. Some colors remain quite similar, while others vary greatly – for example blue, green and orange hues.

HKS is a color system which, like Pantone, is based on different pigment combinations for each color. It is mainly used in Germany where it is used more than Pantone. The HKS system is based on 88 physical colors, each with 39 shades, totaling 3520 colors. Exactly like the Pantone system there are printed color guides on coated and uncoated papers for all the colors and their corresponding number codes.

3.6 Why Are the Colors Never Right?

Most people who have worked with inks and colors know how hard it is to reproduce them just right. Why is it so difficult to achieve color consistency between the monitor and the final print? And why do they look different on different monitors? And why do the test runs almost never exactly match the final results? We have already discussed some of the most important reasons.

First of all, there is a basic difference between printers and printing presses on the one hand, and monitors and projectors on other. The first group uses the CMYK system with inks, while the second group uses the RGB system with light sources. You can't achieve the same range of colors with inks that you can with light sources, and for this reason you will never achieve a really good color match between the two systems.

Secondly, there can be differences between two pieces of equipment using the RGB system and two pieces using the CMYK system. An example can be the difference between a laser printer and an inkjet printer. Both use CMYK, but the laser printer uses ink powder that is burned onto the paper, and the inkjet printer uses liquid ink that is sprayed on. In the same way there can be a large difference between printing presses, especially if they use different printing techniques with different kinds of ink. As soon as you broach the subject of printouts and inks, there are also the different kinds of paper and their widely varying effects on color reproduction to consider.

Last of all, there are differences between two of the same kinds of equipment, such as between two monitors or two laser printers. For example, if you go into an electronics store you will find that the same image displayed on the televisions will differ, although they all transmit the same image containing

PANTONE GUIDE
To pick the right Pantone color, printed Pantone guides are used.

SEPARATING PANTONE COLORS
Pantone colors that are separated to CMYK often give a completely different color. There are special color guides to facilitate this type of conversion.

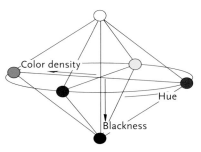

NCS
Natural Color System, NCS, is a Swedish color model that is derived from a visual identification of colors. NCS is used mostly in the textile and paint industries. The NCS model is based on six main colors: black, white, red, green, blue and yellow. It is constructed of divisions into blackness (brightness), hue (color) and color density (saturation) that can be visualized as a double cone image. The division between colors is done in steps that are adjusted according to the eye's way of perceiving colors. There are special conversion guides that translate NCS values into the CMYK model.

the same color values. One of the reasons for this is that the red, green and blue light sources of the monitors can differ from each other.

All this makes it enormously difficult to achieve consistency in colors. RGB and CMYK are "device dependent" color models because the colors will look different depending on the device used. Because these models don't allow for inconsistency among different monitors, prints or processes, they are not appropriate for color management systems. Thus, a color management system that can measure and indicate colors precisely, independently of the device the color is displayed on is necessary.

3.7 CIE – A Device Independent Color System

The CIE-system is the only method to describe colors in an exact and "device independent" way. Commission Internationale d'Eclairage, or CIE, is a color model created by the International Commission on Illumination. The model is based on the results of extensive experiments studying the human perception of color, conducted in the early 1930s. Because each person's sensitivity to color differs, a standard colorimetric observer was created based on the average of the subjects' color perception. It was concluded that human color perception could be described according to three sensitivity curves called tristimulus values. These values, combined with the characteristics of the light falling on a surface and the colors in the light that the illuminated surface can reflect, can be used to very precisely define the color of the surface.

CIELAB and CIEXYZ are versions of the CIE model. CIELAB is a development of CIEXYZ and the system is based on human color perception. Because CIE is based on three different values, you could say that it is three-dimensional, and that it therefore constitutes a certain space – color space. Colors defined in the CIIELAB model are assigned values for L, A and B and in the CIEXYZ model, X, Y and Z, respectively. In the CIELAB system, a movement or change, in the color space (expressed in CIELAB values) is relative to the change in color (expressed in wavelength) wherever in the color space the movement occurs. For example, if you move between two places, or two colors, within the blue spectrum of the color space, the perceived change in color would be identical if the same movement was conducted elsewhere in the spectrum. Regardless of

DIFFERENT COLOR MODELS

Color model	NCS	CIE	Pantone	RGB	CMYK
Meaning	Natural Color System	Commission Internationale d 'Eclairage	Pantone Matching System	Red Green Blue	Cyan, Magenta, Yellow and Black
Purpose	Paint and fabrics	Clear-cut exact definition, determined visually	Spot colors in print	Scanning, image editing, storing	Four-color print
Function	Visual divisions, equal steps	Device independent storage	Pre-defined color proofs, larger color space than CMYK	Additive color model, larger color space than CMYK	Subtractive color model, color space is determined by printing

DIFFERENT DEVICES DIFFERENT RESULTS

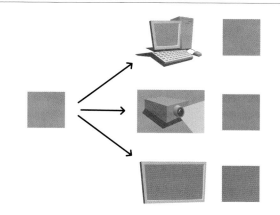

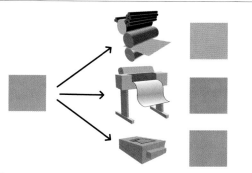

RGB DEVICES

There is a large difference between different devices that use RGB, in spite of their receiving the same signals in. An example can be the difference between a projector and a monitor. Both use RGB but the monitor has a lot of small pixels while the projector has a light bulb whose light passes through the color filter and is projected onto a cloth. This means that the colors are reproduced differently.

CMYK DEVICES

Her can be a large difference between two devices that use CMYK, despite their receiving the same signals in. An example can be the difference between a laser printer and an inkjet printer. Both use CMYK, but the laser printer uses powder ink that is burned onto the paper, as opposed to the inkjet printer that uses fluid ink that is sprayed on. In the same way there can be a large difference between two printing presses, especially if they use different printing techniques using different kinds of ink. This means that the colors are reproduced differently.

IDENTICAL DEVICES DIFFERENT RESULTS

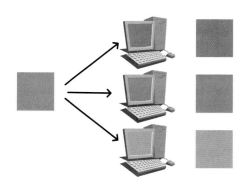

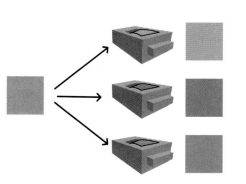

RGB DEVICES

Despite RGB devices being identical, the color reproduction can differ between them. A typical example of this is when you see a number of TV sets in a store and all their images differ from each other color-wise, despite their receiving the same signals. One of the reasons for this is that the monitors' red, green and blue light sources can vary.

CMYK DEVICES

Despite CMYK devices being identical, color reproduction can differ between them. A typical example of this is printers that yield different results, despite their receiving the same signals in. One of the reasons for this is that the printers' inks can vary.

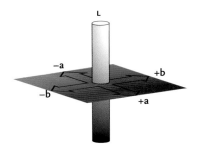

CIELAB COLOR MODEL
CIELAB describes colors with one parameter for the lightness of the color (L), another for green and red (A), and the third for blue and yellow (B).

Different L value, same a and b value

Different a and b, same L value

WHAT AFFECTS L AND WHAT AFFECTS A AND B
The six colors above are defined in CIELAB. In the top row the colors have the same a and b values but different L values. In the bottom row they have the same L value but different a and b values.

where a value change takes place in the CIELAB model, the eye will perceive it as equivalent because the model is based on the eye's perception.

The visual difference between two colors is expressed as ΔE (pronounced delta E). A color change within the color space based on the wavelength, or distance, does not necessarily result in the same ΔE value, because the eye differs in its sensibility depending on the area of the color space. If ΔE is smaller than 1, the eye can't perceive a difference between colors. CIELAB is the model primarily used in the graphic industry when a "device independent" color model is desired, because its definitions of color are based on the eye's perception of colors and the exact physical expression of that.

3.8 RGB Color Standards

The difficulty with an image that is described in RGB is, as we have already discussed, that we can't actually say how it will look. A pixel that is only composed of a full signal in the red channel will of course come out red, but which red is not exactly defined. It will look different on different monitors and printers and you won't be able to tell which version is correct. RGB is at the same time an intuitive way of describing colors in an image. The eye is based on RGB, and the system is the foundation for the monitors, scanners and digital cameras we use in daily production. CIELAB on the other hand makes it possible for us to describe colors and thus a digital image in a precise way. Therefore RGB values have been standardized by relating RGB values to a CIELAB-defined color space.

There are several RGB standards: ColorMatch RGB, Adobe RGB (1998), sRGB, Apple RGB, and others. The various standards have their origins in different areas of use, for example. printing, video, film, TV and monitors. This means that they have their own characteristics and are adapted for different applications. The right RGB-standard has to be selected for the appropriate use. What differentiates the standards is that the base colors red, green and blue are defined in different ways and therefore give different RGB-color spaces. In practice this

LIGHT × SURFACE × TRISTIMULUS=CIE
Normal incoming light is composed of certain wavelengths.

The colored surface reflects some wavelengths better than others.

The eye is differently sensitive to different wavelengths as expressed by the tristimulus curves x, y and z. These correspond to the sensitivity in each of the three cones in the eye of a standard observer.

Multiplying x, y and z respectively with the two other curves will give you three values: X, Y and Z, also known as CIE values.

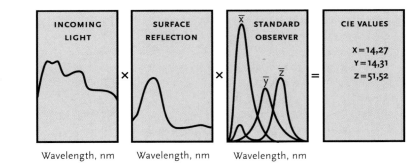

means that the same RGB-value will give different colors in different RGB-color spaces. You can compare this with different definitions for temperature when 20 degrees Celsius and 20 degrees Fahrenheit have the same value but don't describe the same temperature.

The RGB color spaces included in Photoshop are different standards for how RGB is predefined in CIELAB. This means that when you change from and RGB standard to another in, for example, a picture all the RGB values are converted from the old to the new space. This can be compared again with converting a temperature from Fahrenheit to Celsius. The actual temperature remains the same regardless of the number assigned to it. Since different RGB spaces have different color ranges, it is possible to correctly translate some colors from one RGB space to another. The different RGB color spaces largely overlap one another, which means that most colors can be described in all RGB spaces, and translated to them without any problem. However, those colors that lie outside the overlapping sections cannot be translated from one RGB color space to another. For example, with a color space conversion from Adobe RGB (1998) to sRGB, certain colors in Adobe RGB (1998) lie outside the color range of sRGB and hence cannot be described. When such colors are to be described, they have to be changed to another color that can be described in sRGB space. This is taken up further in the discussion on color conversions [*see 3.8.6*].

Most RGB-color spaces have smaller ranges of color than human vision, which is almost entirely represented by CIELAB. The three parameters that define and differentiate various RGB-standards are described below.

3.8.1 RGB Standard Color Range

One characteristic that differentiates RGB standards from each other is how wide their color ranges are. A wider color range means that it can contain more saturated colors. What controls the color range is quite simply how saturated the red, the blue and the green channels are.

In an RGB color standard that is based on 256 shade steps in each channel (red, green, blue) 16.7 million colors can be specified. If the color space is wider there will be a greater distance between colors than with a smaller color range. When an image with highly saturated colors is defined with an RGB standard with a wider color range, problems can arise when it is converted to CMYK, which has a much smaller color range. If you use an RGB standard with a smaller color range, which is closer to a CMYK color range, the changes in colors will be less. Despite this, people usually use an RGB-standard with a larger space in graphic production, for example Adobe RGB. This is because RGB-standards with smaller color ranges often have a wider color range than CMYK but don't fill in the whole CMYK color range, which RGB standards with larger spaces do. The optimal choice in graphic production is to utilize an RGB standard that has the smallest possible color range, but still fills in the whole color range of CMYK [*see 3.13 and 3.5.2*].

3.8.2 The RGB standard's Gamma Value

All the colors in an RGB color space can either be divided up with equal differences in brightness between them, or they can be divided so that there are

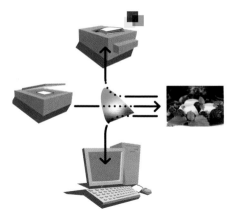

CIE AND RGB
The RGB model that is found in Photoshop is all pre-defined in CIELAB. This means that when you change from a RGB standard to another, all the RGB values in, for example an image, are translated from the old to the new color space. This type of conversion also happens when you are utilizing a device that makes use of CMYK, for example a printer.

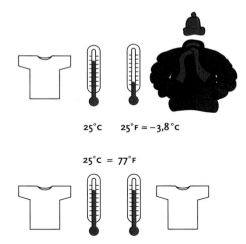

CELSIUS AND FAHRENHEIT
When you change from an RGB model to another, all the RGB values are changed. For example in an image, to the new color space. This can be compared to when you translate a temperature from, or example 25 degrees Celsius, to 77 degrees Fahrenheit. If you don't translate the values between the two RGB standards, it is like saying that 25 degrees C is the same as 25 degrees F.

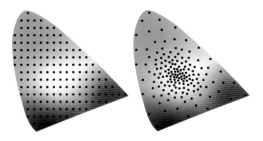

DIFFERENT GAMMAS
All the colors in an RGB color space can either be evenly divided, that is with equally great difference in color between them, Gamma=1, or they can be divided more effectively so that the values are placed more closely together, with less difference in color, where the eye is more sensitive for color variations. This occurs especially in light areas, and the colors can be divided with greater color differences where eye sensitivity is lower, Gamma=1.8–2.2.

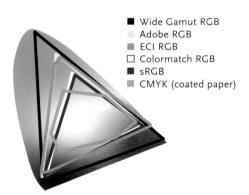

■ Wide Gamut RGB
□ Adobe RGB
■ ECI RGB
□ Colormatch RGB
■ sRGB
■ CMYK (coated paper)

DIFFERENT RGB STANDARDS
The different RGB standards have different color gamuts. They overlap a great deal, which means that most of the colors can be described in all RGB spaces and converted between them without any problem.

more colors, and therefore smaller differences in color can be given in the lighter areas where the eye is more sensitive [*see Prepress 7.7.8*]. We refer to this as using different "gamma values". A gamma value of 1.0 means that the definition of the colors is completely linear, or that all the colors are equidistant from each other in terms of brightness. Normally the gamma value lies at 1.8–2.2 in most RGB standards. This means that the eye's sensitivity has been considered, and more of the 16.7 million steps lie in the lighter color ranges. By taking the eye into account we can divide up the available RGB values where they can best be used and take better advantage of our bits of data and create better conditions for handling images. This is especially important in RGB standards with greater color spaces.

3.8.3 The RGB standard's White Point
Yet another factor where RGB standards differ from each other is the color temperature of the white point. Some color spaces let the whitest white (R=255, G=255, B=255) be 5000 Kelvin ("D50"), while others use 5400 Kelvin ("E"), 6500 Kelvin (D"65") or 6774 Kelvin ("C"), which is a little bluer. Which one is used has little importance since our eye accustoms itself to the white point regardless of its value.

3.8.4 Adobe RGB
Adobe RGB (1998) has a wider color space than ColorMatch RGB and is today the most commonly used RGB standard in professional graphic production. This color space was previously called SMPTE-240M. If you come across images defined in SMPTE-240M, you should use Adobe RGB. Adobe RGB has a relatively wide color space, and only a few monitors manage to display all its colors. Gamma 2.2, D65.

3.8.5 ECI RGB
ECI RGB is a relatively new RGB standard developed by the European Colour Initiative (ECI) and has approximately the same color space as Adobe RGB (1998). Gamma 1.8, D50.

3.8.6 sRGB
sRGB is a standard supported by Hewlett-Packard and Microsoft and is based on the HDTV standard. Hewlett-Packard and Microsoft use sRGB as a standard for non-Post-Script-based flows and for Web browsers. sRGB comes from the color gamut an ordinary PC monitor can display, and this is also its limitation. The color space is much smaller than the RGB color spaces normally used in graphic production and is less suited for images that are to be printed since a large portion of the CMYK color space lies outside it. Gamma ca. 2.2, D65.

3.8.7 Apple RGB
Apple RGB was previously used as the standard RGB color space for Adobe Photoshop and Adobe Illustrator. Its color space is not that much larger than that of sRGB and it is therefore not suitable for graphic production. Gamma1.8, D65.

3.8.8 ColorMatch RGB

ColorMatch RGB is based on the RGB color space of a Radius PressView. Radius monitors are commonly used in professional graphic production and have a relatively small color space, poorly suited for graphic production purposes. Gamma 1.8, D50.

3.8.9 Wide Gamut RGB

Wide Gamut RGB has such a large color space that most definable colors can neither be displayed on a regular monitor nor reproduced in print. 13 percent of Wide Gamut RGB lies outside of the visible area. As with Adobe RGB, it can cause problems when converting from RGB to CMYK because it contains so many colors. Gamma 2.2, D50.

3.8.10 Monitor RGB

Monitor RGB/Simplified Monitor RGB is a method that uses the monitor settings to define RGB color space and is primarily used when you don't work with ICC flows.

3.8.11 CIE RGB

CIE RGB is an old RGB color space that is hardly used anymore. It is still available in Adobe Photoshop, in case you need to open an old image defined in CIE RGB. It has a wider color space than CIELAB. Gamma 2.2, E.

3.8.12 NTSC

NTSC is an old RGB color space used for video. It is available in Adobe Photoshop in case you need to open an old image defined in NTSC. It has a relatively large color gamut. NTSC is the North American standard for TV transmissions. Gamma 2.2, C.

3.8.13 PAL/SECAM

PAL/SECAM is a standard RGB color space used for TV transmissions in Europe and it has a relatively small color gamut. Gamma 2.2, D65.

3.9 Color Management Systems

When working with images in graphic production, it is inevitable that the images will have to be converted between different color systems (e.g. from RGB to CMYK) so that they can be displayed on monitors or reproduced in printers or printing presses. In order to control colors and color reproduction throughout the chain, we need a system which enables us to control how colors are changed when they are converted between different color systems and color spaces.

A color management system converts color values from one device, for example a scanner, to color values from a different device, i.e. a printer, so that the colors reproduced by the printer correspond to those scanned. Where an exact match cannot be achieved, the color management system calculates color values which reproduce the colors of the original as accurately as possible.

WHY WE USE COLOR MANAGEMENT

- So that different devices such as printers, scanners, monitors and printing presses will reproduce colors as accurately as possible

- To make it possible to convert images as accurately as possible between different color models and color spaces.

- To make it possible to simulate different printing results on printers and monitors.

There are three main reasons for using color management systems. The first is to ensure that different devices, such as printers, scanners, monitors and printing presses, will reproduce colors as accurately as possible. The second is to enable images to be converted as accurately as possible between different color systems and color spaces, i.e. from Adobe RGB (1998) to a given CMYK or from Adobe RGB (1998) to sRGB. The third reason is to enable different printing results to be simulated on printers and monitors.

There is a standard for color management, the ICC (International Color Consortium), which contains specifications for how color management systems should work. The standard is the product of extensive cooperation within a group of software and hardware manufacturers from the graphic production industry.

The ICC system itself is based on three different elements. Firstly, the device-independent color space CIELAB, which is the only means to describe colors precisely (it is also known as RCS, Reference Color Space, or PCS, Profile Connection Space). Secondly it is based on ICC profiles, which are correction tables describing characteristics and defects of various devices, such as monitors, scanners, printers and printing presses. They describe how the reproduction of each color in each device differs from given reference values. The third basis of the ICC system is the software Color Management Module (CMM) which calculates color conversions between different color spaces using the values in the ICC profiles.

When working with a color management system, all three of these elements affect the final result. For example, if you scan in an image, the Color Management Module uses the ICC profiles to compensate for errors and defects in the scanner and calculates the values which the scanned colors should have in the device-independent color space.

CIELAB is perhaps the most important building block in the ICC system. It is a device-independent color system, as it describes the appearance of a color rather than telling a device how much of each basic color should be used. RGB and CMYK, unlike CIELAB, are device-dependent color systems, which means that any given percentages in CMYK or values in RGB will look different depending on what device reproduces them. An example of this which we have already mentioned is when the same image appears a different color on different television sets in an electronics store, despite the fact that all of the sets are displaying the same image with the same color values. The same is true of printing presses, where differences can appear because of varying dot gain, print colors, dampening solution, paper, etc.

CIELAB conforms to the eye's perception of a color and is a physically precise description of it. The ICC system therefore uses CIELAB as a reference in order to convert colors from one color system to another.

CIELAB does not replace RGB or CMYK, but rather makes in possible to convert colors precisely and accurately between these systems. If the television sets in the example above had used color management systems, every set would have received all of the colors in the program defined in the signal as CIELAB colors. The CIE Lab values would then have been converted using unique ICC profiles in each television set to RGB signals, which would be unique for each device. These values would then have compensated for the defects in each device, and the colors would have looked the same on all of the sets in the store.

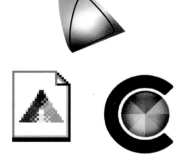

THE ICC SYSTEM'S COMPONENTS

- The device independent color space, CIELab
- ICC profiles
- The color management model
  (CMM, Color Management Model)

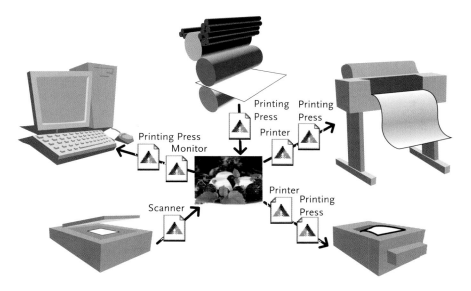

Every device in the production has its characteristics and weaknesses. You can measure these characteristics and sage them in an ICC profile.

To simulate print results on the screen you should use the monitor's profile to compensate for the monitor's characteristics and weaknesses at well as the printing profiles that contains information about the actual printing conditions. When you combine the two profiles you get a good simulation of the final printed product.

If you want to simulate the print results on a colored printout, you combine instead the printing profile with the printer's profile.

3.10 **How the ICC Profile Works**

An ICC profile describes the color space, the strengths and the weaknesses of a device. An ICC profile also makes it possible to simulate the printed result on a printer or monitor.

When, for example a color is shown on the computer screen, it usually isn't what was intended. Orange may appear a little too red on one monitor. By carefully compensating the orange values to make them a little more yellow for that monitor, all the orange shades will be corrected. ICC profiles can help with this kind of color management.

The profile compares how a device reproduces colors in comparison to a preprinted color chart – reference values (based on CIELAB) tell you what the color values should be. The difference between the two values is the basis for the profile and allows you to generate information regarding color compensation, i.e., how to reach the same value as the reference value on the color chart. Colors whose reference values are not included on the color chart are calculated and interpolated by the Color Management Module using two or more reference colors closely resembling the one in question.

There are several programs on the market for creating device-specific profiles, including Profilemaker from Gretag Macbeth, Colortune from Agfa, Printopen and Scanopen from Heidelberg, and ColourKit Profiler Suite from Fuji. Some products have their own systems for creating profiles – including monitors from Barco and Radius, as well as certain color printers.

There are two types of ICC profiles: input profiles and output profiles. Input profiles are for devices that read in images, such as scanners and digital cameras, while output profiles are for devices that display or reproduce images, such as monitors, printers and printing presses.

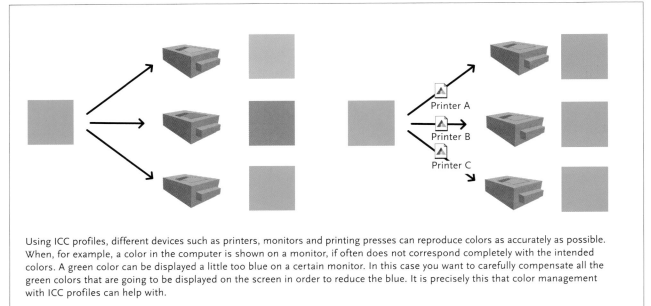

Using ICC profiles, different devices such as printers, monitors and printing presses can reproduce colors as accurately as possible. When, for example, a color in the computer is shown on a monitor, if often does not correspond completely with the intended colors. A green color can be displayed a little too blue on a certain monitor. In this case you want to carefully compensate all the green colors that are going to be displayed on the screen in order to reduce the blue. It is precisely this that color management with ICC profiles can help with.

SIMULATION — HOW IT WORKS

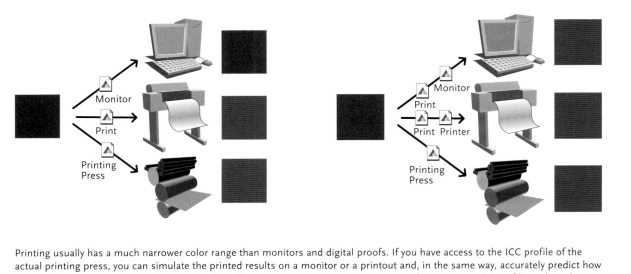

Printing usually has a much narrower color range than monitors and digital proofs. If you have access to the ICC profile of the actual printing press, you can simulate the printed results on a monitor or a printout and, in the same way, accurately predict how the colors will come out. To simulate printed results on a monitor, it is necessary to use the monitor's ICC profile so the colors can be displayed accurately. The profile is then combined with the printing press's ICC profile, which takes into account printing conditions and simulates the printed results. In the same way you can simulate the printed results with a printer.

3.10.1 Creating an Input Profile

To create a profile for an input device you need the software and a standardized color chart with different color reference fields. The program that creates the profile has precisely defined reference values in CIELAB for each color on the chart. The color chart is printed, displayed or scanned on a particular unit and each result is given an RGB value, which is then compared to its respective reference value in CIELAB. The result is a conversion table that is stored in an ICC profile.

For example, to create a profile for a scanner, you scan a color chart on photo paper or transparent film, and the scanned digital color chart is compared filed by field to the respective reference values. For two different scanners you will normally get two different RGB values for the same reference color field. This may be because they use different light sources, color filters, optics, etc. These two RGB values can still be converted to the same correct CIELAB values by using the CIELAB values in each scanner's ICC profiles. Correction with ICC profiles permits two different scanners to give the same result.

For scanners there are color charts for both reflective and transparent film from leading film manufacturers such as Agfa, Kodak and Fuji. They use varying emulsions in their films and papers, which produce different results when scanned. For example, when you scan images photographed with transparent film by Fuji, you have to use a profile developed with color charts on transparent film from Fuji in order to accurately determine the correct compensation value. In practice this means that you should produce many ICC profiles for just one scanner so you can choose the right ICC profile for the particular kind of original you are using.

The appearance of the color charts is defined in the ISO standard IT8 (ISO 12641). Most manufacturers of profiling software have their own charts based on IT8. Color charts consist of up to 252 color reference fields with primary, secondary, tertiary colors as well as gray tones. The color charts of the different manufacturers differ because they use their own color fields in addition to those defined in IT8. This helps manufacturers to better characterize the weaknesses of their particular devices.

HOW TO CREATE AN INPUT PROFILE
To create an ICC profile for a scanner or a digital camera, you need a standardized test chart that contains a number of fields and different reference colors. A digital file is included with the test chart with the exactly defined reference colors in CIELAB for each reference color field on the test form. The test form is scanned or photographed so that every reference color field gives an RGB value which is then linked with its respective reference value in CIELAB. The result is a conversion table that is saved in an ICC profile.

3.10.2 Creating an Output Profile for Printers and Printing Presses

Profiles for output devices such as printers or printing presses are generated by outputting or printing a standardized color chart (ISO 12640). As opposed to a color chart for an input profile which is a physical slide or photocopy, the color chart of a printer or printing press consists of a number of digitally described reference fields. There are a total number of 928 digitally defined color fields, as defined in CMYK values. The color chart is then printed out. The results are measured with a spectrophotometer, and these measurements in CIELAB are compared to the CMYK color reference values and stored in an ICC profile.

Just as with two different scanners, two different printers or printing presses can yield different results when they print the same reference colors. In the case of printers or printing presses, they will have differing CIELAB values for the same reference color field in different contexts. This may be because of different papers, inks, printing techniques, alignments, etc.

Using every printer or printing press's unique ICC profile, the program can correct the colors at different CMYK values so the result will be the same CIELAB value. This means that in theory two different printers or two different printing presses will show the same results despite their differences.

Just as with different types of film or photo paper giving different results with input devices, the end product with printers and printing presses are affected by the choice of paper. This means that ICC profiles should also take into account the kind of paper being used. An ICC profile for the selected paper should be produced. Printing houses usually provide one ICC profile for coated and one for uncoated paper. When printing a high quality product, a test run should be done on the exact paper to be used and an ICC profile created especially for the test sample.

3.10.3 Creating an Output Profile for Monitors

To generate an output profile for a monitor you start with a number of reference colors defined in RGB values. The reference colors are displayed on the monitor, and a spectrometer is used to measure color values directly off the screen in CIELAB values. The results are compared to the RGB color reference values and stored in an ICC profile. Two different monitors can yield different CIELAB values, with the same RGB reference values. This can be because of differences in phosphorous, techniques, greater use, etc.

The unique ICC profile for every monitor can help correct the RGB values, which will result in the same CIELAB value. Thus, in theory, two different monitors should be able to show the same results.

3.10.4 Standard Profile or Custom Profile?

Some manufacturers deliver ICC profiles with products like scanners and printers. These are generated profiles for the particular product model and do not take the strengths and weaknesses of the individual product into account and can provide varying results. Because of this, it's better to work with profiles created for a specific device in a specific environment. For example, even if a company only has monitors of the same make and model, you should still generate profiles for each monitor in order to achieve the best possible results.

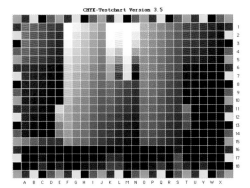

IT8 – COLOR TEST CHART
The appearance of the color test charts is defined in the ISO standard IT8. Most manufacturers of profile software have their own color test charts based on IT8. The color chart displayed above comes with Logo Profilemaker Pro.

SPECTROPHOTOMETER
A spectrophotometer measures the spectral composition of a particular color in printer outputs, proofs, prints and on the monitor display. The measurement values can be used to create profiles for color management systems, for example ICC profiles.

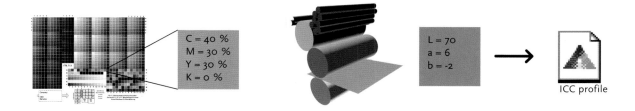

C = 40 %
M = 30 %
Y = 30 %
K = 0 %

L = 70
a = 6
b = -2

ICC profile

HOW TO CREATE AN OUTPUT PROFILE

To create an ICC profile for a printer or printing press, you use a standardized test chart (ISO 12640) that is composed of a number of digitally defined reference color fields. The test chart contains the exactly defined reference values in CMYK that is printed out on a printer or printed on a printing press. Every reference color field is measured with a spectrophotometer and its color value iin CIELab is linked with its respective CMYK value to a conversion table that is stored in an ICC profile.

For offset printers there are also standardized ICC profiles generated by ECI (European Colour Initiative) and Gretag Macbeth. These are based on the international ISO standard 12647-2 for process control for offset printing. There are profiles for different types of paper, and the profiles are regularly updated [*see Printing 9.11.10*].

When producing advertising, standard profiles are also used. The same advertisement is often printed in so many newspapers that it is impractical and risky to create a digital file for the advertisement with an ICC profile custom made for every newspaper and printing house.

For one standard profile to be effective, all printing houses must adjust their processes accordingly. For the Swedish press for example, the newspaper producers in Sweden have created a standard profile that all the newspaper printers conform to. The German research institute, FOGRA, also furnishes standard profiles for the German press.

3.11 **Creating Effective Color Management**

The right conditions are necessary in order to create an effective color management system. One requirement is equipment and software that is suited for color conversion between different devices using ICC profiles. Another requirement is that the equipment be handled and installed in the correct manner throughout the whole graphic production process. We will deal with three steps: stabilization, calibration and characterization.

A basic assumption for all color handling is that you have stabilized and calibrated devices in your system. This means that the equipment gives the same previously decided results the whole time. Before achieving this there is no point in creating an ICC profile or carrying out color management since the result will still not be predictable as long as the equipment gives varying results. An ICC profile describes a specific piece of equipment under certain

AN OUTPUT PROFILE CONTAINS INFORMATION ABOUT

- The printer/printing press's characteristics (i.e. contrast, dot gain, etc.)
- The inks' characteristics and range
- The actual color characteristics of the actual paper
- Gray balance and separation type (UCR/GCR)

PROGRAM FOR CREATING ICC PROFILES

There are several programs on the market for producing ICC profiles:

- Profilemaker from Gretag Macbeth
- Colortune from Agfa
- Printopen
- Colourkit Profiler Suite from Fuji

A MONITOR PROFILE CONTAINS INFORMATION ABOUT

- The monitor's characteristics (i.e. color range, gamma, etc.)
- The monitor's actual settings (i.e. light strength, white points, etc.)
- Surrounding light conditions

You can find standard profiles here:

- **ECI** (www.eci.org) – standard profiles for offset and gravure printing for a number of different paper qualities.

- **Newspaper producers** (www.ifra.com) standard profiles for newspaper printing (coldset).

A STABLE ENVIRONMENT IS IMPORTANT
The ICC profile is not only unique for the respective devices, but also for the conditions that rule when the actual measurements are being decided, for example which paper you should use in the printer, or how much moisture should be in the room with the presses. The ICC profile describes the device's color range as well as its characteristics and weaknesses under specific conditions. For an ICC profile to be effective, when using the profile you have to aim to recreate the conditions that existed when the profile was made.

conditions. If these conditions are not met the ICC profile will not apply. If one of the ICC profiles does not apply in a color management system, the system does not work. All equipment such as scanners, printers, monitors and printing presses must yield the same results over a period of time for a color management system to be functional.

3.11.1 Stabilization

Stabilization involves making sure that all printing units consistently provide the same results. Inconsistencies can occur because of mechanical errors or fluctuating environmental conditions, like humidity and temperature. Stabilization of the environment, equipment and materials is very important to get dependable results over time.

3.11.2 Calibration

Calibration involves adjusting the equipment to predetermined values so that all devices are coordinated – for example, if you set a value of 40 % cyan hue in the computer, the value for cyan will also be set to 40 % on the printer, in the proof or the imagesetter. The various units often come with calibration software or tools. When you calibrate a monitor, you often also do a characterization with whose help you create an ICC profile for the monitor.

3.11.3 Characterization

Characterization involves creating an ICC profile for a specific device. The device should be calibrated and the environment, materials and other conditions should be stable before the characterization is carried out. The characterization happens by printing out, scanning or displaying an IT8 color chart and measuring how the results are reproduced on a certain device. The ICC profile created describes the characteristics of the device and its defects, and makes it possible to compensate for these.

3.12 Color Management in Practice

In order for color management with ICC profiles to work practically, all the units involved, such as monitors, digital cameras, scanners, printers and printing presses, must be stable. This means that they give the same results every time they are used. They should also be calibrated, that is their basic installations are correctly done, and the same goes for when their ICC profiles are created. When these demands are met, a graphic production flow can be color managed, with the colors being corrected and converted between different color systems. Color conversion is done with a color management module using an ICC profile. Below we will go through the various steps of the process.

3.12.1 Getting the Right Colors in Print

When working with images photographed or scanned in RGB mode, you are using RGB color spaces predefined in CIELAB. The camera or the scanner's RGB values are compensated for and converted by using the ICC profile and the Color Management Module for CIELAB values. These can then be translated into the RGB values you have chosen to save the image in, for example Adobe RGB (1998). The image's colors correspond to reality as well as possible in the CIELAB defined color space you have chosen to work with. The various RGB color spaces have different characteristics exactly like the CIELAB since every RGB value refers to a CIELAB value. The image can then be saved in whatever format supports the ICC profiles.

3.12.2 Color Management of Monitors

When previewing a print on the monitor, you must take into consideration the monitor's way of displaying the image – i.e., you must make certain adjustments based on the monitor's ICC profile. This is done so the strengths and weaknesses of the monitor will be compensated for and the image will be correctly displayed.

3.12.3 Color Management for Color Printers

The ICC profile for the color printer is used to color convert images and RGB colors to CMYK for printing out so that the printer's weaknesses can be compensated for. Normally conversion occurs when printing out. Conversion can also be done manually in Photoshop for each individual image, which is then converted to CMYK and adjusted for printing.

3.12.4 Color Management for Printing

Color management works in the same way with the ICC profile for color conversion to CMYK for printing presses.

3.12.5 Simulation of Printing

Printed products normally have a much smaller color space than a monitor, and original images in RGB mode. Even printers can usually produce more saturated colors and greater contrast than a printing press.

You can calibrate your system based on experiences with similar prints. Such "simulation" is, of course, not an exact procedure, but it is fairly simple and it works relatively well.

One way to calibrate using the simulation method is to print out and view on the monitor a document that has already been through the printing process, and set your units according to its appearance. You can do this from, for example, Adobe Photoshop, Indesign and Acrobat [*see Image Editing 5.3.1, Layout 6.9.7, and Prepress 7.5.2*]. The idea is to adjust the software and monitors so that the screen display is as consistent to the printed product as possible. In the same way, the color printer and proof can be adjusted to simulate the final print result. A more precise method is to take a final print and adjust the units to the corresponding values. By combining the information in the two profiles you will be able to achieve a good simulation of the final print on the monitor. If you want to simulate the printed result in a color printer output, you combine the printer profile and the output profile instead.

Simulation requires that the monitor or color printer that will show the simulation have a wider color space than the printed product in order to display it correctly.

If you don't have access to a spectrophotometer, you can set the monitor using a program and your eye to create an ICC profile that will yield good results. In Mac the program is included in the system. In Windows the program is installed in Adobe Gamma that is a correlating function to Adobe Photoshop. Just like most professional programs that are used together with a spectrophotometer, the calibration and characterization of the screen is done with the same process. The result is a good ICC profile. Remember that it is only valid as long as the monitor is calibrated in the same way as when the profile was created. Do not adjust the monitor's settings if you are not going to make a new ICC profile. Below you can see how you do this step by step for both Mac and Windows.

MAC OS

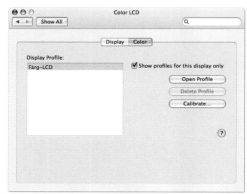

In Mac OS there is the function to set the monitor under APPLE MENU → SYSTEM PREFERENCES... → MONITOR → COLOR.

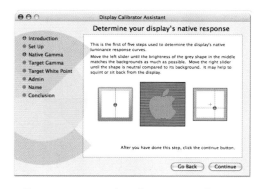

1. By answering a number of questions and using the eye as a measuring instrument, the program can determine how the monitor will behave.

2. Assign the monitor's GAMMA VALUE to 2.2. This will determine the basic contrast and lay the foundation for the ICC profile that will be created.

3. Assign next the color temperature, TARGET WHITE POINT, that whatever is white on the screen should have. It usually works best for printed products if you set it at 6,500 K (D65).

4. Lastly, the program creates a correction table for the monitor in the shape of an ICC profile that automatically sets the control panel. Everything that is displayed on the monitor now "passes by" this profile.

WINDOWS

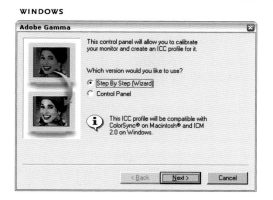

There is no built-in function in Windows. Instead you have to install Adobe Photoshop and then Adobe Gamma is also installed. The program is found under START MENU → ADOBE GAMMA → CONTROL PANEL. Use STEP BY STEP installation.

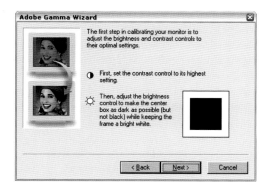

1. First the monitor is calibrated. Follow the directions and set the controls on the monitor.

2. By answering a number of questions and using the eye as a measuring instrument, the program can determine how the monitor will behave. Assign the monitor's GAMMA VALUE to 2.2. This will determine the basic contrast and lay the foundation for the ICC profile that will be created.

3. Assign next the color temperature, HARDWARE WHITE POINT, that whatever is white on the screen should have. It usually works best for printed products if you set it at 6,500 K (D65).

4. Adobe Gamma creates a corrections table for the monitor in the shape of an ICC profile that automatically sets the control panel. Programs like Adobe Photoshop look there and then display the images via the right ICC profile.

3.13 **Color Conversion**

Color conversion is when colors are converted between two color systems or color models. The values of the original colors are calculated to new values in order to adapt them to a new color space. This color conversion can be done in several ways, and a number of factors influence the process. All conversions are done via CIELAB, an exact color system.

When you generate an ICC profile you base it on a number of predefined reference colors. The profile compares how a device reproduces colors in comparison to a preprinted color chart – reference values (based on CIELAB) that tell you what the color values should be. The difference between the two values is the basis for the profile and allows you to generate information regarding color compensation, i.e., how to reach the same value as the reference value on the color chart. Colors whose reference values are not included on the color chart are calculated and interpolated by the color management module using two or more reference colors closely resembling the one in question.

The color management module is extension software that calculates the color conversion between different devices using ICC profiles. Apple ColorSync is the most common color management module and is always delivered with Apple's operating system. LinoColor is used with Windows. Many manufacturers like Kodak, Heidelberg and AGFA have their own color management modules. All software that needs to convert or edit colors uses a color management module for color conversions. For example, scanner software uses a CMM when scanning an image, and image-editing software uses a CMM when converting the colors into CMYK.

When the various manufacturers decide how their particular color management module should manage conversions, they all base their decisions on the following:

- All neutral (gray) colors should be maintained when converting
- The contrast should be as high as possible after the conversion
- When converting, all devices should be able to represent all the colors. In other words, all the colors should be within the possible color space of the device

Some parts of the color space are difficult to convert and can cause problems. For example:

- Light colors can be "flattened", or blended together, when the color management module tries to create the highest possible tonal range. The same problem occurs with very dark tones.
- Saturated colors cause problems when they are outside a device's color space. They have to be translated into the device's color space in order to be reproduced. That process always changes the color in question and, in addition, may change other colors within the color space.
- Color bordering the device's color space and covering large areas can lose nuances when they are converted.

A graphic production flow is color managed by correcting and converting colors through different color systems.

Color conversions are managed by the color management module using the ICC profiles for the various devices. The profiles describe each device's color range among other things.

By combining the ICC profile for a printer or screen with the ICC profile of the print, you can simulate the print on the printer or screen.

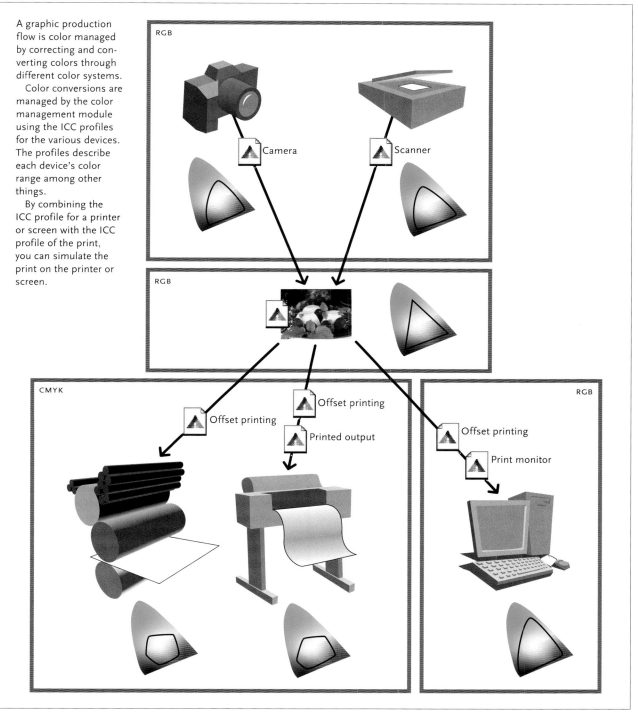

There are four different ways for Color Management Modules to handle colors. The main difference among them is the way they manage translating colors into a device's color space. The four means of conversion are the following:

- Perceptual conversion
- Absolute conversion
- Relative conversion
- Saturated conversion

3.13.1 Perceptual Conversion

The perceptual method of converting colors is mainly used when converting photographic images. When an image is converted, the relative distance in the color space, ΔE, is maintained. Colors outside of a device's color space are moved into the range of the device, but those colors already within the space are moved as well, in order to maintain the relative differences among all the colors. The human eye is more sensitive to differences in colors when they are viewed together than when viewed individually. For example, we can easily detect fine differences between colors when they are placed next to each other whereas when they are viewed separately we have a hard time knowing if it's the same color or not. Perceptual conversion maintains slight differences in color and is therefore the recommended method for separating photographs. The word perceptual refers to how the brain and the eye work together to perceive colors.

3.13.2 Absolute Conversion

The absolute color conversion method is primarily used when simulating prints with a proof print system. The colors outside of the proof print system's possible color space are moved inside it, while those already within are not changed. Tonal differences between the colors within the possible color space and those on the border will then disappear. The method is appropriate in situations where it's impossible to reproduce colors as precisely as possible, as with a proof print system. To avoid the problem of losing tonal differences, you should strive for a color space in the proof system that is greater than the one for the print.

3.13.3 Relative Conversion

Sometimes a perceptual conversion can cause images to lose contrast and saturation. In those cases a relative conversion may provide a better result. The relative distance, ΔE, among colors outside of a device's possible color space is maintained after they have been moved inside. The colors within the color space maintain their values. The colors that are moved are converted into a color as close as possible to the original color by maintaining their brightness. The relative distance between two colors in the periphery of the color space changes and the two colors can now provide essentially the same value.

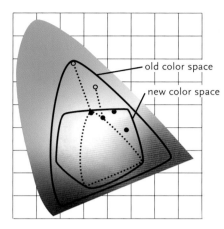

RELATIVE COLORMETRIC COLOR CONVERSION

When converting relatively, the relative distance delta E is preserved, between colors outside the device's possible color space, even after they have been moved in. The colors that lie within the color space keep their values. The colors that have been moved are converted as closely as possible by keeping the colors' brightness. Delta E between two colors in the color space's outer edge is changed and two colors that earlier were different can in general give the same value.

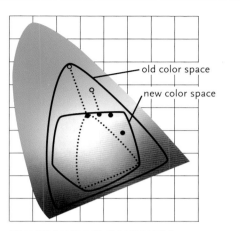

ABSOLUTE COLORMETRIC CONVERSION

With absolute colormetric conversion, the colors outside the device's possible color space will be moved in, while colors within preserve their values. Differences in hue between the colors that lie outside of the possible color space and those that lie on the edge will then disappear.

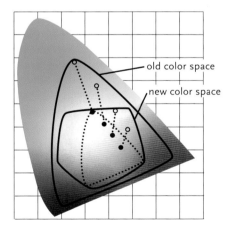

PERCEPTUAL CONVERSION

With a perceptual conversion the relative distance in the color space is preserved between the different colors, delta E. The colors that lie outside the device's possible color space are moved in, but even those that lie inside it are moved so that the relative color differences remain.

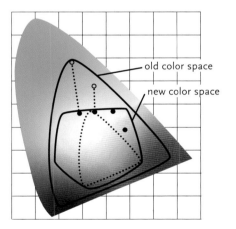

SATURATION CONVERSION

With saturation conversion as much saturation as possible is preserved. This is achieved by changing the relative distance between colors, delta E, but keeping the same saturation. You will thus get maximum saturation since each pixel will retain its saturation value regardless of whether it lies outside or inside the possible color space.

IS THE PRINTING PRESS AN UNSTABLE FIGHTER JET?
The printing press is like an unstable modern
fighter jet – you are contstantly making corrections
and adjustments according to printing conditions.
This means that the result always varies throughout the edition.

3.13.4 Saturation Conversion

When working with object-based images, the preferred method of conversion is saturation conversion. The method strives to provide a conversion with as high color saturation as possible. The relative distance between colors, ΔE, is changed, while the saturation is maintained. This allows each pixel to maintain its saturation value regardless of whether it is within or outside of the possible color space of a particular device.

3.14 Problems with Color Management

Problems can arise in color management with devices not giving stable results via a stable process, and problems can also arise from inconsistencies in ICC standards themselves. We will begin by looking at problems with devices and the color management process. Although the process must be totally stable, all devices will give varied results over time, no matter how new they are. The equipment must be continually monitored and calibrated. But there will be still be small misalignments and variations over time. One of the greatest culprits is the printing process. The printing press is often the piece of equipment most difficult to keep constant – printed results vary all the time, even within one printing. Printing with a printing press has been compared to steering a modern unstable fighter plane. You must continually make corrections and adjustments during the printing process itself. When the printed product begins to veer away from optimal results and you make necessary adjustments, it takes time for the results from that adjustment to show, and then you may have to counter adjust. This, combined with the instability of the other equipment, means that a color management system can never be exact.

Although the ICC is a standard, the different programs used to develop profiles provide different results despite following the same ICC specifications. These problems are a result of the fact that the ICC standard's specifications are not precise enough. Because the standard was developed by many different interested parties from various fields, it has not been tightly monitored. Instead, there has been room for different companies to adjust the standards in order to get optimal results with their particular products.

04.

digital images

What resolution should images have in order to be printed? Should you use TIFF, EPS or JPEG images? Can you use PDF format for images? Can I save an image in such a way that it will take up less memory without sacrificing quality? What is a duotone image and how do you make it? How many megapixels should my camera have to make images I can use in print? Which file format is best for extracted images? How much can I enlarge an image? Which file format works best for a graph or a diagram? Does an image lose more information each time I save it in JPEG format? How do you achieve the best quality with a digital camera?

PHOTOGRAPHY IS CARRIED out mainly with digital cameras. To achieve high image quality with digital photography you first have to understand how digital images work and also understand and be able to manage the camera. In this chapter we will go through digital image theory from the ground up. We will take a closer look at digital photography and different types of cameras. We will go over how the camera is constructed, how it works, how it creates a digital image, and we will compare the different kinds of files that a camera can deliver. We will also give some tips on how you attain good image quality with your digital camera.

If you are photographing with film, the images have to be scanned into the computer to be turned into digital form. Scanners are divided principally into flatbed scanners, film scanners and drum scanners. When you scan images with a scanner, you come into contact with concepts such as color range, color compression and gamma. Resolution, screen frequency, scaling factor and sampling factor are other concepts of central importance. We will explain the meanings of these terms and go into how to scan images.

But first we will start by looking at the basic types of digital images and file formats. There are two main types of digital images: object graphics and pixel graphics. Object graphics consist of mathematically calculated curves and lines that create surfaces and shapes, while pixel graphics are images consisting of pixels of different colors, squared to picture elements. Pixel graphics are used

OBJECT GRAPHICS
Object graphics consist of curves and lines. Images can be enlarged without affecting the quality.

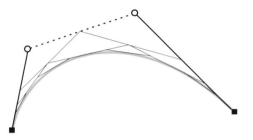

BEZIER CURVES
This is how a bezier curve is created. A number of anchor points determine the shape of the curve. Object graphics are mainly based on bezier curves.

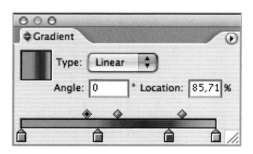

GRADIENT
In Adobe Illustrator you can create tonal transitions between two or more colors.

mostly for photographic images. We will also go over terms such as color mode, resolution and different file formats as well as explain image compression.

4.1 Object Graphics

Logotypes, news graphics and illustrations are examples of images that often consist of object graphics. Object graphics can include simple curves, straight lines, circles, squares, typefaces and other graphic objects. These can in turn have outlines of varying thickness and be filled with different colors, patterns and gradients. Object graphics are sometimes wrongly labeled "vector graphics." This term is derived from a time when vectors were used in graphic software. Simply speaking, a vector is a straight line between two points. In this technique, a series of short, straight lines is used to create the illusion of a curve. When you enlarge such images, however, the straight lines become visible and the curves appear jagged. Today object graphics are based on Bezier curves, named after a mathematician at the French car manufacturer, Renault. Bezier curves are softly bent curves that can assume any curved shape.

Object graphics consist of filled-in areas with outlines. Mathematical values tell the computer to draw a certain type of line or curve from one point to another in the image. You get a very exact figure with a perfectly sharp outline that can be enlarged without affecting the quality. Only the limitations of the printer or the monitor you use affect the image quality. Object graphics use very little memory because only the location and design information must be defined – very simple vales. This also applies to the colors used in object graphics, which are also expressed numerically.

Object graphics are based on a number of basic components.

4.1.1 Outlines and Lines
Lines and outlines in object graphics can assume any color. You can also specify how thick the lines should be, the style of the lines, (solid, dotted, etc.) and the shape of the corners: curved, pointed or squared.

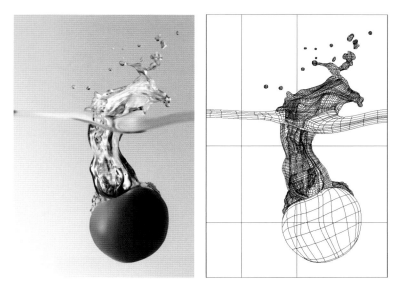

ADVANCED OBJECT GRAPHICS

Using Illustrator's function MESH, many life-like images can be created, but the work is time-intensive. On the right you can see the actual mesh the image is based on. At every meeting point of two lines a color and how far it extends is indicated.

4.1.2 Fill

Curved and closed objects can be filled with colors, color shifts and patterns. The colors are expressed numerically in terms of the ink coverage required for the respective printing inks. You can select fill patterns and color shifts from a predetermined menu.

4.1.3 Patterns

A pattern consists of a small group of objects repeated in a square pattern. It is easy to make your own patterns that you can then use in your illustrations.

4.1.4 Gradients

Color shifts are transitions among several colors at set distances. Gradients can either be linear or circular.

4.1.5 Knockouts

A curve that is placed within a closed object – a circle within a square, for example – can be extracted as a knockout. In this example, the extraction means that a circle knocks out a transparent hole in the square. As a result, whatever you put behind the square will be visible through the circular hole [*see a knockout in the star in the image to the right*].

4.1.6 Superimpositions and Transparency

Objects can be made transparent and/or combined with underlying objects using different software tools.

CREATING OBJECT GRAPHICS

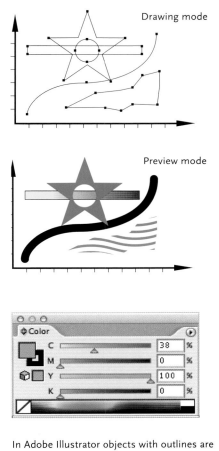

In Adobe Illustrator objects with outlines are created in an invisible coordination system. Using the color palette you can provide the graphics with different attributes such as fill, width, outline, knockout, pattern and tone. Palettes also exist for such settings as line, gradient, transparency, pattern, etc.

Line art with a low resolution becomes jagged. It can be improved by converting it into Bezier curves.

Line art is converted into object graphics in a computer program, in this case Adobe Illustrator, using the function OBJECT → LIVE TRACE.

The result is an image with sharp outlines that can be enlarged as much as desired. The image can also be edited, for example, in Adobe Illustrator.

Photographs can also be converted into object graphics – but with a different result.

Adobe Illustrator divides up the image into a number of colors consisting of monochromatic and curved surfaces.

The image is posterized. In this case, we have divided the image into 17 different colors.

4.2 Applications for Object Graphics

Object graphics are created in illustration software such as Adobe Illustrator and Macromedia Freehand for printing as well as Macromedia Flash for the Web. There are also programs that take pixel graphics and convert them to object graphics. Adobe Streamline and Freesoft Silhouette are examples of such programs. They are usually used to convert pixel-based logotypes into object graphics so they can be used in all possible sizes without loss of quality. Adobe Illustrator and Macromedia Flash also contain simpler versions of this software.

4.3 File Formats for Object Graphics

Object graphics are usually saved in EPS or PDF picture format. However it is also common to use the format of your illustration software, such as the AI-format from Adobe Illustrator. Object-based formats such as WMF, EMF, SVG and SWF, are used in office applications and on the web. Below are descriptions of the most common forms.

4.3.1 PDF

PDF format is the most practical for object-based images. Most layout programs manage and set up images in PDG-format.

PDF files can contain both pixels, typeface and curved objects, and handle all graphic effects that can be shown in illustration software.

PDF format has, as well, the advantage that with the free program, Adobe Reader, everything with images can be opened, scanned and printed out. This also makes it possible to handle images from any PDF file, and, for example, make comments and corrections using the tolls in Acrobat, or publish it on the web. You can even set a password on the file for security. PDF files in general use little memory space, and pixel-based images can be compressed.

You can use PDF format in Adobe Illustrator and still make use of all the capabilities of the software when you open the file for editing. When PDF files are adapted to allow full editing capacity in Adobe Illustrator, the files become a little larger.

PDF formats are not always supported by older layout programs or by RIPs. In such cases the EPS format could be a suitable alternative.

4.3.2 EPS

Encapsulated PostScript, or EPS, manages both object graphics and pixel graphics.

The EPS file consists of two parts: a low-resolution preview image, and a PostScript-based image that can contain both objects and pixels. The preview image (PICT) is used when placing the image in the page layout software.

The preview image is in PICT format for Macintosh and BMP for Windows. It can be in black and white or color, but always has a resolution of 72 ppi (pixels per inch) since that is the standard resolution for a monitor.

The objects in the EPS file are independent of the size of the image and therefore require the same amount of memory for any size image. However, if you have created an object-based image with large width and height saved in EPS format, the file size may be larger since the preview image takes more memory, at the same time as the preview image has greater resolution. If you have little memory available for object-based EPS images, you can either choose to compress the format before saving the mage in order to get a smaller preview image, or choose a black and white preview image. In this case the preview image will be a little jagged and you won't be able to see the colors, but the quality of the printed image won't be affected. Adobe Indesign can show EPS-based images with high quality on the monitor by using the high-resolution part of the file instead of the preview image.

4.3.3 Illustrator – AI

Adobe Illustrators own file format is used for object-based images, but can also contain mounted pixel images.

Adobe Indesign can mount images in Adobe Illustrator format. In Adobe Indesign you can also directly paste in images that were cut from Adobe Illustrator, with the possibility of editing them in a layout application.

The Illustrator format is used principally as a working format before the illustrations are done, and you want to have a file using minimal memory with

---

OBJECT GRAPHICS +/–

+ Contain an unlimited number of colors
+ Can be rescaled without compromising image quality
+ Easy to edit without compromising quality
+ Don't take up a lot of memory
– Cannot be used for photographic images

PDF +/–

+ Can be opened by everyone
+ Is the same for Mac and Windows
+ Files use little memory
+ Can include fonts
+ Is managed like ordinary PDF files
+ Can be protected with a password
+ Can include ICC profile
– Cannot be managed by older layout programs

EPS +/–

+ Commonly used
+ Can be mounted with most layout applications
– Takes up somewhat more memory than illustration application files
– Does not retain all the editorial features of the illustration application
– Different file formats for Mac and Windows
– Required an illustration or layout program to be viewed
– Only newer file versions can include fonts

ILLUSTRATOR +/–

+ Uses little memory
+ Can use all editing features
+ Can include fonts
+ Can include ICC profiles
– Cannot be managed by all layout programs

PIXEL GRAPHICS
Digitalized photographic images consist of tiny squares of color, called pixels. The eye cannot perceive the pixels unless the image is greatly enlarged.

OILS IN THE COMPUTER
In programs like Corel Painter you can paint and draw images that look like they have been made with pencils, watercolors or oils.

all the editing features. Illustrator images are commonly saved in EPS or PDF formats before you mount them in a layout application.

4.3.4 WMF and EMF

WMF (Windows Metafile) and EMF (Enhanced Metafile) are image formats for simpler object graphics that are used in Windows settings. They are supported by most office applications. They are however, very limited in their ability to render graphics and should be avoided in graphic production.

4.3.5 SVG

Scalable Vector Graphics, SVG, is a file format for object-based images for the web. SVG format is completely based on XML and supports as well JavaScript and filter effects for dynamic and interactive images with sound and animation.

The format is not intended for making printed products, can be exported from Adobe Illustrator. SVGZ is a compressed variation of SVG.

4.3.6 DWG and DXF

DWG (short for Drawing) is a standard format to store drawing files produced with a CAD application, for example, Autocad. DXF files are often used to transfer Cad files.

Cad files are in general built up of object graphics and are used in places such as packaging production for designs in packaging. The files can be imported to Adobe Illustrator and make up the foundation of packaging design.

4.3.7 SWF

SWF format (Shockwave Flash) is used for object-based animations and interactive images created by Macromedia Flash for the web. The format is not intended for printed products.

4.4 Pixel Graphics

A pixel graphic is divided into tiny squares of color, almost like a mosaic. These tiny squares of color are referred to as pixels from the words PICture ELement.

A pixel-based image can be created in different ways:

- With help of a scanner that reads in the physical original such as photographic film (slides or negatives), photographic paper prints, drawn illustrations, signatures, early types, etc.
- With help of a digital camera that directly creates a pixel image when taking the photograph.
- You can also create pixel-based images directly in the computer with different design applications such as for example, Corel Painter or Adobe Photoshop.

Below we will go through the most important concepts in pixel graphics and image handling: image resolution, color modes that pixel images can exist in, file formats, compression, image management, sharpness, touching up, aggregate exposure, etc.

4.5 Applications for Pixel Graphics

The overwhelmingly most popular application for pixel-based management is Adobe Photoshop. It is used equally by the most advanced professionals as well as by eager amateurs. A limited version exists for home users, called Adobe Photoshop Elements. An alternative for professional image handling is Photo Retouch Pro from Binuscan. This does not contain as many functions, but it is very powerful for making adequate color corrections of images.

There are also some applications created to automatically adjust images. Intellihance from Extensis and Photo Perfect from Binuscan are two such programs. The automatic adjustments that these types of programs do are often good, but do not replace manual adjustments in a professional setting. Manual image handling also give the advantage that you have to make a decision about every image's adjustments, which is necessary to reach an high and even image quality. Fotostation from Fotoware is an example of an image bank program that also has functions for automatic image handling in the larger work stream, for example in daily newspaper production. Paintshop Pro from Corel is an intermediate alternative to Adobe Photoshop.

Painter from Corel is another application for pixel graphics, but that is completely adapted to painting and drawing illustrations with very realistic tools for things like watercolors, markers, oil paints and different materials.

There are even hundreds of simpler programs that can manipulate pixel-based images, but that are not suited for professional graphic production.

4.6 Color Modes

Pixel-based images can be black and white or color and contain different numbers of colors. One usually says the images have different color modes. The simplest color mode is line art, which only contains two colors: black and white. Some other example of color modes are grayscale images like black and white photographs, duotone images for tinted black and white images, indexed color images for the web, images in RGB mode for image editing, and CMYK images for four color printing.

BIT DEPTH FOR EVERY PIXEL
Pixels in images can be assigned to different amounts of memory, known as bit depth. Depending on how much memory the pixels are assigned to, a corresponding number of colors can be shown. In practice this includes everything from 1 bit in line art with two colors to 16-bit RGB images where there are 16 bits in each pixel for red, green and blue, and they can show 65,536×65,536×65,536 = 280 billion colors. Below is a table that describes how many colors different bit depths can give:

1 bit	→	2^1 →	2 colors
2 bits	→	2^2 →	4 colors
3 bits	→	2^3 →	8 colors
4 bits	→	2^4 →	16 colors
5 bits	→	2^5 →	32 colors
6 bits	→	2^6 →	64 colors
7 bits	→	2^7 →	128 colors
8 bits	→	2^8 →	256 colors
10 bits	→	2^{10} →	1 024 colors
12 bits	→	2^{12} →	4 096 colors
14 bits	→	2^{14} →	16 384 colors
16 bits	→	2^{16} →	65 536 colors

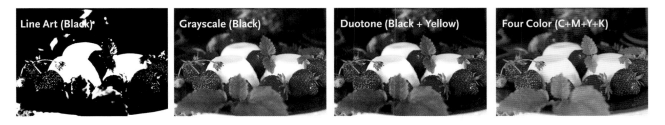

COLOR MODES
Here are examples of the same image in different color modes. You can also see which printing colors are used in the respective color mode.

Line art images are composed of completely black and completely white pixels without any mid-range tones. They require higher resolution the better the print quality you want. The resolution is adjusted according to the paper:

Laser printout, newsprint	600–800 ppi
Fine, uncoated paper	800–1,200 ppi
Fine coated paper	over 1,200 ppi

GRAYSCALE IMAGES
Grayscale Images are composed of pixels in black, white and different shades of gray. Grayscale is suitable for black and white photographs or pencil drawings.

GRAYSCALE

A black and white digital image consists of pixels in different shades of gray. The scale in between black and white is divided into a number of steps.

Normally digital grayscale images consist of 256 different tones. As a result, the eye cannot perceive any distinct steps in the grayscale.

Here is a "grayscale" for a duotone image with black and cyan. The darkest areas are black and the brightest are white. Because the scale between the black and white is tinted in a color, the image maintains its contrast compared to a grayscale image.

Every pixel in the image requires different amount of memory depending on which color mode the image is saved in. The necessary memory is expressed in bits per pixel; the more bits per pixel you have, the greater the number of different hues and colors a pixel can assume.

4.6.1 Line Art

Line art means images that only contain black and white pixels. They are described with a one or a zero and only take up one bit per pixel in memory. Examples of such images are one-color logotypes or graphic illustrations like woodcuts. Screen fonts (the images of typefaces displayed on the computer monitor) are line art images of letters [see Layout 6.5.2]. Texts and images transmitted via fax are translated into line art.

Line Art can be found in Adobe Photoshop under IMAGE → MODE → BITMAP.

4.6.2 Grayscale Images

A grayscale image contains pixels that can assume tones ranging from 0 to 100 % of a particular color. The tonal range from white (0 % black) to black (100 % black) is divided into a scale with a number of different steps. This makes grayscale mode appropriate for black and white photographs or marker drawings that contain mid-range tones but are composed of one color.

The tonal scale in print from white (0 % color) to black (100 % color) is divided in digital images into a scale with a different number of steps, usually 256, that is 8 bits or one byte, how many depending on how much memory is allotted to each pixel. The darkest point in the image receives the digital intensity value of 0 and the lightest receives a value of 255, and all the gray nuances get values in between. 256 is enough for our vision, which needs around 100 gray tones in a linear grayscale, and 256 tones gives enough margins for simpler image management.

The grayscale can be found in Adobe Photoshop under IMAGE → MODE → GRAYSCALE.

4.6.3 Duotones – Tinted Grayscale Images

As the name duotone indicates, two printing inks instead of one are used in these instances. If you want to reproduce fine details in a black and white image, make it softer or tint it a color other than black, you use duotones. Usually you print with black plus one spot color of your choice. To ensure that the image does not become darker when the second ink is added, the black tones have to

IMAGES WITH TINTS

DUOTONES
A duotone image has white and black parts and the scale is between is tinted in color.

FAKE DUOTONE
A grayscale image printed on a tinted area is called a fake duotone. The white parts of the grayscale image get the color of the tinted area.

GRAYSCALE IMAGE IN COLOR
A grayscale image can also be printed using a spot color instead of black.

be lightened correspondingly. Image-editing software calculates the relationship between the first and second printing inks. Of course, you can also print with two spot colors instead of black and one spot color. If you print a grayscale image with three printing inks, it is called a tritone image, when it is done with four inks it is called quadtone.

When converting a grayscale image into a duotone image, the same pixel image is used for both printing inks. From a technical point of view, the same grayscale image forms the basis, but at output the image is separated into two colors – the black printing ink and the spot ink. Information about the spot

DUOTONE SUMMARY

- Pixel-based grayscale image printed with two colors.
- The relationship between the two colors is determined by curves.
- Works in EPS-, PDF- and Photoshop-format.
- Orientation of halftone screens is important.

CREATING A DUOTONE IMAGE

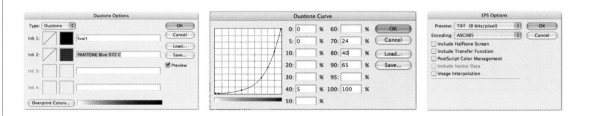

DUOTONE OPTIONS
When creating an image in duotone mode in Adobe Photoshop, you start with a grayscale image and IMAGE → LAYER → DUOTONE COLOR. There are a number of pre-selected duotone combinations to choose from. If you want to create your own you have to start by selecting which colors you would like to print the image with. You do this by clicking on the color sample. Then a menu pops up the choose colors from.

DUOTONE CURVE
To change a printing color's amount in different shades, you can give this curve a different shape by clicking on the color's curve symbol and then modifying the curve. You see the result in the tonal scale at the bottom of the window. You can also create triplex and quadruplex images by defining three or four colors and curves.

Remember that the printing colors chosen in Adobe Photoshop must be defined with the exact same name in the layout document.

SAVING THE DUOTONE IMAGE
The duotone image has to be saved in EPS, PDF or Photoshop format. No special adjustments need to be made.

colors is also added to the file, but duotones do not really take up that much more memory than black and white images.

It is important that the two halftone images output from a duotone image have the correct screen orientation. This means that the angles should be spaced to avoid moiré [*see Prepress 7.7.9*]. The program from which you are outputting the images can adjust the screen angles.

"Fake" duotones are black and white images printed over a colored tint area. You can choose to print a grayscale image with a spot color. Fake duotones, like the choice to print an image with a color or color combination other than black, is done most simply with a layout program [*see inset at Layout 6.8.3*]. A duotone image should be saved in EPS, PDF or Photoshop format. The TIFF format does not work with duotones.

4.6.4 RGB

Red, green and blue, or RGB, are the colors used to scan a color image [*see 4.12*]. These are also the colors the monitor reproduces. Therefore, when images are previewed on the monitor – multimedia presentations, for example – the RGB mode is usually used. Each pixel in the image has a value for how much red, green and blue it contains. The eye perceives this combination as a certain color [*see Chromatics 3.3*]. You could say that an RGB image consists of three separate pixel images. Technically, these are three images in the grayscale mode that represent, respectively, red, green and blue. Because of this, an RGB image takes up three times as much memory as a grayscale image of the same size and resolution.

This construction means that every pixel in an RGB image in an 8-bit configuration can assume $2^8 \times 2^8 \times 2 = 256 \times 256 \times 256 = 16.8$ million different shades.

Just like in a grayscale image the value 0 means no light at all and 255 means maximum light. The combination red=0, green=0, and blue=0 yields black, or no light, and red=255, green=255, and blue=255 yields white, maximum light.

If instead you work with a 16-bit configuration, that is 16 bits for red, green and blue respectively, each pixel can assume many, many more shades: ($65,536 \times 65,536 \times 65,536 = 2.8 \times 10^{14} = 280$ billion).

In order for an RGB image to be printed, it has to be translated into the printing inks, cyan, magenta, yellow and black, known as four-color mode. This conversion is called print adjustment or separation [*see Prepress 7.4*].

RGB can be found in Adobe Photoshop under IMAGE → MODE → COLOR.

4.6.5 LAB

Lab is based on the CIELAB system [*see Chromatics 3.7*]. CIELAB is based on the colors being given in terms of lightness (L-value), along with two color values. The color values are stated between green and red (the a-value), and blue and yellow (the b-value). The LAB system makes it easy to adjust a color's lightness (L) and nuance (a and b) independently of each other.

Normally one works with an 8-bit image depth in the LAB mode, which together with the construction of the mode means that every pixel can assume $2^8 \times 2^8 \times 2^8 = 256 \times 256 \times 256 = 16.8$ million different colors.

The LAB mode has as wide a color range as the human eye, that is much larger than a normal digital image. That means that a normal digital image

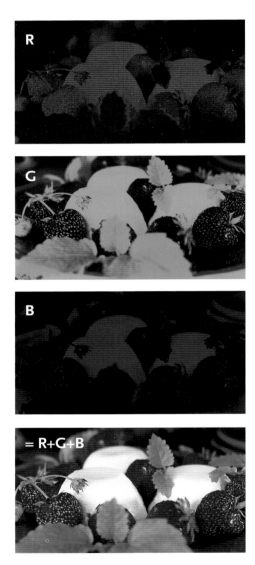

RGB MODE
The RGB mode is based on the combination of light from three colors. The eye perceives this combination as color.

whose colors have a much narrower range, only utilizes a fraction of the color spectrum. A digital image in the LAB mode utilizes normally 256 tonal steps in the L file, but only about 50 tonal steps out of 256 in the a and b files. This in turn means that the image only contains about 256×50×50=640,000 shades out of a possible 16.8 million different colors. If the picture is instead configured in the RGB standard, which is better adapted to the image's color range, more of the possible tones will be used.

An image in the LAB mode should therefore be configured for 16 bits in order to have more possible colors within the image's range. A LAB image in an 8-bit configuration does not have the same margins for image handling as an RGB image because of fewer color tones in the image. Such images should be converted to 16-bit configurations before working with the image in order to preserve as much of the quality as possible.

LAB mode is found in Adobe Photoshop under IMAGE → MODE → LAB-COLOR.

4.6.6 CMYK

When printing photographic images or other color images, the ink colors cyan, magenta, yellow and black are used; this is know as four-color printing. The transition from RGB mode to CMYK mode is called conversion. Each image in the four-color mode technically consists of four separate grayscale images. Each one of these defines the amount of each respective printing ink used during the printing process. A four-color image takes up 33 % more memory than the same image in RGB mode because it consists of four separate files, rather than three. The transition between RGB mode and four-color mode is called print adjustment or separation. Theoretically every pixel in a CMYK image can assume one of 256×256×256×256=4.3 billion different colors, but since an image during print separation is being transferred from an RGB image with 16.8 million colors, the latter is the maximum number of shades a CMYK pixel can assume. In practice there are even fewer colors in CMYK files because of printing and

CMYK MODE
The CMYK mode is based on combining the four printing inks by printing half-tone dots on top of each other. The result is a color image.

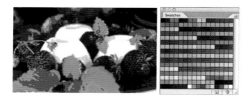

INDEX COLOR MODE
This image contains 256 colors, which is not appropriate for printing. To the right is the image's color palette when it can show 256 colors. Index color mode is mainly used on the Web for simpler images such as illustrations, colored dots, etc.

therefore CMK mode has a narrower color than what RGB mode has. CMYK mode is found in Adobe Photoshop under IMAGE → MODE → CMYK-COLOR.

4.6.7 Index Color Mode

Occasionally, you might want to use only selected colors in a digital image. You might do this because you want to keep the file size down or because the image is displayed on a monitor that can only manage a limited number of colors. Index color mode is used in these instances. GIF images for the Web are created in index color mode, for example.

An image in index color mode can display up to 256 different colors. This number of colors is defined as a palette on which each palette box contains a color and a number. This means that all the pixels in a particular image have a value between 1 and 256, based on the color palette. Therefore, in index color mode, an image only contains one pixel image of the same size as a grayscale image], plus a palette. Usually you start with an RGB image, the colors of which are approximated as closely as possible by the 256 colors in the predefined index palette. You can also use palettes with fewer than 256 colors to further reduce the image file size, for example 128 colors – 7 bits, 64 colors – 6 bits, or 32 colors – 5 bits. This is often done for Web pages. Indexed images are usually not appropriate for color photographs, which contain far more than 256 colors. Index color mode is found in Adobe Photoshop under IMAGE → MODE → INDEXED COLOR...

8 OR 16 BITS PER CHANNEL

Normally when you scan and edit digital images each pixel is saved with 8 bits, which allows for 256 different tones. A pixel in an RGB image made up of three channels is therefore saved with 3×8 bits = 24 bits. It is called a 24-bit image.

When you carry out image editing on an image, information is destroyed. In order not to have loss of quality when information is destroyed, it may be desirable to have several tones, more information, in the images. This is done by increasing the bit-depth, that is the number of bits per channel and per pixel. Adobe Photoshop handles, in addition to the normal 8 bits per channel, 16 bits per channel.

Working with 16 bits per channel naturally yields twice as large image files compared with the normal 8 bits per channel. 16-bit image therefore require more storage space and more RAM in the computer when editing images. A pixel in an RGB image with 16 bits per channel receives a total of 3×16 = 48 images. It is called a 48-bit image.

Adobe Photoshop can handle images in grayscale, RGB, Lab multi-channel and CMYK modes, with 16 bits per channel.

16-bit mode can be saved in Photoshop, PDF, TIFF, PNG and Photoshop Raw formats

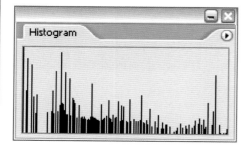

8-BIT IMAGES AFTER IMAGE EDITING
The gaps in the histogram show gaps in information that has occurred during image editing.

16-BIT IMAGES AFTER IMAGE EDITING
The large number of tones that a 16-bit image contains means that the histogram is evenly distributed, even after heavy image edting.

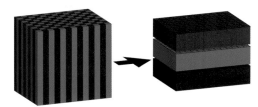

CHANNELS AND LAYERS
RAW format is normally only one channel, but with 10–14 bits (1,024–16,384 hues) per pixel that are converted to pixels with three channels to each bit, which together builds 16.7 million tones. During conversion the values of nearby pixels is also included in the calculation.

PIXELS IN RAW FORMAT IS IN R, G OR B
In most cameras' RAW format files, each pixels represents only one of the colors red, green or blue. The color that each pixel represents is determined by a given order. During RAW format conversion these single-channel pixels are then turned into regular three-channel pixels.

4.6.8 RAW Format

Some digital cameras can store images in RAW format. In this image mode, every pixel has received its information directly from the camera's image sensors and contains all the image information that the camera is able to capture. RAW format stores information in a special way. Images in RAW format are usually composed of one file as opposed to RGB, for example, which has a file for each color. In RAW format mode, each pixel represents instead only one of the colors red, green or blue. Which color each pixel represents is determined by a given order, for example every third pixel could be green.

HOW MUCH MEMORY IS USED IN DIFFERENT IMAGE MODES?

COLOR MODE	CHANNEL	BITS/PIXELS	COLORS
Line Art	1	1 bit per pixel	$= 2^1 = 2$ tones; black and white
Grayscale	1	8 bits per pixel	$= 2^8 = 256$ gray tones
Index Color	1	(from 3 to) 8 bits per pixel	$= 2^8 = 256$ colors
Duotone	1	8 bits per pixel	$= 2^8 = 256$ gray tones*
RGB (8 bits)	3	8+8+8=24 bits per pixel	$= 2^8 \times 2^8 \times 2^8 = 256 \times 256 \times 256 = 16.8$ million colors
RGB (16 bits)	3	16+16+16=48 bits per pixel	$= 2^{16} \times 2^{16} \times 2^{16} = 65,536 \times 65,536 \times 65,536 = 2.8 \times 10^{14} = 280$ million colors
CMYK	4	8+8+8+8=32 bits per pixel	$= 2^8 \times 2^8 \times 2^8 \times 2^8 = 256 \times 256 \times 256 \times 256 = 4.3$ billion colors**
Lab	3	8+8+8=24 bits per pixel	$= 2^8 \times 2^8 \times 2^8 = 256 \times 256 \times 256 = 16.8$ million colors***
Raw format	1	8 to 14 bits per pixel	$= 256$–65,536 colors per pixel****

* The image is still based on a gray scale pixel-based image.
** Since the image originates in RGB mode that has 16.8 million colors and no more colors are created during print adjustment, we still get 16.8 million colors.
*** In practice no more than 256×50×50=640,000 are normally used.
**** Is recalculated to 8 or 16-bit RGB image during Raw format conversion.

A CALCULATION EXAMPLE
An image that is 10×15 cm and has a resolution of 300 ppi contains 120 pixels per centimeter (1 inch = 2.54 cm). This means that it continas in total (10×120)×(15×120) = 2,160,000 pixels. Since 8 bits are 1 byte, when the image is uncompressed, it is now easy to calculate the file size for this image for different image modes. Line art = 264 Kbytes, Grayscale/Index/Duotone + 2.1 Mbytes, RGB = 6.3 Mbytes, CMYK = 88.4 Mbytes, Lab = 6.3 Mbytes, Raw format = 2.1–3.7 Mbytes.

8 pixels

0,00228 inches

IMAGE RESOLUTION
A pixel-based image always has a set resolution (pixels per inch, or ppi.) In the example above, the image has 8 pixels/0.0228 inches = 350 pixels per inch, or 350 ppi.

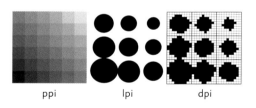

ppi   lpi   dpi

PPI, DPI, AND LPI

- **Ppi** – Pixels per inch. Resolution of a pixel-based digital image. A simplified rule of thumb is that the value will be double the scanning density (lpi).

- **Dpi** – Dots per inch. Exposure points per inch in a printer or typesetter. The value should be at least 10 times higher than the value of lpi.

- **Lpi** – Lines per inch. The number of raster lines 9raster points) per inch in print. It's called screen density. High screen density (lpi) gives amore detailed image. The value is limited by the paper and printing technique.

Every pixel is stored normally in 10, 12 or 14 bits, compared with 3×8=24 bits in RGB mode, which results in 1,024 to 16,384 possible shades per pixel in RAW mode. Exactly how RAW format is constructed varies according to the camera and camera manufacturer [*see Digital Images 4.11.6*].

Photoshop RAW is not the same thing as RAW format in a digital camera. It is instead a relatively uncommon transport format for digital images.

4.7 Resolution

When scanning, you must specify the resolution of the image. Two things determine the scanning resolution: the screen frequency you wish to print with, and whether or not you need to change the size of the image. The screen frequency is determined by the printing method and paper you use. If you assume that a pixel-based image is printed in a certain size, the image will consist of a certain number of pixels per centimeter or per inch (ppi). The resolution of an image is measured in ppi or pixel per centimeter ppcm (1 inch = 2.54 cm).

The higher the resolution the more pixels per centimeter, the more detailed the image can be reproduced. The fewer pixels per inch, the larger the pixels will be and the less detailed the image will be when reproduced.

An image that is constructed of up to 300 pixels in width and is one inch wide will have a resolution of 300 ppi.

If the resolution of an image is low, the pixels will be large, and you will clearly see that the graphic consists of a mosaic-like pattern. At a higher resolution, however, the eye cannot perceive that the image is made up of pixels. There is an appropriate high-level resolution for most images; if you make the resolution higher than that, you will get a better quality image but it will take up more storage space.

4.7.1 The Right Resolution for Images

The relationship between the image resolution and the screen frequency of the print is called the sampling factor. It has been determined that the optimal sampling factor is 2 – i.e., the resolution of the image should be twice as high as the screen frequency. For example, an image that will be printed with a screen frequency of 150 lpi (lines per inch) should be scanned with a resolution of 300 ppi.

However, experience has shown that the optimal value of the sampling factor varies with scanning density. With lower scanning density, as in for example newspaper printing, especially with one-color printing, it is important to not have a too low sampling factor. If the sampling factor is less than 2, image quality will be compromised, although it is difficult for the eye to perceive this until the sampling factor starts to get below 1.7. If the sampling factor gets down to around 1, the pixels created by the scanning process will be clearly visible in the printed image. On the other hand, increasing the sampling factor above 2 will not result in a better image. Instead, the image file will just take up a lot of memory and can become awkward to work with.

With line art images are not screened when output, which means you don't define resolution according to screen density and the sampling factor [*see below.*]

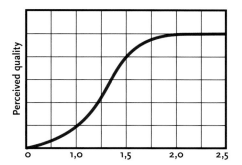

THE SAMPLING FACTOR
Increasing the sampling factor above 2 will not result in a better image. Instead, the image file will just take up a lot of memory and can become awkward to work with in the computer.

CM VS INCH
Normally images' and printers' resolutions and screen densities are given per inch (ppi, dpi,lpi). Some places the values are given per centimeter (ppcm,dpcm, lpcm). This table could be helpful for conversion between these different methods.

Per inch	Per centimeter (standard lpcm value)
50	20 (20)
60	24 (24)
72	28 (28)
75	30 (30)
85	33 (34)
100	39 (40)
120	47 (48)
133	52 (54)
150	59 (60)
175	69 (70)
200	79 (78)
220	87 (87)
300	118 (120)
350	138 (140)

Inside the parentheses are the lpcm values that are normally used.

RECOMMENDED SCREEN FREQUENCY

Below is a list of the recommended screen frequency for the different paper types and printing methods.

Paper	Screen Frequency		Printing methods	Screen Frequency
Newsprint	65–100 lpi		Offset	65–300*lpi
Uncoated	100–133 lpi		Gravure	120–200 lpi
Coated, matte	133–170 lpi		Screen	50–100 lpi
Coated, glossy	150–300*lpi		Flexographic	90–120 lpi

* *Water-free offset, otherwise approximately 200 lpi.*

4.7.2 **The Right Resolution for Line Art**

Line art are images are not screened when output, so the resolution rules of pixel-based images don't apply [*see Prepress 7.7*]. Line art requires a high resolution so that the image does not appear jagged due to all the pixels. The printing process determines the level of resolution needed. Around 600 ppi is appropriate for laser printouts and simpler prints. 1,000 to 1,200 ppi reproduces most details in a sheet-fed printing press on uncoated paper. Optimal print conditions and coated paper require more than 1,200 ppi for best results. When scanning a pre-printed and screened black and white image in the line art mode, you need to increase the resolution to 1,200–1,800 ppi to maintain the shape and size of the halftone dots, depending on the screen frequency. Keep in mind that the upper range of the printer determines the maximum ppi you can print with. For example, a 1,000 ppi line art image printed on a printer with 600 dpi will not look better than a 600 ppi line art image.

4.8 File Formats for Pixel-Based Images

Pixel-based images can be saved in a number of file formats. Some of them have more or less become industry standards. They are primarily differentiated by which color mode they can handle as well as the level of features they are capable of. In the table you can see which formats handle which color modes. The most common image file formats are Photoshop, EPS, PDF, DCS, TIFF, PICT, BMP, GIF and JPEG. The two formats generally used in graphic production are TIFF and EPS. PDS and JPEG are also well suited and commonly used formats, but require a certain care since their quality can vary because of compression. Photoshop format is becoming more popular, but isn't useful for every situation.

4.8.1 Photoshop Format (PSD)

This pixel-based image is primarily used during the actual editing of the image. Some of the advantages of Photoshop, also called PSD, are that you can save the images in files and even save so-called alpha-files, adjustment files, mask channels, tranparency, etc. Photoshop also supports 16-bit files, which is an advantage when you are working with touching up images. It also supports several color files, needed when you are using four-colors together with spot colors in an image, for example.

In modern versions of Adobe Indesign and Quark Xpress, you can mount images saved in Photoshop format directly, but often TIFF or EPS is a better choice since these formats use up less memory. This is important if you have large quantities of images to save. The advantage with saving images in Photoshop format is that you can use the same images for printing as were used in image editing, with all the Photoshop functions intact. Many other image applications besides Adobe can manage Photoshop as well.

ICC profiles can be embedded in Photoshop images [*see Chromatics 3.10*].

4.8.2 TIFF

Tagged Image File Format, or TIFF, is an open image format for pixel-based images. The file consists of a file header and information describing the image content, size and how the computer should read the file – a kind of instruction manual for how to open the image. TIFF images have the advantage of being able to be LZW-compressed directly from Photoshop [*see 4.9.2*]. The TIFF format also differs from Windows to Macintosh, but most applications manage files suited for both platforms. The file formats are open, which means that with help of the layout program, you can more easily manipulate the appearance of mounted TIFF images, for example by adjusting the contrast or the colors in the images.

TIFF handles line and grayscale images in RGB and CMYK modes. The format supports alpha-files, which means that you can save markings. They also support clipping paths and layers. However, not all layout applications can support clipping paths and layers in TIFF images.

ICC profiles can be embedded in TIFF images. The TIFF format supports 16 bits per channel.

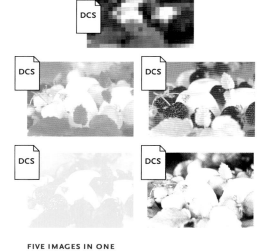

FIVE IMAGES IN ONE
Images in DCS format are divided up into five separate files – one low-resolution preview image in RGB mode and one high-resolution grayscale file for each of the four print colors.

4.8.3 EPS

Encapsulated PostScript, or EPS, manages both object graphics and pixel graphics. This file format is used both with Adobe Illustrator and Adobe Photoshop. There are a number of useful functions in the EPS format for pixel graphics. Images can be extracted with clipping paths and the file format can store information about the halftone screen type and screen frequency as well as transfer functions for print adjustments.

The EPS file consists of two parts: a low-resolution preview image, and a PostScript-based image that can contain both objects and pixels that are principally used for printing. Adobe Indesign uses only the high-resolution part of the EPS image, even for previewing images.

The high-resolution part of the EPS file can be JPEG-compressed without losing any of its EPS functionality. EPS file formats are different for Windows and Macintosh, among them the previewing function which is PICT format for Macintosh and TIFF for Windows.

EPS handles lineart, grayscale, RGB and CMYK mode as well as object graphics. ICC profiles can be embedded in EPS images.

4.8.4 DCS and DCS2

Desktop Color Separation, or DCS, is a version of the EPS format for four-color images that is no longer commonly used. DCS has all the functions that EPS has. The major difference is that a DCS file is divided into five parts: a low-resolution preview image in PICT format, and four high-resolution images, one for each printing color (C, M, Y and K). DCS is therefore sometimes called a five-file EPS.

One advantage with DCS is that the prepress company or printer can send low-resolution images to the designer or editor who places the images into the document. The high-resolution images simply replace the low-resolution ones when the document is output. If outputting one component color, for example cyan, only the part pertaining to to cyan in the image file is sent to the printer via the network and as a result the output is faster than it would have been if the entire image file would have been sent. A little warning when it comes to DCS: because the file consists of five parts, there is increased risk that part of the file will disappear or be damaged. Then the image cannot be used.

DCS2 is a development of the DCS format enabling you to save an image in a certain number of files based on the number of colors the image contains. For example, if you have a four-color image with two spot colors the image is saved in seven separate image files: a low-resolution preview image, and six high-resolution images, one for each printing color (C, M, Y, K, Spot 1 and Spot 2) DCS2 is an appropriate format when creating artwork containing spot colors, commonly occurring in production involving packaging.

ICC Profiles can be embedded in DCS images.

4.8.5 PDF

Portable Document Format, or PDF, manages both object graphics and pixel graphics. PDF combines the best characteristics of EPS and Photoshop formats. In addition, is better standardized and can be read across all platforms. PDF

PSD +/−

+ Handles 16 bits, transparency, layers, layer masks, adjustment layers, typefaces, etc.
+ Handles most color modes
− Cannot be read in simpler image programs
− Cannot be compressed
− Cannot be mounted in earlier versions of Quark Xpress

TIFF +/−

+ Color, contrast, and brightness can be modified in the page layout software
+ Can be LZW-compressed
+ Slightly smaller file size than EPS
− Cannot contain clipping paths
− Cannot handle halftone screen information

EPS +/−

+ Can be extracted with channels
+ Can be stored with information about halftone screens
+ Can be stored with information about transfer curves
+ Safe, because it is encapsulated
+ Can be divided into five files (DCS, Desktop Color Separation), see below
+ Can be JPEG compressed
+ Manages duplex mode
− Cannot be modified in the page layout software
− File size is slightly larger than TIFF

DCS AND DCS2M +/−

The file type has the same functionality as EPS, but is divided up into five partial files.

+ The low-resolution part can be easily be transfered
− Risk of losing partial files

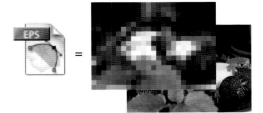

BOTH HIGH AND LOW RESOLUTION
An EPS file is made up partly of a low-resolution preview image as well as the image information that can consist of both objects and pixels.

+ Can be read by everyone
+ Handles most color modes and functions
+ Normal PDF functions can be used.
+ Can be compressed with and without loss

JPEG +/−

+ Takes up very little space
+ Degree of compression can be varied
− Compression quality loss

JPEG 2000 +/−

+ Takes up very little space
+ Degree of compression can be varied
+ Can do lossless compression
+ Can compress parts of the image
+ Can save spot color channels
− Compression quality loss
− Cannot be handled by all programs

format can contain both pixel and object graphics, as well as fonts, ICC information, clipping paths, layers, alpha-files, transparency and more.

Pixel information can be compressed with both lossless (ZIP) and lossy (JPEG) compressions. Therefore you should be careful to not compress files too much when using PDF files.

Adobe Photoshop can manage pixel-based images in the PDF format and Adobe Illustrator prefers to store object-based images in the PDF format.

Images in the PDF format can be read both in Adobe Reader and Acrobat. Because of this the receiver of an image does not have to have the image application. That makes the PDF format appropriate for editing work, especially since using Adobe Acrobat you can both draw and write editing comments on PDF files. You can also secure the file with a password so unauthorized users are prevented from using them.

PDF format manages most color modes: line art, grayscale, RGB, LAB, CMYK and indexed colors. ICC profiles can be embedded in PDF images. The PDF format supports 16 bits per channel.

4.8.6 JPEG

The Joint Photographic Experts Group, or JPEG, format is a compression method for images that also works as its own image format. The advantage to the JPEG format is that it is the same on all computer platforms. JPEG works for grayscale, RGB and CMYK modes, but cannot save alpha files. ICC profiles can be embedded in JPEG images [see 4.9.6].

4.8.7 JPEG 2000

JPEG 2000 is the successor to JPEG and has an array of additional functions. It was chiefly developed to give better image quality to highly compressed images with low resolution, for example web images, but it works also with printed images. JPEG 2000 files can also be compressed with lossless compression methods.

JPEG 2000 manages the color modes grayscale, RGB, Lab and CMYK. In addition, it supports 16-bit modes, 8-bit transparencies, alpha-files and spot color files.

JPEG 20000 also allow you to, through the creation of an alpha-file, determine which parts of an image will be compressed or not. This can be used to avoid damaging an image in critical areas. The technique is called ROI (Region of Interest).

JPEG 2000 is not supported by all image and layout applications.

4.8.8 Raw Format

When advanced digital cameras capture an image with the help of an image sensor, you can store the file that the image sensor created without making a conversion to traditional RGB. This is of interest since the conversion the camera does automatically doesn't take motifs into account, which means that the conversion that occurs isn't optimal. You can choose instead to carry out the conversion in Adobe Photoshop, for example.

If you don't allow the camera to perform the conversion, the file will contain all the image information the camera can create. This in turn must be converted in the computer from the camera's special file construction, called raw format, to a common RGB file before it can be used in image management and layout. This is called raw format conversion, and allows the possibility of better taking advantage of the uniqueness of the image, and thus achieving the highest possible quality. A raw format file can be compared to a negative when you take photographs with film, and raw format conversion can be compared to scanning in the negative and then prioritizing how the tones and colors of the negative should be handled.

Raw format files contain many more shades than a normal RGB image, but at the same time take up less memory. Thus it may be advisable to store in raw format and later convert the files according to different needs.

Raw format files usually build on a file with only one file containing red, green and blue pixels respectively, normally stored with 10, 12 or 14 bit color depth [*see 4.11.6*].

Raw format files are constructed in different ways in different camera models. For this reason conversion programs have to have conversion filters for the specific type of camera's raw format file.

4.8.9 DNG

Since raw format differs from camera to camera, it could lead to problems in the future with storing raw format files. This will partly be due to some files not containing the information about which type of camera they come from, and partly because certain camera models and their files formats will be outmoded and the image management applications will no longer have conversion filters for them. This will make it difficult to obtain a correct conversion. Adobe has therefore developed a standard for how raw format files can be stored, Digital Negative, or DNG. The camera's raw format file can without loss of information be converted to DNG in order to insure that in the future the raw format files can be converted without the conversion program needing information about the construction of raw format file of the actual camera.

4.8.10 PSB

A version of Photoshop format that supports very large image files, PSB files only work from Photoshop CS version and on.

4.8.11 PICT

Picture File, or PICT, is exclusively a Macintosh format. It is used internally in the computer for icons and other system graphics. It is also used to create low-resolution mounting images in EPS and OPI systems. PICT images are not appropriate for print production and are primarily used for line, grayscale and RGB images. They also handle object graphics.

ICC profiles can be embedded in PICT images.

COMPARISON BETWEEN IMAGE FORMATS

POSSIBLE COLOR MODES FOR THE VARIOUS IMAGE FILE FORMATS

- **TIFF** – line art, grayscale, index, RGB, Lab, CMYK

- **EPS** – line art, grayscale, duotone, RGB, RMYK

- **PDF** – line art, gray scale, duotone, index, RGB, Lab, CMYK

- **JPEG** – grayscale, RGB, CMYK

- **PICT** – line art, grayscale, index, RGB

- **PSD** – grayscale, duotone, index, RGB, Lab, CMYK

- **GIF** – index, maximum 256 colors

THE CONSTRUCTION OF IMAGES BASED ON FILE FORMAT

- **TIFF** – File head and bitmap file

- **EPS** – Encapsulated PostScript information and preview in PICT

- **DCS** – Like EPS, but the preview and the high resolution CMYK part is divided up into five separate files

- **GIF** – Color palette and compressed bit map information

- **JPEG** – Visually reduced and Huffman-coded

4.8.12 GIF

Graphic Interchange Format, or GIF, is a file format primarily used on the web. An American ISP, CompuServe, originally created the GIF format to make images small enough to be easily sent via telephone lines. A GIF image is always in index mode, can consist of line as well as grayscale images and can contain anywhere from 2 to 256 different colors. The number of possible colors is determined by how many bits are assigned to a pixel: 1 to 8 bits are possible. The colors are selected from a palette, which can be adjusted to the actual color content of the images or be drawn from set palettes for Macintosh or Windows. There is also a set palette for the web that represents a combination of Macintosh and Windows palettes. It dates from when computers couldn't show more than 256 colors and Macintosh and Windows only had 215 of these in common [*see Index Color Mode 4.6.7*].

4.8.13 PNG

Potable Network Graphics, or PNG, is a file format for pixel images that is used mainly for web publishing. PNG was created as a successor to the GIF format, and in some situations TIFF as well. In principle PNG can manage all the functions of GIF format such as index colors, transparencies, interlacing, etc. However, PNG images may not contain animation – another image format has been created for these, MNG. But PNG has many more functions. PNG manages also alpha-files for transparent masks – for example shadows – and supports color management also since it can store images in sRGB. The PNG algorithm is freely used and often yields more effective compression than with other lossless methods. The PNG format supports 16 bits per file.

4.8.14 MNG

MNG is a version of PNG format that can contain animation.

4.8.15 BMP

BMP is short for "bitmap" and is an image format that is standard in Windows. It is used for monitor graphics and office programs like Microsoft Word and Excel.

BMP format supports line mode, grayscale, RGB and indexed modes, but not CMYK.

Images in BMP format are normally stored in 4 or 8-bit modes and can be compressed with sequential coding.

4.8.16 PCX

PCX is an image format for pixel-based images in a Windows environment, and can be used in most office programs, but is less suitable for graphic production.

PCX format supports images in line, grayscale, RGB and indexed modes, but not in alpha-files.

PCX images can be stored in 1, 4, 8 or 24-bit modes and can be compressed with sequential coding.

4.8.17 Photoshop RAW

Photoshop RAW is a file format for transporting digital images between different applications and computer platforms. Images in Photoshop RAW format can be in grayscale, RGB, CMYK (with alpha-files) as well as several file modes and Lab (without alpha-files). Photoshop RAW format supports 16 bits per file.

This format should not be confused with raw files from digital cameras.

4.9 Compression

Pixel-based images often take up a lot of storage space in the computer. Most of the time this is not a problem, but when transporting images, particularly via network and telephone lines, it is important to minimize the memory used to ensure fast transmission times. Therefore images are usually compressed. There are two types of image compressions: lossless and lossy. Aside from these, there is also the possibility of using certain common file compression programs, which can be used on all file types.

Lossless image compression reduces the size of an image file without reducing image quality. When the image is uncompressed, it will look exactly like it did before compression. From a purely technical point of view, the description of the way in which the image is digitally stored is simplified. There are many types of compression methods that are lossless, for example sequential coding, LZW, Huffman, ZIP and CCITT. Different file formats make use possible by different compression methods. The methods are described a little more in-depth below, and the appropriate file formats given.

Lossy image compression is a type of compression that remove information from the image. Generally, they remove information that cannot be perceived by the human eye. It can be a matter of tiny changes in a color or details in a surface that is mostly one color. You could say that you are simplifying the image. If you compress an image too much, however, you can remove too much information. The loss in quality is clearly visible; the image loses sharpness and begins to look like it is constructed of monochromatic fields of different sizes.

It is important the remember that even if the lossy compressions is not visible, usually so much image information has been lost that generally the image can only tolerate very careful image editing. Therefore it is usually recommended that lossy compression be used only when image manipulation has been completed.

4.9.1 Run Lenght Encoding, RLE

A simple type of lossless compression is run lenght encoding. It is used for line art, which only consists of black and white pixels. Normally the code states the color of each individual pixel. A row might look like this; black, black, black, white, white, white, white, white, white, white, white, white, white, white, white, white, black, black, black, black, black, black. If the image is compressed with sequential coding, the row would be defined like this instead: 3 black, 14 white, 6 black. This takes up considerably less memory. Normally, images consist of many continuous parts of the same color, which means that compression can save a lot of space.

B B W W W W W B B B B B B B B B W W
W W B B B B B B B B B B W W W W B B B B

2 B 5 W 10 B 4 W 10 B 4 W 4 B

RUN LENGHT ENCODING
When several pixels in a row are identical, less memory is necessary when stating sequences of pixels (2 5 10 4 10 4 4) than when stating the color of each pixel (1 1 0 0 0 0 0 1 1 1 1 1 1 1 1 1 1 0 0 0 0 1 1 1 1 1 1 1 1 1 1 0 0 0 0 1 11 1 1). This is the basis for sequential coding.

BEST QUALITY FOR A CERTAIN FILE SIZE
Generally, a better image quality is achieved if you work with high resolution and heavier compression than if you work with low resolution and lighter compression, if the resulting file will have the same size. This is because the 8×8 pixel groups of JPEG compression will end up being smaller for higher resolution.

Sequential coding can be used in BMP and PCX format.

PackBits is another lossless compression method that uses run lenght encoding for compression of TIFF files in Adobe ImageReady.

4.9.2 LZW Compression

LZW compression (after the scientists Lempel, Ziv and Welch, who developed the method) is another lossless compression method.

LZW can be used in graphic production for images saved in TIFF, PDF, GIF or PostScript formats. LZW can manage line, grayscale, RGB, LAB, and CMYK images.

If you use LZW compression on grayscale, RGB or CMYK images, their size is diminished to about half the original size. LZW is somewhat more effective is the image is in Lab mode. Then the image can go down to one fourth the original size. Most effective is when the image is made up of large surfaces of the same color, for example with line art and LZW compression the file can be reduced to approximately one tenth the original size.

4.9.3 Huffman Coding

Huffman coding is a mathematic compression method and is used in a modified version in fax machines. The method is used also as a lossless step in JPEG compression.

LZW COMPRESSION AND FILE SIZE

Uncompressed line image
= 321 KB

Uncompressed four-color image
= 2,100 KB

Here are examples of how LZW compression affects the file size of an image. LZW compression is loss-less and has the greatest effect on line art while grayscale and color images re only compressed to half their original size.

Same image LZW-compressed
= 66 KB

Same image heavily
JPEG compressed = 61 KB

4.9.4 ZIP Compression

ZIP compression is also a lossless compression method. It is mainly used for images in PDF format or images included in a PDF file, but it is also supported by TIFF format. This method has the best effect with images containing large surfaces of the same color.

4.9.5 CCITT

CCITT is short for the French spelling of International Telegraph and Telekeyed Consultive Committee. They developed an array of lossless compression methods to use in transporting black and white images over telephone lines, for example in faxes. CCITT compression is used for line art in PDF format and is also supported by PostScript.

4.9.6 JPEG

The most common type of lossy image compression method is JPEG. JPEG compression allows you to set the amount of information that can be removed from the image and thereby control the level of image compression. At the lowest levels of compression – when the image loses the least information, for example in Adobe Photoshop – the file is reduced to about 1/10 of its original size and the loss cannot be perceived with the eye. When an image is compressed more you would perceive the change if you compared the two images, a strange pattern of squares,

REPEATED JPEG COMPRESSION

When you open a JPEG-compressed image and then save it in JPEG again, the image does not have loss of quality on the surface – as long as you haven't chosen a heavy JPEG compression. If you have edited the image before saving it again, those parts of the image that have been changed will be reduced in quality from the repeated compression. Adjusting curves or changing the images resolution are examples of such editing.

JPEG +/−

+ Reduces file size significantly
+ Works in all computer platforms
+ Can be used in EPS and mounted directly onto the page
− Removes information in the image
− Takes longer to open and save

JPEG COMPRESSION AND FILE SIZE

Lossy compression may sound dangerous but the fact is you can JPEG-compress without any visible difference in the end result. Of course, heavy compression is visible but if you're compressing lightly it is very difficult to notice a difference. In addition, you have a lot to gain in file size, which might be a great advantage when storing or transmitting images via the Internet. (The partial enlargements above are shown 3 times their original size.)

Uncompressed image, 2,100 KB

JPEG lightly compressed, 840 KB

JPEG medium compressed, 165 KB

JPEG heavily compressed, 61 KB

The key to JPEG compression is that the image is divided into smaller blocks 8 pixels wide and 8 pixels high, that is a total of 64 pixels. Within the block the compression program reduces the differences in lightness and color between the 64 pixels. This simplifies the image and can be stored with less memory.

Unfortunately JPEG cannot take into account where the details are found in the image, which means that the blocks are placed evenly over the whole image. Thus they are equally large regardless of the image's resolution and the evening out within the block is done extensively across the whole image.

If the compression is too great, the blocks are visible since the evening out between the different blocks increases and the blocks are perceived as large pixels. The effect of too heavy JPE compression becomes more noticeable the lower the resolution of the image, since in this case the pixels and blocks would be larger.

JPEG COMPRESSION IS CARRIED OUT TECHNICALLY IN FIVE STEPS:
1. The image is divided into blocks of 8×8 pixels.

2. The color range of the image is then converted from the original RGB or CMYK to a new color range with luminance and chromaticity value. Luminance is of the greatest importance for our visual impression of the image, and therefore the luminance values are prioritized during compression.

ORIGINAL PICTURE

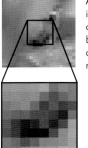

JPEG

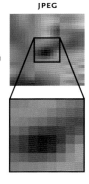

At JPEG compression the image is divided into bocks of 8×8 pixels. Within these blocks, differences between color and brightness are reduced.

3. A "discreet cosine-transformation" (dct) is applied to each block of pixels. This is a mathematical operation that means that the median luminance and median chromaticity of every block is calculated. The value of all the pixels in the block are then described according to how their luminance and chromaticity deviate from the median.

4. Now the actual compression will begin. The program that performs the compression reads which degree of compression has been chosen (for example "low quality" in Adobe Photoshop). The deviation of the pixels for luminance and chromaticity are then rounded off. The greater the compression, the greater the rounding off will be. The more rounded off the values are, the less room will be needed to store the pixels. This is the lossy part of JPEG compression.

5. Finally the image file is compressed a second time with the newly rounded off values being compressed by a lossless mathematical method, usually called Huffman coding.

a so-called JPEG artifact. The word artifact means that it is formed by humans and therefore is not a natural part of the motif [*see Image Editing 5.3.5*].

If you edit an image in JPEG format, it will be compressed every time it is saved. Therefore, images that will be edited repeatedly should not be saved in JPEG format.

JPEG compression is most visible in images with high resolution. JPEG compression is supported by file formats JPEG, TIFF, PDF, and EPS. Unfortunately you cannot simply see from a TIFF, EPS, or PDF file if it contains compromised information. With TIFF files JPEG compression should be avoided, since not all applications support TIFF files with JPEG compression.

JPEG files are only supported by RIPs with PostScript level 2 or later. All modern layout and image applications support JPEG, as well as web browsers and other Internet programs. However, JPEG images seldom work in CMYK mode in web browsers and similar applications.

FILE FORMAT

		AI	BMP	DCS	DCS2	EMF	EPS	GIF	JPEG	JPEG 2000	PCX	PDF	PICT	PNG	PSD	SVG	TIFF	WMF
SUITABILITY	Web							●	●	●				●		●		
	Print	●		●	●		●		●	●		●			●		●	
	Office Program		●			●			●		●	●					●	●
COMPOSITION	Pixels	●	●	●	●		●	●	●	●	●	●	●	●	●		●	
	Object	●				●	●					●	●			●		●[5]
	LowRes. Preview			●	●		●											
	1 file per channel			●	●													
PLATFORM [3]	General format	●		●	●		●	●	●	●		●		●	●	●		
	Mac OS format												●				●	
	Windows format		●			●					●						●	●
FUNCTION	JPEG-compr.						●[8]		●			●[8]					●	
	Wavelet-compr.									●								
	Lossless compr.		●[8]							●[8]	●[8]	●[8]					●[8]	
	16-bit mode									●		●		●	●		●	
	Transparency									●		●		●	●			
	Alpha channels		●									●	●[1]		●		●	
	Adjustment layer														●			
	Layer											●			●		●[4]	
	Extractions path			●	●		●					●			●		●[7]	
	ICC support	●		●	●				●	●		●	●		●		●	
	Screen freq. set.			●	●		●[6]											
	Metadata						●	●	●	●		●		●	●		●	
COLOR MODE	Line art		●				●	●			●	●	●	●			●	
	Grayscale		●	●			●		●	●	●	●	●	●	●		●	
	Duotone						●					●			●			
	Index		●					●			●	●	●	●	●		●	
	RGB	●	●			●	●		●	●	●	●	●[2]	●	●	●	●	●
	Lab	●					●			●		●			●		●	
	CMYK	●		●	●	●	●		●	●		●			●	●	●	●
	Spot col. channel				●					●								

1. *Only one alpha channel* 2. *16 or 32 bits, not normal 24 bits* 3. *Indicates the platform's bound version – which does not prevent the file from being opened in other platforms* 4. *Is only supported in Photoshop* 5. *No bezier curves – only vectors (straight lines)* 6. *Is not supported by Illustrator* 7. *TIFF supports the functions, but not all layout programs handle these* 8. *Compression can be done*

When a digital camera saves an image file, information is also stored about the date, time, aperture, brightness, exposure time, flash setting and much more. The information is called EXIF (Exchangeable Image File Data). This information can be valuable if you want to find the source of a possible problem with the image. The information can also be used in certain programs for automatic adjustments – for example object distortions in the image. Examples of EXIF information:

Filename: IMG_0737.JPG
FIF_APP1: Exif
Main Information
Make: Canon
Model: Canon PowerShot G6
Orientation: left-hand side
XResolution: 180/1
YResolution: 180/1
ResolutionUnit: Inch
DateTime: 2006:05:16 11:21:18
YCbCrPositioning: centered
ExifInfoOffset: 196
Sub Information
ExposureTime: 1/200Sec
FNumber: F4,0
ExifVersion: 0220
DateTimeOriginal: 2006:05:16 11:21:18
DateTimeDigitized: 2006:05:16 11:21:18
ComponentConfiguration: YCbCr
CompressedBitsPerPixel: 5/1 (bit/pixel)
ShutterSpeedValue: 1/202Sec
ApertureValue: F4,0
ExposureBiasValue: EV0,0
MaxApertureValue: F2,0
MeteringMode: Division
Flash: Not fired(Compulsory)
FocalLength: 7,19(mm)
MakerNote: Canon Format: 916Bytes (Offset:942)
UserComment:
FlashPixVersion: 0100
ColorSpace: sRGB
ExifImageWidth: 3072
ExifImageHeight: 2304
ExifInteroperabilityOffset: 1882
FocalPlaneXResolution: 3072000/284
FocalPlaneYResolution: 2304000/213
FocalPlaneResolutionUnit: Meter
SensingMethod: OneChipColorArea sensor
FileSource: DSC

CustomRendered: Normal process
ExposureMode: Auto
WhiteBalance: Auto
DigitalZoomRatio: 3072/3072
SceneCaptureType: Standard
Vendor Original Information
MacroMode: Off
Self-timer: Off
Quality: Super-Fine
FlashMode: Off
Drive Mode: Single-frame
Focus Mode: Single
ImageSize: Large
Easy shooting mode: Manual
Digital Zoom: Off
Contrast: Normal
Saturation: Normal
Sharpness: Normal
CCD Sensitivity: AUTO
MeteringMode: Evaluative
FocusType: Auto
AF point selected : Unknown (8197)
ExposureProgram: Program Normal
Focal length of lens: 7,1875-28,8125(mm)
Flash Activity: Off
Long Shutter Mode: Off
Photo Effect: Off
Sequence number(Continuous mode): 0
Flash bias: 0 EV
Image type: IMG: PowerShotG6JPEG
FirmwareVersion1.00
Image Number: 1070737
Owner name: Robert Ryberg
ExifR: R98
Version: 0100
Thumbnail Information
Compression: OLDJPEG
ResolutionUnit: Inch
JPEGInterchangeFormat: 2548
JPEGInterchangeFormatLength: 6875

4.9.7 JPEG 2000

JPEG 2000 is a compression method that can compress both lossless and lossy files. In addition, it can compress different parts of the image differently. With lossless compression the images will be reduced to half their uncompressed mode. Tests have shown that JPEG 2000 yields at least 20 percent better compression than JPEG. The best effect JPEG 2000 has had in comparison to JPEG is with heavily compressed images at low resolution, for example on the web.

This compression method uses the so-called Wavelet technique. Where ordinary JPEG images give a checkered impression when compressed too heavily, the Wavelet technique gives a grainy, unfocused impression. A file that has been compressed with JPEG 2000 can be transported between computers progressively, which means that the image will become more detailed and uncompressed as more and more of it is received. This is an effect you often see on the Web.

4.10 The Digital Cameras

Digital cameras are constructed using the same optic techniques as film-based cameras, but where the film used to be is now replaced by an image sensor in digital cameras. The image sensor registers the light that is reflected off the subject and is read in red, green and blue components (RGB).

The advantages with digital photography compared to photography using film are many: it is easily to decide right away if the image turned out well, it is easy to adjust the exposure when you can see the consequences of the adjustments, you save a lot of time, it costs nothing to take a number of alternative pictures, there is no effect on the environment from film rolls or film developing, the image is digitalized directly inside the camera which means that you do not need to scan the image in with a scanner and the image will be immediately available for further digital reworking.

Digital camera technique, practically speaking, yields the same image quality as film photography does. There are however some aspects of the two techniques where they differ:

Better digital cameras are more expensive than corresponding film cameras. The image sensor in almost all digital cameras is smaller than the surface area of photo film. This means that for optical reasons you won't get the same short-range depth of focus that you can get with film cameras. You also run the risk of greater color refraction errors. The subject also needs to have shorter focal length to give the same wide angle as with a film camera.

Digital cameras have a poorer dynamic range than film cameras, which means that they have more difficulty reproducing tones in the darker areas of an image and create a lot of noise in tricky light situations.

Digital photography is less sensitive to the color temperatures of light since an electronic white balancing of the image can be done.

Digital cameras are usually marketed according to the maximum number of pixels the camera can capture, which shows the maximum image size that can be shown on a monitor or as a print. The measure is given as the number of megapixels, that is how many million pixels the image can maximally contain.

FILE SIZE AND MEGAPIXELS

Below we see the file size that can be created with digital cameras depending on the camera's maximum number of pixels as well as how large these images can be made in maximum printed screen frequencies of 150 lpi. Note that these are theoretical sizes. How large an image can be created in reality depends largely on the image's quality. Some advanced studio cameras can also give 4 or 16 exposures for the same image, which creates a large image file.

TYPICAL MEGAPIXEL VALUES	APPROX. WIDTH (PIXELS)	APPROX. HEIGHT (PIXELS)	FILE SIZE* (MB)	WIIDTH (150 LPI)	HEIGHT (150 LPI)
0.3 megapixel	640	480	0.9	5,4 cm	4,1 cm
0.5 megapixel	800	600	1.4	6,8 cm	5,1 cm
0.8 megapixel	1,024	768	2.3	8,7 cm	6,5 cm
1.3 megapixel	1,280	1,024	3.8	10,8 cm	8,7 cm
2 megapixel	1,600	1,240	5.7	13,5 cm	10,5 cm
3 megapixel	2,050	1,550	9.1	17 cm	13 cm
4 megapixel	2,400	1,600	11.0	20 cm	14 cm
5 megapixel	2,600	2,000	14.9	22 cm	17 cm
6 megapixel	2,800	2,100	16.8	24 cm	18 cm
8 megapixel	3,500	2,300	23.0	30 cm	19 cm
11 megapixel	4,000	2,700	30.9	34 cm	23 cm
14 megapixel	4,550	3,100	40.4	39 cm	26 cm
22 megapixel	5,400	4,100	63.3	46 cm	35 cm
83 megapixel	10,400	8,000	238.0	88 cm	68 cm

* File size for an uncompressed image in RGB mode.

In reality this does not tell us however about the image quality the camera can attain.

An image photographed with a digital camera that has fewer pixels but has good quality optics and electronic components, can give better quality enlargements than a camera with a greater number of megapixels and low quality optical and electronic components. For this reason cheaper consumer cameras can have the same or higher megapixel values than professional cameras that are much more expensive.

Technical image parameters such as gray balance, the amount of noise in the image, the color correspondence with reality, the tonal reproduction in darker areas and the sharpness of the image are more important measures of image quality for digital cameras. These factors are difficult to gauge however, from the specifications of the manufacturer, and can be better determined by testing the camera.

You can divide digital cameras into six kinds depending on how advance they are and the image quality they provide: web and cell phone cameras, compact cameras, semi-compact cameras, system camera-like cameras, system cameras and studio cameras.

COMPACT CAMERAS

Typical characteristics of compact cameras:

- Don't have interchangeable optics
- Have viewfinders or only displays
- Store the images usually only in JPEG format
- Usually lack manual brightness
- Have poor optics
- Produce a lot of noise in the image

SEMI-COMPACT CAMERAS

Typical characteristics of semi-compact cameras:

- Do not have interchangeable optics
- Sometimes have electronic viewfinders with a small display
- Can produce raw format or uncompressed files
- Has manual brightness and exposure
- Has sharper focus and optics that let in more light
- Produce little noise in the image

SLR CAMERA-LIKE CAMERAS

SLR camera-like cameras have the same functions and produce the same image quality as semi-compact cameras, but in appearance they resemble SLR cameras and have a lens with a greater focal length, which, however, cannot be changed.

SLR CAMERAS

Typical characteristics of SLR cameras:

- Have interchangeable optics
- Have mirror reflex viewfinder
- Can produce raw format or uncompressed files
- Have all the possibilities of manual settings
- Have a medium-sized image sensor
- Produce little noise
- Often have mechanical shutters

4.10.1 Web Cameras and Cell Phone Cameras

Web cameras are computer accessories for video conferencing or simple still photography. Cameras are often built into hand-held computers and cell phones. Sometimes they also have simple video cameras built in. Images from these types of cameras are usually not of high enough quality to use in print. Better cameras in these categories deliver images that are good enough for the Web. Their resolution usually lies between 0.3 and 3 megapixels.

4.10.2 Compact Digital Cameras

The simplest and cheapest type of digital cameras is meant for the consumer market and can fit into an ordinary pocket. They are cheap but don't give very high image quality. The images are at their best on certain monitor screens, photocopiers or printed in smaller format because of their low resolution and low image quality. Normal resolutions lie between 5 and 7 megapixels. The cameras are normally completely automatic regarding focus and exposure.

4.10.3 Semi-compact and SLR-Like Cameras

There is a kind of larger compact camera which, like the consumer camera, has optics that cannot be changed. This is usually called the semi-compact camera.

SLR-like cameras have the same function and deliver the same image quality as semi-compact cameras, but they look like SLR cameras because they have a longer lens, which however cannot be changed as on a SLR camera.

The lens on this type of camera allows in more light, it is more "light tolerant", and has a sharper focus than on compact cameras.

Some of these types of cameras have an electronic viewfinder, of the same kind as many video cameras, and is used like an ordinary viewfinder, but what you see in the viewfinder is shown on a small, low-lit display.

This kind of camera has a flash shoe for attaching an external flash, and images can be saved in raw format or some other uncompressed format. There is an array of manual setting possibilities for exposure via shutter time, aperture, brightness and so on. In other words, these cameras can be controlled in order to attain a relatively high image quality.

The length of the lens in digital cameras, as in video cameras, is usually specified as to how great the difference is in enlargement between the wide angle and the longest telephoto. On SLR-like cameras it is typical to have a zoom lens with 10 times enlargement, which can be compared to semi-compact cameras and compact cameras that usually have a zoom of up to 3–4 times enlargement. A typical resolution for this kind of camera is around 8–10 megapixels.

4.10.4 SLR Cameras

Digital SLR cameras are similar to traditional SLR cameras, but where there used to be film an image sensor now sits.

Handling a digital SLR camera is very much like handling a traditional camera. What makes a digital SLR camera different from a simpler digital camera is that the lens is interchangeable and in general is of very high quality. The image sensor is also larger which allows for shorter depth of focus in the image

CELL PHONE AND WEB CAMERAS
Cameras in telephones and Web cameras generally have too low lens and sensor quality to produce images that can be used in print.

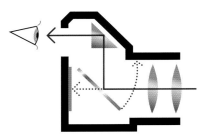

MIRRORS AND SENSORS
Mirror reflex technique, which most SLR cameras are based on, means that the light passes through the lens via a mirror and a prism, and reaches the eye via the lens finder. In the lens finder the same image is then shown as will reach the sensor, though usually lightly cropped.

When the photograph is taken, the mirror folds up and the image reaches the sensor. Since the mirror is open before the photo is taken the subject cannot be shown on the screen before the picture is taken.

and this also means that the image can be sharper. These cameras often have a mechanical shutter to regulate exposure time – the time when the light hits the image sensor – as opposed to simpler cameras which regulate the exposure electronically.

These cameras have what is called a mirror reflex view finder, which means that when you look through the viewfinder you see the subject through the camera's lens via a mirror. It folds up when the photo is taken, and the light through the lens hits the image sensor instead. Since the mirror sits in front of the image sensor in a SLR camera, the first time the image can be shown on the display is after exposure.

Resolution with digital SLR cameras is between 6 and 14 megapixels.

4.10.5 Studio Cameras

The largest and most expensive variation of the digital camera is the studio camera. It is meant for professional use where the demand for image quality is very high. This type of camera has the highest resolution and produces the best image quality. It is often built out of a camera body of a medium-format camera for film, where a digital camera back is used.

Most modern studio cameras work in the same way as SLR cameras, but with larger image sensors and better optics.

IMAGE SENSOR TECHNIQUE

CCD, APS OCH CMOS
The image sensor is based on a large number of light-sensitive cells. Each cell is created the base for a pixel in the final image.

The sensor is based on one of two common techniques: CCD, (Charge Coupled Device) or APS (Active Pixel Sensors).

In the CCD sensor, each cell "senses" the intensity of the light and then sends a signal from each cell, one at a time, to the image processor, which converts the strength of the signal to a digital value for each pixel.

The APS sensor gives a digital value for every pixel directly in the image cell. The most common type of APS sensor uses CMOS technique (Complementary Metal Oxide Semiconductor).

CCD and CMOS are generally equally good techniques, but they differ in certain aspects, which is why they are used in different types of cameras. CCD has traditionally produced less noise in the image but uses more electrical power, while CMOS sensors can be made smaller and are predicted to become cheaper. CMOS sensors are used today in advanced cameras as well.

BAYER MATRIX OR FOVEON
There are two techniques for how the image sensor is constructed to understand red, green and blue. Traditional sensors are constructed with a color filter in red, green or blue in front of every cell. Each cell can thus only comprehend one of the image's three components. The cells are placed in a systematic order, usually GRGB in what is called a Bayer matrix.

When the image is then registered, the image processor or

Bayer matrix, wich is used in almost all digital cameras on the market.

the program that is in charge of raw format conversion counts the image's pixel value so that every pixel receives a value for red, green and blue by also determining the values of the surrounding image cells.

A new alternative sensor technique is Foveon, which involves each cell giving an R, a G and a B value directly. Since the cells let in red, green and blue light to different depths in the cells, the respective color values can be read. Theoretically this allows for a greater richness in detail in the image than with the same number of cells in the image sensor than with the Bayer matrix.

Some studio cameras use a multi-shot technique where an exchangeable color filter with either R, G or B is placed in front of the cells in the image sensor and an exposure is made, whereupon the color filter is exchanged for one of the next color and a new exposure made for R, G and B separately.

Sometimes studio cameras can also move the image sensor a little between each exposure in a series exposure, so that in this way you can achieve an even higher resolution when 4 or 16 exposures are placed together in an image file.

Usually you connect this type of camera directly to a computer for storing image files and controlling the image on the monitor. Some cameras require being connected to a computer, while others can be used independently.

A variation of the studio camera is the so-called three-shot camera which can only be used on a tripod for completely still objects. It has a black and white image sensor where the cells are equally sensitive to red, green and blue. Instead of having cells that are sensitive for each of the colors red, green and blue, there is a large revolving filter with one red, one green and one blue section that sits in front of the image sensor. One exposure is done first for one image component, and then the filter is rotated the next color and an exposure is done for the next image, and the same for the last component. Finally the images are placed together to form and RGB image. In this way the image sensor is fully utilized and the result is one image with very high clarity and low noise.

Studio cameras with the highest resolution have image sensors with image cells placed in a row instead of in a matrix. They are only suitable for product photography in a studio. The exposure is then done as the image sensor moves along the image plane. The image sensors then register the image in a way that is similar to how a plane scanner works and the exposure time is very long.

This technique is considerably slower than normal and the exposure time (input time) can take up to several minutes. In exchange, it gives a considerably higher resolution and often better image quality than what ordinary cameras can achieve. Exactly like with a scanner, you can set the desired resolution. This type of camera can create RGB images which in 8-bit configuration take up 240 megabytes. It is generally more expensive than the other types of cameras. The price is usually tens of thousand of dollars.

4.11 Digital Photography

When you take a digital photograph there are a number of things that affect image quality. We will follow the path of the image through a digital camera from the subject to the memory card, and see how the image is affected by the different steps it goes through along the way.

4.11.1 The Lens Determines the Angle of View
An image is the registration of the light that is reflected off a subject in a certain instant. The light is captured through the lens of the camera, a row of glass plastic lenses polished and ordered in an ingenious manner. The lens in digital cameras uses the same type of optics as traditional cameras. The properties of the lens are stated as the largest aperture and focal length. The focal length is stated as the camera's angle of view, for example shorter focal lengths mean wide angle and longer focal lengths mean telephoto. Digital cameras are all built differently. And for this reason it is difficult to compare lens angles of view through the focal lengths. Therefore you calculate the focal length of a digital camera lens as that of a lens with the same focal length of a corresponding 35-mm film camera to get the angle of view. Wide angle, short focal lengths, are then 15–35 mm, while telephoto, or long focal lengths are 85 mm and upwards.

STUDIO CAMERAS
The largest and most expensive version of digital cameras is usually meant for professional use in the studio where the demand on image quality is very high. This type of camera has the highest resolution, best electronics and optics and produces the best image quality.

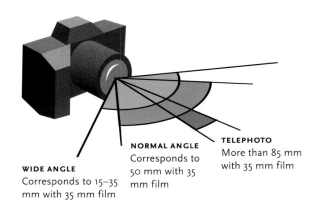

WIDE ANGLE
Corresponds to 15–35 mm with 35 mm film

NORMAL ANGLE
Corresponds to 50 mm with 35 mm film

TELEPHOTO
More than 85 mm with 35 mm film

ANGEL VS FOCAL LENGTH
The normal subject correspond to the eye's angle of view. A shorter focal length yields a wider viewing angle (wide angle) and the subject is perceived as being farther away. A longer viewing angle (telephoto) yields a narrower viewing angle and you perceive the subject as being closer. Digital cameras are often compared to traditional cameras with 35 mm film to have a common frame of reference point.

REFRACTION ERRORS
A typical error with digital cameras, especially when photographing with wide angle, is refraction error. It expresses itself in halo effects in m agenta and green in the corner of the image. The error can to some degree be corrected with RAW format conversion.

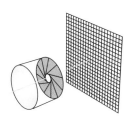

ONE SHOT TECHNIQUE
Most types of digital cameras capture the image in a CCD matrix with a short exposure.

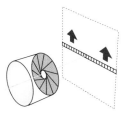

SCANNER TECHNIQUE
Older digital studio cameras can be constructed with a row of CCD cells that slowly sweeps across the motif. These cameras cannot photograph a moving subject.

At around 50 mm we are talking about a normal lens, which corresponds to the angle of view or the eye.

4.11.2 The Aperture Controls the Amount of Light

With the lens aperture the camera regulates the intensity of the light that reaches the image sensor. The aperture is a circular curtain whose opening can vary in size. The aperture value is usually given with an "f" in front of it. A large hole (low aperture value, for example f2.4) lets in a lot of light and a little hole (high aperture value, for example, f22) lets in less light. By varying the aperture opening you can reach an average amount of light with an adequately long exposure time. The aperture also affects the image in such a way that the smaller the aperture, the deeper the area in the deep field will be in focus. A larger aperture results in a shorter depth of field, and brings out the subject with a blurrier foreground and background.

4.11.3 The Shutter Controls the Exposure Time

Using the shutter the camera regulates the amount of tide that is allowed in to the image sensor. The shutter is a curtain that opens and shuts in front of the image sensor. Simpler cameras have so-called electronic shutters. This only means that the time the signal from the image sensor is registered is controlled electronically, during which time the sensor is hit by the light from the subject.

4.11.4 The Image Sensor Registers the Image

The image sensor corresponds to the film in a traditional camera. The image sensor is made up of a large number of light-sensitive cells. Each cell registers the incoming light and turns it into an analogue electronic signal. The electronic signals are then translated into a digital value. To get good image quality the image sensor has to have as a large a dynamic range as possible, that is be able to register differences in tonality in as both as light and as dark areas of the subject as possible.

Normally an image sensor is used where each cell either gives and R, G or B value, a so-called Bayer matrix, or a system is used where every image cell gives both an R, G and B value, a so-called Foveon sensor.

The image sensor in almost all digital cameras is smaller than the surface of traditional film, which is why the depth of field is much larger with film and other focal lengths are needed in the lens of a digital cameras.

4.11.5 Buffer Memory, Image Processor and Memory Card

When the image is registered by the image sensor it is stored in a buffer memory and passes through the image processor before it is stored in the relatively slow memory card. The order in which the image passes through the processor and the buffer memory varies from camera to camera.

The buffer memory is a quick RAM memory whose speed and size determine how quickly a new image can be taken and how many images can be taken in quick succession. If the image passes through the processor before the buffer memory, the cameras speed is also influenced by the speed of the processor. Eventual compression to JPEG format can also mean that going through the processor will take a longer time.

The image processor converts the raw registered file to regular RGB values for each pixel, and makes necessary adjustments for brightness and contrast, adding sharpness or makes other adjustments. After that any necessary JPEG compression is done. Since sharpness occurs before JPEG compression, in some cameras it may be appropriate to let the camera do some sharpening while saving the JPEG file in order to beast take advantage of the sharpness the exists in the raw file before the JPEG compression reduces detail in the image.

Finally, the image is saved on a memory card. If the image is saved in raw format, it is not affected by the image processor before it has been saved on a memory card [*see The Computer 2.6.5*].

Memory cards exist in many forms, but in general they are all equally good. Besides the memory size, the card's writeability and readability are the most important factors when choosing a memory card.

4.11.6 Saving Images in JPEG, TIFF or RAW format?

It is normal to save images in JPEG format in digital cameras. In compact cameras JPEG is often the only available file format for images. The point of using JPEG is of course to be able to store as many images as possible on the memory card. The drawback with this is that the image is compressed, often quite a lot, and loses a lot of quality in such a way that adjustments disappear afterwards.

The more advanced compact cameras can also save in TIFF format, which doesn't have any damaging effects during storage. This is preferable to JPEG format if you want to attain higher image quality.

Slightly more advanced digital cameras can save the raw digital images just as the image sensor registered them before they were converted by the image processor to an ordinary RGB image, and without affecting the images in any way. This digital file is usually called a raw format file (RAW) and should be regarded as the negative of a digital camera. This type of file contains the most image information and offers the possibility of the highest image quality.

Raw format files have to be converted in the computer to RGB format in order to make any changes to the image. Conversion allows you to prioritize the tones and colors of the image to produce an image with the highest quality, somewhat like when scanning in a negative.

An image saved in raw format allows you to prioritize how the image sensor's image information will be used in the best way. This happens inside the computer when the image is converted from raw format to a normal RGB image. For example with raw format conversion you can bring out details in dark areas, correct brightness or compensate for optic errors in the camera lens. This conversion can be compared to the choices and prioritizing that is done when scanning in a slide or a negative. Conversion from raw format to RGB files is called raw format conversion. A normal RGB file is made up of three components – one red, one green and one blue – where one pixel is saved with bits for each component, totaling 24 bits. This means that a pixel can accept one of the 256 tone values for each component.

Most digital cameras have an image sensor that registers the image as one component despite the fact that in the image sensor there are three types of

FILE FORMATS IN THE CAMERA

JPEG
+ Takes up little space
− Produces low image quality

TIFF
+ Produces higher image quality
− Takes up a lot of space

RAW FORMAT
+ Produces the highest possible quality
+ Allows the possibility for adjustments afterwards
− Takes up relatively a lot of space
− Requires RAW-conversion

RAW FORMAT CONVERSION
In order to be able to edit and print an image that was photographed in raw format, it has to be first converted to a traditional three-channel RGB. The conversion is similar to scanning a physical image, but occurs in a program for example Adobe Camera Raw.

FILE ENDINGS FOR RAW FORMAT FILES

- Canon .crw
- Nikon .nef
- Olympus .orf
- Fuji .raf
- Kodak .dcr
- Minolta .mrw och .thm
- Pentax .pef
- Panasonic .raw

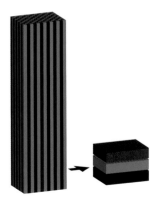

RAW FORMAT CONVERSION
A Raw format file is made up of one channel with many bits worth of color depth, for example 12 bits = 4,096 shades. This is normally converted to three-bit RGB channels with 256 colors each.

image cells that are sensitive to either re, green or blue. Image information in this one-component file is normally stored with 10 to 14 bits per pixel. This means 1,024 to 16,384 possible tonal values.

One image in 14-bit raw format from an ordinary 6-megapixel camera takes up approximately 9.8 megabytes, and if it is converted to an 8-bit RGB image, it will be approximately 16.8 megabytes. Some cameras compress the raw format files without damaging them in order to save memory, which in practice yields somewhat smaller raw format files. Image cells in the image sensor are placed in a systematic pattern (Bayer matrix), most often in green, red, green, blue order (GRGB). The number of green pixels in raw format files is therefore twice as many as the red and blue, which usually results in the converted images having less noise in the green components. A newer technique for image sensors called Foveon is based on each pixel registering red, green and blue information. Each pixel thus produces a RGB value directly which theoretically leads to greater richness in detail and raw format conversion from GRGB to RGB isn't necessary. There are also certain types of studio cameras with so-called three-shot technique that deliver an ordinary RGB image directly [*see 4.10*].

PHOTOGRAPHING WITH QUALITY

TIPS FOR THE HIGHEST DIGITAL PHOTO QUALITY
Below are a few technical photo tips to get the best image quality

- Avoid low light that adds noise and long exposure times.
- Avoid slow shutter speeds that either cause the subject or the camera move during the exposure.
- Use a tripod for longer exposure times.
- Adjust brightness manually against a white or gray surface.
- Include a grayscale in an image or a series of images that are photographed in the same light.
- Use the display as a viewfinder to more easily determine the exposure.
- Use the histogram in the camera to create an image that takes advantage of the whole color range in the digital image. [Image: Histogram in the camera]
- Use the exposure compensation to create a good histogram.

- To get an even color range in the image, avoid photographing in direct sunlight.
- Have good planning since many digital cameras have a lag time for turning on, focusing and setting the exposure.
- The depth of field cannot be as shallow with most digital cameras as it can be with film cameras.
- Choose a low ISO value in the camera to avoid noise.
- Store images in raw format or possibly TIFF.
- Avoid JPEG format.
- Turn off the "Digital Zoom" function.
- Avoid turning on the sharpness in the camera (light sharpening can be good for JPEG storage).
- Avoid the camera's highest resolution.
- Don't use the camera's built-in flash indoors.
- Extreme angles of view can result in color refraction errors or spherical distortions.

- Do not reset image numbers if you don't want to write over previous image numbers.

TYPICAL FLAWS IN IMAGES FROM DIGITAL CAMERAS

- Noise in the image, especially in dark areas
- Poor tone reproduction, flat surfaces
- Narrow color range in the image
- Digital moiré
- Errors in color refraction
- Poor image focus
- Wrong gray balance
- Unnatural colors
- Loss from JPEG compression
- Over sharpening done in camera
- Interpolation damage done by digital zoom
- Shaking and moving focus
- Dead pixels

There many tools to implement raw format conversion, for example Adobe Photoshop's tool Camera Raw or Capture One from Phase One.

Raw format files can also be converted to a camera independent raw format called DNG, Digital Negative [*see 4.8.9*].

4.11.7 ICC profiles for digital cameras.

Every digital camera, like other graphic equipment, has its own unique characteristics that you many want to pay attention to in order to achieve the right colors. To this end an ICC profile for the camera can be created. However the light varies in every photo situation and color temperatures differ. In practice this affects the image more than the camera's characteristics. If an ICC profile for the camera is to be used, a profile must be created for every photo session.

Incamera from PictoColor is a system to create ICC profiles and color correct digital photographs. The system is based on a test chart being taken along with one of the pictures. The image with the test chart is then opened in Incamera and a grid is placed over the test chart. The program creates an ICC profile for the actual photo session. The other images photographed in the same light can then share this GB-ICC profile. By assigning a correct ICC profile to an image you can correct the image's colors so that they correspond to the actual subject's colors correctly.

4.12 Scanners

In order to transfer original images to the computer for viewing and editing, you use a scanner, which reads the original image and converts it into a digital image. There are several types of scanners, according to the physical original artwork that is to be scanned in. The three main types of scanner are: drum scanners, film scanners and flatbed scanners. Flatbed scanners are sold in a number of different price and quality levels, from simpler models for home use for under a hundred dollars to professional equipment for tens of thousands of dollars. Some simpler scanners are combined with writing and fax functions. There are even some models especially adapted for quick scanning of black and white documents and are equipped with feeders. Film scanners cost from a few hundred dollars to tens of thousands of dollars. Drum scanners were very expensive, but generally speaking are no longer sold. They have been replaced instead by professional flatbed scanners.

When scanning an image, the scanner divides the surface of the original image into a checkered pattern, in which every little square corresponds to a scanning point. The denser the bitmap you select, (the higher the resolution), the more image information the scanner will record – resulting in a larger file. Each scanning point is converted to a picture element (pixel) in the computer. The scanning resolution is measured in the number of pixels per inch (ppi) [*see 4.7*].

The scanner illuminates each point with white light. The light that is reflected (if you are using reflective art) or transmitted (back lit, if you are using transparent art) from the scanning point will pick up the color from the respective point on the original image. The reflected or transmitted light is then divided into three components – red, green and blue, by color filters, providing the RGB value for any given color with the help of light-sensitive CCD cells.

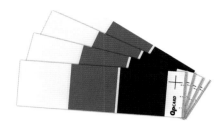

GRAYSCALE FOR DIGITAL PHOTOGRAPHY
When taking photographs the brightness scale left at the bottom of the image is used to balance the brightness in connection with raw format conversion or image editing.

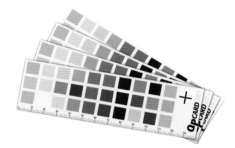

COLOR SAMPLES GIVE THE RIGHT COLOR
By having a special color sample chart in the image, the image and all other images photographed in the same light can be automatically color-corrected.

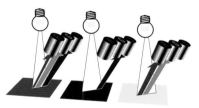

THE PRINCIPLE OF SCANNING
The scanner illuminates a surface with white light and the reflected light is divided into three components – red, green and blue – by color filters. The combination of the reflected light translated into RGB vales stating the particular colors.

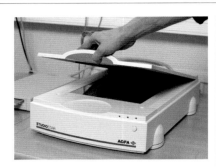

FLATBED SCANNER
The original artwork is placed on a flat glass plate.

DRUM SCANNER
The original artwork is mounted on a glass drum.

FILM SCANNER
A film scanner scans slides or film negatives.

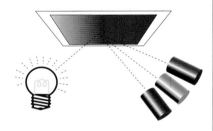

SCANNING IN A FLATBED SCANNER
The light from the lamp is reflected in the original and continues to the CCD cells.

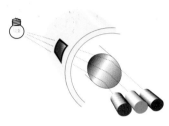

SCANNING IN A DRUM SCANNER
The light passes through the original film and continues through the rotating drum. After that, the light is led via a mirror to the CCD cells or photo multipliers.

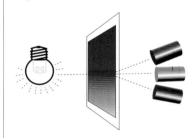

SCANNING IN A FILM SCANNER
Scanning in a film scanner is similar to using a drum scanner but the film stays still during scanning.

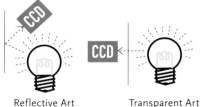

Reflective Art   Transparent Art

SCANNING
When an image is scanned, light is either reflected or transmitted through the original image. Reflective images reflect the light while slides or negatives let the light through.

The electronics of the cells then translates the analogue electronic impulse given of by the light intensity, just like a digital camera, to digital numeric value. In front of every cell is color filter that lets each cell give a value for either red, green or blue. In this way you get every pixel's RGB value. The intensity of the basic colors determines the basic numeric values.

4.12.1 Flatbed Scanners

The original artwork is placed on a glass plate on a flatbed scanner, which works fine if you have non-bending originals. The maximum of the originals is usually A4 or A3. Slides and negatives are often taken out of their frames before scanning.

Scanning with a flatbed scanner occurs with the help if CCD cells [*see below*] that align themselves along the original image. This means that an entire line in the original is scanned at the same time.

The optical resolution of a flatbed scanner varies from 600 ppi and a narrow color range, to 5,000 ppi and a color range of over 4 density units in the most advanced scanners [*see 4.13.2*]. The more expensive plane scanners in the floor model are no longer made, in principal, since the number of negatives and slides that have to be scanned in has been reduced dramatically.

4.12.2 Film Scanners

There is a type of scanner completely adapted for scanning transparent art, that is slides and negatives. This type of scanner is called a film scanner. It normally scans one picture at a time.

There are models that only manage small film images (35 mm), and some that manage mid-range film format, 4.5×6 cm, 6×6 cm, 6×9 cm, and some that manage all the way up to large format film such as 12×25 cm.

In these canners the film is hung in freely in the air from a holder.

There are also scanners that are based on a technique where the film is bent as if round a cylinder and thus held at the correct distance from a rotating scanner head in a more exact way.

The resolution in these scanners varies from 3,000 ppi to 8,000 ppi.

4.12.3 Drum Scanners

The drum scanner gets its name from the large glass drum on which the original artwork is mounted for scanning. The maximum size of the original varies depending on the manufacturer, but is usually A3 (11" × 17"). For obvious reasons a drum scanner can only scan flexible original images. If, for example, you want to scan a book cover, you have to photograph it first. Otherwise you have to scan it in a flatbed scanner. Slides have to be taken out of their frames before they are mounted on the glass drum. Drum scanners are usually very large and expensive but provide high quality and productivity. They are generally used by prepress service providers and commercial printers who need to produce high-quality results in large volumes.

Drum scanners scan images by illuminating them and reading them with a read head containing photo multipliers or CCD cells [see inset on previous page], which sense the intensity in the reflected/transmitted light. The drum rotates at high speed while the read head moves slowly along the surface of the image. Images in a flatbed scanner are read by a number of CCD cells that move forward in measured steps along the surface of the original image, scanning an entire row of the image at one time.

Resolution in a drum scanner reaches just over 10,000 ppi. The drum scanner is no longer manufactured, in principle, since the number of negatives and slides being scanned has diminished sharply.

4.12.4 Photomultipliers CCD Cells

The quality of the photo multipliers or CCD cells in a scanner is important for ensuring the correct translation of light signals. Photo multipliers used to be used more in high-quality scanners, but today all modern scanners use CCD cells since they achieve equally good quality but are cheaper. CCD cells used to have difficulty distinguishing tonal differences, especially in the darker parts of an image and in professional scanners they need to be chilled to reduce the amount of noise in the image. CCD cells also have a tendency to age, which reduces their ability to reproduce colors and tonal transitions precisely.

MOUNTING WITH GEL/OIL
To achieve extra high image quality, avoid what are known as Newton rings and diminish the effect of scratches on the film when you scan negatives and slides, you can mount transparent art on the scanner's glass surface by placing a thin layer of oil or gel on it first, This type of mounting is relatively unusual.

The image above shows how Newton rings can appear.

QUALITY OF THE SCANNER
The quality of the scanner is determined by:

- Mechanical and electronic factors
- Photo multipliers or CCD cells
- Range
- Number of bits per basic color
- Resolution
- Image scanning software

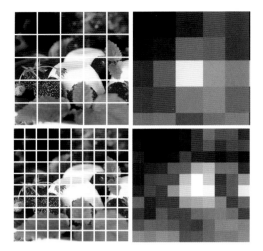

SCANNING IMAGES
When scanning an image, the scanner divides the surface of the original image into a checkered pattern in which every little square corresponds to a scanning point. The denser the bitmap you select, (the higher the resolution), the more image information it will record – resulting in a larger file. Each scanning point is converted to a picture element in the computer, also called pixel. The scanning resolution is measured in number of pixels per inch (ppi).

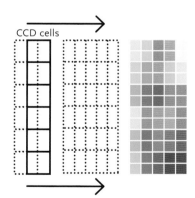

CCD cells

WHAT DOES RESOLUTION 1200 × 600 MEAN?
In some scanners the maximum resolution is indicated as higher in one direction than the other. This is because the row with CCD cells can be moved in smaller steps than the row's own resolution. The scanner can thus scan in more tightly in one direction than the other. At the highest resolution two pixels beside each other will be the same.

4.12.5 Precision and Sharpness

The mechanics and electronics of the scanner are crucial in determining the precision you can scan images with. The optical precision affects color reproduction and sharpness, while the mechanical precision is important to ensure that the image capture is consistent over time. Poor optical precision results in dirty color reproduction and blurriness, while poor mechanical precision can cause striping and misregistration.

4.12.6 Tonal Range

The "range" of a scanner refers to its ability to reproduce the tonal range of an original image, including tiny color changes. The range of the scanner is limited by the sensitivity of its photo multipliers or CCD cells. To understand the limitations of a scanner's tonal range you can compare it to the tonal range of an original artwork. For example, a slide has a maximum tonal range of 2.7 density units [see 4.13.2]. A scanner with a lesser tonal range than the original can never reproduce it in an optimal way. A scanner with less tonal range may not be able to perceive tonal nuances, particularly in dark areas of an original image, resulting in a digital image with uneven tonal transitions and a lack of contrast. Advanced scanners have a tonal range (Dmax), which normally is about 4, meaning that it can handle different types of original artwork and take advantage of all the tones in the original image.

4.12.7 Bits per Color

Most scanners can scan more than 8 bits per color, R, G, and B, even if the final image contains 8 bits per color. The number of bits assigned to each color is usually referred to as the "bit depth" of a scanner. There are scanners with bit depths of 10, 12, or 14 bits per color. This means that instead of just 256 tonal steps, as with 8 bits, a bit depth of 14 allows for 16,384 tonal steps, and 16 bits allows for 65,536 tonal steps. When you scan 16 bits for each color, you talk about 48-bit scanning (3×16 = 48).

Scanning more tones than the final image needs means that you get extra information when scanning. The eye is not able to perceive all these steps, but the extra bits can store important information about an image that is particularly sensitive, like shadow details in a dark image, for example. Some scanners can use a larger bit depth when scanning to supply a 16-bit digital image. This gives a better departure point for image editing than an 8-bit image [see 4.6.5].

4.12.8 Scanner Resolution

Another indicator of a quality scanner is its resolution. A high-quality scanner can capture images at more than 5,000 ppi. High resolution is important when you want to enlarge an image considerably. For example, a regular small-format slide (24×36 mm) that you want to enlarge ten times has to be scanned with a resolution of 3,000 ppi in order to maintain an acceptable image quality and to be printed with a screen frequency of 150 lpi.

It is important to differentiate between optical and interpolated resolution. Optical resolution is the actual resolution that the scanner gives. Interpolated resolution is a mathematical increasing of the image's resolution that is calculated in the scanner based on the optical resolution the image was scanned with. This doesn't mean that the image has more detail, only higher resolution. Interpolated resolution should therefore not be used, and the only reliable measure of the resolution of the scanner is the optical resolution.

Some scanners can however achieve a higher resolution by scanning the image several times over.

4.12.9 Noise Level
A scanner produces noise in the image just like digital cameras. Noise expresses itself like a kind of extra graininess in the image. Noise increases when the scanner and the CCD cells get heated up. The most advanced scanners have built-in cooling systems to minimize the problem.

4.12.10 Speed
One factor that doesn't really affect the quality of the final image but can still be important is the speed of the scanner, in terms of both previewing and scanning high-resolution images. A fast scanner is more enjoyable to work with and results in higher productivity.

4.12.11 Image Scanning Software
Most scanners come with advanced programs which allow you to set different specifications for the scanning process. A good image-scanning program should include a range of setting for scan resolution, separation and print adjustment, and selective color correction with the ICC profiles.

You gain both quality and production time by adjusting the settings as well as possible when scanning. A poorly scanned image can be hard to edit afterwards. Sometimes it is impossible.

You should also be able to adjust settings for batch scanning (though not with film scanners). Most scanners are supplied with the manufacturer's own scanning software. One popular separate program is Silverfast from Lasersoft.

4.12.12 Single-Pass and Three-Pass Scanners
Most scanners can capture the red, green and blue color components simultaneously. This is called single-pass scanning. Some scanners, known as three-pass scanners, scan colors one by one. A single-pass scanner is therefore almost always three times as fast as three-pass scanner. Another advantage to single-pass scanning is that you will have better registration between the colors.

4.12.13 ICC Profiles for the Scanner
Every scanner has its own unique characteristics. Every machine is unique and the characteristics differ even between machines of the same make and model. One may, for example, make a certain red nuance for yellow and light, while another makes the same red nuance for blue and dark. To still get the correct colors in the scanned image, that is so the scanned image will look like the original image, you have to compensate for the scanners flaws. The scanner has to be color corrected. This is done by filtering the color values of every image through a compensation table in the form of a so-called ICC profile [*see Chromatics 3.10*].

A SPECTROPHOTOMETER
A spectrophotometer measures colors in a very precise way. It is used to measure printed sample surfaces or sample colors on a monitor when you create an ICC profile.

DENSITY OF DIFFERENT ORIGINALS

• Print (newsprint)	d0.9–d1.0
• Paper copy	d1.8
• Print (coated paper)	d1.8–d2.2
• Negative	d2.5
• Slide	d2.7
• Reality	over d3.0

TONE COMPRESSION IN PRINT
Because toner range is lower in the print than in reality, it must be compressed. When you compress, tones are lost and you need to prioritize which tones are most important.

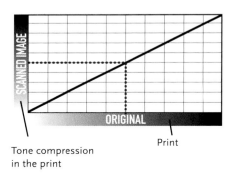

Tone compression
in the print

TONE COMPRESSION IN SCANNING
In the diagram we wee how the tonal range of the original is compressed in scanning to match the print's tonal range. The X and Y axes indicate the tonal range of the original and the scanned image respectively.

The ICC profile for the scanner is created by a carefully prepared test chart of the different photo papers and films from different manufacturers, such as Fuji or Kodak. These charts contain several hundred test surfaces with different colors that are scanned in. Using the ICC application the color values of the different test surfaces are compared to those that have been scanned. The program then automatically creates an ICC profile. The ICC profile is subsequently used by the scanner application on each image that is scanned. If you were to scan a test chart with the new ICC profile, all the colors would be correct.

Programs and test charts for the color correction of scanners are sold together with a measuring device, a spectrometer, and are relatively expensive. One example of this equipment is Eye-One from Gretag Macbeth.

4.13 Scanning Images

In the following section we will review what you need to know about scanning images into a computer, including the definitions of tonal range, tone compression, and gamma. Resolution, screen frequency and sampling value are other terms of central importance. Finally we will go through how you actually scan in an image. To begin with we will look at what you should keep in mind when working with different type of original images.

4.13.1 Original Images
Original image refers to the original material that is scanned into the computer to create a digital image. An original image can be a paper print (reflective art), a slide or a negative (transparencies), or even a hand-drawn illustration, etc.

Different original images are appropriate for different situations. When you intend to print an image in large format or partially enlarge an image, it is important to select large originals. The maximum resolution of the scanner set limitations on how much you can enlarge an image. If the scanner has a low resolution, you will not be able to enlarge an image very much. The size of the original is particularly important when using slides or negatives because the grain of the film can become clearly visible if the image has to be enlarged too much.

Different original also have different life spans. A Polaroid picture will probably only keep its quality for a couple of years, while a correctly treated black and white paper print stored in a cool, dry and dark place can survive or more than 100 years.

4.13.2 Tonal Range in Original Images
The tonal range refers to the number of tones that can be captured by a particular type of original. Slide films have the highest tone range of the materials discussed here, and are often used as originals when scanning because they contain the most information. Tonal range is expressed in density units, and is a measurement of the maximum contrast between the lightest and the darkest areas of an image. An original slide usually has a tone range of 2.7–3.0 density units. By contrast, a print on a fine, coated paper has a tone range of around 2.2 density units, a print on newsprint paper has a tone range of approximately

0.9 density units and print on paper based on a negative has a tone range of around 1.8 density units.

The color range of reflective art is about 2 density units, but has usually been well adjusted when copied from the negative to paper, which is why it is most often very easy to scan and reproduce reflective art in print despite that the margin in the color range is very small. However, the small margin makes it not possible to bring out the details in the image. Instead you have to use the image just about the way it looks as a photo original.

The fact that the reflective art's size is approximately the size of the final print also makes copying it easier and puts less of a demand on the scanner.

4.13.3 Quality of Original Images

A good physical original image is as close to the desired end result as possible. Details and colors that aren't in the original image can't magically appear. The less that has to be adjusted when scanning and handling the image, the better the final result will be.

Besides the image having all the colors, gray balance is important. The original should contain as little color balancing as possible. You can attain this end by making sure that the film type and color temperature are appropriately matched.

All photographic film yields some graininess in the image. If you use a more light-sensitive film, or compress the film, that is under expose and overdevelop it, the grain will be extra large. Grain may be desirable in some pictures, but it is hard to take away when handling the images if you don't want it.

The size of the original also affects the possibilities for good image quality and what it as a digital original image can be used for. The larger the original, the easier it is to get good sharpness and richness of detail. The original image must also be sharp of course, and free of dust and scratches.

4.13.4 Take the Motif Into Account

To use the image information in the best possible way, you can control the tone compression and prioritize certain areas of the image, giving them a higher tonal range than other. You should assess each image before scanning it in order to decide which parts of the image to prioritize. For example, if you have original artwork with a lot of detail in the dark areas, you can prioritize the tone range of those dark areas and compress the lighter areas more, thus preserving the important information in the image.

We have divided images into three categories or motifs: snow images, mid-range images and night images. A snow image is bright overall and has a lot of detail in the bright areas. The mid-range image has details mostly in the mid-range areas. A night image is a dark image with lots of detail in the dark areas.

4.13.4 The Gamma Curve

You can adjust the tone compression of an image with the help of a gamma curve. The gamma curve allows you to see how the tone values of the original artwork are translated into tone values for the print. A linear gamma curve does not affect the translation of tones, while gamma curves with various curvatures control the translation of tones in different ways.

SNOW IMAGE
The snow image is bright with many details in the bright areas of the image.

MID-RANGE IMAGE
The mid-range image maintains detail mainly in the mid-range areas of the image.

NIGHT IMAGE
The night image is a dark image with many details in the dark areas.

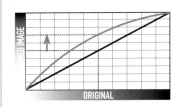 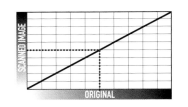 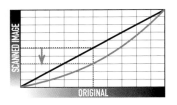

GAMMA LESS THAN 1.8
The images below are scanned with the recommended gamma curve for snow images.

GAMMA EQUALS 1.8
The images below are scanned with the recommended gamma curve for mid-range images.

GAMMA HIGHER THAN 1.8
The images below are scanned with the recommended gamma cure for night images.

SNOW IMAGE
The snow image maintains detail in the bright areas of the image but compromises the level of detail in the dark areas.

SNOW IMAGE
The snow image loses part of its detail in the bright areas of the image.

SNOW IMAGE
The snow image loses all of its detail in the bright areas of the image.

MID-RANGE IMAGE
The mid-range image loses part of its detail in the dark areas of the image.

MID-RANGE IMAGE
The mid-range image maintains detail in the mid-range areas of the image but compromises the level of detail in the dark and bright areas.

MID-RANGE IMAGE
The mid-range image loses part of its detail in the bright areas of the image.

NIGHT IMAGE
The night image loses detail in the dark areas of the image.

NIGHT IMAGE
The night image loses part of its detail in the dark areas of the image.

NIGHT IMAGE
The night image maintains detail in the dark areas of the image but compromises the level of detail in the bright areas.

The gamma value states the orientation and the position of the gamma curve. Normally, a gamma value of 1.8 is recommended for mid-range tones, because it approximates how the human eye perceives color. A night image, on the other hand, has to be scanned with a high gamma value so that the details in the dark areas of the original will appear in the print. The trade-off is reduced detail reproduction in the bright areas of the image. A snow image should be scanned with a gamma value less than 1.8 so that all the detail in the bright areas of the original image is reproduced in the print. The quality o the details in dark areas of the snow image will be compromised somewhat as a result.

4.13.6 Enlarging Images When Scanning

If you want to enlarge the entire image or even partial areas of an image in relation to the original, you have to take this into consideration when selecting the scanning resolution. The relationship between the size of the original image and the print is called the scaling factor. If, for example, you are printing an image at three times the size of the original, the scaling factor will be 3. This means you must have three times the scanning resolution as you would if the image was printed in the same size as the original. Sometimes this is given with 300 percent scaling.

Most scanners take care of the resolution on their own if you choose the final size and resolution or screen frequency you want the image to have. In the cases where you choose the screen frequency you often set the sampling factor first – that is the relationship between the resolution and the screen frequency. It should be 2.

MAXIMUM ENLARGEMENT
Maximum scaling factor = maximum resolution of scanner/image resolution
(for example 4 = 1,200/300).

4.13.7 The Optimal Scanning Resolution

The scanning resolution is determined by multiplying the screen frequency, the sampling factor and the scaling factor. For example, if you have an image you want to print with a screen frequency of 150 lpi at 170 % of the original size, the optimal scanning resolution will be 150×2×1.7 = 510 ppi. You should select the resolution on you scanner that is closest to the optimal value in order to get fast, good scanning. In this case, you would probably select 600 ppi, as the preset resolutions are usually expressed in even hundreds. Keep in mind that the

OPTIMAL SCANNING RESOLUTION
Optimal scanning resolution = screen frequency (lpi) × sampling factor* × scaling factor (%).

The sampling factor should be 2.

SCREEN FREQUENCY AND IMAGE FORMAT

Screen frequency	A6	A5	A4	A3
500 ppi/250 lpi	4	5	6	7
350 ppi/175 lpi	3	4	5	6
240 ppi/120 lpi	2	3	4	5
170 ppi/85 lpi	1	2	3	4

FILE SIZE IN UNCOMPRESSED RGB:

1 – ca 2,25 MByte	5 – ca 36 MByte
2 – ca 4,5 MByte	6 – ca 72 MByte
3 – ca 9 MByte	7 – ca 144 MByte
4 – ca 18 MByte	

As soon as you change the size of digital images the resolution and thereby the screen frequency is affected. The table shows the relationship between file size/image format and image resolution/screen frequency. In a digital image enlarged 200%, for example from A6 to A4, the resolution is cut in half and it can only be printed with a maximum of half the screen frequency of the original image. An image scanned in the A6 format for 250 lpi, i.e. 500 ppi, can e enlarged to A5 for 175 lpi, A4 for 120 or A3 for 85 lpi (=number code 4 above).

resolution of the image equals double the screen frequency, while the scanning resolution equals the resolution of the image multiplied by the scaling factor. In the example above, the image resolution would equal 300 ppi, and the scanning resolution would equal 1.7×300 = 510 ppi. Most scanning applications have a function that automatically calculates the optimal scan resolution if you provide the screen frequency and the scaling factor.

4.13.8 How Much Can the Scanner Enlarge an Image?

Your ability to enlarge images is determined by the final desired resolution and the maximum scan resolution of the scanner. The maximum scan resolution is the smallest unit of length that the scanner head is constructed for. If a scanner has a maximum resolution of 4,800 ppi, it means that it can scan an original image at a maximum of 4,800 dots per inch.

Using the previous example, and assuming that the scanner has a maximum scan resolution of 4,800 ppi, an image that is printed at 150 lpi requires an image resolution of 300 ppi if we are using the optimal sampling factor of 2. This means that you can maximally enlarge the image 4,800 ppi/300 lpi = 16 times. In other words, an image that is going to be printed at 150 lpi and read with a scanner resolution of 4,800 ppi can be enlarged 1,600 % at most. If you are scanning in a small image's negative in this manner, it can be enlarged from 24×36 mm to 38.4×57.6 cm, that is larger than A3.

If you are scanning an image that you want to print in a large format, it makes sense to use a large original image. If the original image you use is too small, you run the risk of not being able to enlarge it enough. Small images' negatives are normally not enlarged to over A3 size, usually not over A4 and snapshots are seldom enlarged at all.

4.13.9 Using a Scanning Application

When scanning an image the work is done through an application that controls the scanner and lets us adjust the settings to how we want the image scanned. The scanning application can be a separate program, or it can be part of the programs in Adobe Photoshop.

Before scanning a preview is done that shows how the image is placed in the scanner. By previewing you can choose the areas that are to be scanned and how. Now is when you can adjust the contrast, set the black and white point, adjust saturation and color balance, as well as choose a suitable gamma value for the actual type of motif. Many applications also have automatic settings.

If you are scanning in a slide and more particularly a negative, the scanner should have ICC profiles set for the types of film being scanned since colors and tones vary between film types. The scanning will be made noticeably easier with good film profiles.

It is important to scan the image in as closely to the desired result to facilitate any further editing, and attain the highest possible image quality.

Scanning applications usually have setting for sharpness. This function should not be used. Sharpness should be done manually instead at the end of image editing and during print adjusting.

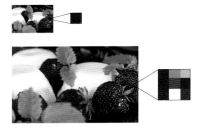

TO ENLARGE IMAGES
If an image is enlarged three times its size, the resulting image requires 9 pixels for an area of the motif that only required 1 in the original size. Thus, it takes 9 times more memory to store and edit the enlarged image compared to the smaller one.

TO CREATE A SCANNED IMAGE WITH THE HIGHEST QUALITY

- Remove dust and dirt thoroughly from the original
- Make the best basic adjustments possible in the scanning application
- Color correct the scanner with an ICC profile
- Supply the image in 16 bits to get as many nuances as possible
- Supply the image with the RGB profile Adobe RGB (1998)
- When scanning film: use an ICC profile for scanning adjusted for the actual film that is being scanned
- When scanning with very high resolutions with a drum scanner and a flatbed scanner oil mounting may be necessary

Above are examples of an image with different scaling factors. Research shows that enlargements up to 120% provide a good result. With enlargements of more than 120% you'll get a clearly visible quality loss. The effect is most evident in diagonal outlines, for example in the upper corner of the open lid. Generally, great enlargements result in blurriness and extreme enlargements in clearly visible pixels.

The scanner program handles most of the calculations needed for resolution. Normally you do a basic setting for what sampling factor you want to use. It should be set at 2. Then for every image you should set what screen frequency the image is going to printed with and also what percentage of the original image the scanned image will have. If the image is going too be twice as large, the size should be set at 200 %. However, different scanning applications vary regarding these settings.

4.13.10 Scanning Several Images at Once

If you are using a flatbed or a drum scanner, it is possible to place several images beside each other on the scanning surface. Certain film scanners can do the same function using and automatic film feeder. The scanning application should be able to handle batch scanning, which means that adjust the setting for each individual image, after which the scanner can scan the images automatically in sequence. With batch scanning you don't have to sit and wait by the scanner

CROPPING AND STRAIGHTENING
When an image is scanned it can easily happen that the image needs to be straightened in the image-editing program to be straight. In Adobe Photoshop rotating and cropping can be done in one step with the cropping tool by rotating the corner of the cropping outline.

The image is 1,382 KB

The image is 957 kByte

The image is 627 kByte

The image is 479 kByte

The image is 380 kByte

The image is 297 kByte

The image is 182 kByte

The image is 116 kByte

The image is 66 kByte

EXAMPLES OF IMAGES WITH DIFFERENT SAMPLING FACTORS
Above are examples of the same image with different sampling factors. Research shows that a sampling factor above 2 does not result in a better image, just a larger file size. It has been determined that a sampling factor slightly higher or lower than 2 provides the optimal relationship between file size and image quality. The effect of a low resolution in relation to the screen frequency (low sampling factor) is most evident in diagonal outlines, for example in the upper corner of the open lid. Generally low resolution results in blurriness and extremely low resolution in clearly visible pixels. These images are screened at 100 lpi to make the effect of a low resolution clearly visible.

BATCH SCANNING
In most scanning programs you can choose to automatically scan several images that have been placed in the scanner. After a pre-scanning all the images in the preview, each are given their own cropping and scanning settings,  and then all the images are scanned in one sweep.

to manually start the scanning of each image, and this can make the scanning process much more efficient.

If the scanner can't do batch scanning and the images are so alike that the same scanning settings can be used, all the images can be scanned as if they were one digital image. Adobe Photoshop can then automatically divide up the scanned image into the separate images and rotate these. The command for this can be found under: FILE → AUTOMATE → CROP AND STRAIGHTEN PHOTOS.

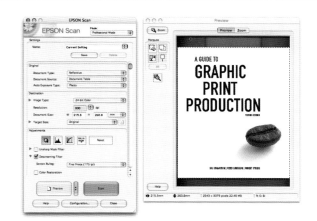

... A FACSIMILE

If you want a printed copy of a facsimile, that is a thumbnail image of another printed but don't have the original document, then you have to scan the printed copy. After that there are a few other things you should thing of to obtain the best possible quality.

Color printing: Scan the image in color (RGB). Use descreening when scanning. Indicate the screen frequency the printed product is probably printed with. The follow the normal work steps to edit the printed image. If possible you should use a printing setting with a lot of GCR [see Prepress 7.4.4].

Black and white: Black and white original artwork often turns out best if you scan it in line art. The scanned images should contain 1,200–1,800 ppi in the final size. The advantage with using line screen is that the facsimile will not be rasterized and the text in the facsimile will be relatively readable. Remember to scan the image at a light setting if possible, since there is no compensation in bit map for dot gain when printing.

If the facsimile is to be made smaller than the original, you should use grayscale instead and carry out the image editing as usual.

Facsimiles without gray or color tones are best scanned as bit map image the same way as the black and white images described above.

Facsimiles turn out best if you use the original digital file and create an EPS or PDF file. Then the images will be rasterized correctly for the new printed product and the text will be reproduced in the best possible manner in only black and without rasterizing [see inset at Layout 6.8].

... AN ALREADY PRINTED IMAGE

If you are forced to scan an image for printing that has already been printed once, you run a large risk that there will be strong moiré patterns in the image.

To avoid or minimize this, the scanning application's function for "descreen" is used. The scanning will thus take a longer than normal time and the image will be a little blurry, but this will make it possible to use the image in print again.

Sometimes it is suggested that you scan the image a little on the diagonal to avoid moiré patterns, but in practice this method yields little or no effect since the moiré problem mainly happens because of the screen frequency of the printed product.

When printing with FM screen frequency this kind of moiré poses no problem. Descreening can, however, still be needed.

... A SIGNATURE

A signature looks most natural if it isn't rasterized when printed. You also want the signature to look sharp around the edges. The best way is thus to scan the signature in line art or bitmap. An image in line art is not rasterized when photo-copied or printed. The resolution when printed for this kind of image should be around 1,000 ppi.

If you want to color the signature, the simplest way to do it is by choosing a color for the image in the layout application. Then it may be rasterized, but still have much sharper edges than if it were scanned in grayscale or RGB.

05.

image editing

What are the most common flaws in a digital image? How do you know if the image is of good enough quality? How do you correct the most common errors in an image? How do you extract an image? How much sharpness should you add to an image?

DIGITAL IMAGES ARE CREATED and edited by just about everybody today. With the aid of digital cameras, scanners and cell phones with cameras and widespread image-editing programs in ordinary computers, large amounts of digital images are created. This means that the traditional reproduction companies have almost disappeared. Those who edit digital images are not always as experienced and focused on image-editing as before. At the same time higher demands are placed on image-editing when the only existing original is a digital one and you don't have a chance to go back to a negative or a slide if the image is going to be used over again.

Unfortunately, the fact that an image is digital seldom means that it is of high enough technical quality to be printed. For this reason it is always necessary to proof and in general even adjust digital images before they are printed, even if the image originally comes from a "professional" supplier.

In order to proof and adjust images properly you mainly need the right knowledge, but you also need good methods as well as an idea of what you are trying to achieve. What characteristics should the digital image have to be considered of good quality? How can a technical standard for images, that is specifications for the technical demands placed on an image, be helpful to effectively attain evenly high-quality images [see 5.8]?

In this chapter we are going to go through working with images from the ground up. We will go over how you can proof an image for quality and work with adjusting the image and retouching and the most important tools for this work. We will also go over digital photography and scanning images. In connection with this we will look at digital cameras and scanners. The large amount of images we create also necessitates storing them in an archive. We will therefore look at how you give images the right information in order to be easily found.

But first let's look at what makes an image good.

5.1 What is a Good Image?

What makes an image good partly depends on subjective opinions, but above all it depends on physical and psychological parameters.

Images with high quality are photographed in an optimal way, utilizing the possibilities afforded by a digital file, and free of damage. Technically speaking, the digital original image should have the highest possible resolution and be adjusted and retouched in a careful and correct manner.

It can be important that the colors of the image be natural. This may mean, for example, that food should look appetizing, reference colors be the right colors, i.e. that grass should be grass green, or that the color of a car should match the original finish.

One of the most important factors for the final quality we experience, is that images, when they are in a printed product, are all produced equally well. This would include, for example, contrast, graininess or color range. Images that do not harmonize with each other affect the quality of the printed product and images very negatively.

5.1.1 How to Create a Good Original Image

Since digital cameras are used so widely today, more and more images are stored, including even film photographs, in digital format for future use. This means that our original images have become digital. Today images can be scanned, photographed with digital cameras, come from a CD with royalty-free images, or be obtained from a digital image archive. For this reason we don't often know if the image is a good original, and therefore we have to go through a number of steps to make sure this is so.

First, we have to verify that the image is not damaged or limited, then we have to adjust the image to get as much out of it as possible in terms of colors, contrast, etc., as well as to create a homogeneity between different original images. After these steps we usually retouch the image to add, remove, draw out or hide details in the subject. When this is done, we have a good original image, technically speaking, but we also have to name and label and the image so it will be searchable and have the information and rights attached to it.

Working with digital original images goes smoothly if the images are not bound to a certain kind of printing or some other use, such monitors and so forth. If they aren't it means you can reuse a digital original for different projects and purposes. When you go to use a digital original image again you can adjust it for a specific printing process, separate it or adapt it to the Internet.

5.1.2 Requirements for a Digital Original Image

In a digital original image the colors and tones must be correct and flaws like dust, etc. should be retouched and eliminated. Even other manipulations and adjustments should be done so that the image can be of visibly high quality.

The digital original should be stored in a mode that is not adjusted for printing, that is in RGB or CIELAB. If CIELAB is used the image should be prepared and stored in 16-bit format so that enough colors are included with the image.

Resolution and size of the image should be big enough so that it can be reused in any imaginable context. Even if the image is meant to be small for its first use, you often choose to create and archive a larger image so that in the future you will have the freedom to use the image in another setting that requires a large image.

The images are often stored in an uncompressed 8-bit RGB and then the image's size is usually stated in megabytes. For uncompressed files this amount is proportional to the number of pixels in the image. An uncompressed RGB image intended for A4 in highest screen frequency is, for example, around 36 megabytes, and for A3 it is double. In extreme circumstances where the images must be able to be used in the largest picture size with highest screen frequency, files of up to 250 MB can be appropriate. However, you seldom create digital images in sizes over 150 MB.

A digital original image shouldn't be sharpened to a large degree. Instead, sharpening should be done when making any adjustments for printing [*see Prepress 7.4*].

Finally, the original image should be labeled in a logical way that facilitates searching and identifying. All the information about rights and the photographer should be stored in the image's IPTC field.

5.2 Discussing Image Quality and Images

When you want to communicate about image quality, it is important to use clear language. If you send comments about an image asking someone else to adjust it, just saying "make the tree better" or "the image has to jump off the page" isn't enough. How should the tree be changed? How should the whole image be adjusted?

It is best to describe what should be done and where in the image. You should use concepts such as lighter/darker, higher/lower contrast, increase/decrease saturation, neutral gray, sharper/blurrier, remove/add/move, yellower/bluer/redder, etc. Specify also where in the image this is to occur, for example in the dark areas, in the sky, in the entire image, black spots/white spots, in everything red.

Describe also, if you can, the intended result, for example "increase saturation in the ball so that it will be the same color as the pail."

It is simplest and clearest to make comments about the image by drawing and writing comments on the image itself. This can be done both digitally and on the physical image. To work digitally is of course convenient, since you can then simply send comments via the Internet.

CLEAR CONCEPTS
To indicate how an image should be adjusted it is important to use clear concepts such as, for example, lighter/darker, increase/decrease saturation, neutral gray, sharper/blurrier, remove/add/move, yellower, bluer, redder.

"Lighter"　　"More saturated"　　"Yellower"

"Darker"　　"Less saturated"　　"Bluer"

PDF format can be saved from both Adobe Photoshop and Adobe Illustrator. If you make notes with the NOTES TOOL in Adobe Photoshop, VIEW → SHOW ANNOTATIONS, these are included as commentaries in the PDF file which can then be read by anyone opening the file in Acrobat. You can in the same way use Sound notations, which means that, via a microphone, you can input spoken comments that can then be listened to in Adobe Acrobat. The comments can be imported back into Adobe Photoshop from PDF files, but this function has not been fully developed, so these comments are best read via Adobe Acrobat.

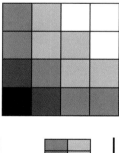

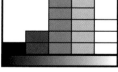

WHAT DOES A HISTOGRAM SHOW?
A histogram is a bar graph (bottom) where the horizontal axis represents a tone scale and the height of the bars represents how large a part of the image (top) is, i. e. how many pixels is made up of the respective tones along the scale.

In working with digital images PDF files and communication functions in Adobe Acrobat are an appropriate tool. You can circle the parts of the image in question and comment on them, place stickies, etc. [*see Layout 6.12.2*]. If you have access to Adobe Photoshop and if the file is saved in TIFF, PDF, or Photoshop format you can add and read comments directly there.

Using PDF format also makes it easy to receive and look at images without having special programs that, for example, can only handle Adobe Photoshop or Illustrator format.

If you don't have access to Adobe Acrobat, you can make comments on a printed copy. Remember not all color copies give the correct colors, which is why you can't assume the results of these copies will correspond to the colors in the digital images. If you are working from a printed photo you can place the photo in a copy machine and then write and draw your comments on the copy. You can also place transparent paper over the photo and write and draw on it.

5.3 Proofing Images

Digital images are seldom perfect. Before you use a digital image in production it has to be proofed. Even if it is delivered by a photographer, obtained from a professional photo archive or has been adjusted by someone at an earlier stage, for example by a photographer, it will often contain technical errors and should be checked. We will look more closely at the more common errors and how they are discovered so that you will not have any surprises during production or even when you look at the finished printed product. We will also give suggestions for the most appropriate safeguards. The most common flaws are too low resolution, the image is already in CMYK mode, large discrepancies between images, incorrect black and white points, poor saturation in the images, discoloration, blurriness or over sharpness in the image, wrong natural colors, the image contains JPEG or interpolation damage, color tones are missing in the image or there is moiré, grain or noise in the image.

Checking the technical quality of a digital image consists mainly of looking at the image on a monitor or in a printout. You can also make good use of tools such as those in Adobe Photoshop.

5.3.1 Proofing Images in the Computer and in Printouts
To easily make a sure decision as to the quality of an image it can be good to use some tools in an image-editing program. We will begin with Adobe Photoshop.

When you judge details in a digital image it should be shown at 100% of its size on the screen. Then every pixel in the image is shown with a pixel on the monitor, that is all the information in the image is shown. In Photoshop you can do this easily by double clicking on the magnifying glass. It will say 100% in the lower left of the program window.

A useful thing to help judge is to isolate the color channels: red, green and blue, or cyan, magenta, yellow and black if the image is already adjusted for printing. This is when many of the errors that first show up in printing can be caught on the monitor.

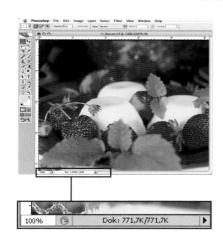

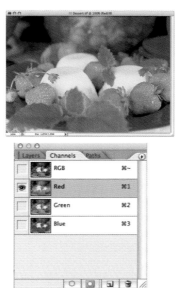

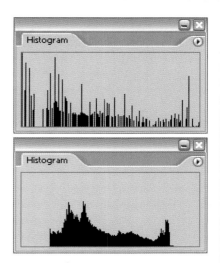

100% IMAGE
When you are going to check the details in a digital image, it should be viewed at 100% of its size. Then every image pixel will be shown by a monitor pixel. In Photoshop you can set this by double clicking on the magnifying glass. 100% shows in the lower left corner of the program window.

ONE IMAGE – SEVERAL CHANNELS
An effective way to judge the quality of an image is the separate the color channels: red, green and blue, or cyan, magenta, yellow and black.

GOOD TONE?
The histogram gives good information about the distribution of tones in the image. If the histogram has too many and too large gaps the image is damaged. If the peaks don't cover the whole histogram the image has too low contrast. You can also show a histogram for the separate channels in the image.

To view the image's histogram gives good information about the distribution of tones in the image. You can also show the histogram for different channels in the image. Choose WINDOW → HISTOGRAM in Adobe Photoshop to see a histogram.

If the image that is going to be proofed is in RGB mode, you will find it useful to use VIEW → PROOF COLORS in Photoshop. Then you will see the image as it will be when it is adjusted for printing, that is transferred to CMYK mode.

To simulate printed colors on the screen the printer's ICC profile has to be selected in the menu EDIT → COLOR SETTINGS... → COLOR SPACE → WORKING SPACES in Photoshop. In addition, the screen has to be color calibrated. Printouts can be good for easily judging the quality of digital images. So that the printout will be reliable, you will have to use a printer with good resolution and color range. Normally this would be an inkjet printer.

The printer also has to be calibrated to ensure that the colors the printer shows reproduce the digital image's colors accurately. When you go to proof an RGB image you would normally want to take advantage of the printer's maximum color range in CMYK to reproduce the image's RGB mode's even larger color range. Sometimes this is called an RGB printout even though the printer is based on CMYK.

In digital images there are some typical errors that you should watch out for. Here are the most common:

- The RGB image lacks or has the wrong ICC profile
- The image is in CMYK mode
- The image has too low resolution
- The image has JPEG damage
- Tones are missing from the image
- There are specular highlights
- The low lights lack detail
- The image has interpolation damage
- The image contains digital noise
- The image is blurry in some way
- The image has been over sharpened
- The image contains moiré from the screening frequency
- The image is extracted sloppily

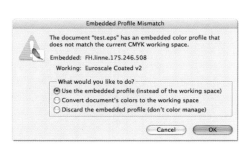

EMBEDDED PROFILE OR WORKING PROFILE?
If an image has an embedded profile that is not the same as the one chosen as its working color space, a warning window appears when the image is opened. You should choose to keep the image's profile and not change to the one for the working color space.

You can also simulate printing's more limited range by additionally compensating the printout by using the printing house's ICC profile. This makes it possible to predict how the image will look in print. If the printout is produced by someone else, it is important to know if is simulating offset printing when the image is judged.

When you look at printouts you should also use lighting where a color temperature of 5000 Kelvin is used [*see Chromatics 3.4*].

5.3.2 RGB Images Lack or Have Diverging ICC Profiles
When an image is opened in Adobe Photoshop a warning window can pop that says the image doesn't have an embedded ICC profile. This means that there is no definition of RGB values in the image in CIELAB, which means in turn that the colors are not device independent [*see Chromatics 3.6*]. You should then choose to embed the profile you have chosen to use as a working color space. This means that the colors will be defined in CIELAB and become device independent.

In some images there is an embedded profile that is the same as that chosen for a working color space. In that case the warning window will appear when the image is opened saying that the image has a diverging embedded profile. In this mode you should choose to retain the profile embedded in the image file since the colors are already defined in CIELAB and therefore device independent. Otherwise you run the risk that the image will lose tones during conversion because the different color spaces have different ranges.

5.3.3 The Image is in CMYK Mode
It is very common to receive images for production saved in CMYK mode from different places such as image banks, photographers, old projects and so on. When an image is converted from RGB to CMYK it is print-adjusted for a specific combination of printing and paper using an ICC profile. This means that all CMYK images are optimized for some kind of printing conditions. If you are going to print a CMYK image on some other paper and/or another printing press than what it is adjusted for, the image will look different than expected. The image can be adjusted for example for a newspaper printing press meaning it will have very low maximum color amount and will b very light to compensate for the high dot gain. This means it will look light and without contrast on, for example, a higher quality sheet-fed offset printing press using coated paper.

If you know what ICC profile the image was originally print-adjusted with, the image can be print-adjusted to the new paper and/or the new printing press with relatively good results. You will then use both the original ICC profile as well as an ICC profile that describes the new printing conditions. This is called CMYK to CMYK conversion.

In Adobe Photoshop this is done in two different ways depending on whether the original ICC profile is built into the file or not. If the ICC profile is not built in, the conversion is done by first selecting the CMYK profile the image has originally been print-adjusted with, in the menu EDIT → COLOR SETTINGS··· → COLOR SPACE → WORKING SPACES. Then you change the mode of the image to RGB, or Lab under IMAGE → MODE. Note that when you convert the image from CMYK to RGB it will not get back the larger color space that the original RGB color image normally would have. If needed you can therefore make adjustments to the image in that mode. Then you adjust the image for printing with the new conditions in the usual way you print-adjust RGB images. This means that you set the ICC profile for the new printing conditions under CMYK, in the menu EDIT → COLOR SETTINGS... → COLOR SPACE → WORKING SPACES. Then you change the image mode to CMYK color under IMAGE → MODE.

If the ICC profile the image originally has been print-adjusted with is embedded in the image file, you can convert the image to the new printing conditions by going into Photoshop under EDIT → CONVERT TO PROFILE... and there choosing the ICC profile for the new printing.

WRONG CMYK-PROFILE
Here you can see what happens if you haven't used the right ICC profile for printing adjustments (bottom half).

SIZE AND RESOLUTION

TOO LOW RESOLUTION
This image has too low resolution, 100 ppi. The resolution of the image should be double that of the screen frequency, 175 lpi × 2, when it is mounted in 100% size on the layout program, that is 350 ppi.

105 cm, 72 ppi

IS THE IMAGE BIG ENOUGH?
It is hard to determine the resolution of an image directly from a digital camera. Often the resolution is low, but the image size large.

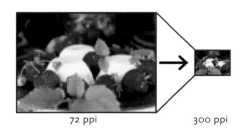

72 ppi   300 ppi

TOO LOW RESOLUTION – REDUCE THE IMAGE SIZE
If you take an image from the Web it has a resolution of 72 ppi, which is too low a resolution for printing. If you reduce the size of the image to a quarter of the size it will have a resolution of 300 ppi which is enough for most printing conditions.

RIGHT RESOLUTION – RIGHT SIZE
Using IMAGE → IMAGE SIZE... in Adobe Photoshop you can reset the resolution to what is needed for printing, and then you can see how large the image will really be. Note: do not have "Change image resolution" checked off.

If you don't know which ICC profile an image has been print-adjusted with, it is especially important to adjust the image's brightness. An appropriate tool for this is IMAGE → ADJUSTMENTS → CURVES in Photoshop. First convert the image to RGB or Lab mode the then make the adjustments so the image looks good. The image can be print-adjusted after these adjustments using the ICC profile of the printing house itself.

5.3.4 Too Low Resolution

A common problem is that digital images have too low resolution to be printed in the size desired. The decision as to an image's printing quality is based on whether or not the resolution is high enough. Otherwise the image will appear blurry. If an image with very low resolution is printed you risk the pixels making up the image being large enough to be visible.

A general rule of thumb is that the resolution of a digital image should be twice the screen frequency in print when traditional screen frequency is used.

An image that is published on a web page has a resolution of approximately 72 ppi. An image that is going to be used in print has a considerably higher resolution. For an image from a web page to have 300 ppi, which is a typical resolution for a printed image, it has to be reduced to a fourth of the size it had on the web page.

HOW JPEG ARTIFACTS IS REDUCED

1. Here is part of an image with clear JPEG artifacts shown in 330% scale.

2. Choose FILTER → NOISE → REDUCE NOISE... in Adobe Photoshop and check off REMOVE JPEG ERRORS.

3. This is the result after using REDUCE NOISE... A certain amount of blurriness remains, but the damage is reduced.

4. Some people prefer a light sharpening to reduce the blurriness that remains and a little noise to further hide the damage.

The quality of an image with too low resolution is improved somewhat if you let an image-editing program increase the image's resolution. This is called interpolation [*see 5.4.5*]. Using interpolation you cannot magically produce details that are missing from the image, but the problem of low resolution is somewhat reduced.

You should note that monitor dumps should not be interpolated despite the fact that they have a low resolution. Keep this low resolution even in print.

You can be fooled when images from a digital camera are often very large in terms of dimensions, but have a very low resolution. You have to check the image with IMAGE SIZE in Adobe Photoshop and adjust it for the resolution the image should have in print. Then you will see the actual dimensions of the image so you can decide if it can be used as large as you need when printed.

5.3.5 JPEG Artifacts

With JPEG compression information is always removed from the image and compression damages can be disturbing, especially in areas with small details and high contrast, as well as where there are diagonal lines. Damages show up as solid blocks of color in the image.

To know if the image has been damaged by compression, you can either print it out on a printer with high resolution or inspect at it on a computer screen.

Inspection of an image on the screen should be done with an enlargement of 100 % or 200 % in an image program. Then you can see all the pixels in the image correctly and can see if it has disturbing JPEG artifacts. Try to look at the image in the separate red, green and blue channels, especially where there are soft tones such as the sky in our example or where there are diagonal contours with high contrast.

HOW IS IT COMPRESSED?	QUALITY	PERCENT OF THE ORIGINAL FILE	NEED FOR REPAIR?
Pure JPEG compression in Photoshop	12 (max)	35 %	Normally does not need to be repaired
Pure JPEG compression in Photoshop	10 (max)	15 %	May need to be repaired
Pure JPEG compression in Photoshop	9 (high)	10 % or less	Repairs are recommended, but the image may be too damaged
Photoshop EPS with JPEG compression	max quality	30 %	Normally doesn't need to be repaired
Photoshop EPS with JPEG compression	high quality	15 %	Probably needs to be repaired
Photoshop TIFF with LZW compression	–	60 %	Does not need adjustments since LZW does non-damaging compression

SHOULD THE JPEG IMAGE BE REPAIRED?
The more compression the greater the probability that damage in quality will be great enough to require repairs in Photoshop. Too much compression can even render the image unusable. Comparing the file size in JPEG format with an uncompressed file gives a good indication of the size of the damage. The size of the uncompressed file can be checked in Photoshop or by resaving the image uncompressed. The above values give indications as to need for repairs.

PROGRAMS FOR REPAIRING JPEG-ARTIFACTS

- The filter REDUCE NOICE... in Adobe Photoshop
- Alien skin Image Doctor: www.alienskin.com – plug-in program for Adobe Photoshop
- JPEG Fixer: www.vicman.net – independent program
- Photo Retouch Pro: www.binuscan.com – independent image editing program

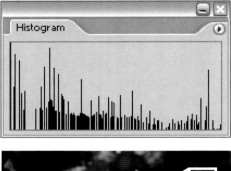

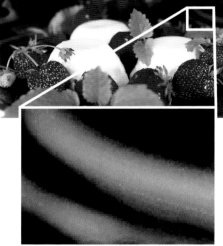

SPARSE HISTOGRAM = RISK FOR BANDING
After too extreme image editing the image may have lost tones and runs the risk of banding or blockiness in the soft tonalities. You can determine this either by checking the image's histogram to see if it is sparse, or you can see banding if you separate the image's three channels, here (bottom) the green channel.

You can also open the image in an image-editing program and compare the open image's file size with the compressed file and get an indication of the quality. You can also do this if the image is EPS or TIFF format. If you use Adobe Photoshop you can look in the lower left corner in the program window when the compressed image is opened to see the file size. You can also use IMAGE → IMAGE SIZE... and compare the value for pixel dimensions with how much space the file takes up on the hard drive. The difference between the compressed and the uncompressed files' sizes is also influenced by the image's size and the richness in detail.

If you want to repair JPEG damages in an image, you can use FILTER → NOISE → REDUCE NOISE and check off REMOVE JPEG ARTIFACTS. Alternatively, you often get a good result with FILTER → SHARPEN → SMART SHARPEN... in Adobe Photoshop and experiment to find the right values. You can even do UNSHARP MASK with a large radius and add a little noise afterward to regain a natural appearance. Otherwise the image can look a little "plastic."

One way to reduce the visible effect of damage to the image is to reduce the image's size in the layout since then the JPEG damage's visible 8×8 pixel groupings will become less obvious [*see Digital Images 4.9*].

Image text JPEG damage: It is easier to see when you look at the separate color channels in the image, especially at soft tones such as the sky, in our example, or in diagonal contours with high contrast.

5.3.6 Missing Colors in the Image

With image-editing tones always disappear that were in the original digital image. Normally this doesn't make any difference since a certain margin exists. If the image-editing is comprehensive or is done wrong, so many colors disappear in the image that the quality suffers. Then banding occurs or blockiness.

Look for the phenomenon in the separate red, green and blue color channels of the image, and even study the image's histogram for each color. If the histogram is sparse, especially in light colors, there is a large risk that bands will be visible in the printed image. The lost colors cannot be recreated. The banding effect in large detail-free areas with missing colors, for example a clear blue sky, can be reduced to a certain degree with the aid of a sharpening filter.

5.3.7 Specular Highlights

Poor coverage, that is lack of tones, is visually easier to accept in dark areas than in light areas of the image, which is why it is important to include all the tones in the image's bright parts.

In some images the lightest parts have lost all their tones completely. Such areas are natural in many images, for example in a shiny spot, but should be very small. When they are large they appear as white spots.

In some cases this is acceptable – for example if the sun or a spotlight is in the image. Generally, however, it is better to slightly underexpose an image than to risk specular highlights.

In Adobe Photoshop you can use IMAGE → ADJUSTMENTS → LEVELS... to find specular highlights. Check off Preview and hold down the Option key at the same time as you click on the white arrow under the histogram when the arrow all the way to the right of the scale. Everything that is shown as white is completely white.

5.3.8 Interpolation Damages

If an image has too low resolution you can let the computer increase the resolution by adding pixels to the image and trying to calculate how these new pixels should look. This is called interpolation. You can't magically create details from nothing, which is why this method is always worse than scanning or photographing the image again with a higher resolution. Even when scanning or digitally photographing this type of damage can occur since you can sometimes choose resolutions that are higher than what the equipment can actually manage, optically speaking. In a digital camera this is called digital zoom and should always be avoided.

5.3.9 Grain and Digital Noise

In images that are scanned and greatly enlarged the grain of the film appears gritty. This is hard to avoid without photographing with film that has smaller grain. Usually it would be film with a lower ISO value.

Even digital cameras and scanners yield a kind of grainy texture in the image, called noise. This shows up either in the form of color noise where pixels in the image have a strong red, green or blue color cast, or quite simply there is a variation in the brightness that makes the image appear grainy. This happens with digital cameras mainly in the dark areas of the image or in images that have been photographed under weak light with a highly light sensitive setting.

To minimize the effect of simpler noise you can use Adobe Photoshop's built-in tool for noise reduction under FILTER → NOISE → REDUCE NOISE... This is a powerful tool to remove noise from digital cameras. You can also use FILTER → SHARPEN → SMART SHARPEN... and begin with the values with a radius and threshold around 3 and experiment.

If it is a question of color noise you can try to convert the image to Lab mode and just edit the alpha and beta channels as above so as to not affect the rest of the image.

Another trick that can be combined with the above is to duplicate the layers of the image and give the uppermost layer a moderate amount of opacity.

There are also several plugins for Adobe Photoshop for noise reduction.

Another way to reduce noise with digital photography of stable objects is to set the camera on a tripod and take several identical photographs.

Since the noise occurs randomly different images will look different. The images can then be combined with each other by placing them in separate layers in the image-editing program and then making them semi-transparent.

5.3.10 Sharpening the Image

A sharp image has steep transitions between dark and light details in the subject. The transition between dark and light surfaces can occur in as short a distance as between two pixels. Blur means that the image lacks these steep tonal transitions between light and dark parts and the image thus cannot reproduce the finest

WITH AND WITHOUT INTERPOLATION DAMAGE
Images can have the correct resolution but the resolution may have been interpolated up in the scanner, digital camera or computer. The effect can be experienced as a grainy blurriness with traces of the jagged pixels that were found earlier in the lower resolution.

SHARP AND BLURRY TONAL TRANSITIONS
Blurriness means that the image lacks steep tonal transitions between the light and dark areas and thus the image cannot reproduce the finest details. The steep tonal transitions that are necessary between dark and light details in the image happen instead in the form of tonalities across a number of pixels (left). In this example sharpness has been increased too much so that edge effects from steep tonal transitions have appeared.

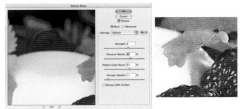

NOISY IMAGE

Digital cameras often deliver pixels in the image with the wrong colors, known as noise. It appears either in the form of color noise where the pixels in the image get a strong tinge of red, green or blue, or quite simply as a variation in lightness that yields graininess in the image.

NOISE REDUCTION PART 1

Adobe Photoshop's built-in tool for noise reduction under FILTER → NOISE → REDUCE NOISE... is a powerful tool for removing noise from digital cameras.

NOISE REDUCTION PART 2

To decrease color noise you can use FILTER → BLUR → SMART BLUR... and then choose directly EDIT → FADE ASMART BLUR and choose MODE: COLOR.

NOISE REDUCTION PART 3

Or you can duplicate the image's mode and in that mode add a lot of Smart unsharp and then blend the modes by giving the right amount of lower opacity to the upper layer.

NOISE REDUCTION PART 4

Noise distributes itself randomly. This means that if you have multiple identical exposures you can place these in several layers and reduce the opacity of the uppermost layer to reduce the noise.

NOISE REDUCTION PART 5

A variation of part 4 can be combined advantageously with FILTER → NOISE → REDUCE NOISE... in Adobe Photoshop.

details. The sharp tonal transitions required between the light and dark details in the image take place instead as tonal transitions across a number of pixels.

Blurriness can happen in different ways. Mainly we talk about three types of blurriness: shaking blur, motion blur and lens blur.

When the camera moves during exposure the image will not be sharp. This phenomenon is called shaking blur. It is especially common in digital cameras, which, because of lower light sensitivity than traditional cameras, use longer exposure times. With a long lens (telephoto or zoom) shaking blur can happen even more easily.

Shaking blur is detected when the image is sharper in one direction than in the other. It is most easily seen in thin lines in the subject that retain their sharpness if they go in the same direction as the shaking, or in small contrast-rich sharp details that form a streak, such as glare, in the direction of the shaking.

During long exposure times the subject may have time to move. This is called motion blur. Motion blur is like shaking blur, but only part of the image is affected. Either the camera has remained still and the main subject has become blurry, or the camera has followed the subject and the background has motion blur. The phenomenon is detected in the same way as shaking blur. In some types of images motion blur is an intended effect and not an error.

When the focus has not been correctly adjusted during photographing you talk about lens blur.

No matter which type of blur you have in the image, you cannot adjust or correct for the error, meaning that blurry images in principle are unusable.

In emergency cases you can improve visibly blurry images' sharpness somewhat with the tool FILTER → SHARPEN → UNSHARP MASK in Photoshop. You have to use a relatively high value for Radius in Unsharp Mask because the tonal transitions are wider than in sharp images. You can experiment with a value of 2–5 pixels. Another way to be able to use blurry images is to make the image significantly smaller, which means that the tonal transitions in print are shorter and appear sharper

5.3.11 Over Sharpening

Over sharpening occurs when you let a digital camera, scanner or image-editing program add too much sharpness or when you happen to sharpen an image that was already sharpened in the computer. When this happens the undesired edge effects appear – halos and black borders around the edges in the image. Unfortunately this is an error that can't be corrected with really good results.

One method you can try, if you want to erase strong edge effects without affecting other details and surfaces, is to make a selection marquee on all the edges before putting on Gaussian blur filter. This is done by selecting and copying the whole image, creating a new channel and pasting on the image there. On the grayscale image that is created in the new channel you use FILTER → STYLIZE → FIND EDGES. With an eraser tool, for example, Gaussian blur filter, Curves or Levels, the channel can then be edited to control the width and size of the edges. Then the channel is loaded as a selection marquee under SELECT → LOAD SELECTION… and then applying Gaussian blur filter with a radius of about 1.

LENS BLUR
Blurriness because the camera wasn't focused correctly appears as an even blurriness as compared to with a short depth of field where the foreground and background are blurry while the subject is sharp.

SHAKING BLUR
Blurriness because the camera was not steady during exposure appears as if everything in the image is being pulled in one direction. Look at details, for example glare, that form lines.

BLURRY BECOMES SHARP
If you greatly reduce the size of blurry images the tonal transitions will be shorter when printed and the image will appear sharper.

OVER SHARP
Images that have been sharpened too much can get halo effects around the edges and they may appear hard and grainy.

RASTER BY RASTER
When scanning in images that have traditional screen frequencies you will get scanning moiré effect. The scanner's pixel matrix interferes with the rasters in the image. The pattern doesn't show up sometimes until you print the image, that is when the image is rasterized one more time.

FINDING POORLY DONE EXTRACTIONS
Poorly done extractions are mainly visible with hair or fuzzy areas that have an unnatural edge against the background. Or else you see parts of the old background that have been extracted.
  In Adobe Photoshop the transparent part of the image is normally shown against a checkered pattern. To better judge an extraction, the background should be made black or white instead. You can do this under REFERENCES → TRANSPARENCY & GAMUT, or by placing a black or a white layer behind the subject.

5.3.12 Moiré from scanned screen frequencies

If you scan in images that have traditional screen frequencies and then print them you will get a moiré effect. Sometimes this shows up first in print, but often you can detect it in the digital image.

Most scanner programs have a so-called descreening function (Descreen) that helps with this type of problem. The method makes scanning very slow, but reduces the risk of moiré.

5.3.13 Poor Extractions

Images that have extractions always have to be proofed to make sure they were done carefully. Poorly done extractions are most noticeable in hair and fuzzy motifs, but sometimes the old background is visible too.

Extractions can be made in different ways: filling in the background with white, making the background transparent, or using paths.

When you open an image that is extracted with paths in Adobe Photoshop, the image does not appear as if an extraction was made. Instead you see the entire image. To see the clipping path in the image you have to select it in the paths palette. The path shows up as a thin line in the image, but it is hard to see the outcome of the extraction.

The best way to check an extraction is to print out a proof of the image. Then the parts that were not enclosed by the path are hidden and it is easy to judge how the extraction looks.

If the extraction was made by filling out the undesired background with white, that is erasing everything in that part of the image, it is easier to check the quality ot the extraction on the screen. Choose to look at the image in at least 100% scale. Even with this method a printed proof of the image is useful for judging. Then you can easily see how well the image has been extracted and the image's tones against white.

If the image has been extracted using a transparency, the transparent part is normally shown with a grid in Adobe Photoshop. It is easier to judge the extraction if the background chosen was white instead. This is done under EDIT → SETTINGS → OPACITY AND PRINTABILITY.

For the same reason as when making extractions against white, it is a good idea to print out an image proof in order to make a qualified judgment.

When making an extraction against white or with a transparency, it is important to check that the tonality that is created with the subject against the background is carried out well, so that it looks natural and the transition is not too fuzzy or too abrupt. Sometimes shadows have also been retouched into the image. Extra care should be paid to proofing these things so that they look natural and correspond to other extracted images that may be placed next to each other in the layout.

5.4 Adjusting Images

Once you have checked that an image doesn't have any serious errors it has to be adjusted. This work means cropping, rotating and adjusting the resolution at the same time as you try to optimize the image's quality. You adjust contrast color, color cast and gray balance.

5.4.1 Creating the Best Image Quality

When you adjust images you do it to optimize and increase the image's quality. The problem is that there is a series of steps during the adjustment work that makes information, for example details and colors, in the original image get lost. This means that the adjustment has to happen in such a way that the information that gets lost doesn't affect the quality negatively. Despite that the steps from a technical standpoint "destroy" the image, the final result gives the impression of a better image.

Because of this you should minimize the number of adjustment steps and carry them out in the right order to avoid repeating them. You should also avoid too large adjustments when editing an image. For this reason the adjustment of an image's brightness, contrast and colors should be done to the greatest degree possible at the time of scanning or raw format conversion [*see Images 4.8.8*]. At that point a base image with the best quality possible is created so larger adjustments for these things will be unnecessary.

In Adobe Photoshop you can avoid problems with information getting lost during image adjustments if you use an adjustment layer. (LAYER → NEW ADJUST-MENT LAYER). This is a tool that means you can try out a number of adjustments.

WORSE BUT BETTER

Unadjusted image

Adjusted image

TO DESTROY AND IMPROVE AT THE SAME TIME

On the left is a recently scanned, unedited image without any loss of information. The histogram under the image describes its distribution of tones along the entire range, dark tones to the left and light tones to the right. The height of the columns describes the number of pixels for each tone. To the right is the same image after it has been edited. In the histogram under the image, you can see that quite a number of tones have disappeared from the image – gaps occur in the histogram. The image becomes "lossy" because it loses image information. However, it still looks better to the eye. As soon as images are edited, some image information disappears. It is not a problem unless you edit the image too much. If it is edited repeatedly or in the wrong order even more tones disappear and the image will end up with a loss of quality.

RIGHT IN — RIGHT OUT

Take the opportunity to adjust the image as well as possible at the raw format conversion stage or when scanning it in. This yields both better quality and quicker and easier image editing.

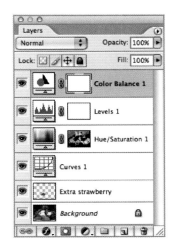

ADJUST SIMPLY AND WITH THE BEST QUALITY

By using adjustments layer, layer masks and layers you will get the highest quality and the greatest flexibility when image editing.

ADJUSTING IN THE RIGHT ORDER

When adjusting an image without adjustment layers the following order should be used to give the image the right quality, make the job go smoothly and avoid steps having to be repeated. When adjustment layers are used steps 4–7 can be done afterward without lowering the technical quality.

1. Rotate and adjust the perspective of the image

2. Crop the image

3. Adjust the image's resolution and size

4. Adjust the color balance
   IMAGE → ADJUSTMENTS → COLOR BALANCE...

5. Adjust the black and white points
   IMAGE → ADJUSTMENTS → LEVELS...

6. Adjust the brightness and contrast
   IMAGE → ADJUSTMENTS → CURVES...

7. Adjust the saturation and specific colors in the image
   IMAGE → ADJUSTMENTS → HUE/SATURATION...

8. Give the image extra overall sharpness
   FILTER → SHARPEN → UNSHARP MASK...

9. Save the original digital image

ROTATE WITH A RULER

Draw a line with a ruler alongside something that should be horizontal. Then choose EDIT → TRANSFORM → ROTATE. The correct rotation angle will then be chosen and you just need to click OK for the image to be correctly rotated.

CHANGING SIZE AND RESOLUTION INSTANTLY

When cropping in Adobe Photoshop the size and resolution of the image can be set by stating the dimensions and resolution in the Options palette.

without its being applied to the final image before you are satisfied with the result. The effect of several adjustment layers is carried out all at once instead of via a number of steps in sequence, which means that less information in the image is destroyed. With the aid of what is know as a layer mask (LAYER → LAYER MASK) adjustment layers can also be applied to parts of an image.

Another way to avoid problems with information being used up during adjustment work, is to choose during scanning or raw format conversion that the image be stored with 16 data bits per pixel and channel versus the normal 8 bits. A 16-bit image can produce one of 65,536 colors versus 256 colors per pixel and channel for 8-bit pixels. The margins will then become much larger in image editing and you won't have to worry as much about the image being ruined during adjustments. When the image is adjusted and ready it can be converted to 8 bits per channel to be saved in some normal image format. You will then have an image where 256 colors per channel are represented and if you look at the images histogram there will be no gaps.

To get as effective image editing as possible, you should carry out the adjustments in a certain order. The order we recommend goes by the following basic steps:

Reduce and crop the image first to its final contents and size – then the rest of the work will go faster and easier. Then make all the adjustments that are needed so the image will be right.

Necessary general changes should be done first, that is those that affect the whole image and whose effect isn't changed by the subsequent step.

Then the adjustments that only affect parts of the image are carried out.

5.4.2 Rotating and Adjusting the Image for Perspective

If the image needs to be rotated do it first. You should avoid rotating the image in layout. Do it instead in an image-editing program both to get the best image quality and to get faster printouts.

In Adobe Photoshop you can easily rotate images by using the measuring tool. Draw the measuring tool along something to be horizontal, for example the horizon, the edge of the floor or something similar. Then select EDIT → TRANSFORM → ROTATE. The right angle of rotation will than be chosen and you can just click on "OK" to get the image rotated correctly.

WRONG PERSPECTIVE
You can correct errors in perspective in an image by adjusting the cropping unevenly. In order for this to work, you have to check off Perspective in the Options palette. When the image is then cropped it will be stretched into a normal right-angled image. (The correction does not work, however, if you have the cropped area "hidden" in Photoshop.)

The cropping tool can be used to straighten crooked images. You just have to grab the image outside one corner so the rotation marquee appears and then turn the image straight. You can even adjust perspective errors in the image by adjusting with cropping unevenly. Once the image has been cropped the image is stretched to a normal right-angle image. To make this happen you have to check off Perspective in the Options menu. The correction won't work, however, if you have cropped the area outside the boundaries of the document.

5.4.3 Cropping the Image
After rotating the image unnecessary parts of the image are taken away by cropping. This is done so that you won't have to work with, and then later send and save, a larger image than necessary. A smaller image is faster to edit, particularly if there are several layers or 16-bit mode is used. Remember that if the image is going to be used as a bleed, it has to be big enough so that 5 millimeters bleed can be cropped away from the edge of the page.

If you want you can choose to not permanently remove the cropped areas, and instead hide them. You do this by, after making a selection marquee as to what to crop using the crop tool, you choose hide instead of remove in the Options menu. However none of the cropping will be saved in memory.

5.4.4 Decreasing an Image's Resolution
If you need to decrease an image's resolution, there are several ways to do this. Ideally you should decrease resolution in whole integers of the original resolution, that is reduce to half, to a third, to a fourth, etc. to retain the highest quality.

When cropping in Adobe Photoshop the size and resolution of the image can be set by stating the dimensions and resolution in the OPTIONS PALETTE.

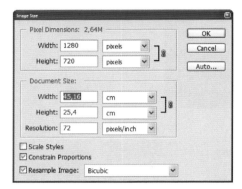

CHANGING SIZE
To change the size and resolution of an image use Image size in Adobe Photoshop. Remember to check off Change image size.

CHANGING RESOLUTION IN LINE ART
If you have to change the resolution of line art it should be done by first going to the image mode Grayscale with the resolution kept the same, then doing a bicubic change resolution and then returning to the image mode drawing mode by selecting IMAGE → MODE → BITMAP.

In Adobe Photoshop the tool used is IMAGE → IMAGE SIZE… to change images' resolutions. The method to Change resolution should be Bicubic.

When the image's resolution is reduced by bicubic interpolation, the image loses sharpness. Therefore it may be appropriate to give the image extra sharpness [see 5.4.12]. This can be done with the Unsharp Mask filter after the image's resolution has been decreased or you can choose Bicubic sharpen as the method to Change resolution. The advantage with Unsharp Mask is that you can visually regulate the amount of sharpness while Bicubic sharpen can in some cases yield an over sharp image.

You can use the cropping tool in Adobe Photoshop to adjust the image's resolution. The setting for this pops up in the Options menu. There is also the possibility here for setting the size of the image to which the image will automatically be scaled when cropping occurs. This measurement can be stored as a tool presetting to facilitate scaling images to, for example, A5 size or 2 or 3 columns' width. The method for Change Resolution that you selected under IMAGE → IMAGE SIZE… is used.

5.4.5 Increasing an Image's Resolution

If a digital image has too low resolution there are four alternatives: Let the image keep its low resolution and accept the low image quality; or scan in, raw format convert or rephotograph the image with a higher resolution; or reduce the image's size to thereby increase the resolution; or finally, increase the image's size via an image-editing program.

Increasing the image's resolution with an image-editing program means that the computer guesses with the help of mathematical formulas how the pixels that are added should look. This is called interpolation. Interpolation means that you get a poorer image than if you scanned or photographed the image with a higher resolution from the beginning, and therefore you should resort to this only if there are no other alternatives.

If the image is photographed with a digital camera in raw format the best way to increase the image's resolution is to do it simultaneously as raw format conversion since an interpolation is done at that time.

The image-editing program guesses during interpolation how the pixels should look by looking at the colors of pixels nearby in the image. It is simplest to use IMAGE → IMAGE SIZE in Adobe Photoshop. You can then choose the advantage of Bicubic Smoother as the method for Change Resolution for the best result when you increase an image's resolution.

There is also an array of programs and plugins for Adobe Photoshop that are intended for giving higher image quality when resolution is to be increased in an image. Some examples are Genuine Fractals from Lizardtech or Pxl Smartscale from Extensis. Another way to increase an image's resolution with a somewhat better result is to use bicubic interpolation but to make the increases in many small increments. The method is usually called stepwise interpolation. You can use an increase of about 10 % per step, until you achieve the desired resolution. You can make a function macro for this to your advantage in Adobe Photoshop [see 5.8.4].

After the resolution has been increased in an image, the image often becomes blurry and you have to add extra sharpness [*see 5.8.4*].

5.4.6 Adjusting Color Casts

An image with an erroneous gray balance will wind up with what is called a color cast, which means that the entire image will appear to be tinted a certain color, for example a greenish tint. This will be disturbing in natural reference colors like skin, grass, oranges and so on, and even more so in tones that should be neutral gray such as asphalt or concrete, for which our brains are very sensitive in deviations in colors.

Sometimes it can be difficult to see if you have the correct gray balance. The Histogram palette (WINDOW → HISTOGRAM) in Adobe Photoshop can be very helpful in this case. By selecting SHOW ALL CHANNELS in the Histogram palette you can see if all three colors R, G and B fill out the whole tonal scale in a uniform way. If, for example, only the histogram's blue channel shows peaks in the image's lightest channels it means that the image's lighter parts are blue.

There are tools in Adobe Photoshop with whose help you can change the gray balance of an image and eliminate eventual color casts: LAYER → NEW ADJUSTMENT LAYER → COLOR BALANCE... or alternatively, IMAGE → ADJUSTMENTS → VARIATIONS... where the Variations tool is found. Also the LEVELS TOOL and CURVES tool have functions to create neutral gray tones, which can be an easy way to get the right gray balance.

In COLOR BALANCE you can affect the respective colors with a control, while under VARIATIONS you see a number of variations of the image with different compensations for color casts. Under variations you can also change the image's brightness. All the colors on the image's surface are affected together (as long as you haven't made a selection marquee on a certain area to make it the only one affected.) In VARIATIONS you can also control the cases where you just want to have an effect on low, medium or highlights.

When you are going to work with gray balance you should set the Info palette so that you can see the RGB value. This is done under WINDOWS → INFO. Find a part of the image that should be neutral, a gray surface in other words, and move the cursor across the surface. Check in the INFO palette if the three colors, R, G, and B have approximately the same value. Set the sample size to 3×3 or 5×5 pixels in the OPTIONS menu for the EYEDROPPER TOOL. Adjust the whole image with one of the above tools until the part of the image that should be neutral has attained the same RGB value. When you have achieved a gray balance in the most important parts of the image the whole image should be adjusted correctly. If light but varying color temperatures have appeared in different parts of the image you may need to do gray balance adjusting locally in the image.

Another way to adjust the gray balance is to work with the gray balance eyedropper. In the LEVELS palette and in CURVES there are several eyedropper tools. The middle one is the gray balance eyedropper. It is used by clicking on a surface of the image that should be neutral gray and this automatically adjusts the image's gray balance. The surface can be light or dark, but the result is best if the surface is made up of midtones. In practice the RGB values vary from pixel

- On uncoated paper dark images are often hard to reproduce well,

- while light images work well on both uncoated and coated paper.

- On uncoated paper the surface is raw and screen frequencies coarser.

- Therefore avoid images with too much detail.

- Colors do not become as saturated on uncoated paper.

- Coated paper is necessary if you want to give the image the highest contrast.

- Choose very bright white paper if exact correspondence of colors is important.

COLOR CASTS GIVE INCORRECT GRAY BALANCE

The upper half of the image has a color cast that is clearly visible on the white paper. In this case R, G and B have different values.

CLICK AWAY COLOR CASTS

Color casts are most visible on surfaces that are supposed to be a neutral gray such as pavement or the plastic crates in this example. On these surfaces you can adjust the color cast with a mouse click by using the GRAY BALANCE EYEDROPPER under LEVELS... or CURVES...

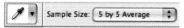

Click on the eyedropper on the TOOLS PALETTE. In the Options menu at the top the choice SAMPLE SIZE will pop up. Set it at 5×5 pixels to more easily get a correct adjustment of the color balance when SET GRAY BALANCE EYEDROPPER is used.

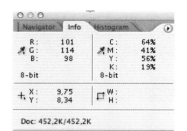

RGB – SAME VALUES MEAN GRAY

By looking at the vales for R, G and B in the info palette when you hold the curser over part of an image that should be neutral gray, you can see if the image has a color cast. In this case the image has a green cast – the value for G is considerably higher than R and B.

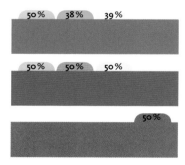

CMYK – SAME VALUES MEAN NOT GRAY

If you indicate the CMY values to get neutral gray these values will not be the same. They will instead follow the gray balance of the actual print (top). The reason for this is that printing colors are not ideal.

In printing the gray balance is usually judged by comparing a surface that is printed with only black (bottom) with a surface made up of a neutral blend of the three color inks, C, M and Y. This neutral blend can vary between different printing techniques and therefore you have to know the gray balance of the actual printer.

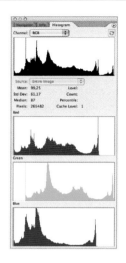

HISTOGRAMS REVEAL COLOR CASTS

If the histograms for the respective colors have different size gaps at the ends it means that the image has a color cast.

ACHIEVING BALANCE

Color balance is the most common tool for adjusting a color cast. It also exists in adjustment layers.

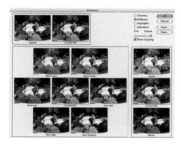

POINT AND CHOOSE

The VARIATIONS TOOL makes it possible to point at the new appearance you want the image to have until you are satisfied.

to pixel, even on the neutral surface of a photograph, which is why it usually requires a few attempts before you get an acceptable result.

By placing the neutral gray card in the image when photographing it, you facilitate the work of adjusting eventual color casts. The gray card doesn't have to be in all the images in a series photographed in the same light, since the setting for one gray balance adjustment can be saved and used in the other images.

5.4.7 Setting the Black and White Points

One typical error is the image not utilizing the whole tonal scale. The parts that should be black are instead dark gray and those that should be white appear light gray. This makes the image appear washed out and without contrast. We say that the black and the white points are defective. Often the black and white points are visibly defective but sometimes you need the help of a histogram, a diagram that shows how the tones are divided up in the image. To adjust the black and white points the Levels tool should be used in Photoshop under LAYER → NEW ADJUSTMENT LAYER → LEVELS…, or, alternatively, IMAGE → ADJUSTMENTS → LEVELS…

BLACK AND WHITE POINTS

You can adjust black and white points in the image by using LEVELS. Click on AUTO or adjust manually according to the procedure below.

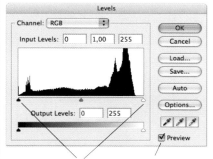

Press the ALT KEY and click on the white or black arrow to read the white or black points.

PREVIEW must checked off in order for this to work.

C =	12 %
M =	12 %
Y =	12 %
K =	3 %

C =	7 %
M =	5 %
Y =	5 %
K =	3 %

WHAT IS WHITE?

The brain decides what is perceived as white in an image. The motif determines the interpretation. If the brain knows that a certain area of an image should be white it is perceived as white even if it's not, as in the image above. To take advantage of what printing makes possible and create maximal contrast in the image so it doesn't appear grayish, the image's lightest point should be made as light as the printer allows, and the darkest parts as dark as the printer allows.

CHECKING WHITE POINT

When checking the white point only the entirely white parts of the image are displayed as white – everything else is black. The reverse applies when the black point is checked

By interpreting the histogram you can draw a whole lot of conclusions as to how the image looks and what might need to be adjusted.

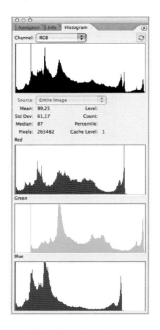

In Adobe Photoshop's HISTOGRAM PALETTE you can see a histogram of the image as a whole, but you can also choose to see a histogram for each channel, in this case, R, G and B.

A histogram that lacks tones at the ends is black or white point flawed.

If the histogram is sparse this means that there are many tones missing and there is a risk of banding.

If the histograms of the three channels have different size gaps in the dark or light parts of R, G and B, it means that there is a color cast in the image.

A normal image should have an even histogram that fills out the whole scale and tapers gently at either end.

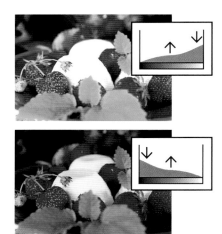

A histogram that does not end at the bottom and ends relatively high instead is a sign of incorrect exposure.

If the histogram ends high in the light end the image is overexposed and large parts of the image are completely white or almost so. You say there are specular highlights in the image.

If the dark parts end high it means the image is underexposed and large parts of the image are black or dark without any details in the dark parts. The histogram should be adjusted in the direction of the arrow to get close to the distribution in the normal image. Both these types of images are difficult to take measures against in the computer since lost tones in the subject can't be brought back.

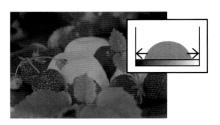

In an image where the histogram has spaces at the ends the lightest and darkest tones are missing. The whole tonal range is simply not being utilized. The result is that the image seems gray. This can be adjusted for example with LEVELS.

In an image with soft tonal transitions the midtones have a larger representation than in normal images. This is most easily adjusted with CURVES.

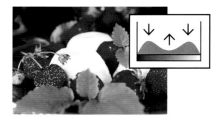

In an image that seems hard most tones are in the dark and the light parts and few are in the middle parts. This is normally adjusted with CURVES.

Here the histogram's bars should be divided up the whole length from black to white and optimally level off toward the zero level in each end of the histogram. If there are gaps at the end of the histogram the entire tonal scale has not been utilized.

The white triangle under the grayscale image under the histogram in Levels is placed where the lightest tones in the digital image are found and the black arrow is placed where the darkest tones are found.

In order to see which parts will be completely white or black you can hold down the option key and hold in the mouse button with the cursor on the triangles you adjust the white and black points with. Then the surfaces of the image that are completely white or black will be shown. Note that "Preview" cannot be checked off in certain versions of Photoshop for this function to work.

In an RGB or grayscale image in 8-bit mode the whole color range should be taken of advantage of so that the absolutely darkest tones anywhere will have a value of 0 and the value 255 is represented in the lightest highlights. The image's RGB value can be read off in the Info palette when you drag the cursor over the image.

Often it is enough to use the automatic correction for the black and white points ("Auto" in the Levels palette). Technically it works so that it looks for the lightest and the darkest parts of the image and sets them as white and black points respectively, and gaps in the ends of the histogram are avoided. The function also exists as a ready menu command under IMAGE → ADJUSTMENTS → AUTO LEVELS.

The automatic correction can work in three different ways that are set under Options in the Levels palette.

In the automatic adjustment's simplest form the image's color balance is not affected. Instead, only the brightness of the image, meaning all three channels are adjusted together and the channel that contains the lightest parts determines the white point and the channel with the darkest determines the black point. This option is called "Improve monochrome contrast" and is found under IMAGE → ADJUSTMENTS → AUTO CONTRAST.

With the other type of automatic adjustment you can also let each channel in the image be adjusted individually by selecting "Improve contrast by channel."

The third version of automatic setting of the black and white points in the image is called "Find dark and light colors."

The last two are stronger adjustments that can both decrease and increase color casts in the image so you have to be watchful of the result when the adjustments are used.

You can also choose "Snap neutral midtones" when these functions are used. This means that Photoshop tries to keep the parts that are neutral in the image as neutral despite the fact that the channels are being adjusted individually.

IMAGE → ADJUSTMENTS → AUTO COLOR is equal to using IMAGE → ADJUSTMENTS → LEVELS, selecting "Snap neutral midtones" under OPTIONS and then using AUTO.

The value of the clipboard governs how many of the image's black and white pixels should be ignored in the darkest and lightest parts respectively with automatic adjustments. The value of the clipboard should be set at 0.01–0.05%

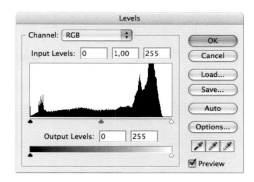

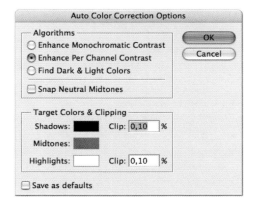

AUTOMATIC CORRECTIONS

Under OPTIONS in the LEVELS PALETTE, there are three types of automatic corrections for black and white points:

- ENHANCE MONOCHROMATIC CONTRAST does not affect the image's color balance, just the image's brightness, that is all three channels are adjusted together and the channel that contains the lightest parts sets the white point while the channel with the darkest value sets the black point.

- ENHANCE PER CHANNEL CONTRAST adjust each channel in the image individually. Give color changes.

- FIND DARK & LIGHT COLORS also adjusts the contrast in the image. Gives color changes.

These functions are found also directly under IMAGE → ADJUSTMENTS and are called AUTO LEVELS, AUTO CONTRAST and AUTO COLOR respectively.

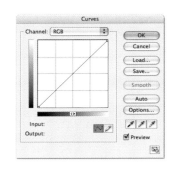

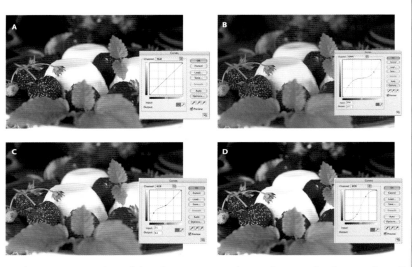

BRIGHTNESS AND CONTRAST

By using CURVES in Photoshop you can adjust the brightness and contrast of the image. To some extent you can also adjust the white and black points.

When the curve's shape changes the image's appearance changes accordingly. In this case, a flatter curve provides a "softer" image and a steeper curve a "harder." Keep in mind that the beginning and end stay in the same place, thus the white and black points are not affected.

A: The image is not adjusted thus the curve is straight. **B:** The image has been "softened" by flattening the mid-section of the curve. Black and white points are not affected.
C: The dark areas of the image have been brightened. The rest of the image is not affected.
D: The image has been made "harder" by sharpening the mid-section of the curve.

BEFORE ADJUSTING

AFTER ADJUSTING

MORE UNSATURATED IMAGE
Often digital images do not have as saturated colors (top) as they could have (bottom). The colors of the image appear grey.

for images of good quality. When scanning poorer quality originals or using an older scanner a value of 0.1 or just above may be necessary.

By clicking on the white, gray and black windows, the black and white points and the goal values for R, G, and B are set for "Shadows," "Midtones" and "Highlights." These should be 0, 128 and 255 respectively.

5.4.8 Adjusting Brightness and Contrast

In most images you will probably just want to adjust brightness and contrast, sometimes for only some of the tones in the image. You may just want to adjust the dark areas and keep the rest of the image intact.

An image can be too soft or have too harsh contrast. This applies either to the whole image or parts of it. An appropriate tool in Adobe Photoshop for adjusting brightness and contrast is to create an adjustment layer: LAYER → NEW ADJUSTMENT LAYER → CURVES... When working without an adjustment layer you use IMAGE → SET → ADJUSTMENTS → CURVES...

In CURVES there is also an Auto-function. This is identical to the Auto-function in the LEVELS tool and adjusts the black and white points, but without showing any histogram. For this reason it is easier and safer to use LEVELS when you want to test the automatic adjustment.

ADJUSTING CERTAIN COLORS

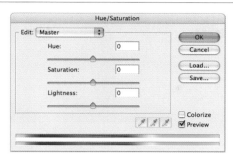

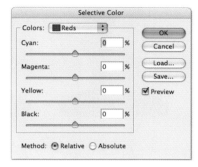

TAKE A TRIP THROUGH TIME
In SELECTIVE COLOR or HUE/SATURATION you can change the colors in the image. You can even make strawberries unripe!

THE EASIEST WAY
HUE/SATURATION is the easiest tool for adjusting individual colors. For example, check off green if you want to change green colors.

In the color scale at the bottom of the window you can set how large a range of colors should be affected.

THE EXACT WAY
SELECTIVE COLOR makes it possible to adjust individual colors in a more exact way, but is a little harder to handle.

5.4.9 **Adjusting Certain Colors**

Sometimes you might want to adjust particular colors in an image after you have adjusted the gray balance. Often it is natural reference colors like skin tone, the color of the grass, the sky, etc., that need to be corrected. Another common problem in images is that the colors are watered down.

The tool LAYER → NEW ADJUSTMENT LAYER → HUE AND SATURATION... are suitable for adjusting this. An alternative tool is LAYER → NEW ADJUSTMENT LAYER → SELECTIVE COLOR...

The tool gives the opportunity to adjust each color's saturation, hue and brightness separately. You can choose, if you want, to change all the colors of the image at the same time, or only one individual color such as changing a strawberry from red to green. If you want to make all or parts of an image black and white, hue and saturation can be used by decreasing the overall saturation to as low as it goes.

5.4.10 **Adjusting Parts of the Image**

Sometimes you might want to make adjustments in certain parts of the image, for example on a face or an object. In this case you have to make a selection marquee for the area you want to change. You can do this in Adobe Photoshop by outlining it with the LASSO tool, the RECTANGULAR or the ELLIPTICAL MARQUEE tool, the MAGIC WAND or QUICK MASK [see 5.5].

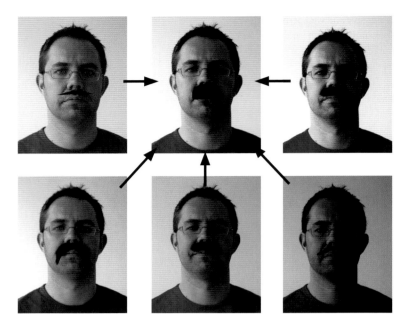

When working with images with similar motifs or images that will be presented together, particularly portraits, you should choose an image as a reference for adjusting all the other images. You should keep the image on the screen and check it against each other image that is adjusted. If you have repeat images in the same style, for example product images, the same reference image should always be used.

A QUICK MASK is a mask that can be modified afterward. A mask hides part of the layer that the layer mask belongs to so the masked portion becomes transparent. The mask can cover unevenly and the masked surfaces thus can have different degrees of transparency. Layer masks can therefore be used as a flexible means of hiding parts of a mask when you are creating things like montages, or for extracting images.

If you are doing tonal or color adjustments with ADJUSTMENT LAYER you can choose which part of the image should be affected by using a Layer Mask. (LAYER → ADD LAYER MASK) in the adjust layer so it only changes part of the image. All the adjustments that are made are connected to the mask, which means that the adjustments are only carried out in the unmasked area [see 5.5].

5.4.11 Homogenizing Images

Making images technically the same in a printed product is more important than high quality in each individual image. The human brain is very sensitive to deviations, but it is more tolerant toward general flaws. If an image with the correct color balance is placed beside an image with a slight color cast, we experience it as more disturbing than if all the images had a slight color cast. We talk about the homogeneity of the images.

The dilemma is that images can come from everywhere and each and every image be of high quality, but when they end up beside each other they can give an impression of low image quality because of how much they differ from each other. This is in regard to, for example, the images' colors, contrast, graininess, brightness or photographic angle.

Not having the images technically homogeneous is one of the factors that most affects the impression they give of quality or lack of it. No matter how

AVOID PIG'S FACES
A simple rule of thumb is to use approximately 15 % more yellow than magenta when reproducing the skin tone of fair-skinned people.

expensive and well printed a printed product might be, and no matter how high the quality of each image, the overall quality will seem poor if they are not technically even. Therefore it is very important to adjust your images in relation to each other when editing to avoid their appearing of poor quality as a whole.

To determine if the images are homogeneous you should open the images together on the monitor, or print them out beside each other on a proofsheet.

The most effective way to adjust the images so they become homogeneous, is to find an image with the appearance desired, and use this one as a reference on the monitor during editing. Use this as a baseline and adjust the other images accordingly so that they are as close as possible to the reference image regarding colors, skin tones and contrast. To saturate the color tones you can use the alpha and beta values in the Lab system.

The easiest way to convert an RGB image to grayscale is to change the mode under IMAGE → MODE → GRAYSCALE. After this operation usually the black and white points have to be adjusted. Many people feel, however, that this method does not yield the best result, especially for skin tones. There are some alternative ways:

One way is to convert the image to Lab mode. Then you can choose to use only the brightness channel from the image and let it become the grayscale image to be used by selecting DIVIDE CHANNEL in the CHANNELS palette. Photoshop creates three separate grayscale images from the Lab image's three channels. Use the image that has an L at the end of the file name – that is the one that will serve as the new grayscale image.

Another way is to use the function IMAGE → CALCULATIONS and then combine the red and green channels at 40 percent. Select MULTIPLY and NEW CHANNEL. This way around usually provides good contrast in skin tones. A new channel with the new grayscale version of the image is created. Then use DIVIDE CHANNELS in the CHANNELS palette whereby four separate images in grayscale mode are saved. Use the image that doesn't have R, G or B at the end of the image name.

An easier version is quite simply to divide up the image directly into channels directly from the RGB image and save the green channel. This usually also gives good skin tones but distorts the color representation in the grayscale image somewhat more. To create a grayscale image out of only one of the RGB channels in this way generally yields more noise that the other methods, but the green channel is still the best starting point for this method since in part is gives nicer skin tones, and digital cameras usually produce the least noise in this channel.

5.4.12 Sharpening

The last step in adjusting images is to sharpen them. When an image is experienced as blurry this means that it is lacking in steep enough transitions between the dark and light tones on either side of an edge. Instead of having a steep transition the edge is made up of a soft tonal transition. When you sharpen an image you make the soft tonal transitions steeper that otherwise make an image blurry. This type of artificial sharpening is carried out by most digital cameras to varying degrees.

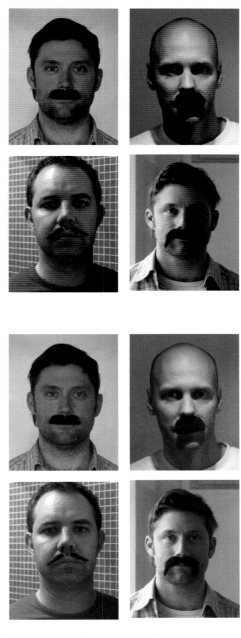

WHEN IT IS HARD TO MAKE THEM ALL ALIKE
If it is hard to make portrait images homogeneous one trick is to make them all gray scale or duplex images instead. This is especially effective in portraits with different appearances where otherwise variations in skin tones and lighting would be distracting.

Here are examples of soft and sharp transitions in an image. The difference between adjacent areas determines if it should be an outline that needs sharpening (sharp transition) or a tonal transition (soft transition) that should remain as it is.

UNSHARP MASK in Adobe Photoshop has three settings: AMOUNT, RADIUS and THRESHOLD.

The three factors amount, radius and threshold can be illustrated as in the figure to the right.

- RADIUS is a measurement of how large blurry areas of the image have to be for the sharpening to take place. The measurement is stated in amount of pixels that the blurry transition is wide, in this case four pixels. Only the areas around the selected radius are sharpened.

- THRESHOLD determines how different the brightness values between two pixels must be before they are considered edges and are sharpened. The measurement is stated in the minimum difference between tonal steps necessary for the tonal transition to be sharpened. With the threshold function you can fine-tune the settings to avoid sharpening intentionally grainy surfaces.

- AMOUNT is simply the value of how much an image should be sharpened. If the sharpening amount is too high, it can cause a distracting outline effect.

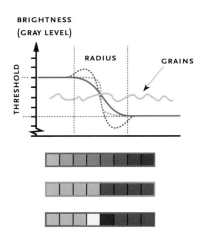

- Here is a row of pixels from an blurry area of an image (blue). A blurry area means that the transition between light and dark is soft (the blue, flat curve).

- In order to sharpen the image, try to make the soft transitions steeper (green curve).

- If you sharpen the image too much, a halo effect occurs along the outline (red curve).

The second image above has been sharpened too much. It causes a distracting effect around outlines because a light line becomes visible on the light side of an outline and a dark line on the dark. Below is an example clearly depicting the contrast effect.

Sharpening occurs in two ways and can be done at two stages during image production. The first type of sharpening refers to giving the image a basic sharpness so the digital image will contain the best conceivable basic quality to produce a good original digital image that will be lasting enough for archives. The second type of sharpening occurs before printing or before web use to compensate for the blurriness that comes about through printing and rasterizing [see 7.4.7].

Images photographed with good digital cameras, with good optics and the sharpness correctly set, do not need very much basic sharpening, while images photographed with poorer preparations need more sharpening. Basic sharpening should always be done with care so that you don't damage the image. In certain digital cameras and scanners there are functions to add sharpness, but you shouldn't use these. Sharpness should instead be added in the computer where you can both see the result and have the option of several settings. The exception is in digital cameras where you can save in JPEG format. Then light sharpening in the camera can be justified since this sharpening is done before the image is compressed [see Images 4.11.5].

FILTER → SHARPEN → UNSHARP MASK... is the best sharpening tool in Adobe Photoshop. The same filter also exists in many other image-editing programs. The tool has three setting possibilities: RADIUS, THRESHOLD value and AMOUNT.

When an image is going to be given sharpness you have to adapt the sharpness to how sharp the digital image is to begin with. In UNSHARP MASK this is taken into account in the RADIUS setting. How short the tonal transitions are will be stated clearly there, in number of pixels, for sharpening. Long tonal transitions are included as a rule in natural tonalities in the subject and should not be sharpened. If you instead set for a small radius the image will not be affected at all. The radius must therefore be adapted to the image's sharpest tonal transitions.

The radius for scanned images, or images taken with simple to moderately digital cameras should be between 0.8 and 1.6. In images photographed with digital cameras of studio quality sharpening is often done with 0.1 – 1.3 pixels radii. When sharpening an image that is going to be displayed on a monitor and with a computer projector, for example on a web page, the radius is appropriately set to 0.3 pixels.

It is only edges that are sharpened. The question is how large tonal differences there should be between two surfaces for the transition between them to be considered an edge.

If you sharpen with too small tonal differences, phenomena such as digital noise will also come into the image, or grain in photographic film or natural textures on the surface of the subject will be sharpened and result in an unnecessarily coarse appearance.

Therefore you set a threshold value for how large the differences will be for sharpening to occur. The threshold value in UNSHARP MASK in normal cases is around 3–9. If the image is very grainy you can raise the threshold to around 20–30. The measurement Threshold Value is stated as the difference in gray tonal values needed so that the transition between surfaces can be counted as an edge. Since the image is made up of 256 tonal steps from black (0) and white (255) the

THRESHOLD value is stated as how many of those tonal steps at a minimum must differ to determine if the tonal transition should be sharpened.

How steep the tonal transitions should be made during sharpening is determined by the AMOUNT setting. If you specify too low a value for AMOUNT the image is given too little extra sharpness. When you set too high a value for AMOUNT an extra dark edge will appear on the dark side and a light edge will appear on the light side. Such phenomena are called haloes. The AMOUNT should in, general, lie between 100 and 200 %.

We have given recommendations of values that can be used in UNSHARP MASK. You should, however, experiment to find out which settings best fit each individual case. As far as very blurry images go, it can be difficult to give extra sharpness with the above values. This is because the small difference between RADIUS and THRESHOLD doesn't exist in such blurry images. You can try with a larger RADIUS and a lower value for AMOUNT. It is important when you evaluate images on a monitor that the display signal be 1:1 or 100 %. With this signal it means that every pixel in the image will be shown as a monitor pixel. Thus you have the best conditions for judging the image.

Normally UNSHARP MASK is applied to the image in its entirety in RGB mode. There are, however, some alternative procedures and tools. If you first convert the image to Lab colors and than add sharpness in the BRIGHTNESS CHANNEL this enables you to add a little more sharpness than normal without it yielding any negative effects. This way you will not have any problems with color noise or that you inadvertently sharpen variations in color, something that at times occurs with normal sharpening. When converting to Lab mode you should always switch to 16-bit mode first.

A simpler version that gives the same result is placing UNSHARP MASK on an RGB image and going directly to EDIT → FADE UNSHARP MASK... and select MODE: LUMINOSITY. You can even diminish the effects there of the newly applied sharpness by selecting different values for OPACITY.

A trick that can be used to place sharpness just around edges and not, for example, on top of noise on smooth surfaces, is to select all the edges with a marquee tool before the UNSHARP MASK is applied. This is done by selecting the entire image, creating a new channel and pasting in the image there. On the grayscale image that is created in the new channel use FILTER → STYLIZE → FIND EDGES. With, for example, the ERASER TOOL, GUASSIAN BLUR, CURVES or LEVELS, the channel can then be edited to determine the width and size of the edges. Finally, the channel is loaded as a selection marquee under SELECT → LOAD SELECTION and choose channel, then apply the UNSHARP MASK. It could be easy to create a function macro for these steps.

There are also many other tools on the market for sharpening images such as Focal Blade from Thepluginsite.com. This is a plugin program that works with Adobe Photoshop, as well as with other applications. Such plugins offer the ability to carefully control sharpness for better results.

TOOLS IN PHOTOSHOP

The TOOL PALETTE in Adobe Photoshop hides a large number of optional tools. By holding down the mouse on the tool that has the little arrow in its lower corner the different options appear as below. You can also hold down the Alt key and click on the tool to change between the different options. To choose one of the different tools directly you can click on the letter on the keypad that is to the right of the tool's name.

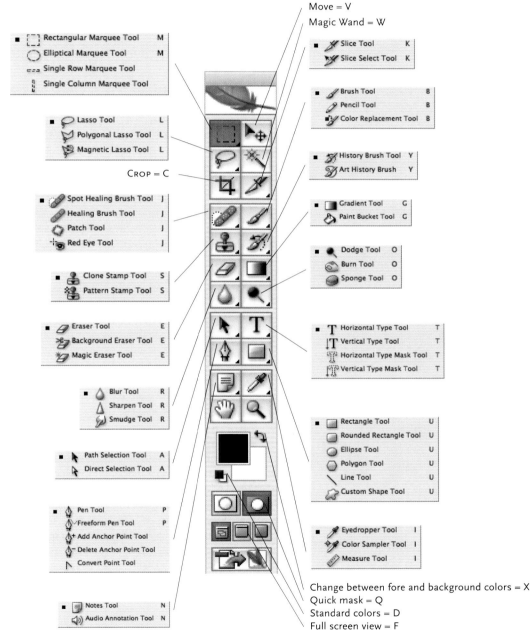

Move = V

Magic Wand = W

■   Rectangular Marquee Tool   M
○   Elliptical Marquee Tool   M
  Single Row Marquee Tool
  Single Column Marquee Tool

■   Slice Tool   K
  Slice Select Tool   K

■   Lasso Tool   L
  Polygonal Lasso Tool   L
  Magnetic Lasso Tool   L

■   Brush Tool   B
  Pencil Tool   B
  Color Replacement Tool   B

CROP = C

■   History Brush Tool   Y
  Art History Brush   Y

■   Spot Healing Brush Tool   J
  Healing Brush Tool   J
  Patch Tool   J
  Red Eye Tool   J

■   Gradient Tool   G
  Paint Bucket Tool   G

■   Clone Stamp Tool   S
  Pattern Stamp Tool   S

■   Dodge Tool   O
  Burn Tool   O
  Sponge Tool   O

■   Eraser Tool   E
  Background Eraser Tool   E
  Magic Eraser Tool   E

■   Horizontal Type Tool   T
  Vertical Type Tool   T
  Horizontal Type Mask Tool   T
  Vertical Type Mask Tool   T

■   Blur Tool   R
  Sharpen Tool   R
  Smudge Tool   R

■   Rectangle Tool   U
  Rounded Rectangle Tool   U
  Ellipse Tool   U
  Polygon Tool   U
  Line Tool   U
  Custom Shape Tool   U

■   Path Selection Tool   A
  Direct Selection Tool   A

■   Pen Tool   P
  Freeform Pen Tool   P
  Add Anchor Point Tool
  Delete Anchor Point Tool
  Convert Point Tool

■   Eyedropper Tool   I
  Color Sampler Tool   I
  Measure Tool   I

Change between fore and background colors = X
Quick mask = Q
Standard colors = D
Full screen view = F

■   Notes Tool   N
  Audio Annotation Tool   N

5.5 Retouch and Photoshop Tools

Beyond the basic proofing and adjusting an image might need to be changed or improved in other ways. We usually speak of retouch and manipulations. This can mean anything from removing dust or other imperfections to creating a large collage. Photoshop offers a large number of tools and functions and we will go over those that are most important for retouches. If you want to learn more about how the tools are handled we recommend Photoshop's help function.

5.5.1 The Options Bar

Right under the Menu Bar is the OPTIONS bar in Photoshop. It show different contents depending on what tool you have chosen. There are usually several settings possibilities for the tool you have chosen. You should try out different ones to see what possibilities they afford with the different settings.

5.5.2 Size and Texture

All painting tools in Adobe Photoshop, for example PENCIL, BRUSH, CLONE STAMP, ERASER, etc., can be set for size and texture, or how soft the edges given by the painting tool should be. This is set in the OPTIONS bar. In this bar you can also choose specific settings that control colors, i.e. how transparent they are and so on.

5.5.3 Marquee Tools

LASSO is the normal tool used to encircle an area you want to edit. By holding down the OPTION key straight marquee lines can be clicked out. To use a marquee along an edge you can use MAGNET LASSO to an advantage since it can sense the edges and help make the selection in the right place. For simple selections you can use RECTANGULAR or ELLIPTICAL MARQUEE tools.

In the OPTIONS bar FEATHERS and SMOOTH can be set as a selection marquee for both RECTANGULAR MARQUEES and LASSO.

Another tool to create selection marquees with is the MAGIC WAND. You use this to make a selection marquee with similar colors in a nearby area. When you click with it on one color, that color and others like it will be governed by TOLERANCE in the OPTIONS bar.

By holding down the shift key and clicking on the area that has not been selected you can expand the selection marquee. If you want to diminish the selection hold down the option key and select the areas that you don't want to be selected.

SELECT MARQUEE → COLOR RANGE has similar functions to MAGIC WAND but works on the entire image and has possibilities for more specific settings. It can be useful for creating a selection marquee for a certain area in an image, for example a colored background or an object of a certain color.

Selection marquees can be saved under SELECT → SAVE SELECTION... Saved selection marquees are, technically speaking, grayscale images and are shown as channels in the channels palette.

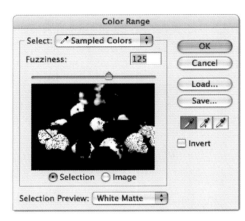

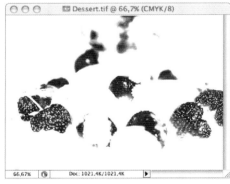

SELECT EVERYTHING OF ONE COLOR
The tool COLOR RANGE in Adobe Photoshop makes it simple to select everything in an image that is a certain color. If you choose to preview it as above, only selected areas of the image are visible as you adjust the settings.

5.5.4 Quick Mask

To quickly and easily make a selection marquee in an image you can use QUICK MASK. Click on the right QUICK MASK symbol in the TOOLS palette. Paint either over the parts of the image that are to be selected or that are not to be selected, depending on how Photoshop is set. You can use whatever paint tools you like when you create the mask, including GRADIENT. This means that you can create selection marquees that give effects of varying degrees, depending on how much coverage the mask you create provides. Click on the left QUICK MASK symbol to go back to normal mode. Then the selection marquee for the mask you created will show. You can also click on the QUICK MASK symbol when you have a selection marquee you want to save in the form of a mask, which makes it possible to modify the selection marquee with a paint tool.

5.5.5 History Brush

The HISTORY palette is a function that saves all the steps that have been carried out when editing an image. With the HISTORY BRUSH you can go back in the process in specific areas of the image, to see how the image looked at different stages. First you specify how far back in the process you want to go by making a selection marquee in the HISTORY palette. Then you paint that area that you want to go back in with the HISTORY BRUSH.

5.5.6 Clone Stamp and Healing Brush

When you are going to retouch something out of an image and replace it with a surface that is the same as another part of the image the CLONE STAMP is an appropriate tool.

It is often used to take away, for example, grains of dust, birthmarks and such. It works by copying a surface from another part of the image. Select CLONE STAMP. Hold down the OPTION key and click on the part of the image that will be replicated. Then you can paint with this part wherever you like in the image. The place you got the surface from is shown with a little cross in the image.

For careful retouching choosing the OPTIONS palette mode is extra important. This means that you can effectively limit you cloning to either darker or lighter details in an area, for example dust or birthmarks.

One tip is to create a new layer in the OPTIONS palette. Then you can easily adjust cloning afterward as well as hide the layer to compare it with the original image.

The HEALING BRUSH is a more sophisticated, but hard to handle tool, of the same type. It is best suited for when you are repairing a surface with homogeneous colors and brightness.

5.5.7 Blur, Sharpen and Smudge

If you want to make an area in the image blurry you use the BLUR tool that looks like a teardrop. You paint blurriness with it. The more you paint the blurrier it gets. The tool is very useful to take away the edge effect or for toning down details. The SHARPEN tool is in the same place as the teardrop, and it looks like a pencil point. It has the opposite function, that is it increases sharpness. Unfortunately it doesn't yield very high quality results. To sharpen a detail it

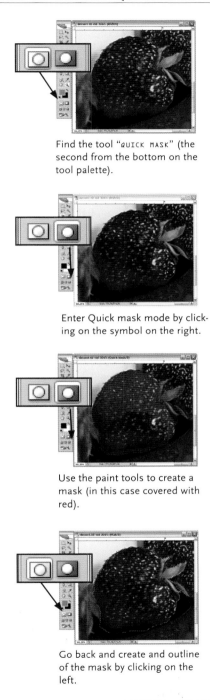

HOW TO CREATE A QUICK MASK

Find the tool "QUICK MASK" (the second from the bottom on the tool palette).

Enter Quick mask mode by clicking on the symbol on the right.

Use the paint tools to create a mask (in this case covered with red).

Go back and create and outline of the mask by clicking on the left.

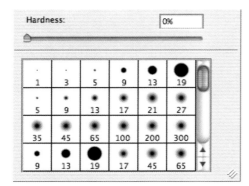

PAINTBRUSH AND PENCIL
In the OPTIONS MENU for PAINTBRUSH and PENCIL in Adobe Photoshop you can select different brush shapes and sizes as well as create your own shapes. These can be layered and given varying hardness as well.

SAVING SHADOWS
Images where parts of the image have been underexposed, for example subjects that have been photographed against the light or that have been photographed in strong sunlight, can be hard to adjust. The SHADOW/HIGHLIGHT tool is very powerful in situations where you want to bring out details that are in shadow or reduce the "exposure" of highlights.

is better to make a selection marquee and use UNSHARP MASK. The finger symbol is used to smudge parts of the image as in a pencil drawing.

5.5.8 Dodge, Burn and Sponge Tools
DODGE and BURN are two tools taken from a photography darkroom. They work in the same way as if you were dodging part of an image (making it lighter) or burning it (making it darker) when you make a copy on negative photo paper. The DODGE tool can, for example, be used for lighting up eyes that have ended up in shadow.

The SPONGE tool soaks up color and makes the image's colors less saturated.

5.5.9 Brush and Pencil
The BRUSH and PENCIL tools are used for painting. The pencil paints well only for complete color coverage and hard edges, while the brush can paint with different transparencies, textures, opacities and flow. Which characteristics you want to have are set in the OPTIONS palette. By setting lower opacity the color will not give complete coverage. By setting a lower flow, the brush will have the same effect as a sprayer, that is the longer you spray on a certain point, the more color coverage you will have. This can be appropriate if you want to create a shadow, for example.

Another important setting for brushes is LAYER. There you can, for example, choose to only let the brush affect the hue of a surface. This means that you can paint over a pair of green eyes with blue color, but only affect the eyes' hue without completely covering their surface with color or affecting their brightness.

5.5.10 Pen Tool
The PEN tool is used to create Bezier curves for selecting with paths. Bezier curves can also be used to smoothly create selection marquees by choosing MAKE SELECTION in the PATHS palette.

5.5.11 Gradient
The GRADIENT tool creates a soft blend between two colors. Which colors it is going to blend are set in the TOOLS palette as foreground and background colors. This tool is very useful in QUICK MASK to create a selection marquee that softly blends into an unselected surface.

5.5.12 Match Color
To create homogeneity between different RGB images, for example portraits or product images, the function IMAGE → ADJUSTMENTS → MATCH COLOR... is used. With MATCH COLOR... you can let Photoshop automatically adjust the colors in an image from a reference image that acts as a standard for how all the images will look. How much the images are influenced by the reference image's appearance can be adjusted in the function. You have to either have a reference image open, or have previously saved the image statistics from a reference image to use for comparison. The image statistics are reference values that other images can be matched to without a reference image needing to be opened and analyzed.

5.5.13 **Shadow/Highlight**

A valuable function for adjusting wrongly exposed images is IMAGE → ADJUSTMENTS → SHADOW/HIGHLIGHT... The tool lets us adjust light and dark areas of the image in such a way, which, if properly handled, can compensate to poor lighting conditions during photography. Unfortunately the tool does not exist as an adjustment layer.

5.5.14 **Blur Tool**

It is not unusual for you to want to make parts of an image blurry, for example a background, a surface with unwanted details, a grainy or noisy image, or if you want to simulate a movement in the image. Under FILTER → BLUR there are

LAYER BY LAYER

ADJUSTING EASILY AND WITH THE BEST QUALITY

By using ADJUSTMENT LAYERS, LAYER MASK and LAYERS in Adobe Photoshop you get both the highest quality and greatest flexibility when editing images. LAYERS can contain parts of images that are placed on top of each other or made up of tone and color adjustments that are applied to the underlying layer. These are known as ADJUSTMENT LAYERS, which in turn can be changed later on without affecting the quality of the image. Layers can be hidden and shown at any time, change their order of placement, blended in different ways and adjusted to different transparencies. LAYERS and ADJUSTMENT LAYERS can even be partially hidden or hidden to varying degrees using LAYER MASKS, which in turn can be hidden or shown.

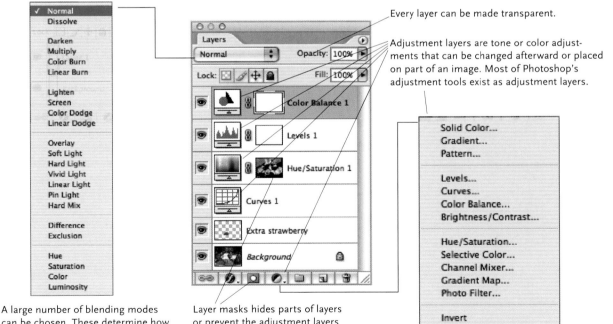

Every layer can be made transparent.

Adjustment layers are tone or color adjustments that can be changed afterward or placed on part of an image. Most of Photoshop's adjustment tools exist as adjustment layers.

A large number of blending modes can be chosen. These determine how the respective layers are to be blended with the underlying layers.

Layer masks hides parts of layers or prevent the adjustment layers from affecting parts of the image.

The image's memory requirements are affected by layers, channels, saved selections and layer masks as well as 8 or 16-bit modes, different compressions, etc. Here we have tested with an 8-bit RGB image in A4 size and 300 ppi saved in Photoshop format:

Original image	26.1 MB
With a saved selection/alpha channel	26.4 MB
CMYK mode	33.5 MB
CMYK mode with ICC profile	34.0 MB
With three adjustment layers	51.9 MB
With a layer in 25% size image	59.2 MB
With a layer mask	57.5 MB
16-bit mode	54.0 MB
With three layers in full-size image	104.4 MB

Different file formats also give different size files:

EPS format	36.2 MB
Uncompressed TIFF file	27.0 MB
Photoshop format	26.1 MB
ZIP compressed PDF	27.9 MB
LZW compressed TIFF	14.7 MB
JPEG highest quality	5.5 MB

(Observe that an image with several details, with few details, other selections, layer masks, etc. can give different file sizes.)

several different functions. The most important are GAUSSIAN BLUR··· LENS BLUR··· SMART BLUR··· MOTION BLUR··· and RADIAL BLUR···

GAUSSIAN BLUR··· can be viewed as the normal tool if you want to create a blur in a selected part of the image. LENS BLUR··· gives a more realistic simulation of blurriness, for example a short depth of field from when the photograph was taken, and is best if you want to create a blurry background in the image. SMART BLUR··· lets the edges keep their sharpness, while more even surfaces in the image are affected, which is why this tool is most appropriate for removing noise and graininess. MOTION BLUR··· is appropriate if you want to give the impression of an object moving in a certain direction, while RADIAL BLUR··· is good if you want to give the impression that the wheel of a car is going around, for example.

5.5.15 Layers

Working with LAYERS is useful when you retouch or create a collage. This is also true when you create graphics made up of many different objects, for example image, text, subject, shadow, etc., that you want to keep separate until you are done.

The possibility of using LAYERS in Adobe Photoshop means that the image is made up of different strata where the different parts of the image can be put. Parts of the different layers can be partially transparent and have soft edges to blend in a natural manner with the layers underneath. Each layer can also be made transparent in varying degrees and blended using different methods with the underlying layer. For example, a black surface in a layer can be made transparent and multiplied with the underlying layer to create a natural shadow. Which characteristics a layer provides is set in the LAYERS PALETTE. Layers can also be grouped in LAYER installations or linked to each other for easier handling.

Images that contain LAYERS should be saved in Photoshop format.

5.5.16 Adjustment Layers

The adjustment layers function, LAYER → NEW ADJUSTMENT LAYER, makes it possible to make unlimited use of the basic adjustment tools such as CURVES, COLOR BALANCE, HUE AND SATURATION and LEVELS in Adobe Photoshop without the information becoming damaged and the quality in the images negatively affected. ADJUSTMENT LAYERS are presented as an ordinary layer in the LAYERS palette and can also be created and handled from there. Several adjustment layers can be placed on each image and can either affect all the underlying layers or be linked to one specific layer. ADJUSTMENT LAYERS have the advantage that the effect of every adjustment layer is shown beforehand on the monitor, but is not carried out in the high-resolution image before it is printed out or the layers are merged. All the different effects carry the same weight before the composite effect is carried through on the image, which means the information in the image is retained in the best way. If two adjustment layers cause opposite effects no change is carried out, out as opposed to when the layer effects are laid on manually. When done manually each step affects the image's quality in a specific way, whereby the image loses information and then, if the step is cancelled out by another change, the image loses even more information. By using adjustment

The classic way to extraction an image, that is to remove the background around the subject, is to use a selection path. The path is a Bezier curve that gives a very sharp edge to the selection that in a subject with fuzzy edges or with a lot of detail, for example fur, can look unnatural. The images extracted with a path can be used in all layout programs.

1. Start with an image in which the object you want to extract has sharp contours.

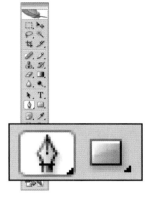

2. Select the PEN TOOL from the TOOL PALETTE.

3. Create a path with the pen tool. The path can circumscribe one or many objects. For best results, place the path somewhat inside the edge of the object you want to extract.

4. Save the path by double clicking on WORK PATH in the floating palette PATHS. Give the path a clear name. You can save several paths in an image only use one for a selection.

5. Choose to use the saved path as CLIPPING PATH. A low value on the number of discrepant pixels results in a slower rasterizing process. A value of around 8–10 is usually recommended.

6. Save the image as PDF, EPS ord PSD.

7. Voila! The image is displayed as a selection when you place it in the page layout application or output as a selection according to the path you created. The entire digital file is however intact and visible if the image is edited in Photoshop (step 3).

If you want to extract where the edges of the subject are soft and can be blended into the background, you can make the extraction with the help of a transparency. The most flexible way to work is to use a layer mask to create the transparency. Since the image is built of layers you can also add shadows to this type of image. Images extracted with transparency cannot always be used in older layout programs.

1. Start with any image. The object can have edges that are to be given a soft transition into the background.

2. Create a new layer mask. Click on the layer mask to select it and then color the image black in the areas where you want the image to be transparent. Erase the black areas or paint white to reduce transparent areas.

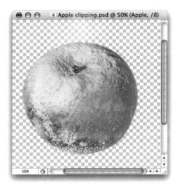

3. The transparent surfaces are previewed with a checkered pattern. Test the extraction by creating a layer behind that you fill in with a color.

4. Save the image in Photoshop format and check the layers box.

5. Voila! The image is ready to use. In the layout the image is shown extracted and the soft edges can be toned into surface such as tinted areas or other images.

6. When the image contains transparency, you can also put layers behind the object to create a shadow, for example.

7. The shadow can be created using regular paint tools.

8. A semi-transparent shadow can be blended with background surfaces in a natural way.

layers the original image can, in other words, be kept in its own layer with all the information intact.

5.5.17 Masks in Layers

One more way to flexibly edit images is to use vector masks, layer masks, and clipping paths. These masks work like selections that hide all or portions of a layer so that it becomes transparent, without the hidden parts being eradicated. Instead, they remain intact even if they are temporarily not visible. The mask can easily be deactivated temporarily whereby the whole layer becomes visible. By using masks instead of a regular selection marquee, the selection's shape and placement can be changed afterward and whatever is hidden or affected by the mask can be changed.

A vector mask is a path that hides part of a layer. Paths always have the advantage that, like other Bezier curves, they can be revised and they take up an insignificant amount of memory.

With a layer mask all or part of a layer can be hidden and can be made completely or partially transparent. A layer mask can also be put on an adjustment layer so that the adjustment layer only affects that part of the image that the layer mask shows, while other parts of the image remain unchanged by the adjustment layer.

Layer masks are carried out, technically speaking, by a grayscale image in the same way as ordinary selection marquees, and can thus be revised as a grayscale image by clicking on the layer masks and then using all the regular tools. This means also that every layer mask takes up as much memory as a grayscale image of the same size and resolution.

When you use a clipping mask you permit the contents of one layer to mask the layer on top by having all the surfaces that are transparent in the underlying layer hide the contents of the layer above.

5.5.18 Extraction Techniques

Extracting an object in an image means that you take out the background so that the object lies free. There are several ways to create this type of extraction: against white, with paths or with a transparency. They yield different results and some methods work only in certain layout programs.

The easiest method for extracting against white, is based on simply making the whole background in the image white. This means, consequently the object always gets a white background and cannot be placed naturally over another image or tinted area. One advantage with this method is that the transition between the object and the background can be made soft and natural, for example when you have a short depth of field. You can easily keep a natural shadow or add one as if the object were photographed against a white background. Another advantage is that the method works in all file formats.

The most usual method for extracting with paths is based on clipping paths in Photoshop. With the PEN tool you create a Bezier curve around the desired object. You can also create additional curves to make holes in the extraction, for example if you are extracting a ring. The path is saved in the PATHS palette and then the path is chosen as a CLIPPING PATH in the palette menu. When a path is chosen as a clipping path in Photoshop, you need to set a deviation value. The value affects accuracy and speed during printing. When the image is prepared for desktop printing, a value of 2–5 is appropriate, while a value of 7–10 is more appropriate for offset printing.

The edges of an extraction become very sharp with a clipping path. When an image is extracted with a path the background shows in the digital image but isn't visible when mounted in a layout or when printed. That means that you can go back to the original image by deactivating the path. Extracting with paths works in EPS, DCS, PDF and PSD file formats.

A third way to extract is with transparency. This makes it possible to have a see-through background at the same time as having shadowed objects in an image. In addition, the transition to transparency can make the transition to the background softer so the image has a more natural look. A shadow in the image can be made semi-transparant and blended with an image lying behind it, or with a colored area in the layout for a natural appearance. This type of extraction requires that the image is saved with transparency and that the layout is in Adobe Indesign since other programs cannot completely handle images with transparency. The file format for images that handle transparency in this way are PSD and PDF.

If you work in PSD format transparency can be created with LAYER MASKS, which means that, as when you make extractions with CLIPPING PATHS, you can change the placement of the extractions in the image afterward, or return to the original image by deactivating layer masks.

In images with complex edges in the object to be extracted, for example in the case of woods or hair, it can be very difficult and demanding to create a path or mask by hand and maintain a natural effect. In Photoshop there is the EXTRACT filter that helps with this work and gives us an image with an extracted object against a transparent background. An alternative is a plugin from Corel as an alternative that is called KNOCKOUT. It can be used in earlier Photoshop versions or in other programs that support Photoshop plugins.

EXTRACT helps with automatically selecting edges and removing the background. You draw with the EDGE HIGHLIGHTER TOOL on the edges of the object you want to extract, then click inside the part you want to extract with the FILL TOOL. The filter will trace the edges and extract the filled parts of teh image. What remains will have transparent edges and will thus be suitable for advanced collages or montage in Indesign in PSD format with the transparency preserved.

5.6 **Naming and Tagging**

Given that most original images today are digital there is a real need to be able to locate images. Therefore it is very common to save your digital images in some form of digital archive. Regardless of how you save your images, it is necessary to have some kind of good information about the images that make finding them possible and that shows facts about them. Information about files and images that are being archived is usually called meta information. For help we have the file name plus an array of fields with textual information that can be stored embedded in the image file.

DATA ON DATA
A large number of file formats allow data about the file, called meta data, to placed in the file.

The information is invisible except for when you choose to show it in, for example, Adobe Photoshop or an image archive program.

The information can be about copyright concerns, subject of the image, contact information, when and where the image was created, etc.

Usually this data is structured according to an international standard called IPTC.

5.6.1 Naming Files

In most cases it is important that the image name describe the image content to facilitate locating, handling and using the files, etc. An image name in the style of "Image 1" is not of any use. A name in the style of "Food Report 1" is of course better, but doesn't differentiate for example between the image of raw vegetables and the image of the chef.

A good file name can cover many of the needs as to giving providing information about the image. In the file name you can put the project name or number, for example, the subject, image number, the photographer's initials and a simple code as to permission rights of the image. In some contexts it can be important to specify whether or not the image is Web ready, print ready, low resolution, etc. Even this information can be included in the file name.

An important advantage of using the file name for giving information about the image is that the file name is searchable in all kinds of computer systems without needing any special archive program. The disadvantage is that you can easily end up with complicated file names.

5.6.2 File Information

In many file formats for images there is support for storing detailed text information about the image embedded in the image files, known as meta information.

Keywords can be provided here that describe the image, categories and so forth, which facilitate locating and archiving. There are also text fields that can give additional information about the image, for example a description of the image, image text, the creator, when the image was created, as well as where and perhaps most important of all – under what circumstances the image may be used.

The information that should always be given is the creator, the user rights and what is shown in the image.

The standard for how this text information is built is called IPTC (International Press Telecommunications Council) after the organization that together with NAA, Newspaper Association of America, formed it.

The meta information that is added to the image according the IPTC standard is embedded in the file with an XML-based technique called XMP (eXtensible Metadata Platform), developed by Adobe. The meta information in this form becomes searchable by archive programs [*see Layout 6.15.4*].

The meta information can be advantageously added to images directly after photographing and as soon as they enter the computer. In Adobe Bridge and many camera and archive programs this type of information is added to several images at one time, which makes the work easy. You can also often create templates for meta information which simplifies things even further.

In images photographed with digital cameras, text information about the camera settings, exposure, etc. is stored in the image according to a standard called Exif [*see Digital Images 4.10*]. Exif information is also readable by archive programs. When an image is edited in Photoshop, a history log, detailing the editing history, can be included in the document's XMP information. The history log is activated under PREFERENCES → GENERAL.

PREVIEWING PRINTING COLORS IN PHOTOSHOP
In adobe Photoshop you can preview printing by choosing VIEW → PROOF COLORS.

CAN ALL THE COLORS BE PRINTED?
By choosing VIEW → GAMUT WARNING in Adobe Photoshop all the areas of the image that don't lie within the color range of the printing process and thus would change during the color separation are highlighted.

Both Exif information and the history log can be of good use if later on you want to detect how any technical errors in the image may have arisen.

You can add meta information to files in Photoshop, PSB, TIFF, JPEG, EPS, PNG and PDF format. If you work with Photoshop in Mac OS the information can also be added and read in files in other formats that are supported by the application, with the exception of GIF.

5.7 Adjusting the Image for Printing and the Web

Images are normally adjusted and retouched to become digital original images. A well-adjusted image lends itself to being used in different contexts. When the image is going to be used it has to be adjusted to the right size and to the use it is intended for, for example printing or showing on a monitor.

5.7.1 Adjusting the Image for Printing

Before an image can be printed it has to be adjusted for its intended use. There are mainly three adjustments that you should make: Conversion to CMYK, size change and sharpening. When the image is converted to CMYK mode you take into consideration the characteristics and shortcomings printing has, and compensate the image for these. You can, for example, convert the image in Adobe Photoshop before it is placed in the layout. You do this by choosing IMAGE → MODE → CMYK COLOR. The image is then adjusted with the ICC profile that has been chosen for CMYK in WORK COLOR SPACES under EDIT → COLOR SETTINGS... [see Prepress 7.4].

The size adjustment is done to facilitate the handling of images in layout. The image's size can be adjusted in Adobe Photoshop with IMAGE → IMAGE SIZE...

Images also need to be adjusted for sharpness. This is because the rasterization process makes images blurry. The lower the screen frequency the blurrier the image will be. This becomes especially important, for example, in newspaper print, which has relatively low screen frequency [see Prepress 7.4.7].

Size adjustment and printing adjustment can also be done automatically when producing a PDF file. If a PDF file is produced in Indesign the image can also be cropped during PDF production. Doing it this way however, means that no print-adapted sharpening is added to the image after the size is reduced.

When you do image-editing this should be done in RGB or Lab modes. If you know what type of printing the image is going to be used for, it can be of interest and of value to preview how the image will be adjusted to the printing process since the color range of printing is narrower.

To this end, there is the possibility of previewing the printed result by choosing PROOF COLORS in the VIEW MENU in Adobe Photoshop. Then the image will be shown on the monitor as if you had print-adjusted it by going to CMYK mode. You can also choose to preview the image's channels for printing plates by going to VIEW → PROOF SETUP. Adobe Photoshop uses the ICC profile that was chosen under CMYK during WORKING COLOR SPACES under EDIT → COLOR SETTINGS...

All the RGB image's colors will be transferred within the printable color range during printing adjustment. The colors that lie outside the color range can be affected undesirably. Therefore you can identify these areas so you can

adjust them manually. They are highlighted on the screen by choosing VIEW →
GAMUT WARNING.

If you drag the cursor across the image you can let the INFO palette show
te CMYK values even if the image is in RGB or Lab modes. If you then come
across an area with colors outside the printable range, a yellow triangle will
appear at those color values.

5.7.2 **Adjusting Images for Monitor Viewing and the Web**
There are principally four adjustments you need to do to adjust pixel-based
images for viewing on a monitor or with a projector, for example when being
used for the Web. These adjustments are resolution, color mode, file format
and sharpness.

To begin with, the resolution that has been set in the image has no effect
on monitor and Web publishing. The size of the images is measured only in
the number of pixels in width and height. The monitor that shows the image
has a certain resolution and controls how wide the image really will be on the
screen. It is often said that monitors have a resolution of 72 ppi. In that case, an
image that is 72 pixels wide will be one inch wide when it is shown, that is 2.54
cm. Most modern monitors have higher resolution than this, which is why in
reality the image often becomes smaller. In practice this is often less important
since the whole web page will become smaller in terms of measurements on a
high-resolution monitor, thus the image will become the right size on the page,
proportionally speaking. If the image is going to be shown with a projector, its
width and height should be adjusted to the projector's resolution, for example
1024×768 pixels.

When editing images for the Web you should always look at the image in a
100% viewing scale on the monitor. This also gives an indication of how large the
image will be on the monitors of people surfing the Web. Since the resolution
cannot be controlled it doesn't matter what resolution you choose for the image.
It can, however, be appropriate to set the resolution to 72 ppi for the image if,
for example, you want to print out the image and then have it approximately
the size it is on the screen, or if you want to be able to get information from an
image bank program as to whether the image has low resolution in case it will
not be suitable for high-resolution printed products.

When you are going to adjust an image's color mode, there are principally two
color modes for images on the Web: RGB for photographs, as well as indexed
mode for simpler illustrations, logotypes, image-based texts, etc. Color management for the Web is difficult, not to say impossible. Web browsers such as
Microsoft Internet Explorer do not handle ICC profiles. In addition, the majority of Web users do not have color-corrected monitors. However, most monitors
are to some degree adapted to sRGB, which is why you should work with sRGB
as a WORKING COLOR SPACE in Adobe Photoshop, to get as good an idea as possible
about how the colors will end up looking on the Web users' monitors.

Which file format should be chosen for an image depends on what type of
image it is. RGB images are saved in JPEG format. The images are compressed
as hard as possible to create memory-skimping images, and the compression
grade has to be adapted to each image's appearance. JPEG2000 is also a file

FILE FORMATS FOR THE INTERNET
On the Web images in RGB or indexed mode are
used. CMYK or Pantone do not work. Only a few
file formats work:

- JPEG
- GIF
- PNG

NO RESOLUTION FOR THE WEB
For images that are produced to be shown on the
screen the resolution is not of importance. Only
the image's size calculated according to the number of pixels determines how large the image will
be when shown on the screen and whether or not
the quality is good enough.

format that is well adjusted to Web images, but not all Web browsers handle this image format.

Indexed images are saved in GIF or PNG8 formats. PNG does not function, however, in older Web browsers.

The last adjustment that should be done on images intended for monitor screen viewing is sharpening. This should be carried out after the other adjustments so that it can be given the right level of sharpness [*see 5.4.12*].

5.8 Editing Images Effectively

Editing images in terms of proofing, adjusting and retouching can be done with more or less good quality results. Image editing can also be carried out more or less effectively. Effective work methods mean that the work goes faster and you can ensure that the editing is done correctly and with even results.

Effective image editing is based on knowing what you have to check for in the digital image, finding the best and easiest work steps, and taking advantage of the tools you have at hand in the best way when carrying out image adjustments.

5.8.1 Image Specifications and Reference Images

The best way to make image editing effective is to naturally do as little as possible to every image. To minimize work it is important to have the best possible material to start with. By setting simple and clear demands on those who deliver the digital raw images you can make this easier. A good tool is written specifications that state in what shape you want the digital images to be delivered to you from photographs, scanned images, image archives and retouches.

An example of the contents of such specifications could be the demands you place regarding resolution, size, file format and compression, color mode and ICC profile. The specifications can also contain information as to which adjustments are expected to be carried out and which not: for example gray balance, black and white points, retouches and sharpening. Above and beyond the technical image demands, it can be very helpful in minimizing uncertainty and time in finding the right images if the images' names and file information are as correctly created as possible.

When you want to build homogeneity with other images or just explain what style you expect, it can also be suitable to look at the sample images of photographers and other suppliers.

Image specifications and sample images are also valuable to use for proofing and carrying out adjustments with a defined goal. If you are building an image archive, the archived images should also always follow image specifications so that everyone will easily know the technical quality of the images in the archive.

5.8.2 Following the Right Work Steps

In having a predetermined order for the steps in editing images you can turn the work into a routine. Routines make the work go faster and you progressively learn to fine-tune your hand. Basically, your working order should consist of checking basic errors, adjustments, retouching, naming and labeling and finally storing images in an appropriate file format.

Making a checklist of what should be proofed and adjusted and in what order can be helpful for finding a good and effective routine. Then you should consider how each step can be carried out in the easiest way. Often you can use keyboard shortcuts or functions macro for the main work steps.

5.8.3 Keyboard shortcuts

There are always work steps that are often repeated in image editing. One good way to make the work more efficient is to let these be carried out as automatically as possible.

Using shortcuts instead of the mouse and menu choices is very important to achieve an efficient workflow, but is also important for good ergonomics. Most tools in Adobe Photoshop have shortcuts linked to them. If you need a shortcut that is not already provided, you can easily create a new one under EDIT → KEYBOARD SHORTCUT... Even existing shortcuts can be changed this way.

The working order you have defined can be reflected in the shortcuts so that you, for example, can always carry out you proofing steps with the function keys F1, F2, F3 and so forth, while actions and tools can be given their own shortcuts.

5.8.4 Actions

A series of work steps in Adobe Photoshop can be recorded and saved in an action. By playing back an action the same work steps can then be carried out on other images. Actions can be used to carry out the same editing steps on several images. The actions palette, where actions are recorded and edited, is found under WINDOW → ACTIONS.

5.8.5 Droplet

One way to carry out an action is to create a droplet in Adobe Photoshop under FILE → AUTOMATE → CREATE DROPLET... A symbol is then created on the desktop of your computer. When an image is placed on this symbol the image is opened in Adobe Photoshop and a certain action is carried out on the image. After that the image is named and saved in a predefined way.

5.8.6 Batch Editing

The function macro can be carried out on all images in a folder using the command FILE → AUTOMATE → BATCH... In Adobe Bridge you can also choose a number of images and carry out a function macro on these.

Batch editing can be very useful when you want to carry out work steps that don't require you to look at the image. Some examples can be when you want to do a raw format conversion to a number of images in the same way, set the resolution for a number of images or put on the adjustments layers that are needed in the image to continue editing. These work steps can also be carried out together in the same function macro to good advantage.

Another useful form of batch editing that can be done in Adobe Bridge is to rename the images in a batch. You can give the group a new file name that might

TURNING ON THE IMAGES ON A DROPLET
Adobe Photoshop makes it possible to "record" a series of activities that are done to an image and this recording can then be "played back" in another image and the same editing work will be carried out on it. This kind of recorded activity is called an ACTION. It can also be activated by a DROPLET which can be turned on by an image and the image editing that the droplet represents will be carried out on that image.

contain the original name, adding on a project name or number, the date and an automatically generated ordinal number [*see Layout 6.15.5*].

5.8.7 Saving the Tool Presets

The values you set for a certain tool in Adobe Photoshop can be stored as a tool presetting in the WINDOW → TOOL PRESETS. The tool can then be reused with the saved settings. The CROP TOOL can in this way, for example, be preset for different sizes and resolutions. Different settings for BRUSHES, CLONE STAMPS and ERASERS can be stored as well. For example, you can save a setting for a CLONE STAMP that only affects the areas that can become lighter when you remove wrinkles, or a brush that only affects the hues used for changing lip and eye colors.

5.8.8 Working Flexibly

By introducing more flexibility in your work you can achieve higher efficiency. Photoshop adjustment layers offer a means to a flexible work process since they provide a way to edit a document without loosing the ability to change or undo earlier steps.

Adjustment layers give both higher quality and more working flexibility than using the same tool separately. Layer masks give greater flexibility when you wan to make an adjustment for just part of an image. By storing the image in Photoshop format, the image is saved with ADJUSTMENT LAYERS and LAYER MASKS, which means that the image can easily be adjusted later without loss of quality.

By scanning in or raw format-converting the image to 16-bit mode and editing the image in that mode, even more flexibility is achieved, since greater margins are created for new adjustments.

The HISTORY PALETTE also gives freedom to adjust later on. There is a list shown in the HISTORY PALETTE that contains all the steps carried out on the image. You can let the image return to the appearance it had just when a certain step was being carried out on it. By choosing ALLOW NON-LINEAR HISTORY under HISTORY OPTIONS... in the HISTORY PALETTE you can remove one step that had been carried out earlier, so the image looks out as if the step had never been taken. By selecting a step in the list and choosing the HISTORY BRUSH TOOL, you can restore parts of the image to how it looked when the selection had just occurred. By fixing it a version of the image is stored that you can return to even if the history is no longer there to show how the image looked before.

5.8.9 A Good Computer Helps

When you work with 16-bit mode, adjustment layers, layer masks, layers, non-linear histories, etc. you easily end up with image files that take up a lot of memory and processor space. This is especially true if you work with large images. Thus a computer with a lot of RAM, a fast processor, and a quick hard drive facilitate the work considerably. A fast internet connection can also make things easier.

A large monitor is also valuable since it makes it easier to find space for tool palettes without having to hide them when they are not being used. An alternative is to connect an additional small monitor to the computer for your tool palettes. You can also hide all the tool palettes but still continue working with the chosen tool by pressing the Tab key. Also, program arrays can be hidden by pressing the F key. By pressing this twice, the menu array and the icon array at the bottom of the screen are hidden as well. The image is then shown in full screen mode.

06.
layout

Should the fonts be in Truetype or Opentype format? Can you combine Mac and Windows in the same project? How do you check the layout document before printing? How do I choose ink that will be right for printing? How can manuscripts be prepared so that the typography goes smoothly? What is XML? How do you convert Pantone colors to CMYK? How do you spot varnish? How do you make an image bleed? What is the difference between a double-page spread and a center spread? What can I do to make sure that my tint area will be the right color in print? Why isn't Word a good layout program? Which settings and preparations can I do to expedite the layout work?

THE PERSON WHO PREPARES layout documents for printed products has to be aware that it isn't enough to just create an attractive layout. It is at least as important for the document to be easy to output, create plates from and be suitable for printing. A document that isn't correctly produced can cause increased costs, delayed production, or the finished printed product not coming out as you planned.

In this chapter we will go through everything that is important to know when you produce a layout document for printing. Some important areas are manuscript work, image editing, and logotypes as well as the choice of colors and color combinations in the layout. We are going to look at how you avoid common pitfalls in layout work and how you can work with proofs.

In this book we will not deal with typography from an aesthetic point of view, but some terms and typographical definitions may be good to know. We will go through typefaces in this chapter, the handling of fonts and the construction of fonts. We will also look at different styles of typefaces and some software for handling fonts.

Finally, we will go over what you should think about when you are checking your layout document and when you leave it for printing.

First we will look at the different programs for layout work, what preparations you can make and what help exists to work effectively.

6.1 **Layout Work**

In graphic print production the person who creates the original, the layout, has a broad task. This can include receiving original text, original images and illustrations, checking material, mounting it all into a layout document, creating the typography, and creating PDF files for proofing, putting in the corrections, creating the printouts and making the original print, often in the form of a print-adjusted PDF file with high-resolution images. The layout process is a crucial point for the whole graphic print production flow.

Layout documents are created with software such as Adobe Indesign and Quark Xpress. In the layout document the manuscript text is mounted from a word processing document. The text lies embedded in the layout document. The text is then given the right typography in the layout program using fonts that are linked in with the document. The fonts are not embedded in the layout document. The same thing is true of images that are also placed in the layout, but are linked to the document. The only thing that is embedded in the document is a low-resolution image. You can also draw object-based graphics in the layout program using a simple drawing tool. Both typography and drawn objects are colored in with color combinations that you create in the layout program or with spot colors that are taken from a library that comes with the layout program. All the colors that have been chosen are embedded and stored in the layout document.

Printouts can be made directly from the layout document, in which linked images and fonts are embedded in a Postscript file that is sent to the printer. Instead of sending the Postscript file to the printer it can also be transformed to a PDF file via, for example, Adobe Acrobat Distiller. The PDF file can contain the linked images and fonts that have been used. If you work with Adobe Indesign you can create a PDF file directly from the layout program.

It is important to choose an appropriate layout program and install it well to have a flexible work tool You can also simplify and make layout work more effective by working with ready-made layout templates. We will begin by looking at layout programs that are suitable to work with.

6.1.1 **Choosing Layout Software**

When choosing layout software it is important to choose a program that is normally used in the profession so that it will be easy for others to receive and continue working on the files. It is also important to choose a program that fits graphic production well.

The main software for doing layouts and producing pages is Adobe Indesign, Quark Xpress, Adobe Pagemaker and Adobe Framemaker. Adobe Illustrator is also used for the layout of single pages and for packaging, for example. There are also simpler layout programs that are normally not used in professional graphic print production, such as Microsoft Publisher and Corel Ventura.

Layout programs are used to design pages and bring together text, typography, illustrations and images on finished pages. They can import most text and image formats that are intended for printed production. They are also used

---

A BELOVED CHILD HAS MANY NAMES

We are writing about layout in this book. This is the process of arranging text and images into complete pages in a printed product. Graphic design in general, means the creative work done prior to the layout of the pages, that is the design which establishes the basis for the layout. The border between design and layout is, however, rather fluid.

If the printed product has few or no images and the work mainly involves setting the type, for example a novel, the process of laying out the pages is sometimes called text- or page formatting.

for making high-quality printouts or producing digital printed originals in the form of PDF files.

What makes a layout program suitable for these tasks is its capability for designing, typography, image and color editing as well as its support of the page description language, Postscript, that is used in graphic print production [*see Prepress 7.1*].

Programs such as, for example, Microsoft Word, Corel Wordperfect, Microsoft Powerpoint and Microsoft Excel are not based on the page description languages PDF or Postscript. They are lacking in or have poor support for four-color and spot colors. They also have very poor typographical proofing capabilities and usually don't give warnings for missing fonts, but instead replace them with others automatically. They don't handle important file formats or images that are used in graphic print production either. The placing of text and graphics can be changed automatically by the program and make the layout unpredictable. These factors make them expressly unsuitable for use in print production. This does not mean that the programs are bad in and of themselves, only that they are not appropriate for making printed originals.

If you receive a document prepared in one of these programs you should transfer the content to a layout program you are going to use for printing. From a purely technical standpoint however, even these programs can set the foundation for a fully functional printed original in the form of a PDF/X file, but if you use one you should be watchful and check things as you go.

SOFTWARE FOR GRAPHIC PRODUCTION
Different programs are used to create pixel and object-based images, text and pages. Even if the programs to some extent overlap, it's better to use a program designed for your particular assignment to obtain the best result. For example, it is better to stay away from doing page layout in word processing programs.

6.1.2 Planning the Layout

Before you create the layout document the page format (size) must be decided. It is also appropriate to decide on the volume (number of pages), as well as the type of paper since it can affect how broad the spine of the printed product will be and the color values in the layout. The binding also affects the layout, such as how images can be placed over the two-page spread. A good tool for planning is to make a page plan with page sketches.

It is also important for layout work to choose which and how many print colors will be used, for example single color four-color or spot colors.

With some productions it can also be important in layout work to know how the pages will be placed on the printer's sheets. You can then get an imposition plan from the printer that shows what pages are going to be printed together. This can, for example, be used for planning how spot colors will be used, but also to discuss how eventual delivery of pages to the printer will be prioritized if not everything can be delivered at the same time. The imposition plan also shows where center and double-page spreads occur [*see 6.10*].

6.1.3 Making Templates and Setting the Basic Structure

Working with templates of different types in layout work is a good way to create structure. They give a common setup and an effective way to work with manuscripts and layouts if you are several people. In the layout document you can create templates for standard settings, for example in the design of documents and page templates, library and object templates, as well as typographical templates.

6.1.4 Document Templates and Master Pages

For most kinds of documents you can create a template document. When you create a new working document from these the document is given all the important default settings you have worked out in the template. In a template document there can, for example, be many finished pages with different page margins or column spacings. On the template pages there can even be reoccurring objects such as page numbers and page headers.

6.1.5 Library and Pull-outs

In what is called the library, image and test frames, with or without content, or groups of these can be stored and easily reused by dragging them out onto the pages.

In Adobe Indesign there are also pull-outs, or snippets, that functions as slightly more advanced library objects, and can be saved as separate files in the computer and then pulled directly out onto the page.

6.1.6 Typographical Templates, Object Templates and Color Squares

Typographical settings for paragraphs or separate characters can be saved as piece or character format. These can then easily be applied to other texts that can be given the same settings. If you change the format of a character or a paragraph, this change will be carried out everywhere in the text where this format is used.

It is possible to save color combinations as general formats, known as color swatches, that can be applied to objects and changed in the same way as paragraph and character format for text.

In Adobe Indesign there are also object format templates, which means that all the settings for a frame, for example a frame line, transparency, shadow and recessed margins, can be stored as a format that can be applied to another frame and be changed centrally in the same way as a paragraph format for text can be changed.

6.1.7 Default Settings

An appropriate thing to do in this context is to make the default settings in your layout programs so you will get the basic typography, frame and tools that you want. Paragraph style, character style, color swatches, object style, etc. are saved in the default settings. This assures that these templates are included in all new empty documents. In Adobe Indesign the default settings for tools and palettes and their placement on the screen can be saved as work spaces. Indesign can, in addition, store PDF and printer settings, which considerably facilitates the production of PDF files and printouts.

6.2 Text Manuscript

Text is a fundamental part of almost all graphic communication and is also the part that needs the most editing and proofing. Therefore it is important to work in such a way as to facilitate the editing and corrections that have to be done. When you produce text that is going to be placed in a printed product, a manuscript, the text should be checked for content, proofread and approved before it is mounted in a layout document. A manuscript approved this way functions as an original for the text – original text.

An original text should also be adjusted to the layout so that the body text fits and so that headers, for example, fit on one line. It should also be saved in a file format that is secure, open to editing and can be imported into different programs.

Original text is produced in word processing programs and is given typography and placement in a layout program.

6.2.1 Appropriate Software for Word Processing

Microsoft Word is the absolutely most common word processing program. Word Perfect from Corel is used in some situations in Windows-based computers, while Apple Works (earlier known as Claris Works) is used in some circumstances on Macintosh. An alternative is OpenOffice's word processing program Writer that is completely cost-free to use and exists for Mac OS, Windows and other operating systems. It is compatible with other office programs' files (www.openoffice.org).

6.2.2 Appropriate File Formats for Text

Original text is saved in mainly two types of format. The files are either saved in the word processing software's own format, for example, Word format, or it is saved in an open file format such as RTF or ASCII format. The open file formats are relatively independent of the programs or the computer platforms they are created or used in. This means you avoid problems with, for example, odd characters when transferring between different programs and platforms.

6.2.3 Program-specific Text Files

Program-specific text files such as Microsoft Word files, for example, can contain all the functions and the refinements of the original program. Problems can sometimes arise when they are transferred between different computer platforms.

The more recent the version of the word processing program you use, the more functions in the program that will be supported by the program's file format. The fact that the file format for text files is developing in this direction can create problems since the layout program being used to mount the text has import filters that support the word processing file.

Files from earlier versions of word processing programs create almost no problems and are to be preferred. They are also preferable if you want someone to be able to open the file in another word processing program.

In addition, the files of new programs can contain functions that are valuable to include in the layout such as tables, footnotes, etc. that can be imported to the layout program. For example, tables from Microsoft Excel can be imported to Adobe Indesign.

6.2.4 ASCII format

American Standard Code for Information and Interchange, ASCII, is a standard for digital information, especially text. When is comes to storing text, ASCII

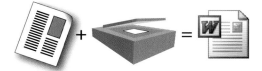

OCR – SCANNING TEXTS FOR WORD PROCESSING
If you have a text on paper and need to transfer it to a digital text file, you can use an OCR program. Such a program interprets a scanned image of the text and translates it to an ordinary text file. You can do the scanning with a regular tabletop scanner. OCR stands for Optical Character Recognition.

OCR is used for digitalizing manuscripts in paper form or digitalizing, for example, a company's incoming mail and making them easy to distribute internally at the same time as making the data searchable in a database.

The results of OCR interpretation of a text are not perfect. Many errors in the translated text depend a lot on typography, print quality and scanning quality. But in combination with the correct spelling function in a word processing program and proofreading, digitalizing large amounts of text from paper in publishing houses can save a lot of time. A typical OCR program is Omnipage from Nuance. Adobe Acrobat also works for converting image files with scanned text to searchable text in the form of memory-saving PDF files where the text is based on fonts instead of pixels like in the scanned image of the text.

Unicode is a modern standard for storing and providing characters and is used in different file formats. It handles a little over 1.1 million characters, divided up into 17 "layers" with 65,536 characters and is aimed at being able to handle all the written languages of the world. Today we have been able to identify approximately 100,000 characters from al the know alphabets.

Unicode is supported by all modern operating systems such as HTML and XML code and is also the base in Opentype fonts.

is originally based on each character being saved with 7 bits, and therefore handles up to 128 different characters in one text. A setup with 128 characters is not enough for all the digits, upper case and lower case letters, as well as special symbols that are needed in a text. That is why this version can sometimes cause problems. More modern versions are based on saving every character with 8 bits and thus handling 256 characters.

ASCII format can be read in most programs managing text, and usually has the file ending "txt". An ASCII file is often called a plain text file since it only contains the actual text and not any information about the text's design.

6.2.5 RTF Format

RTF, Rich Text Format, is an open format that, along with text, contains codes for typefaces and simpler typography. RTF is a common format that was created to make it easy to move text files between different programs while retaining typographical information. The RTF format can also store names in paragraph and character format, which is important in order to create links between manuscript documents and layout documents.

6.3 Mounting Text

Text manuscripts are normally imported into the layout program, placed in the typeface and then edited to fit the existing space. The images that lie inside the text document cannot be imported to the layout program. In other words it is not a good idea to place images in word processor programs, they only take up unnecessary space. All typographic work and layout done in the word processing document are, as a rule, done in vain. In Adobe Indesign the manuscript file can be linked to the layout in the same way that images and text in the layout can be updated if the manuscript file has been changed.

If you run into problems with importing text files in certain formats you should see if it is possible to update the import filters in use in the current program. You can also try to first save the word processing file according to an earlier version of the word processing program, or test saving it in RTF or text format before mounting it.

When you mount text in the layout it can be a time-consuming job to select the right typography for the paragraphs, words and characters that are to be specially formatted. Information needs to be sent from whoever wrote the manuscript to the person doing the layout as to what type of typography is requested for certain words and characters and for each paragraph. Delivering the information takes time and can easily lead to typographical mistakes. To provide a safer and quicker typography process you can let the text be structured and marked up in the manuscript stage. Then what kind of text is paragraphs and, for example, headers, quotations, etc. is indicated and can easily be given the right typography when mounted in the layout.

There is an array of different techniques for structuring and marking up text before doing the layout to facilitate setting the text in type. This can be done by assigning the text a given structure, using built-in or project-specific format

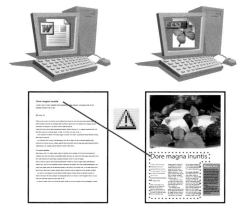

When images are mounted in a layout program a link to the image file is created. When text manuscript is mounted, the actual text is placed in the layout document and eventually revised. In Adobe Indesign a link is also created to the manuscript file. This means that if the manuscript file is changed it will be shown with a warning triangle in Indesign's links list. You can choose to update the link whereby the text in the layout document is replaced with the updated manuscript text.

templates in the word processing document, and using special tags for Adobe Indesign or Quark Xpress, or coding texts in XML format.

6.3.1 Using the Structured Manuscript

If you are consistent in use of paragraph and character formatting already in the manuscript text, this formatting can be used for creating the layout. When importing to Adobe Indesign or Quark Xpress the paragraph and character style is translated to the format as defined in the layout document. By naming the paragraph and character alike in the word processing and layout document the translation will be done completely automatically. In order for the translation of the format between the word processing document and the layout to be successful, the text has to be stored in Microsoft Word or RTF format.

Another way to set text in type in the layout more effective, is to have a given structure of the order of the different elements in a text. Then in Adobe Indesign CS2 or later, you can let paragraph format follow a sequence automatically, for example so that the first paragraph is the heading, the second is the subheading, the third is the introduction, the fourth is the body text without indentation, the fifth and so on will be the body text with indentations. This method works equally well on a partial text, for example from a subheadline to the next, i.e. on paragraphs in insets or tables. The method is based on the current paragraph format's containing settings for whatever the following paragraph format will be.

In typography, you mark the paragraphs you want and click right on the paragraph format in the paragraph formatting palette that is to be used (control click in Mac OS without the double click mouse). For example, choose APPLY → HEADING → AND THEN THE FOLLOWING. This method can give you very quick typography for the text and works well when texts are introduced structurally in the same way.

6.3.2 Using Tagged Manuscript Text

In both Quark Xpress and Adobe Indesign there is support for handling marked text, also called "tagged" text. Marking text is based on each part of the text being provided with a code, tags, or whichever of the layout document's paragraph or character formats will be utilized in the text. The text is saved in ASCII format. In Quark Xpress, Xpress Tags are used and in Indesign, Indesign Tags are used. Xpess Tags also make it possible to direct other things in the layout from the codes in the manuscript document. The coding is similar to the way text is marked up for a website using HTML.

6.3.3 Using Manuscripts in XML Format

XML, or eXtensible Markup Language, is a code language for logically tagging a text's different existing parts according to the content, for example, which are headings, introduction or image captions. The XML file describes which text elements are found in the text, but contain no information about the typographical design of these. Text coded in XML format can be imported to and from Adobe Indesign and Quark Xpress, but can also be used for other purposes, for example for the Web or in cell phones.

THE TEXT ON THE LEFT AS INDESIGN-TAGGED TEXT

```
<ParaStyle:Heading2><CharStyle:Entrynumbers>6
.3.1<CharStyle:>Using the structured manuscript
<ParaStyle:Body without indent>If you are consist-
ent in use of paragraph and character formatting
already in
```

EXCEL FILES IN THE LAYOUT

Transferring a table or diagram from Excel to Indesign or Quark Xpress can at times be a little difficult. Here are three ways to go about it:

- Export to PDF and mount as an image
- Import the table in Illustrator and create a new-diagram-design. Mount the Illustrator image.
- Import the table in the layout program and use the table tools to give it a nice design.

THE TEXT ON THE LEFT AS XML CODE

```
<cookbook style>
    <chapter number>
        6.3.3
</chapter number>
</heading_3>
    Using the manuscript in XML format
</heading_3>
<body text>
    XML, eXtensible Markup Language, is a code
language for logically marking up the parts of a
text in according to content, for example, what is a
heading, introduction or body text.
</body text>
</cookbook_style>
```

When you import the XML file in the layout program is when you decide how each text element shall be designed. In the layout program the XML marking words are linked with headings, for example, together with a paragraph style giving them their design. In XML marked text links to images can also be found so that these are mounted automatically.

Working with the XML format in layout work lends itself well to storing large amounts of text, which is subsequently structured and made up of contents that are frequently repeated, for example, in production of catalogues or reference works. Since in the XML file you don't state the design of the text, the format is also useful for material that is going to be published in different media such as print, on the Web or used in cell phones.

6.3.4 Linking the Layout to Text Databases

If there are larger amounts of text in a database there can be a direct link between the layout program and the database. This method of working is suitable for catalogue production, for example, where changes in the database can be carried out in the layout and changes of the text in the layout can be carried over to the database.

6.3.5 Working With Text Editing Parallel With Layout Work

In a traditional layout workflow the text is produced by a writer who leaves an original text with an artworker who then mounts the text in the layout, selects a typeface and produces a PDF file or printout that the writer and others review. But we live in a world where production has to happen more and more quickly, which means layout work and text editing often have to happen in parallel. There are various solutions that make this method of working easier.

The simplest solution comes built into Adobe Indesign. When the text files are mounted in Indesign a link to the text file can be created, exactly the same as what happens to the images when they are mounted. Just like when the images are changed, you receive a warning if, for example, corrections have been made in the text manuscript after it has been mounted in the layout. You can then choose to update the text whereby the changed text is mounted in the layout. If the manuscript is pre-formatted to correct the character and paragraph format, and no textual or typographical changes have been done to the layout program after mounting, the corrected manuscript file can simply be re-imported and replace the earlier mounted text.

If changes have been made to the text in the layout, the text can be exported to a new manuscript document in RTF format. If you then import it again and thereby create a link, other people can go in see the changes that have been done in the text and make new changes. However site-specific typographical adjustments, for example, kerning and tracking cannot be exported and imported via RTF format.

There are also other solutions for working with text and layout in parallel where the writer can edit and correct the typeset text in place on the layout. You can also adjust the text for the available space. Either this can happen directly in the layout program, where the overall layout can also be affected, or in a specially adapted editing program where only the text in the layout can be edited.

PARALLEL WORK USING INCOPY
There is a sister program to both Quark Xpress and Adobe Indesign which makes it possible for an editor or copywriter to edit the text without risking changing things in the layout. In the sister program to Indesign, Incopy, the layout can also allot different texts in the layout document to different people for editing. The texts will then be temporarily locked to the layout workers, who can still continue working in parallel on the rest of the document. When the editing is finished the layout worker's document is updated and he or she resumes command of the layout.

These kinds of editing programs exist for both Adobe Indesign and Quark Xpress: Adobe Incopy and Quark Copydesk. All adjustments having to do with text and typography can be done in these programs without images, objects and text frames being affected. The programs also make it possible to edit the text in simplified, word processor-like views.

Adobe Indesign can also allow for different elements of the text to be edited in Adobe Incopy by different writers in parallel, while the layout is edited by the layout worker, for whom the text is locked. In Adobe Incopy comments can also be added to the text, which can be read in Indesign and vice versa. Adobe Incopy can also create low-resolution PDF files for proofreading, where these comments become comments in the PDF file and can be read in Adobe Acrobat.

When larger groups of writers and layout workers are working together, for example on a newspaper, larger editorial systems are used to keep track of a large number of manuscripts, who is working with them and if the are mounted, etc.

6.4 Typefaces, Fonts and Typography

One of the most important components of graphic design and layout is typography. The typeface that creates typography is stored in fonts – digital typeface files – that are linked in the layout document. When printing out or creating print-ready PDF files, they are embedded together with images and graphic elements in Postscript and PDF files, respectively. We shall take a look at what a font is, the file format they can be saved in, how you can preview typeface and find the right type and how you create subsequent typography easily.

6.4.1 Type and Font

To begin with, it's important to understand the difference between a typeface and a font. Typeface is the term for the design of a set of characters, for example Garamond. Font is historically the name for a set of lead type with typeface shapes, while today it is the name for the digital font files that have replaced lead type. Typefaces can come in a number of typestyles, such as bold, narrow or light. Font refers to the character set in one or several styles stored in the digital form.

There is no standard that says which type should be included in a typeface in a font. Some fonts do not contain letters for all western European languages, or both upper case and lower case letters. Some fonts only consist of a number of symbols or special symbols and not ordinary letters. Each key on a keyboard represents instead a symbol or a special character.

If you work with languages other than western European ones, for example eastern European or Asian languages, special fonts for the characters of these languages are often necessary since some typefaces can only hold a relatively small amount of characters.

There are a number of different types of files for storing fonts, for example Opentype, Truetype and Postscript Type 1. Fonts that are saved in Opentype can contain up to 65,000 different characters and therefore have the possibility of including all the language versions and typestyles of a specific typeface in the same font.

FONT, TYPEFACE, FONT FILE

TYPEFACE
Appearance of the "characters". A set of typefaces is characterized by the design given by the originator.

TYPESTYLE
Variation of a typeface, for example bold or italic.

FONT FILE
A data file containing a typestyle, for example Helvetica bold.

FONT
Collection of font files that contains the same typeface, for example normal, bold and italic of the typeface Helvetica.

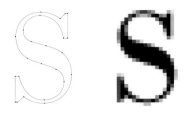

All font file types contain an object-based printer font. Postscript type 1 also contains a pixel-based screen font.

TYPEFACE CATALOGUES
Catalogues are very useful and are given out by most font manufacturers.

HOW DO FONTS LOOK?
In Extensis Suitcase fonts in the computer can be previewed on the screen.

6.4.3 Choosing a Typeface

When you are choosing a typeface it is easiest to choose from font samples, printed samples of a typeface. You can order catalogues or buy books with font samples from most font suppliers. If you don't have any catalogue you can either choose a typeface directly from your monitor or print out your own font samples.

Both Mac OS and Windows have built-in support for the most commonly found font files. To get a quick image of how a typeface looks it takes only a double click on the font file. In Windows a window opens with font samples that are suitable for printing out. In Mac OS a window opens in the program Font book. If you want to print out a font sample you can choose the font file in the Font book and then make a printout.

For those who want to print out more advanced typefaces it is a good idea to organize a page in Adobe Indesign or Quark Xpress. Put in it all the characters and sizes you are interested in. One hint is to format all the text with a paragraph format. Then you can easily change the typeface for the whole page, by changing it within the paragraph format and then printing out different typefaces with you own design.

Older versions of Window (Windows 98, NT 4 and older) and Mac OS Classic do not have any built-in support for showing Postscript fonts. For these you need free software from Adobe called Adobe Type Manager (ATM) [see 6.4.9].

6.4.4 Working with Typography Templates

In most printed products the typography will be identical throughout the entire printed product. This can be true of headers, insets or body text. Instead of hand marking a paragraph of text and manually choosing all the settings for such things as font size over and over, you can gain a lot by creating typography templates. This can be done in all layout programs. In typography templates an array of settings is selected and then applied to the characters or the paragraphs repeatedly. Typography templates save both time and increase quality of the type when you are guaranteeing that all of the body text of the document, for example, will be set in exactly the same way. In addition, the use of a typography template allows rapid subsequent changes in the typography. If, for example, you want to change the typeface of all the headings in the whole document, you change the template so that the change will be carried out automatically everywhere in the layout that the template has been used.

Typography templates can be imported from one document to another. If you use the Book function in Adobe Indesign it also makes it possible to synchronize typography templates between several documents so that body text typography, for example, is identical in all the documents that are put in the book.

In Quark Xpress these typographical templates are called Typography Templates, and in Indesign they are called PARAGRAPH STYLES and CHARACTER STYLES. The settings that can be stored are for both characters and paragraphs, for example face size, points, space between letters, color, line spacing, kerning and tracking, character width, raising and lowering, setting for how the Opentype functions should be used, syllabification rules, margin settings, how the paragraphs are held together, number of rows at the beginning and end of the paragraphs, initial letters, encapsulated format, numbered and bullet lists, etc.

6.4.5 How to Install Fonts

Font files can either be installed manually directly in the computer's operating system or with the help of a font manager application. To activate a font file manually you only have to place it in the right folder in the hard disk. For Windows this folder is FONTS inside the WINDOWS folder. It also works if you add fonts via the CONTROL PANEL. Then Windows will copy the font files automatically to the right place. In Mac OS there is a corresponding folder in LIBRARY. Remember that Mac OS has several libraries. If you put a font in a user's library the characters will only be available when the user is logged on. If you put the font file in the computer's general LIBRARY the character will immediately be available for all the computer's users. If you have installed any of Adobe's graphic programs, there is also a font folder in the program's installation folder. If the fonts are placed there they will only be available in the Adobe program.

If you use a font manager application, it places the font files in the right places and checks which ones are active at the moment.

6.4.6 Activating Fonts without Installing Them

In Mac OS there is a built-in font manager called Font book. You can create groups in it, for example specific projects, and easily activate the font files you want to use temporarily. In Windows, and if you want more advanced font management functions, in Mac OS, you can use a program such as Suitcase from Extensis. Along with the functions that are found in Apple's Font book, there are functions in suitcase to automatically activate fonts and manage conflicts when you try to open several versions of the same typeface.

Using Suitcase, you can activate the fonts you need while working without restarting the program, or even installing the fonts in the right place in the computer. Just as in Font book you can create groups of fonts so that with one stroke you can activate and deactivate all the fonts that belong to a certain production, project or customer. Extensis Suitcase can also activate the fonts automatically in certain programs such a Quark Xpress, Adobe Indesign or Illustrator, if you so wish. This means that when you open a document in the program that uses fonts that are not installed in the computer, Suitcase tries to open these automatically. In order for this to work you have to install a plug-in. This function is handy but, for example, in the case of a printing house that receives documents from customers, it also means that you lose control over exactly which font file that is going to be activated since you often have very many similar fonts available in the computer at the same time.

6.4.7 Finding the Right Characters in the Font

A font normally contains many more characters than what is shown on the computer's keyboard, To reach these characters in all their versions, and the hidden characters you can hold down different combinations of keys on the keyboard, for example Alt+a letter. These combinations can be hard to remember. There is some help for finding hidden characters. For symbol fonts that do

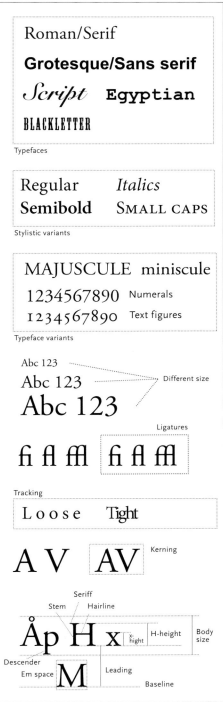

TYPOGRAPHIC TERMS

Roman/Serif
Grotesque/Sans serif
Script Egyptian
BLACKLETTER

Typefaces

Regular *Italics*
Semibold SMALL CAPS

Stylistic variants

MAJUSCULE miniscule
1234567890 Numerals
1234567890 Text figures

Typeface variants

Abc 123
Abc 123 Different size
Abc 123

Ligatures

fi fl ffl fi fl ffl

Tracking

L o o s e Tight

A V AV Kerning

Seriff
Stem Hairline
Åp H x x-height H-height Body size
Descender
Em space M Leading
Baseline

ScalaSansPro-Bold
Type: OpenType
Family: ScalaSansPro-Br
Screen font: ScalaSansPro-Br
Printer font: N/A
reen font location: C:\WINDOWS\Fonts\ScalaSansPro-Bold.ot
Inter font location: N/A

Version: Version
Foundry: 2005 Martin Majoor.

ABCDEFGHIJKLMNOPQR...
abcdefghijklmnopqrstuvw...
1234567890!@#$%^&*()
Twenty years from now
you will be more
disappointed by the things
that you didn't do than
by the ones you did do.
So throw off the bowlines.
Sail away from the safe
harbor. Catch the trade
10

PRINT OUT YOUR FONTSTYLES
In font managers like Extensis Suitcase it is possible to print out sample of font styles.

not contain regular letters some of these tools are necessary to find the right character.

In Adobe Indesign there is the window, GLYPHS, that gives a good overview of all the characters that make up a font. This window also shows special functions in Opentype fonts where several characters, for example, different versions of one character, are linked together.

Adobe Indesign has, in addition, its own function, TYPE → INSERT SPECIAL CHARACTER, to insert, for example, a copyright symbol or a blank character.

In Microsoft Word there is a similar function for inserting special characters. You find this under TEXT → INSERT SPECIAL CHARACTER.

There are also tools in the computer's operating system for finding special characters and inserting these. In Mac OS there is a function that can be used for all programs under EDIT → SPECIAL CHARACTER... In Windows there is corresponding help under PROGRAM → ACCESSORIES → SYSTEM TOOLS → CHARACTER SETTINGS.

6.4.8 Keeping Fonts Organized

When you are working with many different fonts at once, it is easy for the folders where the active fonts are stored to get disorganized. In addition, many installed and active fonts mean the menus where you choose typefaces in the layout program grow very long. Many active fonts can also take up a lot of your computer's valuable allocated RAM, which diminishes performance.

One good way to create order among fonts and to not utilize more fonts than you need at the time, is to use extensions that can group and activate fonts.

FIND THE RIGHT KEY

INDESIGN
The palette WINDOW → TYPE & TABLES → GLYPHS, gives a good overview of all the glyphs that are included in a font. This window also shows special functions in Opentype fonts where several characters, for example different versions of a character, are linked together. Adobe Indesign has, in addition, its own function, TYPE → INSERT SPECIAL CHARACTER, to insert, for example, a copyright symbol or a space between letters.

MICROSOFT WORD
A similar function for inserting special symbols in the manuscript is found under INSERT → SYMBOL...

MAC OS AND WINDOWS
In Mac OS you can easily show a font and most important, find where on the keyboard and with what combination of keys, under EDIT → SPECIAL SYMBOL (Alt, Shift, etc.) you can get a certain symbol.

In Windows the corresponding aid can be found under PROGRAM → ACCESSORIES → SYSTEM TOOLS → SYMBOL SETTINGS.

Examples of these are the program Suitcase from Extensis or Font book that is included in Mac OS.

When you use tools such as Suitcase or Font book you can sort your font archives into different folders in an organized manner. You should choose a way that fits in with how you yourself work with typefaces. If you remember them by name you should arrange them in alphabetical order. You can also sort them according to appearance, for example, according to the typeface family they belong to – Romanesque/serif, grotesque /sans serif, script and so on. Or you can perhaps choose a third alternative by sorting them according to manufacturer: Adobe, Monotype, Agfa, etc. If a lot of people make use of the same fonts, you can store them on a server that is available to everybody and that everybody can activate fonts from. If you want to gain full control over font management in a larger organization, Extensis, for example, has a special server/client program to centrally control how all the users can attain and activate fonts. This can be good for keeping the licenses for the fonts in order and for guaranteeing that everyone has access to the exact same version of a font.

6.4.9 Adobe Type Manager – ATM

Adobe Type Manager, or ATM, is a utility from Adobe used primarily to improve handling Postscript fonts in earlier operating systems. From Mac OS X or Windows 2000 and on there has been built-in support for displaying Postscript-based fonts on the monitor. If you use an older operating system such as Mac OS 9 (also Mac OS X Classic), Windows 95, 98 or NT 4.0, ATM is necessary for getting support for Postscript fonts. You can then use ATM Light, which is downloaded free from Adobe's website (www.adobe.com).

Among other things, ATM makes it possible for printer fonts to be displayed in large sizes on the screen. It also makes printing with Postscript fonts on non-Postscript-based printers possible. This means that in these operating systems you reach the character's contour paths in illustration programs such as Adobe Illustrator.

Despite having ATM installed, you need screen fonts for Postscript fonts in earlier Mac OS, otherwise the computer won't find the corresponding printer fonts. Another reason for having screen fonts despite having ATM installed is that the pixel-based characters in a printer font are clearer on the screen in small sizes as opposed to characters generated from printer fonts by ATM.

6.4.10 Where Do You Get the Fonts?

There are thousands of fonts in existence today, and new ones are constantly being created. The main suppliers of fonts are Adobe and Monotype, but there is also a large number of smaller suppliers with both good and exciting typefaces to offer.

You usually buy fonts from a wholesaler or directly from the supplier via the Internet. Each typestyle can be bought separately or in the form of larger typestyle collections where other versions are included.

There are also many fonts you can get for free and that can be downloaded from the Internet. When it comes to the fonts that are free on the Internet, use them somewhat cautiously since they sometime cause problems when ripping.

SORT WITH SUITCASE

Suitcase makes it possible to sort fonts in an accessible way and use them from a server. You should sort them according to how you think they should be grouped logically, for example, alphabetically, according to appearance, or character family by creator.

Displayed above is the Adobe tool for letting you know whether fonts can be included when handing off material.

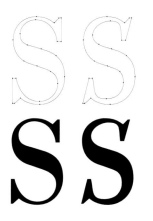

MODIFYING FONTS
Printer fonts are based on Bezier curves. It makes it easy to change the shape of the font (by modifying the Bezier curves) while maintaining the quality.

DISTORTIONS IN THE LAYOUT PROGRAM
Object-based fonts let you adjust characters in the layout program in terms of width and height, or warp them, color them and add effects.

It is easy to copy fonts and it doesn't require any registration number or password as when installing most other programs.

Despite it being normal for fonts to be copied, especially when you deliver material for further editing, there are certain copyright rules regarding copying [*see Legal 11.7*].

6.4.11 Creating, Modifying and Converting Fonts

You can create you own fonts or modify what you already have with special font programs. Fontlab, Fontlab Studio and Fontographer are the most common programs for this. You can design the font directly in the program, using scanned sketches or importing object-based information from Adobe Illustrator, for example. You can also add information about kerning and tracking, or add Opentype functions to these programs to save a font file in final form in a free-choice format.

This type of program can also be used if you want to convert fonts between different computer platforms, for example from Macintosh to Windows, or between different font styles. This may happen because certain RIPs don't allow Truetype format in the fonts, or it can depend on your having to change platforms in layout work between Mac OS and Windows. There are also simpler and cheaper conversion programs such as Transtype.

If you want to modify the characters in a typeface a few times or use some characters to form a logotype, you don't need to work in this type of program. Instead you can take advantage of the fact that the font is made up of curves. In programs like Adobe Illustrator or Indesign you can simply reform the letters to character contours that can then be modified freely as with any other illustration.

6.5 Font File Formats and Functions

There are three normal file formats that are stored in traditional Truetype or Postscript Type 1 and the newer Opentype. They differ technically and in the refinements they offer. All three function well in modern graphic production, even if the format Truetype has a reputation for causing problems with older graphic equipment.

We will go through the fonts' basic functions, the file formats they are saved in and how they differ.

6.5.1 Opentype

Opentype is the modern file format for fonts that has been developed by Adobe and Microsoft together. The format has many advantages. One is that the same font file is used for Mac OS and Windows. In addition the fonts are made up of only one file, not of two as fonts in Postscript Type 1 format are.

Opentype fonts are built on a standard called Unicode that uses 16 bits to save each character, which means that each font file can contain approximately 65,000 different characters. This means that every conceivable typestyle and character can be collected in one file. Therefore Opentype lends itself well to working with a text that is going to be produced in many different language versions or with a typography that uses many typestyles. This is something that

OPENTYPE IN INDESIGN
Adobe Indesign can manage all the functions of Opentype fonts such as, for example, capital letters, superscript and subscript, and decorative symbols as needed.

PROS AND CONS WITH OPENTYPE
+ Same file type for Mac and Windows
+ Only one file per font
+ Supports up to 65,000 characters in one file
+ All typestyles in the same font
+ Includes more advanced typography

− Problems can arise in certain older RIPs if the Truetype version is used.

would otherwise demand several fonts of the same typestyle where you would need to be able to handle languages with special characters.

Opentype fonts also make advanced typography possible since the font can contain several versions of the same character – for example different typestyles at the beginning and the end of a word, or versions of the same character depending on what text size you use. Since Opentype fonts have a larger character setup, you can also have several different ligatures available.

Adobe Indesign has complete support for all the Opentype functions. Quark Xpress can use Opentype fonts, but lacks support for most functions that Opentype include.

There are two versions of Opentype fonts. They are based on either Truetype or Postscript techniques. For printed production the same thing that was true for Truetype fonts is true of Opentype fonts based on Truetype: that certain older RIPs can have problems with it even though this seldom occurs. Opentype in Postscript format works, however, even with older RIPs.

6.5.2 Postscript Type 1

Postscript Type 1 is the basis for the three current versions of Postscript and was launched in the mid-eighties. A Postscript Type 1 is actually made up of two font files. One is a screen font with information about character widths, kerning information as well as a low-resolution pixel-based screen version of the font, the other is a curves font, also called printer font that depicts the character's shape using Bezier curves.

The screen font is used when the font is going to be printed out or shown on the screen in larger sizes. The file format is different for Mac OS and Windows. In Windows the outline font has .pfb file endings (Printer Font Binary) and the screen font has .pfm (Printer Font Metrics).

The screen font contains a character setup that is saved in a string – small pixel-based images in black and white that are used to show typestyles in small sizes on the screen.

SEVERAL VERSIONS OF THE SAME CHARACTER
Fonts in Opentype format can contain several versions of each character, for example superscript and subscript, capitals or embellished characters, or versions adapted for large or small grades.

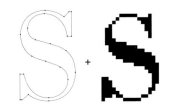

POSTSCRIPT TYPE 1 FONTS
Postscript Type 1 fonts consist of two parts, one object-based printer font and a second pixel-based screen font. Now you can also use a printer font on the screen.

There are often several screen font files for every printer font file. There are a number of sizes, for example, 10, 12, 14, 16, 18 and 24 point type.

Screen fonts are suitable for showing characters as clearly as possible in small sizes despite the screen's low resolution. Screen fonts for one typeface family in Mac OS can be saved in a special type of folder called a font suitcase.

In Postscript Type 1 font each character is represented by 8 bits. This means that the font can contain a maximum of 256 different characters. Therefore different font files are necessary for, for example, bold, narrow, small or capital versions as a well as language versions of the same typeface.

6.5.3 Truetype

Truetype fonts are made up of one file. Font file types were developed originally by Apple and were introduced in 1991. Now it is supported both by Mac OS and Windows, although the file formats are different in each. Mac OS also supports, however, Truetype fonts in Windows format. Truetype is completely based on curves, b-spline curves, and also has one curve font and now a separate pixel-based screen font such Postscript Type 1.

In certain older RIPs Truetype fonts have a tendency to cause problems when ripping. Truetype supports almost all Postscript Level 2 RIPs and all Postscript 3 RIPs. However, certain printers and reproduction companies have problems with Truetype fonts.

When you save a layout with Truetype fonts such as a PDF file, the fonts are converted, which means that the printout also works on a RIP that does not support Truetype.

6.5.4 Kerning Tables

In every font, information is saved about the distance between each combination of two characters in a text, for example between A and V. These are known as kerning values and are saved in the font. If you are not satisfied with these pre-defined values you can change them how and where you want in the text. If you want to carry out these values overall you can create your own kerning tables in Quark Xpress. In Adobe Indesign there are two possibilities. Either you can use the kerning values built into the font, know as metric kerning, or you can choose optic kerning where Indesign "looks" at how much space is needed between every character. This optic kerning often diminishes the need for manual adjustments of the font's kerning. If you still want to make such adjustments you can use plug-ins that provide this function, for example Cool Kerning from Knowbody.

6.5.5 Hinting for Better Printouts

When you print out characters in small sizes on a printer with low resolution, for example a laser printer, sometimes the small parts of the letters are hard to print out correctly. This may depend on the thin line in a character being as thin as 1.5 exposure points wide. The number of exposure points per inch, (dpi) is a measure of the printer's resolution. Should the printer create the thin line with the aid of one or two exposure points on the printout? The difference is 50 % thinner or 50 % thicker, and changes the appearance of the typeface. To help the

---

OTHER FILE FORMATS

D-FONTS
In Mac OS a special version of Truetype fonts is used as a system font internally in the computer. These are called d-fonts. They shouldn't be used for graphic design and do not work on other computer platforms.

FON
Fon files are bitmap fonts that are used in Windows programs to draw nice-looking fonts in very small grades on the monitor. These are not used in circumstances other than within the program.

MULTIPLE MASTER
Multiple Master, MM, is a development of the Postscript Type 1 format that was launched by Adobe. Multiple Master fonts can be correctly scaled typographically in width and in weight. Font file types that stopped being developed in 1999 still work if you install the extension program ATM Light from Adobe if you use Windows, but the font type is not sold any longer.

aaaaaaa
aaaaa

ANTI-ALIASING

Anti-aliasing allows the fonts to be better reproduced on the screen. A font's contour lines are softened with gray scale tones of the color used. Using anti-aliasing means that viewing on the screen is slower.

Anti-aliasing can be activated in Adobe Indesign.

Here we see how anti-aliasing looks. The character on the right has not been anti-aliased. If you use Indesign and your screen typography looks like this you can activate anti-aliasing under PREFERENCES → DISPLAY PERFORMANCE... → ENABLE ANTI-ALIASING.

CLEARTYPE IN WINDOWS

Cleartype is a technique from Microsoft that can be used in Windows for evening out text on the screen. It is an expanded version of version of anti-aliasing that takes advantage of the

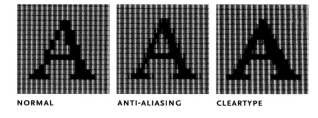

NORMAL **ANTI-ALIASING** **CLEARTYPE**

capacity to determine each screen pixel's red, green and blue lights individually to create smoother character forms, even in small grades. Normal anti-aliasing handles each pixel as a whole. Cleartype is activated under CONTROL PANEL → MONITOR → APPEARANCE → EFFECTS → USE FOLLOWING METHOD FOR EVENING EDGES OF CHARACTER TYPEFACE → CLEARTYPE.

UNICODE

Since Postscript Type 1 and Truetype fonts are based on 8-bit techniques and therefore contain a maximum of 256 different characters, these font file types do not have the capacity to hold all the characters that are needed in one single file. Special fonts have therefore been developed that can, for example, contain the special typestyles necessary for Easter European languages. The same thing is true of course for type version such as bold, italic, etc. To solve this, the international standard Unicode was created. It is based on 16 bits per character, which makes it possible to define up to 1,114,112 different characters within one font. It allows at the same time for each character takes twice as much memory space as earlier 8-bit fonts. Opentype format supports Unicode and can contain up to 65,000 different characters in one font. Windows from version 2000 and Mac OS X support Unicode. Adobe programs have built-in support for Unicode.

COOLTYPE

Adobe programs have a built-in font manager called Cool Type. This makes it possible, among other things, that within Adobe's program you can use fonts in Windows format in Mac OS.

---

printer's RIP make the best choice there is a suggestion setup in the font. Such a suggestion is called a "hint". All fonts for graphic production are hinted.

Truetype and Opentype have greater possibilities for more exact hinting than Postscript Type 1. Postscript Type 1 is built on simpler hinting, but lets the RIP do more thinking work, which means that typography created with Postscript Type 1 fonts can get better hinting with upgraded RIPs than with older RIPs.

6.6 **Pitfalls with Fonts**

There are some typical pitfalls and normal problems regarding fonts that you should avoid, for example when fonts are missing or the font's ID number collides with that of another font.

6.6.1 **Missing fonts**

Layout documents done in Quark Xpress or Adobe Indesign, for example, contain links to the fonts that are used in the layout. If you want to see how the layout will look on the screen, print it, or create a PDF file for printing, the fonts have to be activated in the computer. This can create problems if, for example,

FONT HINTS

Displayed above is a letter. The thin line of the letter is 1.5 dots wide. A "hint" determines if one dot (see letter to the left) or two dots (see letter to the right) should be used for the best possible result.

a document is going to be printed out from a computer where the fonts are not accessible.

To avoid this problem it is appropriate for whoever has done the layout to save the document as a PDF file when it is being sent for printing or for proofing since the fonts can then be included. If the PDF file is created so that it follows the standard format PDF/X [*see Prepress 7.2.6*] the fonts have to be included in the file. This means that the receiver does not need to have the fonts used available in his or her computer in order to be able to see and print out the document correctly.

If you try to open a layout document without having the typeface used available, you will receive a warning about this with the choice of canceling the opening of the file, or replacing the missing fonts with some that are available. Therefore it is common to include the fonts when you send a layout document to someone else for further editing or printing. This is also important because different versions of what appear to be the same font can cause unexpected line and page breaks.

The receiver must, in most cases, have the license for the font in question to use the typeface in his or her document. Inserting fonts in a PDF is, however, permitted from a license standpoint. Some font manufacturers take advantage of the opportunity that exists to block their fonts from use in PDF files but this is very unusual.

6.6.2 Different Typefaces with the Same Name

Some typefaces exist in many different cuts: these are versions designed by different typographers but with the same name. That means that one cut of Garamond is most likely not like another. If you replace a missing font in a document with a font with the same name you can get some differences if it is not exactly the font that was used when the document was created. Fonts can also contain unique adjustments of, for example, kerning values, but others build on the same original font.

6.6.3 Font Identification Numbers

Technically all font files have been assigned a unique ID number, a font ID. This makes it easier for the computer to keep the different fonts that are installed separate. Unfortunately it can happen that two fonts get the same number and problems arise when they are active simultaneously. What happens are usually called typeface collisions or ID number conflicts.

Software such as Extensis Suitcase solves this problem automatically. It can also be solved manually by activating one font or opening the font in a font-design program and giving it another ID number.

6.6.4 Mac and Windows Fonts

Truetype and Postscript Type 1 fonts exist both in Mac and Windows versions. This can cause problems when transferring documents between platforms. However, Mac OS manages Truetype fonts from Windows if they have been installed in the program's own font folder. If you want to be sure to avoid platform problems with fonts you should use Opentype fonts.

6.6.5 Truetype Fonts

In some older RIPs that are based on Postscript Type 2 [*see Prepress 7.7.6*] problems with printing out Truetype fonts can arise. It used to be said you should avoid Truetype in graphic production. In modern RIPs this poses no problem.

6.6.6 Bold or Italic in the Layout Program

In some layout programs such as Quark Xpress you can choose typestyles such as "bold" or "italic" from the style menu. In such a case the program looks up the font's corresponding bold or italic style and uses it. This also means that if later on you don't have a bold version of the printer font available you will get undesired results when printing out. Normally in this case the non-bold version will be used instead, but without any warning of a font change occurring. In other words, you should avoid using this function and instead choose the bold typestyle in the font menu. If Adobe Indesign is being used, this problem cannot arise since the function of choosing "bold" or "italic" doesn't exist and right from the beginning you have to choose the right typestyle.

6.7 Images

There are two main kinds of image file: object graphics and pixel images [*see Digital Images 4.1 and 4.6*]. Graphics such as diagrams, news graphics, and the like are saved as object graphics, as long as you don't want them to look painted or drawn. Logotype should be object-based and not saved as pixel-based images. This means that they are described by mathematical curves and that you can rescale them without losing quality. Logotypes that are saved as pixel-based images should be transferred to curves [*see Digital Images 4.2*].

Object-based images are normally saved as EPS or PDF files from programs like Adobe Illustrator or Macromedia Freehand. Adobe Indesign also handles object-based images saved in Adobe Illustrator's own AI format. This gives the advantage that the file can keep the drawing program's own editing ability and functions such as layers, filter effects, etc.

Photographic images and hand-drawn illustrations that are meant to reproduce pen and pencil strokes and the underlying structure are saved as pixel graphics. Pixel-based graphics most often come from digital cameras and scanners, or from drawing programs such as Corel Painter. They are normally edited in Adobe Photoshop. The images are usually saved in the standard formats TIFF, EPS or PDF that can be mounted in, for example, Quark Xpress, Adobe Indesign or Adobe Pagemaker. Image files can also be compressed, in general with JPEG or LZW compression [*see Digital Images 4.9*].

Pixel-based images can also be saved in Photoshop's own format, PSD, that has also become standard in many other programs. The image can then retain the functions that are possible in Photoshop, such as masks, adjustment layers, etc. Files in PSD format can be mounted in Adobe Illustrator.

6.7.1 Images in CMYK or RGB?

When you scan images with a scanner or take photographs with a digital camera the RGB system is used for describing colors. In order to make it possible to

KEEP TRACK OF IMAGE COPYRIGHTS
Remember that images can be copyright protected or only be bought for limited use. Unlawful use can be expensive mistakes.

print the images they have to be converted so their colors are described in the CMYK system (the color system that is used for print). This is done during print adjustment. At that time the images are converted while they are being optimized for the halftone dots, paper and the printing process they will be printed with [*see Prepress 7.4*].

This print adjustment of the images can be done before the layout so that the images you mount in the layout are in CMYK mode. But you can also mount the images in RGB mode and let the images be print adjusted after the layout work when managing the print-ready PDF files.

The advantage with mounting the images in RGB mode is that you don't adjust the images to a certain printing situation, but instead can change, for example, the type of paper without affecting the layout. This method of working means you can even use the same layout document for several different types of printing. If you want to work with RGB images in the layout you have to discuss this with your printer first.

You can also combine CMYK and RGB images in the layout. This means that RGB images are adjusted at a later stage during the handling of the PDF file while the CMYK images remain untouched.

If you work with Adobe Indesign you can easily check if the images you have mounted are in CMYK or RGB mode by selecting an image and studying Color image in the Information window. You can also see there which ICC profile has been embedded in the respective image files. This is important to be sure that the CMYK images are print adjusted for the printer you are going to use, that is with the right ICC profile. An alternative for seeing if the images are in CMYK or RGB is to study LINK INFORMATION for each image or do an FILE → PREFLIGHT... where Indesign gives a warning for all the RGB images that are being used.

6.7.2 Rotating or Skewing Images

It is easy to affect images in the layout program by rotating or skewing them. But if you do this type of adjustment on pixel-based images each printout will take a much longer time since the RIP in the printer has to calculate the adjustments in the high-resolution images with every new printout. Therefore you should do these kinds of adjustments to your images in the image editing program before mounting them in the layout.

6.7.3 Optimal Image Size

When you mount images in a layout program you decide what size they will be in print. This means that the resolution of pixel-based images is affected by the size you give the image in the layout. If you make the image smaller the resolution will increase when the pixels in the image are packed more tightly together. If you enlarge the image the resolution will decrease when the pixels are stretched out and become larger. If the resolution gets too low the image's quality will suffer. Therefore you should already, before beginning with the layout, make an image manuscript and decide what size the images will be used in and during image editing adjust the images to a resolution that is double that of the screen frequency in print.

If you are unsure as to the screen frequency the printed product will be printed with, you can let the images have a resolution of 300 ppi/120 ppcm, which is enough for all types of printing and screen frequencies.

Today storage space and transfer speed are seldom any problem, which is why 300 ppi/120 ppcm usually works well, though at times it can be an unnecessarily high resolution. The resolution of the images can also be automatically lowered later on when producing the PDF file for printing. [*see Prepress 7.2.6*].

6.7.4 Low Resolution Placement Images – OPI and DCS

If you are working with large images requiring a lot of memory space and have limited storage space, slow network transfers or slow computers an alternative can be to provide low resolution copies of the images for the layout. You then place the low-resolution copies of the high-resolution images in the layout and the images are replaced by the corresponding high-resolution ones before printing.

The advantages with using low-resolution images for layout work are faster transferring of images via Internet and somewhat faster mounting in the layout. The disadvantage with working with low-resolution copies of images is mainly that you are locked to one workflow and eventually to one supplier. There are even a number of more practical disadvantages: careful mounting of the images is made more difficult since you can't see all the details of the image. It is difficult to judge the final image quality from the low-resolution image. It is useless to carry out image editing on the low-resolution images. You cannot create a high-resolution PDF file for printing without the high-resolution files. If you change the name of the low-resolution image the replacement doesn't work with the high-resolution images when printing out.

The many disadvantages with the increased capacities of computers and networks makes work with low-resolution copies of images more uncommon today.

There are two ways to work with low-resolution copies of images. Either an OPI system is used – Open Prepress Interface – or a DCS format is used on four-color images.

The OPI system is a server-based special program which automatically creates low-resolution copies of high-resolution images. These are mounted in the layout and when a printout of the document is then made via the OPI system, the low-resolution images are automatically exchanged for the high-resolution images. The OPI system is found exclusively in prepress companies and printing houses.

The other alternative for working with low-resolution copies of images is to save the images in DCS format – a format that is a version of the EPS format [*see Digital images 4.8.4*]. DCS files are four-color images that are divided into five separate files – one low-resolution and four high-resolution, one four every printing color. DCS is therefore sometimes called five-file EPS. The low-resolution image can then be used for the layout work. When you print out or create a PDF the low-resolution images are replaced by the high resolution ones. When you work with DCS you don't need any special system as in OPI solutions.

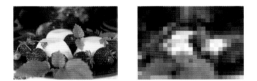

HIGH-RESOLUTION AND LOW-RESOLUTION IMAGES
Sometimes you talk about low and high-resolution images in conjunction with the layout. High-resolution images are images with enough resolution for printing. Low-resolution images are placement images for layout work with a resolution that is far beneath what is needed for printing, often around 72 ppi. This resolution is also enough for screen presentations in Microsoft Powerpoint or for the Web.

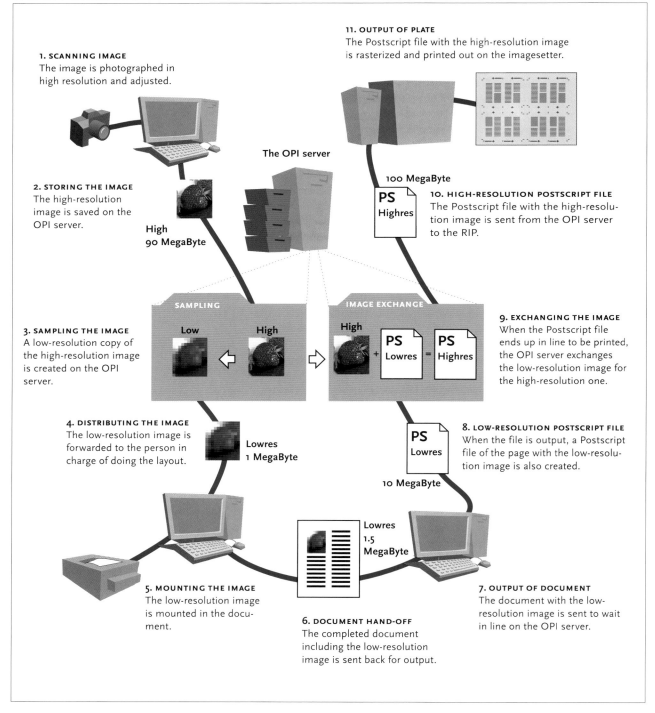

1. SCANNING IMAGE
The image is photographed in high resolution and adjusted.

2. STORING THE IMAGE
The high-resolution image is saved on the OPI server.

The OPI server

High
90 MegaByte

SAMPLING

Low   High

3. SAMPLING THE IMAGE
A low-resolution copy of the high-resolution image is created on the OPI server.

4. DISTRIBUTING THE IMAGE
The low-resolution image is forwarded to the person in charge of doing the layout.

Lowres
1 MegaByte

5. MOUNTING THE IMAGE
The low-resolution image is mounted in the document.

6. DOCUMENT HAND-OFF
The completed document including the low-resolution image is sent back for output.

Lowres
1.5 MegaByte

7. OUTPUT OF DOCUMENT
The document with the low-resolution image is sent to wait in line on the OPI server.

8. LOW-RESOLUTION POSTSCRIPT FILE
When the file is output, a Postscript file of the page with the low-resolution image is also created.

PS
Lowres

10 MegaByte

IMAGE EXCHANGE

High   PS
        Lowres

PS
Highres

9. EXCHANGING THE IMAGE
When the Postscript file ends up in line to be printed, the OPI server exchanges the low-resolution image for the high-resolution one.

100 MegaByte

PS
Highres

10. HIGH-RESOLUTION POSTSCRIPT FILE
The Postscript file with the high-resolution image is sent from the OPI server to the RIP.

11. OUTPUT OF PLATE
The Postscript file with the high-resolution image is rasterized and printed out on the imagesetter.

6.8 **Mounting Images**

When an image is mounted, or placed, in a layout program, a low-resolution copy of the image is created in the document. This low-resolution image has a direct link, to the high-resolution image. When the document is printed out the program searches, using the link, for the high-resolution image and lets it replace the low-resolution one. The link works with the image file's name and location in the file structure of the computer. Therefore you should not rename image files or move them to another folder after mounting them in your layout program. If you change the location of the image files in the computer or the server after mounting them in the layout program the image link will be broken. You can then update the link by telling the program where the image files are located. Image links are often broken, for example, when you deliver your document to a service provider for further editing. The receiver must then update the image links so that everything will be correct.

You can check that all the image links are consistent by going to WINDOW → LINKS in Adobe Indesign, OTHER → IMAGES in Quark Xpress and FILE → LINKS in Adobe Pagemaker. You can also update image links here by clicking on update and telling the program where the image files are located.

Layout programs cannot edit images but can, among other things, change their location size, dimensions and vertical position, as well as to a certain degree affect their colors. In Indesign, however, you can open and edit the images directly in Photoshop, which after editing will update the layout.

6.8.1 **Embedding Images in the Layout Document**
In Adobe Indesign and PageMaker you can embed mounted images directly in the layout file instead of linking them. You should, however, avoid embedding larger image files in order to avoid large, unwieldy documents. For simpler types of templates, however, embedding can simplify handling when you don't risk losing linked images, for example with logotypes or business card templates.

A disadvantage with embedding images in the layout document is that you won't make corrections in them without first exporting the images.

Indesign automatically embeds pixel-based images that are smaller than 48 kB in size. Indesign doesn't show, however, the symbol that the image is embedded before you have manually chosen to embed the file.

6.8.2 **Reducing and Enlarging the Image in the Layout**
If you mount an image with optimal resolution and then decrease the size the resolution will be higher than necessary. This, however, does not affect the quality of the image. The image will, however, take up more memory than is necessary.

If you enlarge the image the resolution is reduced and you risk getting such low resolution that the image quality suffers. You usually can expect to enlarge an image in the layout program up to 115–120 % without notable quality reduction. This holds under conditions where the resolution is optimal at 100 % size.

Let us take an example: An image that has a resolution that yields a sampling factor of 2 when rasterized is enlarged to 150 % in the layout program. The

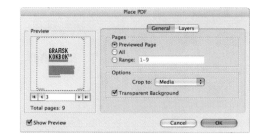

MOUNTING PDF IN INDESIGN
PDF files can be mounted as images in layout programs. Adobe Indesign affords the possibility of choosing which page, in a multi-page PDF, you want to mount.

MAKING A FACSIMILE AS A PDF FILE
In order to make a facsimile – that is an image of another printed product – the best way is to create a PDF file from the printed product's layout document. If you scan in the other printed product in gray scale or RGB or take a screen shot of the page, all the typography included will be rasterized. A PDF version of the printed product combines font-based typography object-based graphics and pixel images, which yields the best quality. EPS format also works, but there are several advantages to the PDF format, among other things the fact that fonts can be embedded in PDF files [*also see Digital images 4.13 about scanning facsimiles*].

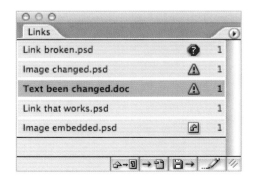

LINKED OR NOT LINKED, THAT IS THE QUESTION
Adobe Indesign's link list shows if the links work, are broken, if a linked image or text is changed or if an image is embedded in the layout document. By clicking on the symbols in the lower edge of the window the faulty links can be dealt with.

In Adobe Indesign you can create a duotone image of a mounted color or of a gray scale image. With a color image the image is mounted and the desired duotone color is set as a tint inside the frame with the DIRECT SELECTION TOOL and in the TRANSPARENCY PALETTE, LUMINOSITY is set as the method. With a gray scale image the above is done first with black as a tint to create a black and white image. Then a frame is created that is filled in with the duotone color and placed behind the image. Finally the image frame is selected with the SELECTION TOOL and MULTIPLY is set as the method for the image frame's transparency

From a gray scale image a fake duotone image can easily be created in Indesign. Give the frame a tint. Then select the actual image in the frame with the SELECTION TOOL and MULTIPLY is set as the method in the TRANSPARENCY PALETTE.

sampling factor will than be decreased to 2/1.5=1.33, which is entirely too low. If we decide to allow a sampling factor of 1.7 this means that we can enlarge the image to 2/1.7=1.18=118 %. Somewhere around here lies the boundary for a clearly visible reduction in quality and therefore we usually say that in a layout program you can enlarge an image up to 115 %.

For gray scale images, however, you should be a little more careful. In such cases you shouldn't enlarge more than 105–110 %. The reason is that gray scale images are printed with only one color ink and thus only one screen frequency. Color images are built up of four separate screen frequencies, each in its own gauge, which thus camouflages a lower resolution better.

If you use Adobe Indesign as a layout program you can see the resolution an image has after you have changed its size by looking in the Information window and studying EFFECTIVE VALUE of PPI. This means that you can mount images in any resolution and then adjust the size until the resolution is good enough. This facilitates, for example, when images come from digital cameras where images often have a resolution of 72 ppi, but are very big as to width and height.

If you want to enlarge the image you have four alternatives: scan it, photograph it again at a higher resolution, lower the screen frequency of the printing, or accept lower quality or interpolate from a higher resolution in an image editing program. The interpolation will not yield the same quality as if the image had been scanned in with the correct resolution, but you get a better result that printing out the image with too low a resolution [see Digital Images 5.4.5].

6.8.3 Viewing the Images in Low or High Resolution

When images are mounted in the layout program a low-resolution copy is created in the document for both pixel-based and object graphics. In certain contexts, because of lack of detail, it can be hard to place and crop the images exactly. In these cases it is possible in both Adobe Indesign and Quark Xpress to select a view of the true high-resolution or object-based image. It facilitates placement and cropping considerably, especially if you increase the viewing scale (zoom in) greatly. Viewing with high resolution is, however, demanding on the computer and can make the program work a little slowly. Therefore you should only do it on images where it is really necessary.

6.8.4 Printouts in High or Low Resolution

When printing out you can, in most layout programs, choose if you are going to print out the document only with the low-resolution image copies created by the layout program, or if the high-resolution images are going to be printed out. If you print out the low-resolution images the printout will be considerably faster but the image quality will suffer. If you want to be able to judge the image quality from a printer meant for this purpose, the printout usually has to be done with the high-resolution images.

The fastest printout is when you don't print any images at all. In that case the layout program usually replaces the images with gray squares instead.

6.9 Color

When you go to choose colors according to design, illustrations, typography, etc. in your layout, you have to decide if you are going to work with spot colors, four-color or both.

A spot color is a special ready-made blend of printing ink in a certain color that is printed with its own printing plate. Spot colors exist in a large number of different colors and the most common system for spot colors comes from Pantone and is called Pantone Matching System, PMS [*see Chromatics 3.5*].

Four-color is the four printing inks in four-color printing, CMYK (cyan, magenta, yellow, black). By combining the four printing inks in different proportions you can create thousands of different colors [*see Chromatics 3.4*]. You call them four-color combinations even if in practice you don't blend the actual printing inks with each other. Instead we print them beside and on top of each other.

6.9.1 Choosing Colors From Printed Color Guides

When it comes to color in design, illustrations, typography, etc., color reproduction on a monitor corresponds poorly with that in print. For this reason, when choosing colors for this type of use, you should choose them out of a color guide regardless of whether you are working with four-color or spot colors. Print guides are printed products where different colors and color combinations have been printed. Color guides show how a certain spot color or four-color combination will look printed.

You should always remember to look at a color guide in the right light and use a color guide that has been produced on the type of paper you are going to print on since both four-color combinations and spot colors yield different

PRINTED COLOR GUIDES

PANTONE GUIDES
In order to choose the right Pantone color you use printed Pantone guides.

COLOR GUIDE FOR CMYK
You should not select colors based on what they look like on the screen. Instead, you should use a color guide printed on a paper similar to the one you will be using. In the color guide, you will also find the colors' CMYK combinations.

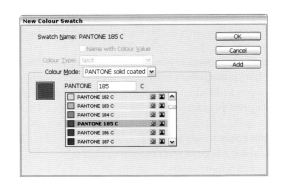

WHAT DOES "X052" MEAN IN THE FOUR-COLOR GUIDE?

In color guides the percentages are usually stated in a simpli-fied way with four symbols. The respective symbols stand for a percentage and are indicated with 0–9 or X where, for example, 9 stands for 90 percent and X stand for 100 percent. The order in which the colors are given varies between the dif-ferent color guides, and usually is indicated at the beginning of the color guide. If the color guide is based on the European standard that colors are given in YMCK order, that is from light to dark. Some printers present the colors in CMYK order in their color guides instead, since this is the order in which the printing inks are most commonly talked about. If we follow the Europa scale order the combination X052, for example, would mean 100 percent yellow, 0 percent magenta, 50 percent cyan and 20 percent black, which results in a dark green color.

WHAT DOES "CVC" MEAN IN PANTONE COLORS?

Pantone colors often have a lettered code following the number of the color, for example "185C". The code indicates if the color is printed on coated (C = Coated), uncoated matt (M = Matte) or uncoated (U = Uncoated). If CV stand in front of the colors when you go to choose the color in your computer program, it means that the color is a screen simulation (CV = Computer Video). 185 CVM thus means a screen simulation of print on coated matt paper of the Pantone color 185.

COLOR CHIPS

There are Pantone guides and four-color guides that come with color samples that you can tear out. These can be practical to send to the printer when you want to be sure that the colors will come out as you intended when printed.

colors on different paper. For this reason there are color guides for coated paper and for uncoated paper as well as for newsprint.

Color guides for four-color are often constructed in 10% increments for each printed color. In this type of printed color guide you can see exactly which color combination you are should choose to achieve a certain color.

If you use four-color combinations you should preferably use a color guide that has been printed at the printing house you are going to use. Such a color guide should be printed under the same conditions (paper, ink, color order, screen frequency and machines) you are going to use for your printed product.

There are different types of color guides. There are color guides for spot colors that contain percentages of the respective spot color. There are color guides for spot colors that contain the four-color combination that most closely resembles the spot color.

6.9.2 Four-color Together with Spot Colors

Sometimes you might want to complement a four-color print with spot colors, for example combining normal four-color images with exact colors in texts, logotypes or tint areas.

If you are going to work with spot colors together with four-color you should find out how many inks the printer's printing presses can print with. If, for example, the printer's printing presses only have four printing units and therefore can only print four colors, one after another, a printed product that is to be printed with a spot color in addition to the four-color process will need to be printed twice in a row in the same printing press. This affects the price dramatically. Many printers have printing presses that can print with five, six or eight inks. If you print a printed product with four-color and two spot colors in a six-color press you can print all six colors at once.

6.9.3 Converting Spot Colors to Four-color Values

Adobe Pagemaker, Adobe Indesign and Quark Xpress can convert spot colors to four-color combinations automatically by stating that every spot color used is to be printed with four-color. It is not certain that the same four-color values used will be like those in a color guide with spot colors and four-color combinations shown as corresponding with each other. The result is usually good, but if you want control over which four-color combination will be used you should go through the spot colors yourself and put in four-color values chosen from a color guide.

Since layout programs contain a large number of pre-defined spot colors to choose among, and since the programs themselves can convert spot colors to four-color combinations, this means that you will be tempted to choose colors for you four-color printed product from the spot color squares on your monitor. This is not a good solution. Printed four-color guides should be used [see 6.9.1]. In addition, you risk forgetting to convert the spot colors to four-color.

6.9.4 Converting Four-color Values to Pantone Colors

If you have a four-color value and want to find the closest possible Pantone color you should preferably take a printed Pantone guide and compare it with a printed sample of four-color combinations with the correct lighting.

If you don't have a printed sample available, you can get help from Adobe Photoshop. Photoshop can select the Pantone color that most closely resembles the actual four-color combination you have. You begin with setting the actual four-color values in the color selector by clicking on the color square for the foreground color in the tools palette or in the color palette. Depending on whether the paper you are going to print on is coated or uncoated, you choose Pantone Solid Coated or Uncoated under Color library and Photoshop shows the Pantone color that is closest to the four-color combination.

6.9.5 Saving the Color Combination as a Color Swatch

Once you have decided to use specific combinations of CMYK in the color scale for your layout, you can save these as color squares in the layout program. Each color square can then be used to apply just that color combination to different objects in the layout. If you then change the color combination, you change the color square and all the objects that are colored in with that color square get the new combination of CMYK. This really makes things easier when you want to change a color combination in an entire printed product.

CONVERTING A SPOT COLOR TO FOUR-COLOR

- Use a color guide that shows the Pantone color against the CMYK combination that is closest to it.

- Use a Pantone color guide and compare yourself the actual color against the color squares in a four-color guide. Find the CMYK combination that is most like the spot color.

- Check off SEPARATION in the color definition for spot color in Quark Xpress or choose CMYK as COLOR TYPE for SPOT COLOR in Indesign.

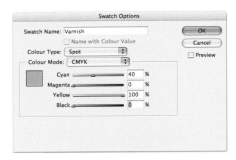

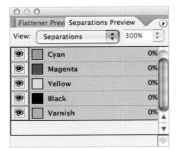

When you are going to varnish a specific surface in printing, it is done most easily by defining a special spot color for the varnish. The part that is to be varnished should be stated so that that varnish is printed over those objects and colors.

Without simulation

With simulation

WITH AND WITHOUT PREVIEW
By simulating printed colors on the monitor you get a chance to predict how the printed colors will appear.

You can also create tones in different percentages of the color square. These can be saved as tonal color squares. These also change their color composition if the original combination of CMYK in the color square is changed.

6.9.6 Varnish is Defined as an Ink in the Layout

Sometimes you may want to use varnish on certain objects in your printed product, known as partial varnishing, to create a special effect, for example, on a logotype [see Finishing and Binding 10.3]. In your original document you work with varnish in the same way you do a spot color. Define a special color for the varnish and state which objects should have that color (varnish). Spot colors can also be placed in object or line art images that indicate where the varnish will be placed.

To facilitate the layout work the object with the varnish can be placed in its own layer to be easily hidden. It is important that the varnish be defined so that it prints over all the other colors.

6.9.7 Handling Colors Using ICC in the Layout

When you work with layout you will naturally want the colors on the screen to resemble the printed colors as closely as possible. In order for this to be possible three things are required: that the screen's display of the colors be correct, that you have information regarding the printer's ability to reproduce colors and that the layout program be installed to simulate printing.

To get the screen to display the correct colors it is necessary for you to have a monitor that is good for this [see The Computer 2.4.5] and that the monitor be calibrated [see Chromatics 3.11] so it shows exactly the colors you ask it to show.

Information about the printer's ability to handle colors is found in the printer's ICC profile. Printing houses often have current ICC profiles that can be downloaded from their website.

To get the layout program to simulate the appearance of print the printer's ICC profile should first be installed in the computer. Then you should activate the color management in the layout program. In Adobe Indesign this is done under EDIT → PROOFS COLORS. In Quark Xpress the extension Quark CMS must first be activated, then you go in under SETTINGS → QUARK CMS and check off color handling active. Then the printer's ICC profile is chosen as the current ICC profile for CMYK. In Adobe Indesign this is done under EDIT → COLOR SETTINGS... WORKING SPACES → CMYK. In Quark Xpress this is done under SETTINGS → QUARK CMS → DESTINATION PROFILES → COMPOSITE PRINTOUT. In Adobe Indesign you can also choose if the blackness in the printing and the whiteness of the paper should be simulated. This is done under VIEW → PROOF SETUP → CUSTOM...

Finally, the simulation should be activated. You do this in Adobe Indesign by selecting PROOF COLORS under the VIEW MENU. In Quark Xpress preview comes on when the choice of COLOR HANDLING active is made earlier.

When these steps are carried out, then all the colors in images, tint areas, typography, etc. are shown simulated according to the printer's ability to show colors. If the simulation of print black and paper white has been chosen in Adobe Indesign, these will also more closely resemble the printed result.

The ICC profiles you have chosen for simulation are given in the layout document if the color manager is active when the layout is saved. This is done if the document is opened on another computer so you can also see colors on the screen there in the same way if color handling, simulation and the same profiles are activated.

If the color manager is activated and the Indesign document does not have a profile embedded when it is opened, you will be asked if you want to assign ICC profiles for RGB and CMYK. You should always assign an ICC profile for RGB so that other users of the document will be able to see the same RGB colors.

Assigning profiles and activating color management and simulation does not change the content of the file's images or colors. Instead it only affects viewing things on the screen and, if you wish, also print adjustments for the eventual production of a PDF file or a printout on a color printer. If images in RGB mode or colors of objects in RGB values are used in the layout document and then a PDF file is exported in CMYK mode, all the images and objects in RGB will automatically be print-adjusted to CMYK with the chosen ICC profile [*see Prepress 7.4*].

6.10 Pitfalls in Managing Colors

There are some typical errors that can arise when managing colors in the layout document and that can cause problems when the document is sent to the printer. They involve mainly how spot colors are handled. We will go through the most common pitfalls here.

6.10.1 Removing Unused Spot Colors

Every printed color is printed with its own printing plate in the printing press. If you work with four-color images and two spot colors the document will be printed with six colors – CMYK for the images as well as two spot colors.

If sketches were done with different spot colors at the time the design was made, it can easily happen that some object still has a color left that was not intended to be used. It may be hard to see on the screen if two objects are very close in color.

Each of the printing colors used will be printed out on its own printing plate at the printing house. The risk is that even the objects with spot colors you decided not to use will get their own printing plates.

Occasionally it may happen that printing plates will be printed out for all the printing colors in the document regardless of whether or not they are used in the layout. There is a great risk that you will be forced to pay for the printing plates that are not needed. If nothing else, confusion will be created at the printer's as to which printing colors to use.

In communicating with the printer you must clearly state which spot colors you want to use in printing.

Unused colors should therefore also be removed from the layout document before sending it to print. In Adobe Indesign there exists the possibility of selecting all the unused color squares in the color box and then deleting them. If any of these colors are used you will get the question as to which one you want to replace it with.

REMOVE UNUSED COLORS

In Adobe Indesign's window COLOR SWATCHES, you can choose to SELECT ALL UNUSED colors, which then can be erased. This is a simple way to avoid problems when printing.

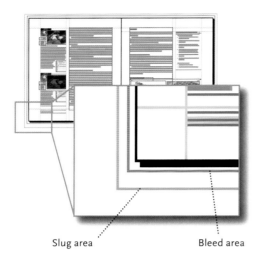

Slug area   Bleed area

If you deliver print-ready PDF files to the printing house you can, in Adobe Acrobat Professional, check which process colors are in the document by choosing ADVANCED → OUTPUT PREVIEW → SEPARATIONS.

If the PDF file is exported directly from Adobe Indesign the used spot colors are removed along with the file.

6.10.2 Spot Colors That are not Color Separated

It is usual for the designer to sketch the layout with spot colors or to choose his or her colors in the form of spot colors, even if only four-color will be used in printing. Before printing you have to check that all the spot colors have been set for separation to four-color. If not, all the objects that are in spot colors will not be included in the print since they do not contain process colors that the print is being made from. A better way to do it is to always choose hues for process colors from the printed four-color guides.

6.10.3 Naming Spot Colors Alike

When you work with spot colors in illustrations it is important for spot colors to have the exact same name in illustrations as in the layout document. Normally all the spot colors are imported from illustrations to the layout document where you can easily see if there are two spot colors with similar names. In such a case it is important to adapt the name of the spot color in the illustration as well as subsequently removing all the unused spot colors from the layout document.

6.10.4 Being Careful with Ink Amounts

When you make four-color combinations you should remember not to make combinations that contain too much ink. Theoretically the maximum ink coverage is 100+100+100+100=400 % color. Depending on the printing process and the paper you cannot really print with more than 220 to 340 % ink. A fine, sheet-fed print can usually take approximately 340 % ink coverage, while a newspaper print is usually limited to approximately 240 % coverage. You can get the exact values from you printer [*see Printing 9.5.2*].

6.11 Pitfalls in the Layout Work

There are a few typical errors you should avoid in the layout. Many have to do with the risks associated with using four-color, but there are also pitfalls of a more technical character. We will go through the most common ones here.

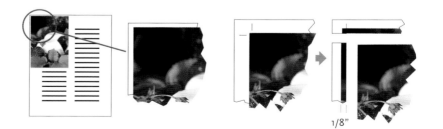

1/8"

PART 1
You will always get a certain variation in color composition on the printed sheets and even between the left and the right side of a sheet. That is why you should avoid placing objects or images with sensitive colors across a two-page spread.

PART 2
You will never get a 100% registration between two separate pages. That's why you should avoid placing objects or images diagonally across a double-page spread.

PART 3
You should also avoid thin lines that bleed across a two-page spread. Thicker lines are less sensitive to misregistration.

6.11.1 Bleeds

Images or tint areas that reach all the way to the paper edges are called bleeds. It is important that these objects stretch slightly outside of the page format so that they will remain as bleeds after the printed product has been cropped and finished and bound. If objects do not extend outside the format there is a risk that they will not reach all the way to the edge of the page after it has been finished and bound. As a consequence, there will be a white, unprinted area between the image or the tint area and the paper edge. Because printing and finishing and binding are never exact, a safety margin (bleed) is required. A bleed of at least 1/8" is recommended.

The cover should be made like one large document with the front and back covers and the spine. When you make a cover that will be placed on a binder, the bleed should be approximately 3/8".

If the layout is done in Adobe Indesign a ruler guide for the bleed can be set to facilitate mounting the object that bleeds. The ruler guide can also be used for printouts and PDF production to include bleeds in a simple way.

6.11.2 Crossover

Sometimes you want to place an image or other object across a spread. Often during printing, the two pages of the spread will be on different sheets or on different parts of the same sheet, not printed immediately next to each other [*see Finishing and Binding 10.12*]. Spreads that are printed this way are called double-page spreads.

When the final print is finished and folded, it can be difficult to get perfect registration between the two pages. Avoid placing particularly delicate objects, such as small texts or thin rules, on two-page spreads.

Images placed diagonally across the spread are also very sensitive to small color changes. The color combination in the print often wanders a bit through-

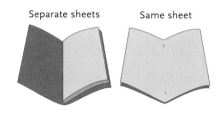

Separate sheets   **Same sheet**

SPREADS
The left spread consists of two separately printed sheets (double-page spread). The right spread consists of pages from the same sheet (a center spread).

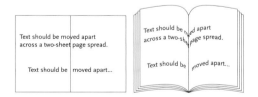

TEXT ACROSS THE PAGE SPREAD
When you place text across two separately printed sheets, the text should be moved apart during layout work so that parts of the text will not disappear or be difficult to read across the page spread after the pages are stitched together. This is especially important with glued or stitched bindings. The phenomenon can also affect images.

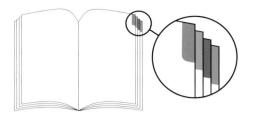

Color variations can occur on different parts of a sheet, vary throughout the edition and even between different makereadies. This means that sensitive four-color combinations, tertiary colors, can yield different results throughout the edition. If the surfaces that use four-color combinations lie so that they are seen beside each other, for example as a thumb tab or a tint area bleed, the effect can be disturbing.

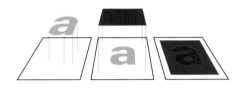

THE PROCESS COLORS ARE TRANSPARENT
This is the premise for the subtractive color combination and it means that a printed object will be visible through the component color printed over it.

ALSO BLACK IS TRANSPARENT
A tint area consisting of 100 % black ink will not be able to cover objects consisting of any of the other component colors. It requires a rich black tint to get full coverage.

out the run and also between different makereadies. Thus, two different parts of an image, placed on adjacent pages, can differ in color. This can be readily apparent with sensitive images or objects.

When you place text across a spread, the text should be moved apart so that parts of the text don't disappear or be hard to read after the pages are stitched together.

6.11.3 Color Variations

When you print, the degree of inking, the amount of ink transferred to the paper, often varies throughout the run. The degree of inking can vary between different parts of a sheet and shift a little throughout the edition, and even between different makereadies. Thus, the same four-color combination that reoccurs in a layout can easily yield different results in the same printed product, for example between different pages in the printed product. If the surfaces that use the four-color combination are placed in such a way that they are seen beside each other, for example as thumb tabs or a tint area bleed, the effect can be disturbing.

6.11.4 Rich black and Overprints

If you place a tint area that only contains 100% black beside a dark part of a photograph in a printed product, it will look pale. This is because the darkest parts in photographs contain both 100 % black and larger amounts of cyan, magenta and even yellow. Process colors, even black are always transparent, which means that the more inks you print on top of each other, the darker the result.

If you place a color photo against a black tint area you should make the tint area darker that you can get with only 100 % black. To make a black surface extra dark in the print, you usually make a rich black color combination that contains 100 % black and approximately 50 % cyan and/or magenta. If you just add to the magenta you get a little warmer black color. If you just add a little cyan you get a somewhat colder color. It is important that the cyan and magenta areas are shrunk, made smaller than the black tint area, so they are not visible in case of misregistration [*see Prepress 7.4.8*].

Another occasion when it is appropriate to choose a rich black tint area is when it should cover other objects on the page. Process colors are, as we have said, transparent. This means that a printed object that lies under a tint area in a process color can shine through. A tint area that is only made up of black will not cover other objects enough.

Most layout programs' base settings are that all objects except for those printed in 100 % black will knock out a hole in any object placed beneath them in a layout. This means that the topmost object will be printed directly on the white paper. Objects in 100 % black print over underlying objects, that is they have the underlying objects' ink under them. This means that if a black text partially lies on top of a photograph the overlapping part of the text will have the photograph's cyan, magenta and yellow behind it, but not where the text lies on the white paper by itself. In such cases you may need to control the overprint manually, either by making the text rich black or by knocking out for the text where it overlaps the image.

SHADES OF BLACK
By mixing 100% black with 50% cyan and 50% magenta you get a richer black tint than if only using black. With only cyan and black, the shade will also be rich black but with a cooler effect. With black and magenta you will get the corresponding rich black but with a warmer tint.

If you do not want 100 % black ink not to print over underlying objects you can control it in several ways. A simple way is to set the color to 99.9 % black whereby the RIP will not understand it as 100 % and not print over objects. The blackness of 99.9 % black in print is the same as 100 %.

6.11.5 **Text and Tint Areas**
When you go to print several colors on top of each other some degree of misregistration will occur. In large objects such as images, illustrations, tint areas, or large text it is hardly noticeable, but in objects such as text in a small scale, fine line patters, or illustrations with fine detail misregistration is quite visible. The result of this is objects that appear blurry. Adding color to small text or line patterns with four-color combinations can be unsuitable. If it is important for text or line patterns to have a certain color it is better to print them with a special spot color instead. The same phenomenon can occur if you make use of negative (white, unprinted) text or line patterns against a colored background or in an image. In such cases you should instead choose a strong process color,

Text consists of thin lines. If the text is colored using many component colors like in this one, it is easy to get misregistration.

It is safer to set the text in one of the component colors or in a spot color because it is impossible to get misregistration.

You shouldn't use Romanesque typefaces for small-sized, negative text against a colored background because the fine lines in the letters are distracted by

A larger grotesque typeface with thicker lines looks better.

If you place text on a monochromatic background, you will not get misregistration. It is always safe to set negative text on areas that only consist of one color.

MISREGISTRATION IN TEXT
Avoid coloring small text with four-color combinations because it is easy to get misregistration.

NEGATIVE TEXT IN FOUR-COLOR TINT AREAS
Avoid small-sized, roman typeface in negative text on tint areas consisting of many component colors.

AREAS PRINTED WITH ONE COLOR ARE SAFE
To avoid misregistration in negative text, you should set it against a monochromatic background.

for example black, or a spot color for the background. If you still place negative text against a background (image or tint area) printed with several colors, it is best to choose a sans serif typeface. Serif typefaces have fine lines, called hard strokes that risk disappearing completely in print if misregistration occurs. How great the misregistration will be differs a good deal between different printing methods. Newspaper print has more misregistration than a normal sheet-fed offset press. [*See Printing 9.5.2*].

6.11.6 Transparency and Drop Shadow

Both Quark Xpress and Adobe Indesign handle transparency in the layout and in mounted images. The programs can also create see-through shadows behind objects. These functions often cause problems, however, when ripping, since older RIPs do not support transparency. This can be eliminated if before printing you create a PDF/X file [*see Prepress 7.2.6*]. Then the transparency is replaced with many high-resolution, pixel-based images that give the same result.

6.11.7 Moving Documents Between Mac OSX and Windows

Sometimes it can be necessary to transfer a document from one computer platform to another, for example from Mac OS to Windows.

Some problems whose files generally move without any problem between Mac OS and Windows are Adobe Indesign, Illustrator, Photoshop and Acrobat, Microsoft Word and Excel. Quark Xpress and Microsoft Powerpoint move relatively problem-free between different platforms as long as you use the same version of the program. Image files such as JPEG, TIFF, EPS, PDF, PSD, GIF, PNF and others are identical or generally are usable without any problem in both platforms.

What can cause problems even when these programs and file types are used are the fonts that are used by the document. Postscript and Truetype fonts differ between Mac OS and Windows and when changing platforms can, for example, cause unwanted line breaks and page breaks. One way to avoid this is to use Opentype fonts since these are based on the same file format for all platforms.

6.11.8 Moving Documents Between Different Programs

When you need to convert files from one program to another certain problems can arise. When moving between different versions of a program, it almost always works to open an older file in a newer version of a program, while the reverse can mean that certain functions disappear, cause problems, or may not be possible at all. Converting between different programs also often works well, for example from Quark Xpress or Adobe Pagemaker to Adobe Indesign. With certain combinations of programs special plug-ins can make converting possible. However, certain limitations can exist in any file version that is brought in by the imported program. Indesign can, for legal reasons, only convert Quark Xpress documents from version 4 and earlier. There exist, however, plug-ins that can convert from newer versions of programs.

When converting, some functions from the original document can get lost or unwanted phenomena can occur. It is therefore better to build the document from the ground up in the new program. Then you avoid changes and can make

SMALLER FILE SIZES FOR LAYOUT DOCUMENTS
When work has gone on for a while on a layout document, the file size may have grown and the file may take more space to store and be slower to work with, even you haven't added material to the file. In most layout programs the file size of a document can be reduced by saving the document using the function ARCHIVE → SAVE AS...

good use of the new program's special functions and way of constructing the document.

6.12 Proofing

Reviewing the text, typography and layout is called proofing. Throughout the project you can review text, typography and layout using printouts of the manuscript or layout page. Proof prints can also be made to good advantage with PDF files using Adobe Acrobat's comments functions. It is important, however, for the text to already have been proofread for tone, style, language, grammar, and proper spelling before it is put into layout.

6.12.1 Proofreading on Paper

Proofreading symbols must be clear and follow standard conventions (the international standard ISO-5776) to avoid misunderstandings and simplify communication and the changes that have to be carried out. Even though standards and traditions for proofreading symbols exist, differences exist in how the symbols are used and in some cases symbols may need to be adjusted or found for special situations. Proofreading symbols are also carried out a little differently in different languages. For this reason it is important to be consistent in how you use your proofreading symbols so the receiver will understand them easily.

Symbols are made in the text where the correction should be made. New content and instructions are placed in the margins and have a circle around them. Underlining is done to indicate change of typestyle, for example changing to italic.

When it comes to proofreading layout there are no specific rules, rather you just work with a combination of arrows, lines and descriptive comments. What you are checking for is typography, placement and accuracy in the placement of objects.

In proofreading it is most practical to write in changes with colored pencil so it is clearly visible in black text.

6.12.2 Proofreading with PDF and Acrobat

In Adobe Acrobat there are several tools for indicating and handling correction of texts and layout directly in PDF files – notation tools, drawing tools, crossing out pens, stamps, etc. The tools can of course also be used to indicate corrections in photographs and illustrations in PDF.

In Adobe Acrobat there are also functions to list all the proofreading comments, respond to the comments, see who wrote in which corrections and check off the corrections that have already been carried out.

Proofreading functions do not exist in Adobe Reader, but can be activated in a PDF file when it is created in Adobe Acrobat Professional 7. Then the proofreading tools can be used in Adobe Reader 7 as well.

Adobe Acrobat also contains functions to create the workflow for handling proofs of PDF files. The PDF file can be placed on a Web server and emailed to everyone who is to check the PDF file. Proofreading comments are then sent from everyone involved in the same PDF file on the Web server. Then only the

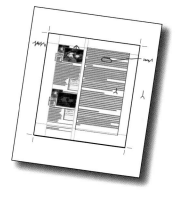

MAKE LAYOUT PROOFS ON LARGE PAPER
Print out layout proofs on larger paper to leave space for corrections. If it is tight the corrections can be numbered and explained on a separate sheet.

WHAT SHOULD BE CHECKED IN THE TEXT?

- Language/tone/style
- Factual content
- Spelling
- Syllabification
- Hyphens and spaces between letters
- Page and image references
- Pagination
- Consistency of typography and symbols

TIPS FOR PROOFREADING TEXT

- Remember that many errors can be searched for and replaced in word processing and layout programs
- Use the dictionary and an authoritative style manual for help

WHY SHOULD YOU LEARN ACROBAT'S PROOFING TOOLS?

Sending PDF files as proofs usually means saving considerable time and money. Adobe Acrobat has a number of proofing tools that are meant to replace physical drawing and writing. If you want to have clear communication between those working on layout and the person reviewing the pages, it is a good idea to learn to use these tools. The alternative is to attach PDF files to an email and write comments in the message. The risk then is obviously that some things will be difficult to explain easily in writing. It can be get confusing as well if a page is sent back and forth several times. It is better to draw, write and show ideas in approximately the same way as you do on paper – directly on the page. In addition, the comments are saved directly in the actual file so that there can never be any mixing up of different versions.

COMMENTS

The COMMENTING TOOLBAR contains the usual tools for adding proofing marks. Below we will look at what they are.

DRAWING MARKUPS TOOLBAR
There are different tools to circle things, make arrows and so on.

HIGHLIGHTING
To clarify exactly which part of the text a comment refers to you can easily make a highlight selection, underline or draw a line above the text.

STAMP TOOL
It can be used for extra clarification.

ATTACH A FILE AS A COMMENT
Attachments, for example a Word or html document, can be placed on the page.

RECORD AUDIO COMMENTS
You can also place sound clips on the page. It is easy to record a comment with the tool directly in Acrobat.

NOTE TOOL
The most common tool is the NOTE TOOL. By clicking on it the comments are showed in a window.

COMMENTS
All text-based comments for a page can also be shown as a list under the COMMENTS TAB. Observe that a comment has gotten a reply. You can also cross off comments when, for example, you have carried out a desired correction.

OPTIONS
All comments can be gathered to print out, for example. You can also export and import comments, see inset to right.

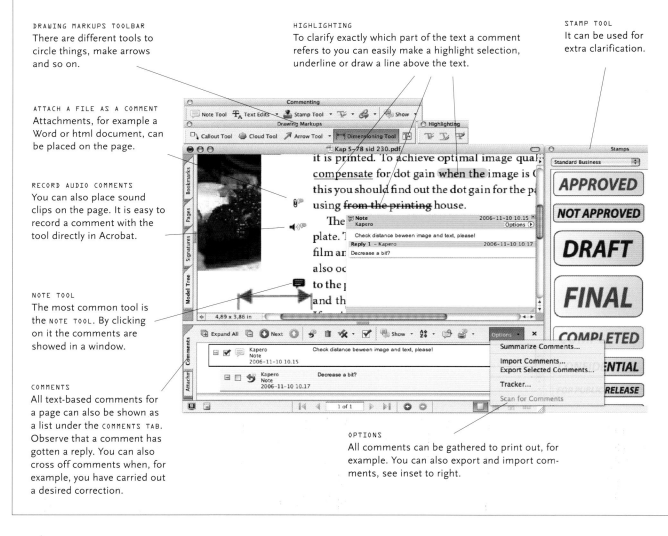

HANDLING PDF PROOFS

There are several ways to handle the exchange of comments using Adobe Acrobat. The easiest is to add comments in the PDF file and send it directly to someone, for example as an attachment with email.

To send comments more quickly than sending the whole PDF file, you can choose to only send back the comments in the form of a small file where only the comments themselves are saved. Such a comment file is called .fdf and can be sent with an email or directly from Adobe Acrobat. When the receiver double clicks on the comments file the original PDF file opens in Acrobat and the comments are put in place.

ADMINISTRATIVE PROOFING ROUNDS

Sometimes there is more than one person who is reviewing a document. In this case there are two functions for handling proofs for several people built into Adobe Acrobat Professional. Both are based on the person who is sending out the PDF file asking a number of people to do proofing. The receivers only need to have the simpler program version of Adobe Acrobat.

The first function lies under FILE → SEND FOR REVIEW... → SEND BY EMAIL FOR REVIEW... The PDF file is then sent as an attachment by email to those who have been asked and comments are then sent back to the send in the form of small comments files. All the comments are collected in the original file at the sender, who can then see everyone's comments and see who said what.

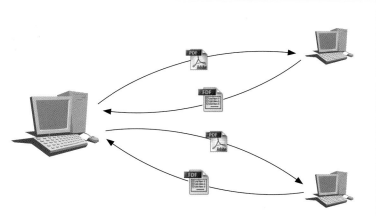

SEND BY EMAIL FOR REVIEW...
With email as a distribution method, only the person who has asked the others to do the proofing can look at all the comments from the different participants. The comments are sent back by Adobe Acrobat as small comments file.

SEND FOR WEB-BASED VIEWING...
In Adobe Acrobat there are tools to place the PDF file on a special type of Web server. This makes it possible for several people to make their comments in the same PDF file and see other people's comments, then making their comments on those comments in turn, directly in the Web browser.

FREE COMMENTS TOOLS

In the free version of Adobe Acrobat Reader there are normally no tools for making comments. Some PDF files can, however, activate these tools which lie hidden in Adobe Reader. This is very useful if you send proofs to people who only have free versions of Acrobat. To create such a PDF file you open the file in Acrobat Professional and choose COMMENTS → ENABLE FOR COMMENTING IN ADOBE READER...

Delete	℘	the ~~type~~ font	the font
Insert	type	the ⌄font	the type font
Let it stand	stet	the ~~type~~ font	the type font
Reset in capitals	cap	the type font	THE TYPE FONT
Reset in lowercase	lc	THE TYPE FONT	the type font
Reset in italics	ital	the type font	the *type* font
Reset in small capitals	sc	See type font.	See TYPE FONT.
Reset in roman	rom	the (type) font	the type font
Reset in boldface	bf	the type font	**the type font**
Reset in lightface	lf	the type (font)	the type font
Transpose	tr	the (font type)	the type font
Close up space	⌒	the ty pe	the type
Delete and close space	℘	the type fo nt	the type font
Move left	⌐	⌐ the type font	the type font
Move right	⌐	the type font	the type font
Run in	run in	The type font is Univers. It is not Garamond.	The type font is Univers. It is not Garamond.
Align	‖	the type font the type font the type font	the type font the type font the type font
Spell out	sp	③ type fonts	Three type fonts
Insert space	#	the⌄type font	the type font
Insert period	⊙	The type font⌄	The type font.
Insert comma	⌄	One⌄two, three	One, two, three
Insert hyphen	⌃=⌃	Ten⌄point type	Ten-point type
Insert colon	⊙	Old Style types⌄	Old Style types:
Insert semicolon	⌃;	Select the font⌄ spec the type.	Select the font; spec the type.
Insert apostrophe	⌄v	Baskerville⌄s type	Baskerville's type
Insert quotation marks	⌄/⌄	the word⌄type⌄	the word "type"
Insert parenthesis	(/)	The word type is in parenthesis.⌄	The word (type) is in parenthesis.
Insert en dash	⌐N⌐	Flush⌄left	Flush–left
Insert em dash	⌐M⌐/⌐M⌐	Garamond⌄an Old Style face⌄is used today.	Garamond—an Old Style face—is used today.
Start paragraph	¶	⌄The type font is Univers 55.	The type font is Univers 55.
No paragraph indent	no ¶	⌐ The type font is Univers 55.	The type font is Univers 55.

comments themselves are sent, in the form of a memory-saving FDF, so the transfer will be very fast. There is also the possibility of using a built-in email function in Adobe Acrobat. In that case the PDF file is sent as an email attachment that is opened in Adobe Acrobat. Even here it is only the corrections themselves that are sent back and not the whole PDF file.

From all the PDF files in Adobe Acrobat you can export comments and corrections as an FDF file that can be sent back to the PDF file created. When the FDF file is opened where the PDF file was created, the comments are placed automatically in the PDF file.

6.13 Proofs

Before a layout document of a PDF file is sent to print, the material needs to be checked from a technical standpoint. Is the file usable? You check that the fonts and the links to the images are working. You also need to check the material from a technical perspective. That is when you check that overprints and knock outs are done correctly, that the right printing colors are being used in the right places, that the images have the correct resolutions and color modes, that you have worked with bleeds, etc.

To help you with these checks there are tools in the layout program or separate proofing programs, known as preflight programs. You can also proof on the screen, and printouts are also a good help.

6.13.1 Printouts for Proofing

One good way to technically proof your layout is to make printouts on a laser printer. Printouts on a color laser printer make it possible to check that the right colors have been used in the right places. The color correspondence is usually too poor to judge how the colors and images will look in print. On a laser printer the quality of the typography is often lower than on a black and white printer, but in exchange the image quality can be judged better. Laser printers can generally simulate the printer's colors well if they have been properly set and the color handling for the printout is correct.

If you print out on a paper that is larger than the final format you can take advantage of this to check if the bleed is correct and use cropping marks to indicate how large the final format will be.

You can also choose to print out thumbnail images on printouts using the layout program's settings or through the printer driver routine. In this way you can get an overview of all the pages of the document or cover to check that all the pages are there and that all the material is in place.

By creating a separate printout of your layout you can also check overprinting and knock outs. If you print out one page per printing color and per page you can check that there are no printing colors defined in the layout that shouldn't be there.

6.13.2 Checking Printing Colors

If you want to check how many printing colors are being used in the layout and that the colors are ending up in the right place, you can most easily use the function FILE → PREFLIGHT... in Adobe Indesign. You can also make a PDF file that you open in Adobe Acrobat Professional and check by choosing ADVANCED → OUTPUT PREVIEW → SEPARATION. At this point the content for the respective printing plates will be shown in black. If you use Adobe Indesign you can choose WINDOW → OUTPUT → SEPARATION PREVIEW for the same effect. This yields the same result as if you, as mentioned above, made a separate printout on a printer.

To be able to predict more easily what in the layout document will be printed over, in Adobe Indesign you can preview overprinting on the monitor by choosing VIEW → OVERPRINT PREVIEW. The program will show on the monitor how other printing colors "shine through" the black color and make it darker where overprinting occurs.

MANUAL DOCUMENT REVIEWS

Preflight programs check a number of things. But many of the technical problems can be avoided by checking the document itself, at the same time many things cannot be checked using preflight programs. Below are a few tips as to how and what you can check to achieve good technical quality in your document.

IMAGES

- Have high enough resolution, but not unnecessarily high. Images should have a resolution measure in pixels that corresponds to double the screen frequency measured in raster lines.

- Don't crop an image too much in the layout. Do it in the image-editing program, or crop it in the PDF export in Indesign.

- Images must be in RGB mode or print-adjusted for the exact printing process by using the printer's ICC profile.

- Object-based images have to keep the right gray balance and maximum saturation (for example 320 %).

- If the images in the PDF file are in RGB mode or Lab mode, you have to find out if the printing house can handle this. Never have the images in indexed mode (GIF format, BMP).

- If Jpeg images are used, check that they are not compressed too much.

- All image links have to work and the images delivered along with the open layout document if it is being delivered.

COLORS

- Remove all unused spot colors from the document.

- Check that no spot colors exist in the document if the printer only uses CMYK.

- Check overprinting (black should normally print over).

- Use the right gray balance for four-color gray (not the same values as C, M, Y).

- Make sure that the maximum saturation is not exceeded in inked tint areas, lines, typography, etc. (for example 320 %).

- Avoid designing thin lines and such in several printing colors to avoid misregistration.

TYPOGRAPHY AND FONTS

- Include fonts in the PDF file that is sent to press. Alternatively deliver it with all the fonts used (even those that are used in images and logotypes) if you send an open layout document.

- Don't use bold, italic or printer fonts via Quark Xpress functions.

- Small text and special serif fonts shouldn't be printed in combinations of several printing inks to avoid misregistration.

- Small text and special serif fonts shouldn't be set as negatives against a tint area or image built up of several printing inks.

- Set the text with printer fonts in object-based images, or make sure the fonts are sent along with the document.

THE PAGE

- Add 1/8"–1/4" bleed for image bleeds and objects. For the cover of a binder the bleed should be at least 3/8".

- Construct the whole cover over the spine like a double-width page including the width of the spine.

- Deliver the right number of pages to the printer. Remove unused pages in the document.

- Remove unused objects outside the page in the document.

- Avoid lines thinner than 0.3 points, do not use "hairline".

- Ask the printing house about how the images that are on a full spread are going to be mounted in a larger castoff of the printed product.

6.13.3 Preflight of the Layout Document

The word "preflight" is borrowed form the aviation world, and refers to the pre-flight check a pilot performs on an airplane before takeoff. In the graphic print production industry, preflight refers to the review of digital documents before they go into production. Special preflight software is used to check documents against a standard checklist. The technical prerequisites of a document include images being correctly linked with enough resolution, fonts being set, colors being correct, etc. In Adobe Indesign and Quark Xpress a simpler preflight can be carried out directly in the program. Adobe Indesign's preflight function is limited to checking fonts and links and sending a red flag if the document contains RGB or Pantone colors, requires certain plug-ins or contains transparency. It does not give a warning, however regarding image resolution. For Quark Xpress there are extensions that make it possible to do a preflight review, for example QC from Gluon.

A more thorough preflight of layout documents can be done with external programs. A more secure way to do preflight, however, is to check the PDF file that makes up the original print. Everything decisive for printing can be reviewed there. Adobe Acrobat and Enfocus Pitstop contain advanced preflight functions [*see Prepress 7.2.7*].

6.14 Sending Documents to Print

When the layout document is finished it is time to send it to print. Traditionally the actual layout file from, for example, Adobe Indesign is sent to the printer, together with fonts and any high-resolution images.

If you have access to all the high-resolution images you can produce a high-resolution PDF file that contains layout and has all the images and fonts embedded. It is a more secure and more effective method of working that also entails that whoever creates the layout can technically control the actual material before it is sent to print. You eliminate the steps that arise when the printer creates a PDF from the open document, which means that you reduce the number of steps, create greater effectiveness and reduce the risk for error [*see Prepress 7.2.2*].

When you send "open documents", layout documents with images and fonts to the printer, the printer opens the layout file in the same layout program that it was created in. This makes it possible to carry out late changes at the printing house without the originally created layout needing to be involved. It still involves risks, however. Even if the fonts are sent to the printer there is still the risk of unwanted line breaks and page breaks. Image links can be broken and the layout can be changed in other ways. But one of the most important problems with letting the printing house carry out changes is that you as the customer may not have access to the final version of the document. This is the reason for one of the most common errors when printing printed materials: the final print is made from the uncorrected document.

Making use of a PDF file reduces the risks of the above named problems, but also reduces the opportunity for making late changes at the printer's, even if some adjustments can be made in the PDF file. If changes are made in the PDF

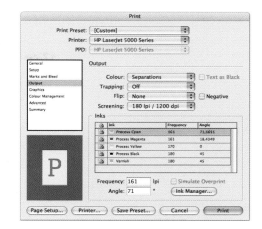

All the printing colors are shown.

Only the printing color magenta is shown.

CHECKING THE PRINTING COLORS
If Indesign or Acrobat is used separate printing colors, known as separations, can be previewed directly on the monitor. The function is found under OUTPUT → SEPARATIONS PREVIEW.

By looking at one color at a time you can check that overprinting and knock outs occur where you want. In the example we see that the magenta plate has been knocked out for the yellow text, while the black text is printed over the magenta color.

The printouts you send must be the absolute latest version, no changes can be made in the document after printing it out. Otherwise the risk exists that at the service provider they will "correct" back to the wrong version.

PACKAGE
Package is the name of the function that exists in Indesign and Quark Xpress for gathering together layout documents and all the mounted images and fonts used with a table of contents in one file. The function is meant to be used before you send the document on to, for example, a printing house, but is also useful when archiving a completed project since all the images, regardless of the network and the disks they are mounted from, are collected in one folder.

PREFLIGHT IN INDESIGN
There is a simple built-in function in Adobe Indesign that can check that all the links to images are unbroken, and that the document's fonts are active. It sends a warning also if there spot colors or extensions have been used. It cannot check, however, the images' resolutions and other graphic pitfalls. The function works best when you want to make a quick check before creating the PDF file for printing.

file, the problem comes up that the changes many not have been carried out in the layout document and you end up with the same problem as above with reprinting. Since direct changes to the layout document can be made quickly, creating a new PDF file and sending it to the printer is the better way to go.

Regardless of which procedure you use, you should gather your material and inform the printer as to the expected results in a clearly stated way.

6.14.1 Including a "dummy"
If you deliver open files to the printer you should always include a PDF file or printouts of the layout. Ordinary black and white printouts are good enough. The PDF file or printout must be from the very last version of the document. Printouts are one way for those who create the layout to check for themselves that the document that was sent is correct, in addition to giving the printer a good chance to detect possible errors at an early stage if the layout and typography are not the same when they open the document file.

If the layout document involves a printed product that requires more advanced finishing processes, it can be good to furnish the printer with a prototype (dummy) that shows how the final printed product is meant to be. If the printing colors, type of paper, surface treatment and such that is to be used in the printed product varies from page to page, if the document contains many pages, is sent several times or is made up of many separate documents, it may be appropriate to send along a page plan to the printer.

This should show a list or a miniature image of the pages in the printed product along with the necessary information.

6.14.2 Collecting Documents, Images and Fonts
When you send open layout documents to the printers it is important to make sure that all the material is included. Therefore you should begin to assemble all the files that belong to the document, for example, image, illustrations, logotypes and fonts. Quark Xpress, Adobe Indesign and Adobe Pagemaker have functions for saving the document, collecting together all the pertaining objects and placing these in a folder. In Adobe Indesign the function is found under FILE → PACKAGE... When you use it, it first checks that the document is correct, a preflight check, and then it places it in a folder together with images, fonts and a report. The function is also available for viewing the result of a preflight check under FILE → PREFLIGHT...

In Quark Xpress material is gathered together by going in under ARCHIVE and choosing PACKAGE. Then the document is gathered together with images in the designated folder. In addition, a report is created that contains information about all the fonts, images and colors that are used as well as any further information about the document.

In Adobe Pagemaker there are two similar functions. One is carried out under FILE → SAVE AS, by choosing SEND OUTPUT SOMEWHERE ELSE under COPY. Then the document with images and trapping information, but no report, is submitted. The second function is found under TOOLS → PLUG-INS → SAVE FOR SERVICE BUREAU, and is much more developed. A report is created at the same time as the typestyle is saved along with it.

6.14.3 Delivering Files

If you are delivering files over the Internet, in general you should compress all your files. The most common type of file compression is ZIP compression that works on both Mac OS and Windows.

Generally it is also good to compress all files that belong to a document into a single file. You should, however, remember that if you send files via email there may be limitations as to the size of the attachments.

When you are sending material on a CD or DVD for further editing it is important to mark the material clearly. The files should also be labeled and structured so that you can find your way around easily in the material.

6.15 Structuring and Archiving

The person doing the layout sits at a junction in the graphic process. This means that there are often an extensive number of files to be managed. For this reason it is important to create a good order among the material and the files and make it as simple as possible to find things in the material. This is especially important when there are several people that need to work with the material. This makes it crucial to structure and name all the material in the same way.

6.15.1 Working in Conjunction with a Server

The foundation for storing your material in a common and structured way is saving it on a server and working in conjunction with that the whole time. Today's cable computer networks and servers are so powerful that this delivers the same performance as storing files right in your computer. In many systems you can also choose to synchronize files so that selected folders and files are also stored as copies in your own computer. This allows for somewhat faster handling and makes the files available if the network is not accessible, for example on a laptop. One important advantage with working with a server is also that the material can more easily be securely backed up regularly and automatically.

6.15.2 Storing Files in a Structured Way

To easily locate material, a clear structure is needed that makes it easily for you to find your way through it. How the file structure is built is determined by how you work. For example, customer names or years can make up the top level, and then you can place things in folders according to your respective printed production projects. If you have large amounts of files for each printed product, these in turn may need to be sorted in folder. In project folders there could be folders for manuscripts, administrative project documents, layout files, proofs, print originals, etc. the more levels and folders you build up for you storage, the more structure, but also the more clicks it takes to find respective files.

To simplify things when everybody is working with the same sub-folders for their respective projects, you can create a folder template with empty, correctly names sub-folders that can be copied for every new project.

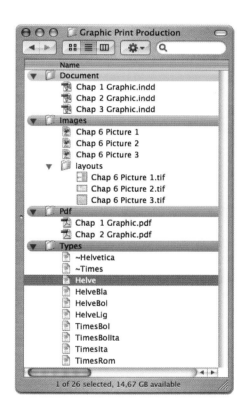

KEEPING THINGS IN ORDER
In order to make everything easy to find, work on, archive and work together with others on, it is important to create a clear structure of all the files in the project. The simplest way is to make the structures the same for all projects. In Mac OS X you can also color coordinate files and folders to locate them easily.

6.15.3 Naming Files and Folders

Folders and files should be names in a consistent and clear manner, which everyone involved can follow and understand. An important way to think in conjunction with naming files is that sub-files are most easily sorted alphabetically in a folder. This means that whatever comes first in the name becomes what dictates the sorting. It also means that if several files or folders have the same beginning for their file name, they will all be grouped together when you sort by alphabetical order, which means that you may not need to sort them in sub-folders if you are only dealing with a small number of files.

Naming is also decisive for easily finding files using the computer's built-in function for file searching. You may therefore choose to include important information in the file name such as, for example, the project number, language, customer's name, format, type of printed product, season, the initial of the layout person, or other information that you often have to look for. The information can of course be well stated with abbreviations as long as they are clear.

With the file name, BS_AD_NYT_HALFV_0123_NH_#3-IND you could, for example, be able to read that it is the third version of an Indesign file for Boston Shoes and that it is an advertisement in the New York Times in vertical half-page format with the project number 00123 and the layout was done by Neil Howe. All this information is easily found in the computer and all advertisements for this company are grouped together and organized according to newspaper and then format when you arrange the files alphabetically. On the other hand, the file in this example will not be sorted by layout, person or version number since the project number is stated first.

Stating the version clearly is important so that the latest version will always be used. Using version numbers and the like is a good way. The time of when the file was saved is not secure enough since it can be changed if the file is only moved or copied. Indicating versions with, for example, "new" or "final version", can easily lead to misunderstandings when later versions are created.

6.15.4 Metadata and Keywords

Files can also be given extra file information, known as metadata. In image files these often follow the IPTC standard [see Image Editing 5.6.2].

METADATA
Many file formats, especially for image, allow information about the file to be added. This information can be read off, searched in and edited in different types of archive programs, but also in programs like Adobe Indesign, Illustrator and Photoshop.

Adobe has also constructed a technique called XMP (Extensible Metadata Platform) in its program, which means that files from Indesign, Illustrator, Photoshop and others can be given keywords and meta-information. It can be used to link, for example, keywords and categories, contact information, copyright information, instructions, etc. to files. This information is searchable in archive programs and media banks.

6.15.5 File Managers

In both Windows and Mac OS there are built-in functions to search for files and show thumbnail images for certain types of image files. The search occurs mainly in the file name. You can search for certain types of files, file creation dates or dates of changes and so forth, but can also search using text content in certain types of text files.

To search for and enter metadata into files you need a special file manager. If you use Adobe's program suite, such a program, called Bridge, is included. Some other programs with similar functions are Mediadex, Fotostation, Portfolio, etc. You can look for files and in Metadata. If you use Bridge together with the other Adobe programs, you are given the possibility of easily mounting found images or automatically carrying out Photoshop editing directly from Bridge.

This type of program can also build up a database locally across the files found on the server and in some programs even in external media such as external hard disks, CDs and DVDs. This makes the search very fast, but also makes the search possible in metadata for files that exist, for example on a DVD in a security cabinet, as long as the content was catalogued earlier by the program.

The programs also have functions to write in metadata in one or several files at a time. They can also create preview images for a large number of file types. Some programs also have sophisticated functions for renaming large numbers of files.

6.15.6 Digital Asset Management System

If you are several people working together and have large numbers of files on a server that you want to be able search through quickly, it may be wise to have a digital asset management system. Some standard programs with such functionality are Cumulus from Canto and Fotostation from Fotoware. These build up a searchable database with all the file information, known as metadata, about the files that are stored in the media bank. The information can then be easily kept current and the search will be very fast via a client program that all the users are given.

If you want to make large numbers of files accessible via the Web, this type of media bank is also appropriate. Both Cumulus and Fotoware have extension modules for Web publishing of the content in the management system.

The system can create thumbnail images of files itself, and generate different resolutions of image files in the management system via downloading.

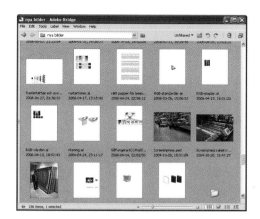

FILE MANAGER
In a file manager you can search for and show images and other documents. Often you can also search for and edit files' metadata. An example of such a program is Adobe Bridge that is included with Adobe's program package Creative Suite.

DESIGN PLANNING

1. Balance an environmentally responsible approach with the client's and/or product's needs. Can an innovative material or process be used? Will the client be supportive of this experimentation and accept the risks involved?

2. Understand the product life cycle for the entire project, from the materials used to the disposal, reuse, recyclability, and biodegradability of the product.

MATERIAL SELECTION

1. Minimize the amount of material in your design.

2. Specify high-recycled post-consumer waste (PCW) content.

3. Design for recyclability to avoid disposing of the waste after use.

4. Specify paper made from sustainably harvested timber, or specify kenaf, hemp, straw or other tree-free fibers.

5. Maximize the use of recycled and biodegradable materials. Design so that a material can be recycled into something of greater or equal value first, such as turning cotton scraps into fabric, before converting them into paper.

6. Specify materials that minimize or eliminate the use of hazardous chemicals (such as chlorine) in the production process.

7. Keep a library of "Best Recycled/Tree-Free/Chlorine-free" paper samples. File them from best to good (best being TCF or PCF, then ECF, and with a high PCW content of 50–100 %, then 30%+).

PRINT PRODUCTION

1. Ask whether your printer has an environmental policy. Choose printing methods which minimize wastes and conserve water and energy. Can the project be done electronically, from digital to plate, avoiding the need for film negatives and related processing chemicals, etc.?

2. Replace foil stamping or thermography (which are not recyclable) with embossing or debossing. Use a non-toxic color instead of one which contains a heavy metal. Go through your Pantone® book and "X" out all the toxic colors, so you'll be discouraged to spec them.

3. Reserve coatings and laminations for use on long life-cycle projects, where protection, as well as aesthetics, is the intent.

4. Solid ink coverage increases the amount of chemicals required to de-ink reclaimed paper. Use screened areas of a darker color to minimize ink coverage, or choose a paper that has an interesting texture and color for a desired effect.

5. Frequently specify PCW recycled and non-chlorine bleached paper, and encourage your printer to stock it as standard. This simple act has a tremendous ripple effect.

6. Make the most of your press sheets – even if it's to make book marks. Use leftovers of press runs for pro-bono work.

7. Avoid waste by working with your printer to determine sheet size and grain direction before finalizing your design.

07.

prepress

How do you check to see if all the pages are in the right place before printing? Why can't a printed product have 15 pages? What is PDF/X? Why does the print never turn out like the contract proof? Can you approve print colors on a monitor? Can I reject my printed product if I don't have a contract proof? What happens when I convert an image from RGB to CMYK?

PREPRESS IS A RATHER GENERAL catch-all name for all the work steps that are carried out before you begin with the actual printing. Repro is an older term that has often been used for prepress. The dividing line between prepress and image production is unclear and in practice creates a number of problems and misunderstandings regarding who is responsible for what. Before, there were so-called prepress providers who took care of both prepress, layout design and image production, something which contributed to the confusion as to what prepress actually was.

Today layout design is generally done by advertising and in-house departments as well as specialized companies. Image production has begun to move over to photographers or specialized image-retouching providers. So what is prepress? In this book we have chosen to define prepress as those phases of work and technology that are necessary to create print-ready digital files that can serve as the basis of print production.

In actuality prepress is really the phases involving the creation of high-resolution PDF-files, making images and documents print-ready, controlling imposition and screen frequency, as well as technologies such as Postscript, PDF, JDF and different types of contract proofs. A large part of the prepress work is automated today and often done at the printing house.

Since the borders between all these areas are fluid, some parts of prepress are completed by people working in layout or image production. The important

POSTSCRIPT-CODE

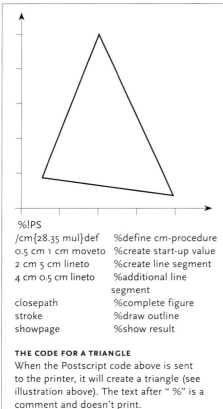

```
%!PS
/cm{28.35 mul}def       %define cm-procedure
0.5 cm 1 cm moveto      %create start-up value
2 cm 5 cm lineto        %create line segment
4 cm 0.5 cm lineto      %additional line
                         segment
closepath               %complete figure
stroke                  %draw outline
showpage                %show result
```

THE CODE FOR A TRIANGLE
When the Postscript code above is sent to the printer, it will create a triangle (see illustration above). The text after " %" is a comment and doesn't print.

thing is that who does what is defined, which important phases of production are required and what kind of competence is needed to take responsibility for them.

7.1 **Postscript**

A page description language (PDL) is a graphic programming language that describes the layout and appearance of a page. When printing a document, the file format used to create it (i.e., Quark Xpress, Adobe Indesign, Microsoft Word) has to be translated to a file format that the Raster Image Processor (RIP) or imagesetter can understand. A PDL is used to describe the elements a page contains (text, images, illustrations, etc.) and the location of these elements on the page to the processor or printer. It also enables the RIP to translate the page description into halftone screens.

A number of different page description languages have been developed by different manufacturers. Today's graphic production industry uses software and hardware from many different manufacturers, so the ideal page description language is one that works with all machines, regardless of the brand, and allows them to communicate freely with each other. Some examples of such page description languages are AFP from IBM, PCL from HP or CT/LV from Scitex. However, Postscript from Adobe currently dominates the market, and has therefore become known as the de facto industry standard. Postscript is an open standard, which means that other companies besides Adobe can use Postscript. In graphic production where programs and machines from different manufacturers have to be able to communicated with each other, it is absolutely necessary to have a PDL that is manufacturer-independent.

Postscript started out as a programming language, but for our purposes it's easier to think of it as a system consisting of several different parts. The system has three main components: translation of files into Postscript code, transfer of Postscript code, and processing (rasterizing) of the Postscript code.

Postscript code used to be based on 7-bit text files (ASCII), but can now be saved as 8-bit binary code [*see Binary integers, page 29*]. Postscript exists today in three versions: Postscript Level 1, Postscript Level 2 and Postscript 3 [*see 7.1.7*]. Postscript 3 is the latest version and contains enhanced capabilities compared to earlier versions.

Adobe created a book called "The Postscript Language Reference Manual", which contains complete Postscript specifications for those who want to make Postscript-based machines or programs. Unfortunately, problems with so-called Postscript "clones" often occur with both RIPs and printer drivers. Postscript is a form of programming code, and this means that there isn't one clear-cut way to describe a layout in Postscript code. Different programs are good in different ways in creating Postscript files. The problem usually shows up as changes to the original line arrangement when a file is saved and rasterized. Therefore it is recommended to use vendors that sell the original Adobe systems.

You can also save a document in Postscript format without sending it to a printer. Doing this "locks" the appearance of your document. You cannot open the document from the Postscript file, nor can you edit the Postscript file. If you want to make changes, you have to make them to the original file and save it as a completely new Postscript file. Some programs, like imposition and trapping programs, are based on the Postscript format. A document must first be saved as a Postscript file before it can be edited with these types of programs. It should be noted that these programs only allow you to add or remove information from a document, not change the actual content of the document.

Even if PDF file are mostly used in today's work flows, functionality is still completely based on the underlying capabilities that are in Postscript. Many documents are converted to Postscript before they are converted to PDF with Acrobat Distiller, or RIPs in the printer use Postscript code to process all print-outs, including PDF files that are sent to the printer.

7.1.1 Postscript is Object-Based

Postscript is an object-based page description language, which means a page is described based on the objects it contains. The objects in a particular Postscript file – be they typeface or graphic objects like lines, curves, shades, patterns, etc. – are all described with mathematical curves. An image that consists of pixels – a scanned photograph for example – is stored in Postscript file as a bitmap with a Postscript file header.

Because the objects in Postscript are based on Bezier curves, you might assume that you can shrink or enlarge the pages without losing image quality. This is partly true – if there are no pixel-based images in the file, you can enlarge or reduce without a problem. However, if a pixel-based image is included in the file, you cannot enlarge the page without reducing the quality, as enlarging a bit-mapped image lowers its resolution [*see Digital Images 4.7.1*].

7.1.2 Creating Postscript Files

Every time you output a document from the computer to a Postscript-compatible printer, a Postscript file is created. It contains all the information of what the page will look like when it is printed. Instead of outputting a file to an output device, you could choose to save it as a Postscript file on the hard disk using a similar procedure.

There are essentially two ways to convert a file to Postscript, depending on the type of program you are translating it from. The most common way is to create the original files in Postscript-based programs like Adobe, InDesign, Adobe PageMaker, Adobe Framemaker, QuarkXpress, Adobe Illustrator, and Macromedia Freehand, among others. These programs translate the actual file to Postscript when you output it and when you want to save the output as a file. Today all graphic software can, oon principle use PDf directly, which is why it is usually unnecessary to first create a Postscript file.

However, if you are using a non Postscript-based programs such as Microsoft Word, the computer's own printout functions must be used to create Postscript. The computer must have Postscript-based a printer driver installed and a Postscript Printer Description, or PPD. This gives the program access to information about the specific output device you are using, including its resolution, page setup, etc., and the Postscript file is adjusted accordingly. If a physical Postsript printer is connectd to the ocmputer with USB there is a large chance

LOOKING FOR POSTSCRIPT ERRORS
Previously it was quite usual to find Postscript
errors. It is no longer as common, but if one
occurs you can try the following:

- Print out the document without images. Then
  you will notice if iit is one of them causing
  problems.

- Try printing out the pages separately. Then you
  will discover which page the problem is on.

- Try changing the font to see if one of the fonts
  is the problem.

- Try creating a PDF/X file and print it out
  instead.

that a printer queue will be created with the right PPD file installed.vOtherwise the PPD file has to be installed manually. The easiest way to create Postscript files from Microsoft Office is to have Adobe Acrobat installed, otherwise. Then this functionality is added to the Office programs so you can create PDF files directly from the program. If needed these can be resaved to Postscript in Adobe Acrobat very successfully.

7.1.3 **Postscript RIPs**
RIP stands for Raster Image Processor. It is a special program that is installed on a computer to handle printouts. Sometimes the RIP program is integrated into the printer itself. A Rip consists of two main parts, a Postscript interpreter and a processor translating the pages into raster images (bitmaps).

Documents created in programs like Quark Xpress and Adobe Indesign are describes using the format specific to that particular program. In order to look at a document on the screen, the program's code has to be translated into a language the screen can understand. When outputting your document, the program code is translated into Postscript code with the adherent settings. The RIP receives the Postscript information, interprets what needs to be done on the page and performs all the calculations. When an entire page has been calculated, including images, typeface, logotypes, etc., a bitmap, i.e. line art for each print color (four for a CMYK print, for example) is created [*see Digital Images 4.6.1*]. The bitmaps (based on ones and zeros) than let the imagesetter know which exposure dots should be exposed [*see 7.7.6*]. When printing separated films, each page is calculated four times, one for each color.

The more complex a page is, the longer the calculations and rasterizing takes. A complex page might contain numerous fonts, complicated illustrations with several layers of information, vector-based images with many anchor points, rotated or scaled images, or images that were not cropped in the image editing application but in the desktop publishing application. Such pages can take a long time to rasterize even if the file size is small. On the other hand, exposure in the image setter always takes the same amount of time, regardless of the file size or the complexity of the document.

7.1.4 **Postscript and Typeface Management**
When using Truetype typeface, every character must be transformed into a Postscript-based object graphic. When creating a Postscript file for output or to be saved for further editing, you can include the fonts with the file or choose to use fonts that are already stored in the output device. In Postscript 2 output devices, there are 35 standard fonts, while Postscript 3 Output devices have 136. If it is a recurring print using the same fonts, it might be easier to have the fonts downloaded in the output device. This allows the Postscript file to be smaller and therefore faster to create, move and output. If the printed product is to be done repeatedly using the same typeface, it can be best to have the fonts stored in the printing unit. Thus the Postscript files will be smaller and therefore faster to create, transport and RIP print [*see 7.7.4*]. But most printed products vary and it is more common to include the typeface in the Postscript file so you get the correct typeface when printing.

7.1.5 Postscript Level 1

Level 1 is the basis for the three current versions of Postscript and was launched in the mid-eighties. The two latter levels are based on the same page description language as Level 1, but each subsequent version contains additions and improvements. The different levels are compatible with ach other, a Postscript 3 RIP can convert a Level 1 file and vice versa. On the other hand information is lost when you go from a higher to a lower level. Postscript Level 1 is a relatively simple page description language, compared to the other two. For example, Level 1 does not support color management [*see Chromatics 3.1*].

7.1.6 Postscript Level 2

Not until Level 2 could Postscript products support color management. Earlier, some specially designed products from different manufacturers supported color management, but with the advent of Postscript Level 2, all products were able to support CMYK color mode and images in RGB and CMYK. New functions were also added, including support by device-independent color models (CIE), improved screening techniques, compression and decompression filters, and increased support for the unique functions of specific printers.

7.1.7 Postscript 3

One important difference in comparison to older versions is that Postscript 3 is a lot faster in processing pages when printing output. A multi-page document can even be automatically divided up and processed in parallele by several RIPs to reduce ripping time. This is especially important when printing individual copies digitally, where RIP printing has to happen at least as fast as the printer can output.

From Postscript 3 version 3017 that was released in January 2006, an later, a Postscript printer can also handle PDF file that contain transparent objects, extra color channels and 3D objects and print these out correctly. This allows you to avoid the often problematic tendency of flattening of transparent objects that happens when one page is converted to PDF for digital and offset printing. Since is will take a long time for all printing houses to have RIPs with the new version of Postscript, it is recommended for now to deliver files for printing in PDF format without transparencies. A good standard for this is PDF/X [*see 7.2.6*]. Modern layout programs can also "flatten" transparencies with RIP techniques resulting in the same appearance when the PDF file is created. Note that Postscript files, regardless of the version, cannot contain transparencies. This means that PDF must be used if you want to retain transparency in the files that are sent to the printer and that the PDF file must be created directly from the layout program, not via a Postscript file and Acrobat Distiller. Examples of layout programs that can work completely with transparent objects are Adobe Indesign and Adobe Illustrator.

7.2 **PDF**

PDF, an abbreviation for Portable Document Format, is a file format created to move advanced contents between computers in a simple manner. Adobe launched PDF format in 1993, but it didn't have its break-through in the graphic production industry until the late 1990s and among general users not until a couple of years after that. PDF format is now an open standard, which means that programs that use PDF technique can be freely developed.

A PDF file can contain many different things. Besides graphic content like text and images, there can also be video, sound 3-D graphics and interactive software for filling out forms are included. PDF lends itself well to a wide variety of file formats for such diverse uses as graphic production, transferring photographic images and CAD drawings, handling proofs, e-books, blank forms and multimedia presentations.

PDF can be opened without access to the program that created the contents since it is all included in the file. The only thing you need is the free application Adobe Reader, which can cones pre-installed in many computers or some other PDF reader software. In Mac OS there is a built-in support for PDF directly in the operating system. Everyone who works with a special program and needs to show the results to others who don't have access to that program can use PDF.

PDF is closely related to Postscript since both describe the contents of a file as objects or vectors, exactly like Adobe Illustrator, for example. As described above the PDF format is, however, more developed and can contain several items. It is also standardized better than Postscript. Where Postscript can describe one thing in many different ways, PDF can describe it more simply and only one way. This is a large advantage when printing out pages where there is less risk that different printers behave differently. PDF can be said to have taken over Postscript's roll in graphic production, even if Postscript language technically speaking is still in all printers. Today PDF is the basis of all graphic design work flow and software. It has also become the de facto standard for submitting advertisements and submitting originals to printing houses all over the world.

7.2.1 **Programs for PDF Files**

With few exceptions, Adobe's Acrobat program series is used to look at, edit and print PDF files. Depending on how the PDF file is made, more advanced functions can also be activated in the program such as certain correction tools. Adobe Reader can however not be used to create new PDF files.

There is also a special version of Acrobat aimed at larger companies that need volume licenses to make PDF files from Microsoft Office software. It is called Acrobat Elements and has the same function as Adobe Reader, but installs PDF tools as well in Office programs.

For those who need to be able to create new PDF files or other change existing files, but don't need advanced functions to create blank forms or handle graphics, there is Acrobat Standard. In this program you can, among other things, create links between different pages, different documents and even to

PROGRAM	FIND	FILL IN FORMS	EDIT SECURITY SETTINGS	CREATE FORMS	COMMENTS	ACTIVATE COMMENTS IN READER	PREFLIGHT AND PREVIEW OUTPUT	PDF/X SUPPORT
Reader	•	•						
Acrobat Elements	•	•	•					
Acrobat	•	•	•	•	•			
Acrobat Professional	•	•	•	•	•	•	•	•

Adobe has developed an entire program family around the PDF file format. The most common programs are:

- Adobe Reader – reads PDF files
- Adobe Acrobat Elements – create PDF files from Office programs. Is only sold as volume license
- Adobe Acrobat – creates and edits PDF files
- Adobe Acrobat Professional – checks and edits PDF files for professional graphic production
- Adobe Acrobat 3D – provides 3D sketches

other pages on the Internet. In this way you can create interactive documents from outside a file that was meant to be printed matter in its final form. Acrobat Standard also has a number of very useful support functions to work with digital editing and there is the capability of signing and approving files. You can also make changes in existing texts and images [see 7.2.8]. Acrobat Distiller Standard comes with the software. This makes it possible to create PDF files from all the software that can print out.

Acrobat Professional is the version that should be used by anyone working with graphic production. It contains powerful working tools to control, correct and color convert PDF files before printing.

The support for the PDF/X standard only exists in this version.

Acrobat Professional includes Acrobat Distiller Professional to create PDF files which makes it possible to show PDF files even from, for example, Quark XPress.

Acrobat 3D is a version of Acrobat designed for CAD program users. 3D graphics can be handled in the second version of Acrobat too, but in this version 3 dimensional content can be adjusted with an array of advanced tools. This version installs PDF functionality in ordinary CAD programs too.

7.2.2 **Creating PDF Files**
PDF files can be made principally in two ways: either through a built-in support in the application you are working in (for example Adobe Indesign or Adobe Illustrator) or with the help of Adobe Acrobat. For Microsoft Office and ordinary CAD programs, for example, Adobe can automatically install a script that makes it very easy to export PDF files directly from the program with one click. Otherwise you have to write a Postscript file that then has to be converted to

PDF using the Adobe Acrobat Distiller program. In this way you can create PDF files from all the programs that are able to print on a Postscript printer. Quark XPress has a built-in "PDF export" that automatically creates a Postcript file and then converts it to PDF using Adobe Acrobat Distiller in one step. If you use one of Adobe's graphic programs Indesign, Illustrator or Photoshop, there is also built-in support ro creating PDF/X files suitable for printing [see 7.2.2].

When you create a PDF file you have to choose which parameters the file should be created from. Acrobat Distiller, the PDF export function in Microsoft Office, the CAD programs and Adobe's graphic program are installed together with a number or pre—defined adjustments, known as Job Options. The point of this is to easily create PDF files adjusted for different purposes such as presentations, editing or printing. These Job Options affect a number of different parameters, for example resolution, compression, fonts and color handling. If the PDF files is only going to be used to viewing on a monitor you can reduce resolution and compress the images to keep the file size down. If the file, on the other hand, is to be used for printed material, you should allow the images to have a higher resolution and no transparency. If you are working in Adobe Indesign you can also state if mounted RGB images should be converted to CMYK with an ICC profile when exported to PDF.

7.2.3 Adjusting for Proofs

Adobe Acrobat also has a function for adapting existing PDF files for different uses. The function is found in the ADVANCED MENU and is called PDF OPTIMIZER. This function is useful above all when you want to save a low-resolution copy of a high-resolution PDF printed copy, which is useful when you want to send a proof to someone who cannot receive large files. Since the low-resolution PDF file is created from the print-ready PDF file this will be a safe and secure way of working when both files are identical except for the resolution of the images they contain, for example.

7.2.4 Security Settings

When you create a PDF file you can also designate different security settings that protect the file in different ways, PDF files can be protected with a password to control who can read or change them. It is possible to allow or prohibit printing, changes, copying of text and images as well as limit the possibility of adding or changing notations or the fields of blank forms. If you allow printing you should think about whether the user can then create a new PDF file using Acrobat Distiller. The new file will then not contain security settings at all and will thus be able to be completely controlled by the user. In practice this means that you should not allow printing if the contents of a PDF file is of a sensitive nature.

It is also possible to open an existing PDF file in Adobe Acrobat Standard or Professional and add security settings. These settings can be saved in Policies which subsequently can be applied to the PDF file of your choice so access to it can be limited. One Policy is created in Acrobat by following a Wizard where you either make use of a password or a Digital ID and then state which type of access limits you desire. Acrobat and PDF standards also have support for advanced ciphering or electronic ID. Which makes it possible for PDF to be used in work with very high secrecy demands, for example in companies that handle sensitive financial information.

Once you have opened a PDF file with limited security settings, an orange icon of a padlock shows down at the bottom of the document window's left corner. By clicking on this icon the exact limits placed on the document will be indicated. You can even check which security settings a certain PDF file has by looking under FILE → DOCUMENT PROPERTIES... → SECURITY.

When sending a PDF file to a graphic production company for production you should set the security specifications to allow for any and all changes because you might need them to make last-minute corrections. In contrast, when sending a PDF file for review and proofing it is often appropriate not to permit changes to the file. However, you should allow for the person reviewing the document to add notes and copy text in order to paste it into an email message or a file in Microsoft Word for example.

7.2.5 Different Kinds of PDF Files

PDF format has been developed over the years at the same pace as Adobe Acrobat, which continually has been able to handle more and more advanced content. For this reason, the specification for PDF format has been given a version number. Earlier versions of PDF format (PDF 1.1 and 1.2) were hardly usable for printed originals since their handling of color and fonts were not strongly defined enough. PDF version 1.3 was the first version that practically speaking was useful for printed originals and is still recommended as the standard for PDF files headed for print production.

Today there are no strict technical limitations in order to use PDF for print production. The problem is more the opposite. PDF format can do o much more besides being the print original, thus possibly creating problems in graphic production. A fill-in form or a presentation with a video clip is an example of something that is not part of graphic design work. For this reason most printing houses and newspapers have stated specifications of how they want PDF files to be set up for their production.

7.2.6 PDF/X

With the aim to simplify all printed production and minimize the risk of technical problems when leaving something for printing, an ISO standard for PDF files for graphic production has been developed. It is called PDF/X. A PDF/X file is an ordinary PDF file except it has been produced according to the standardized production criteria for graphic security production. The criteria are available in the form of adjustment files for creating PDF files in the same way there are installation files for creating PDF files for e-books, for instance. This means that PDF/X files can be created directly from most modern software applications that produce PDF files for printing.

The criteria regulate a long row of technical parameters. The thinking behind this is that PDF files will thus be completely standardized and can be expected to always function and behave exactly the same in all printers and systems. The PDF/X standard also prevents the occurrence of a number of non-allowed

SECURITY SETTINGS IN ADOBE ACROBAT
Adobe Acrobat can set limitations and use identification for PDF files. Identification can be via a password or an advanced coded ID control according to one of the standards that exist on the market for digital ID. A setting for limitations can then be saved in a policy.

We have made a policy for A Guide to Graphic Print Production when PDF files are being sent as proofs. Limitations can be, for example, that the document can only be printed out in low resolution or that no changes can be made in the file.

PDF VERSION	ACROBAT VERSION	IMPORTANT GRAPHICS SPECIFICATIONS
1.3	4	Spot colors, overprint
1.4	5	Forms function
1.5	6	Transparence, layers
1.6	7	Moving 3D graphics

VERSIONS OF THE PDF FORMAT
Every time specifications for the PDF format are updated, Adobe also has released a new version of Acrobat to which these specifications correspond according to the above.

PDF/X standards are based on PDF 1.3 in order to be able to functions even with older versions of Acrobat as well as older printers and RIPs.

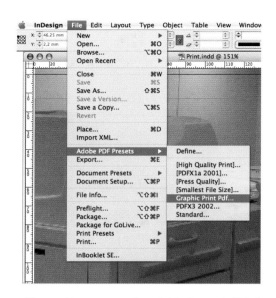

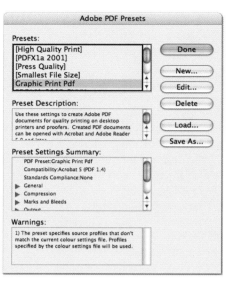

1. The graphics programs from Adobe have a built-in function for creating PDF files so you don't need to use Adobe Acrobat Distiller. Here is shown the PDF export function in Adobe Indesign. You can either create your own PDF export setting or use one of those that come with the program.

2. When you are creating your own PDF setting, you can either start from an existing setting or create one that is completely your own. PDF settings are the same in all Adobe programs. This means that if you create a setting in Adobe Indesign it also pops up in Adobe Illustrator and Adobe Acrobat Distiller.

3. Regardless of which program is used to create a PDF file, you can choose to adjust the resolution in the images and eventually add compression as JPEG or ZIP.

It is usual for images to have needlessly high resolution if you scale them down in the layout. In this example the resolution is reduced in all color and grayscale images that have a higher effective resolution than 350 ppi to 300 ppi. In addition, all the images are compressed with ZIP compression to reduce the size of the PDF file without affecting the image quality.

In Adobe Indesign you can also choose for the parts of the image that are not visible to be cropped in the PDF file, which creates a smaller file.

4. The example shows how it looks when you save a PDF file from Adobe Indesign. This is where you choose how much bleed will be included in the PDF file. Crop marks and page information are also normally included. If you use another program to first create a Postscript file and then convert to PDF with Acrobat Distiller these settings are made when you create the Postscript file.

5. When you export a PDF file from Adobe Indesign you can indicate an ICC profile for the kind of printing that is going to be used. By choosing CONVERT TO DESTINATION (PRESERVE NUMBERS), RGB images are automatically separated to CMYK using the chosen ICC profile. Images in CMYK mode and other objects such as tint areas and illustrations in CMYK colors are left untouched. This can be a good way to work if you want to use RGB images in the layout, but the printing house wants PDF files with only CMYK.

6. Since Adobe Indesign and Adobe Illustrator can work with transparent objects, these may need to be "flattened" to be able to be printed on an ordinary printer. In the example we also base our PDF export setting on the ISO standard PDF/X that does not allow transparent objects in the file. Transparency flattening simply means that the areas of the page that contains transparent objects are recreated into small, very high resolution images in the PDF file. Therefore it is important for the setting HIGH RESOLUTION to be used so that the result will be good when printed out.

The ISO standard PDF/X exists in a few different versions and specifies in a detailed manner how a PDF file shall be furnished to work painlessly in graphic production. A PDF/X file is an ordinary PDF, but it is created according to a strict set of guidelines.

PDF/X-1 VS. PDF/X-3
There are two principle types of PDF/X files: PDF/X-1 and PDF/X-3. What differentiates them is what colors are allowed in the file. PDF/X-1 can only contain CMYK and spot colors. PDF/X-3 can in addition contain RGB. PDF/X-3 files may therefore need to be separated before they are printed.

THE MOST IMPORTANT GRAPHIC REQUIREMENTS IN PDF/X
PDF/X sets a variety of demands on the PDF file to make it safer to print from. Some examples are:

- No layers
- No interactivity
- No transparency
- Fonts must be included
- Colors must be kept in order (RGB, CMYK and ICC profiles)

PDF/X DOES NOT REGULATE EVERYTHING
There are a number of factors that PDF/X does not set requirements for since they vary among different kinds of printing. For this reason they have to be set manually. Here are some of the most important:

- The images' resolution
- Number and indication of printing colors
- Maximum total number of colors
- Bleeds
- Crop marks

functions such as layering, interactivity, transparency and other things that are not suitable for printing. Note that most security adjustments make the file unacceptable as a PDF/X file. The standard does not regulate files that are specific to a certain production, for example the measure of sampling points and image resolution are still decided independently.

The PDF/X standard exists in two main varieties: PDF/X-1 and PDF/x-3. One exists for files where all the colors are already print-ready so that they only contain print colors such as CMYK or Pantone colors. Three also allows RGB as well as CMYK and Pantone, and is suitable for a work flow where the images are adjusted for CMYK at the printer's. There is also another ISO standard called PDF/A which exists for long-term storage and various digital documents.

7.2.7 Proofing PDF Files
A PDF file that is prepared for printing should be proofed at the time it is being made and before it is put into production at the printing house, that is both by the person creating the PDF files and the person receiving the advertising material at the newspaper or the printer's. Proofing can be divided into two steps: content check and technical check. The content control means that you inspect the file in Adobe Acrobat and ten print it out. Printing it provides a control for technical flaws that other tools might no detect such as dropped lines, spelling errors and making sure that all the parts are included. You can use the loupe tool to easily magnify parts of the pages. For technical checks you can use Adobe Acrobat Professional. The program contains an array of useful tools for this. The most important is ADVANCED → PREFLIGHT... and ADVANCED → OUTPUT PREVIEW... → PREVIEW SEPARATIONS.

By using PREVIEW: SEPARATIONS one color channel, that is the contents of one printing plate, can be proofed separately. This is a good way to check for knock outs and black overprinting [see 7.4.8], or deep black printing [see 6.1.4] which is hard to gauge on the monitor. You can also let Acrobat Professional Color in all the places on the page that have overprinting or rich black printing. There is also the possibility of controlling the parameters for total ink amount (see 7.4.3) in dark areas. For certain printing techniques it can be of the greatest importance that no surface has more ink than what is permitted, for example in newspaper printing where there is often a maximum allowed ink amount of 240 %. By stating a value for the maximum ink amount the surfaces in the files that don't stay within the allowed limits are colored in.

There is also a function ADVANCED → OVERPRINT PREVIEW. By activating this function the view on the monitor is adjusted to simulate how it will look when printed on a printer or at by professional printing house. If a test is white and lies within an image, but has the adjustment for overprint, it will disappear with this adjustment and black type over an image will allow some of what lies under to it show through, just like with printing. Use this function while turning off the black in OUTPUT PREVIEW to get an exact idea of how black overprinting will behave when printed.

For handling Pantone colors there is the INK MANAGER function if, for example, if a Pantone color comes with two different names or to indicate if a Pantone color is a glaze or total coating. Another important function is FIX HAIRLINES.

This converts lines that are too thin and can be hard to print or it can make sure that all the lines in the document get the least possible amount of thickness.

With the PREFLIGHT function all the technical parameters in the file can be checked, for example image resolution, color layers, maximum amount of ink permitted, the occurrence of Pantone colors and typefaces included. It is also possible to check more advanced things, for example to make sure that no text is smaller than eight points and contains more than one ink color. In Adobe Acrobat Professional there are pre-checked adjustments to choose from as well as the possibility to easily create your own. There are also pre-set adjustments for verifying that a file follows the PDF/X standard. If the file contains technical errors a list of explanations is presented, other wise the file will not be approved. For advertising departments and printing houses that accept PDF files for printing there is accessory software to Adobe Acrobat called PitStop Professional from Enfocus. The program has a preflight function similar to the one built into Acrobat Professional, put can in addition take measures against a number of errors that the check encounters. In Acrobat Professional you can take steps against simpler errors as well. But usually it is best to take care of any errors in the original layout or image files and create a new PDF file.

7.2.8 Editing PDF files

Although PDF files are essentially locked in terms of editing, you can make certain small revisions. The degree to which you are able to edit a document is determined in part by the security settings assigned to the PDF file when it was created. In general, revising PDF files is not recommended, but at times it can be necessary for simpler last-minute corrections. Some useful revision tools in Adobe Acrobat Professional are the texture tool, the object tool as well at the cropping tool.

To make changes in the text you use the touch up text tool. A limitation on revisions of the text is that the information necessary no longer exists in a PDF file created for graphic production. The advantage to this is that you can no longer end up with the typeface out of line. The disadvantage is that it is not practically possible to make large changes in the text since each line is a unit unto itself. The exception is PDF files created to be used as e-books. There is additional information in these files as to what lines should connect to the whole document since the text has to be adjusted to the width of each screen so that you don't have to turn the pages to read a long line, for example on a pocket PC.

Text editing can be easily done in Adobe Acrobat. It is limited, however, in that you can only make changes to individual lines – i.e., you cannot change the line arrangement. You can add a new line within the text, but line breaks and hyphenation have to be done manually. To edit text in Acrobat, you have to have the correct typeface installed. If you don't, the typeface of the edited text will be replaced with another typeface from the computer you are using. Text editing in Acrobat is normally not recommended and should only be done minimally and when absolutely necessary. Any significant changes to the text should be done in the original file.

THINGS TO CHECK IN PREFLIGHT
Below are some things that can be practical to check in Preflight:

- The file follows the requirements of the PDF/X standard
- The resolution of the images is adequate
- Do not use spot colors
- The number of colors used should not exceed the limit
- The size of the text is not too small
- Lines are not too thin

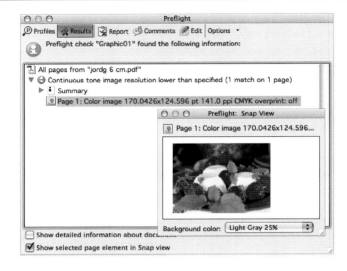

PREFLIGHT – PART 1

Adobe Acrobat Professional has a built-in technical control function called PREFLIGHT. To do a check you begin by choosing PREFLIGHT → PROFILES – the setting that decides what is going to be checked. It is simple to create your own profiles if, for example, you check that all the colors are CMYK or that images have a certain resolution.

PREFLIGHT – PART 2

When you double click on a preflight profile the check is carried out and a list of possible problems is shown. In the above example two images in the document had lower resolution than what was specified in the profile "A Guide to Graphic Print Production". To easily find exactly which image is being viewed, a miniature image is shown in the window SNAP VIEW.

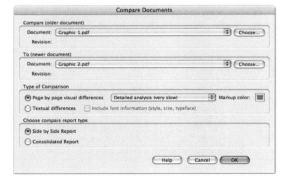

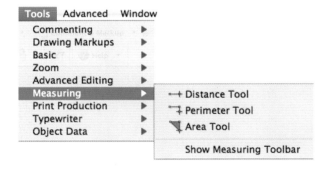

COMPARE DOCUMENTS

If you have a made new PDF after making a spelling correction, for example, and you want to be sure that nothing else has been changed on the page, you can use the Compare document palette. Then all the things that differ between documents are highlighted.

CHECKING DISTANCES

If you want to check the distances on the page there are three different measuring tools that make it simple to do one last check that a table has the right dimensions or that an area of type really is on the right page.

OUTPUT PREVIEW — PART 2

OUTPUT PREVIEW also has two WARNINGS, functions for helping determine haw the black ink will behave when printed. SHOW OVERPRINTING colors in all the black objects that are overprinted. RICH BLACK ink in all the objects that use deep black. No functions in OUTPUT PREVIEW affect the content of the file.

OUTPUT PREVIEW — PART 1

The palette Output preview assembles many clever functions. Under Simulation profile you choose the ICC profile that will simulate the printed result if you want to make use of "Soft Proof", the technique where the monitor's colors simulate the printed result. Under SEPARATIONS there is a function that is similar to INFORMATION in Adobe Photoshop where you can measure with the curser anywhere on the page and see the color values. At the bottom of the screen is the function to check TOTAL AREA COVERAGE of printing ink. If you type in a value, for example, 330 %, all parts of the page that exceed this value are highlighted.

FIX HAIRLINES

If you are concerned about certain lines on the page being too thin to work well in print, you can use the FIX HAIRLINES PALETTE and specify that lines under a certain thickness should be thickened, and they will be adjusted in the PDF file.

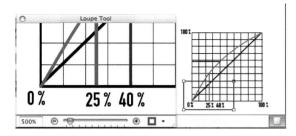

CHECKING WITH THE LOUPE TOOL

The LOUPE TOOL is a handy enlargement function when you want to quickly check small texts, for example, and don't want to zoom in the whole page.

Images and object-oriented graphics can be altered in Adobe Acrobat using the "Touch-Up" tool. The tool allows you to mark the images you wish to change. Images can then be moved, cropped, removed or copied and pasted into other parts of the document. You can also open individual images or illustrations in Adobe Photoshop or Adobe Illustrator, edit them, and save them directly into the PDF file, which will automatically update itself with the changes. Adobe Professional can also use these two programs to edit the contents of a PDF file. You use the "Touch-Up" tool and indicate which image you want to change. Context click for Mac or right click for Windows on the side of the object and select EDIT. If the object is a pixel-based image, it will open automatically as a temporary image file in Adobe Photoshop, and if it is object graphics, for example text or logotype, it is opened as a temporary object in Adobe Illustrator. Exactly which program should be used is configured easily in Acrobat's settings. The object or the image can then be edited independently and when the image is closed in the external program, the changes are automatically made in the PDF file. This can be useful if an RGB image, for example, needs to be converted to CMYK, or text in an illustration changed. Images and objects can also be moved.

With the cropping tool the page can be cropped, for example to take away the gutters and crop marks, or to just keep part of a page. Either you run the tool across the page just like in Adobe Photoshop, or you give the exact measurements. PDF format uses four different page-size indicators, known as page boxes. With the cropping tool you have to choose which of these you want to affect. Normally it is the page size box that regulates the outermost edge of a PDF file. There are also a content box, a gutter box, and a cropping box, depending on exactly what you want to do.

7.3 JDF – Job Definition Format

Today there is an increased need of automation and communication between different systems for graphic production and administration. At the same time graphic production often takes place in mixed environments with systems from different manufacturers. For this reason Heidelberg, Man Roland, Agfa and Adobe began a collaboration, with the goal being to produce a standard to facilitate communication between administration and production systems.

The standard is called JDF – Job Definition Format, and starts with the PDF-based flow of production. It is partly based on Adobe's PJTF (Portable Job Ticket Format), that ties the information around the prepress work to the files themselves, for example, layout, trapping and ripping, and partly based on CIP3's PPF (Print Production Format), whose task is to allow information exchange between the different production steps, for example imposition, printing and finishing and binding. JDF covers both of these areas. JDF defines how the information should be structured in a job specification. The job specification is saved in an independent XML format and can be seen as a digital work order whose task is to link together administrative systems with different production systems. The idea is that with the help of JDF you can tie together the whole work stream, from the initial information on how the work that is placed in

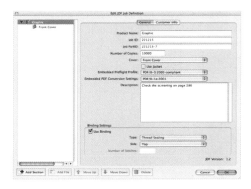

PDF SUPPORTS JDF
JDF defines how the information should be structured in the job definition, which is saved in an independent XML format. Adobe's PDF format supports JDF and makes it possible to create and edit information about the assignment. You find it under TOOLS → PRINT PRODUCTION → JDF JOB DEFINITION.

the administrative system is to be executed, to the steering of the production system (for example number of pages, folding and cutting). Production systems should also be able to exchange information between themselves (for example ink coverage, folding and cutting). JDF makes it possible for different systems to communicate with each other and therefore can be used to define and control different processors. In this way you achieve a higher level of automation at the same time as you attain increased control and follow-up of production. The vision is that the printer pulls out an offer in its business system and the customer points in his or her PDF file to the offer in question. When the PDF arrives at the printer, the JDF file is created and filled with the information about the offer that is linked to the offer number. In this way all the information falls in place automatically and can be used for directing the flow of production.

The standard has been divided up in a number of areas so that suppliers of prepress, printing and binding and finishing do not have to pay attention to the parts they are not involved in. The JDF file consequently contains basic facts (for example size of the print run, format, number of pages, inks, paper) as well as information about prepress, printing and finishing and binding. In addition, it contains information about what is done with the files in a log. This is called JMF – Job Messaging Format – a standard to send status information within different systems, for example in order to gain control over where the different products are in the flow of production and if anything has gone wrong. Acrobat 7 contains an order form to generate order information according to the JDF standard.

The difficulty with JDF is that it requires standards so that all the information that is being tracked by all kinds of suppliers in the system, from the printing presses to finishing and binding and administrative systems. Therefore there are few users who have been able to completely utilize the benefits of the JDF system. It is being most fully exploited within finishing and binding, and printing. In these areas there is a tradition of automation and a limited number of dominating companies that are large enough to steer the development of the JDF system. But in order to achieve the vision with JDF it is necessary for the manufacturers of business systems (MIS –Management Information System) to fully support JDF. The same progress has not been made in this area, probably because many of these companies do not specialize in graphic production and they are often small specialty companies who do not have the resources to manage such comprehensive development

The responsibility for JDF's development has today been taken over by CIP4 – International Cooperation for the Integration of Processes in Prepress, Press and Postpress – which is the new name for what was earlier known as CIP3. CIP4 is commonly run by all the suppliers of different systems within graphic production and in this way guarantee its independent development.

7.4 **Adjusting for Printing**

When you look at an advertising campaign in which the same image appears in a newspaper, a weekly magazine, on a billboard downtown, or on a bus, etc., you should be aware that all these pictures are adjusted specifically for each

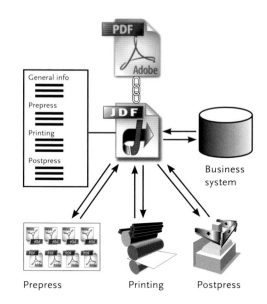

JDF ENABLES THE EXCHANGING OF INFORMATION
The JDF file contains basic facts (for example print run, format, number of pages, inks, paper) as well as informaton about prepress, printing and finishing and binding. In addition, it contains information about what is done the file during the production process.

JDF makes it possible for different systems to communicate with each other and therefore can be used to define and control different processes in the production. This way you obtain a higher level of automatization while, at the same time, increasing the control over and follow-up of the production.

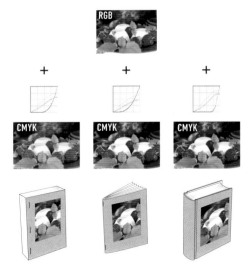

An image needs to be separated using a unique curve, ICC-profile, for each printing occasion. As a result, the same image has to be adjusted and edited differently depending on its intended use. A color-separated image is therefore difficult to use in a situation different from what it was originally intended for.

WHAT AFFECTS THE CMYK CONVERSION?
The three main factors to consider when converting/adjusting for printing are:

- Paper stock
- Printing process
- Halftone screens

TO SET VALUES WHEN CONVERTING INTO CMYK

- Gray balance
- GCR/UCR
- GCR and maximum ink coverage
- Dot gain
- Color standard

purpose. Technically, they are actually five completely different digital images, treated and adjusted for their respective purposes. Generally a digitized image that has been adjusted for printing can only be used for the type of product it was created for.

Color reproduction in printing is principally affected by three factors: ink, paper and the printing process. Actual pigments can never exactly reproduce theoretical colors. The closer they correspond to the theoretical values, the closer they will come to looking identical. At the same time, different printing processes require different characteristics to succeed. This makes it difficult to get comparable results with different techniques. The thickness of the ink layer caries between different printing techniques and paper types, and is decisive as to what color range you can print with. The more ink you can lay on the paper the larger the color range and the better the color reproduction will be. The shade of paper, its surface structure and printing properties affect color reproduction to a large degree. There are few types of paper that are completely white. Most have a light coloration while others, for example pink paper used in some newsprint, control the gray balance in pictures. The paper and the printing process limit that maximum amount of colors that can be used [see 7.4.4]. Paper and printing technique are also the principal factors that influence dot gain in the printing process. When you print you always get a certain amount of misregistration. Misregistration can vary between different printing techniques, and can also depend on what kind of material you are printing on. Certain printing techniques have limitations as the smallest halftone dot that can be printed on it, which influences how finely shaded the colors can be in print.

Different papers, printing techniques and inks also require that the images and documents be adjusted to the specific prerequisites necessary for the printed product. If you print on unusual material, in general the adjustments made will be more elaborate and less standard than if you were printing on paper. This demands a higher level of competency for the process and for the materials being printed on, and the printer must make the correct adjustments for knocking out, trapping and overprinting.

When you prepare original art for printing means that you must first choose colors from the correct color guide [see Layout 6.9.1]. Adjusting images for printing is also sometimes called four color separation and in general is done with ICC profiles and converting the images from RGB to CMYK. This conversion can be done directly in Adobe Photoshop or in the production system of the printing house before making the printing plates. When converting images from RGB to CMYK, they are also adjusted for the specific print process and material that will be used. The three main factors to consider when converting/ making adjustments for printing are paper type, printing process and halftone screen type. All three set special requirements on how the conversion should be done. The most important separation parameters are color standard, gray balance, maximum ink coverage, UCR, GCR and dot gain. If you work using ICC profiles, in practice you don't need to be confronted with these parameters since they are built into the ICC profile itself. It is still good to have an understanding of how they work, since they form the basis of four-color separation and give a good understanding of which printing conditions yield what results and how.

When you create an ICC profile, you put in values for these parameters, therefore anyone creating an ICC profile for printing has to have a deep understanding of how these parameters influence the printed result.

Sometimes certain manual printing adjustments not covered by an ICC profile or the image, are required, especially with unusual printing conditions. This would be regarding extra sharpness and compensation for tonal transition. We will go through the different parameters and what they entail.

7.4.1 Color Standards

When you convert an image into CMYK, you need to consider the color standard used. Different countries and parts of the world use their own definitions of the printing colors cyan (C), magenta (M), yellow(Y) and black(B). In the United States for example, SWOP is standard, whereas in Europe the European Color Initiative is used. Within these color standards there are different options based on paper type and printing method, such as Eurostandard Coated for a coated paper printed with colors according to the European Color Initiative. When you convert into CMYK you set the color standard used when printing and the image will be converted according to the color characteristics of these particular printing inks.

New color conversion techniques have been developed recently based on more colors than the four traditional process colors, resulting in the need for six-, seven-, or eight-color conversions. These processes make possible a greater tonal range and are capable of reproducing a considerably larger part of the color spectrum. The printed images resemble the original ones more closely as a result. Often the four primary colors, CMYK, are used with ad additional two three, or four colors. Hexachrome is the most common of these new techniques and is based on six colors, CMYK plus the additional colors green and orange. For these kinds of separations special separation programs are needed.

7.4.2 Gray Balance

If you print with equal amounts of the three colors, C, M and Y, this will result in a surface that is not neutrally gray, although theoretically it should be. This has to do with the color of the paper, the fact that the printing inks don't stick to each other completely (and therefore, the order in which the printing inks are applied to the printed surface also matters), the differences in dot gain among the printing inks and because of uneven pigments and transparency in the printing inks.

If the gray balance is not correct, natural reference colors in images such as grass, sky, or skin tone will look off. An image with an erroneous ray balance will have to adjust the image to adjust for the above-mentioned discrepancies. A common value for gray balance is 40 % cyan, 29 % magenta and 30 % yellow. This combination usually provides a neutral gray tone on regular coated sheet-fed press paper.

BLACK AND WHITE IN FOUR-COLOR
A black and white image can be converted and printed with CMYK to get softer tones and a better depth in the image. In this case, it is particularly important to use the correct gray balance value because it's easy to get color casts.

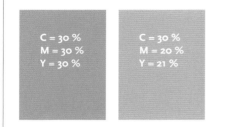

C = 30 %
M = 30 %
Y = 30 %

C = 30 %
M = 20 %
Y = 21 %

NEUTRAL GRAY
In practice, a CMY combination of 30/30/30 will not come out as a neutral gray. A CMY combination of 30/20/21 however usually comes out neutral gray.

RIGHT AND WRONG GRAY BALANCE
The left image has the correct gray balance whereas the right image has the wrong gray balance and, as a result, a distracting color cast.

SHEET-FED OFFSET PRINTING ON COATED PAPER
Here is an example of gray balance values sheet-fed offset printing on coated white paper.

C	0	5	10	20	30	40	50	60	70	80	90	95	100
M	0	3	4	11	20	29	38	48	58	68	78	83	88
Y	0	4	5	12	21	30	39	49	59	69	79	84	89

NEWSPRINT
Here is an example of gray balance values for coldset printing on uncoated newsprint.

C	0	5	10	20	30	40	50	60	70	80	90	95	100
M	0	2	4	10	19	28	37	47	57	67	77	82	87
Y	0	1	3	8	17	26	35	45	55	65	75	80	85

C 92 % M 93 %
Y 75 % K 83 %

Total 343 % ink

C 75 % M 84 %
Y 99 % K 12 %

Total 270 % ink

MAXIMUM INK COVERAGE
The image above has high ink coverage in the dark areas, is based on the four process colors, and has a total ink coverage of 343 %.

7.4.3 UCR and Maximum Ink Coverage

In regular four- color printing you have four colors (CMYK) and each component color at a full tone achieves a tonal value of 100 %. With each color at 100 % you could, theoretically, get a total ink coverage of 400 % (for example in a black tint area, consisting of 100 % cyan, 100 % magenta, 100 % yellow and 100 % black), although this is impossible to achieve in practice [*see Print 9.5.16*]. Coverage of 400 % is undesirable anyway, as too much ink can result in smudging, and in digital printing it can mean that the toner doesn't adhere properly to the paper.

One of the most important settings when an image is separated, that is when it is converted from RGB to CMYK, is to limit the total ink coverage in the image's dark areas. The principle for this is called UCR, Under Color Removal. Thus, in the image's dark areas the amounts of cyan, magenta and yellow are reduced and the amount of black ink is decided. If you allow a maximum ink coverage of 300 %, this means that none of the image will contain more than 300 % ink when it is printed. Other parts of the image will be affected also by how you choose to use black ink in the dark areas. It a dark area is built up with a lot of black ink, less cyan, magenta and yellow are used. The opposite is also true.

Depending on the type of paper and printing methods, the total amount of ink coverage is usually limited to between 240 % and 340 %. Under certain circumstances the maximum ink coverage can sink as low as 150 %, for example when printing on sheet metal, glass or plastic. If the printed product is to be given a protective varnish, [*see Finishing and Binding 10.3*] directly in the printing press, then this can mean that more ink may be used on the paper since the drying time is shortened. But on certain types of paper just the opposite can be true. Where the limits for total ink coverage lies for a certain printing process, is a value you have to find out through testing in practice.

7.4.4 GCR and UCA

If you print the colors C, M and Y with the correct gray balance you will get a neutral gray hue. This ink combination can be substituted with black ink and you will still get the same gray color. Even colors that are no neutrally gray consist of a gray component. If we take an example consisting of C=90 %, M=25 %, Y=55 %, the gray component of this color composition is C=25 %, M=25 %, Y=25 %. If you substitute this gray component with black (K=25 %) and mix it with the remaining amount of cyan(C=65 %) and yellow (Y=30 %) you will, in theory get the same color.

This type of substitution is called Gray Component Replacement, GCR. You can vary the level of GCR so that you only substitute some of the gray component with black. In the above-mentioned example, this might mean substituting a smaller portion of the gray component, for example C=10 %, M=10 %, Y=10 %, with K=10 %, than mixing the black ink (K=10 %) with the remaining portions of cyan, magenta and yellow (=80 %, M=15 %, Y=45 %). In a color image this means that you can use black printing ink and replace the gray component completely, or partially in the entire picture.

In reality equal amounts of cyan, magenta and yellow do no result in a neutral gray tone. Depending on the paper and the printing process the exact value of the gray balance can vary [*see 7.4.2*]. This value is also the basis for the common gray component that is replaced when you work with GCR.

The purpose of GCR is to reduce the total amount of ink used without changing the color. This makes it easier to reach gray balance in print and thereby get a more even print quality. GCR conversions also result in fewer problems with smudging in the printing press because the total amount of ink in the press is reduced. Images that are particularly sensitive to color changes should therefore be converted with GCR. Black four-color images, i.e., black white images based on the four process colors, are one example of sensitive images.

When you substitute black for other colors, the darkest tones of the image can look washed out. To avoid this, you can add a little bit of color to the darkest tones. This is called Under Color Addition, or UCA. This adjustment is normally used sparingly since too much ink in dark areas can be counter productive and do the opposite of what was intended by making it hard to achieve a neutral black color in the printing press.

7.4.5 Dot Gain

Dot gain is a technical print phenomenon wherein the size of the halftone dots increases during the printing process. In practice, this means that an image that has not been adjusted to account for dot gain will appear too dark when

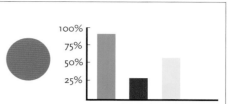

Above color combination consists of C=90 %. M=25 % and Y=55 %. The total ink coverage is thus 170 % (90+25+55).

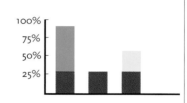

The color combination has a common gray component consisting of C=25 %. M=25 % and Y=25 %. The gray component is replaced with the corresponding amount of black, i.e. K=25 %.

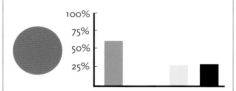

The result is a color combination with a considerably lower total ink coverage but with the same final result. Total ink coverage will in this case be 120%.

ADVANTAGES WITH GCR
Some advantages with GCR are:

- Easier to achieve and maintain gray balance in the print and thereby an even print quality.

- The print is less sensitive to smearing because ink amount is lower.

- Possible to get more accurate colors using low maximum ink coverage.

IMAGE WITHOUT GCR

CMYK

=

CMY

+

K

If GCR is not used, no black component color is generated.

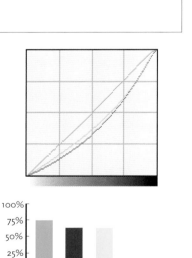

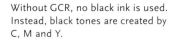

Without GCR, no black ink is used. Instead, black tones are created by C, M and Y.

IMAGE WITH LIGHT GCR

CMYK

=

CMY

+

K

With light GCR some parts of the primary colors' common gray component is substituted with black printing ink.

IMAGE WITH MEDIUM GCR

CMYK

=

CMY

+

K

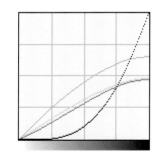

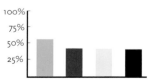

Medium GCR means that a large part of the primary colors' common gray component is substituted with black printing ink.

IMAGE WITH MAXIMUM GCR

CMYK

=

CMY

+

K

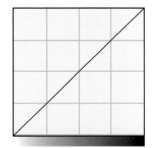

With maximum GCR all parts of the primary colors' common gray component is substituted with black printing ink.

IMAGE WITH UCR

CMYK

=

CMY

+

K

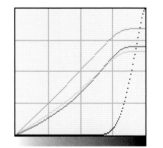

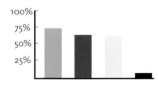

UCR substitutes the common components of the primary colors with black in the neutral, dark areas of the image.

WITH OR WITHOUT GCR

Normally, images with or without GCR should provide identical results. But if the amount of printing ink varies or is uneven in the printing press, an image converted with GCR will be less affected.

An image without or with light GCR mainly consists of the primary colors. It's therefore considerably more sensitive to color fluctuations in the print and even minor changes can give the image a noticeable color cast.

Because an image with GCR consists of fewer tones comprised of the primary colors, the gray balance is not as affected by color fluctuations in the print. This means that the same image printed on different sheets remains identical.

ADJUSTING FOR DOT GAIN
The image to be printed need to be adjusted according to the dot gain that occurs in the printing process. A non-adjusted image will print too dark. In the example above, you find a non-adjusted image (above) and an adjusted image (below).

DOT GAIN

it is printed. To achieve optimal image quality in print, you must therefore compensate for dot gain when the image is CMYK converted. In order to do this you should find out the dot gain for the paper and printing process you are using from the printing house.

The size of the halftone dots increases when they are copied to the printing plate. This is only applicable to negative film and plate. If you are using positive film and plates, the opposite effect takes place – the dot size decreases. Dot gain also occurs in the printing when the ink is transferred from the printing plate to the paper. Different papers have different characteristics that affect dot gain and therefore the conversion has to be adjusted to account for these factors. If an image is erroneously adjusted – i.e., for a fine, coated paper (which has a low dot gain) when it will be printed on newsprint paper (which has a high dot gain) – the image will print too dark. The printing process also affects the degree of dot gain. Roll offset is characterized, for example, by a greater dot gain than sheet-fed offset, if you are printing with the same quality paper. A higher screen frequency always yields a greater dot gain than a lower screen frequency, under the assumption that you are printing with the same process on the same kind of paper. There is also an optical dot gain, caused by the way the light is reflected on the paper.

Dot gain is usually measured in 40 % and 80 % tones. A common value for dot gain is around 23 % in the 40 % tone for a 150 lpi screen and coated paper (negative film). Dot gain is always measured in absolute percentage units. Using

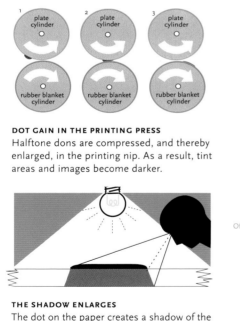

DOT GAIN IN THE PRINTING PRESS
Halftone dons are compressed, and thereby enlarged, in the printing nip. As a result, tint areas and images become darker.

THE SHADOW ENLARGES
The dot on the paper creates a shadow of the reflected light that is often larger than the dot itself.

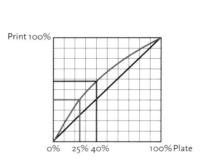

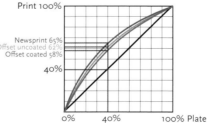

HOW TO MEASURE DOT GAIN
You can measure dot gain with a densitometer and a color bar. Dot gain is usually measured with 40 % and 80 % tones as reference values.

Dot gain is always stated in absolute percentage units. Thus a dot gain of 19 % means that a tint area of 40 % will result in a 59 % tone in the actual print.

To define a tint area as 40 % in the print, you draw a horizontal line from 40 % in print until the line intersects with the curve stating the dot gain. From the point of intersection you then draw a vertical line down to the film axis, which states the value. In this case you have to correct a 40 % tint areas to 20 % so it will turn out right in print.

the above example, this means that a 40 % tone in the film will result in a 63 % tone in the actual print (40 % + 23 % = 63 %).

7.4.6 Minimum Highlight Dot

Minimum Highlight Dot indicates the smallest percentage point at which a certain printing process, with a certain screening frequency on a certain type of paper can manage to achieve. Most normal printing methods can manage to reproduce such light tones that you can create a tonal transition that disappears into white without seeing a jagged edge. This is the prerequisite for light areas in an image to be reproduced successfully. In certain printing procedures, such as flexography on aluminum sheeting or screen printing on cloth, it can be difficult to reproduce the lightest tones, if you don't want to use a very large screening frequency. Sometimes it can be so difficult that all tones below, for example 10 %, disappear. It thus is impossible to create a tonal transition to white or to reproduce very light areas of an image without unsightly jagged edges appearing. In a color image jagged edges can also appear in different parts of the image because of different printing inks which can cause sudden color shifts in light areas. If you still wish to print an image with a printing process that cannot best reproduce light-colored tones, you can manually darken the lightest areas of the image. With color images all the printing inks in light areas will have to be slightly darker than the original tonal range, which will usually darken the entire image quite a bit. In such cases layout and image choice should be carefully selected.

7.4.7 Sharpen the Image

Images in computers are usually sharpened a little to look good when printed. One reason for this is to compensate for the printing process (screening frequency, misregistration, wet ink on the paper), all if which will somewhat blur the image. The second reason is because most of us are used to seeing sharpened images in print. Unsharpened images can be perceived as unfocused, even if they are true to the original.

Since softening in the printing process differs for different printing methods, the images have to be sharpened to different degrees, depending on how they are to be printed, if you want to attain optimal results. An image that is to be printed with a high screening frequency on good paper in sheet-fed offset doesn't need to be sharpened as much as an image that is to be printed in the newspaper where there is more misregistration and lower screening frequencies. It is also important that the different adjustments for sharpening as well as the amount should be controlled. Sharpening thresholds show up more readily with higher screening frequencies, which is why for finer printing a well-defined but short threshold should be selected, while for a daily newspaper a less clear but relatively longer threshold can be chosen.

7.4.8 Knocking out, Trapping and Overprinting

When one object is placed on top of another (for example text over a color field) you can choose to print the one directly on top of the other, or to knock out a hole in the color block in the exact shape of the object to placed over it, which

MINIMUM HIGHLIGHT DOT
We see what happens here if you don't compensate an image for the minimum highlight dot (middle image). The lightest tones in the original image (above) do not get reproduced and you get washed out areas in the image (see the gray scale under the image). In the two lower images we have simulated that the smallest percentage point for minimum highlight dot is 7 %. When you compensate the image (bottom image), the lightest point is given this value (see the gray scale under the image).

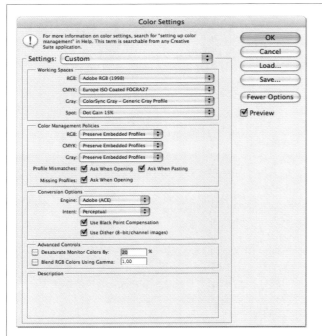

ICC PROFILES

The most important step for making it possible to print an RGB image on paper is separating the colors to CMYK color values. This is done easily in Adobe Photoshop by changing the color mode from RGB to CMYK. You can even do this when a PDF, for example, is saved from Adobe Indesign. The result is the same, so it is a question of workflow as to how you want to do it. ICC profiles and settings in the program determine how the separation will be carried out, that is exactly which CMYK color values a certain color should be built up with. ICC profiles for print are exactly like other ICC profiles, a corrections table to attain the right colors in a certain printing press. But ICC profiles for print have, in addition, setting that specifically determine how much black in k coverage there will be and how much maximum ink coverage there will be in one place. By choosing the right ICC profile for the printing process you are going to use, you will get optimal CMYK color values in the separated image. The image above shows the dialogue window for making the color settings in Adobe Photoshop.

ADOBE BRIDGE

In the Adobe Bridge program you can make sure that all the Adobe programs in the computer have the same basic settings as far as color conversion goes. This is done under EDIT → CREATIVE SUITE COLOR SETTINGS. The simplest way is if you set it up in Adobe Photoshop and then use Adobe Bridge to synchronize these with Adobe Illustrator and Adobe Indesign.

WORKING SPACES

The first frame is called WORKING SPACES. Here is where you set the ICC profiles that will be the program's base setting. In the example we have set ADOBE RGB (1998) as our presetting for RGB images.

The most important setting is the ICC profile for CMYK. In the example we have set Fogras ICC profile for ISO-based sheet-fed offset printing. This means that if I then change color mode in an image from RGB to CMYK, this IICC profile will be used along with all the rules and settings that accompany the profile. It is also very important to set the right ICC profile before you go from RGB to CMYK.

COLOR MANAGEMENT POLICIES

The next frame is called COLOR MANAGEMENT POLICIES and is unimportant in the sense that the settings do not affect how the image is separated. It is here that you set how the program will behave if you want to open an RGB image, for example, that does not correspond to the program's basic settings.

By clicking off ASK WHEN OPENING you avoid the dialogue window that asks if you want to convert the image's RGB setting to the program's basic setting or not.

CONVERSION OPTIONS

The third frame, CONVERSION OPTIONS, should be set as in the example. MOTOR decide which conversion program should be used in the calculations between RGB and CMYK. It used to be important to use different kineds of these programs, depending on if ICC profile used was created with a program from Agfa or Heidelberg, for example. Today Adobe's own conversion programs works in practice with all ICC profiles.

INTENT is a very important setting that determines how the conversion process should handle colors that there isn't "room for" in the new image. An example is if an RGB image contains stronger colors than what is possible to reproduce when the image is converted to CMYK colors.

The method PERCEPTUAL is used to advantage when converting from RGB to CMYK. It retains all the details of the image's strongly colored areas and should thus be preset here. The COLORIMETRIC method is used mainly in the more unusual scenario where you need to convert a CMYK image to another type of CMYK.

ADVANCED CONTROLS

The frame ADVANCED CONTROLS has two powerful tools for adjusting the monitor image, but does not affect the content of the actual image files. The settings installed in this dialogue window can, as with most other settings in Adobe programs, be saved. It is easy to work with several pre-installed settings, for example if you are working with several printing houses and need to go back and forth often.

Color Settings

For more inform...
management" in...
Suite applicatio...

Settings: Cust...

Working Spaces
RGB:
CMYK: ✓ Europe ISO Coated FOGRA27
Gray:
Spot:

Color Management
RGB:
CMYK:
Gray:

Profile Mismatches:
Missing Profiles:

Conversion Option...
Engine:
Intent:

Custom CMYK...
Load CMYK...
Save CMYK...

Other

ColorSync CMYK – Generic CMYK Profile
Europe ISO Coated FOGRA27
Euroscale Coated v2
Euroscale Uncoated v2
Japan Color 2001 Coated
Japan Color 2001 Uncoated
Japan Color 2002 Newspaper
Japan Standard v2
Japan Web Coated (Ad)
U.S. Sheetfed Coated v2
U.S. Sheetfed Uncoated v2
U.S. Web Coated (SWOP) v2
U.S. Web Uncoated v2

150-Line (Pantone)
Canon CLC500/EFI Printer
Generic CMYK Profile
KODAK SWOP Proofer CMYK – Coated Stock
KODAK SWOP Proofer CMYK – Newsprint
KODAK SWOP Proofer CMYK – Uncoated Stock
Photoshop 4 Default CMYK
Photoshop 5 Default CMYK
SWOP Press
Tektronix Phaser III Pxi

OK
Cancel
Load...
Save...
Fewer Options
☑ Preview

Advanced Controls
☐ Desaturate Monitor Colors By: 20 %
☐ Blend RGB Colors Using Gamma: 1.00

Description
Europe ISO Coated FOGRA27: Uses the FOGRA27 press characterization. It is designed to produce quality separations for standard ISO printing using: 350% total ink coverage, positive film and coated paper.

Custom CMYK

Name: Custom Inks for blach & white images

OK
Cancel

Ink Options
Ink Colors: Other
Dot Gain: Standard 20 %

Separation Options
Separation Type: ● GCR ○ UCR
Black Generation: Medium
Black Ink Limit: 100 %
Total Ink Limit: 300 %
UCA Amount: 0 %

Gray Ramp:

Ink Colors

	L*	a*	b*	
C:	58,3	−28,5	−42,6	
M:	44,9	75,2	−2,0	
Y:	87,6	−13,1	91,6	
MY:	41,9	62,2	49,9	
CY:	54,6	−35,0	42,1	
CM:	25,5	30,9	−26,4	
CMY:	23,4	23,6	22,3	
W:	93,0	−0,4	1,5	
K:	7,4	1,3	−0,1	

OK
Cancel

☑ L*a*b* Coordinates
☑ Estimate Overprints

There is a function in Adobe Photoshop to manually create your own ICC profiles for printing. To reach this function you have to check off MORE OPTIONS in the color settings window. In the list above CMYK profiles you can then choose CUSTOM CMYK.

In the dialogue window that then appears you can indicate which type of CMYK colors are going to be used along with a number of settings. These are the same as existed in Adobe Photoshop since the first version, long before there were ICC profiles. Or you can specify the CMYK colors with your own CIE LAB values, which you can get from a spectrophotometer by measuring a print. This together with the setting for dot gain provides enough data to be able to create a complete ICC profile.

Finally, you can set two separation parameters: maximum black ink coverage, and maximum ink coverage in one place. This can be done either with GCR where you indicate how much black ink will replace cyan, magenta and yellow in neutral colors, or with GCR where, by giving a limit of the total ink coverage in the image's darkest areas you achieve the same result. Since Adobe created the settings the GCR method is preferable since then you will gain more control in Adobe Photoshop.

A real ICC profile program can utilize more than a thousand premeasured CIE LAB values to create an adjustment for a certain printing process and yield in more exact profiles by far compared with this built-in ICC generator.

Printing houses usually don't use this function in Adobe Photoshop. Instead they have professional special programs to create ICC profiles. The functions can however, in some emergency cases, be justified in using. An example would be if no professional ICC profile or professional ICC profile program was available and there was a special need.

VALUE GUIDELINES FOR SEPARATION	NEWSPRINT	UNCOATED PAPER	COATED PAPER
Screen frequency	65–100 lpi	100–150 lpi	150–200 lpi
Dot gain	ca 28–30 %	ca 22–24 %	ca 18–20 %
GCR/UCR	high GCR	low/medium GCR	low GCR/UCR
Ink coverage	240–260 %	280–300 %	320–340 %

will then be printed on an unprinted (white paper) surface. When you choose the first alternative, so-called overprinting, the color of the text is blended with that of the color block to form a new color. If you choose the second alternative, so-called knocking out [*see inset below*] the text will take on the color you defined with the layout program. If you don't indicate otherwise the layout program usually uses knocking out. If you print several colors on top of each other, you will always get some amount of misregistration among the colors. The reason is that the dimensions of the paper are altered width-wise as well as length-wise during the printing process. If you have utilized knocking out, the misregistration will show up as a white or discolored gap between the object and the background, for example between the text that lies against the color field and the color field itself. Small misregistrations can be bothersome. The problem is greatest in roll offset printing and flexography, where the paper roll undergoes large changes in dimensions and can easily go off course sideways. Misregistration also happens with other printing techniques, but is not as noticeable as in roll offset printing or flexography. To avoid this you have to utilized trapping or overprinting.

Trapping means you let one object get big enough to overlap another object. One example is one color field lying on top of another color field. So that there won't be a white gap between the two, you spread one color field so that it lies up against the other. The word trapping is usually used as a catch-all term for the functions of spreading and choking. Spreading means that the overlying object is made larger while choking means that the knockout, that is the hole, is shrunk. Both functions create an overlap between the object and the background, which prevent any gap from occurring in the event of slight misregistration. The degree of trapping is determined by the size of the misregistration during the printing process. The greater the misregistration, the greater the trapping. The overlap (or the border as it is often called) that is a result of spreading and choking, means that the object and the background are printed on top of each other to

KNOCKOUT AND OVERPRINT

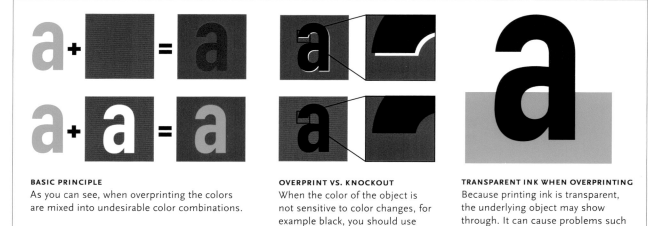

BASIC PRINCIPLE
As you can see, when overprinting the colors are mixed into undesirable color combinations.

OVERPRINT VS. KNOCKOUT
When the color of the object is not sensitive to color changes, for example black, you should use overprinting to avoid gaps.

TRANSPARENT INK WHEN OVERPRINTING
Because printing ink is transparent, the underlying object may show through. It can cause problems such as in the image above.

a certain degree, and construct a new, darker color. This means that you will get a visible edge that may be bothersome. Often such an edge is still preferable to a white gap. A small difference in lightness of color between and object and the background means that the edge will be less visible than if the difference in color were great. The color of the edge will in such a case be noticeably darker than both the object and the background. The darkest parts of an object or a background determine what shape the eye will see. Therefore usually the lightest parts are spread or choked to avoid the eye perceiving that the object has changed shape. If you choke a yellow background under dark blue text, the text will retain its optical form. If on the other hand, the dark text were to be spread, it would be obviously distorted. It is also important that the spreading only occur on the parts of the object that lie against the color field so the object doesn't change shape in the parts that lie against white. In the accompanying image we have for simplicity's sake used to different processing colors. Of course trapping works if the object and background are composed of several colors as well. Trapping occurs in such a case with the different colors as dictated by necessity. If the colors of the object and the background are the same when the colors are placed together during the printing process, trapping isn't necessary. If you have two objects that are multi-colored at the same time as one of the objects has higher value of many colors, trapping isn't necessary either.

When the difference in lightness between a dark object and a light background is large enough, it is simplest to use overprinting. With black text overprinting is always recommended. It is impossible to get misregistration between objects. It is always faster for printing out pages. Overprinting is also usually advisable for thin lines or small text, as long as it doesn't require major changes in the colors of the lines or the text.

With trapping the dimensions of the object are somewhat altered. This effect is more noticeable the smaller the object is, since trapping is equally great regardless of the size of the object. For this reason overprinting should be used as far as possible instead of trapping with small objects. Black text against a color field or an image and continues onto a white background will change colors if you print using overprinting. The part of the text that lies on the color background will urn out darker than that part lying on a white background. If you wish to avoid this, you should instead knock out the black text. Then the whole text will be printed against a white background and thus be the same color.

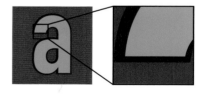

STYLISTIC CHANGES IN DARK OBJECTS
The eye can easily register changes in the shape of dark objects. To avoid distracting shapes you should, as in the case above, shrink the background. In the upper example, the dark text has been trapped, causing a distracting shape.

OVERPRINT SMALL TEXT
You should overprint small text to avoid changes in shape when knocking out and trapping.

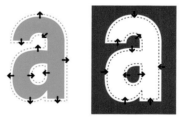

MISREGISTRATION WHEN KNOCKING OUT
With knockouts and misregistration you will et white or miscolored gaps.

TRAPPING AND CHOKING
When trapping, the object is enlarged. Choke requires that the knockout be shrunk.

DISCOLORED OUTLINE
When trapping and choking you will get a discolored outline. If two objects have similar shades the area of overlapping will have a darker shade, which sometimes can be distracting.

ONLY TRAP HALF OF THE OBJECT
To avoid getting discolored objects, you should only trap where necessary.

TRAPPING IS NOT NECESSARY
If an object and a background have a similar combination of process colors, the gap that appears at misregistration will get a similar color. That's why you don't need to trap or choke the object or the background.

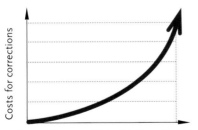

COSTS OF MISTAKES
One mistake always costs money. The earlier you can correct it the less it will cost.

The adjustments for trapping are no longer done with the program where you produced the original, for example Quark Xpress or Adobe Indesign, but are stead done when printing at the printing house. There are two methods. Either trapping is carried out in a PDF file which is then sent tot the printer, or else trapping is done automatically in the printers RIP software during printing. The most common way is trapping with a RIP program. Exactly how trapping is done varies between manufacturers, but the most common is that the pages automatically undergo trapping according to preadjusted general rules. Trapping then becomes an automated process that occurs at the same time as the printed product is printed. The document is trapped according to set valued and rules. It is difficult to give a general recommendation as to what value should be used. The reason is that values are different for every printing process and paper type, in the same way as dot gain curves. Tapping values usually are at 0.1 to 0.5 dots, depending on the printing process.

For more complex production, for example packaging where many different colors, lithopone, etc., are used, there are special programs where all the trapping on the page can be controlled and manipulated individually. The most common program for this is called Art Pro and is used by many packaging printers.

7.5 Proofing and Contract Proofs

Before you produce your printed product it is important to review the text, images and layout to ensure that everything will be correct when printed. The later in the production process you discover errors, the more expensive and time-consuming it is to correct them. The prepress state is actually your last chance to check your document before you begin printing. This is also when you need some sort of final approval of the document before going to press. Today there are many available ways to review and proof the original document. You can use PDF files and review everything on a computer screen, you can print out proofs with a laser printer in color or black and white, and you can create various analog or digital proofs. With particularly important productions, you can even make a proof in a printing press before the edition is printed. This is expensive, but justified in certain cases. If nothing else is used, you can also create some sort of a contract proof for the final check. Such proofs are also called "chroma", "proof" or "color proof". PDF files and laser printers are suitable for an initial proof before the contract proof is reviewed, but sometimes these types of proof are used as a final check.

All of these review and proofing procedures serve the same purpose: to ensure that every step goes as planned. The method you choose depends to a large degree on how high quality you are seeking, but it also depends on practical factors such as cost and time frame. The following sections will cover the pros and cons of different reviewing procedures and what they are best used for.

7.5.1 What Should be Checked and by Whom?
Checking the original before going to print is the common responsibility of the client, the producer of the original artwork and the printing house. As the cli-

ent it is therefore important to know what responsibility one has and what one should check. In principle you can say that the client has the main responsibility for checking that the content, layout and colors are correct, while the printing house is responsible for carrying out technical controls and insuring that the original artwork and the proofs are correctly adjusted for the printing process and the paper. The one who produces the original artwork is responsible for making sure the layout and images represent the content and concept of the client's wishes, and that the original artwork is technically suited for reproduction in print. This responsibility does not take away any of the printing house's responsibility to check for and eventually prevent any mistakes. In the end it is always the printing house's responsibility to not begin printing before all the checks have been made and the original artwork is determined to be technically correct from a printing perspective. Layout and content however are always the responsibility of the client.

7.5.2 Soft Proofs – Proofing on the Screen

Soft proof is a term for checking and text and images on the computer screen. In general print compatible PDF files are used. The advantage with this method is that it is cheap and quick since you don't have to make print-outs that you may have to send to different people.

If you are going to check colors on the computer screen it is important for it to be carefully calibrated. The screen uses an additive color system (RGB) while printing uses a subtractive one (CMYK) [see Chromatics 3.3 and 3.4]. Therefore you cannot rely one hundred percent on the screen being an exact replica of the printed document. With good screen calibration and with help of the printer's ICC profile, you can however attain a surprisingly close match between the computer screen and the printed document. At the same time the color verification of the two will not be good enough to correct the printed product regarding color and images. In order to do this you have to print a pre-printing proof.

Using a soft proof you can check most things, however. It is important to check typography, image placement, illustrations, logotypes and text. You can also check spelling and line arrangement, format, type area, bleeds, image handling and touch ups.

ICC PROFILES FOR SOFT PROOFS
In Acrobat it is easy to choose the ICC profile that corresponds to the printing process you want to simulate on the monitor under ADVANCED → OUTPUT PREVIEW... All the ICC profiles available on the computer are shown on the list. By clicking on SIMULATE INK BLACK the colors shown on the monitor are adjusted to give an appearance of how they will look in print. Also by clicking on SIMULATE PAPER WHITE the bright colors on the monitor are adjusted to reflect the color of the paper.

7.5.3 Laser Printer Output

Laser printer outputs are primarily used to review typography, check the placement of images, illustrations and logotypes, and to fact-check text and correct spelling. Laser printers also allow you to check hyphenation, line arrangement, format, type area and bleeds. Color laser printer outputs are not recommended for checking images since they do not correspond closely enough color-wise with printing. If you are going to use a laser printer output as a final control versus a printing house's printed proof, you cannot later claim any errors in the printed product regarding color and images. The advantage is that you save time and money without contract proofs, but in general these costs are not great compared to the cost of printing.

To get a good idea of how the page will look you can do the printout on a Postscript-based printer in black and white. Ideally the printout should be the same size the printed product will be. If you do a color printer output, you can also check that all the elements on the page have approximately the color you want (remember that this method is not the most accurate way of doing this). You can check that the color conversions are correct by making a four-color separated laser printer output. For a regular four-color page you should get four printouts per page, one for each printing color. If you are printing with spot colors you don't want, you've probably forgotten to separate one or more colors in your document, or have neglected to delete the colors you decided not to use. In four-color separated laser printer outputs, you can also check trapping and overprinting.

7.5.4 Preflight Software –Technical Controls

The word "preflight" is borrowed from the aviation world, and refers to the preflight check a pilot performs on an airplane before takeoff. In the graphic production industry, "preflight" refers to the review of digital documents before they go into production. Preflight is a technical control to check that the digital original documents are correct and ready for the right printing process, paper and finishing and binding. Generally this is done by the printing house.

Certain preflight functions are used which check the document step by step following a special checklist. The actual control is done either on the layout document with InDesign or Quark Xpress or PDF files. Eventual corrections are then done in the programs where documents, illustrations and images are created, for example Quark Xpress, Adobe Illustrator or Adobe Photoshop. In some cases you can also correct PDF files directly.

Preflight review might seem like an unnecessary step, but most digital documents sent to production arrive with errors that must be corrected. Preflight programs help catch these errors as early as possible, reducing the risk of delays and cost overruns.

7.5.5 Contract Proofs

By contract proof we mean a color printout that will simulate how the printed product will look. These proofs used to be made with chemical printed proofs that were produced from the graphic films that were necessary to expose printing plates. The different methods that were used could not be adjusted to a specific printing procedure, but instead followed their own standard. Then the printer would have to try to replicate the contract proof as closely as possible. The manufacturers of these systems have in many cases been able to give their names to contract proofs in general. Old names such as Chromalin, Chroma and Colorart still exist.

The term contract proof comes from the idea that there is a legal contract between the client and the printing house. In practice this means that it will be difficult to lodge any formal complaint if the client does not have a reviewed and approved contract proof to refer to.

The contract proof will ensure that any prepress work has been correctly carried out, and will function as the last checkpoint before the printing plate is

CONTRACT PROOFS
In principle you can say that proofs fulfill three important functions:

- Checking colors and images as well as the final proofing of the product as a whole

- A legally binding contract between the customer and the printing house

- A guideline for the printing house as to how the final product should look created. It is also used as the guideline and the standard for the printing house as to how the client expects the end result.

Today the contract proof is produced by some kind of advanced color printer, usually an inkjet printer. This kind of color output can be produced in two ways. Either you can let the printer make as good a printout as it is capable of, or you can use the printer to simulate the appearance of the print from another device, usually a printing press. The first way is used to check RGB image and is then called an image proof, or print after the colored prints photographers always used to make. A contract print on the other hand, should simulate the appearance of the final print. This can also be done in two ways. Either the printout will be adjusted according to some kind of printing standard, for example the ISO standard for print on coated paper or a general setting for a newspaper, or the printout will be adjusted for a certain paper in a certain printing press. All settings for simulating print are done in the printer using ICC profiles [*see Chromatics 3.12*].

Most printing houses recommend creating a contract proof. If you as a client decline to do this you are limiting your options if you are not satisfied with the printed product. In some cases it may be justifiable to bypass this step, particularly in the interest of time. If you are doing a repeat run you can use a printed product from an earlier run as a reference. If you decide no to make a contract proof you should be clear with the printing house on who will be responsible for what. If you have high standards regarding color, you should definitely make a contract proof.

If anyone other than the printing house produces the contract proof, a very close dialogue is necessary between the producer of the proof and the printer. A contract proof should always contain measuring grids that make it possible to check the proof technically. Otherwise it is more difficult afterward to determine whether it is the print, the contract proof or the digital original that is at fault when the final result doesn't turn out as expected. Many printing houses and repro companies also use these measuring grids for a running control that the contract proof as produced is technically correct before it is shown to the customer. This is important to the customer since it is impossible to determine if a proof that appears good has been correctly done. As a customer you should always ask how closely the printout is adjusted to your own print.

7.5.6 Limitations of Contract Proofs

You should be aware that you can never attain a one hundred percent match between the contract proof and the printed product. This is because the contract proof is produced by other processes, with other machines, with different inks and often on different paper. Still, you can come very close by making sure the equipment is calibrated and if you are using the printer's ICC profile.

At the same time there are certain limitations that may be difficult to circumvent regarding certain errors.

The first is quality and characteristics of the equipment used for printing the contract proof. Some machines have a relatively low resolution, can only use shiny white paper and vary widely in their colors during a print run. The term contract proof is used for output produced using all types of printers

If you have high demands on image quality, you should make special image proofs to check the images. If image quality is of lesser importance, it may be enough to check them on a well calibrated screen. The more knowledge about images and reproduction, the more things can be checked on the screen.

DIGITAL PROOF SYSTEMS

INKJET TECHNIQUE
Inkjet printers have become very common as proof printing systems. They have a resolution of up to 2,880 dpi and can print out on most kinds of paper up to A-2 format.

DYE SUBLIMATION TECHNIQUE
There are also special proof systems based on dye sublimationp technique, also known as thermal transfer technique. These systems can show traditional screening, have a resolution of up to 2,540 dpi, and can also print out with some Pantone colors.

possible. The choice of equipment is therefore important for the final result to be good enough.

The second important factor is how the equipment has been maintained. Many professional printers need a lot of attention to produce a stable and first-class result. Now all graphic production companies have good routines and express responsibility for care and calibration of their equipment for contract proofs.

Contract proofs are often done on the supplier's standard paper, which means that you are limited regarding paper choice. This paper is often white and shiny. If you have chosen a coated, calendared paper with high whiteness for your production, the resulting of the contract proof can be very close to the final result. If, on the other hand, you have chosen an uncoated paper, that is a little matte and yellowish, the colors may vary widely between the proof and the printed product. In many contract proof systems you can now make use of the chosen paper or something similar, which is recommended. Certain printing techniques, paper types and inks can be very difficult, not to say impossible, to simulate in contract proofs. Offset printing on coated paper is the easiest to reproduce in a contract proof system. Other printing techniques such as gravure, flexography or screen printing are considerably more difficult to imitate, especially if you are printing on more unusual materials such as plastic, glass or metal. This means that you can set considerably higher demands on the consistency between a contract proof and the offset print than with any other method.

Most contract proof systems cannot simulate PMS colors, which means that in general you are limited to the four-color processing cyan, magenta, yellow and black. If you use PMS colors, you can create a four-color proof instead, with some of the process colors, or four-color separate the PMS colors when you print out the contract proof. This of course won't give the correct color impressions, but you can make sure that everything is there, and that it looks approximately like it should. This kind of contract proof should be completed with a printed reference (for example a PMS color swatch from a color chart). This reference would show how the actual color would look in reality.

7.5.7 Press Proofs

To press proof means to print some sample copies of the print in the printing press before the actual edition is printed. Press proofs are sometimes made on a different printing press than the one used for the edition, but because they are created on similar equipment, press proofs provide the most accurate projection of the final result though the colors may vary somewhat. With digital printing it is easy and cheap to print out single copies and produce a contract proof. In offset and other printing situations it is expensive and time-consuming but naturally gives the closest to the final result.

When producing books with high standards for image reproduction, especially coffee table books, it is usual to gather only images on one large sheet and make a contract proof of these in a real printing press.

CONTRACT PROOF   PRINT

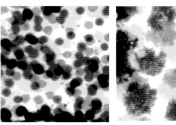

DIFFERENCES BETWEEN
CONTRACT PROOFS AND PRINTS
Most contract proofs that are used today can not be shown with traditional halftone screens. Here we can see dots from a contract proof and a real print close up. The contract proof is shown with inkjet technique and the print is shown with traditional screening.

7.6 **Imposition**

Imposition is the step where you arrange the pages on the printer's sheet to fit the eventual finishing and binding and utilize the paper in the best way. When you print you always try to use the printing press's format as effectively as possible and use the largest paper format possible. At the same time it is important to fill the printed surface as well as possible so that there won't be any costly waste of paper. The printing press is the costliest unit per hour in the graphic production process. You should try to minimize the time spent in the printing press. Paper is the one most expensive material used for creating the printed product. Imposition is in other words decisive in being economical in printing. As well as printing press format and paper format, there are five parameters that affect imposition:

- *The printed product's final format* – The format of the printed product decides how many pages there will be room for on the printing surface and thus determines how imposition shall be done.

- *The number of pages in the printed product* – If the number of pages is grater than the number of pages that can be fit onto both sides of the paper, you will have to execute many makereadies. The number of pages thus determines imposition.

- *Fiber direction* – In order to have durable stitching and attractive printed products, the fiber direction of the paper has to run lengthwise along the sine or fold. Thus fiber direction influences how the pages will be placed on the paper.

- *Finishing and binding equipment* – the machines you use in finishing and binding can at times be limited as to how large a sheet format can be used. Folding machines can be restricted as to how many folds they can make [*see Finishing and Binding 10.10*]. Certain finishing and binding equipment also require a gripper edge, an extra "lip" that is used for the machine to grab onto the sheet. All these different parts affect and determine how jmposition shall be done.

- *Stitching method* – Different stitching methods place the sheets together in different ways – the sheets are placed inside each other in signatures, or one after another in sheet order. How they are stitched in relation to each other affects how they are placed on the sheet. Thus stitching method influences imposition [*see Finishing and Binding 10.12*].

With all of these factors taken into account, you will try to attain the most cost-effective imposition as possible, with a minimum of paper use and time in the printing press. How the pages are imposed in relation to each other is done using an imposition dummy. This means that you, for example take on or several A4-sheets of paper and fold them in the way the printed product

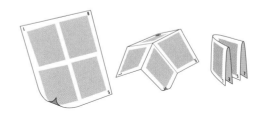

IMPOSITION SCHEME
An imposition scheme is used to show which pages should be where.

DIFFERENT TYPES OF IMPOSITIONS

The printing press is the costliest unit per hour in the graphic production process. You should try to minimized the time spent in the printing press by utilizing large paper sheets and as much space of the paper sheet as possible. Most printing presses have maximum format of 4, 8,16 or 32 pages, depending on the sheet size used.

When printing a book or booklet, for example, several pages are arranged next to each other on the same printer's sheet. The arrangement of the pages on the sheet is called imposition and varies according to the paper formats the printing press can accomodate.

As an example to illustrate the different imposition variations, we are using an 8-page 8 ½″ × 11″ booklet, which consists of two 11″ × 17″ sheets, folded in the middle and stapled together with two staples in the fold.

Each 11″ × 17″ sheet accommodates four 8 ½″ × 11″ pages, two on each side. After taking the off press processing into consideration, an 8-page booklet can be imposed in two different ways: by folding and stapling two separated 11″ × 17″ sheets or by cross folding, stapling and cutting clean one 19″ × 25″ sheet.

IMPOSITION FOR AN 8-PAGE, 8 ½″ × 11″ BOOKLET
FOR AN 11″ × 25″ PRINTING PRESS

If a printing press's largest format is 11″ × 17″ you need to impose for four 11″ × 17″ pages. You will have to execute four makereadies in the printing press because each 11″ × 17″ sheet runs through the printing press twice, one for each side of the sheet. When the print run is completed, you will end up with two 4-page 11″ × 17″ sheets with two 8 ½″ × 11″ sheets on each side of the sheet. The sheets are then folded, one by one, and stapled into an 8-page 8 ½″ × 11″ booklet.

IMPOSITION FOR AN 8-PAGE 8 ½″ × 11″ BOOKLET FOR A 19″ × 25″ PRINTING PRESS

If a printing press's largest format is 19″ × 25″, you need to impose for two 19″ × 25″ pages. You will have to execute two makereadies in the printing press because each 19″ × 25″ sheet runs through the printing press twice, one for each side of the sheet. When the print run is completed, you will end up with an 8-page 19″ × 25" sheet with four pages on each side of the sheet. The sheet is then right-angle folded and stapled into an 8-page 8 ½″ × 11″ booklet.

IMPOSITION FOR AN 8-PAGE, 8 ½″ × 11″ BOOKLET FOR A 23″ × 35″ PRINTING PRESS

If a printing press's largest format is 23″ × 35″ you need to impose for one 23″ × 35″ page. You will only have to execute one makeready in the printing press because each 23″ × 35″ sheet runs through the printing press twice, one for each side of the sheet, but without changing the printing plate. Pages 1,8,4 and 5 are imposed on one half of the 23″ × 35″ sheet and 2,7,3 and 6 on the other. After the 23″ × 35″ sheet has been printed on one side, it is turned over and the other side is printed with the same plate, a procedure called halfsheet work, or work and turn. When the print run is completed, you will end up with a 16-page 23″ × 35″ sheet with eight pages on each side of the sheet. The sheet can then be divided into two identical 8-page sheets, right-angle folded and stapled into an 8-page 8 ½″ × 11″ booklet.

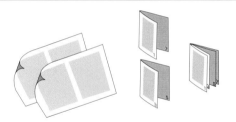

8-page booklet made from two 11″ × 17″ sheets.

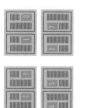

8-page booklet made from one 19″ × 25″ sheet.

Four printing plates   Two printed sheets

Two printing plates   One printed sheet

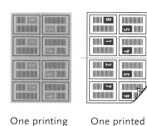

One printing plate   One printed sheet   The sheet is divided into two parts

THE INK SETTINGS AFFECT THE IMPOSITION

If all the pages in a printed product are not printed with the same amount of compound colors, it is generally cheaper to print on different printing presses. For example, because a cone-color printing press has a lower cost per hour than a four-color printing press you are better off printing one-colored pages in a one-color printing press, etc.

When you produce the originals you can, if you know in advance the format the product is printed with, study the imposition and take advantage of the ink settings. Let's use the example of the 8-page booklet. It should be printed with black ink except for page 3, which is in four colors. The side of the print sheet that contains page 3 has to be printed in a four-color printing press. In the examples below, you can use four-color on all pages placed on the same side of the sheet as page 3 without generating additional costs (we have not taken the costs for color separation into consideration).

In an 11″ × 17″ printing press, the entire page that contains page 3 has to be printed in a four-color printing press. Even if page 6 only contains one color, it will also be printed in the four-color printing press.

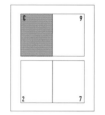

In a 19″ × 25″ printing press, the entire page that contains page 3 has to be printed in a four-color printing press. Pages 2, 6, and 7 are thus also printed in the four-color printing press.

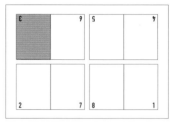

In a 23″ × 35″ printing press, all the pages of the booklet are on both sides of a 23″ × 35″ sheet. All the pages on the entire sheet have to be printed in a four-color printing press regardless of whether they contain color or not.

BUDGET AND IMPOSITION

You should always try to impose the pages as inexpensively as possible, which means minimizing the time spent on the printing press. If we use an eight-page folder as an example, a 23″ × 35″ press would probably be the least costly printing press format. The cost is dependent on the volume of the run and the hourly charge for the printing presses. A 23″ × 35″ will be more cost effective than a 19″ × 25″ or 11″ × 17″ press for a larger run (one thing that takes longer). For a smaller project a 19″ × 25″ press might be better – it might take longer in a 19″ × 25″ press than a 23″ × 35″, but the hourly rate is much lower and the total cost will come out less. The makereadies don't really differ in the actual time needed, but the 19″ × 25″ press requires twice as many makereadies as the 23″ × 35″ press. The illustration shows a comparison of the production times for the different printing presses.

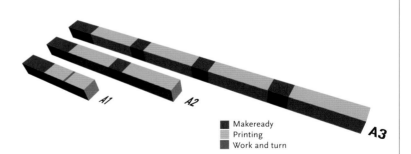

Makeready
Printing
Work and turn

PRODUCTION TIME SPENT IN DIFFERENT PRINTING PRESSES

Illustrated in the image above is the production time spent in the different printing presses producing an 8-page booklet. The budget affects which type of printing press should be used and thereby also the imposition. The choice of format is determined by the cost per hour in the printing press.

MANUAL IMPOSITION
Imposition used to be done manually. The individual page films were taped to a large montage film. To make sure the pages were placed correctly, the mounting was done on a light table

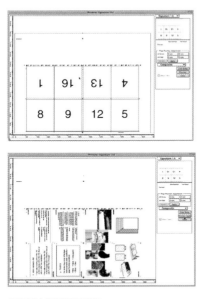

DIGITAL IMPOSITION
When digitally imposing the pages, they are mounted on a digital printer's sheet. Above is an example of two such impositions.

will be folded. This creates a little copy of the printed product which you then paginate. When you then unfold the sheet you will see how the pages should be placed in relation to each other.

Along with placing the pages in the imposition, you also impose a number of aids for printing and finishing and binding in the form of marks and bars. They are placed out along the edges of the sheet of paper and are used for adjustments and checking the printing and finishing and binding.

Imposition is done with special impositions programs where separate digital pages in the form of PDF files or pre-rasterized pages are placed into the program, and it creates a digital printing image which corresponds to the entire printing format that is to be printed. In imposition programs you can save the impositions that are created in the form of templates, with all the accompanying marks and bars. In this way you can build up a library of templates that encompass the impositions you usually use. When you use imposition templates your work with imposition becomes very efficient – you load the template into the program and import the separate pages and then the imposition is done.

If you are using graphic film in the printing process, that is every page in the printed product has been printed out on separate film, you have to do the imposition by hand. The pages are then placed according to and imposition plan, and then imposed with the help of tape onto a larger transparent piece of film. A different film montage is done for each printing color and page on the sheet. The montage places very a high demand for exactness to get good registration between the different colors when printed. This is still very unusual today.

There are a number of main types of imposition that everybody uses to minimize paper consumption, time in the press and also take finishing and binding into account. We will go through the most common types of impositions.

7.6.1 Gang-Up

Depending on how many copies of the product you place on a sheet, this imposition is referred to as a 2-up, 3-up, etc. these impositions are usually used if the product only has one or two printed pages. You want to impose as many copies of the pages as possible on a single sheet of paper, in order to minimize the time you project spends on the printing press. For example, if your printed product consists of an 8 ½″ × 11″ sheet and is to be printed in a 19″ × 25″ press, you can impose the print 4-up. Printing a product gang-up can be done in combination with some of the imposition methods mentioned below.

7.6.2 Prima-Secunda

The most common imposition is called prima-secunda. With a prima-secunda imposition a separate imposition and set-up of printing plates is done for each side of a printer's sheet – the prima side and the secunda side. In sheet-fed offset a makeready is executed for each side of every printer's sheet, that is two makereadies per sheet. The sheets are placed so that the first page of the printed product lies on the prima side of the printer's sheet, and the printed product's second page lies on the secunda side of the sheet.

TYPICAL IMPOSITIONS

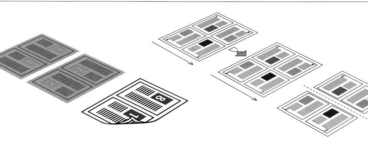

GANG-UP
Here you can see a 2-up and a 4-up imposition.

FIRST FORM – INNER FORM
Each side of the printed sheet will need one makeready. Thus, you will need two imposed film sets per printed sheet.

HALFSHEET WORK (WORK AND TURN)
You place a first form imposition on one half of the sheet and an inner on the other. When the entire run is printed, the sheets are turned over and run through the printing press a second time. That way, both pages of the sheet can be printed with only one makeready – i.e. without changing the printing plate.

7.6.3 Work and Turn (Halfsheet Work) and 2-Set (2-Up)

Work and turn work and 2-set are two imposition techniques based on a situation where the sheet has space for at least twice as many pages as the printed product contains. These methods place a first form imposition on one half of the sheet and an inner on the other. This gives you a version of the 2-up, also called a 2-set or 2-on, because you get two printed products from one sheet. When the entire run is printed, the sheets are turned over and run through the printing press a second time. That way, both pages of the sheet can be printed with only one makeready – i.e., without changing the printing plate. Even if the printed product has four colors on one side and only one color on the other, it can still be cost effective to use this type of imposition instead of doing two makereadies in two different printing presses.

Work and turn, or halfsheet work as it is also called, is the most common of these two types of imposition. The printing press grips the same edge of the paper when printing both the front side and back of the sheet. With the 2-set technique, the same gripper edge is not used for both sides. Instead, the sheet is turned over for the second run in the printing press and the gripper edge is moved to the other side of the sheet, making it more difficult to align the front and back sides of the print. In this case, even something as minor as having slightly different-sized sheets of paper in the press run can cause misregistration.

7.6.4 Signatures and Sheet Order

When you plan to bind a printed product with metal stitching, glue binding or thread sewing, you generally use right-angled folding. For metal stitching, right-angle folded sheets, called signatures, are inserted into each other. For glue binding and thread sewing, the folded sheets are placed one after another

SIGNATURES OR SHEET ORDER

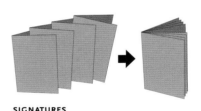

SIGNATURES
The folded sheets (the sections) are inserted into each other. This method is used in saddle stitching, for example).

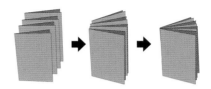

SHEET ORDER
The folded sheets (the sections) are gathered after each other into a bundle. This method is used in glue binding, for example.

Finishing and binding procedures affect how large the sheets can be and what direction the grain must have. You should also take into account the gripper edge and cropping.

When printing large, heavily colored solid colors areas or images you should not impose too many pages on the printer's sheet. That way you avoid the negative impact the different pages may have on each other.

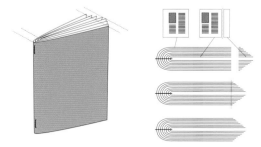

CREEPING
When right-angle folding and especially with signatures, the pages are punched slightly outwards – the closer to the center, the greater the displacement. You can compensate for this problem in the position by successively reducing the size of the gutter (the inner margin) as you progress towards the center spread.

in sheet order. The two variations require two different types of imposition, signature imposition and sheet order imposition. With signature imposition the first and last pages of the printed product will lie on the same side of a printer's sheet, while with sheet order imposition the first and last pages end up on the first and last printer's sheets, respectively.

7.6.5 Crossover bleeds

When you stitch printed products with glue, thread or Smyth-sewn stitching, you can have problems with parts of the images or layout objects lying across the gutter or the inside margin not being visible or being cut away. You can often compensate for this during imposition. Already when doing the layout you can adjust crossover and overlapping of the pages. The person who knows how this is done and is in a position to check the results is the person who executes the imposition. This person is responsible for informing the one in charge of layout if and how any eventual compensation should be made, and the he or she is the one responsible for checking that it was done properly.

7.6.6 Gripper Edge

The gripper edge is the extra distance between the printed text and the edge of the paper that the printing press and the finishing and binding machine grab hold of in order the move the printer's sheet. How large the gripper edge should be and where is should be placed varies from press to press and between finishing and binding equipment.

The printing house know what size gripper edge the printing press needs and even executes the imposition, and can easily make sure the requirement for the gripper edge is met. If the book binder has special requirements for the gripper edge for finishing and binding, they will usually deliver a diagram to the printing house on which they have marked where the gripper edge should be and how large.

7.6.7 Compensation for Creeping

When a sheet is right-angle folded, the center spreads are pushed slightly outwards and the middle pages of the folded booklet are displaced. This phenomenon is called creeping. Creeping becomes even more pronounced when you sue signatures because each additional signature pushes the central one further outwards. When you crop your printed product after it's been folded, the type area of the pages "creep" towards the outer margins more and more as you get to the center spread. You can compensate for this problem by successively reducing the size of the gutter (the inner margin) as you progress towards the center spread. This is done by indicating the thickness of the paper in the imposition program. The program then compensates for the creeping that occurs for a certain thickness of paper with a certain imposition. This will ensure that the printed image is properly oriented and that the margins are consistent on the page throughout the printed product. In compensating for sheet order imposition the gutters are reduced toward the middle of every printed sheet.

7.6.8 Imposition Proofs

Imposition proofs are the last proofs done before printing begins. They have many different names and are usually called everything from blue copy, blues, plotter, digital blue copy to prototype. These proofs used to be produced with a technique where the printed text was shown in blue, which is why they are still often called blue copy, blues, etc., even though the technique is now different.

Imposition proofs are printed out on large inkjet printers as a whole printed sheet true to size. Usually the output is usually printed on one side of printer paper. This means that the printouts for the prima sides of the printer's sheet have to be fastened together with the printouts for the secunda sides to make a double-sided sheet before folding the proofs according to how the printed product will be folded. Before fastening the two sides together, each sheet is usually cut along the cutting marks and that is when crossover bleeds are checked that they bleed correctly. When the proof is folded together, you leaf through it and compare it with the layout dummy and check that all the pages are in the right places.

The goal of the imposition proof is to make sure that the imposition has been executed correctly, that compensation for images across the gutters has been achieved, that crossover bleeds are correct and that the right pages are in place. This is done by folding together the printout to a prototype and checking everything.

Normally the printing house checks and approves the imposition proof since these controls mainly affect their work. Despite that, there are many clients who would like to approve the imposition proof since it is the last review before printing. It is seen as an opportunity to check everything one last time: spelling, images and layout.

There are many reasons why one should avoid making these changes on the imposition proof. First of all, it is way to late to discover spelling, image and layout errors on this proof. These types of errors should have been found

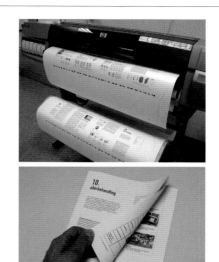

BLUELINES
There are inkjet printers that can print out in large format – as you see here a whole imposition. Today it is the most common type of imposition proof. Sometimes this kind of printout is still called bluelines, an expression from the old blueprints. Blueprints were a special kind of chemical analog proof that were used to check imposition films and their contents.

REGISTRATION MARKS AND COLOR BARS

During the imposition, different marks and color bars are usually added to make the printing and off press processes easier.

- *Color bars:* to check the correct ink coverage in the print.

- *Registration marks:* to check that the different component colors are registered (placed exactly on top of each other).

- *Crop marks:* to show how the sheet should be cut to the correct format.

- *Fold marks:* to show where and in what direction to fold.

- *Collation marks:* to show the order of the sheets [*see Finishing and Binding*].

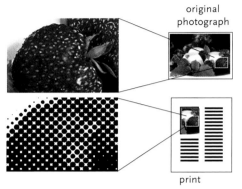

original
photograph

print

CONTINUOUS TONAL TRANSITIONS
In the upper gray scale, we have simulated a continuous tonal transition. The tonal transition is, in reality, not continuous but because the halftone screens are so fine the transitions are not visible.

In the lower gray scale, we show the same tonal transition but with a lower screen frequency. The brain also perceives this example as a continuous tonal transition. You can see that the gray scale is composed of differently sized dots in black and white, the two colors you can print with black printing ink.

HALFTONE SCREEN
– SIMULATION OF GRAY HALFTONES
A printing press cannot produce continuous tones, like in a photograph with smooth tonal transitions. It can only print with color or without color. To reproduce gray tones in print, you use halftone screens instead. Halftone screens consist of small dots in closely spaced rows. Their size varies depending on which tone you want to simulate. Halftone screens deceive the eye into believing it sees continuous tones although only black and white have been used.

on text, image and layout proofs. Secondly, the size of the printouts has low resolution to keep printout times reasonably low. This means the proofs are not appropriate quality for checking hard-to-read text, images and colors are reproduced poorly, and the layout appears inexact.

Above and beyond these factors the client should consider whether it is wise to approve the imposition proof since that means risking taking reponsibility for any imposition errors later on that may sneak in during printing, for example a missing page.

7.7 Halftone Screening

A photograph consists of continuous tones – tonal transitions of color hues. A printing press cannot produce continuous tones. Instead, it combines printed and non-printed surfaces to achieve a similar effect, almost like a stamp. Halftone screens deceive the eye into believing it sees continuous tonal transitions by dividing the printed image into very small parts, which the eye blends to look like continuous tones when the image is viewed from a normal distance. Smaller divisions result in better image quality.

There are two main techniques to fooling the eye with the aid of halftone dots. In one technique the halftone dots are always the same distance from each other and vary in size to create different tones, so-called traditional halftone dots. In the technique all the dots are the same size, and their distance from each other is varied to cover different parts of the surface differently to create different tones. These are called stochastic halftone dots.

A halftone screen consists of small dots in closely spaced rows. The size of the dots varies depending on the tones you want to simulate. In light areas, the dots are small; in dark areas the dots are larger. The denser the dotted rows are, the higher the "screen frequency". A high screen frequency means the image is divided into smaller parts (smaller dots in the halftone screen) and, as a result, you will get finer tonal transitions and finer detail in printed images. A black surface has an ink coverage of anything between 1 % and 99 %, depending on the shade of gray. If the surface is half-covered with halftone dots you will have 50 % coverage.

Halftone screens are created by the printers software, a Raster Image Processor (RIP), when you print out a document. Most suppliers of RIP's use their own halftone screening technique, which means that the halftone dots are built up in different ways, depending on which RIP the halftone screens are created by.

7.7.1 Halftone Dot Types
With traditional halftone dots the eye is fooled into perceiving different tones by placing the halftone dots at the same distance from the center, but whose size can vary and thus can cover different size areas of the paper. Small dots create light tones while large dots create dark ones. When the halftone dots are made larger they can grow together and cover the whole surface with color.

Not all "dots" are round. Dots can be round, elliptical or square, though round dots are most common. Depending on the printing method, and some-

The different halftone dot shapes have different characteristics, visible in fine tonal transitions.

ELLIPTICAL DOTS:
Suitable for images with many types of objects, for example skin tones and products in the same image. Elliptical halftone dots have a tendency to create patterns.

SQUARE DOTS:
Can be used in detailed images with high contrast, for example images of jewelry. They are worse with skin tones.

ROUND DOTS:
Are appropriate for light images, such as skin tones. Worse for images with detailed shadowed areas.

The choice of dot shapes can also depend on the printing process.

Diamond halftone dots

Elliptical halftone dots

Square halftone dots

Linear halftone dots

Round halftone dots

---

times on the printed product, square or elliptical dots might be a better choice. The corners of square dots meet at a tonal value of 50 %. The eye can sometimes perceive this transition in softer shades. Round dots work the same way, but meet at a darker tone, approximately 70 %. Because of their shape, elliptical dots meet at two different tonal values, 40 % where the pointed ends meet and 60 % where the long sides meet. You will thus get two critical points of interaction in the tonal transitions and elliptical dots can sometimes create lines in the image where the dots meet. There are halftone screens that combine different dot shapes in different screen percent values. Agfa Balanced Screening (ABS), for example, combines round and square dots in order to get the benefits of both shapes.

Some example of raster techniques for traditional rasters are Agfa Balanced Screening, Irrational Screening from Heidelberg and Co-Res Screening from Fujifilm.

7.7.2 Frequency Modulated Screening – Stochastic Screening

The big difference between stochastic screening and traditional halftone screening is that the number of dots per surface unit varies, rather than the size of the dot. The name used by the graphic production industry, "stochastic screening", is somewhat incorrect, however. Stochastic means random, and the screens are not random. A better name for this technique is Frequency Modulated screening, or FM screening.

ELLIPTICAL DOT CRISIS
Because of their shape, elliptical dots meet at two different tonal values, 40 % where the pointed ends meet and 60 % where the long sides meet. You will thus get two critical points of interaction in the tonal transitions causing linear patterns.

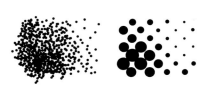

PRINCIPLE DIFFERENCE
In FM screening, the halftone dots are the same size but the distance between them differs. In traditional screening, the halftone dots have the same distance to each other but differ in size.

BUILDING GRAY TONES
In the FM technique to the left, the exposure dots are spread out in the cell. In the traditional to the right, the dots are collected in the center. Both halftone screens have the same gray tone, approximately 17 % (11/64).

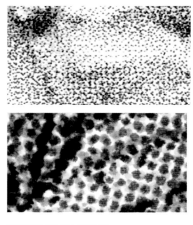

UNDER THE MAGNIFIER
In the enlarged screens above, you can see the difference between FM and traditional screening.

In FM screening, all halftone dots are the same size. The halftone dots are approximately the same size as the smallest dots in traditional halftone screening. A dark area in a traditional halftone-screened image contains large dots, while the same area in an FM screened image contains a large number of dots instead. It may seem like these dots are randomly placed within the screen, but in reality, a program places the dots according to mathematical calculations. Different dot sizes are available for different types of paper. Smaller dot sizes are used for paper with a smoother surface, which requires a higher output resolution. Larger-sized dots are more appropriate for low-quality paper and low-resolution printing. The sizes available depend on which RIP is being used. Do sizes can vary between 14 to 41 micrometers. The measurement micrometer means a thousandth of a millimeter and is usually indicated with the unit µ. The smaller dot sizescan be used on paper with a smoother surface and larger dot sizes are better suited for paper with more uneven surfaces.

FM screening generally allows for better reproduction of details than traditional halftone screening. This is particularly evident when using FM screens on low-quality paper where you would otherwise have relatively low screen frequency. On the other hand, tinted areas and soft tonal transitions can appear blotchy with stochastic screening. With this type of screening, there are no screen angles, and therefore no problems with moiré or distracting rosettes. As with traditional halftone screening, different manufacturers have developed their own versions of this technology, including Cristalscreening from Agfa, Prinect Stochastic Screening from Heidelberg, and Staccato Screening from Creo/Kodak. These all work in the same way in principle, though they different with different halftone dot-generating algorithms.

7.7.3 Hybrid Halftone Dots
There are halftone dots that combine traditional and stochastic halftone technique to take advantage of the best of both techniques – the stochastic halftone dots' capability to reproduce fine details and the traditional halftone dots' ability to depict middle tones without patchiness. These are called hybrid halftone dots. The build for example on stochastic halftone dots in light and dark tones, and traditional halftone dots in middle tones. Different suppliers have their own variations of hybrid halftone dots, for example Sublima from Agfa, Maxtone Hybrid Screening from Creo/Kodak, and Prinect Hybrid Screening from Heidelberg.

7.7.4 Other Screening Techniques
In addition to the above-mentioned techniques, there are other specialized screening techniques like line screening and divided halftone dots. The former technique is built on lines that vary in width to create different tones in the image. The latter technique divides each normal-sized dot into four smaller dots, giving the impression of double the screen frequency with the same tonal range in the large halftone cell. A screening technique that is sometimes used is the printer technique. For example with certain inkjet printers you can not only vary the size and frequency of the halftone dots, but also their density, that is how thick a layer of ink is placed on the paper. This means that you can work

with a lower printing resolution than with traditional halftone dots without losing quality or the number of tones that the halftone dots can reproduce.

7.7.5 Screen Frequency and Dot Size

The screen frequency is a measurement of the number of halftone cells per line. It is measured in lines per inch, or lpi (sometimes this is denoted as l/in, lines per inch, or l/cm, lines per centimeter). The lower the screen frequency, the larger the halftone cell and, consequently, the larger the halftone dot. This means that a halftone dot with a 50 % coverage in a 60 lpi screen is four times as big as the same halftone dot in a 120 lpi screen.

The higher the screen frequency, the finer the details in the resulting image. The paper and printing method used help determine what screen frequency you can print with. Paper suppliers usually provide screen frequency recommendations for different types of paper. The printing house can also provide this information. If the screen frequency is too high for a certain kind of paper, you run the risk of blurring the halftone dots, which will result in a loss of detail and contrast in the print. 175 lpi is the common screen frequency and 20 micrometers is a typical dot size for high-quality products like brochures and annual reports and 85 lpi is a common screen frequency and 40 micrometer is a typical dot size for low-quality products like newsprint.

7.7.6 The Structure of the Halftone Dot

When a traditional halftone screen with a certain screen frequency is built, an area is defined for every halftone dot, known as a halftone cell. Within this area the dots can vary in size depending on how large a surface the dot should cover, that is what halftone is to be created. When a halftone dot fills half the surface of a cell, for example, it gives it a 50 % tone and when the whole cell is filled it gives it a 100 % tone.

The halftone dot builds up a number of exposure dots. The smallest size that a halftone dot can be is the size of an exposure dot. The largest size is when the whole cell is filled with exposure dots. Every exposure dot can only be black or white, that is print or not print. For traditional halftone screening the halftone dots are constructed from the center and out into the halftone cell. In FM screening it is inside the halftone cells that the number of halftone

HYBRID SCREEN
Hybrid screening combines traditional and FM screening.

LINE SCREEN
Often used for effect, the line screen method generally provides low image quality. The screen consists of lines rather than dots.

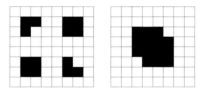

DIVIDED HALFTONE DOTS
If you have a screen with divided halftone dots, the screen derives from four separate units within the halftone cell (left). The cell maintains its number of gray tones but the resolution appears to have doubled. Compare it to the traditional screen with one single unit (right). Both examples show a 20 % gray tone.

VARIATION IN DENSITY
In some inkjet and sublimation dye printers, a screen technique is used that not only varies the size and frequency of the halftone dots, but also their density. This refers to how thick a layer of ink is placed on the paper.

RECOMMENDED SCREEN FREQUENCY
Here is a table of screen frequency recommendations for different paper qualities and printing techniques:

PAPER	SCREEN FREQUENCY	PRINTING METHODS	SCREEN FREQUENCY
Newsprint	65–100 lpi	Offset printing	65–200 lpi
Uncoated	100–150 lpi	Gravure printing	120–200 lpi
Coated, matte	150–175 lpi	Screen printing	50–100 lpi
Coated, glossy	150–200 lpi	Flexographic printing	90–150 lpi

50 lpi   100 lpi   175 lpi

SCREEN FREQUENCY

Screen frequency is stated in lpi, lines per inch, and is a measurement of the number of halftone cells per inch. The lower the frequency, the larger the halftone cell and the halftone dot. Above are examples of different screen frequencies. At 50 lpi the eye is still able to perceive the halftone dots but at 175 lpi the surface is perceived as a continuous tone.

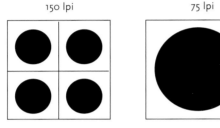

150 lpi   75 lpi

SCREEN FREQUENCY DIVIDED IN HALF

If you divide the screen frequency in half, the halftone cell will be four times as big. As a result, a halftone dot in the same gray tone will be one fourth the size in a 150 lpi screen compared to the 75 lpi screen.

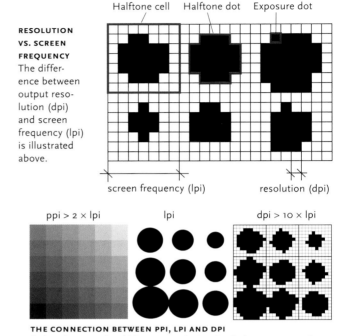

RESOLUTION VS. SCREEN FREQUENCY The difference between output resolution (dpi) and screen frequency (lpi) is illustrated above.

Halftone cell   Halftone dot   Exposure dot

screen frequency (lpi)   resolution (dpi)

ppi > 2 × lpi   lpi   dpi > 10 × lpi

THE CONNECTION BETWEEN PPI, LPI AND DPI

A digital image should have a resolution (ppi) that corresponds to double the screen frequency (lpi). When you go to print out the page to a plate or on a printer, an output resolution (dpi) that is at least 10 times as large as the screen frequency (lpi) is required.

LINES PER INCH VS. LINES PER CM. Normally screen frequency is given per inch (lpi) in the U.S. In other parts of the world it is more usual to give screen frequency per cm.

PER INCH	PER CM.	L/CM. VALUE THAT IS USED
50	20	20
60	24	24
72	28	28
85	33	34
100	39	40
120	47	48
133	52	54
150	59	60
175	69	70
200	79	78
300	118	120

points are varied to cover different surfaces and thus simulate different tones. The size of the halftone dots in FM screening corresponds in principle to the size of an exposure dot.

The number of exposure points that are used to build up a traditional halftone dot decides its size and what tone it will simulate. If a traditional halftone dot only has room for four exposure points in every cell, the dot can only show 5 tones, that is white (no black exposure points), light gray (one of the four exposure points black), medium gray (half of all the exposure points black), dark gray (3 of 4 exposure points black) and black (all exposure points black). In practice you need more tones to simulate a continuous tonal transition. One recommendation is usually that you need 100 tones to be able to simulate a continuous tonal transition.

7.7.7 Screen Frequency and Visual Resolution

When you create continuous tonal transitions with halftone screening, there are two aspects of the eye you have to consider. First, what is the resolution of a halftone screen that the eye requires so as to not perceive the dots, or in other words how small the halftone dots have to be. Second, what the smallest differ-

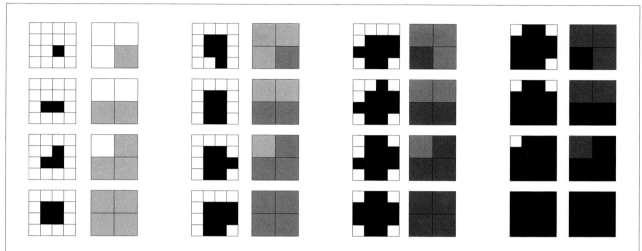

2 DENSITY LEVELS REQUIRE HIGHER PRINTING RESOLUTION THAN 5 DENSITY LEVELS
Inside a halftone cell, the halftone dot is constructed by exposure dots that fill the cell from the center and outwards always following the same pattern. The number of exposure dots that fit in the cell determines the number of sizes a halftone dot can assume, i.e., the number of gray tones the halftone screen can simulate. The halftone dot shown can simulate $4 \times 4 + 1 = 17$ tones (+ 1 is derived from the unfilled halftone cell). In some inkjet and sublimation dye printers, a screening technique is used that not only varies siize and frequency of the halftone dots, but also their density, or how thick the layer of ink is on the paper. This means that you can work with a lower printing resolution than with traditional screening without losing quality or the number of tones the screen can reproduce. In the example above we see a halftone screen with five density levels compared with a traditional halftone screen that has two density levels (black and white).

ence in lightness between two tones is that the eye can perceive. Halftone screens deceive the eye into believing it sees continuous tonal transitions by dividing the printed image into very small parts, which the eye blends to look like continuous tones when the image is viewed from a normal distance. Through practical testing it has been shown that at least 100 different gray tones are necessary so that the eye will experience a scale from black to white as continuous.

A traditional halftone screen must have higher resolution than what the eye can perceive and FM screening has to have smaller points than what the eye can perceive. How high the screen frequency has to be or how little the halftone dots have to be is determined by the eye's resolution ability. This can be stated with the eye's angle of resolution as the smallest angle where the eye can see the difference between a black and a white line.

This angle is created by the triangle that is formed by the distance between two of the eye's light receptors (rods and/or cones) as well as their distance from the pupil. Normally this angle is about 0.025 degrees. Since the eye's resolution ability builds on the assumption that the eye can see details that take up a certain angle of the field of vision, the eye's ability to see halftone screen lines increases the closer one gets to the halftone screen. This means that the more closely one looks at a halftone screen, the higher the screen frequency it has to have to avoid the eye perceiving the halftone dots. From a normal viewing distance,

35 cm, it is necessary for the halftone screen to have a higher screen frequency
than 84 lpi or 33 l/cm [*see accompanying illustration*]. If you are going to look
at something from further off, for example a large painting from a distance of
1.5 meters, 20 lpi is enough.

In the same way you can calculate how small the dot size has to be in FM
screening so that the eye will not perceive the dots, but since such small dots
are used in FM screening it is seldom a problem.

7.7.8 Tonal Range

Tonal range refers to the maximum number of gray hues you can get with a
particular screen frequency and output resolution in the imagesetter. The relationship between the screen frequency and the output resolution determines
the tonal range that can be reproduced. The number of tones is determined by
the number of exposure dots that can fit in the halftone cell. The number of
exposure dots per halftone cell is determined in turn by the screen frequency
chosen and how high a resolution the printer or imagesetter you are printing
an output on is set for. Printing resolution is measured in dpi, (dots per inch),
the number of exposure dots per inch. When you use an imagesetter or printer
you can often choose the resolution – normal resolutions are 1,200, 2,400 or
3,600 dpi. The higher the screen frequency you choose the higher the printing
resolution you have to choose to get enough exposure dots per halftone cell.
Higher printing resolution gives better tonal range. That is a larger number of
tones that the halftone screen can reproduce.

The gray hues of the computer and the imagesetter are created according
to a linear function: each gray hue represents an equal-sized step in the total
tonal range. By contrast, the eye's perception of gray hues is logarithmic, which
essentially means that the eye is differently sensitive in different parts of the
grayscale – it can m ore easily distinguish tonal differences in the lighter part
of the spectrum than the darker part. Thus, in order to compensate for the
more sensitive parts of the eye, you have to be able to reproduce approximately
65 linear hues. It is difficult to determine the exact number of hues needed, so
it is recommended that you have at least 100 hues per component color, and
therefore that you select an output resolution capable of producing that number
of shades given the desired screen frequency. That means that in a halftone dot
every halftone cell has to be built of at least 10 × 10 exposure points, which gives
us 101 possible hues. (10 × 10 plus the empty halftone cell).

To use the previous example you can calculate a tradition halftone screen's
tonal range with the help of the printer resolution and the screen frequency. For
example take a 175 lpi screen, a resolution of 2,400 dpi, and a tonal range of 189
tones, which is enough to fool the eye. If you were to choose a setting of 1,200
dpi, and set the imagesetter at 175 lpi screen frequency, it could only reproduce
48 tones, which is why this alternative is not to be recommended. With an 85
lpi screen frequency as in today's newspapers, the printer resolution of 1,200 dpi
would give the screen 200 tones, which is more than enough.

For example a 175 lpi halftone screen printed with 2,400 dpi and a tonal range
of 189 tones. The same screen would, if you could vary the exposure dots' density
in five levels, yield 753 tones. Five levels of density would then make it possible

SCREEN FRE- QUENCY LPI	SCREEN FRE- QUENCY L/CM.	LEAST VIEWING DISTANCE
20 lpi	7,9 l/cm	146 cm
40 lpi	15,7 l/cm	73 cm
85 lpi	33,5 l/cm	35 cm
133 lpi	52,4 l/cm	22 cm
150 lpi	59,1 l/cm	20 cm
175 lpi	68,9 l/cm	17 cm
200 lpi	78,7 l/cm	15 cm

distance in cm: 15 22   35   73   146

SCREEN FREQUENCY AND VIEWING DISTANCE

When you choose screen frequency you will want a screen where the halftone dots are so small that they are not visible when you look at the pirnt from a normal distance. How large "normal" distance is depends also on what type of printed product you are making. A large poster in the city, for example, has a larger viewing distance than a brochure. The image and the table show what the minimum required screen frequency is for a certain viewing distance so the halftone dots will remain invisible.

SCREEN FREQUENCY AND THE EYE'S RESOLUTION ABILITY

When you choose halftone screen frequency it should be greater than the eye's resolution ability so the halftone dots will not be visible. The eye's resolution ability is calculated by first calculating how far the distance is between the white and black lines as defined by the angle of resolution. This distance is the same as the thickness of the lines. This is done with the help of the viewing distance, (in this case 35 cm) and the angle of resolution (0.025 degrees).

Dbw = Distance between black and white lines
Vd = Viewing distance = 35 cm
Ar = Angle of resolution = 0.025 degrees
Dbw = Vd × tanUV = 35 × tan 0.025 = 0.015 cm.

The distance between the black and white lines is then multiplied by 2 to get the distance between 2 black lines.

Dbb = Distance between two black lines
Dbb = 2 × Dbw = 2 × 0.015 = 0.030 cm

Distance between two black lines (Dbb)

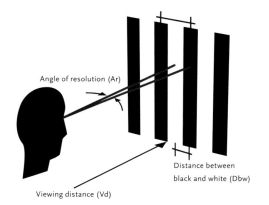

Angle of resolution (Ar)

Distance between black and white (Dbw)

Viewing distance (Vd)

To calculate the highest screen frequency (lines per unit of lenght) where the screen dots are still visible, you take the distance between the two black lines and invert it, in other words take 1 and divide it with the distance. This gives you the eye's resolution ability, which is the same as the highest screen frequency where the eyes sees the screen from that distance.

R = Eye's resolution ability = Lowest screen frequency
R = 1/Dbb = 1/0.030 = 33 l/cm = 84 lpi

When you choose screen for this viewing distance, the screen frequency has to be higher than the eye's resolution ability so the halftone dots will remain invisible.

With the formula below you can calculate the maximum number of tones a traditional halftone screen with a specific frequency can have at a certain printing resolution:

Number of tones = (print reso./screenfreq.)^2+1

If you want a tonal range of at least 100 gray tones we recommend using a 100 lpi screen and a 1,200 dpi output resolution. If you would like to increase the resolution even more, 2,400 dpi takes you a lot further than a 200 lpi screen.

Certain printer techniques can create exposure dots, and thus halftone dots, with varying density. In such cases you don't need as high printer resolution since the same halftone dot can take on a number of different tonal values. The number of tones that can be reproduced can then be calculated with this formula:

Number of tones
= (print reso./screenfreq.)^2 × (g–1) +1

g = number of levels of density (no color at all included) that the halftone points can take

This means that if you work with a screen technique that has five density levels you can halve the output resolution compared with a traditional screen technique with the same screen frequency and still retain the tonal range.

For example, a 175 lpi screen output with 2,400 lpi gives a tonal range of 189 tones. The same screen would, if you can vary the exposure dots density in five levels, give 753 tones. Five density levels would then make it possible to reduce the output resolution to 1,200 dpi and still get 189 tones.

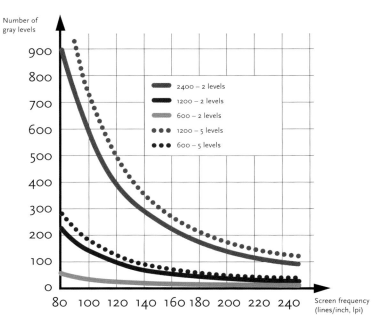

to reduce the printing resolution to 1200 dpi and still get 189 tones. This means that if you work with a halftone technique that has 5 levels of density, including no color at all, you can halve the printing resolution compared to tradition halftone screens, and still keep the same tonal range.

With a printer it is important to set it for as high a resolution as the number of tones you can get in the exposure dots' density. At the same time you don't want to have a higher resolution than necessary since this lengthens the printing time considerably without visibly better results.

When you work with a computer it is important that it can show more than one hundred tones. A grayscale image on the computer generally consists of 256 gray hues, that is more than more than the 100 tones necessary for the eye. The extra tones are needed since the image loses information in the imagesetter and at times you will want to make bigger adjustments of certain tones in the image. Normally 256 are plenty, but with extreme touch ups and much repeated image editing on the same picture, it might happen that you have used up so much information that the image is damaged. In certain parts of the image there wouldn't be enough tonal range to reproduce the image well [*see Image Editing 5.3.6*].

7.7.9 Screen Angles
The traditional halftone dots are placed in rows so that they build lines, screen lines. The brain can easily perceive patterns involving 0 and 90-degree angles. Halftone screens are therefore tilted at 45-degree angles to make patterns less obvious. When printing with four colors, the screen for each component color is placed at a different angle in order to avoid a moiré effect [*see below*]. Because

17 gray levels
(4 × 4 + 1)

50 gray levels
(7 × 7 + 1)

101 gray levels
(10 × 10 + 1)

145 gray levels
(12 × 12 + 1)

HOW MANY GRAY LEVELS ARE NECESSARY?
A halftone screen has to be able to create enough gray tones to show continuous tonal transitions. The number of gray levels necessary is determined by the eye's ability to perceive tonal transitions. If you start with the smallest tonal transition that the eye can perceive, you will get a guideline of 100 gray levels.

When a screen has to few gray levels, as in the two top images, you will get a step-effect in fine tonal transitions. In the images it is particularly visible in the shadow behind the tomato. More gray levels than 100 do not lead to higher quality, compare with the two bottom images, only longer printing time.

You can calculate a traditional halftone screen tonal range using the printing resolution and the screen frequency. For example, a 175 lpi screen printed with 2,400 dpi gives a tonal range of 189 tones, which is enough to fool the eye. If you were to have a printing resolution of 1,200 dpi, a 175 lpi screen only gives 48 tones, which is why this alternative is not recommended. With a 85 lip screen, which is typical for newspapers today, the printing resolution of 1,200 dpi would give 200 tones in the screen, something that is more than enough.

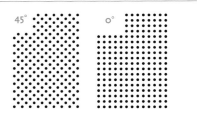

PATTERNS AS PERCEIVED BY THE BRAIN
The brain is easily distracted by patterns, particularly those involving 0 and 90-degree angles. To make patterns less obvious, halftone screens are therefore tilted at 45-degree angles.

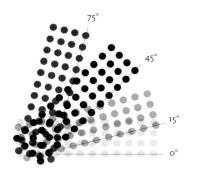

SCREEN ANGLES OF THE PROCESS COLORS
Black is the most distracting color for the brain and its screen is tilted to 45 degrees, the angle that distracts the brain the least. Yellow is the least distracting color for the brain and its screen is tilted to 0 degrees, the angle that distracts the brain the most.

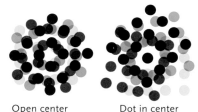

Open center   Dot in center

HALFTONE SCREEN ROSETTES
When the screen angles used in printing are well-registered, the resulting print has a rosette-like pattern. There are two main types of rosettes: those with an open center and those with a dot in the center. Which one is better is disputed.

ink is tilted to 45 degrees, the angle that distracts the brain the least. Yellow has the lowest contrast, so its screen get the "worst" screen angle, or 0 degrees. The angles of the cyan and magenta screens are oriented as close to 45 degrees as possible, in opposite directions. For offset printing, the recommended screen orientations are 45 degrees for black, 15 degrees for cyan, 75 degrees for magenta and 0 degrees for yellow. This gives you an even displacement of 30 degrees among the three most visible colors. These suggested angles only apply to offset printing. Other printing methods like screenprinting or gravure printing require different orientations. It happens that in offset printing you might not use the traditional screen angles. You would instead set black at 0 degrees, despite what is written above. This is because the printing conversion of images from RGB to CMYK only uses black in the really dark parts of the image. In these dark parts the screen lines are not very visible, as the surface coverage nears 100 %. In such a case you could put cyan or magenta at a 45 degree orientation. This technique is well suited for images and helps you avoid problems with halftone screen rosettes [*see below*], but can in turn create disturbing patterns in, for example, color fields.

7.7.10 Screen Rosettes

When the screen angles used in printing are well-registered, the resulting print has a rosette-like pattern. If you look closely at a printed image, this rosette pattern is more or less visible to the naked eye, depending on the ink coverage and the color combination of the print. Although rosettes might be distractingly obvious in some parts of a printed image, this is considered a "normal" screen phenomenon, unlike moiré. In general, the lower the screen frequency, the more visible the rosettes. Today it is usual to not use traditional screen angles with traditional halftone screening to avoid the problem of halftone screen rosettes [*see 7.7.9*]. Stochastic rasters lack patterns among themselves and therefore do not produce halftone screen rosettes.

All analog proofs, and some digital, allow for a sharp reproduction of halftone dots, and rosette patterns can be very evident as a result – even though they may not appear that way in final print. For example, if you want to do an analog proof of a newspaper advertisement at 85 lpi, (a low screen frequency), the rosette pattern might be distracting when reproduced in sharp detail on the fine paper of the proof. When the advertisement is actually printed on low-quality newsprint, however, the dots will not appear as sharp and the rosettes will not be as evident.

7.7.11 Moiré

Proper orientation of the screens is very important for ensuring a quality print. Improperly set screen angles can result in an effect known as moiré. Moiré is an obvious, regularly occurring pattern in the print, which can be easily perceived by the eye. It is very distracting. Today's halftone screening techniques avoid moiré by assigning each component film a slightly different screen frequency. Often the screen angles are also adjusted to compensate for this effect. This makes it considerably more difficult for the different halftone screens on the films to interfere with each other. When you scan images that have been printed with traditional halftone screens, it is usual to get moiré when the images are printed. This is because the images in the newly scanned printed product already have halftone screens and the old ones interfere with the new halftone screens. Most professional scanners have filters to reduce the risk of this occurring [*see Digital Images 4.13.9*].

Sometimes you will also find moiré in isolated parts of an image, an effect called "object moiré". This is not the result of an error in setting the screen angles, but because patterns in the image coincide with those of the screens. Object moiré is relatively unusual but does occur occasionally in sensitive images like checkered or patterned fabrics, for example. A similar phenomenon can be observed when someone appearing on a TV screen is wearing a checkered or patterned suit.

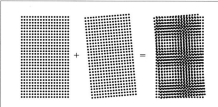

PATTERNS THAT AFFECT EACH OTHER
Moiré is a regular pattern that occurs when two individual patterns are placed on top of each other. It is easily perceived by the eye and can be very distracting in the print.

WRONG SCREEN ANGLES CAUSE MOIRÉ
If an image is output with improperly set screen angles, moiré can be visible in the print.

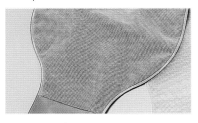

OBJECT MOIRÉ
Sometimes patterns in an image coincide with those of the halftone screens and cause object moiré.

08.

paper

Why is it difficult to flip through some printed products? What is the difference between coated and uncoated paper? Which paper provides the best image quality? What is cardboard? Why do some paper types turn yellow? Is there a major price difference between different types of paper? How do you calculate the spine width? Why do some printed products crack in the spine? Which paper should you choose if you want it to last for a long time? Are bleached papers less environmentally friendly?

THERE ARE A NUMBER of different grades of paper, which are used for different purposes. In this book we will limit our discussion to those used for graphic production, known as "fine papers." A paper's characteristics are of vital importance to the final printed result. Therefore you should select the paper as early as possible in the production process, preferably even before starting to work on the original artwork. This allows you to make all necessary adjustments to the production according to the paper selection, optimizing the quality of the outcome. Too often it happens that the paper is selected too late or that the decision is changed right before going to press. Many people also select paper without thinking about the consequences it will have on the printed product. The choice of paper affects, among other things, readability, the production of the original artwork, text and image quality and reproduction, as well as the quality and durability of the printed product. Since paper is sensitive to temperature and humidity, it is also important to think about how the paper is handled. The paper's characteristics are determined during production, and are influenced by such things as kinds of wood and any fillers used in the paper pulp. In this chapter we will begin with what you should think about when you choose a paper, and then go through the most important qualities and concepts, and what importance they have on the eventual printed product. We will also look at other areas like the handling and production of paper.

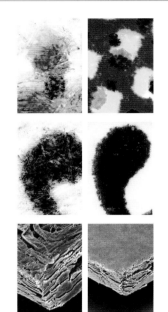

UNCOATED VS COATED
In the images above, you see uncoated (to the left) and coated (to the right) paper. When the paper is coated, the optical characteristics and printability of the paper improve. You can use a higher screen frequency and get a higher gloss in the print because the paper absorbs the ink more quickly and evenly.

CONTRAST
With the uncoated paper (simulated bottom) you will not obtain the same contrast as with a coated paper (top).

8.1 Coated or Uncoated

Commercial printers commonly distinguish between coated and uncoated paper. Coated paper can be further divided into additional categories depending n the amount of coating it has: lightly coated, medium coated, highly coated or art paper. Coated paper has a smoother surface which gives it a higher printing quality. Examples of coated papers include paper used for brochures, art books and magazines. Examples of uncoated papers include stationery, photocopying paper and the paper used for paperback books. Most uncoated papers are surface-sized in order to ensure good surface bonding strength. Uncoated paper is not necessarily cheaper than coated.

8.2 Matte/Silk or Glossy

The surface of the paper can also be calendered to obtain a higher sheen. A coated paper can be matte or glossy. Uncoated paper can also be calendered. A glossy paper gives a good reproduction of images and colors while text readability is poor because of distracting reflections. To achieve greater readability books with a lot of text are often printed on matte and/or uncoated paper. Matte coated textures have been developed, called matte silk. The texture is smooth, but non-reflective, which means that paper treated with this coating will produce prints with a combination of high image quality and readability.

8.3 Wood-free and Wood-pulp

This classification is mostly based on how the paper is produced and is increasingly of lesser importance in modern graphic print production. Wood-pulp paper has a shorter life span, poorer surface strength and is not very white, but it does have higher opacity and bulk. Wood-pulp papers are generally less expensive than wood-free papers. The terms wood-free and wood-pulp are primarily derived from customs regulations that assign different tariffs to the different types of paper. Different countries have different standards for what is considered wood-free and wood-pulp respectively, with the result that this distinction is not as commonly used today.

8.4 Paper or Cardboard

Cardboard is a stiff paper product. Paper manufacturer usually define cardboard as a paper with a weight greater than 80 lbs. If a paper exists both in a lighter paper weight and in heavier cardboard weight, the cardboard version is called fine cardboard. This type of cardboard is produced in the same way as paper.

Cardboard produced in special cardboard machines is called graphic cardboard. There are two types of graphic cardboard: multi-layered board and solid board. Multi-layered board is made up of several layers of different types of pulp. Solid board is also made up of many layers, but all the layers are the same type of pulp.

8.5 Plastics and Foils

Sometimes you may want to print on plastic or foil instead of paper. Plastic is chemically stable, insensitive to moisture and temperature, strong and flexible, easy to work with, and inexpensive. For these reasons plastic has, in recent years, had a breakthrough as a printing material, primarily in the packaging industry.

There are two kinds of plastic: thermal plastic and hard plastic. Thermal plastic is solid at room temperature but soften when heated and becomes malleable, returning to its original state when cooled. Thermal plastics can easily be applied to different surfaces, for example to packages that are shrink-wrapped. Hard plastics on the other hand are sensitive to heating. They melt and lose their shape when exposed to too high temperatures. Hard plastic are often used for different sorts of containers.

The most important difference in the context of printing between paper and plastic is that paper is porous, and therefore an absorbent material. This means that the printing ink seeps into the paper. When you print on plastic the printing ink lies on top of the plastic. In practice this means that it takes longer for the ink to dry. It is also difficult to print several colors on top of each other, and you have a greater risk of smearing.

When you print on plastic you have to therefore use different printing inks from what you would use on paper. Printing on plastic also places certain demands on the binder in the printing ink so that the ink will adhere properly to the surface. It is also important that the ink not contain solvents that can corrode that plastic. Different plastics can have different chemical properties that make it difficult to standardize a printing ink for plastic.

RAG PAPER
If at least 25% of the paper pulp is made up of cotton fibers, the resulting paper is called rag paper. Tag paper is characterized by durability and a comfortable smoothness, (it resembles fabric a bit), which it gets from the cotton fibers. Rag paper is appropriate for certain types of special prints. Foiling, for example, is one type of print often done on rag paper.

PRINTING ON TRANSPARENT PLASTIC
Since transparent plastic cannot reflect light, it is important to place white printing ink, a white coating, under the décor that is to be printed.

OXIDATION DRYING
When you print on plastic and foil, the printing ink lies on the surface of the material. For this reason you have to use printing ink that dries via oxidation, a chemical reaction that occurs when the ink comes in contact with oxygen. This process takes significantly longer than when you print with ordinary ink on paper. It can take three days before the ink has dried thoroughly.

8.6 **Paper Format**

The most usual paper formats in Europe are based on a series of standard formats where the A-format, A0, A1, A2, A3, A4 and so on, are the most usual. In the A-formats the relationship of the length of the page to the width is 1:√2 (the square root of 2 is approximately 1.414.) This means that a page that is 210 millimeters wide would be 210 × 1.414, or 297 millimeters long. The A-formats

A IN E IN C IN B
A paper in the A-format fits into an envelope in the E-format, which fits into a C-envelope, which fits into a B-envelope.

CUTTING CHARTS

This chart shows how many pages one can expect to get from some standard U.S. paper sizes.

TRIMMED PAGE SIZE (INCHES)	NUMBER OF PRINTED PAGES	NUMBER FROM SHEET	STANDARD PAPER SIZE (INCHES)
4 × 9	4	12	25 × 38
	8	12	38 × 50
	12	4	25 × 38
	16	6	38 × 50
	24	2	25 × 38
4 1/4 × 5 3/8	4	32	35 × 45
	8	16	35 × 45
	16	8	35 × 45
	32	4	35 × 45
4 1/2 × 6	4	16	25 × 38
	8	8	25 × 38
	16	4	25 × 38
	32	2	25 × 38
5 1/2 × 8 1/2	4	16	35 × 45
	8	8	35 × 45
	16	4	35 × 45
	32	2	35 × 45
6 × 9	4	8	25 × 38
	8	4	25 × 38
	16	2	25 × 38
	32	2	38 × 50
8 1/2 × 11	4	4	23 × 35
	8	2	23 × 35
	16	2	35 × 45
9 × 12	4	4	25 × 38
	8	2	25 × 38
	16	2	38 × 50

PAPER FORMATS

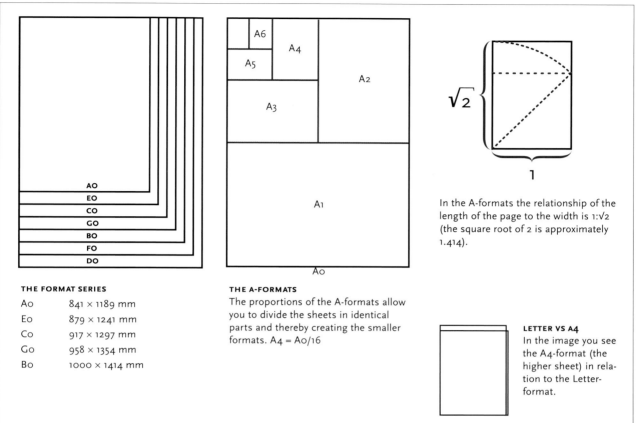

THE FORMAT SERIES

A0	841 × 1189 mm
E0	879 × 1241 mm
C0	917 × 1297 mm
G0	958 × 1354 mm
B0	1000 × 1414 mm

THE A-FORMATS
The proportions of the A-formats allow you to divide the sheets in identical parts and thereby creating the smaller formats. A4 = A0/16

In the A-formats the relationship of the length of the page to the width is 1:√2 (the square root of 2 is approximately 1.414).

LETTER VS A4
In the image you see the A4-format (the higher sheet) in relation to the Letter-format.

AMERICAN AND EUROPEAN PAPER FORMATS

The American and European paper formats differ. In the United States they are based on basis weights.

EUROPE	SIZE (MM)	SIZE (INCH)
A0	841 × 1189	33 $1/8$ × 46 $3/4$
A1	594 × 841	23 $3/8$ × 33 $1/8$
A2	420 × 594	16 $1/2$ × 23 $3/8$
A3	297 × 420	11 $3/4$ × 16 $1/2$
A4	210 × 297	8 $1/4$ × 11 $3/4$
A5	148 × 210	5 $7/8$ × 8 $1/4$

USA	SIZE (INCH)	SIZE (MM)
Letter	8 $1/2$ × 11	216 × 279
Ledger, Tabloid	11 × 17	279 × 432
Demy	17$1/2$ × 22$1/2$	445 × 572
19 × 25	19 × 25	483 × 635
23 × 35	23 × 35	584 × 889
25 × 38	25 × 38	635 × 965

Basis weights for standard papers.

BOOK 25″×38″	BOND 17″×22″	COVER 20″×26″	GRAMMAGE (G/M²)
30#	12#	16#	44
40#	16#	22#	59
45#	18#	25#	67
50#	20#	27#	74
60#	24#	33#	89
70#	28#	38#	104
80#	31#	44#	118
90#	35#	49#	133
100#	39#	55#	148
120#	47#	66#	178
33#	13#	18#	49
41#	16#	22#	61
51#	20#	28#	75
61#	24#	33#	90
71#	28#	39#	105
81#	32#	45#	120
91#	36#	50#	135
102#	40#	66#	158
91#	36#	50#	135
110#	43#	60#	163
119#	47#	65#	176
146#	58#	80#	216
164#	66#	90#	243
183#	72#	100#	271

are based on A0, which has a surface of 1 square meter and a width-to-length ratio of 1:√2. For example, when you divide an A0 sheet in half across the long side, you get two A1-sheets, each with a surface area of half a square meter and the same width-to-length ratio.

In the United States stock paper sies are much less standardized and are based on a combination of the size of the presses most commonly used and the most popular trim sizes for books, for example, Bond, Book Text and Cover. There are also a number of other formats, for example, Tabloid, Broadsheet, Berlin Format, Magazine Format and Catalogue Format. In the office environment Letter is a normal format.

8.7 Basis/Substance Weight

A paper's weight is called basis weight and in the U.S. is given in pounds per ream (500 sheets) calculated on the basis size for a specific grade of paper. For example, a 60 pound (#60) book paper is a paper for which 500 sheets at the basis size of 25″ × 38″ weighs 60 pounds.

This measure is often used a little sloppily to indicate the paper's thickness. A paper's weight in grams per square meter [g/m²] is called grammage substance, or gsm, and is the most common measure of a paper's weight outside of the United States. When talking about an 80-gram paper you are referring to a paper that weighs 80 grams per square meter. So, what does an 80-gram A4-sheet weigh? As explained above, you get 16 pieces of A4 for from a single A0-sheet. He A0 sheet is 1 square meter. This means that the A4-sheet weighs 80 g divided by 16, or 5 grams. Normal photocopying paper usually weighs 80g/m², newsprint 45g/m² and a standard offset printing paper between 80 and 150 g/m². Paper with a greater weight than 170 g/m² is called cardboard. Paper with a greater weight than 400 g/m² is called board.

8.8 Density and Bulk

Density describes a paper's compactness and is defined by the relationship between the thickness of the paper and its weight [g/m³]. A paper with a low density is therefore light and thick (porous), while a paper with high density is heavy and thin (more compact).

BASIS WEIGHT TO GRAMMAGE
Formula to convert basis weight to grammage:

$$\frac{\text{Basis Weight} \times 1406,5}{\text{Basis Size}} = \text{g/m}^2$$

BULK
A paper with high bulk is pourous while a paper with low bulk is compact. If you have two paper types with the same surface weight but different bulk, the one with the higher bulk will feel stiffer. Sometimes you have to reduce the surface weight, for example to lower the distribution cost. Then it is common to choose a paper with a higher bulk so that the printed product won't feel "flimsy".

Bulk is the same thing as density, although the reverse. It describes the relationship between the thickness of the paper and its weight, and is expressed in the U.S. as pages per inch (ppi). This may range from 200 to over 1,000 ppi, depending on the type of paper, its basis weight and finish. Bulk is a measure of how voluminous a paper is. Paper with a low ppi is thin, heavy and compact, whereas paper with a high ppi is lightweight, thick and porous.

When using glue binding, paper with a higher bulk is preferred to that with a low bulk. In order to ensure a strong binding, the glue has to penetrate into the paper, which is easier with a porous, high-bulk stock. Papers with a high bulk generally feel stiffer and thicker than low-bulk papers with the same weight.

8.9 Surface Smoothness and Formation

Surface smoothness is a description of the surface characteristics of the paper. Paper with high surface smoothness has a fine surface, while paper with low surface smoothness has a rough surface. You could compare it to a sandpaper being with coarse or fine.

Formation has to do with how evenly the paper pulp is distributed during paper production. If you hold up a piece of paper to a light source and it looks even- i.e. without "clouds" – the paper is considered to have a good formation. Good formation is important for good print quality, especially with offset printing, because of the paper's absorption of the oil component of the ink [*see Printing 9.5.6*]. Offset printing on a paper with a poor formation manifests blotchiness in the color, especially in flat even tint areas.

8.10 Brightness and Whiteness

A paper's brightness describes how much light is reflected by its surface. Whiteness refers to how large a part of the white light that falls on the paper is reflected by its surface. The paper's brightness is important in order to print text and images with high contrast. You can increase the brightness of paper during its manufacture by bleaching it and adding special colors and pigments. The technical term for brightness is luminance or Y-value. Brightness is measured by how much light a paper reflects from a special lamp with a wavelength of 457 Nanometers. Whiteness is measured in CIELAB.

8.11 Opacity

Opacity means non-transparency and is a measure of how much light penetrates the paper. The opacity depends on how well light is spread and absorbed by the paper. You can say that it describe how little print is seen through the paper it is printed on. A paper that is 100% opaque is completely non-transparent. Paper with high opacity is, in other words, less transparent, and paper with low opacity more transparent. An example of a paper with low opacity is wax paper. High opacity is often preferred for printed matter because you don't want text and images showing through both sides of a page.

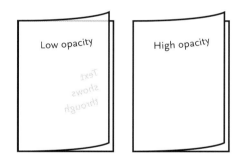

LOW VS HIGH OPACITY
In practice, opacity is a measurement of how little the printed image from one side of a paper show through to the other side. Paper with high opacity is, in other words, less transparant and paper with low opacity more transparent.

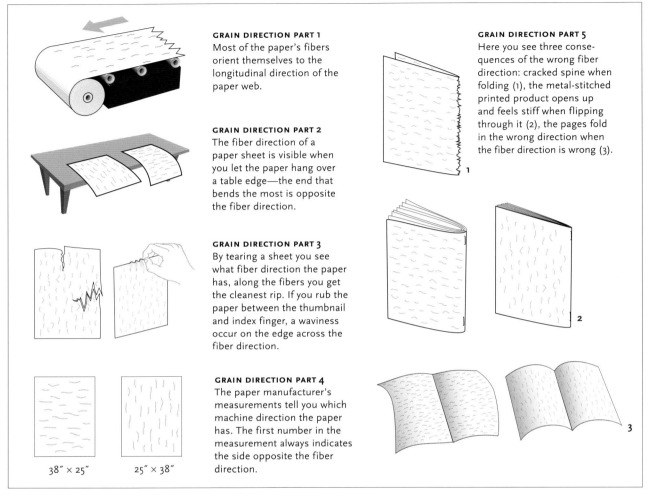

GRAIN DIRECTION PART 1
Most of the paper's fibers orient themselves to the longitudinal direction of the paper web.

GRAIN DIRECTION PART 2
The fiber direction of a paper sheet is visible when you let the paper hang over a table edge—the end that bends the most is opposite the fiber direction.

GRAIN DIRECTION PART 3
By tearing a sheet you see what fiber direction the paper has, along the fibers you get the cleanest rip. If you rub the paper between the thumbnail and index finger, a waviness occur on the edge across the fiber direction.

GRAIN DIRECTION PART 4
The paper manufacturer's measurements tell you which machine direction the paper has. The first number in the measurement always indicates the side opposite the fiber direction.

38″ × 25″   25″ × 38″

GRAIN DIRECTION PART 5
Here you see three consequences of the wrong fiber direction: cracked spine when folding (1), the metal-stitched printed product opens up and feels stiff when flipping through it (2), the pages fold in the wrong direction when the fiber direction is wrong (3).

1

2

3

When printing ink is applied to paper its oil component sinks into the paper, allowing the pigment to stick to the surface of the paper [*see Printing 9.5.6*]. Similar to a grease stain on paper, this oil can negatively affect the opacity and the pigment can show through to the other side. This primarily applies to newsprint where the oil component of the ink is relatively high. Therefore in selecting a paper it is important to remember that the opacity of printed paper is lower than that of unprinted paper.

8.12 Grain Direction

When the paper is manufactured, most of its fibers orient themselves to the longitudinal direction of the paper web. This direction is usually referred to as the paper's grain direction. Paper is approximately twice as stiff across the grain direction as along it, and therefore it is easier for paper to bend in that direction. You can take advantage of this trait when trying to figure out the grain direction of a particular piece of paper. Let the paper hang over a table edge – the end that bends the most is opposite the machine direction. You can also pinch along the machine direction. Machine direction is important in certain printing methods. If it is difficult for the paper to bend and follow the intended path through the printing press, there is more of a chance that problems will occur when running the press. In this case, you could want to load the paper so that it bends easily, with the grain direction opposite the printing direction. It is also important to have the correct grain direction when folding paper. If you fold opposite the grain direction, the fibers are broken down and it looks as if the paper is cracking. Folding paper along the grain direction will give you a fine, smooth crease instead. The paper manufacturer's measurements tell you which grain direction the paper has. The first number in the measurement always indicates the side opposite the grain direction. Consequently, a paper with the measurement 25″ × 38″ has a grain direction opposite its short side. Conversely, a paper with the measurement 38″ × 25″ has the grain direction opposite its long side.

8.13 Dimensional Stability

Because paper has a fiber direction and the fibers have particular dimensional characteristics, the paper takes on these characteristics. Wet paper fibers shrink and bond less lengthwise as they dry. When paper fibers shrink simultaneously while drying, the paper web tightens in the machines direction and causes tension in the paper structure. The tension is higher in the fiber direction. Because the fibers' dimensional change is higher in the opposite direction and because there are no particular tensions across the paper web, the paper is much more inclined to change dimension opposite the fiber direction. Thus the paper changes asymmetrically when exposed to variations in humidity. This phenomenon means that you always get misregistrations in different directions in wet offset printing.

However, a paper with good dimensional stability maintains its shape comparatively well throughout the entire print run and thereby reduces the risk of misregistration.

8.14 Strength

Paper can be strong in different ways. There are tensile strength, tearing strength, bursting strength, surface strength and Z-strength. For the printing process it is important to have a paper with high tensile and tearing strengths so the paper does not give way in the middle of printing. Surface strength measures the paper's strength perpendicular to its surface, and is important so that the surface does not get damaged during printing, resulting in burls. Bursting strength is important for paper bags and various kinds of packaging. Z-strength is the

- What "feel" do you want to communicate with the printed product?
- What is the expected life span?
- How much can it cost?
- What is more important, the readability of the text or image quality?
- Which screen frequency and tonal range should it have?
- Which printing method should be used?
- How should the printed product be off press processed?
- How should it be distributed?
- How important is the environmental impact for the buyer?

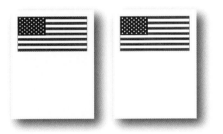

PRINTING ON COLORED PAPER
When you print on colored paper, the images have to be adjusted according to the color of the paper. In some cases it's impossible to avoid problems.

PAPER PRICES DIFFER

- Paper sheets are more expensive than paper on a roll.
- Glossy papers are more expensive than matte or silk papers.
- Wood-free paper is more expensive than wood-pulp paper.
- Colored paper is more expensive than white.
- Paper with cotton fibers, rag paper, is more expensive than papers without.

integral strength of the paper and describes how well the paper holds together, which is important, for example, in many uses of cardboard.

8.15 Age Resistant and Archive Paper

A paper's age resistance is principally its tendency to withstand yellowing or fading and its ability to retain its strength over time. Paper's age resistance is affected by what type of pulp it is made of and what ingredients it contains. All paper ages since the fibers do break down. This process can be prolonged by manufacturing the paper a neutral PH value, and by using calcium carbonate as filler. The paper's longevity is affected also by how it is handled, and the temperatures, moisture and light it is exposed to.

Paper made from mechanical pulp, (wood-pulp), yellows relatively faster than paper made from chemical pulp, (wood-free), which stays relatively unaffected for a long time. An example of paper with low age resistance is newsprint, which is made from mechanical pulp and therefore yellows rapidly. Wood-free paper keeps its color better than wood-pulp paper.

There is an international standard for age resistant paper (ISO 9706) to indicate paper's physical durability over time. This kind of paper is used, for example, for different records and documents that are to be archived read in several hundred years. Notice that this standard only applies to the paper's physical longevity, not its tendency to yellow or its ability to retain its original color.

For extreme uses there is also archive paper. It is very durable and can be folded at least 150 times on the weakest grain direction. Archive paper contains cotton or linen fibers as well. These fibers are longer and stronger than ordinary wood fibers that are used in traditional paper production.

8.16 Choosing a Paper

There are hundreds of different grades of paper in a number of different varieties. The choice of paper affects the feel of the printed product and its appearance and can be decisive for the printed product's communicative message, but there are also other things it is important to consider: What will the printed product be used for and what is its intended lifespan? How much should it cost? Which will have priority: text or images? What print technique and type of finishing will be used? How will it be distributed? How will it affect the environment? Does the printing technique make any specific requirements? All these aspects influence the choice of paper in different ways.

8.16.1 The Feel and Appearance of the Printed Product

The choice of the paper is very important in creating the feel you want your printed product to have. Your printed product has an intended purpose – for example, you want to sell something or give information or create a profile. The paper can have a large influence on what a printed product communicates "between the lines." When you go to choose a paper it might be good to look at other printed material that has been done. The quality of the paper is usually stated in the printed product's colophon, the general information about the printing house and other facts which are usually found at the beginning or the end of a printed product. You can also contact the paper distributors and ask them for paper samples or a paper dummy, (for printed products with many pages).

The feel and the appearance are affected first off by three things: the surface of the paper, the color and the thickness. Regarding the surface, a distinction is commonly made between coated and uncoated paper, as well as whether the finish is matte or glossy. Coated paper can be further divided into additional categories depending on the amount of coating it has: lightly coated, medium coated or highly coated. Highly coated paper is also sometimes called art paper. Remember that the surface of the paper influences its thickness, its stiffness and opacity (how non-transparent a paper is.) Coated, glossy paper is, as a rule, thinner and less stiff and has lower opacity than uncoated paper with the same basis weight. So with glossy paper you can go up in basis weight and in this way achieve a higher opacity and stiffness.

There are many colored papers to choose between as well as other special papers that are transparent, patterned, etc. Colored papers are in general somewhat more expensive, but with smaller runs it seldom makes a major difference in the total printing cost. When you choose a colored paper it is important to think how the colors and images that will be eventually printed on the paper will be affected by this color. Colored paper is usually uncoated.

The thickness of the paper influences to a large degree how it feels to hold and leaf through the finished printed product. When we talk about thickness it is important to keep in mind that two different qualities of paper with the same basis weight can be of different thicknesses. Thickness is related to how porous or voluminous the paper is; this is usually referred to as the paper's bulk. If you have two papers of the same quality the thickness is in direct relation to their basis weight, that is a paper with a higher basis weight is thicker than a paper with a lower basis weight. The basis weight also affects the stiffness of the paper. The stiffness of the paper is usually said to increase three times as much as an increase in basis weight. If you choose a basis weight twice as heavy, the paper will be six times as stiff. When you choose between glossy and matte finish the thickness is also affected. Glossy paper has been compressed between rollers during the calendering process and thus is thinner and not as stiff as matte paper. With a paper dummy you get the best idea of how the finished printed product will turn out and how it will feel to leaf through it. A dummy is also good for seeing how thick the printed product will be. Dummies can be ordered from paper manufacturers.

8.16.2 The Life Span and Uses of the Printed Product
The life span of the printed product is directly related to its intended uses and the choice of paper. As the paper ages its characteristics will change. What happens first is that paper yellows with age and it loses strength. A typical example is newsprint, which doesn't take long before it yellows, and it tears easily when it gets old. This doesn't matter so much with a daily newspaper; it is a perishable good, but in other circumstances aging paper can be disastrous. As a rule of thumb, papers made from wood pulp are more sensitive to aging

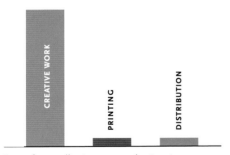

Costs for small print runs and print size.

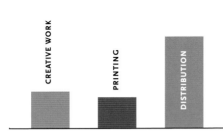

Costs for large print runs and print size.

PRICE PER UNIT
The costs for a printed product are distributed differently depending on the print run. With a small print run, the cost for creative work, for example image, text and graphic design, greatly affects the total cost while distribution costs dominate large print runs.

PAPER STOCK
It is usually worthwhile to use the papers the printing house normally uses and has handy in stock.

than wood-free ones. In the same way it is also the case that uncoated paper is more sensitive to aging than coated.

If it is important for the printed product to last a long time there are two different kinds of paper to choose between: age resistant and archive. For age resistant paper there is an international standard called ISO 9706. This type of paper will normally last several hundred years without its characteristics being noticeably altered However you still have to consider how the papers longevity will be influenced by how it is handled and how much it will be exposed to sunlight. Archive paper has a higher strength than age resistant paper since cotton fibers are added to it.

There are also papers that are specially adapted for specific purposes. For handbooks that are used daily in industrial environments there is extra strong paper. Paper containing linen works well if you need a paper that is dirt resistant. There is also moisture resistant paper that is well suited for outdoor use, such as for books or posters. Along with these there is paper that is difficult to tear, useful for example in envelopes that contain sensitive material.

8.16.3 Costs and Print Runs

When choosing paper you should keep in mind the aspect of cost. A basic rule is that the larger the print run the greater the share paper cost will take up in total production cost. With larger runs, for example 50,000 copies or more, a relatively small difference in price between two qualities of paper can still amount to a large difference in the total cost of production. With small runs up to a few thousand copies, smaller differences in price can still be considered insignificant. The fact is that the most usual qualities of paper do not vary more than fifteen percent from each other in price. However, the price differential between some specialty papers can be significantly.

If another basis weight of a certain paper quality is chosen, the price is generally influenced proportionally to the change in basis weight. If the basis weight is halved, then the paper will cost approximately half as much. Hence with larger runs, a paper with low basis weight but with high bulk, that is thick and porous, is often chosen. The paper will be cheaper but will still feel as thick as paper with a higher basis weight.

When you talk about print runs, it is also important to figure the size of the printed product: that is the number of pages. Even the format of the printed product will affect paper consumption. Certain unusual formats make it difficult to utilize the printed sheet optimally so much of the paper goes to waste. Small changes in format can therefore make a big difference in paper consumption. The printing house can give advice regarding choice of format.

You usually buy paper from the printer you engage. Therefore it is important to consider the price of the paper is also affected by the agreement the printer has with the different paper distributors and which quantity the printing house buys of a certain paper. The price of the same paper can for this reason vary between different printing houses. If you want to know the price difference between different papers you can ask the printer to calculate different paper alternatives.

8.16.4 Readablity vs. Image Quality

For high quality images a bright white, coated paper works best, preferably with a glossy finish. The whiteness and gloss of the paper give a high contrast between the printing ink and the paper and make the colors and tonal variations even clearer and more distinct. The coated surface allows a more even transfer of ink in the printing press and you can use a lot of printing ink to further increase the contrast between the ink and the paper. With coated paper you get an even higher resolution since it allows printing with a high screen frequency.

However, when it comes to printed products in which text information is more important you have to abandon this ideal. Too much contrast between the paper and the printed text can cause eyestrain for the reader. Therefore, a slightly yellow-toned paper is generally recommended for printed products with a lot of text. The paper should also be matte or even uncoated in order to avoid distracting reflections. The eye's ability to comprehend text can be up to eighty percent better with an uncoated paper as compared to a coated one. Textbooks are an example of a type of product usually printed on uncoated, yellow-toned papers. This is when you are talking about papers with high readability. It is important to choose a paper with high opacity for printed matter so the text and images on the back of the page don't show through and distract. Uncoated paper most often has a high enough opacity. Coated and glossy paper with high whiteness and low basis weight can lead to problems with opacity. Be sure and choose a paper with a high basis weight.

If images and text are equally important, you can compromise with a coated matte paper that combines the most important characteristics for good image and text reproduction. If you want you can even have the printing house put on a partial varnish for the images to give them a higher gloss and to get better image quality. Another way is to actually choose two different qualities of paper for images and text in the same printed product. This requires however that you create a layout with text and images on separate pages. In old books you can often see this arrangement. That was because they used to print pages of text and pages of images on different printing presses.

You can also attain high image quality on uncoated paper. This however requires more experience and more precise adjustments of the printer for the images. You must also take greater care in subject matter. Lighter images are considerably easier to reproduce with a high quality than dark images. Pictures with a lot of detail, especially in the darker areas, are also very hard to reproduce. When you print on uncoated paper it is also difficult to achieve a precise reproduction of the original as far as colors, contrast, sharpness and resolution go. This doesn't mean that you will have to experience the images as inferior; it just means that you won't have to strive to recreate an exact original. Many systems for preliminary proof runs have problems using uncoated paper, making it harder to do quality controls.

Uncoated grades of paper call for greater dot enlargement in printing and with that lower contrast in the images. This is something you have to consider when you are preparing images for printing. Often so-called achromatic repro is used too, which diminishes the total ink layer in the images and therefore increases the contrast when printing on uncoated paper. As opposed to a coated paper, you will

READABILITY
A text printed on a glossy paper (left) might be difficult to read because the light is reflected. On a matte paper the light spreads out more and provides a more pleasant reading for the eye. A yellowish or greyish paper provides even better readability.

RECOMMENDED SCREEN FREQUENCIES

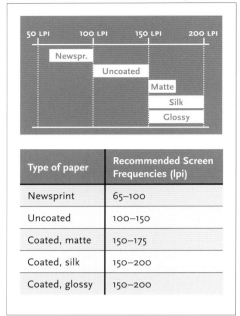

Type of paper	Recommended Screen Frequencies (lpi)
Newsprint	65–100
Uncoated	100–150
Coated, matte	150–175
Coated, silk	150–200
Coated, glossy	150–200

also have to print with a lower screen frequency, which means that the images will have a lower resolution. One alternative can be to ask the printing house to use a stochastic screen, which gives a significantly better resolution than a traditional screen with low screen frequency. Paper distributors have recommendations for different screen frequencies for their various grades of paper.

If you print images on colored paper or a paper with a low whiteness, be aware that it is difficult to compensate for the color of the paper in the printing process, and you will often get a lesser quality image as a result. Also keep in mind that colored text and illustrations can come out wrong when printed on colored paper.

8.16.5 Printing Technique

Some printing methods require that the paper used have a certain machine direction in order to ensure smooth operation of the printing press. Different printing methods also have limitations as to the thickness and sheet size of the paper. Offset printing, for example, requires a paper with a high surface bonding strength. The viscous printing ink used in wet offset printing has a tendency to rip the paper fibers and, at the same time, the water used in the process weakens the paper. In dry offset, there is no water to weaken the paper but the ink has a higher viscosity [*see Printing 9.5.2*]. Gravure printing, on the other hand, requires that the paper have a very smooth surface to avoid problems with the application of the ink.

Printers who print with digital printing presses will recommend papers based on their own proof runs, and you should contact them for information before you begin production. Xerography techniques (laser printer outputs or copying) work best with a slightly uneven paper surface, and uncoated paper is often recommended. This is because the toner powder used in these processes has difficulty adhering to coated paper. You cannot use regular coated offset paper in a laser printer, but paper manufacturers have developed special paper with a coated feel just for xerography machines. In turn, these special papers are ot particularly appropriate for offset printing. This type of paper does not absorb

WEIGHT STATED IN GRAMMAGE FOR A PRINTED PRODUCT IN A4 FORMAT

	NUMBER OF PAGES (2 PAGES=1 SHEET)							
g/m²	2	4	6	8	12	16	24	32
70	4,38	8,75	13,13	17,50	26,25	35,00	52,50	70,00
80	5,00	10,00	15,00	20,00	30,00	40,00	60,00	80,00
90	5,63	11,25	16,88	22,50	33,75	45,00	67,50	90,00
100	6,25	12,50	18,75	25,00	37,50	50,00	75,00	100,00
115	7,19	14,38	21,56	28,75	43,13	57,50	86,25	115,00
130	8,13	16,25	24,38	32,50	48,75	65,00	97,50	130,00
150	9,38	18,75	28,13	37,50	56,25	75,00	112,50	150,00

GRAMMAGE SUBSTANCE

the oil component of the offset printing inks and the pigment has difficulty adhering to the paper surface as a result [*see Printing 9.5.6*].

8.16.6 Finishing and Binding of the Printed Product

Folding is affected by the kind of paper. You have to remember to fold the paper in the direction of the grain to ensure a smooth fold. If you fold against the grain, the fibers will break and it will look as if the surface of the paper is cracked. If the grain direction has ended up going the wrong way, you can score the paper before folding to minimize fiber breakage [*see Finishing and Binding 10.11*]. Wrong grain direction can cause adhesion problems in gluing as well [*see Finishing and Binding 10.14 and 10.15*].

Thick or stiff papers always have to be scored before they can be folded. Scoring means that the fibers are pressed together along a line where the fold will be. Scoring acts like a hinge and facilitates folding. After the paper is scored the fibers are easily displaced when folded and do not resist bending. Coated paper over 150g/m2 and uncoated over 200g/m² should be scored before folding.

If you are using the glue binding technique when binding your printed product you can have problems with coated and glossy paper. The pages can have a tendency to loosen from the spine. The reason is coated paper doesn't absorb the glue as well as uncoated paper. The strength of the binding is greater the higher the bulk of the paper, that is the thicker and more porous it is. Thicker paper simply has a larger surface area for the adhesive, and the paper's porous nature makes it easier for the adhesive to penetrate the paper, creating a deeper, sturdier bond. If you use coated paper you should therefore use paper with a higher basis weight or consider thread stitching your printed product. Paperbacks are a typical example of a printed product where the combination of uncoated paper and a glued binding work well [*see Finishing and Binding 10.14*].

If you want to achieve a very high gloss with glazing, you use coated paper. Glazing uncoated paper does not create any sheen, yet it does provide good protection against dust and dirt.

Laminating uneven paper surfaces and uncoated papers is not advisable. The result will be a dirty gray and the lamination may have trouble adhering to the paper. Choose instead coated and/or glossy finishes.

8.16.7 Distribution and Weight

If you are creating a printed product that is to be distributed via postal mail, it's important to keep postage rates in mind when choosing paper. Selecting paper with a lower weight might help you avoid a lower postage rate and save you a lot of money. It is also important to think along these lines if you are going to use envelopes or some other type of packaging. It's always good to make sure the envelope is the right size. Odd sized envelopes outside of the standard format can take a long time to be delivered.

8.17 Paper and the Environment

According to the Worldwatch Institute, the use of wood over the last half century has more than doubled, and the consumption of paper has increased nearly

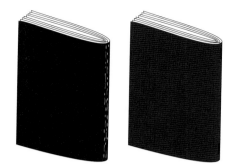

RISK FOR CRACKS
When folding a coated, printed paper across the spine, it easily cracks. To avoid the problem, you either need to score the paper before folding or choose an uncoated paper. Uncoated paper types are not as sensitive to cracking.

six-fold. "The less than one-fifth of the world's population who live in Europe, the U.S., and Japan, consume over one-half of the world's timber, and more than two-thirds of its paper. In the next fifteen years, global demand for paper is expected to grow by half again." This contributes to an expanding economy, but the ecosystem on which it depends is taxed. The signs of stress are evident in shrinking forests, falling water tables, eroding soils, rising CO_2 levels, rising temperatures, and disappearing plant and animal species.

8.17.2 Recycled

Just because a paper is recycled doesn't mean that it's the most environmentally preferable. Paper mills have been recycling their own waste and trimmings from envelope converters for many years. This is referred to as *post-industrial waste*.

Alternative solutions: To truly close the loop, paper must first go to the consumer, be put in the recycling system, and then processed back into pulp for papermaking. This recycled material is *post-consumer waste*.

In addition to relieving solid waste problems, specifying the highest post-consumer recycled paper (or tree-free alternatives) for every job is probably the most significant act a graphic design studio can make in the battle against global warming. Forests "eat" and store carbon dioxide (a greenhouse gas), thus removing it from the atmosphere where it can cause harm.

Today there are so many options that specifying 100% recycled paper with at least 30% post-consumer waste (PCW) should be the minimum standard. Remember that the higher PCW content you use, the more you are helping to build an environmentally based economy.

8.17.3 Chlorine-free

Chlorine bleaching is probably the single most devastating part in the production of paper. Chlorine is used to dissolve wood lignin (the sticky material that holds cellulose fibers together) and to bleach the fibers white. The chemical byproducts that result from the interaction of the chlorine, lignin and cellulose fibers are some of the most toxic substances ever created. Studies have conclusively found a strong link between the production of chlorine-bleached paper products and dioxins, carcinogens capable of causing cancer, reproductive disorders, deformities and developmental problems in children, and impaired immune systems. Because they don't break down, dioxins persist in our air, water and soil, contaminate the food chain, and accumulate in the bodies of wildlife and humans.

Alternative solutions: To fully understand chlorine-free papers in detail, it is important first to define terms.

- *Totally chlorine free* (TCF) is paper made with 100% virgin wood fibers manufactured without adding any chlorine or chlorine derivatives. No harmful dioxins, furans, or other organochlorines result, so collection and disposal of these toxic compounds is unnecessary. If a paper is TCF, it is a virgin grade and contains no post-consumer waste.

- *Processed chlorine-free recycled* (PCF) paper is also made without adding chlorine or chlorine derivatives. Because paper recovered from the solid waste stream and used in making recycled paper may have been chlorine bleached in its first life, the end product cannot be guaranteed totally chlorine-free.

- *Elemental chlorine free* (ECF) paper is manufactured without using elemental chlorine gas as a whitening agent. These papers are typically processed with chlorine dioxide or other chlorine compounds, which some paper makers believe to be less harmful to the environment than elemental chlorine gas. Although lower levels of chlorinated dioxins and furans are found in the mill's effluent and other related chlorinated compounds are reduced, they are not eliminated. Also, chlorine dioxide bleaching methods use 20 times more water and energy than chlorine-free processes.

- *Non-deinked post consumer waste* is recycled waste paper that has not gone through the bleaching process the second time around. Chemicals used in the papermaking process are minimized since the inks are left in the slurry, resulting in a delicate peppered appearance in the final sheet.

- *Oxygen delignification and ozone bleaching* are totally chlorine-free processes used to separate lignin from wood fibers, and to bleach and whiten pulp. Mills using oxygen or ozone bleaching can send the effluent to a recovery system, where the organic material is burned to produce energy and metals and minerals are filtered out, thus closing the loop.

  Hydrogen peroxide, which bleaches by oxygenating, is the preferred agent because no harmful byproducts result from its use. This process has been the bleaching agent of choice for newsprint and groundwood. Although stigmatized a decade ago for producing dull paper, the brightness of the pulp needed for fine printing and writing papers has and continues to improve.

8.17.4 Alternative (non-wood) fibers

While recycled stocks help alleviate solid waste problems, deinking post-consumer paper waste still involves using harsh chemicals and results in by-products of toxic sludge. Although recycled papers contain an increasing percentage of post-consumer content, most are supplemented with virgin wood pulp to enhance tensile strength. The sources: forests (some old growth) and tree farms.

Estimates indicate that as much as half of the 12 billion acres of forests that once covered the earth's surface have already been destroyed. In the last 35 years, wood consumption has doubled, and paper use has more than tripled. Trees do produce consistent fibers, but they take a long time to grow, require a large amount of bleaching and chemical processing, and present industrial harvesting methods that are far from environmentally sustainable.

alternative solutions: Recognizing the urgent need to conserve and preserve the world's forests, a new industry is developing around "tree-free" papers. These are made from fast-growing fiber crops such as kenaf and hemp; agricultural wastes, such as vegetables, corn and cereal straw, coffee grounds, and banana stalks; industrial wastes, such as recycled currency, denim scraps, cotton textile rags and factory trimmings; and flax, bagasse, bamboo, and seaweed.

Of these, kenaf is one of the most promising. A member of the hibiscus family, it shoots from seed to 15 feet high in just five months. An acre of kenaf can yield up to 11 tons of usable fiber per year. An acre of forest produces only 4–5 tons of usable fiber in 20–30 years. The kenaf fiber has better strength and performance than that of wood, and because it has a lower lignin content, it requires fewer chemicals and less energy to process. A vigorous plant, kenaf requires a minimum of fertilizers, pesticides and water compared to conventional row crops. Large-scale farming uses chemical fertilizers and pesticides that run off and pollute rivers, lakes, estuaries, oceans and underground water.

Once the backbone of American industry, hemp was "outlawed" in 1935, a move backed by special interest groups such as DuPont and the Hearst Corporations in order to capitalize on their own synthetic and wood-based fiber markets. In spite of its environmental and industrial advantages, the industry still struggles with overcoming hemp's association with marijuana. Like kenaf, hemp (cannabis) is a hardy annual plant requiring minimal water, fertilizer or pesticides. It produces 3 to 6 tons of usable fiber per year. Unlike wood, it requires minimal chemical processing in the treatment of the fibers for papermaking. Because its manufacturing process can be acid-free, hemp paper offers outstanding archival potential (it is said to hold up for 1,500 years).

While many predictions show a diminishing wood supply, an incredible 2.5 billion tons of agricultural wastes around the world are available annually. Converted to 500 million tons of pulp, agricultural wastes such as wheat straw could yield enough fiber to supply 1.5 times the world's paper products consumption. The production of pulp from straw can be totally chlorine-free and acid-free, and the solid waste by-product can be safely used as feed or fertilizer.

Although printing on recycled paper was problematic in the 70s, the technology of producing these – and the newer alternative fiber – papers has greatly reduced or even eliminated the issues. Printers now find most recycled stocks print as well as their virgin competitors. Recycled papers, like virgin papers, will take ink differently and range in brightness and price as well, depending on the grade and the finish. Additionally, some recycled and alternative fiber papers come in rolls for web printing. Ask your printer or local paper distributor to help you with specifying the best environmental paper for your project.

The biggest drawback to many of these papers is availability. Because the market is not fully matured and a number of the manufacturers are small mills, distribution is usually limited to minimum quantities or the price is higher than their virgin counterparts. Still, the papers are worth the pursuit – and the additional cost, if any. Remember that when you specify these papers, you help build a market for them, and then it is only a matter of time before demand allows pricing to drop, and availability to become more widespread.

8.18 Handling of the Paper

Since paper is composed of cellulose fibers, it is a living, or rather an organic, material. This means that paper is sensitive to moisture and temperature changes, among other things, and that its characteristics can be altered because of its sensitivity. For this reason handling and storage of paper is important so that you can be certain that the paper will be able to be used as intended.

8.18.1 Paper and Moisture

When paper fibers are exposed to moisture they expand. When they are dry they shrink. They change mainly in width whereas their length basically remains the same. In practical terms this means that a sheet of paper changes most across the grain direction. You can count on the change in dimension being three times as great across the fiber direction as along it. The thickness of the fibers can change by up to thirty percent.

Large variations in moisture content lead to lasting damage to the paper which in turn leads to problems when it is used. Even minor changes in moisture content can lead to lasting changes in dimensions since paper that has gotten damp and then dried out again does not retake its original dimensions. This can sometimes lead to misregistration during printing. Paper with different surface treatments on the front and back is extra sensitive to moisture since the fibers will react differently. Many have surely experienced this when they have bought postcard that have been kept outside at seaside resorts. The moisture has caused the cards to bend.

8.18.2 Storage of Paper

When you store paper it is important that the air have the right humidity. The humidity is tied to temperature, so it is also important to check the temperature at the storage location. Humidity in the air is defined by how much water a cubic

THE FIBER CHANGES...
The thickness of the pribers can change up to three times at increased humidity.

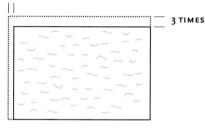

1 TIME

3 TIMES

... THUS ALSO THE SHEET
Because of the change in dimensions of the fiber when exposed to humidity, the paper sheet changes its dimensions. The change is three times as great across the fiber direction as along it.

PAPER AND HUMIDITY

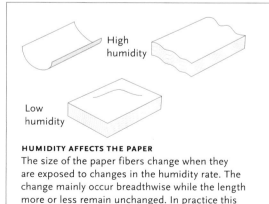

High humidity

Low humidity

HUMIDITY AFFECTS THE PAPER
The size of the paper fibers change when they are exposed to changes in the humidity rate. The change mainly occur breadthwise while the length more or less remain unchanged. In practice this involves a number of problems.

PROBLEMS WITH TOO LOW HUMIDITY

- The edges of the paper contract, the sheets bulge out in the middle.
- Changes in dimensions, unevenness, misregistration.
- Increased risk for dusting.
- More brittle paper, harder to score.
- Static electricity crates problems during laying on and cleaning away.

PROBLEMS WITH TOO HIGH HUMIDITY

- The edges of the paper expand, the sheets warp.
- Changes in dimensions, unevenness, misregistration.
- Extended drying time for printing ink.

A typical problem with paper occurs in connection with variations in temperature during transport, especially when it is cold outside. In this case it is important to give paper time to get acclimatized to room temperature before you begin to use it. Below you find the time to acclimatize for paper at various differences in indoor and outdoor temperatures.

- 10 hours at a difference of 10° Celsius
- 30 hours at a difference of 20° Celsius
- 55 hours at a difference of 30° Celsius
- 70 hours at a difference of 40° Celsius

PRINTABILITY
Printability is the sum of the paper's characteristics that creates the prerequisites for high print quality.

- The pores of the paper make it possible to absorb the printing ink properly and avoid smearing (the ink smears on the following sheet). At the same time, you don't want the print to go too deep and become visible from the backside of the paper.
- The surface of the paper shouldn't restrict the contact between the printing form, the printing surface in the printing press and the paper.
- The paper has to have an adequate surface strength to prevent paper fragments from tearing off, causing pickouts in the print. The pickouts are white spots in the print and are primarily visible in monochromatic tint areas.
- Porous paper absorbs the incoming light and provides high opacity.
- The brightness of the paper is important because it provides a high contrast between print and ink.

meter of air holds at a certain temperature. It is measured with a hygrometer. It is usually recommended that the relative humidity for offset paper be 50 percent at 20 degrees centigrade. With these conditions you minimize the risk of dimensional changes of the paper. Paper for photocopying, laser printing or digital printing is adapted to a lower relative humidity since it is exposed to high temperatures in the xerographic process. A relative humidity of 30 percent at 20 degrees centigrade is usually recommended. Only a few degrees shift in temperature can affect the condition of the paper, so it is important to have a controlled temperature and humidity during all times of year.

Another important factor is light. It affects the color of the paper, and the paper's aging process a well. For these reasons the paper should be stored protected from light.

8.18.3 Transport of Paper

When paper is transported it is also important to think about changes in humidity and temperature. A typical problem with paper occurs in connection with variations in temperature during transport, especially when it is cold outside. In this case it is important to give paper time to get acclimatized to room temperature before you begin to use it. If, for example, the paper has been transported at minus 10 degrees Celsius and it has to get acclimatized to 20 degrees centigrade, it takes about 50–60 hours. This time should be taken into account when ordering paper.

Paper manufacturers usually pack paper in polythene covered wrapping so it will keep a constant moisture content during transport, but during longer transporting this protection may not be completely enough, and the moisture content can be affected. While the paper is getting acclimatized you should let the protective wrapping stay on.

8.19 What Paper is Made Of

When making paper you start out with pulp. Pulp consists of cellulose fibers extracted from wood and are often made in special paper pulp factories. The paper mills then buy the pulp and refine it to pulp stock by beating it. Then the paper itself is made in paper machines and rolled up on huge rolls. Finally the paper receives its post treatment: the surface is finished and the paper is cut into its final shape.

8.19.1 Paper Pulp

There are two types of paper pulp; chemical and mechanical. The raw materials are made up of pine, birch and spruce trees. The trees are cut down, sawed into logs, stripped of their bark and chopped into chips. When making chemical pulp the cellulose fibers are extracted from the wood by boiling it with chemical ingredients. To make mechanical pulp, the wood is ground to extract the cellulose fibers. Chemical pulp usually consists of a mix of long-fibered pulp from coniferous trees (about 2–3.5 mm) and short-fibered pulp from deciduous trees (about 1–1.5 mm), whereas the main raw material for mechanical pulp is fiber from coniferous trees, primarily spruce.

PAPER PULP HAS DIFFERENT PROPERTIES

	Mechanical	Chemical	Recycled
Utilizing raw materials	+	-	++
Energy requirements	-	+	+
Life span	-	+	-
Recycling possibilities	-	+	-
Opacity	+	-	+
Bulk	+	-	-
Strength	-	+	-
Stiffness	+	-	-

WOOD-PULP/WOOD-FREE

- Paper pulp consisting of more than 10% mechanical pulp and less than 90% chemical pulp is called "wood-pulp paper."

- Paper pulp consisting of less than 10% mechanical pulp and more than 90% chemical pulp is called "wood-free paper."

During paper production, these short-fibered and long-fibered pulps are usually mixed together; the proportions depend on what characteristics the paper needs to have. The fibers of coniferous trees are relatively long, and they bond quite securely to each other because they tend to have several points of contact. This results in a stronger paper. Fibers of deciduous trees, which are a bit shorter and therefore form a somewhat weaker bond than coniferous fibers, are useful for better opacity.

Paper pulp consisting of more than 10% mechanical pulp and less than 90% chemical pulp is used to make a paper called "wood-pulp paper," while paper produced from pulp consisting of less than 10% mechanical pulp and more than 90% chemical pulp is called, oddly enough "wood-free paper." Wood-free print paper is strong and very white, and is used for most types of printed prod-

PAPER PULP

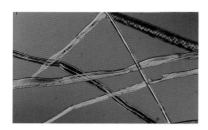

PULP FROM CONIFEROUS TREES
Pulp from coniferous trees is long-fibered. The fibers are around 2–3.5 mm.

PULP FROM DECIDUOUS TREES
Pulp from deciduous trees is short-fibered. The fibers are around 1–1.5 mm.

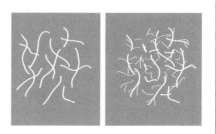

CHEMICAL VS MECHANICAL PULP
Chemical pulp consists of a mix of long-fibered pulp from coniferous trees and short-fibered pulp from deciduous trees, whereas mechanical pulp consists of fiber from coniferous trees, primarily spruce. The mechanical pulp provides high opacity and bulk, whereas the chemical pulp provides high surface strenght.

ucts. Wood-pulp paper often has a slight yellow-grayish tint and is used for publications like newspapers and catalogues. Wood-pulp paper yellows more quickly than wood-free. By adding less mechanical pulp to the chemical pulp, you increase the bulk and opacity of a paper while maintaining the whiteness and capability for good image reproduction. Doing this lessens the differences between wood-free and wood-pulp paper.

The production of chemical pulp requires approximately twice as much wood as mechanical pulp. This is because various waste products are boiled off in the chemical process. Mechanical pulp better conserves our forest resources. On the other hand, energy can be extract from the chemical process, which can then be used for paper production.

About 45% of America's total paper consumption is recycled. Every ton of recycled fiber can replace the paper pulp of about twelve trees. Recycled fibers are not as strong and don't have the same properties of new fibers, but they can be used in a number of different areas. Cellulose fibers can be recycled five or six times and provide good raw material for new paper given the right process. In recent years, fine papers consisting of 100% recycled fibers with good runnability and printability have appeared on the market. When paper pulp is made there are three steps left in paper production: Stock preparation, going through the paper machine and post treatment.

8.19.2 **Stock Preparation**
During stock preparation the paper pulp is refined and prepared for the paper machine. The stock is made up of paper pulp, water, filler and chemicals. The composition of the stock depends on what characteristics you want the paper to have. The cellulose fibers in the pulp are beaten to give the paper the characteristics you want. Beating it makes for better bonding among the fibers, and results in stronger paper. You can also add filler, sizing agents and color. The most usual fillers are ground marble or limestone ($CaCO_3$) and clay. These ingredients improve the opacity and the color of the print on the paper. The fillers also provide the paper with softness and elasticity. Sizing agents like alum and rosin make the paper more resistant to water absorption. They also help prevent ink from being absorbed into the paper and spread sideways, a phenomenon called "feathering." Stock preparation is also the time to add color or other special effects like flower petals, bits of paper, etc.

PAPER PULP HAS DIFFERENT PROPERTIES

THE STOCK
The stock is the mixture of ingredients required to make a particular paper. The stock consists of:

- Water
- Fillers
- Color
- Fibers
- Sizing agents

BEATEN CELLULOSE FIBERS
Beating the fibers in the stock preparation makes for better bonding among the fibers, provides many points of contact, and results in a stronger paper.

8.19.3 The Paper Machine

At the entrance of the paper machine, or "headbox," the pulp stock is about 99% water. The most extensive draining of the stock takes place in the twin-wire where the water is sucked up by two straining-cloths. The wire moves at high speed, which means that the paper has a very short time to be drained. In order for the paper pulp to reach the speed of the wire, the pulp has to accelerate from the headbox. This acceleration causes most fibers to orient in the direction of the machine. This causes the paper to manifest different characteristics lengthwise and crosswise, which in turn affects the dimensional stability.

It is the pulp flow from the headbox that determines the weight of the paper. By varying the flow and concentration of the stock that is poured out onto the wire, you can crate paper with different weights. The "formation" of the paper is also created on the wire.

After the wire section, the paper is fed into the press section. This consists of a press cylinder that uses filters to remove more water. You can affect the bulk of the paper in the press section. In the next step, the paper is dried. The drying level depends on what the paper will be used for. Paper intended for sheet-fed offset printing, web-fed offset printing and photocopying all have different drying levels, for example.

THE PAPER MACHINE
Here's a basic sketch of a paper machine. The stock is poured out onto the wire in the headbox. The paper is drained in the wire 35–50%. In the press and dryer section, the paper is dried 90–95%. After that, the paper can be glazed and rolled up on a roll.

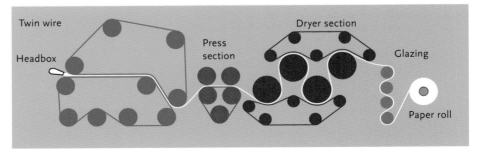

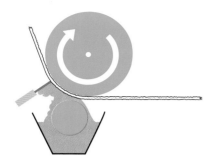

SHEET COATING
The coating consists of a binder (starch or latex) and a pigment (fine kaolin clay or calcium carbonate) and is applied to the paper in a thin layer. In addition, other ingredients are added to provide various characteristics. The process of coating paper can be compared to evening-out the surface with putty and a putty knife.

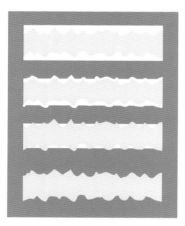

MORE OR LESS COATING
The layer of coating can be thicker or thinner. You see a highly coated paper above and uncoated below. The thicker the coating, the higher the print quality.

ROLL
The paper is rolled up on enormous rolls in the end of the paper machine.

If the paper is to be surface-sized, it is first dried in a dryer section. After that it is surface-sized in a size press and then dried again in the dryer section. The paper is surface-sized to give it a strong surface that can take the pressure it is exposed to when the ink is added in the printing press [*see Printing 9.5.15*].

8.19.4 Post Treatment

The post treatment a paper receives is determined by what paper quality and surface characteristics it is intended to have. A post treatment that is executed in the paper machine is a "machine finish" or "calender finish." During this process, the paper is pressed to an even thickness and given a smooth surface to ensure quality prints.

To make the paper even more suitable for printing, it can be coated. The process of coating the paper can be compared to evening out the surface with putty and a putty knife. The coating itself consists of a binder (starch or latex) and a pigment (fine kaolin clay or calcium carbonate). In addition, other ingredients are added to provide various characteristics. Coating improves both the optical and print qualities of the paper. You can also use a higher screen frequency when printing because the surface of the paper is smoother [*see Prepress 7.7.5*] Coated paper absorbs ink more quickly and evenly, and the prints will have a glossier finish.

Paper can also be glazed to give it a very high gloss. Glazing provides for better image quality but reduces opacity and stiffness. During glazing, the paper is rubbed between different pairs of cylinders. This process is called calendering. Finally the paper is taken up on rolls or cut to sheets, depending on its intended use.

09.
printing

When is digital printing appropriate and when is offset printing appropriate? What printing technique is cheaper for large print runs? Why does the print sometimes smear? Does the digital printing technique limit the paper choice? How is moiré avoided? What happens at a makeready? Why can't a lot of ink be used in flexography? Is the text always converted into halftone screens in gravure printing? How much ink can you add to a printing press and what is the limit?

THE BASIC DIFFERENCE BETWEEN printing press technique and printer technique is that the former always uses some sort of image carrier, printing plates for example. Printing plates are static, which means that every printed product made from the same plates will look alike.

Printing press techniques generally lend themselves best to large print runs and the most common are offset printing, gravure printing, flexographic printing and screen printing. Printers don't use any printing plates which means that every printout can be unique and differ from the previous printout. Printing techniques are better suited for small print runs from approximately 500 copies down to single samples, and the most common are xerographic, inkjet and dye sublimation technique.

When we talk about digital printing we mean in general that the machine that is used is based on the technique of printers, but that it has such high capacity that it can compete with a traditional printing press. The advantages with digital printing is that the contents can vary from sheet to sheet as well as well as having low start-up costs since it does not require extensive makereadies and you don't have to develop film or printing plates. Traditional printing presses require printing plates and take a longer time to set up. They have higher start-up costs, but in general have a higher capacity, which means that thay are more cost-effective with large print-runs.

PRINTED PRODUCT	XEROGRAPHIC	INKJET	SUBLIMATED DYE	PHOTOGRAPHIC
Large posters		Single samples to small runs		
Novels	Single samples			
Coffee table books				
Annual reports, catalogues, magazines	Trial runs			
Price lists	Single samples to small runs, few pages			
Business and visiting cards	Medium quality	Poor quality		
Flyers, Folders & Brochures	Single samples to small runs			
Press proofs		Low to medium high quality requirement, Single samples	High quality requirement, Single samples	
Glass bottles				
Plastic bottles			Shrink wrap, single samples	
Labels and decals	Low quality, single samples to small runs			
Daily newspapers				
Bags				
Photographs		Home products	Home production, Not long-duration	Professional production
Banners	Smaller banners, indoors, on paper, single samples	Outdoors and indoors, textile, plastic and paper, single samples		

SHEET-FED OFFSET	WEB-FED OFFSET	TYPOGRAPHIC PRINTING	GRAVURE PRINTING	SCREEN PRINTING	FLEXOGRAPHIC PRINTING
Medium – large runs				Small – medium runs	
Medium runs	Large runs				
All kinds					
Medium runs	Large runs		Very large runs		
Medium runs	Large runs		Very large runs		
High quality		High quality			
Medium runs	Large runs		Very large runs		
High quality requirement, Single samples					
Labels				Directly to bottle, high quality, no photo images or rasters	
Shrink wrap or labels, high quality					Print directly on the container, low quality
High quality, medium to large runs				Highest quality no photo images or rasters	
	Coldset				
Paper bags, highest quality			Foil bags, high quality	Paper bags, low quality	Plastic bags and paper bags, low quality
				Medium large banners, Outdoors och indoors, textile, plastic och paper, runs in multiples	

In this chapter we are going to go over the different printing press and printer techniques' function and characteristics. Within the framework for the respective printing techniques we are also going to review a number of printing phenomena and how to evaluate the quality of a print. But we will begin with how we choose technique, which parameters are influential and what kind of choices we have when we produce printed products.

9.1 Different Printing Techniques

When you are going to produce a printed product you must choose the technique that fits best, keeping in mind certain prevailing conditions. What mainly affects the choice of technique is layout, format, size (number of pages), quality requirements, and what material you are printing on. In the table below there are a number of typical printed products together with varying conditions and printing techniques. The table isn't intended to be complete, instead it is meant to provide some examples of typical printed products connected with printing techniques.

9.2 Xerography

The xerographic process is a technique that is based on toner and is used, for example, in laser printers, copiers and digital printing presses. They vary enormously in price, and the technique is employed mostly when making from only a few copies up to approximately 500.

9.2.1 How the Technique Works

The principle of the xerographic process is the same regardless of what kind of machine it is used in. The most important moments in the process are: the charging f the photographic conductor, the laser beam exposure, the transfer of the toner particles and heat application. The photographic conductor is made of a material whose electric charge can be affected by light. The process is initiated by a rotating drum, or photographic conductor, which carries either a positive or negative electrical charge (the kind of charge differs depending on the brand). The photographic conductor has the same surface area as the paper that is to be printed on.

The drum is exposed with the help of a laser in the laser printer. In order to expose the entire drum as quickly as possible, a rotating multi-edged mirror is used, often octagonal in shape. Because the mirror rotates, an edge of it can together with the laser beam expose the entire width of the drum at once. The laser beam is only broken when it reaches an area on the drum that should not be exposed.

When as edge of the mirror has exposed a line on the drum, a motor rotates the drum a small step forward so that the next edge of the mirror can expose the next line. The mirror rotates quickly, often several thousand rotations per minute, which makes laser printer sensitive to jolts.

	XERO-GRAPHIC	INKJET	DYE SUBLIMATION	FOTO-GRAPHIC	SHEET-FED OFFSET	WEB-FED OFFSET	LETTERPRESS PRINTING	GRAVURE PRINTING	SCREEN PRINTING	FLEXOGRAPHIC PRINTING
Image Carrier	None	None	None	None	Plate	Plate	Stamp-like form	Engraved cylinder	Screen cloth	Flexographic forms
Print runs	1–1000 copies	1–20 copies	1–5 copies	1–5 copies	500–50000 copies	15000–1000000 copies	50–500 copies	100 000→ copies	10–200 copies	50→ copies
Format	A4–A3	A4 →	A4–A2	A6–A1	A3–Eurosize		A3			
Resolution/ Screen Frequency	Up to 1200 dpi	Up to 9600 dpi	Up to 2400 dpi	300–600 dpi	Up to 200 lpi	Up to 150 lpi	No rasters	Up to 200 lpi	Up to 100 lpi	Up to 150 lpi
Print Carrier	Paper, Overhead-film	Paper, textile, plastic	Paper, plastic, shrink wrap	Photo-paper	Paper, cardboard	Paper	Paper	Special engraving paper	Cloth, paper, metal, plastic, glass	Plastic
Variable data	Parts of a page can vary	Prints out page by page	Prints out page by page							
Print Carrier Format	Sheet or roll	Sheet or roll	Sheet	Roll	Sheet	Roll	Sheet	Roll	Flat and cylindrical forms	Flat for uneven forms
Print characteristics	Limited quality	Large tonal range	Large tonal range	High quality	High quality	Risk of misregistration	Creates a relief	Rasterizes objects and text	Can't show light tones	Can't show light tones

The laser beam's exposure of the drum crates a charged reverse image. The drum is then exposed to toner, small color particles which stick to the charged image (the toner particles are either statically charged or neutral, depending on the brand of printer). The paper is then charged with a higher static value than the charged image on the drum. When the paper passes the drum, the toner is transferred to the paper because it has the higher electrical charge. At this point, the toner is loose on the paper, bound only with a weak electrical charge. The toner is heated and exposed to light physical pressure in order to permanently fix it – or "burn it" – onto the paper. The heat needed to fix the toner is about 200 degrees Celsius. In four-color printers, the above process takes place four times, once for each component color (CMYK).

There are several versions of laser printers that use a number of laser diodes to expose each dot on each line one by one, instead of a laser beam and a rotating mirror. These printers are called LED printer (for Light-Emitting Diodes).

The resolution in a laser printer mainly depends on three factors: the exposure dot of the laser beam, the size of the steps the engine takes, and how small the toner particles are. The exposure dot of the laser beam is determined by the actual laser and by the optics of the laser printer. There are printers that have different resolutions in different directions. This is because the engine can move in steps smaller than the size of the exposure point of the laser, or vice versa. Toner is the factor that currently limits resolution the most. Smaller toner particles mean higher resolution. Toner particles are currently only a couple of micrometers in diameter. In LED printers the resolution is determined by how closely the laser diodes are spaced.

The most common resolution for a laser printer is from 400 to 1,200 dpi.

THE XEROGRAPHIC PROCESS

Regular copy machines and laser printers are based on the same technique, the xerographic process. In the xerographic technique, light changes the charge in a photographic conductor and toner, heat and physical pressure are applied.

What follows is the principle for how a (white-printing) laser printer operates.

THE COMPONENTS OF THE LASER PRINTER
The numbers in the image refer to the following steps for conducting a print-out.

1. The photographic conductor is electrically charged before exposed by the laser beam.

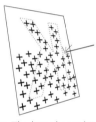

2. The laser beam hits a rotating, octagonal mirror and passes across the width of the photographic conductor, row by row as the conductor is fed forward. When the laser beam hits it, the conductor loses its charge in that particular spot.

3. After it has been exposed to light, the photographic conductor absorbs toner in the charged areas. The toner may have a reversed charge to increase the attraction between the conductor and the toner.

4. The photographic conductor passes the paper, which has the same charge as the conductor but stronger. As a result, the toner is attracted and transferred to the paper.

5. When the toner has been transferred to the paper, it is only fixed to it with a weak electric charge. The toner is further fixed with heat and a light physical pressure.

6. The photographic conductor is cleaned.

LASER PRINTERS
When you are going to work with graphic production you should have a Postscript-based printer. A Postscript printer is often more expensive than a non Postscript-based one. Many of the non Postscript-based printers can be upgraded to Postscript printing.

PHOTOCOPIERS
The original use of the xerographic technique was in the copy machine where it is still most widely used.

DIGITAL PRINTING PRESS, PART 1
The digital print is often based on the xerographic technique and is mostly used for smaller print runs which demand short delivery time. The digital print is also used for test runs and preruns. The prints can usually be delivered within hours.

The ink is dry when the print comes out of the printing press, which makes it possible to postprocess the printed product instantly, without the risk of smearing. Just like common printers, the paper choice is limited but an increasing market is enabling more options. Today there are hundreds of papers to choose from.

DIGITAL PRINTING PRESS, PART 2
Some digital printing presses use liquid ink instead of toner. The ink has the same characteristics as the toner, i.e. it can be controlled by static charge. The most well-known system is Indigo from Hewlett-Packard.

HIGH-VOLUME PRINTERS
Many of these have simple post processing procedures, such as stapling, built in. High volume printers are often used in production of reports, manuals, handbooks and educational materials, in other words printed products that are frequently updated, are printed in smaller runs and have a wide tonal range. The economic breaking point usually lies at around 1,000 copies. The starting costs are relatively low, while the price per unit is high. Most high-volume printers have a resolution of approximately 600 dpi.

9.2.2 **Ink**
The ink you use in the xerographic technique is not a liquid. It is composed of very small particles, toner. Toner particles are today a few thousandths of a millimeter in size and therefore can appear as a thick liquid in their container.

However, since the ink is not a liquid, it does not seep into the paper in the same manner as liquid ink. Instead, it lies on the surface, which you can feel if you feel the printed surface with your hand. Since the toner lies on the surface, and because of the heat conditioning the toner gets from printing and heat fixation, the printed surface is shinier than the paper.

Today toner is usually available in black, cyan, magenta and yellow. And for a number of printers and printing systems there are complementary Pantone

Digital printing is usually based on xerographic technique and used most of all for small print runs with short delivery times. Digital printing is used primarily for short runs with short delivery times. Digitally printed products can often be delivered within a couple of hours. Digital printing s often used for test runs and pre-editions. As with non-digital printers, there are certain limitations in terms of paper choice, but because of the expanding market for digital printing, there are hundreds of papers to choose from today. Digital printing is not likely to replace offset printing or other printing methods within the near future, but instead serves to complement them.

If comparing cost graphs for digital and offset printing, digital printing is characterized by low start-up costs and a high cost per unit. With offset printing, the opposite applies: high start-up costs and a high cost per unit. The high per-unit cost of digital prints is due to the fact that digital printing presses are slow in comparison to offset presses. Expensive service agreements for digital printing presses and the high costs of

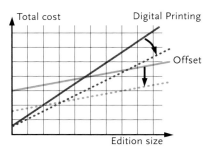

materials (toner, photo conductor, etc.) also contribute to the per-unit cost.

Exactly where the break-even point between digital and traditional offset printing currently lies depends on the type and format of the printed product, though it is usually estimated to be somewhere between 500 and 1,000 units. The future of the break-even point is difficult to predict, but competition from digital printing has accelerated the technical development of offset presses. Since digital printing was introduced, the makeready time of new offset presses has been drastically reduced. At the same time, the cost of materials for digital printing is going down and digital print-

ing presses capable of larger print runs have been developed.

When making cost comparisons between digital and offset printing machinery, you should also keep in mind that there are generally additional costs for film and proofs with offset printing, which are avoided entirely in digital printing.

Because of tough competition among the different manufacturers of digital printing machinery, a lot of time and money has been invested in developing the quality of the finished print – so much so that digital print quality is approaching the standard wet by offset printing. The quality of digitally printed products varies considerably between different providers, however. Providers who have succeeded in getting the best out of digital printers are often pre-press service providers and printers with pre-press departments. The main reason for this is that these providers often have the capability to provide a secure and efficient production process, and possess a staff with a lot of experience in digital graphic production as well as evaluating graphic quality.

colors. For some systems you can even custom order your own colors, if you buy large enough volumes. There are printing technique solutions where you use the xerographic technique but with liquid inks in place of toner. The ink has in this case the equivalent properties of toner, that is it can be controlled with the aid of electrical charges. The most well-known is the Indigo System from Hewlett-Packard.

You can buy toner in ready-made containers called cassettes. They are made to specification for every printer system. Sometimes only the printer manufacturer will supply the cassettes for a specific printer, but sometimes there are several suppliers for the same type of cassette. This is especially true for hone and office printers.

9.2.3 Paper

The paper used for laser printers must have certain characteristics. It cannot be too smooth, like a coated paper, because the toner will have difficulty adhering to the paper's surface. Neither can the paper lose its charge too fast. If it does, the toner will not be attracted to the paper. Finally, it has to e resistant to high

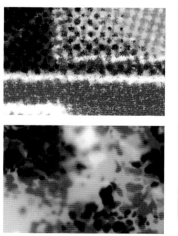

Halftone dots in digital prints are blurrier than those in offset or gravure printing, and the image reproduction of digital printing is of a lesser quality as a result. This is primarily because digital printers print with powder toner instead of liquid ink. Because the halftone dots are divided, the digital prints appear to have a higher screen frequency than they actually do.

Printing with powder toner means that both halftone dots and text become somewhat blurry because the particles don't always end up in the right place. This is the primary reason that text reproduction in digital printing is inferior to offset printing.

temperatures because of how the toner is heat-fixed to the paper surface. The gloss on coated paper can cause smoldering when heated.

The most common laser printers work with paper formats ranging from 8 ½" × 11" to 11" × 17", weighing 20–32 lbs. Papers that are too thick can easily damage the printer. The stiffness of the paper is also important for feeding it through the printer successfully, however it cannot be too stiff to follow the curved paper feed. Because you cannot use coated papers in laser printers, a number of special papers with a coated feeling have been developed.

It is important for the paper to have the right moisture content as well. Moisture content affects how the paper is charged. For example, with a four-color print using xerographic technique, the paper is charged and heated up four times, that is four times for each component color (CMYK). The paper's moisture content will decrease step-wise. If the paper has too little moisture content, it will have too high a static charge, resulting in iit easily getting stuck in the printer. For this reason, paper intended for xerographic processing comes in packaging that retains the proper moisture content. You should avoid taking the paper out of its packaging before you need to use it. The optimal mois-

When creating a digitally printed product, you have the ability to change information on the prints form sheet to sheet. In the beginning, this was considered the breakthrough function of digital printing and was usually called "variable data." The promise of variable data has not been developed to the extent that was hope for yet. At present it is primarily used to address mailings and personalize letters with the names of clients, i.e., "Hi Jim! We heard you recently purchased a new car..." The variable data function is generated with information from a database. It is very important that the database be set up correctly and information entered into it accurately. Database tasks should be done in close collaboration with the provider of your digital printing services.

VARIABLE DATA – HOW IT WORKS
By exchanging parts of the rasterized bitmap with smaller, rasterized bitmaps (which describe the objects on the page), the printing press can change the printed image from sheet to sheet.

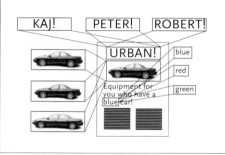

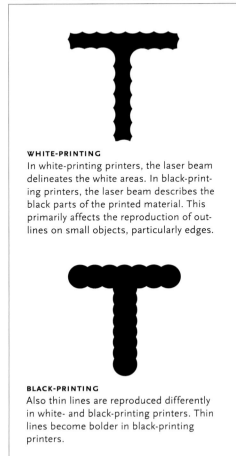

WHITE-PRINTING
In white-printing printers, the laser beam delineates the white areas. In black-printing printers, the laser beam describes the black parts of the printed material. This primarily affects the reproduction of outlines on small objects, particularly edges.

BLACK-PRINTING
Also thin lines are reproduced differently in white- and black-printing printers. Thin lines become bolder in black-printing printers.

ture content for paper being used in xerographic processing differs from, for example, paper being used for offset printing.

The most common laser printers use paper formats between A4 and A3. Certain digital printing presses print from a roll and can print a special long format. Since not all papers are appropriate for xerographic technique, paper manufacturers have produced a line of special papers. Among these are coated papers when offset quality would not be suitable. These special papers are often more expensive than coated papers used for offset printing. Another type of paper frequently used in laser printers is offset pre-printed paper, or "blanks," like letterhead.

There are certain things you need to keep in mind when creating and using blanks in order to avoid problems with staining in the printer. When creating a blank, you need to make sure your paper is suitable for both offset and laser printers. You should avoid layouts with vertical lines and large, heavy tint areas because these can stain the fixation drum. Above all, allow the offset printing to dry completely before using the blanks in your laser printer. This can take up too two weeks.

When using blanks, you should also be aware that it is difficult to get exact registration between the proof and what is printed in the printer. It is difficult to make adjustments to the positioning of where the laser printer print on the paper, and in general, the output will vary approximately +/- 1/24" (1 mm) on the paper.

Most laser printers can be used for printing transparencies as well. You should use the transparency films recommended by the manufacturer, as they will be able to withstand the heat of the fixation process without melting.

9.2.4 Typical Phenomena for the Xerographic Process
Machines made by different manufacturers may utilize different technologies. For example, there is the difference between black-printing and white-printing. In black-printing printers, the laser beam describes the black parts of the printed material on the drum. In white-printers, the laser delineates the white areas – those that are not to be printed. White-printing printers create thinner lines than black-printing printers, which means that the same document printed in both types of printers will produce different results.

9.3 Ink-jet

Ink-jet technology involves small drops of ink sprayed onto a paper surface. Ink-jet technique is used in many different printers for an array of different applications. There are ink-jet desktop printers for office and home use, four-color printers, large format printers, or digital proofs. A simple kind of black and white inkjet technique is often used for printing addresses on printed products. The technique is time-consuming and the printouts are more expensive than those made using other technique, which means that ink-jet is mostly used when producing only a few printouts.

9.3.1 Ink-jet Technology

Ink-jet printing is usually done suing one of two techniques. One method squirts a continuous series of ink drops across the paper. The areas of the paper that should remain white do, as the ink stream is directed away with the help of an electronic field. The second method only sprays the ink on the areas of the paper that should be printed. In both methods, the ink drops are electrically charged and directed by an electric field to the right place on the paper. The drops are smaller if the continuous method is used, giving you a higher resolution and a better tonal range. Ink-jet technique is the printing technique that has the highest resolution. The ink drops are around 10 micrometers in diameter, depending on the manufacturer. Today there are ink-jet printers that have up to 9600 dpi's resolution. When you produce an ink-jet copy you can set the resolution you want it printed at The speed of printing is directly related to what resolution you select. The higher the resolution, the longer the printing time. For this reason you will seldom need to print with the highest resolution, but instead will choose the resolution according to the end-use of the printed product: for example, quick proofs, layout proofs, image proofs, imposition proofs, large format proofs or photographic printouts.

Ink-jet technique is not based on traditional screen frequencies. Instead it uses halftone screening. This means colors are created by varying the amount of ink, that is by placing different thicknesses of ink on each dot. It is difficult to control the exact amount of ink for so many small steps in order to get even tones from cyan to magenta to white. A solution has been to make ink-jet printers that split up cyan and magenta into two separate colors each, one dark and one light. This means that the printing is done using dark cyan, light cyan, dark magenta, light magenta, yellow and black. The result is better tonalization and a wider tonal range.

9.3.2 Ink

The ink used in the ink-jet printer is made up of a combination of approximately 60–90% solvent and various dyes. The solvents usually contain water and polythene glycol or a mix of both. The composition of the dye affects both the function of the printer and the end quality of the printout. One of the most common problems with ink-jet printers is that the ink dries in the nozzle that produces the drops. To avoid that, polythene glycol is added to the water-based inks. The dyes are either pure pigments or dissolved dyes. Pigment-based dyes tend to block the nozzles more but are also less sensitive to light and water once they are on the paper. Pigments allow for heavier color saturation than the dissolved dyes. The dissolved dyes are more sensitive to water and light but do not clog the nozzles.

Ink-jet ink is relatively expensive, which means that for most printers there are a number of ink manufacturers. They are sold in cartridges and for most printers you can buy the colors separately. In certain printers all the colors are contained in one cartridge. This is often not economical because it means you have to replace all the colors even if only one is empty.

INK-JET PRINTER
Ink-jet technique is used in many different printers for an array of different applications. There are ink-jet desktop printers for office and home use, four-color printers, large format printers, or digital proofs.

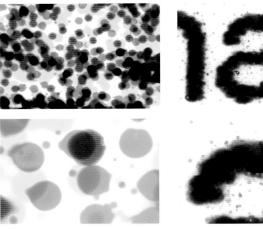

Ink-jet printers generally use a kind of FM screen. The ink is sprayed out on the paper in small drops; each halftone dot consists of several ink drops.

Because of the spraying action of the printer, the outlines of printed text can be blurry. This results in text reproduction inferior to that of the offset method. Note the drops of ink that landed outside of the letters.

LARGE-FORMAT FROM A ROLL
Above is a large-format ink-jet printer. It is only the width of the paper roll that limits the format.

9.3.3 Paper

The type of paper you use with the ink-jet printer is very important, because of the nature of the technology. In some inkjet printers, only the paper supplied by the manufacturer can be used. The biggest problem that occurs is bleeding, when two colors bleed into each other. To avoid bleeding, the ink must dry quickly. The paper has to be able to absorb the liquid components of the ink as soon s possible without the dye following them into the paper. If too much dye is absorbed into the paper, the color density can be adversely affected.

Printing with an ink-jet requires paper that is stable dimensionally, so it does not wrinkle or pucker because of the liquid in the ink. Because most printer manufacturers recommend their own special papers, the selection is relatively limited and the paper itself can be expensive.

9.3.4 Typical Phenomena for Ink-jet Printing

When the ink is absorbed into the paper it not only seeps down into the paper, but it spreads out as well. The effect is called feathering and can be compared to writing with a magic marker on a newspaper. When an ink drop is absorbed into the paper, it increases in size, usually to three times that of the original drop. If feathering is too great, the layer of ink on the paper will be superficial and the tonal range will be negatively affected. The most common reason for extensive feathering is using a paper that is not suitable for ink-jet technique.

9.4 **Dye Sublimation**

Dye sublimation printers, also called thermo-transfer printers, are based on a technique where the ink is bound to a plastic film and is transferred to the paper by heating up the ribbon using a print head or laser. Dye sublimation technique is relatively expensive and is used principally for certain digital proofs or for photographic printouts.

9.4.1 **Dye Sublimation Technique**

The ink in the dye sublimation printer is neither liquid nor powder, but consists of paraffin or wax esters on a ribbon of either polyester film or condensed paper. The colored ribbon is heated by a print head or a laser on the areas where there is to be ink on the paper. The paraffin-based ink melts and is transferred from the colored ribbon to a foil or directly to the paper. If the printer transfers the ink to a foil you have to in a separate step place the foil against the paper and with a heater transfer the ink to the paper.

The print head consists of several small radiators surrounded by porcelain. Each radiator can be heated to different temperatures. This allows you to regulate the amount of ink transferred to every dot in the output. When you use a laser as the heat source it works exactly like a laser printer. The laser beam lights up the dots that are to receive ink and is directed away from the dots that are to receive no ink. The ink on the lighted up areas melts and can then be transferred to the paper or foil.

9.4.2 **Ink**

The colored ribbon comes on a roll and is sold by the color. The dye sublimation printer is based on CMYK, and there are also complementary pantone colors for certain color systems, for example green, orange and blue.

There is only a fraction of the ink from the plastic film than is used on the output. Unfortunately the plastic film can only be used once which makes the output proportionately more expensive. Quite simply, you pay for more ink than you use. The plastic film is usually about 10 mm thick, of which about 4mm is ink.

In the printers that use print heads each radiator can heat up separately to a different temperature. This allows you to influence the amount of ink, that is the thickness of the ink that will be placed on each dot of the output. You can also influence thickness of the ink transferred to each point with laser printers. This done by varying the amount of time the laser beams lights up the dots.

Dye sublimation printers can therefore use both halftone technique, that is different amounts of ink in each dot, and traditional raster screen patterns to create colors You can even work with a combination of both, which means that the printer systems that have complementary colors to CMYK can simulate different Pantone colors.

9.4.3 **Paper**

The choice of paper for dye sublimation printers is relatively open, as long as you pay attention to the roughness of the paper. These printers require a paper

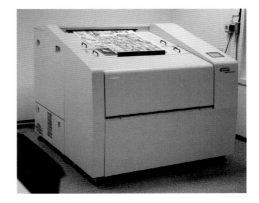

DYE SUBLIMATION PRINTERS
Dye sublimation printers, also called thermo-transfer printers, are based on a techinque reminiscent of old-fashioned typewriters. With dye sublimation printers, however, color is not transferred to the paper by physical pressure (like the typewriter key hitting the ribbon), but by heating the ribbon. The dye sublimation printing technique is relatively expensive and primarily used for certain digital proofs and outputs on photographic paper or transparencies.

with a relatively fine surface, but it does not matter if the paper is coated or uncoated. A very rough surface contributes to lower print quality. In principle this means that you can use most of the papers on the market.

With the printing system that transfers the ink to foil first, you can then laminate the ink onto different materials, for example cardboard, plastic and shrink-wrap (transparent plastic that is used for labels that go around things completely, for example bottles and cans.) The limitations in the choice of materials come from the characteristics of the surface, its thickness (whether or not the material can pass through the laminator), and if it can withstand the heat of the laminator.

9.5 **Offset**

Offset printing is the most common printing technique, and is used for everything from business cards, brochures, magazine and newspapers, to large posters. The basic principle of offset printing is that there are printing and non-printing surfaces on a printing plate. This means that you can only print in full color or no color at all on every dot on the paper [*see Prepress 7.7*].

There are two different types of offset printing: sheet-fed offset and web-fed offset. The names have to do with whether the printing press is constructed to print on cut sheets of paper or from rolls of paper. Web-fed offset is most suitable for large-volume editions from about 15,000 to one million copies, while sheet-fed offset is better suited for about 50 to 50,000 copies.

Within web-fed offset printing technique there is also a differentiation made between heatset and coldset printing. These terms describe if the web-fed offset press has a built-in drying oven, (heatset) or not, (coldset). There is also water-free or dry offset. One reason that water-free is still quite unusual is probably the sway of tradition as well as the fact that regular offset has such high quality that differences between the two techniques are hard to detect.

9.5.1 **How Offset Technique Works**

All offset printing is based on an interaction between ink, water and a printing plate and is called the lithographic principle. Lithographic printing works differently from stamp-type printing, in which the printing surfaces are separated from the non-printing surfaces of the image by differences in surface elevation. In lithography, printed and non-printed areas are separated by their different chemical characteristics.

The non-printing areas attract the water, while the areas that print repel. Because of this, the areas of the plate that print are called hydrophobic (hydro=water) and the non-printing areas that don't are called hydrophilic. In water-free offset printing, the non-printing areas are coated with olio-phobic solution instead.

9.5.2 **Sheet-fed Offset and Web-fed Offset**

The most common printing method in North America is sheet-fed offset, and is used for everything from advertising brochures, annual reports, posters and books, as well as other high quality printed products. It is the traditional tech-

SHEET-FED OFFSET PRINTING PRESS
In the foreground you can see the delivery bay where printed sheets are collected as they come out of the press. The four separate printing units (one for each color) are visible in the background.

nique that gives the highest quality. As the name indicates, printing is done on paper sheets. The size of the sheets is matched with the size of the printing press, from approximately A3 to A0. Sheet-fed presses come in everything from one-color to twelve-color models. This method allows for an enormous selection of paper in terms of both finish and quality. Off-press processing is done in a completely separate step after printing.

Web-fed offset printing is most suitable for large-volume editions. You can rarely do any kind of advanced off press processing with web-fed offset printing; such processing is usually limited to the folding and stitching of printed products. Common web-fed offset products included newspaper, periodicals, folders and other prints of lesser quality.

Heatset gets its name from the fact that the printed material is dried before it is off press processed. The technique is used mainly for production of periodicals, brochures and catalogues. The printed product is dried in an oven whose temperature is set at approximately 200 degrees Celsius. How high the temperature is depends on the speed of the paper feeder. After the oven the paper feeder's temperature is lowered to about 20 degrees with the help of cooling cylinders. There is a phenomenon in heatset printing called curling that occurs from drying the printed product. It manifests itself as rippling in the paper of the printed product. Curling happens because of a combination of high ink coverage, heat in the oven and speed of the paper feeder.

Heatset printing yields much higher quality than coldset printing, but a somewhat lower quality than sheet-fed printing. A typical problem is flaws in trapping (how well the ink colors bind to each other) which can cause secondary colors such as red, blue and green, to be discolored. You also need lower ink coverage in heatset printing in order to avoid curling, which results in a more washed out image.

Coldset gets its name from the fact that the ink dries without the help of an oven. The technique is used primarily in newspaper and advertising flyer production, items that have a short lifespan. Because of the short lifespan combined with the large print runs, a lesser quality paper is used. The combination of the low-grade paper, high printing speeds, as well as off press processing done before the ink is dry, means that the end result will be of much lower quality than sheet-fed offset printing and heatset printing. Along with the lower paper quality, a lower screen frequency is used in printing. A fewer number of ink colors are used under these conditions, to avoid too much smearing and to have fewer problems with registration.

Water-free offset printing essentially functions the same way as offset printing. The difference is that water-free offset printing uses a silicone layer instead of water to differentiate the non-printing surfaces of the printing plate from the printing surfaces. Water-free offset requires special printing plates, coated with a silicone layer. When these coated plates are exposed and developed, the silicone is washed off the exposed areas revealing the printing surfaces of the plate. Water-free offset printing uses ink with a higher viscosity than that used for wet offset printing. Water-free offset presses are often rebuilt offset presses in which tempered cylinders have been added so that the temperature of the ink – and hence its printing characteristics – can be controlled.

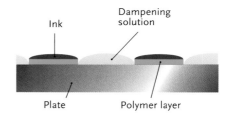

DAMPENING, INK AND PLATE
The printing plate is moistened so the ink willl cling to the polymer surfaces and not the non-printing surfaces. As illustrated above, there is a small difference in level between the printing and non-printing surfaces on the offset printing plate. It is however not this difference that creates the print.

WEB-FED OFFSET PRINTING PRESS
Web-fed offset printing is most suitable for large-volume editions. You can rarely do any kind of advanced off press processing with web-fed offset printing; such processing is usually limited to the folding and stitching of printed products. Common web-fed offset products included news-paper, periodicals, folders and other larger print runs.

In this table the three offset techniques are compared.

PRESS PROCESSING	FORMAT	NUMBER OF COLORS	PRINTING SPEED	SCREEN FREQUENCY	WEIGHT (GRAMS)	INK COVERAGE	AMOUNT OF INK	OFF PRESS PROCESSING
Sheet-fed offset	Open between A3–A0	1 to 10	10000 to 15000 sheets per hour	133–200 lpi	70–300g/m²	360 percent	D 1,4–1,9	Separate
Heatset	Controlled by A-format and number of pages in the press	4 to 5		100–150 lpi	70–150g/m²	320 percent	D 1,2–1,8	Online; folding, glue binding or stapling
Coldset	Controlled by broadsheet and tabloid formats and number of pages in the press	1,2 or 4		85–120 lpi	40–120g/m²	240 percent	D 0,9–1,1	Online; folding, glue binding or stapling

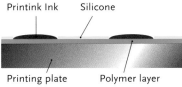

The non-printing surfaces of a water-free offset printing plate are coated with silicone, which repels the greasy ink, making a dampening solution unnecessary.

+ Sharper dots make it possible to print with a higher screen frequency

+ No need to balance the ink/humidity, which speeds up the makeready process

+ Allows for a higher maximum density, which gives you a wider range of colors

+ No dampening solution means less negative impact on the environment

− Pickouts are more common, in part because the ink is more viscous and in part because there is no dampening solution to keep things clean.

− The printing units need to be temperature-controlled, which makes for a more expensive printing press.

There are a number of characteristics that differ from traditional offset:
- You can print with a higher ink density, which results in a higher tonal range.
- Water-free offset allows for sharper printed dots, which means you can print with a higher screen frequency.
- There is a shorter makeready time because you don't have to set the ink and humidity balance.
- Water-free offset is more environmentally sound because it does not require alcohol additives in the dampening solution.
- Pick-outs are more common because of the greater viscosity of the ink and the fact that there is no water to clean off the rubber blanket [*see 9.5.15*].

9.5.3 The Printing Unit

The part of the printing press in which the ink is transferred to the paper is caller the printing unit. A printing unit in an offset press generally consists of three parts: a plate cylinder, a rubber blanket cylinder and an impression cylinder. The construction of the printing unit and its placement within the printing press varies, but for simplicity's sake we will look a four main versions: three-cylinder units, five-cylinder units, satellite units and perfector units.

Three cylinder units are currently the most common units found in sheet-fed offset presses. A three-cylinder unit consists of an impression cylinder, a rubber blanket cylinder and a plate cylinder. This unit prints one color on one side of the paper at a time. For multi-color printing, several three-cylinder units – one for each printing color – are lined up after each other.

Some multi-color printing presses composed of three-cylinder systems can turn over the paper sheets with a converter unit, allowing some of the printing unit to print on one side of the paper, while the rest of the units print on the reverse side. The technique of printing both sides of the paper in one run through the printing press is called perfector printing. A perfector press producing four-color prints on both sides of a sheet in a single run (4+4) would have eight three-cylinder units lined up with a converter unit in the middle.

Five-cylinder units are also used primarily in sheet-fed offset presses. The fine-cylinder unit consists of two plate cylinders and two rubber blanket cylinders with one common impression cylinder. This setup allows the unit to print with two colors on one side of the paper.

Satellite units are mainly in web-fed offset presses, but are also suitable for use in sheet-fed offset presses. A sheet that runs through a satellite system is held with the same gripper throughout the printing press, which facilitates registration between the printing inks. The satellite system generally consists of four plate cylinders, four rubber blanket cylinder and a common impression cylinder. This setup allows the unit to print four colors on one side of the paper. There are also satellite systems with both five and six units.

Perfector units are exclusively used in web-fed offset presses, and print on both sides of the paper in one run through the printing press. This unit has no impression cylinder; instead two rubber blanket cylinders, placed on either side of the paper web, act as impression cylinders for each other.

9.5.4 The Rubber Blanket

Offset printing is an indirect printing method, which means that thee ink is not transferred to the paper directly from the printing plate. The plate cylinder first transfers the print image onto a rubber blanket cylinder, which in turn transfers the image to the paper. The paper passes between a rubber blanket cylinder and an impression cylinder. Since the ink is transferred from the rubber blanket to the paper, its characteristics are very important for the quality of the print.

It is important that the rubber blanket can easily absorb the ink from the printing plate and transfer the ink to the paper. If the rubber blanket has difficulty transferring the ink to the paper, the paper surface can tear, causing what are called "pick-outs," which appear as blotches in the printed areas of

THE PRINTING UNIT

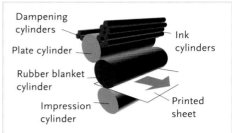

Dampening cylinders · Plate cylinder · Rubber blanket cylinder · Impression cylinder · Ink cylinders · Printed sheet

This sketch shows the basic workings of the printing unit in an offset press. This is how it prints:

1. Dampening solution is added and coats the non-printing surfaces of the printing plate.

2. Ink is added and adheres only to the printing surfaces of the plate.

3. The print image is transferred from the plate to the rubber blanket.

4. Paper is run between the rubber blanket cylinder and the impression cylinder and the rubber blanket transfers the inked image to the paper.

PRINTING UNITS

THREE CYLINDER UNIT
This is the most common type of printing unit used in sheet-fed offset printing. It consists of an impression cylinder, a rubber blanket cylinder and a plate cylinder.

FIVE CYLINDER UNIT
This type of unit is primarily used for sheet-fed offset printing. It consists of two plate cylinders and two rubber blanket cylinders that share a common impression cylinder.

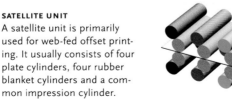

SATELLITE UNIT
A satellite unit is primarily used for web-fed offset printing. It usually consists of four plate cylinders, four rubber blanket cylinders and a common impression cylinder.

PERFECTOR UNIT
The perfector unit is exclusively used for web-fed offset printing. This system does not have an impression cylinder. Instead, two rubber blanket cylinders act as impression cylinders for one another.

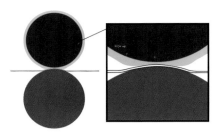

The rubber blanket is pressed in the "nip" between the rubber blanket cylinder and the impression cylinder.

the image. The rubber blanket is subject to wear and damage and has to be changed frequently. Often the rubber blanket appears a little shiny when it is time to change it, and there are a number of phenomena that occur when the rubber blanket is worn out. When the rubber blanket wears out it affects all these phenomena and the print quality is reduced.

- The rubber blanket transfers ink poorly – causing you to compensate by adding more ink to the plate. This is turn leads to problems with ink-dampening balance.
- The dots in the print are blurry – this leads to larger dots with darker print resulting, so-called dot enlargement.
- The rubber blanket doesn't "print" – this means that it doesn't have enough pressured contact with the paper and shows up as patchiness in the print. This can be compensated for by increasing the pressure between the rubber blanket cylinder and the impression cylinder and/ or add in more so-called under packing (paper of different thicknesses) beneath the rubber blanket.

Rubber blankets often need to be changed because of compression. For example, a blanket can be crushed by paper that has inadvertently folded over in the printing press. When this happens, the thickness of paper between the rubber blanket cylinder and the impression cylinder is too great and it compresses the flexible surface of the rubber blanket. A crushed rubber blanket loses elasticity in the compressed areas.

9.5.5 Ink-dampening Balance

It is important to set the ink-dampening balance correctly to obtain good print quality. It's called trying to get the right ink-dampening balance. Too much water creates an excess of emulsified water drops in the ink and can cause small, white dots in the print. This gives a "watery" effect with low density. On the other hand, too little water can cause tinting of the non-printing areas

A commonality between all kinds of offset presses is that they have separate systems of ink cylinders, called the ink pyramid, and the dampening cylinders, called the dampening system. Not all ink pyramids and dampening systems are formed like the picture above, but the differences between different printing presses are relatively small and their overall function is the same.

9.5.6 Ink

The three most important characteristics of printing ink are:

- The chromatic characteristics of the ink, including its purity, its correspondence with the color standard used (The European Scale in Europe of SWOP in the USA), and the color saturation of the ink, such as its liquidity and viscosity
- The drying characteristics on the paper used

The chromatic characteristics of the ink depend on its pigment. Pigment consists of small particles that can be both organic and inorganic in nature. For example, particles used in black pigment include chemical precipitates and

The ink pyramid in a printing press is made up of several types of cylinders with different functions. *The dampening system* in a printing press has fewer cylinders than the ink pyramid but the cylinders are of the same type and perform the same functions:

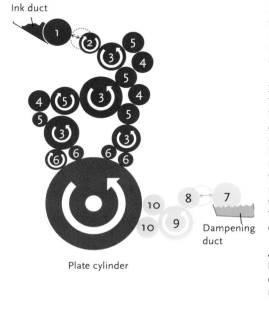

Ink duct

Plate cylinder

Dampening duct

THE INK PYRAMID

1. The duct roller delivers ink from the ink duct to the ink pyramid. The duct roller rotates slowly and is made of steel.

2. The drop roller transfers ink from the duct roller to a distribution roller by "jumping" between the duct and the distribution roller. Thus, it is never in contact with both rollers at the same time. The drop roller is coated with rubber.

3. The distribution rollers make sure that the ink is evenly distributed on the printing surfaces in a thin film. As the distribution rollers rotate they also move side to side, spreading the ink. The first distribution roller picks up ink from the drop roller while the rest pick up ink from the driving rollers. The last distribution rollers transfer the ink to the form rollers. The distribution rollers are usually coated with plastic.

4. Transfer rollers transfer ink between the ink-absorbing and ink-delivering driving rollers. Transfer rollers have a rubber coating.

5. Driving rollers roll against the distribution rollers and either absorb or deliver ink, depending on their placement. Driving rollers are made of plastic-coated steel like the distribution rollers.

6. Ink form rollers transfer ink from the last distribution rollers onto the printing plate. They are rubber-coated.

THE DAMPENING SYSTEM

7. The dampening duct roller is made of chromed steel.

8. The dampening drop roller has a rubber coating covered with a sock of terry cloth or similar material, used for its ability to absorb liquid.

9. The distribution roller is made of steel.

10. The dampening form roller has the same coating as the dampening drop roller, i.e., rubber with a sock of terry cloth or similar material.

soot. Pigments are suspended in a binding agent, which enables them to attach to paper. The binding agent gives the ink its liquid form and provides it with its lithographic characteristics. The physical characteristics of the ink, such as liquidity and viscosity, are also affected by the composition of the binder. The binding agent is also formulated to protect the pigments from dissolving in the dampening solution, which helps prevent toning.

Binding agents used in offset printing inks are made up of resin, alkyd and mineral oil. The combination of these materials helps determine the drying characteristics of the ink. When ink is first applied to paper, the paper absorbs the mineral oil in the ink, causing it to "set." This is considered to be the first phase of the drying process. It is important, however, that the paper does not absorb the pigment as well. If the pigment is absorbed the colors will be less saturated. Hence, the pigment, the alkyd and resin in the ink form a kind of gel on the surface of the paper. This gel is just dry enough not to smear on the next print sheet when the sheets are placed on top of each other in the delivery bay.

ALCOHOL IS ADDED TO THE DAMPENING SOLUTION
Alcohol is added to the dampening solution to help the water spread in an even film over the non-printing surfaces of the printing plate.

DAMPENING SOLUTION
Dampening solution is used in offset printing to:

- Make sure that the non-printing surfaces repel the printing ink

- Keep the plates clean of paper fragments

- Keep the plates cool during the printing process

TONING
Toning occurs when non-printing areas of the printing plate attract ink and become printing surfaces, causing unwanted blotches in the finished print (see background).

The gel dries completely as the alkyd is oxidized. The alkyd undergoes a chemical reaction with the oxygen in the air. This is the second drying phase, called "curing," or oxidation. UV radiation is sometimes used to speed up the curing process. Printed sheets are also sometimes sprayed with drying powder in order to prevent smearing The drying powder actually keeps the sheet physically separate so that the ink on one sheet cannot smear the sheet on top of it, and different grades of powder are used depending on the texture of the paper. Drying powders usually consist of starch or calcium carbonate ($KaCO3$).

9.5.7 Dampening Solution

So that the ink does not stick to the non-printing areas of the printing plate, the plate is dampened before the ink is added with a thin, even film of water. Alcohol is added to the water in order to ensure that it covers the entire non-printing area without creating droplets. Usually, 8 to 12% isopropyl alcohol is added to the dampening solution in order to achieve the desired characteristics for dampening and cleaning printing plates.

To get a good print, thee ink should to some extent be mixed with water before being applied to the printing plate. The water is emulsified in the ink, which results in a mixture of small, discrete drops of the two liquids – a mix of oil and water, so to speak. The dampening solution must also have the correct pH value and hardness in order to work properly (dH°). Hard water contains a number of different mineral salts, which, in large amounts, can cause pigments in the printing ink to dissolve. When the pigments dissolve, they can mix with the water coating the non-printing parts of the plate, thus transferring color to parts of the image that should remain non-printing. This phenomenon is known as "toning." The hardness of the water is regulated by adding a hardness regulator. Optimal hardness of water lies somewhere between 8 to 12 dH°. Too low pH value can lead to problems with the ink drying, and can lead to the surface of the paper coming apart, with pick-outs as a result. This is not good for the printing press either since with too low pH value corrosion can also be a problem. Too high pH value on the other hand, can make it difficult to keep the plate clean during printing. You adjust the dampening solution to buffer, regulate, the pH value. Optimal pH value of the water lies between 5.2 and 5.5.

9.5.8 Control of Ink Coverage

Depending on how the printed product is designed, the actual printed image requires different amounts of ink on different parts of the sheet. Therefore you have to vary the supply of the ink to the printed sheet. With the aid of doctor knives, how much ink will be delivered to different zones of the sheet can be adjusted. Screws controlling the ink allow the printer to specify how much ink should be transferred to the printing plate in different zones across the plate. The ink screws regulate the doctor knife and thereby determine how much ink should be forwarded to the different zones. Large and modern printing presses incorporate a control panel from which you can adjust the position of the screws and, thereby, the flow of the ink. In smaller and older printing presses the print screws are still adjusted by hand.

To facilitate the production of approved print sheets at the start of printing, you have to adjust the amount of ink in the different zones correctly before you start. Modern printing presses have support from JDF, Job Definition Format (earlier CIP3), and can utilize the information once it is launched [*see Prepress 7.3*]. At this point a file is created which contains information about the amount of ink for every zone. The file is created as the system analyzes how much cyan, magenta, yellow and black is contained in the respective zones in the launched digital file. The ink screws and ductor knives in the printing press are controlled with the information in the file, and in this way make the correct ink coverage adjustments, allowing for a faster makeready.

A plate scanner system is the technique that was commonly used to set up the zones in the printing press before the JDF technique was developed. A plate scanner system is also the technique that is mostly used today in printing presses that have no JDF support. The system scans the printing plates before they are mounted in the printing press to provide information about each zone's ink coverage. This information is then digitally transferred to the printing press. This provides you with a fairly accurate presetting of the ink screws and results in a faster makeready. The most efficient way to preset the ink screws is to enter the ink coverage for each zone as specified by the digital file that the print job is based on. There are systems that can analyze this data, convert it for the printing press and use it to preset the ink screws.

The screws on old printing presses were manually preset based on experience and a check of the printing plate or the approved print sheet. When you had gotten the first approved print sheet, it was important to preserve the printing result and the amount of ink coverage throughout the whole printing process. Because changing the amount of ink coverage takes a long time to stabilize in a printing press, unfortunately the amount of ink constantly varied. Unevenness in ink coverage throughout a print run is one of the most common flaws in quality. You have to continually compare the prints with the first approved print sheets and make adjustments in the amount of ink. Controls are done visually, but also adjustments to the different zones are then made according to measurements taken with a densitometer or spectrometer built into the control panel. You begin by taking measurements with the first approved print sheet and then continually measure against this approved print sheet. The control system of the printing press suggests how the ink coverage might be adjusted to obtain the same result. Before this type of integrated system existed, you measured by hand with a densitometer and adjusted the ink coverage with the help of experience.

9.5.9 Sheet Transportation

In a sheet-fed press, the mechanisms that grab the sheets and feed them through the printing press directly affect the final quality of the printed product. This machinery essentially has three main tasks:

- Pick up a single sheet of paper from the paper stack
- Make sure that only one sheet is fed into the press at a time
- Adjust – or register, as it is called – the paper in the machine so that all sheets enter into the printing press in exactly the same way. This is

THE INK DUCT
Printing ink is evenly added to the ink duct and transferred to the duct roller.

INK ZONES
Each number in the ink duct corresponds to a specific ink zone.

THE CONTROL PANEL
The control panel enables the printer to control the ink screws in the different zones. Measuring the different zones against the color bar on the printed sheet will tell you which zones need to be adjusted.

The most common problem in print quality is irregular ink coverage. If you are doing long print runs over the course of several personnel shifts, it is a good idea to take out as many approved print sheets as there are shifts, and place each one in an envelope. At the beginning of each shift the personnel should open their envelope and use this sheet to compare the quality of the run at that time. In this way you can avoid any gradual change in ink coverage.

THE STREAM FEEDER
In an offset printing press, the stream feeder picks up individual sheets of paper from the paper stack and sets them on the feed-board.

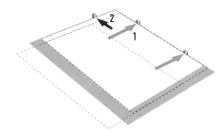

REGISTRATION
Before a sheet is printed it is lined up by its top and side edges. This is important because it ensures that double-sided prints will be properly registered from front to back, and that the registration in the off press processing machines will be consistent as well.

important in order to ensure that the image is printed in exactly the same way. This is important in order to ensure that the image is printed in exactly the same place on each sheet of paper.

The part of the printing press that picks up sheets from the paper stack is called the feeder. There are several different types of feeders but the most common is a pneumatic feeder with suction heads that lift up the sheet. As the sheet is lifted, the heads separate the to sheet from the one below with a blast of air. This ensures that only one sheet is fed into the machine at a time. The feeder takes the sheet it has picked up and places it on the feed board. The paper on the feed board is checked again to make sure there is only one sheet. If more than one sheet is fed into the press at a time, there is a great risk of crushing the rubber blanket.

In order to ensure accurate off press processing of printed products, it is important that the placement of the printed image on the paper sheets is exactly the same throughout the run. If they are not, the accuracy of off press finishing like folds, staples, etc., will be compromised. In order to avoid this, the paper sheets are adjusted, or registered, on the feed board before they continue throughout the printing press. The sheets are registered against two edges, the front edge, called the gripper's edge, and one of the side edges, called the feed edge. The sheets are registered only along two edges because the size of the sheets usually varies slightly throughout a paper stack.

It is important to keep track of the corner formed by the two registration edges. When the sheets are to be printed on both sides, you should make sure that when the second side is printed, the same edges are used to register the paper. Otherwise, it is difficult to ensure that the front and back of the sheets will match up correctly throughout the run As we mentioned earlier, it is also important for the off press processing that the print is registered throughout the run. Because of this, the corner formed by the gripper edge and the feed edge is usually marked on the stack of prints prior to off-press processing [*see Finishing and Binding 10.2*].

9.5.10 Paper

Generally speaking you can use any kind of paper for offset printing. The characteristics the paper should have for offset depends on the kind of printing press used; sheet-fed offset printing or web-fed offset printing (coldset or heatset). Here is a table that describes paper for the different offset techniques.

9.5.11 Production of Offset Printing Plates

The image carrier in offset printing is called the printing plate. When printing with several colored inks, you need a separate plate for each color. This combination of plates is usually called a plate set. There are a number of different types of plates. The most common offset plates are made of aluminum coated with a photosensitive polymer (plastic).

To create printing and non-printing areas the photosensitive polymer is exposed to light. When the coated plates are developed the polymer layer is washed off from the surfaces that are non-printing, revealing the aluminum

In this table the paper for the three offset techniques is compared.

	SHEET-FED OFFSET	COLDSET (NEWSPAPERS)	HEATSET
Weight in Grams	70–300g/m²	40–120g/m²	70–150g/m²
Delivered as	Ready sheets custom ordered for the printed product format and grain direction	Roll with format adapted to the printing press	Roll with format adapted to the printing press
Limitations and problems	Cannot handle thin grades of paper	Requires quick drying times	Curling – paper can ripple during drying
Quality	High	Low	Medium
Supply	Large supply – all papers, some cardboard and also plastic	Very limited supply	Limited supply

surfaces of the plate. Thus the printing surfaces of oliophilic polymer and non-printing surfaces of oliophobic aluminum have been created. The plate's aluminum surfaces are grainy, partly so the polymer will cling to the surface when the plate is made, and partly to create good conditions for repelling water. Water-free offset uses a silicone layer instead of water to differentiate the non-printing surfaces of the printing plate from the printing surfaces.

Offset plate is exposed in a platesetter or CTP (Computer To Plate) as it is called. A platesetter works in principle like a laser printer. Instead of printing on paper with colored pwder, the digital original is exposed directly onto a light or heat-sensitive offset plate. A platesetter has a much higher resolution than a laser printer. An average laser printer has around 1,200 dpi, in comparison with an average platesetter with a resolution of over 3,600 dpi.

A very fine laser beam exposes the areas of the film tat should be exposed according to information in a bitmap. In certain systems the laser beam exposes the dots that are to be printed (positive technique), and in others the dots that are not to be printed are exposed (negative technique). The platesetter's RIP calculates the halftone screens, creating a large bitmap [*see Prepress 7.1.4*] in which every exposure dot in the platesetter is represented by a one or a zero (i.e., exposed or non-exposed surface). If you are printing in multiple colors a separate bitmap is created for each component color in the print.

Most plates have to be developed after they have been exposed. For some plates the laser beam's energy is not enough to complete the chemical process needed to develop the plate. Extra energy is provided by warming the plate in an oven before developing. Developing takes place in a separate machine, the developer. Often a platesetter is built together with an oven and a developer, known as online developing.

To help achieve accurate registration among the different inks, it is important that the printing plates are inserted into the press correctly. The registration pins and holes in the printing plate set the plates properly. The insertion of the printing plate is often done manually, but printing presses with automatic plate changers are becoming more common.

9.5.12 Platesetters

There are three types of setters: capstan or flatbed models, as well as setters with internal or external drums.

The first kind, capstan or flatbed models, are constructed for the plate to lie flat when it is exposed. Exposure is done by a laser beam, which is either switched on and off, or directed through a modulator that can "turn off" and "turn on " the laser beam. The modulator is controlled by information from the RIP file and lets through or directs away the laser beam according to whether the surface should be exposed or not. Then the laser beam hits an octagonal mirror, just like in a laser printer. The mirror causes the beam to sweep across the film in a line. When a line has been exposed, the plate is fed forward and the next line is exposed until the whole plate has been exposed. In a platesetter it is essential that the plate be fed forward exactly and that the mirror rotate exactly.

In the external drum technique, the plate is strapped around a drum which then rotates while the laser beam exposes the plate. The laser, which is either switched on and off, or directed through a modulator that can "turn off" and "turn on " the laser beam, is reflected via a mirror that steps forward along the rotating drum. The plate is exposed row by row. In these platesetters, it is important that the plate is attached to the drum ion exactly the right way and that the mirror steps forward with precision.

In the internal drum technique, the plate is fed into a drum and then "sucked" into place. Exposure occurs with a laser beam that is either switched on and off, or directed through a modulator that can "turn off" and "turn on " the laser beam. Then it is reflected off a mirror, which rotates on a screw inside the drum. The mirror moves step by step along the entire width of the plate. When the plate is exposed, a new plate is fed into the drum and the exposed plate moves on to be developed. The precision of the mirror's movement along the plate is crucial to the success of this technique. It is the only technique in whish the plate remains still while being exposed.

In all types of platesetters, precision and repeatability are very important factors. Repeatability is the platesetter's ability to expose exactly the same way many times in a row. There are registration systems with holes and pins that set the plates properly to ensure good print registration between plates in a platesetter. Proper exposure and development of the plates is crucial to the quality of the final print. Therefore it is important that a platesetter be calibrated and that the developing liquid in the developer is frequently changes. An uncalibrated platesetter can produce completely erroneous tonal values. Old developing liquid loses its ability to develop the film properly, resulting in insufficient or uneven inking.

9.5.13 Types of Plates

There are three principal kinds of plates; Silver-Halide, photopolymer and thermal plates. The different types of plates are sensitive to either light (photo-

PLATESETTER
Platesetters are joined to the development equipment and when the plate is finished it is placed in a stand.

polymer and Silver-Halide) or heat (thermal). Silver-Halide and photopolymer plates are so sensitive that they should not be handled in daylight. Thermal plates, on the other hand, are not sensitive to daylight.

The coating on the aluminum base of the plates has two characteristics: the oliophilic property necessary in order to print, and the photosensitive property necessary for exposure. Often two kinds of materials are combined to optimize both characteristics. It is important for the plates to have an even coating to get an even exposure over the whole plate. All kinds of plates can be over and under exposed. Over exposure of positive plates make the lighter tones darker than they should be, and over exposure of negative plates eradicates the lightest tones. For certain kinds of plates the energy of the laser is not enough to complete the chemical process of developing. In this case heating the plate in an oven creates additional energy.

There are also special development-free plates, which means you can skip the developing process. The three most common techniques are UV technique, thermal technique and inkjet technique. UV technique is based on a laser beam lighting up the plate, and the non-printing surfaces being washed off by the dampening system of the printing press. The thermal technique means that the material on the plate is pulverized from the heat when exposed to a laser beam. After exposure the plate has to be vacuumed so that the residue of the burned material is removed. The inkjet technique is still being developed, and it involves using inkjet technique to spray a printing coating onto the oliophilic aluminum base where dots for the printing surface should be.

DIRECT AND INDIRECT PRINTING PROCEDURES

A distinction is usually made between direct and indirect printing procedures. Direct printing means that the printing ink is deposited onto the paper (or other material) directly from the image carrier. In this case the image on the image carrier has to be reversed so that it prints correctly on the paper, much like the way a stamp works. Examples of direct printing procedures include flexography and gravure printing.

Indirect printing involves transferring ink from the image carrier to a rubber blanket, which in turn transfers the ink to the paper. The print image is correct on the image carrier, and reversed on the rubber cylinder so that it is oriented correctly on the paper. Offset printing is an indirect printing procedure.

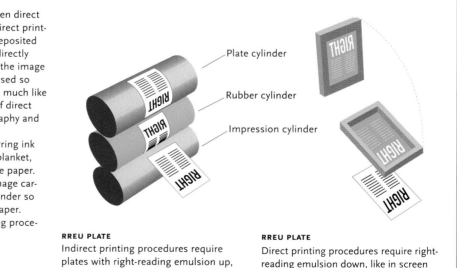

Plate cylinder

Rubber cylinder

Impression cylinder

RREU PLATE
Indirect printing procedures require plates with right-reading emulsion up, like in offset printing as in the example above.

RREU PLATE
Direct printing procedures require right-reading emulsion down, like in screen printing as in the example above.

Before platesetters were developed, graphic film was used and developed in an imagesetter. The developed film was then used to expose printing plates with the help of a UV light. Today taking a detour via film is seldom done, but it is done sometimes in large format offset, flexography and screen printing. There are setters that can produce printing plates for these techniques also, but they are relatively expensive and it has taken longer to phase out film use in these specific areas.

Graphic film consists of a plastic backing coated with a light-sensitive emulsion layer. The unexposed film lies rolled inside a film cassette. Graphic film is exposed in an imagesetter then developed using chemical developers. These chemicals are one of the big environmental burdens of graphic production. Because of this, many film manufacturers have put a lot of energy into developing "dry" films, which don't require the se of hazardous chemicals.

The developed film is then placed on a printing plate and exposed to light. The plate has a light sensitive polymer layer that reacts to the light exposure. The method is reminiscent of the way photographers create contact sheets. After the plate is exposed, it is developed with liquid chemicals.

There is both negative and positive film. When positive film is exposed and developed, all printing surfaces appear black, and all surfaces that are non-printing are transparent. This type of film looks essentially like what the page would look like as output from a laser printer. Exposed and developed negative film comes out exactly opposite – all printing surfaces appear transparent and those that are not to be printed are black.

The offset printing process can accommodate positive as well as negative film, and there are advantages and disadvantages to both. Some commercial printers prefer using positive film while others prefer to work with negative film. Geography seems to play a part in film preference – the United States mainly uses negative film whereas most of Europe uses positive film.

FILMS WITH POSITIVE AND REVERSED IMAGES

Indirect and direct printing procedures require different types of films. Direct printing uses films with positive images, right-reading emulsion up (RREU), whereas indirect printing uses films with reversed images, or right-reading emulsion down (RRED), as they are often called within the graphics industry. This is different than the distinction between positive and negative film that contains the emulsion layer.

The terms right-reading emulsion up and right-reading emulsion down always assume that you are looking at the film from its emulsion side, the matte side. If the print image is reversed, you have a negative film; if the print image is correctly oriented, you have a positive film. Right-reading emulsion up films are also called cliché films.

FILM SETS, MONTAGE AND IMPOSITION OF FILMS

When printing with many colors, you need one film for each printing ink. Such a collection of films is usually called a film set, or in the case of a four-color print, a four-color set.

In a printing press, several pages of the printed product are usually printed together on the same large sheet. This means that the printing plate must contain all of the pages to be printed on any given sheet. When producing film originals, you can either output the individual pages on separate films or on "imposed film." When using many separate films, they are then mounted and imposed manually on a larger film. The final film assembly is used to expose the printing plate. With digitally imposed film, the pages are mounted and imposed on a computer using an imposition program before they are output. This allows you to output an imposed film set for an entire printer's sheet with which you can directly expose the printing plate.

PRODUCTION OF OFFSET PRINTING PLATES

To expose a printing plate with help of film, it is important to place the emulsion side of the film directly against the printing plate. In offset printing the offset plate is then exposed for a certain number of seconds in an "exposure frame." For large format prints, either screen or offset, the film is projected instead onto the large image carrier. It is important to have the timing exact in order for the exposure to come out correctly. Erroneous exposures can result in incorrect screen percent values (too high or too low depending on if the exposure time was too long or too short). Wrong exposures can also prevent halftone dots from transferring to the plate at all. You can determine the correct exposure time by using a control strip. The light source in the exposure equipment ages and its characteristics change over time. Therefore you should regularly check that the exposure times are still accurate. Newer exposure frames automatically revise the time according to the aging of the lamp.

Before the exposure takes place, the film is suctioned to the plate by a vacuum action. It is important that the film is closely and evenly placed against the plate with no air bubbles to ensure an even transfer across the entire plate. It is also important that the plate production takes place in a dust-free environment. Dust prevents the film and plate from lying flush against each other. In addition, larger dust particles can be visible on the printing form, particularly with positive film.

If you are using negative film, the illuminated areas of the printing plate are hardened during exposure. When you chemically develop the printing plate, the unexposed, non-hardened, non-printing areas are washed away. If you are using positive film, the exposed surfaces of the printing form are washed away during development instead, giving you essentially the same results.

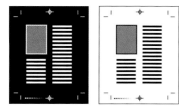

NEGATIVE AND POSITIVE FILM
In negative film, all printing surfaces appear transparent and those that are non-printing are black. Positive film comes out exactly opposite.

SINGLE VS IMPOSED FILM
When working with single pages of film, the pages have to be mounted or imposed manually. They are then taped to a larger film.

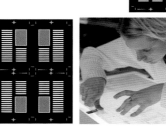

Film Base

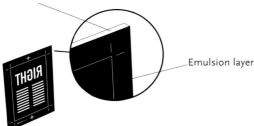

Emulsion layer

FIND THE EMULSION SIDE
If you are not sure which side has the emulsion layer, hold up the film against the light. The emulsion side is matte and the other side is shiny.

You can also try to carefully scratch the corner of the film with a sharp object. On the emulsion side you will be able to scratch off some of the emulsion, on the other side you won't.

The emulsion layer is sensitive to scratches and must not be damaged. Scratches in the emulsion layer will be directly transferred to the printing plate and the print.

PLATE PUNCHER
A plate puncher punches holes in the plate before it's exposed.

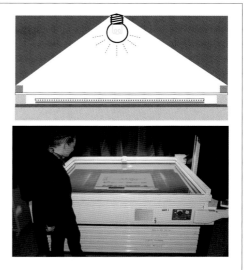

PLATE EXPOSURE
Before the exposure takes place, the film is suctioned to the plate by a vacuum action to ensure that the film and plate are lying flush against each other. The plate is then exposed with the lamp of the exposure frame.

The plate is exposed with ultraviolet light in an exposure frame. When exposing, curtains are used to prevent the light from harming the eye.

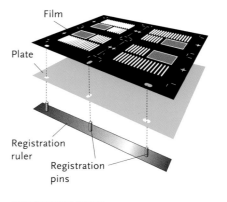

Film

Plate

Registration ruler

Registration pins

REGISTRATION RULER
To be able to keep alignment between the plate and film, you punch holes in them. When mounting and exposing the plate as well as in the printing press, the material is attached to a ruler with pins.

In this table the different CTP-plates are compared

	SILVER-HALIDE PLATES	PHOTOPOLYMER PLATES	THERMAL PLATES
Types of laser	violet laser – 405 nm Argon Ion – 488nm, FD-YAG – 532nm	violet laser – 405 nm Argon Ion – 488nm, FD-YAG – 532nm	IR-laser – 830 nm
Type av setter	Internal drum or flatbed	Internal drum or flatbed	External drum
Sensitive to daylight	Yes	Yes	No
Used by what printing houses	Second most common in both newspaper and other printing	The plate that is most used in newspaper printing	The plate that is used in all forms of printing except for newspapers
Characteristics	Not for very long runs or UV drying colors	Not for very long runs or UV-drying colors	Can be used for very long runs and for UV-drying colors
Resolution	High resolution 200 lpi and upwards	Lower resolution max 175 lpi	High resolution over 200 lpi
Has to be heated up after exposure	No	Yes	Yes

A common problem with light boxes is that the printed image lack in contrast. To achieve higher contrast the motif can be printed on the back, as a mirror image. To gain high contrast and a good result, the back side is usually printed with cyan and/or black. There are also versions with cyan, magenta and yellow.

Different types of plates require different types of laser exposure. There are platesetters with violet lasers – 405 nm, Argon ion - 488 nm, FD-YAG – 532 nm or the IR laser and the violet laser. The IR laser is used with the thermal plate (heat exposure). It is an expensive technique with the laser having a limited lifespan. The laser is never turned off during exposure, with a modulator controlling where the plate should or shouldn't be exposed at every dot. The modulator also has a limited lifespan and has to be changed.

The violet laser technique is used both with photopolymer (light exposure) and silver-halide plates (light exposure) and in cheap in comparison with the IR laser. The technique is built on inexpensive laser diodes, like the ones in a DVD player, with a very long lifespan. The diodes turn on and off at each point on the plate that is to be exposed, which means that no modulator is necessary. The technique is so cheap that it is economically feasible to use a platesetter even for small formats like A3.

9.5.14 Typical Phenomena in Offset Printing
Below we will cover the most common phenomena in offset printing: picking and pick-out, smearing, powdering, toning, reflection and curling. They are all non-desirable, so it is important to understand how they occur in order to minimize their effect.

9.5.15 Picking and Pick-outs
Sometimes small fragments of the paper's surface are pulled off during printing. This is called picking. If these fragments, or "pick-outs" as they are called, land on a printing area on the printing plate, the plate will not absorb ink in

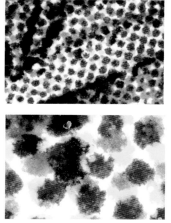

Halftone dots in an offset print are irregular and blurry because of the way they are pressed onto the paper. Offset printing results in a slightly poorer image quality than gravure printing or analog proofs.

Text printed in an offset printing press is sharp and has clear outlines. Offset gives you better text reproduction than gravure printing, but slightly poorer than that of the analog proof.

PICKOUTS
Pickouts are paper fragments that stick to the printing plate or the rubber blanket and cause white dots in the print. They are particularly visible in dark tint areas. You can reduce the sensitivity of black tint areas to pickouts by making them deep black.

STOP THE PRESSES!
When pickouts appear on the printed sheets, you have to stop the press and clean the printing plate.

those places. This results in small, un-printed white dots on the finished print. The same thing happens when the pick-outs get stuck on the rubber blanket. If you are noticing white spots on your prints, you will have to stop the printing press and wipe any pick-outs off the printing plate and rubber blanket. Modern printing presses often have automatic washing cycles to remove pick-outs.

Picking can occur because of poor surface strength in the paper, viscous ink or a printing speed that is too fast. Because of its especially viscous ink and the fact that there is no dampening solution to keep the printing plates clean, water-free offset printing has more problems with picking and pick-outs than wet offset printing.

9.5.16 Smearing

Printed sheets can smear each other if the ink coverage is too high or if off press processing occurs before they have dried sufficiently. This problem can be solved with drying powder or other drying systems. Cyan ink usually takes the longest to dry, and is therefore the most sensitive to smearing.

9.5.17 Powdering

Sometimes ink comes off even though it has dried. This phenomenon is called powdering. It can be because of too much ink being used, and is especially prevalent on silk quality paper. It can appear as a discoloration of a large white area that is adjacent to an area that is heavily tinted. The reason for powdering

1. Correct print image on the printing plate.

2. The paper is compressed as it passes through the first printing unit and the printed image is transferred.

3. The paper gets its original shape back after printing is completed and the printed image shrinks.

4. In the second printing unit, the sheet is compressed and enlarged a little bit more and the print area of the second ink color lands inside the first one.

5. The appearance of the sheet after it has been printed in both units.

The phenomenon called "coning" happens when the print area of the first ink color laid down on a sheet is slightly wider than the print area of the last ink color printed on a sheet. This happens because the paper is compressed as it passes through each successive printing unit. Coning occurs both in sheet-fed and web-fed offset printing.

is that not all the pigment in the dried ink has been bound and a certain amount of the pigment is lying loose on the surface.

9.5.18 Toning

Too little dampening solution can result in toning of the non-printing surfaces of the paper (called a dry run, or tinting). This means that non-printing areas of the printing plate get colored by the ink and become printing areas. Toning can also occur if the water in the dampening solution is too hard, causing the pigments in the ink to dissolve and color the paper.

9.5.19 Reflection

Tint blocks often require a lot of ink, which can cause problems for the rest of the print. Tint areas are also m ore sensitive to changes caused by other areas of the print. These two factors can cause a phenomenon known as reflection or ghosting. "Reflections" of other print areas appear in the tint blocks when the plate cylinder down not have enough time to pick up the large quantities of ink needed for the tint blocks. Reflection is most common in the smaller printing press formats.

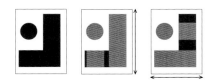

GHOSTING

The phenomenon known as ghosting appears as traces of other printed objects in the printing direction. The image on the left shows the correctly printed image. The two images on the right are printed with different printing directions (indicated by the arrows) to demonstrate the phenomenon of reflection.

9.5.20 Curling

There is a phenomenon in heatset printing called curling that occurs from drying the printed product. It manifests itself as rippling in the paper of the printed product. Curling happens because of a combination of high ink coverage, heat in the oven and speed of the paper feeder. To avoid curling in the printed product you should use an ICC profile that limits ink coverage adequately during printing adjustments. It is important that the ICC profile's limits on inking be extensive enough so that you can still print dense pictures with a lot of ink on both the front and the reverse sides without curling occurring.

9.6 Letterpress

Letterpress printing is the classic printing technique that descends from the Middle Ages wooden block printing and Gutenberg's first printing press. The technique is based on the image carrier having printing areas separated from non-printing by a difference in elevation, just like the stamp. Today's letterpress printing presses use in principle the same technique as when the first printing press was built.

Today letterpress is used mainly for business cards, correspondence cards, invitations, stationery, receipt forms, numbered blank forms, etc., so-called commercial printing. There are three reasons why people use letterpress today. The first reason is because they want to create a printed product with a little bit of an old-fashioned feel. These are printed products like visiting and business cards, correspondence cards , stationery and invitations.

The second reason is that they want to number their printed products, for example blank forms, receipts etc. For this you need a numbering system that gives a new number to every printed piece.

The third and last reason is that you can perform certain off press processing directly in the printing press, such as creasing, embossing, die punching and perforating.

9.6.1 Letterpress Technique

Letterpress printing uses the same principle as the stamp technique with mirror image printing formes. The printing forme is inked and transfers the ink directly to the paper by pressing it against the paper.

There are three main kinds of letterpress printing presses, a division based on their technical solutions. The first variation is called "platen press" and works with a flat printing forme that comes together with a flat impression surface. The most common letterpress printing press, Heidelbergs Vinge, is a platen press.

The second variation is called the "cylinder press" and works with a flat printing forme that prints against an impression cylinder.

The third and last variation is called a "rotary press". In this printing press the printing forme is located on a cylinder and prints against an impression cylinder.

Cylinder presses and rotary presses are not commonly used today.

9.6.2 Printing Blocks and Type

Images carriers for letterpress consist either of set type or printing blocks or both. Today about 60 percent of letterpress is typeset and printing blocks are used for the other 40 percent. It is mainly logotype and such that use printing blocks.

When setting type you build a layout using separate pieces of type, one piece of type for every symbol, and these are placed together, creating a printing mould. You can also complement the typeset printing mould with printing blocks that can't be set in with the other type.

When you use printing blocks you use graphic film and a base material to build the block on. The base material consists of 2 mm thick magnesium

LETTERPRESS PRINTING
Letterpress printing is the classic printing technique that descends from the Middle Ages wooden block printing and Gutenberg's first printing press. The technique is based on the image carrier having printing areas separated from non-printing by a difference in elevation, just like the stamp. Today's letterpress printing presses use in principle the same technique as when the first printing press was built.

Today letterpress is used mainly for business cards, correspondence cards, invitations, stationery, receipt forms, numbered blank forms, etc., so-called commercial printing.

LIKE A STAMP
Letterpress printing uses the same principle as the stamp technique with mirror image printing forms. The printing surface is inked and transfers the ink directly to the paper by pressing it against the paper.

covered with a light-sensitive coating. The graphic film is placed over the light-sensitive surface on the printing surfaces. The printing block is washed, so the non-hardened surfaces are rinsed away. There remains a height difference of about 0.8 millimeters between the printing and non-printing surfaces. When embossing is going to be done, you work with 7 millimeter-thick magnesium blocks, dies, that are etched to a height difference of 3 millimeters. But you also need an impression surface, an upper die that has an etching the opposite of the die, with depressions where the die has raised surfaces, etc. The upper die is made from a special plastic that acts like the die material during exposure only in reverse.

9.6.3 Ink

The ink you use for letterpress printing is exactly like the ink used in offset printing, an oil-based ink consisting of pigment and a binding agent. Today black offset ink and black letterpress ink are used interchangeably in letterpress printing. But there are differences in characteristics between offset and letterpress inks. For example, offset ink does not have to be attracted to the printing form's printing surfaces the way offset ink should be attracted to the printing surfaces of the offset plate. Letterpress ink is more fluid, that is less sticky, and therefore doesn't require the same surface strength that offset paper does. You can also place more letterpress ink on the paper than you can with offset.

Letterpress ink dries exactly the way offset ink does in two stages. First, when it sets and the oil in the ink is absorbed by the paper and the ink forms a gel, and then through oxidation, when the ink reacts to the oxygen in the air.

9.6.4 Paper

Most paper can be used for letterpress printing. The characteristics that are considered so important are a little inconsistent. First and foremost, you want as smooth a paper as possible so the ink will cover completely – will print out which means that glossy paper is preferable. At the same time you want the paper to be compressible and to work a little bit like the rubber blanket in offset so the ink will print out. Unfortunately the compressibility of the paper is diminished with a glossy finish. The paper for letterpress doesn't need to be as high strength as offset paper does. Letterpress also allows for a large choice of paper thicknesses. You can print on everything from the thinnest varieties all the way up to 0.5 mm thick.

It is usual to use a paper with a little rag content for letterpress printing, to give a little old-fashioned feel. It is also usual to print on tag material, since with letterpress you have the possiblilty of simultaneously die punching tags into irregular formats and shapes.

9.6.5 Typical Phenomena in Letterpress Printing

Below we will cover the most common phenomena in letterpress printing. They are all more or less non-desirable, so it is important to understand how they occur in order to minimize their effect.

9.6.6 Problems with "modern" Roman Fonts

When you print with blocks using fonts in letterpress, you should use "classi-cally" cut Roman fonts with somewhat thicker hairlines. Modern carvings of Roman fonts have such fine hairlines that they can lead to problems in printing. The printing mould can have difficulty in transferring such fine lines, which may mean they don't get transferred to the paper at all.

9.6.7 Embossing in Letterpress Printing

To be sure that the ink prints out, that is gives complete and even coverage, the printing mould is pressed into the paper. This can result in an indentation, embossing in the printed product. It used to be considered better quality to have total ink coverage without any feeling of being stamped or embossed. These days it is desirable to have a little feeling of the paper being embossed so you can tell it is letterpress, especially for business or visiting cards, correspondence cards and so on.

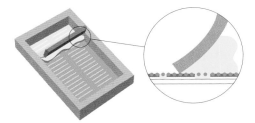

9.7 Screen Printing

The biggest advantage to the screen-printing method is that it allows you to print on almost any material, in any shape or format. The screen-printing method is used to print on porcelain, fabric, metal, and cardboard, amongst other things. The diverse range of products printed using this method includes coffee mugs, clothes, cookie tins and signs, to name just a few.

SCREEN PRINTING
Ink is pressed through the cloth with a ductor blade. The cloth is prepared so that ink is only let through the printing areas.

9.7.1 Screen Printing Technique

Screen printing differs significantly from other printing methods. Instead of a printing surface on a cylinder, screen printing uses thin, fine cloth stretched on a frame, with a different frame, or screen, for each printing ink. Ink is pressed through the cloth with a ductor blade and transferred to the material that is being printed. The cloth is prepared so that ink only seeps through to the print-ing areas, the so-called printing substrate.

In traditional screen printing, that is when you print on a flat substrate, the printing substrate and the screen frame lie still and the ductor blade travels across the screen and presses the ink through the cloth. A screen printing press today is made typically of four frames built together in a row, one for each color. Four printing substrates are printed simultaneously, one in each frame. When the printing in the frame is done, the ink is dried under a UV light. After that the printing substrate is moved to the next screen. Since you are often working with large formats, often the screen printing press is very long. The printing presses have control systems that allow you to quickly increase or dercrease the amount of ink using the ductor blade and the ink supply. A change in the amount of ink occurs right away, in contrast with offset printing where an increase occurs gradually. One of the big advantages of screen printing it that you can print with thicker layers of ink than with offset. This means that you get higher contrast in the printed result. If you print with a large format and light color you don't have to work, as in offset, with mirror image printing on the reverse side to increase contrast.

SCREEN PRINTING PRESS
A screen printing press today is typically made of four frames built together in a row, one for each color. Since you are often working with large for-mats, often the screen printing press is very long.

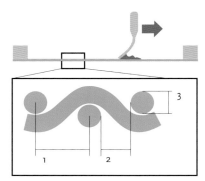

Important characteristics of screen printing cloth:

1. Density of the fabric: measured in number of threads per cm (10–200 is normal)

2. Open printing area: the percentage of the cloth surface that is available for printing

3. Thickness of the threads used to weave the fabric: thin, medium, thick and extra thick

Direction during printing process

Back to starting position

SCREEN PRINTING ON ROUND OBJECTS
The frame and the object being printed are rotated against each other while the doctor blade remains static.

PREPARING THE SCREEN PRINTING FRAMES

SCREEN PRINTERS
The first step in preparing the print-ready screen cloth is to coat it with a light sensitive emulsion. Screen printers using the ink-jet technique write on the emulsion on the printing surfaces with ink or wax. After the emulsion has been cured by ultraviolet light, the non-illuminated parts covered with ink are cleaned.

LARGE FORMATS
Screen printing is appropriate for large formats.

When printing on circular objects like bottles or cans, a method different from traditional screen printing is used. The print surface and the frame move while the ductor blade stays still. The printing surface – a bottle for example – rotates while the frame moves over it at the same speed [*see illustration*]. There are screen printing presses that use similar methods for printing on flat print surfaces. These presses have an impression cylinder that rotates while the printing surface follows the screen.

9.7.2 **The Screen Cloth**
The cloth used is really finely woven net. The net is coated with a screen stencil, which only allows ink to pass through to the printing surfaces. The screen stencil, which consists of a thin film of plastic material, covers the non-printing surfaces of the net while leaving the printing surfaces open. There are different methods and materials for producing screen stencils. In some methods, the screen stencil is already mounted on the cloth before it is exposed, in others the screen stencil is mounted on the screen after it has been created.

Today when you are going to make a new stencil you use a stencilsetter. The cloth is coated with was and a light sensitive emulsion. A laser beam shines on the printing surfaces and when developed the exposed parts of the emulsion and wax are washed away. The non-printing surfaces hardens during development and build a stencil for printing.

In the traditional production methods, screen stencils are made using film also. But as opposed to the above, the stencils are developed with the aid of light exposure using projection cameras. Regular graphic, right-reading positive film is placed on the screen stencil and exposed. The illuminated, non-printing surfaces harden and the printing areas are washed off during development.

Types of screen cloth are usually differentiated by the thickness of the thread used to weave the net, how tightly the net is woven and how large the available printing surface is. Thicker thread and tighter weaving will result in thicker layers of ink on the print. Thick layers of ink require more drying time. The stretching of the cloth on the frame is very important. If the net is not mounted exactly straight, in the direction of the thread and at a right angle to the frame, you can get undesirable moiré effects and interference patterns in the prints [*see Prepress 7.7.11*].

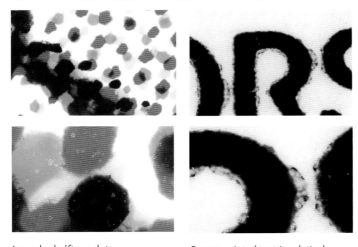

Irregular halftone dots can negatively affect the image quality of screen prints.

Screen-printed text is relatively blurry and of low quality compared to text printed with the offset method.

Advantages and disadvantages with screen printing:
+ Can be used to print on most materials, including thicker paper and cardboard
+ Low waste
+ Water-based printing inks can be used
− Not appropriate for high screen frequencies
− It is difficult to reproduce the entire tonal range with screen printing technique, and fine tonal transitions cannot always be achieved.

Screen cloth can be bought separately but is also sold preinstalled on frames. When the screen stencil is exposed and attached to the tightened cloth, you have to make sure that the noon-printing areas do not have any holes. Holes in the screen are common, and are simply patched up with filler.

9.7.3 Ink
Ink that dries due to the evaporation of solvents is a considerable environmental hazard. Today, more environmentally sound inks are being used, including water-based inks and inks dried with ultra-violet light. With screen printing, it is important that the inks dry quickly, because this method does not allow you to print wet-on-wet. Each component color has to dry before the next one can be added.

9.7.4 Paper and Material
Screen printing is the printing technique with the fewest limitations in terms of what kinds of materials you can print on. In principle you can print on anything that is flat or round.

9.7.5 Typical Phenomena in Screen Printing
Moiré is a typical problem in screen printing [see Prepress 7.7.11]. This is because the fine net of the screen cloth builds a pattern that interacts with the screen patterns and in this way builds an interference pattern. They only way to avoid this is to change the angle of the rasters. For this reason other screen pattern angles are used in screen printing compared with, for example, offset printing.

Gravure printing is an old printing method with roots in copperplates and etchings. It is an expensive technique, financially feasible only for long print runs. Gravure printing presses are web-fed presses, are often large and print at a very high speed. Therefore it is used primarily for periodicals, catalogues, brochures and similar large editions.

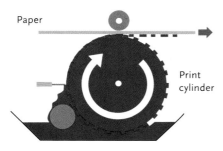

Paper

Print cylinder

THE PRINCIPLE OF GRAVURE PRINTING
The small halftone wells are filled with ink, and a doctor blade removes any extra ink. The ink is transferred from the printing form to the paper in the printing nip.

9.8 Gravure Printing

Gravure printing is an old printing method with roots in copperplates and etchings. It is an expensive technique, financially feasible only for long print runs. Gravure printing presses are web-fed presses, are often large and print at a very high speed. Therefore it is used primarily for periodicals, catalogues, brochures and similar large editions.

9.8.1 Gravure Printing Technique
The gravure technique can be likened to an inverted stamp, where the non-printing areas are higher than the printing areas. Printing plates are not used in gravure printing; the image carrier consists of steel cylinders coated with a layer of copper. The printing areas are engraved (a mechanical procedure) or etched (a chemical procedure) in the cylinder. This gives you halftone screens consisting of small wells. In order to produce halftone dots with different sizes on the paper, the wells vary in size, depth or both, depending on the gravure technique. The wells are filled with ink, which is transferred to the print when the paper is pressed against the printing form by a rubber-coated impression cylinder.

9.8.2 The Gravure Printing Form
Before each new etching or engraving, a new copper layer has to be added to the printing cylinder. The coppering is done using electrolysis with copper sulfate and sulfuric acid.

Gravure is the most common engraving technique done today. The technique is based on a diamond-tipped engraving head, which uses physical pressure to create halftone screens (wells) on the printing cylinder. The printing cylinder rotates as it is being engraved, and after each completed rotation, the graver head inches along the cylinder to engrave the next part of the image. This continues until the entire cylinder is engraved. Gravure cylinders can be engraved using information directly from a digital source. This is known as direct engraving. Before, the engraving was not controlled by a digital file, and was instead read from an opalescent film. The read-head used light to read and transmit the engraving information off the film to the engraving head. Opalescent film was made from graphic film that had information written on it by a photosetter.

Today lasersetters are being developed for engraving. They burn the wells in the copper layer with a laser. To make this possible you have to have a very powerful laser that gives off about 1,000,000,000 watts per cubic centimeter. The advantage with this new technique is that engraving time is reduced enormously, as well as getting away from all the limitations of gravure printing, such as everything having to be screened, including text.

Engraving by etching is an older method. The first step in creating an etching is reminiscent of producing offset printing plates. A light-sensitive gel coats a pigment film, and hardens when exposed to light, capturing an image. The gel is not "binary" like the offset plate – areas can only be printing or non-printing. The gel become more deeply engraved the longer it is exposed. The entire sheet is then transferred to the printing plate, and the unexposed gel is washed off.

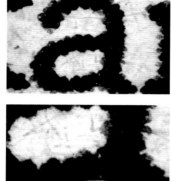

In gravure printing, the reproduction of halftone dots is very precise because they are not pressed onto the paper as they are in offset printing. The image quality is therefore better than that achieved with offset printing.

Everything printed with the gravure technique is built up with halftone screens ("wells"), even solid areas. This means that even the text is rasterised which results in a lesser quality reproduction than offset printing.

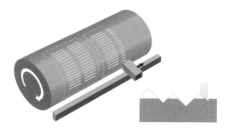

DIRECT ENGRAVING

In direct engraving, the printing cylinder is engraved according to digital information. The engraving is done with a diamond-tipped head whose movement creates halftone wells of differing depth.

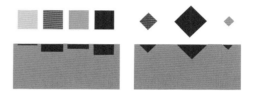

IMAGE CARRIERS FOR GRAVURE PRINTING

On the left is an etched plate used for gravure printing and a print made with it. The figure at the right shows a form for engraving. In the etched plate, the halftone wells are identical in size but differ in color, while the halftone wells in the mould used for gravure printing vary in both size and color.

The actual etching of the copper printing plate then takes place. A liquid that has a corrosive effect on the copper and the gel is used. The engraved gel is gradually dissolved by the corrosive solution. Because the gel is dissolved gradually, the underlying copper printing form will also be dissolved to different levels, depending on how thick the engraved gel layer is at any given spot. This process creates "halftone wells" of different sizes and/or depth.

9.8.3 Ink

Gravure ink cannot be viscous, since it must dry very quickly. In gravure printing you can't print wet-on-wet. Gravure ink contains a volatile solvent (toluene) that evaporates rapidly, causing the ink to dry very quickly. The drying time of the ink is further accelerated by hot air drying systems. The evaporated toluene must be recycled.

9.8.4 Paper

The surface must be even on paper used for gravure printing, otherwise the halftone dots may not be transferred to the paper, so-called missing dot [*see below*]. For this reason calendared or coated paper must be used. The choice is relatively limited, and you usually have to use whatever the printer uses.

GRAVURE PRINTING +/−

Advantages and disadvantages with gravure printing:

+ The printing cylinders last through large-volume runs without getting worn out
+ High volume runs will have low per-unit costs
+ Good image reproduction
− All lines and text are rasterized
− Extensive use of chemicals and solvents in the ink
− High start-up costs (inappropriate for small editions)

9.8.5 Typical Phenomena in Gravure Printing

Below we will cover the most common phenomena in gravure printing. They are all non-desirable, so it is important to understand how they occur in order to minimize their effect.

9.8.6 Missing dot

The missing dot phenomenon appears as patchiness in tinted areas and images. They occur because not all the halftone wells in the printing form succeed in transferring the ink. The result is that there are areas missing ink in the printed product and it looks patchy. Missing dots are caused by unevenness in the paper or problems with ink transfer in the printing press.

9.8.7 Screening of Text

Because halftone wells are used in gravure printing, any printed text will be screened (converted into halftone screens). That mans that from full color surfaces, illustrations, to text is built on halftone screens ("wells"). This means that even the text is rasterized, which results in a lesser quality reproduction than offset printing. It appears most interfering in typeface with small calibrations and fine lines.

9.8.8 Wrong Grain Direction

Gravure printing is used mainly for very large runs. Paper costs are then a large part of the total cost. For this reason layouts are chosen to minimize paper consumption, which means that grain direction is sometimes compromised. This results in the binding having poorer durability and the printed product more difficult to leaf through.

9.9 Flexographic Printing

Flexographic printing is one of the few modern printing techniques that uses the same principle as the stamp. The printing areas are separated from the non-printing by a difference in elevation. Flexographic printing allows you to print on most materials, including paper, cardboard, plastic and metal. This versatility has caused flexographic printing to become particularly popular with the packaging industry and the hygienic paper industry.

9.9.1 Flexography Technique

Flexography uses a rubber or plastic printing surface and a "direct printing" technique, which means that the printing surface transfers the ink directly to the print surface. The printing surface is thus a mirror image of the final printed image. Because the printing surface is made of an elastic material, the impression cylinder has to be hard. This relationship is the reverse of gravure printing, where the impression cylinder is soft and the printing form hard.

9.9.2 Flexographic Plates

There are two main versions of printing plates used in flexographic printing: flexible rubber plates and photopolymer plates. Photopolymer plates are the

FLEXOGRAPHIC PRINTING PRESS
Flexographic printing allows you to print on most materials, including paper, cardboard, plastic and metal. This versatility has caused flexographic printing to become particularly popular with the packaging industry and the hygienic paper industry.

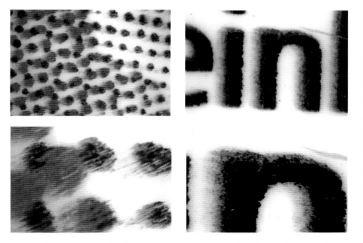

The halftone dots in the flexographic print easily smear because the rubber plate slides against the paper like a stamp.

Text printed with the flexographic technique also smears easily because of the "stamp" principle. This results in text reproduction inferior to that of the offset printing method. Note the flexographic print edge, which is clearly visible inside the contours of the letters.

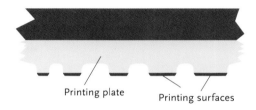

Printing plate   Printing surfaces

THE PRINTING PLATE FOR FLEXOGRAPHIC PRINTING

The printing plate in flexographic printing has elevated printing surfaces, just like a stamp.

FLEXOGRAPHIC PRINTING +/−

Advantages and disadvantages with flexographic printing:

+ Can be used to print on most materials
+ Water-based printing inks can be used
+ Low waste
+ Variable printing format
− The flexographic print edge is distracting
− Difficult to reproduce the entire tonal range with this technique, cannot always achieve fine tonal transitions

most common. The flexible rubber plates consist of a zinc plate which, combined with physical pressure and heat, forms the print-ready plate. The polymer plates are produced by an exposure procedure reminiscent of the production of an offset printing plate. The polymer is photosensitive and the printing surfaces are hardened by exposure to ultra-violet light. Regular graphic film is used for the exposure. The film should be right-reading and negative [*see page 344*]. The unexposed non-printing areas are washed off when the plate is developed.

9.9.3 Ink

Flexography is often used to print on non-absorbent material, so the ink must be able to dry through the evaporation of solvents. The ink is volatile and has to be rapidly transferred from the ink duct to the printing form in order not to dry in the wells of the anilox roller. The ink must have a high liquidity so it can be quickly and evenly transferred to the plate via the anilox roller.

9.9.4 Paper and Material

Flexographic printing is the printing technique that, after screen printing, has the fewest limitations regarding what kinds of materials can be printed on. In principle you can print on anything as long as it is flat or round.

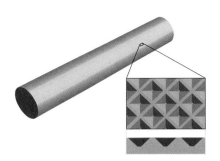

THE ANILOX ROLLER

An anilox roller is covered with small wells that enable it to transfer ink to the printing plate evenly and quickly.

9.9.5 Typical Phenomena in Flexographic Printing

Below we will cover the most common phenomena in flexographic printing. They are all non-desirable, so it is important to understand how they occur in order to minimize their effect.

9.9.6 The Flexographic Print Edge

The print edge in flexography is a phenomenon that appears at the edge of solidly colored areas. Because the ink used in flexography is thin and the printing form is compressible, as edge is visible in flat color areas. The edge occurs because the outline of the area is darker and a small area inside of the outline is brighter than the rest of the area.

9.9.7 Low Ink Coverage on Non-Absorbent Material

When you print on flexographic on non-absorbent material, such as plastic or glass, you can't get as high ink coverage as, for example, with screen printing. With some materials you can't get higher ink coverage than around 150 percent. This means that in principle it is impossible to work with four-color separation and printing. Therefore it is common to work with Pantone colors instead in text and illustrations, and make special separations of color images where you reduce the ink coverage and build up the images with help of a number of Pantone colors instead of four-color.

9.10 Print Makeready

The term "makeready" refers to all the printing-related steps leading up to the first, approved print sheet. Because printing time is so costly, you want this process to take as little time as possible, but there are a number of necessary steps:

- Plate makeready
- Setting the feeder
- Registration of the sheets
- Presetting of ink screws
- Ink-dampening balance
- Registration
- Ink coverage
- Correspondence to the proof

Always strive to minimize the number of makereadies – they can often take more time than the actual print run [see Output 9.6]. What follows is a more in-depth description of the makeready steps.

9.10.1 Plate Makeready

To help achieve accurate registration among the different inks, it is important that the printing plates are inserted into the press correctly. The registration pins and holes in the printing plate set the plates properly [see page 345]. The insertion of the printing plate is often done manually, but printing presses with automatic plate changers are becoming more common.

THE FLEXOGRAPHIC PRINT EDGE

Here you can see what a flexographic print edge looks like (in the dot), as well as a diagram of the ink density across the dot. Because the ink used in flexography is so thin and the printing plate is compressible, an edge is visible in flat color areas. The edge occurs because the outline of the area is darker and a small area inside of the outline is brighter than the rest of the area.

9.10.2 Setting the Feeder
The feeder has to be set to the correct sheet format. The feeder must also be set so that it picks up no more than one sheet of paper at a time.

9.10.3 Registration of the Sheets
It is important that the sheets of paper are accurately registered before going into the printing press. This helps ensure that the image is printed in the same place on every sheet throughout the run, and consequently, that the off press processing will be as accurate as possible.

9.10.4 Presetting of Ink Screws
Making changes to the appearance of the print by adjusting the ink screws is a relatively inefficient process. Therefore it is important that screws are preset as carefully as possible. The ink screws are either set manually or automatically, using information from a plate scanner or from the digital file (JDF) the print is based on.

9.10.5 Ink-Dampening Balance
It is important to set the ink-dampening balance correctly. Too much water creates an excess of emulsified water drops in the ink and can cause small, white dots in the print. On the other hand, too little water can cause tinting of the non-printing areas, also know as "dry-up."

9.10.6 Registration
When printing with several colors, accurate registration is of the utmost importance. Proper registration ensures that the individual printing inks are laid down on top of each other as precisely as possible. Unfortunately, because the format of the paper sheets changes slightly as they pass through the printing press, the press will never achieve 100% registration.

9.10.7 Ink Coverage
The amount of ink transferred to the paper is referred to as the "ink coverage." Proper ink coverage is important; too much ink results in smearing, drying problems and lack of contrast in darker areas of the image. If the ink coverage is too low, the image will appear washed out. Ink coverage is measured with a densitometer [see 9.11.1]. If the ink coverage is too low in a specific area of the print, you have to change the basic setting for that area by adjusting the ink screws.

If the ink coverage of only one of the colors is too low, you can get color casting in the images. When this happens, you say that you have the wrong "color balance." The color balance is checked against gray test marks that become discolored when the color balance is off [see 9.11.7].

9.10.8 Consistency to the Proof
The proof gives the buyer an idea of how the final result will look. It is also important to check that the printed result corresponds, as much as possible, to the proof. Therefore the print is usually fine-tuned against the proof. If the proof and the pre-press work are accurately done, major adjustments should

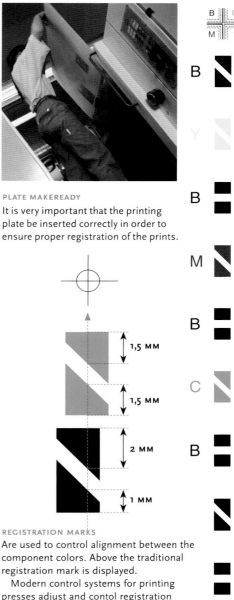

PLATE MAKEREADY
It is very important that the printing plate be inserted correctly in order to ensure proper registration of the prints.

REGISTRATION MARKS
Are used to control alignment between the component colors. Above the traditional registration mark is displayed.

Modern control systems for printing presses adjust and contol registration automatically. To the right, a color control strip with registration marks is displayed. The control is made by measuring the marks along the printing direction. If two wedges of a color (see above) are of the same length, like the cyan wedges, the printing plate is in register. If they differ in length, like the black wedges, the plate is automatically adjusted.

FLEXOGRAPHY
Text printed with the flexographic technique also smears easily because of the "stamp" principle. This results in text reproduction inferior to that of the offset printing method. Note the flexographic print edge, which is clearly visible inside the contours of the letters.

XEROGRAPHY
Printing with powder toner means that both halftone dots and text become somewhat blurry because the particles don't always end up in the right place. This is the primary reason that text reproduction in digital printing is inferior to offset printing.

INK-JET
Because of the spraying action of the printer, the outlines of printed text can be blurry. This results in text reproduction inferior to that of the offset method. Note the drops of ink that landed outside of the letters.

SCREEN PRINTING
Screen-printed text is relatively blurry and of low quality compared to text printed with the offset method.

OFFSET
Text printed in an offset printer is sharp and has clear outlines. Offset gives you better text reproduction than gravure printing, but slightly poorer than that of the analog proof.

GRAVURE PRINTING
Everything printed with the gravure technique is built up with halftone screens ("wells"), even solid areas. This means that even the text is rasterised which results in a lesser quality reproduction than offset printing.

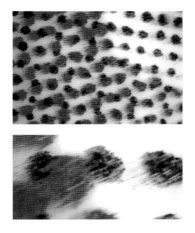

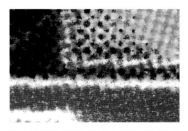

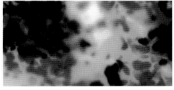

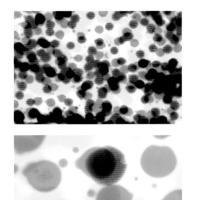

FLEXOGRAPHY

The halftone dots in the flexographic print easily smear because the rubber plate slides against the paper like a stamp.

XEROGRAPHY

Halftone dots in digital prints are blurrier than thoe in offset or gravure printing, and the image reproduction of digital printing is of a lesser quality as a result. This is primarily because digital printers print with powder toner instead of liquid ink. Because the halftone dots are divided, the digital prints appear to have a higher screen frequency than they actually do.

INK-JET

Ink-jet printers generally use a kind of FM screen. The ink is sprayed out on the paper in small drops; each halftone dot consists of several ink drops.

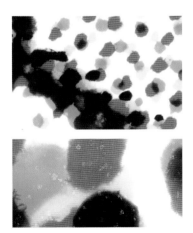

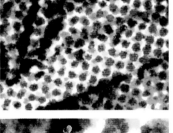

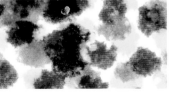

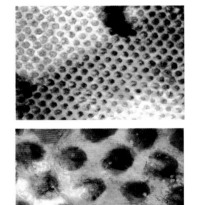

SCREEN PRINTING

Irregular halftone dots can negatively affect the image quality of screen prints.

OFFSET

Halftone dots in an offset print are irregular and blurry because of the way they are pressed onto the paper. Offset printing results in a slightly poorer image quality than gravure printing or analog proofs.

GRAVURE PRINTING

In gravure printing, the reproduction of halftone dots is very precise because they are not pressed onto the paper as they are in offset printing. The image quality is therefore better than that achieved with offset printing.

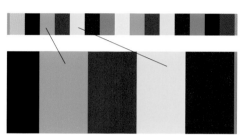

FIELDS WITH SOLID TONES
The density of solid tones is measured against the corresponding fields on the color bar.

THE DENSITY OF DIFFERENT PRINTING TECHNIQUES

	C	M	Y	K
Sheet-fed offset	1,6	1,5	1,3	1,9
Heatset	1,4	1,4	1,2	1,6
Coldset	1,0	1,0	0,9	1,1
Gravure printing	1,3	1,3	1,2	1,5

Measured with polarizing filter.

CONTROL STRIP
The control strip enables technical quality measuring of the print.

not be required to reach a high level of consistency between the proof and the print [*see Chromatics 3.12.5*].

9.11 **Checking Prints**

When printing, you should always include a color bar on the print sheet to measure, proof and control the quality of the print. Checking prints is a prerequisite for generating the values that will help you adjust the pre-press work (the production of originals and image, for example) according to the requirements of the print. The instruments used for measuring today are the densitometer and the photospectrometer.

9.11.1 **Density**

Density is a measurement of how much of a light sent out is reflected on the surface of a printed product. The less light reflected, the higher the density value. It is measured in units of density, 10 percent reflection of the light gives a value of 1. One percent reflection gives a density value of 2 and 0.1 percent reflection gives a density value of 3. The density is measured with a densitometer on the measuring strip's whole color strip; whole color density is being measured. Density is used to determine a list of different parameters: the amount of ink, trapping, dot enlargement, along with other things.

The amount of light reflected on a printed surface is diminished the more ink is placed on the paper, that is how thick the ink layer is. But the strength of the pigment in different inks and the reflectance of different papers give different density. This means that density is not an absolute measure of the thickness of the ink. Instead it can only be used to give measurements between different printed products that have the same paper and ink. There are different color filters in the densitometer, which make it possible to measure the different printing colors, cyan, magenta, yellow. The reflectance of newly printed ink differs some from dried ink. Therefore there is a polarization filter in densitometers that reduces the difference in density between dry and non-dry ink.

9.11.2 **Amount of Ink**

Density is a measurement of how much ink is applied to the paper by the printing press. If the ink layer is not dense enough, the print will look matte and washed out. Too much ink and the halftone dots will bleed and spread, resulting in poor contrast in the print. Excess ink can also cause drying problems that lead to smearing. It is therefore important to use an amount of ink for the paper you are printing on. The printer should test this. A densitometer is used to measure the solid tones of the color bars, the full-tone density. There is at least one solid tone for each printing ink on the color bars.

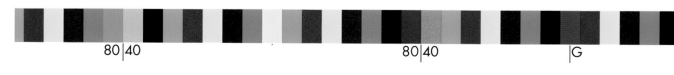

80|40   80|40 |G

While printing, you want to use as much ink as possible, while maintaining the contrast in the dark areas of the print. In order to calculate the optimal ink coverage, you measure the elative print contrast, which is the difference in density between a 100% tone and an 80% tone, divided by the density of the 100% tone (a 70% tone is usually used for newsprint). Optimal print contrast is reached when the difference in density between the 80% tone and the 100% tone is at its highest, and the density of solid tones is at its highest without a high dot gain. The ink density that provides optimal print contrast also provides optimal ink coverage. A polarization filter should be used when measuring the tones with a densitometer. This procedure is called NCI measurement (Normal Color Intensity).

9.11.3 Dot Gain

When dot gain occurs during the production of the printing forms, it means that the size of the halftone dots change when they are copied onto the printing form. Dot gains in the printing process occur when the ink is transferred from the printing form to the rubber blanket, and from the rubber blanket to the paper. The ink is pressed out into the actual printing nip and the halftone dots are slightly enlarged, which results in darker tint areas and images. There is also an optical dot gain that is dependent on how light is reflected by the paper stock. If you are working with graphic film, you will get a dot gain when using negative film, whereas you will get a dot reduction when using positive film. The total dot gain of the final print consists of the value of the dot gain/dot reduction during the production of the plate, plus the dot gain from the printing process and the optical dot gain. The dot gain from the printing process has the greatest impact overall.

Dot gain means that the printed result will be darker than the original, and you should therefore compensate for it. In order to compensate accurately, you will need to know, with the help of ICC profiles, the dot gain for the printing process, the paper and the halftone screen that you plan to use. Printers should conduct regular checks of the dot gains and density values and document their values to make sure the printing process is stable. An image that is not adjusted to compensate for the dot gain will print out considerably darker than intended.

Because the dot gain curve is a continuous curve, it is enough to state the dot gain for one or two tonal values. The dot gain is primarily measured in the 40% tone and sometimes also in the 80% tone. A common value for a dot gain is around 19% in the 40% tone for a print with 150 lpi on a coated paper (negative film). Dot gain is always measured in absolute percentages. This means that a 40% tone in the film or the computer will be 59% in the print (40% + 19%) if you have a 19% dot gain.

RELATIVE PRINT CONTRAST
Relative print contrast is defined according to the formula:

$$\frac{D_{100} - D_{80}}{D_{100}}$$

D_{100} = Density of a solid tone of a color

D_{80} = Density of an 80% tone of the same color

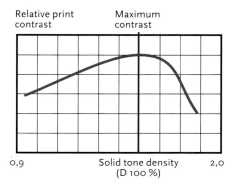

NCI MEASUREMENT

The solid tone density can be found where the curve hits its peak. This is the optimal solid tone density, which will provide the maximum contrast between the 80 % tone and the 100 % tone.

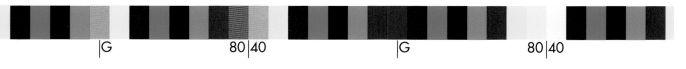

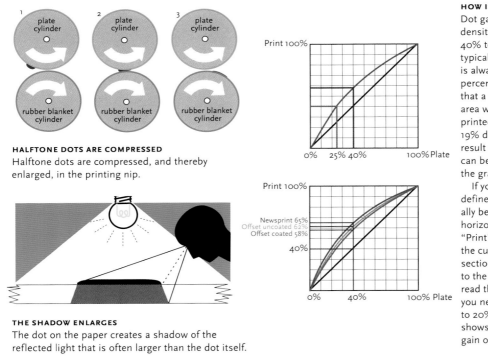

HALFTONE DOTS ARE COMPRESSED
Halftone dots are compressed, and thereby enlarged, in the printing nip.

THE SHADOW ENLARGES
The dot on the paper creates a shadow of the reflected light that is often larger than the dot itself.

HOW IS DOT GAIN MEASURED?
Dot gain is measured with a densitometer and color bars. 40% tones and 80% tones are typical reference values. Dot gain is always measured in absolute percentage units. This means that a 19% dot gain in a 40% tint area will come out as 59% in the printed image. The effect that a 19% dot gain has on the printed result over the entire tonal range can be observed in the curve of the graph.

If you want to know how to define a tint area so it will actually be 40% in the print, draw a horizontal line from 40% on the "Print" axis until the line meets the curve. From the point of intersection, draw a vertical line down to the "Plate" axis, where you can read the correct value. In this case, you need to adjust a 40% tint area to 20%. The diagram on the left shows a comparison of the dot gain on different types of paper.

Factors that affect the level of dot gain in printing include paper grade, printing process and screen frequency. Uncoated paper stock generally results in a higher dot gain than coated. Newsprint has an even higher dot gain. Paper manufacturers generally provide information about the dot gains of their different paper grades. The type of printing process also affects the level of dot gain. Web-fed offset printing, for example, is characterized by a higher dot gain than sheet-fed offset printing (printing on the same stock). Screen frequency affects the level of dot gain as well. A higher screen frequency always results in a somewhat higher dot gain, assuming the same printing process and paper.

9.11.4 Maximum Ink Coverage

Maximum ink coverage refers to the maximum amount of ink you can apply to a particular paper with a certain printing method. It is expressed as a percentage. For example, if you were to print with 100% coverage of all the four printing inks (CMYK) on top of each other, you will wind up with 400% ink coverage. However, that much ink cannot be used without smearing. Different types of paper can absorb different amounts of ink, so testing the paper you intend to use is important. For example, the maximum ink coverage for a coated, glossy paper is around 340%, whereas the maximum ink coverage for newsprint paper is closer to 240%. With flexographic printing the value can be as low as 150%. The value for tha maximum ink coverage affects printing adjustments and should be put in the ICC profile [*see Prepress 7.4.3*].

9.11.5 Minimum Highlight Dot

The lightest tone, that is the smallest halftone dot that the printing press can reproduce on a certain paper with a certain screen frequency, is called the minimum highlight dot. Depending on printing technique, screen frequency and paper, the first minimum highlight dot can lie between 1% and 20%. If you don't compensate for the first minimum highlight dot, disturbing overexposed areas occur in the lightest parts of images or tinted areas. The phenomenon becomes even more apparent the higher the value of the minimum highlight dot.

Different printing techniques and different printing surfaces have different conditions for reproducing light tones in print. At the same time screen frequency is a parameter which to a large extent influences the value of the first printing dot. The finer the screen frequency printed the smaller the halftone dots. It is also harder to reproduce if you get a high value for the first printing dot. Flexographic and screen printing have the greatest problems with the first printing dot. There are printings in flexography that have their first printing dot at 20%. The minimum highlight dot is measured by printing test strips with fields of the finest tones. The value is obtained by checking with a magnifier at which halftone the raster is correctly reproduced.

You can compensate for the minimum highlight dot by adjusting in the print-ready image what is white and giving it the same raster halftone as the minimum highlight dot. All the other light tones will be darker from this adjusted "white" tone on. This results in the printed product having nothing completely white in the image. It is experienced as less disturbing tan the overexposed fields that occur if you haven't compensated for the minimum highlight dot.

In sheet-fed offset printing, where you have made the printing form with CTP, you can get all the halftone dots into print, even the finest. This means that you won't have to compensate the material. In flexographic printing with such a high value as 20% for the first printing point, you should wonder what kind of images you should use or if you should have images at all [*see Prepress 7.4.6*].

9.11.6 Trapping

Offset printing inks have more difficulty bonding with other wet inks than to paper. Offset printing is normally done "wet-on-wet," which means that all the necessary ink colors are printed directly on top of each other before they have time to dry. "Trapping" refers to how much ink bonds with, or is "trapped" by, wet ink already laid down on the paper. The level of trapping can be measured using a densitometer. Color bars specify measurements for trapping in which the solid tones of two printing inks have been place on top of each other. Their combined density is compared with the densities of the corresponding individual solid tones. If the two tones completely bonded together, there would

MINIMUM HIGHLIGHT DOT

Here is an example of what happens if you don't compensate for the minimum highlight dot or the smallest halftone dot possible to reproduce (second image). The brightest tones in the original image (first image) are not reproduced and cause disturbing overexposed areas in the lightest parts of images or tinted areas (see gray bar under the image). When compensating (third image), the brightest dot is given the same value as the minimum highlight dot (see the gray bar under the image). In the second and third image, we have simulated a value of 7% for the first printing dot.

	SHEET-FED OFFSET	HEATSET	COLDSET	GRAVURE PRINTING	SCREEN PRINTING	FLEXOGRAPHY
Minimum highlight dot	1 %	1–3 %	1–5 %	1–6 %	4–10 %	2–20 %

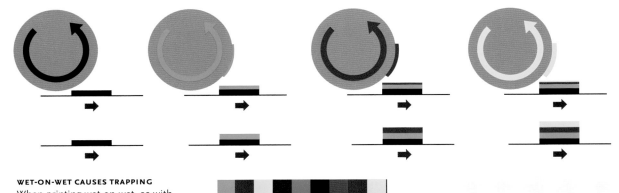

WET-ON-WET CAUSES TRAPPING
When printing wet-on-wet, as with four-color prints in offset, the inks don't bond to each other fully. Problems increase with each successive ink printed. In the upper row you can see the actual result of a four-color wet-on-wet printing, while the lower set shows what the result would look like if the inks bonded to each other fully.

TRAPPING FIELDS
Trapping can be checked against the trapping fields of the color bars. These fields contain two inks, printed one on top of the other.

CALCULATING TRAPPING
Trapping is measured against the trapping fields as shown in the example above. The formula for calculating the trapping is:

$$\frac{D_{1+2} - D_1}{D_2}$$

D_{1+2} = The density of the area with two inks printed on top of each other, measured with the second ink's filter in the densitometer.
D_1 = The density of the first ink in a solid tone field measured with the second ink's filter in the densitometer.
D_2 = The density the second ink in a solid tone field measured with the second ink's filter in the densitometer.

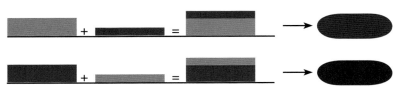

THE PRINTING ORDER AND THE TRAPPING EFFECT
If cyan is printed before magenta, the cyan layer will be thick and result in a cold, bluish, full tone color. If, on the other hand, magenta is printed first, the resulting tone will be more purple-blue.

be a trapping value of 1000%, but normally it lies between 70% and 87%. When there are low levels of trapping the print seems washed out, for example red colors appear orange and blue appear purple. There are often visible problems with trapping in heatset printing.

9.11.7 **Gray Balance**
In theory, if you were to print with equal amounts of the three primary colors C, M and Y you would get a neutral gray. However, in practice, you will get what is known as "color cast". This can happen for a number of reasons: the color of the paper, differences in dot gain between the printing inks, the printing inks don't blend completely, or the pigments in the printing inks are not ideal.

GRAY BALANCE

You might get color casts in your print if the gray balance isn't right. For example, here the upper left corner of the image has a cyan cast.

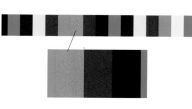

GRAY BALANCE FIELDS

The gray balance can be checked against the gray balance fields of the color bars. Here, CMY-gray is compared to a gray based on only black.

MEDICINE AGAINST INCORRECT GRAY BALANCE

In newsprinting, the printing is controlled by gray balance fields similar to medicine capsules. They are visible in the margin as small, hopefully gray-colored fields. If the

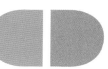

two halves differ in color, one of the component colors CMY is set incorrectly in the printing press.

SHEET-FED OFFSET
ON COATED PAPER

Examples of gray balance values for a coated, white paper.

C	0	5	10	20	30	40	50	60	70	80	90	95	100
M	0	3	4	11	20	29	38	48	58	68	78	83	88
Y	0	4	5	12	21	30	39	49	59	69	79	84	89

NEWSPRINT

Examples of gray balance values for uncoated newsprint paper.

C	0	5	10	20	30	40	50	60	70	80	90	95	100
M	0	2	4	10	19	28	37	47	57	67	77	82	87
Y	0	1	3	8	17	26	35	45	55	65	75	80	85

Gray balance is important because it helps you determine the right mix of colors. If the colors are not balanced properly, you will get a color cast in your printed product. To achieve the correct balance, you must know how the printing press you are using works with the paper, which printing inks and halftone screens you want to use, and adjust the pre-press work accordingly, creating an ICC profile. In order to check if the gray balance is correct, you have gray balance areas that are printed with predefined CMY values and reference fields with the corresponding gray tone, printed only with black, to compare the gray balance fields to. If you have the correct gray balance you will visually get a corresponding tonal value in the gray balance fields as in the black reference fields. This is done with the help of the GCR setting in the ICC profile and results in images that are not at all as sensitive to color shifts [*see Prepress 7.4.4*].

9.11.8 Misregistration

As we mentioned earlier, it is impossible to get a perfect registration of the different printing inks in offset printing; you will always get some misregistration. Misregistration is controlled with the help of registration markers that should line up squarely with each other. Modern control systems have automatic registration control and correction.

MISREGISTRATION

Registration marks are used to check misregistration during the printing process. The registration marks above are the traditional ones. Misregistration causes blurry images and can manifest as discolored edges or gaps in the colored print areas.

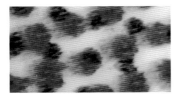

Smearing caused the halftone dots to appear oval in shape.

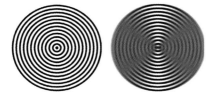

Smearing can be checked using a measuring strip. If the halftone dots are smeared an hourglass pattern will appear (see above right).

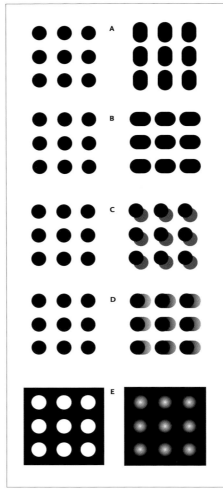

A. Slurring in the printing direction can result when the printing pressure is too high, or when the plate cylinder, rubber blanket cylinder and impression cylinder don't rotate at exactly the same speed.
B. Slurring across the printing direction can be caused by the paper or the rubber blanket.
C. Doubling is often the result of a loose rubber blanket.
D. Smearing can occur because the ink coverage is too dense or because the printed sheets are off press processed before they are entirely dry.
E. Choking can be caused by print pressure that is too high, a poorly tightened rubber blanket, ink coverage that is too high, too little dampening solution, or a combination of these factors.

In such printing techniques as sheet-fed offset, the misregistration is so small that it is not visible to the human eye.

Printing techniqes with great misregistration, you will see discolored edges of gaps on the colored objects. Misregistration can also cause blurry images. You can compensate the digital information for misregistration with so-called trapping [*see Prepress 7.4.8*]. Misregistration differs throughout the printing sheet, and is usually most evident at the outer edges of the printed sheet. That is why you should not fill the entire sheet when your production require high precision and registration.

9.11.9 Dot Deformation – Doubling and Slurring (Mackle)

Dot deformation means that the shape of the halftone dots changes, resulting in a dot gain. The deformation might be a result of problems with the periphery speed relationship caused by mechanical or technical errors in the printing

process. It can also be a result of shortages in the handling of the print material in the printing press.

One such deformation is known as "slurring," when halftone dots are smeared into oval shapes. Slurring can occur when the pressure between the rubber blanket cylinder and the impression cylinder is too high, or when the plate cylinder and the rubber blanket cylinder do not rotate at exactly the same speed. The latter often happens because the cylinders have different circumferences, and consequently, different periphery speeds. This problem can be solved with a makeready: paper sheets placed between the rubber blanket and the rubber blanket cylinder.

Doubling is a phenomenon that manifests itself as a double imprint of halftone dots, one stronger and one weaker. This can be due to a loose rubber blanket, which causes the halftone dots to land in different places on the paper with each rotation of the cylinder.

Oval or double halftone dots affect the dot gain and result in higher surface ink coverage than initially intended. As a result, the entire print image will look darker than it should. There are special fields on the measuring strips (color bars) that allow you to check for slurring and doubling.

9.11.10 Printing Proofs for an ICC Profile

Today images are adjusted for printing with the help of ICC profiles. Profiles are created by proof printing special IT8 test forms on the paper or material you will be printing on. The test form contains up to 300 color reference fields with gray tones, primary, secondary and tertiary colors.

In order for the material that has been adjusted for printing actually works well when printed, the print run must occur under the same conditions that the proof was printed under. It is very important to ensure that the printing press prints the same way the whole time. Then the printing adjustments of material will be optimized for the existing printing conditions It requires small inputs to achieve an approved printed result [see Prepress 7.4].

Because the printed proof lays the foundation for all the printing you do, it is important to print it under optimal circumstances. You will have to take a number of measurements and do quality controls. First you have to make sure the printing press is in good condition. Then you check various parameters: dot distortion, gray balance, first printing dot, slurring and doubling. Then you figure out how thick a layer of ink you can put on the paper, the ink amount.

When all these parameters are under control, you can print an optimal proof as a foundation for creating an ICC profile. During normal production you will wan to print as close to the print proof as possible. If you let the printing vary from time to time it will be impossible to adjust the digital material so that it works in print.

To maintain control during printing equal to what you obtained with the printed proof you have to continually control two parameters during production: density and dot gain. If these two don't stay in the same relation to each other as they did when the proof was printed, you have to look for what's wrong. This is done by going through the other parameters: gray balance, dot gain, trapping, slurring and doubling.

Spectrophotometer is a measuring device used when creating ICC profiles. Profiles are created by proof printing special IT8 test forms on the paper or material you will be printing on. The test form contains up to 300 color reference fields with gray tones, primary, secondary and tertiary colors. The spectrophotometer in the image is mounted to a robot in order to facilitate automatic readings.

9.12 Printing Inks and Environmental Issues

There are four primary factors to consider when discussing the environmental and human health impacts of printing inks: pigments containing heavy metals, such as barium, copper, and zinc; petroleum based, high volatile organic compound (VOC) solvents used as pigment carriers and for enhanced drying; hazardous waste generated in manufacturing and use of the inks; and coatings, which are colorless topcoats designed to provide increased gloss, rub resistance and chemical resistance.

The heavy metals in pigments can contaminate soil and groundwater when leached into the environment through landfills, or wreak havoc in wastewater systems which aren't designed to process such industrial waste. Exposure, especially in large quantities, to these compounds through ingestion, inhalation or absorption can cause genetic disorders, lung irritation, spasms, heart problems or cancer. When deinked, the sludge may be classified as hazardous waste if concentrations of heavy metals and other pollutants are present.

Petrochemical solvents emit VOCs, polluting gasses which react with sunlight and air to form smog, thus contaminating the air we breathe. When evaporating, they can also be an irritant for printshop workers.

U.S. Environmental Protection Agency (EPA) figures estimate that in the U.S., about 44,000 sheetfed offset printers generate more than 60 million pounds of ink sludge annually. This leftover ink, consisting of oil, pigments, solvents and water, is classified as hazardous waste. In addition, an equivalent amount of waste is generated in the manufacture of printing ink – making an estimated 120 million pounds of hazardous waste every year. This waste is often incinerated, releasing more than 300 toxic chemicals and compounds into the air, water and soil.

When considering coatings, air pollution is one of the most significant factors. When printing UV coatings, although they emit little or no VOCs, low wavelength UV light reacts with oxygen, and ozone is created. Workers can also be exposed to radiation if working conditions are unsafe or unmonitored. Aqueous coatings do not undergo chemical reactions to dry, but since they are mainly liquid, vapors are vented into the atmosphere, potentially creating high levels of VOCs. However, this challenge has been resolved in recent years, and low- and non-VOC aqueous coatings are available. In terms of recyclability, aqueous coatings are easier to process than UV coatings. The final answer to the aqueous vs. UV coatings question is a fundamental design issue: is the coating truly needed in the first place?

Avoid colors containing pigments with compounds (e.g., barium, copper and zinc) that exceed the threshold levels listed in Section 313 of Title III of the Superfund Amendments and Reauthorization Action. Generally, these would be colors containing warm reds, and certain flourescent and metallic colors. A list of these inks can be found at www.econewsletter.net. Petrochemical solvents in inks can be largely replaced with agri-based oils such as soy, corn, linseed, tung or canola to reduce VOC emissions and create a safer environment for printshop workers. They are also non-toxic, clean up more easily and need less harsh scouring agents, break down more readily in

Create an environmental policy for your workplace. Include criteria such as:

- Use the blank side of a laser printed sheet for fax paper before recycling to reduce paper consumption
- Buy only U.S. EPA Energy Star rated equipment
- Recycle dead batteries at an appropriate facility
- Recharge and buy recycled toner cartridges
- Turn off machines or use a "sleep mode," which can reduce energy consumption by 25–90%
- Purchase recycled disks and other magnetic media
- Learn what you can about the suppliers you work with. Develop relationships with forward thinking suppliers who can collaborate with new materials and processes, energy- and waste-efficient office equipment and non-toxic supplies. Support local suppliers whenever possible and appropriate.
- Minimize your waste, then recycle as many materials as possible.
- Take advantage of electronic communication to send files, rather than relying on courier systems or faxes. When appropriate, make your presentations via email.

landfills as well as in the deinking and repulping process of paper recycling, and are made of renewable resources (versus petroleum-based, which are finite).

Many printers avow that one advantage of using agri-based inks is brighter colors, which can translate into a more efficient print run with less paper waste and post-run disposal volumes. Today, a wide variety of agri-based inks can be found at competitive prices.

Even though the first agri-based ink that may come to mind is soy (due to some very heavy marketing by the American Soybean Association), there are other types of oils that some inkmakers claim to be superior, such as linseed or tung (which, also, are not as controversial as soybean's bio-engineering issues).

Note that an ink may contain as little as 10–20 % soy or other alternative oil and still be called agri-based, soy-based or vegetable-based, even though the remaining component is petroleum-based. Ask your printer to use the highest agri-based ink possible (up to 100 % is available).

Printing ink waste at offset printers and ink makers can be completely elimi-nated from the waste stream and used to formulate quality recycled ink. A pat-ented process, known as Lithographic Ink Recovery Technology (LIRT), recovers 100 % of the ink sludge once transported as hazardous waste for incineration. Recovery occurs with no solid, liquid or gaseous emissions to the environment and results in three marketable products: ink, solvent and de-ionized water. It is a completely closed loop process. Rich in pigment, even compared to ink manufactured from virgin raw materials, recycled ink generated by the new process has superior printing qualities and generates less process waste.

With current technology, recycled ink is only available in charcoal black, which is a suitable replacement for black ink. In the future, as source separation becomes feasible and market demand increases, process colors (cyan, yellow, magenta and black) will be available so that four-color reproduction with entirely recycled inks will be possible.

COMMUNICATION

1. Find ways to communicate environmental infor-mation to consumers.

2. Educate your clients about the importance and benefits of environmental design considera-tions.

3. Read articles and books, attend conferences on this burgeoning concept. Develop a resource library.

10.
finishing and binding

What binding is cheaper? How do I figure out the spine width? What paper types are suitable for lamination? Can you varnish selected images? How many pages can you staple? Is there a finish that protects the printed product? Is folding and scoring the same thing? Can you laminate uncoated paper? Why do you usually varnish printed products? Why is the grain direction of the paper important when folding?

THOUGH IT IS THE FINAL PHASE of the graphic print production process, finishing and binding has an impact on a project from the very beginning, and should be taken into account when the product is being designed. For example, some types of paper are more appropriate for different finishing and binding processes than others. The imposition of the pages (how they are arranged on the printed sheets) is also determined partly by the finishing and binding desired for the product. Therefore, it is important to decide early on in the planning stages what type of finishing and binding procedures your product will need.

The printed product's intended use affects which finishing and binding processes you choose. A manual that will be used in a garage has to be able to withstand oil and dirt, while a computer manual should be able to lie flat on a table. The choice is affected at the same time by economics and the number of copies printed. A newspaper doesn't have to last more than a day, which means that you would choose a cheap and simple finishing and binding process. With larger printings, you sometimes have to choose a cheaper binding to keep within an economic framework. If you print with web-fed offset printers or intaglio printing, as is usually done with larger runs, the finishing and binding processes are usually connected directly with the printing press: online-processing. This means you will have to select the finishing processes that are available with an on-line system.

Finishing and binding are done at printing houses and bookbinderies. If you are working with a sheet-fed offset printing house, you will often have to take the printed sheets to a separate bookbindery. Bookbinders often specialize in certain kinds of binding, so for different types of finishing and binding processes you will have to resort to different bookbinderies. It is even common for the sheet-fed printing houses themselves to offer some of the simpler off press services. Printing houses that do not have their own finishing equipment usually have close ties with a bookbindery.

10.1 Different Types of Finishing and Binding

Finishing and binding can be divided into three areas: surface processing, off press processing, and binding.

Surface processing includes different stages that affect the surface of the printed product. There are many reasons why printed sheets have to be surface treated. It gives you the opportunity to created visual effects like foiling, create raised areas on the paper, emphasize a picture with partial varnishing or create metal effects with foiling. Often you surface treat a printed product to protect it against wear and tear, or laminate it to increase its folding endurance. It is also common today to varnish the printed sheets in order to be able to finish and bind them more quickly, without waiting for the printing ink to dry.

Cutting and trimming include the stages of book finishing when the paper is physically shaped. Cropping – the printed product is cut and trimmed to get the right format and even edges, die-cutting – the printed product is die-cut into another shape or is given perforations, punching – the printed product has holes punched in it to put it into binders, folding – used to form pages from the printed sheets, and creasing – the printed product is creased to mark a fold.

Binding is the joining of a number of individual printed sheets into a single entity, be it metal stitched brochures, spiral bound manuals, softcover books or hardcover books. The term stitching means how the insert is put together: metal stitching, spiral binding, Smyth-sewn stitching, thread stitching or glue binding. In metal stitching and spiral binding, the cover is attached during the actual binding process. In Smyth-sewn and thread sewing the spine of the insert is sewn together which is then attached to the cover. There are two ways of attaching, or hanging, the cover. In the first version (for softcovers), the cover is glued to the spine of the bound material. In the second (for hardcovers), the first and last pages of the material, called the endpapers, are glued to the insides of the covers. In softcover books the cover is put on during stitching, for example when glue binding softcover books. Hanging a cover is done separately from stitching.

10.2 Before Finishing and Binding

Paper that comes from the manufacturer or that is cropped by the printing house is not perfectly rectangular. The size and shape of the sheets can also very slightly throughout the paper stack. It is important to be aware of that so

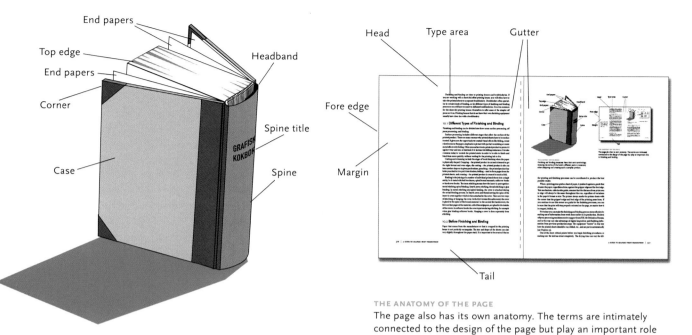

Finishing and binding processes have their own terminology. Knowing the terms of the book's different parts is necessary when designing and creating such a complex product.

The page also has its own anatomy. The terms are intimately connected to the design of the page but play an important role in finishing and binding.

the printing and finishing processes can be coordinated to produce the best possible results.

When a printing press grabs a sheet of paper, it pushes it against a guide that situates the paper, regardless of size, against the gripper edge and the feed edge. This mechanism, called a side guide, ensures that the distance from print area to edge will always be the same throughout the run, regardless of variations in the paper's format or size. The printer always marks the printer sheets with the corner that the gripper's edge and feed edge of the printing press form. If you continue to use this corner as a guide for the finishing processes, you can be sure that the print will stay properly oriented on the page, no matter how it is cropped, folded, etc.

Nowadays you can make the finishing and binding process more effective by making use of information from work done earlier on in production. Modern off press processing machines receive support from JDF, Job Definition Format, and in this way can take advantage of digital imposition and finishing information from previous production steps. The equipment "knows" in this way how the printed sheets should be cut, folded, etc., and are put in automatically [see Prepress 7.3].

One of the most critical points before you begin finishing procedures, is making sure the ink has dried completely. The drying time can vary for dif-

VARNISHING AND THE ENVIRONMENT
Varnishing affects the environment negatively, in part from air pollution and in part because a varnished finish makes recycling paper more difficult. Water-based varnishes are easier to recycle than UV varnishes.

UV varnish contains very or few or no volatile organic compounds (VOC) but have a negative impact on the environment in spite of this. It is the ozone layer that is mainly impacted negatively. As the varnish dries the oxygen reacts with the UV rays and creates ozone.

Water-based varnishes don't undergo any chemical reaction when drying. But their fumes are released into the atmosphere when they are used, and with these fumes are released volatile organic compounds (VOC). Nowadays, water-based varnishes contain very few or no volatile organic compounds (VOC).

ferent printings, but you should allow for three days to minimize the risk of any problems in off press processing.

10. 3 Varnishing

Varnishing is the most common surface treatment and consists of putting a glossy surface on a printed product. Varnish is a liquid just like ordinary printing ink. Varnish can be applied selectively to a printed sheet, called partial-varnishing, or it can cover all of it. It is often applied to the print in the offset press, via a regular inking unit or a special unit just for varnish, or in a special varnishing machine.

Varnishing is used mainly for special visual effects, or to make faster off press processing possible. It can also give extra protection against dirt and wear.

There are three kinds of varnish used: oilprint varnish, dispersion varnish and UV varnish. Oilprint varnish is an oil-based varnish that is applied directly to the print in the offset press. Varnishing with an oilprint varnish is mainly to create a glossy finish, to protect the print against the effects of off press processing and to avoid toning (when the printing ink's pigments color non-printing areas after the ink has dried.) When you want to protect the printed product, you usually choose a matte varnish, which is "invisible." If you want to create a glossy effect you will get a better result with a separate varnishing run once the ink has dried. [*Read about printing ink and drying and toning in Printing 9.5.16 and 9.5.17.*] You can also use oilprint varnish to coat the printed sheets in the offset press for sealing the printing ink, and protecting it from smearing or toning during finishing. This means that you don't have to wait for the ink to dry before off press processing.

Varnishing with dispersion varnish, which is water-based, can also be done directly in the offset press and can give a higher gloss than oilprint varnish. It can also yield a high gloss when it is applied during the same print run as the ink, when it is printed wet-on-wet. Food packaging is a typical use of this technology since dispersion varnish is totally odor-free.

UV varnishing is another common method in which varnish is applied to the print with a special UV varnishing machine. Because the varnish is cured with ultra-violet (UV) light, it can be applied in a thicker layer than the other methods, and thus provide a higher gloss and a harder suface. Varnished sheets should be creased before they are folded to avoid the formation of cracks on the varnish hardened surface.

With all types: oilprint, dispersion and UV, varnish can be applied selectively to certain parts of the image – over images and logotypes, for example. This partial-varnishing method is used for aesthetic effect. If you only varnish the images in a printed product it can create an impression of higher image quality.

To obtain the best results, coated paper is preferred for varnishing. Also keep in mind that fingerprints show up easily on glossy printed products.

10.4 Lamination

Lamination increases protection against dirt, humidity and wear and tear. Lamination is the process of coating a printed page with a protective plastic foil. The method is also used for aesthetic reasons. There are a variety of different types of laminates, including glossy, matte, embossed, and textured, which are used to achieve a glossy, matte or patterned printed product. The most common area of use is book covers, such as this book's, which is laminated with a matte laminate.

A special laminating machine is required, which with water-based glue and heat affixes a plastic foil to the printed product. The paper that is to be laminated should have the smoothest surface possible, preferably coated and glazed for good quality. Laminated sheets can both be creased and folded without the surface cracking (as in UV varnishing) and are not as sensitive to fingerprints (as in glossy varnishing). But laminating costs about twice as much as varnishing and therefore is often replaced by varnish.

10.5 Foiling

Another surface treatment is foiling. It is done for purely aesthetic reasons. You can create metal surfaces, metal inks or extremely matte finishes. The coating is thick and covers all, and so gives the product a unique surface feel. The ink or the metal is transferred from foil to the printed matter with the aid of a warm plate.

10.6 Embossing

When you want to create a relief effect in your printed product you can make use of embossing. Embossing differs from other surface finishes since it is a physical reshaping of the paper. Embossing can cause the print to stand out, positive embossing, or cause it to sink down, negative embossing. There is even a variation called sculpted embossing, where the embossing can have several levels. Embossing is normally done in regular book printing presses.

In embossing, a lower die with raised surfaces corresponding to the embossed shape is pressed into the paper against a resistant surface, the upper die, that has an etching which is the exact opposite of the lower die. The lower die is made of 7 mm thick magnesium, which has been etched to a 3 mm height difference. The upper die is made from a special plastic material. [*See Print 9.6.2*] Most paper can be embossed, but to avoid the formation of cracks along the edges, long-fibered paper is preferred.

Foil embossing is a form of embossing where you apply gilding or shiny ink during the actual embossing. It is done in special printing presses. The lower die is heated and the foil applied to the paper at the same time as it is embossed.

Relief type is another surface treatment that creates a relief in the printed product, but without embossing the paper. You print what will be in relief with special ink. The ink is then heated and raises up, creating a relief. This method is perhaps most common on visiting cards.

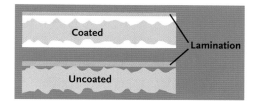

CORRECT PAPER FOR LAMINATION
The paper that is to be laminated should have the smoothest surface possible, preferably coated and glazed, otherwise air pockets under the lamination may occur. Those cause a blotchiness in the lamination.

LAMINATION
The lamination takes place in a lamination machine, which applies a plastic foil over the print using water-based glue and heat.

FOILING
You can also add a gold or silver surface to the printed product, called a foil.

EMBOSSING
You can create relief, changes in the surface of the paper, by causing a print to stand out or sink down. The embossing is executed in special embossing printing presses.

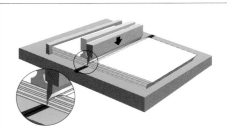

TONS OF PRESSURE
In the cutting machine the blade is pressed down into the paper stack with several tons pressure.

PRESETTINGS AND PRECISION SKILLS
In cutting machines different settings can be saved, for example for the most common impositions. Then the machine just sets itself automatically for the right cropping dimensions. Modern cropping machines have support for JDF and can benefit from digital imposition information when setting the cropping dimensions. In order to cut, two buttons have to be pressed simultaneously to make sure there are no fingers close to the blade.

10.7 **Cropping**

Cropping simply means cutting the paper down to the desired size with some kind of blade. This can be done manually with a special cutting machine or simultaneously with another step in the off press processing cycle.

In sheet-fed productions, it may be necessary to crop a product up to three different times during the production cycle. First, the paper might require cropping in order to fit the format of the printing press. After they are printed, the sheets may have to be cropped again to fit the format of the off press processing machines. In both instances, a single-blade machine is used. In normal single-blade machines different settings can be saved, for example for the most common impositions. Then the machine just sets itself automatically for the right cropping dimensions. Today modern cropping machines have support for JDF and can benefit from digital imposition information and "know" how the printed sheets should be cropped [*see Prepress 7.3*].

In the most common binding methods, (metal stitching and glue binding), cropping is usually the last step of the process. Generally, a three-sided trimmer crops the printed product on the head, tail and fore edge. This final cropping is necessary for several reasons. Multiple pages imposed on the same printing sheet are still attached to each other after they've been folded, either at the head or the tail (this applies if you have right-angle folded sheets with eight or more pages). In addition, the creep requires that the bundle be cut along the fore edge. This way the printed product gets nice, even edges.

The blades used in the cropping machines are sensitive and must be sharpened often. Varnished and laminated papers can damage or blunt the blade. A damaged blade can create a striped appearance along the cropped surface of the printed product.

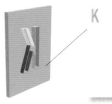

DIE-CUTTING
In die-cutting, a punch die cuts through the paper. In the image, a K is punched into the paper. Die-cutting is used to create dividers for binders among other things.

PERFORATION
You perforate printed products to make it easier to tear off a particular section of that page – a reply card, for example. Perforation is usually done in a letterpress with a special perforation blade or, as illustrated here, with the scoring technique.

10.8 Die-cutting

If you want your printed product to have a shape other than a rectangle, you can have it die-cut. A punch die is created for the shape you want for your product. It is made of a wooden slab in which a thin slot has been milled in the desired shape. A steel band with a sharp edge is place in the slot. The die is then pressed against the printed paper and cuts it to the desired shape. The cost for producing a unique punch die is relatively high for printed products in small editions, but it can be used for reprints.

Perforations are basically used to create a tearing reference, and it is also a form of die-cutting. By punching a dotted line (perforations) in a page, you make it easier to tear off a particular section of that page – a reply card, for example. Perforation is usually done in a letterpress with a special perforation blade, which is pressed into the paper, creating a series of tiny slits. Perforation can also be done in a special punching machine.

10.9 Punching

Paper is punched during finishing so it can be put into binders. The international standard, known as ISO 838, is the standard outside of North America. Within North America, the hole spacing standards are 2 3/4"cc for 2-hole and 4 ¼" cc for 3-hole punching ("cc" stands for center-to-center, and means that the holes are spaced from the center of the hole regardless of its size.) Generally, special drills are used to punch paper when this is done during off-press processing, but you may also be able to purchase pre-punched paper from your paper manufacturer.

10.10 Folding

To get an attractive and durable printed product you should always fold along the fiber direction. If you fold against the fiber direction, the paper is weakened, the fiber is broken down, and an unattractive crack appears in the print

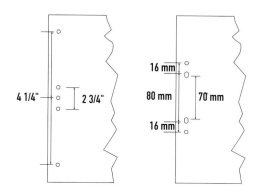

HOLE PUNCHING
U.S. Standard (2 3/4" cc for 2-hole and 4 1/4" for 3-hole punching, left). International standard ISO 838 (two holes, 80 mm apart, right).

DIFFERENT TYPES OF FOLDING
Two examples of right-angled folding: 8-page and 16-page right-angled folding. Three examples of parallel folding: 6-page Z-folding, tabernacle folding and 6-page roll folding.

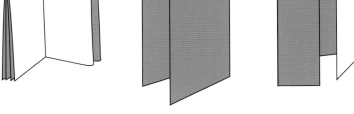
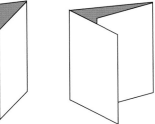

	FOLDER	SPIRAL-BOUND	GLUED SOFT COVER BOOK	SEWN SOFT COVER BOOK	GLUED HARD-COVER BOOK	SEWN HARD-COVER BOOK
FOLDING						
ASSEMBLING						
COLLATION						
METAL STITCHING						
GLUE BINDING						
THREAD STITCHING			*One step*			
CASE WRAPPING						
TRIMMING						
SPIRAL BINDING						
SPINE PREPARATION AND CASING						

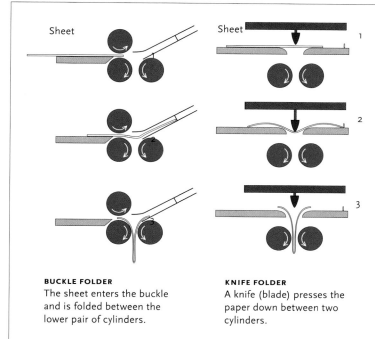

Sheet

Sheet

1

2

3

BUCKLE FOLDER
The sheet enters the buckle and is folded between the lower pair of cylinders.

KNIFE FOLDER
A knife (blade) presses the paper down between two cylinders.

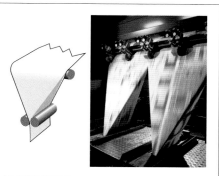

FORMER FOLDER
In web-fed printing, former folders are used to fold the paper lengthwise.

RIGHT-ANGLE FOLDER
A right-angle folder can fold the sheet in two directions – both lengthways and sideways.

SIMPLE BUCKLE FOLDER
Buckle folders are used to make simpler folds, for example to fold letters.

crossing the fold. With wrong fiber direction the binding can also be aversely affected. The product might feel stiff when you try to flip through it, and not want to stay open. Erroneous fiber direction also negatively affects the durability of the binding.

There are two main folding techniques: parallel folding and right-angled folding. Parallel folding, as the name indicates, means that all the folds run parallel to each other. Parallel folding is used when the printed product being processed does not need to be bound. Right-angled folding, on the other hand, means that each new fold is done at a 90-degree angle to the previous one, which can cause problems since every other fold ends up parallel to the grain direction. This method is used mainly for products that are going to be bound and the folds that lie at a 90-degree angle are cut away when the printed product is cropped. Thus problems with folds across the grain direction are avoided. Of course combinations of parallel and right-angled folding can also be applied.

Buckle folding, a technique generally executed by simpler folding machines, is the most common folding method used in sheet-fed print productions. For slightly more advanced folding techniques like right-angled folding, combination folding machines are generally used. Combination folding machines consist of a buckle folder and one or more knife folders. Web-fed printing presses use, for example, former folders, cylinder folders, wing folders and blade folders.

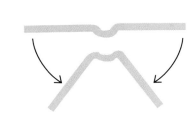

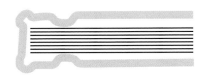

CREASING
The paper is creased in order to reduce the paper's resistance to folding. Very thick paper can be double-creased; two creases are made next to each other.

4-CREASE
Cases are often creased with a 4-crease so the board doesn't crack when it's opened.

SCRIBING
When a paper's weight exceeds 600 g/m², it is scribed or double-creased. To scribe means to make a score in the cardboard. The more the material needs to be folded, the deeper the score.

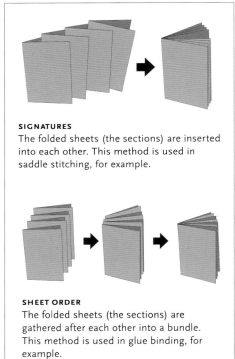

SIGNATURES
The folded sheets (the sections) are inserted into each other. This method is used in saddle stitching, for example.

SHEET ORDER
The folded sheets (the sections) are gathered after each other into a bundle. This method is used in glue binding, for example.

10.11 **Creasing**

When a paper's weight exceeds 150 g/m² uncoated, and 200 g/m² coated, it can be very difficult to fold. To avoid unattractive folds, (coated paper and recycled paper are the most sensitive), heavy paper is usually creased before it's folded. Creasing creates a kind of "hinge" that facilitates a clean fold.

Paper is often creased with the help of a thin steel "ruler" pressed along the fold lines. The crease, that is the indentation itself, should always be in the same direction as the fold. [*See illustration.*] The paper's resistance to folding is reduced along the resultant crease.

Creasing is frequently used for processing cardboard. With very thick cardboard it isn't enough to crease once. Instead several creases should be placed beside each other. Another solution can be scribing, which means to make a score in the cardboard. Covers for books are often creased. The creases in covers prevent damage to the folds and allow the product to open with ease. Creasing is also used to avoid cracking when folding varnished printed sheets,

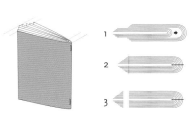

CREEPING
When right-angle folding and especially with signatures, the pages are punched slightly outwards—the closer to the center, the greater displacement. When you crop your printed product in the fore edge, the outer margin will be smaller the closer to the center you get. You can compensate for this problem in the imposition by successively reducing the size of the gutter (the inner margin) as you progress towards the center spread.

CROSSOVER BLEEDS

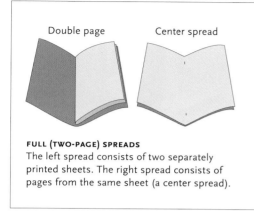

Double page   Center spread

FULL (TWO-PAGE) SPREADS
The left spread consists of two separately printed sheets. The right spread consists of pages from the same sheet (a center spread).

WARNING – CROSSOVER BLEEDS
You will always get a certain variation in color composition on the printed sheets and even between the left and the right side of a sheet. That's why you should avoid placing objects or images with sensitive colors across a bastard double.

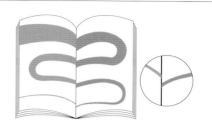

You will never get a 100% registration between two separate pages. That's why you should avoid placing objects or images diagonally across a double-spread.

You should also avoid thin lines that bleed across a double-spread. Thicker lines are less sensitive to misregistration.

or in folding printed sheets across the grain. The crease helps break the fibers lengthwise, thus avoiding an unsightly fold.

10.12 **Signatures and Sheet Order**

When you plan to bind a printed product with metal stitching, glue binding, or thread sewing, you generally use right-angled folding. For metal stitching, also called wire or saddle stitching, right-angled folded sheets, called signatures, are inserted into each other. With other types of stitching, sheets are placed together separately. This is called block stitching. The two kinds of stitching demand different types of imposition layouts: signature and sheet order. Signature and sheet order are done either at the same time as stitching occurs, or at a separate stage before stitching. When a sheet is right-angle folded, a number of spreads are created. These are placed one inside the other roughly the same way glasses are stacked together. Each new spread is placed on top just like each new glass.

COLLATION MARKS
The marks, red in the image, are noted on the imposition. When the signatures are gathered into sheet order, it allows you to check that all folded sheets are included and in the correct order.

METAL STITCHING
Here are two printed products stitched with metal staples. Note how the center sheets creep outwards.

METAL STITCHING

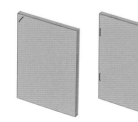

BLOCK STITCHING
Illustrated above is a metal stitching with one staple in the upper left corner (left image) and another two staples along the spine (right image).

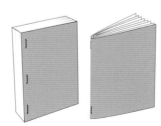

BLOCK STITCHING VS SPINE STITCHING
When using block stitching the sheets are flat whereas in spine stitching the sheets are folded.

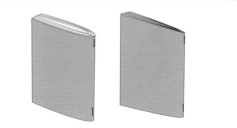

WIRE STITCHED AND FOLDED VS FOLDED AND WIRE STITCHED
If you stitch the sheets into a booklet before they are folded (left image), the pages will be slightly displaced. Compare it to folding each sheet separately and stitching them together (right image).

In the machine the folded sheets are stapled together with metal stitches (staples).

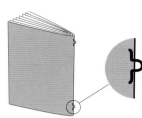

LOOP STITCHES
Loop stitches allow you to put booklets into binders.

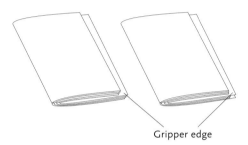

Gripper edge

GRIPPER EDGE
The gripper edge is the edge of the printed sheet that the binding machine "grabs." It is also called the lip. The margin from the gripper edge to the print area has to be somewhat wider than the other margins on the sheet. This edge is necessary when binding because it allows the machine to open the folded sheets. For example, a gripper edge of 7–15 mm is recommended for metal stitching. Folding machines don't need an additional gripper edge.

This means the center spreads are pushed slightly outwards and the middle pages of the folded booklet are displaced. This phenomenon is called creeping. Creeping becomes even more pronounced when you use signatures because each additional insert pushes the central one further outwards. When you crop your printed product after it's been folded, the type area of the pages "creep" towards the outer margins more and more as you get to the center spread. You can compensate for this problem by successively reducing the size of the gutter (the inner margin) as you progress towards the center spread. This will ensure that the printed image is properly oriented and that the margins are consistent on the page throughout the printed product. Digital imposition programs make adjustments for creeping automatically.

10.13 **Metal Stitching**

Stapling papers together with a standard desk stapler is a kind of metal stitching that we've all done. In terms of professional binding, there are two main types of metal stitching. One is block stitching in which metal stitches (staples) are

SPIRAL BINDINGS

WIRE-O BINDING
A type of spiral binding that is useful when the book needs be kept open flat.

SPIRAL BINDINGS
The most common spiral binding above is mostly used for regular notebooks. Below is an example of a Wire-O binding with a cover, providing the product with a flat spine.

DIFFERENT TYPES OF SPIRAL BINDINGS
Spiral- and Wire-O bindings.

placed along one edge or on one corner of the pages. The other is known as saddle stitching, which places metal stitches in the spine of the material.

Block stitching, also called side stitching, is a binding method for simple projects, like internal company publications. Many copy machines and laser printers can even do block stitching, which usually consists or two staples along the left edge, or one at the top left corner of the printed material.

Spine stitching, also called saddle or insert stitching, is used with insert sheets. The number of pages you can saddle together is limited, the suggested number varies, but we recommend a maximum of one hundred pages. Otherwise you will get a lot of creeping and have trouble keeping the product closed.

Today insert stitching is usually done in wire stitching machines. The number of pages is controlled by how many feeder stations there are. A feeder station is necessary for every signature that is going to be inserted. If the printed product is going to have a cover, one feeder station has to be used for this, since a cover for wire-stitched-products is also stitched on. Normal wire-stitching machines crop the printed product at the head, tail and fore edge at the same time as the stitching is done. Simpler wire-stitching machines only crop the printed product at the fore edge.

10.14 Spiral Bindings

Wire-O bindings and spiral bindings are different types of spiral bindings. They are used for manuals and notebooks. Products like these often need to be kept open flat by the user – as when writing in a notebook or following an instruction manual, for example. In this binding process, loose sheets (these can be folded sheets in sheet order cut down to loose sheets) are gathered and punched. The spiral binding is then put in place. There are different methods for this, depending on the type of spiral binding you use. Spirals come in a variety of colors and dimensions. One disadvantage of spiral binding is that it is relatively unstable. A spiral bound product often can't stand upright on a bookshelf, for example, neither can it be supplied with a spine title. The method is also relatively expensive.

10.15 Glue Binding

When a printed product has too many pages for metal stitching, glue binding is often used instead. This method is relatively inexpensive and has the advantage that is provides a spine, for example, for a title. Like most stitching methods, glue binding uses folded sheets in sheet order imposition. But there are also variations where loose, two-sided sheets are used. After the folded or loose sheets of the printed product have been bundled together, the spine is ground down to one to three millimeters, creating a coarse surface that provides a good grip for the glue. It is important that images or text that run across the spread are placed with enough of a margin to account for the grinding down of the spine. Glue is then applied, and a spine reinforcement (in the case of hardcover) or cover is attached. There are also glue binding methods in which the spine is

GLUE BINDING AND THREAD STITCHING
The upper book is bound using the glue binding method. Because the signatures are gathered in a block, the spine will be slightly wider than the insert. When using thread stitching, the folded part of the sheets is not visible since the spine has been ground down.

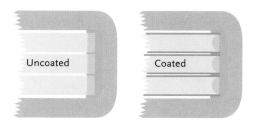

IT IS BEST TO GLUE UNCOATED PAPER
It is more difficult for the glue to penetrate the paper if the paper is coated, printed all the way into the binding or has some other surface treatment. That is why coated papers provide the strongest glue bindings.

not ground but perforated. Glue is pressed through the perforations and into the spine. This type of binding is quite strong.

With glue-bound softcover books (limp-bound) the text block is glued to the cover and is called full-bound. Paperback books are an example of glue-bound products that are full-bound, as are most magazines. Glue binding also occurs in hardcover book production. Extra pages are put on the text block which function as endpapers. These are glued to the inside of the cover and attach the text block in this manner. Nowadays most novels are glue-bound hardcover books.

The gluing process places requirements on the choice of paper. The glue must to a certain extent sink into the paper in order to ensure a strong bond. Uncoated papers with a high bulk are preferred to coated, glossy papers or varnished sheets. If you must choose a coated paper, select a higher weight since glue adheres better to it. It is suggested you use cold adhesive, which works better with coated papers, and avoid placing samples in the page bundle since they can inhibit adhesion [see Paper 8.16.6].

In glue binding it is important that the fiber direction run parallel to the spine. If the fiber direction is wrong, the glue can cause waviness in the gutter. Erroneous fiber direction also negatively affects the durability of the binding and it gets difficult to get the printed product to lie open.

In another glue binding method, glue binding with tape, tape replaces the glue and two separate parts of a sheet are used as a cover. This type of binding has limited strength and durability, and is best used for simpler documentation.

10.16 Thread Sewing

Thread sewing is the traditional bookbinding method. Folded sheets re placed in sheet order, but instead of being glued, the spine is sewn together and builds a text block. First, the first folded sheets are sewn together, then they are sewn together with the next folded sheets, and so on. As with other methods, it is important that the fiber direction run parallel to the spine in order to ensure a strong printed product that is easy to leaf through.

With softcover thread-sewn books, the text block is glued to the cover at the spine. This step is often done in glue binding machines, but without any grinding down of the spine. After the cover is in place, the book is cropped at the head, tail and fore edge. Thread sewn paperbacks are an example of this method.

Thread-sewn text blocks that are to be used in hardcover production are glued to the spine and then cropped at the head, tail and fore edges, before hanging the cover.

10.17 Smyth-Sewn Technique

Smyth-sewn technique is a technique combining thread sewing with glue binding. Price-wise the technique costs somewhere between the other two methods. If you were to flip through the final product, it would appear to be thread- sewn. The actual sewing is performed on a modified folding machine where folding and sewing are done at the same time. The thread that is used is made of a spe-

ENDPAPERS

When you glue text blocks together for hardcover books, four sheets are usually glued onto the front and four sheets onto the back of the text block. Their function is to fasten and thus bind the text block to the hardcover when hanging the cover. These pages are often made of slightly stronger, sturdier paper. They are called endpapers and are frequently colored or patterned, as in this book.

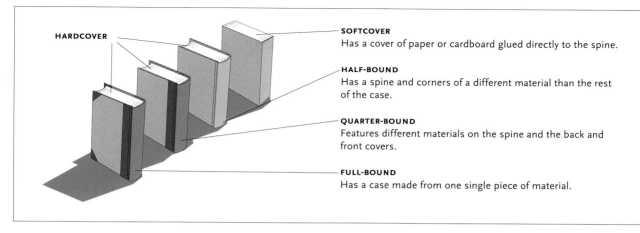

HARDCOVER

SOFTCOVER
Has a cover of paper or cardboard glued directly to the spine.

HALF-BOUND
Has a spine and corners of a different material than the rest of the case.

QUARTER-BOUND
Features different materials on the spine and the back and front covers.

FULL-BOUND
Has a case made from one single piece of material.

cial plastic that melts when heated. When the sheets are folded, needles stitch a thread into the back of the sheets. Each sheet is thus stitched separately. Then the ends of the thread are melted through heating and fastened to the sheets. When all the sheets are sewn, they are gathered and glued together in a glue-binding machine to bundle and sew together all the folded sheets (without grinding the spine). If it is a softcover book that is being produced, the cover is also attached in this step. If, however, it is a hardcover, only the printed sheets are fastened together and the cover is attached separately.

10.18 **Covering**

Covering is the term for when you attach the cover on a softcover book. The cover is generally made of a sheet with a slightly higher weight than the body. Covering is normally carried out in a gluing machine, even when the text block is thread or Smyth-sewn.

The cover should be unglazed and unfinished where the text block is to be glued. If the cover is to be varnished or laminated on the inside, it has to be partially "unvarnished" on the spine where the glue is to adhere. The cover should also have a format at least as large as the format of the uncropped text block, and the fiber direction must run parallel to the spine.

To achieve an attractive and durable product, the cover should be creased. You will get the best results with a "four-crease" technique. A four-crease is literally a total of four distinct creases in the cover: one on either side of the spine, one a few millimeters from the spine on the front cover, and one a corresponding distance from the spine on the back cover. These four creases are the exception to the basic rule that a crease should go in the same direction as the fold. This exception is made in order to give the best possible contact between the body, the glue and the cover. The creases in the cover prevent damage to the folds, and allow the product to be opened with ease, as well as increase the

THE PRICE LADDER OF BINDING
There are many factors that affect the binding choice, for example number of pages, design, usage, and what the printed product can cost. Below is the price ladder of binding, spiral binding being the most expensive and metal stitching the least expensive alternative.

1. Spiral binding
2. Thread stitching
3. Smyth-sewn
4. Glue binding
5. Metal stitching

If you are not sure of what type of binding and paper you want, you can order a product dummy from the paper supplier or the bookbinder.

CALCULATING THE WIDTH OF THE SPINE
If you are using the glue binding or thread stitching technique when binding your product, you need to know how thick the insert is in order to get the correct width of the spine.

$$\text{Width of spine in inches} = \frac{\text{Number of pages}}{\text{pages per inch (ppi)}}$$

HARDCOVERS
Books can be
bound in many
ways. Glue and
thread stitching are
common methods.

adhesion of the glue. Lastly, the covered text block is cropped at the head, tail and fore edges to the final format.

10.19 **Casing in**

Casing in is the term for when the cover is attached to the text block on hardcover (case-bound) books. After stitching, the hardcover-to-be has to go through three steps before it is ready for casing: cropping of the text block, finishing the text block and creating the hardcover.

First the text block is cropped. Cropping is done to give the book nice, even edges and is done by a three-sided trimmer, which trims off the head, tail and fore edge simultaneously. Then the text block is finished with so-called rounding and backing whose job is to diminish the stress between the cover and the end papers when the book is opened. This step is unnecessary with a thickness of less than one centimeter. Rounding means that the text block is formed so that it forms a rounded back (convex) and the front part becomes concave. Backing is a kind of folding of the text block. It is done by pressing together the text block while leaving the last 2 millimeters of the spine free. The free part is then pressed inward towards the text block, from which the spine will take on a mushroom shape with the spine forming the mushroom's head.

After these steps, a gauze strip is glued down the spine of the text block. The strip should hang down approximately 1 ½ cm over the front and back endpapers. This adds strength to the binding.

Before the text block can be attached, or hung, in the hardcover, or case, the hardcover has to be created. It is built of four parts. The cover material is what is printed and is composed basically of a finished, printed sheet. The paper should have a surface weight of 115–135 g/m² and be printed so that the fiber grain runs parallel to the spine. The cover text must bleed enough so that it extends across the cover. Other cover materials used can be plastic, cloth and

BACKING
Backing is a kind of folding of the text block. It is done by pressing together the text block while leaving the last 2 millimeters of the spine free. The free part is then pressed inward towards the text block, from which the spine will take on a mushroom shape. Backing helps reduce the stress on the case and endpapers when opening the book.

OTHER TYPES OF POSTPRESS PROCESSES

JACKET BAND
A jacket band is a thin strip of paper wrapped around a printed product, for example around a stack of printed products or a poster.

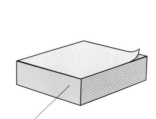

BLOCKING
Blocking is used to create a pad out of a thick bundle of paper sheets. One of the edges of the block is coated with special glue.

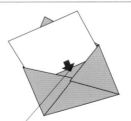

ENVELOPING
Enveloping can be done both mechanically and manually depending on edition size and complexity. Editions of 2,000 copies or less usually benefit from being stuffed manually.

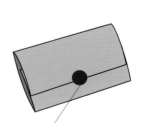

SEALING
One example of sealing is when you close a roll folded printed product with a sticker.

leather. In those cases it is common to use a gilding press to print the cover. With this kind of press you can also create positive and negative embossing, and/or metallic print, use colored foils and/or print with color ink. The other three parts that are glued to the cover material are two parts board, which makes the cover hard and stiff, and the loose spine, a somewhat thinner board used to build the book's spine.

Thread-sewn, hardcover books can be made in a number of different ways, depending on how exclusive they need to be. Full-bound books have a case made from one single piece of material. Half-bound books have a spine and corners of a different material from the rest of the case. For example, half-leather bound books (sometimes called half-French finish) are a version of half-bound. They have spines and corners bound in leather. Quarter-bound books feature different materials on the spine and the back and front covers.

Lastly, the case is rounded at the spine to obtain the same shape as the text block. Then the hanging can be done. When the cover is hung, the front and back endpapers are covered with glue and the text block is put in the hardcover, which is then pressed against the text block. When this is done, the book is pressed with press plates and iron to make sure the book gets its proper form. After that you have a finished hardcover book ready for delivery.

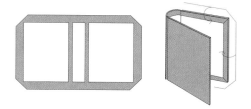

THE CASE IS BUILT OF FOUR PARTS
The cover material is what is printed and is composed basically of a finished, printed sheet. The other three parts that are glued to the cover material are two parts board, which makes the cover hard and stiff, and the loose spine, a somewhat thinner board used to build the book's spine.

THREE-SIDED TRIMMER
In a three-sided trimmer the printed product is cut in head, tail and fore edge.

TO KEEP IN MIND

- It is important that the printed sheets have dried sufficiently before off press processing. If not, the print can smear and ink from one sheet is transferred to another. Tint areas, flat areas with high ink coverage, or images with a lot of color are particularly sensitive. Cyan ink usually takes the longest to dry, and is therefore the most sensitive to smearing.

- To get an attractive and durable printed product you should always fold along the fiber direction [see Paper 12.1.3]. If you fold against the fiber direction, the paper is weakened, the fibers are broken down and an unattractive crack appears in the print crossing the fold. The printed product will also have difficulties remaining closed. When using the glue binding technique, erroneous fiber direction can cause waviness in the paper and decrease the durability of the binding.

- When a paper's substance weight exceeds 80 lbs, it should be creased. If it's not, the surface of the sheet might crack and the product will have difficulties remaining closed.

- When saddle-stitching you should not use sections in order to prevent the printed product from opening itself. The off press processing provider knows what to recommend.

- It is important to have an imposition layout because it allows you to check crossover bleeds and ink settings. You can also avoid printtechnical problems such as ghosting.

- Check with the off press processing provider how much waste, i.e. how many the number of sheets necessary for the off-press makeready, they have estimated. Usually reference copies are included in the estimated waste.

11.
legal BY FRANK J. MARTINEZ, THE MARTINEZ GROUP

Design is often viewed as a mysterious craft by outsiders. In contrast, designers know their work as the creation of communication via the use of visual order and structure. It is only after entering the design profession does the designer learn that design is also a complex business activity balancing interests at the nexus of art and commerce.

THE INCREASING COMPLEXITY of commerce requires that designers have a basic understanding of how the law influences their work and, in some cases, how they create. Good designers, by necessity, become polymaths, developing the valuable skill of learning how to learn. Unfortunately, knowing the law is an elusive pursuit since it is constantly evolving. Both experienced and beginning designers, face legal challenges almost every day of their working life. These challenges come in many forms and frequently occupy many areas of the law simultaneously.

11.1 The Workplace – The Designer as Employee

Upon entering the workplace, a designer is usually confronted with a choice; whether to become an employee or an independent contractor or, to use the well-known, term, a freelancer. Each of these choices places the designer into a different legal status, creating a different set of rights and obligations for the designer. In fact, each term, is a "term of art", a phrase or word signifying the legal status of the individual under state and, more importantly, federal law as it applies via copyright law. Upon accepting a design position there are many factors to be considered when choosing between working as an employee or as a freelancer. Among them are your experience, the nature of the work to be performed and the requirements of the employer. In many cases, the employer will not provide an option and require the hiring of an employee or freelancer.

As a general rule, most employees are "at-will employees." The at-will employee can choose to leave the job for any reason or no reason. Conversely, the employer may terminate the at-will employee at any time, with or without reason. An employment contract alters the at-will status by the consent of the employer and employee and usually identifies terms related to the length of employment, and other conditions under which the employment could be terminated prior to expiration of the contract. Most employees are not offered employment contracts since they are usually reserved for management level positions or those design positions which require unusually sophisticated skills. Each state has its own body of law regarding employer-employee relations and the negotiation and drafting of any employment agreement should be entrusted to an attorney or other advisor who is familiar with employment law in your state. There are some general terms which will apply wherever you are located and they are discussed later in this chapter. However, legally speaking, copyright law makes no distinction as to the contractual status of employees, since, in the absence of an agreement to the contrary, all employees are considered work-for-hire.

11.1.1 The Designer as Work for Hire

Copyright law is very specific in identifying the work made for hire status. Title 17 of the United States Code, Section 101 broadly defines a work made for hire as:

> *"1. a work prepared by an employee within the scope of his or her employment; or 2. a work specially ordered or commissioned for use as a contribution to a collective work, as a part of a motion picture or other audiovisual work, as a translation, as a supplementary work, as a compilation, as an instructional text, as a test, answer material for a test, or as an atlas, if the parties expressly agree in a written instrument signed by them that the work shall be considered a work made for hire…".*

As can be seen, Paragraph (1) states that if you are an employee, all of the work you produce is a work made for hire and is, accordingly, the property of your employer. It is important to note that term "property" is a legal term of art which implies that in addition to owning the work itself, an employer also owns any copyright as well as the right to commercially exploit the work. Care should be taken to recognize that the legal definition of the term employer is broader than it first appears. The Supreme Court has found that an employer could also be defined as a hiring party who has "the right to control the manner and means by which the product is accomplished." Therefore, technically, an employer-employee relationship could arise out of a very informal work relationship. While not initially obvious, Paragraph (2) further permits the contractual creation of the work-for-hire status between two parties who may not be in an employment relationship. As you may have guessed, despite the narrowly defined types of work which the statute defines as being eligible as a work for hire, most freelancers fall into this category.

Being a freelancer has many benefits. Among them is the sense of being in control of your career, choosing whom you work for, choosing where and when to work and in many cases, even earning a larger salary. However, as every experienced freelancer knows, the ownership and control of the work created by them normally remains the exclusive property of their employer. Why? Most freelancers, as a condition of their employment, normally enter into an independent contractor's or freelancer's agreement whereby, both parties agree that the work to be created is work made for hire. The use of such contracts is widespread in the design industry and while they come in many different forms, they all share some basic characteristics. In view of the impact that a contract could have on a designer's career, you should seek some knowledge about the terms and conditions that are likely to exist in a work for hire or employment agreement.

11.1.2 Contracts in Design

There are several myths associated with contracts and their use in design industry. First, there is no such thing as an "ironclad" or "unbreakable" contract. An agreement between two parties is only as good as the intention of the parties. Second, there are no such things as "legal" or "illegal contracts." There are only enforceable or unenforceable contracts. Third, the use of an agreement and negotiating the terms of an agreement with an employer or client is not insulting or adversarial. It's simply a good business practice that clarifies the responsibilities and obligations of the parties. Fourth, a contract that you find in a law book or other self-help guide is nothing more than a good place to start—it is not a substitute for the work of a competent attorney or business professional who understands the needs and circumstances of the designer and the client.

11.1.3 Use of Prior Work in Portfolio

Designers rely on their portfolios to demonstrate their skills and experience. On occasion, the terms of an employment or freelance agreement will restrict or eliminate the ability to show the work you've executed for a former employer. Blanket restrictions may not be enforceable as a matter of law. However, when the work or product shown is not known by the consuming public, or when the client has imposed restrictions upon an employer, prohibiting the use of such work in a portfolio could be reasonable. There are no bright line rules regarding the use of work in a portfolio however, one should always exercise common sense when showing work and claiming responsibility for the design in one's portfolio. Exaggerated claims could be interpreted as misrepresentation or even fraud and could lead to the termination of your employment.

11.2 Copyright

Copyright law is one of the most complex bodies of law in America, surpassed only by the law related to taxation and securities regulation. It has been subject to numerous revisions since it was first enacted into law in 1790. In addition, rarely does a session of Congress pass during which some technical revision or other form of tinkering to copyright law does not occur. Unlike earlier versions of copyright law, registration is not now mandatory for copyright protection since a copyright is deemed to "subsist at the moment of fixation in a tangible medium of expression." In short, when you create a copyrightable work, a copyright arises automatically under federal law. However, registration of a copyright gives the owner of the copyright extra benefits under federal law such as a choice in determining the basis for damages in the event of an infringement and under certain circumstances, even attorney's fees. The rights granted under copyright law are property rights and like other types of property, a copyright can be sold, rented, licensed, or given away. As with any other property right, the ultimate right is the right to exclude and within the context of copyright law, that right is manifested as controlling the right to make copies of the work, hence the term copy-right.

Over the years, the term "writings" has been construed as referring to the expression of original ideas. Now the term encompasses almost any tangible method of expressing a creative idea and has proven to be as varied as the methods of expressing creativity have been. For example, copyright law was enacted prior to the invention of photography. Nonetheless, in 1884 the Supreme Court determined that a photograph of the noted author and playwright Oscar Wilde was protectable under copyright law because the choices made by the photographer and "fixed" in the photograph, evidenced the creative decision-making process. Today, the creative choices expressed in software, web design, multi-media or performance art all comfortably fit within the legal framework developed over 200 years ago.

11.2.1 The Structure of Copyright Law

American copyright law has a constitutional basis. Article I, Section 8, Clause 8 of the Constitution, has been interpreted as requiring that Congress create laws to grant, for limited times, exclusive rights to inventors and authors. This is important because the constitutional mandate requires the balancing of competing interests; stimulating the creation of creative works by appealing to the self-interest of authors. The property rights granted to an author are balanced, sometimes even limited by the interests of the people. When these interests come into conflict, the courts tend to place the public's interest before those of the individual author.

Copyright law was not intended to and, in fact, does not protect creative ideas. It protects the methods by which creative ideas are shown. Stated simply, no rights are granted in the ideas, it only protects how the ideas are expressed. In addition, copyright law will not protect facts or other information that may be in the public domain. Others are perfectly free to use the same ideas, facts or information, provided they do not copy the method of expression previously used by another author.

When viewed as a whole, the complexity of copyright law appears overwhelming. Perhaps an easier way to approach understanding copyright is to view it from the perspective of property rights, that is, a group or bundle of rights that you control.

11.2.2 The Benefits of Registration

Federal registration confers substantial benefits upon a copyright owner. These benefits include a presumption that the copyright registration is legally valid. Thus, in the event of litigation, an infringer must prove that the work is not entitled to copyright protection. The stakes can be very large since, in the event of a willful infringement, the copyright owner has a choice of actual damages or statutory damages of up to $150,000, plus an award of attorney's fees. Accordingly, federal registration should not be overlooked since it provides a significant financial incentive to police infringement. On more than one occasion, infringement and potential damages have not been pursued because the lack of a properly filed federal registration made it too expensive to police infringement.

11.2.3 Registering a Copyright

The Copyright Office is located in Washington, D.C. and is part of the Library of Congress. Registration of a copyright requires the use of an official form which can be obtained online www.loc.gov/copyright. In addition to the official forms, the site contains a large amount of information and notices related to copyright. Of special importance are the Circulars and Brochures. These materials contain a significant amount of material and, in them, you can find an answer for most of your copyright questions. Before you begin, there are some basic considerations which should be helpful in getting started.

First, determine the nature of the work and select the proper form. Read the instructions very carefully, since the Copyright Office has strict rules as to how the form is submitted (printed on both sides) and the nature, number and type of specimens of the work that must be submitted with an application. In addition, no application will be processed without payment of the required fees

The Copyright Office defines the nature of a work very broadly. Accordingly, since you may not find contemporary usage or descriptions on the forms, use the next best term which accurately describes the work you wish to register.

Many of the forms listed in the margins are available for downloading with instructions or in a short form version. The examples noted are not a complete listing of the forms available. Unless you are very experienced, you should also download, read and follow the instructions. If you wish to file a group of works, a compilation of works, serial works or have a large project that involves different types of media, you should consider using an experienced attorney since a defective filing could have serious consequences.

11.2.4 The Author

Like any other specialized endeavor, copyright law has its own language and some of these terms are so unique that you should take time to become familiar with them. For the purposes of copyright, an author could be either the person or persons (joint authors) who created the work or own the work. It is important to understand this distinction since each term denotes a particular legal status. In the case of the designer who is an employee or a freelancer as work for hire, the author is their employer. These distinctions become quite important when registering a copyright, since the author of the work must be identified with accuracy. In addition, the application must note whether the work was created as a work for hire and whether the work was created anonymously or pseudonymously, such as a stage or professional name. Copyright law abounds with cause and effect. When preparing an application, remember that your choices affect the rights and exclusions derived from a copyright registration. Those rights and your ability to use them cascade from and interlock with each other. Don't let the simplicity of a copyright application deceive you. Do some research before you begin or employ an attorney experienced with the process since correcting a mistake can be extremely time consuming, costly and could limit your rights in the future.

11.2.5 Joint Authors

A copyrighted work can and is frequently created by more than one person. In addition, since a company or corporation is a legal entity, a person and a company can also be joint authors. Copyright law places special burdens on joint authors, both with respect to the work as well as the relationship between the authors. Under copyright law, joint authors are co-owners of the copyright to a work. Co-ownership under copyright law has been determined as each owner having a divisible ownership right. A co-author can sell or license his or her rights the copyrighted work. When co-creating a work, you may wish to consider a written agreement or other form of contract that defines the rights of each author. In the absence of such an agreement that provides otherwise, each author has a right to license the work, sell their ownership interest in the work, or a right to create derivative works based upon the original copyrighted work. Disputes between co-authors often arise when the authors haven't considered how they wish to control use or dispose of the work after it's registered.

While each author has a right to license the work, such a right is accompanied by a duty of accounting to the other author. Stated simply, if one author licenses the work to a third party, the licensing author has an obligation to pay a share of the licensing fee and any royalty stream to his or her co-author.

11.2.6 Exclusive Rights Under Copyright Law

Section 106 of the Copyright Statute only identifies six exclusive rights of the owners of a copyright.

While short, Section 106 has been written so as to be extremely broad in defining the scope of exclusivity and, for all practical purposes, encompasses almost every method of use, display or distribution currently known. Of particular importance, is the emphasis placed on the owner's exclusive right to reproduce, copy, perform a work, or to grant a right to others to do the same.

The exclusive rights of a copyright owner can be divided in many ways. For instance, the owner of the exclusive right in a written work can grant one party the right to create a derivative work in the nature of a screenplay while

- **Form TX**, is used for published or unpublished dramatic and non-dramatic literary works (Literary works include nondramatic textual works with or without illustrations. Computer programs and databases also are considered literary works. Plays, dramas, and screenplays are not in the literary works category. Other examples of literary works include fiction, nonfiction, manuscripts, poetry, contributions to collective works, compilations of data or other literary subject matter, dissertations, theses, reports, speeches, bound or loose leaf volumes, secure tests, pamphlets, brochures, textbooks, online works, reference works, directories, catalogs, advertising copy, single pages of text, tracts, games, automated databases and computer programs).

- **Form PA**, is used for published and unpublished works of the performing arts. Such as,
(a) musical works, including any accompanying words;
(b) dramatic works, such as scripts, including any accompanying music;
(c) pantomimes and choreographic works; and
(d) motion pictures and other audiovisual works. Choreography and pantomimes are also copyrightable dramatic works. Choreography is defined as the composition and arrangement of dance movements and patterns usually intended to be accompanied by music. Pantomime is the art of imitating or acting out situations, characters, or other events. Pantomimes and chore-ography need not tell a story or be presented before an audience in order to by copyrightable. Each work, however, must be fixed in a tangible medium of expression from which the work can be performed. Sports, games and physical-fitness exercises are not considered choreographic works.

- **Form SR**, is used for published and unpublished sound recordings (Sound recordings are works that result from the fixation of a series of musical, spoken, or other sounds, but not including the sounds accompanying a motion picture or other audiovisual work. Common examples include recordings of music, dramatic performances, or lectures. Generally, copyright protection extends to two elements in a sound recording:
(a) the performance and
(b) the production or engineering of the sound recording. A sound recording is not the same as a phonorecord, which is defined as the physical object in which a work of authorship is embodied. The word "phonorecord" includes cassette tapes, CDs, LPs, 45 r.p.m. disks, as well as other formats.).

- **Form VA**, is used for published and unpublished works of visual art. (Visual arts are pictorial, graphic, or sculptural works, including 2-dimensional and 3-dimensional works of fine, graphic, and applied art, or advertisements, commercial prints, labels, artificial flowers and plants, artwork applied to clothing or to other useful articles, bumper stickers, decals and stickers, cartographic works, such as maps, globes and relief models, cartoons and comic strips, collages, dolls, toys, drawings, paintings and murals, enamel works, fabric, floor, and wall covering designs, games, puzzles, greeting cards, postcards, stationery, holograms, computer and laser artwork, jewelry designs, models, mosaics, needlework and craft kits, original prints, such as engravings, etchings, serigraphs, silk screen prints and woodblock prints, patterns for sewing, knitting, crochet and needlework, Photographs and photomontages, posters, record jacket artwork or photography, relief and intaglio prints, reproductions, such as lithographs, collotypes, sculpture, such as carvings, ceramics, figurines, maquettes, molds, relief sculptures, stained glass designs, stencils and cut-outs, technical drawings, architectural drawings or plans, blueprints, diagrams, mechanical drawings, weaving designs, lace designs and tapestries).

- **Form SE**, is used for serial publications (such as, newspapers, magazines, newsletters, annuals, journals and any other publication that is issued on a regular basis.).

- **Form CA**, is used to correct or provide additional information given in a registration.

- **Form CON**, is a continuation sheet and can only be used with Forms CA, PA, SE, SR, TX and VA.

granting another party the right to translate the work into another language. In another example, the owner of the exclusive rights to publicly perform a work, can authorize a public performance in Chicago, while reserving exclusive performance rights in the rest of the country. This granting of rights is known as "licensing" and the right granted is known as a "license" and the person or company who is authorized to use another's copyright is the "licensee" of the licensor/copyright owner. The extent to which a licensee may use, perform, display, copy the copyrighted work is normally determined by the terms of the license.

For many years, failure to use the copyright symbol on work of author-ship would result in either the loss of a right to register the copyright or the loss of copyright protection. In 1989 however, the requirement and the arcane rules for the use, placement and display of the copyright notice was entirely eliminated. It is still a prudent practice to display a copyright notice whenever possible since it notifies the viewer as to the owner and the rights claimed. Acceptable displays typically include "© 2006 XYZ COMPANY" or "COPYRIGHT © 2006 XYZ COMPANY". Non-traditional uses or displays of a copyright notice should be approved by legal counsel since the underlying purpose of the copyright notice could be compromised by an unorthodox treatment.

EXCLUSIVE RIGHTS AND THE COPYRIGHT STATUTE

- to reproduce the copyrighted work in copies or phonorecords;

- to prepare derivative works based upon the copyrighted work;

- to distribute copies or phonorecords of the copyrighted work to the public by sale or other transfer of ownership, or by rental, lease or lending;

- in the case of literary, musical, dramatic, and choreographic works, pantomimes, and motion pictures and other audiovisual works, to perform the copyrighted work publicly;

- in the case of literary, musical, dramatic, and choreographic works, pantomimes, and pictorial, graphic, or sculptural works, including the individual images of a motion picture or other audiovisual work, to display the copyrighted work publicly; and

- in the case of sound recordings, to per-form the copyrighted work publicly by means of a digital audio transmission.

11.2.8 **Artist's Rights**

Section 106 (A) of the Copyright statute defines the rights of certain authors with respect to "attribution and integrity." These rights are commonly referred to as artist's rights. The rights defined under the statute are specifically related to preserving the reputation of the artist as it relates the works of authorship as well as, preserving the work itself. In particular, an artist has the right to (a) claim authorship of their work, (b) and the right to prevent the use of his or her name as the author of any work of visual art which they did not create. The statute further grants an artist the right to prevent the use of their name as the author of an artwork in the event the work is distorted, mutilated or otherwise modified in such a way as would be prejudicial to the artist's honor or reputa-tion. Finally and probably most controversial, the statute grants an artist the right to prevent any destruction of "a work of recognized stature", whether the destruction is intentional or the result of gross negligence.

As with any law, there are some exceptions. Modifications of a work that occur through the passage of time or by reason of the nature of the materials used in the work of art, are not considered a distortion, mutilation or an other-wise prohibited modification. Furthermore, any modification which results from conservation or changes which occur during a public presentation such as changes in appearance due to lighting or placement are not considered a prohibited modification of the work of art, unless the modification is caused by gross negligence.

At the outset, it must be noted that these rights are only applicable to works of visual art as defined by the statute and those rights may not apply to any reproduction, depiction, portrayal of a work of one work of art in another work of art. In addition, written works, works of graphic design and all works for hire, are explicitly excluded under the provisions of Section 106 (A). Furthermore the rights granted to an artist under Section 106 are independent and exclusive of the rights granted under a regular copyright. Interestingly, artist's rights under copyright law cannot be transferred or sold. The statute only allows the waiver of the artist's rights in a written document signed by the artist. The waiver must specifically identify the work of art and the uses of the work to which the waiver applies. By law, any right or use not identified with specificity in the written waiver is not granted.

As can be seen, the artist's rights protections granted under copyright law are complex and contain many exceptions and limitations. If you are an artist creating work for installation or display in public spaces, this section of copyright law will be very important to you. If you are designer using or incorporating images or details of known works of art, you should consult with an attorney experienced with these issues since the failure to acquire a waiver or an improper waiver could result in significant liability for your client.

11.3 Fair Use

Within the creative community, the doctrine of fair use is probably the most cited, most discussed and least understood area of copyright law. When discussing fair use, the underlying principle that the people are the ultimate beneficiaries of all "writings and discoveries" is in full view. Section 107 of the Copyright statute states that:

> *"the fair use of a copyrighted work, including such use by reproduction in copies or phonorecords or by any other means specified by that section, for purposes such as criticism, comment, news reporting, teaching (including multiple copies for classroom use), scholarship, or research, is not an infringement of copyright."*

Stated another way, a fair use of a copyrighted work is a use, by another, that is an exception to the exclusive rights of the copyright owner. From a legal perspective, the doctrine of fair use is a defense to a charge of copyright infringement. If this were not the case, the exclusive rights granted to a copyright owner could inhibit creativity; the very purpose of the statute. The important issue in any fair use analysis is an inquiry into the rights of the copyright owner versus the benefits the public derives from the particular use of the copyrighted work.

When faced with determining whether the infringement of a copyrighted work is, indeed a fair use, a court is required to examine the use with regard to the following four factors.

1. The purpose and character of the use, including whether such use is of a commercial nature or is for nonprofit educational purpose;
2. The nature of the copyrighted work;
3. The amount and substantiality of the portion used in relation to the copyrighted work as a whole; and
4. The effect of the use upon the potential market for or value of the copyrighted work.

Despite the statutory mandate, these four factors do not define what constitutes a fair use and they do not create a "rule" for defining a fair use. Each fair use claim is examined on its own merits, the four factors being merely the beginning point of inquiry which should also include a review of the use as it relates to the six different uses noted in the statue, namely, criticism, comment, news reporting, teaching, scholarship and research. Thus a fair use examination ultimately turns on two basic questions; how is the copyrighted work used by another and what is the effect upon the original work and its author?

It's easy to imagine that a newspaper or design magazine is just as motivated by profit as is any tabloid and both are arguably commercial ventures. In such circumstances, the question of what constitutes a fair use in the nature of news reporting turns not on the publication itself, but upon the nature of the use. Pure news reporting, in the absence of libel, will almost always be considered a fair use. However, use of a copyrighted work, which is then "turned" into news, will not be viewed as benign. Use of a copyrighted work in the absence of a profit motive almost always weighs in favor of fair use. However, as with most rules of law, there are always exceptions and not every commercial use of a copyrighted work will be found automatically to be an unfair use. When a copyrighted work is used in a way where the user adds additional value in the nature of creativity, such as use of a copyrighted work in a work of art, a finding of fair use is much more likely. Stated simply, a commercial use of another's work never looks good and a court will inquire as to whether the use has resulted in some sort of public benefit as opposed to mere private financial gain.

The conduct of the user can be quite influential in a fair use examination. Seeking permission to use another's work may be an act of good faith, but contrary to perception, being denied permission to use another's work doesn't mean that a subsequent use isn't a fair use. The Supreme Court has specifically ruled that "being denied permission to use a work does not weigh against a finding of fair use." But, judges are human and are not above reviewing the conduct of the parties in a fair use claim. A copyright owner who seeks to unfairly stifle creativity or legitimate criticism or news reporting may actually broaden the boundaries of what is an acceptable fair use.

In every fair use examination, the nature of the original copyrighted work will be considered. Generally speaking, a court is likely to believe that the more creative the original work, the more protection it deserves. Conversely, the more informational or utilitarian an original work is, the greater the opportunity for a finding of fair use. Thus, works which merely recite factual information are not likely to be considered as creative as a novel or even a biography. Unpublished works will generally be afforded more protection since another's use is likely to alter, if not destroy the original author's market for the work.

Whatever the nature of the use, another key issue is the amount and substantially of the original work used in the second work. Thus, the greater portion of an original work used, the less "fair" the second use becomes. Conversely, the less of the original work used, the more "fair" the second use becomes. However, as can be expected, there is no hard and fast rule to be applied here and there may be cases where the portion of the original work used is small but the effect on the market for the original work is substantial. The key issue will be how "fair" the use is with regard to the author and the market for the original work. Accordingly when the second use adversely impacts, usurps, or replaces the market for the original work, the less "fair" the second use becomes. But not every use that harms another work is prohibited. The copying of an original work in a parody, review or critique which happens to be devastating to the original work may, in fact, be a recognizable fair use.

As can be seen, the doctrine of fair use is utterly devoid of rigid rules and relies instead upon an overall all assessment of the extent and purpose of the use, the actions of the parties and the commercial impact upon the original author. An artist engaged in the creation of an artistic work that incorporate works created by another may have reason to believe that their use constitutes a fair use. A graphic artist may reasonably arrive at the same conclusion, but because the use is for a commercial purpose, might be denied a finding of fair use. The bottom line is that there are no safe harbors and no rule of law that you can rely on entirely. Check with an attorney if you are concerned about using another's work especially if your work is in the nature of entertainment. If you are working in film or music, use of another's work is almost always a problem. Unauthorized sampling or copying is universally frowned upon since the legal liability for a record label, music publisher or film studio can be quite significant. Sometimes it takes a little more effort to create a wholly original work, but almost without exception, it's worth the extra effort.

11.4 Creating Original Work

What is an original work? From a creative perspective, it might be a work that is utterly uninfluenced by another's style or methods. From a legal perspective, original work is work that does not copy a previously created work. Copyright law does not care if a work is "referential" of another's work, it's merely concerned with copying. Works of design that incorporate a preexisting work, if objected to, will always be subject to a traditional fair use analysis. Some designers seem to think that digitizing and manipulating another's work creates a new work. Even transforming another's work by adding new graphic elements, or merging photographic elements from different sources does not create a new work. It simply means that multiple works have been infringed. In addition, it is irrelevant whether the original work is analog or digital. The method of creation and the method of copying are not relevant. An infringement is an infringement.

Almost all works of design are for a commercial purpose. As such, the scope of what may be considered a fair use is likely to be much smaller. That doesn't mean that a work of design can never incorporate another's work, it just makes the fair use analysis more difficult. If you must use another's work, the safest way to proceed is to use the many commercially available resources such as stock photography and other royalty free art.

11.5 Licensing Photography

The use and availability of stock photography has grown significantly with the growth of the internet. Currently, stock photography can be licensed and delivered online. It is important to note that one does not actually buy the work, a use of the work, a license for a particular purpose, is purchased. Therefore, any use outside of the licensed use constitutes an infringement of the work. Occasionally one will hear about "royalty-free" photography or clip art, this is an inaccurate term. When you buy "royalty-free" clip art or photographs, you are actually buying an unrestricted license to use the art.

COPYRIGHT TERMS

- An **architectural work** is the design of a building embodied in a drawing or plan

- An **audiovisual work** consists of a series of related images shown on projectors, viewers or electronic equipment together with sounds

- A **collective work** could be a periodical issue, anthology or encyclopedia, which has a number of contributors, each contribution being independently copyrightable

- A **compilation** is a work formed by the collection and assembling of preexisting materials or date that are selected, coordinated, or arranged in such a way that the resulting work, as a whole, constitutes an original work.

- A **derivative work** is a work based upon one or more preexisting works, such as a translation, musical arrangement, dramatization, fictionalization, motion picture version, sound recording, art reproduction, abridgment, condensation, indeed, any other modification which, as a whole, represents an original work. In addition a derivative work might also include works derived from editorial revisions, annotations, elaborations and other modifications.

- A **joint work** is a work prepared by two or more authors with the intention that their work is to constitute a complete and indivisible work.

- A **literary work** is a work, other than an audiovisual work, expressed in words, numbers or other verbal or numerical symbols regardless of the nature of the material objects which contain them.

- A **pictorial, graphic** and **sculptural works** include two-dimensional and three-dimensional works of fine, graphic and applied art, photographs, prints and art reproductions, maps, globes,

- **charts, diagrams, models** and **technical drawings**, including architectural plans and a pseudonymous work is a work in which the author is identified under a fictitious name.

When commissioning original photography, it is very common for a photographer to retain ownership of the copyright and license the specific use to the client. When commissioning original photography it is important to ensure that your proposed use is properly licensed. Another important task is ensuring that all releases are secured when using locations outside of the photographer's studio and when using live models. If you are using a model who is a minor, ensure that their parent or legal guardians sign the release.

11.6 Using Public Domain Work

Any work for which the copyright or patent has expired is now in the public domain. Any work which was dedicated to the public welfare by the author, is in the public domain. Anyone is free to use any public domain work without fear of infringement. There are several ways to determine whether a work is in the public domain. The United States Copyright Office offers a fee based searching service. If you know the title of a work or its last known owner, it's possible to ascertain whether the work is still protected by copyright. In addition, there are commercial search services such as those offered by Thomson & Thomson or CCH Corsearch. These searches can be expensive, but they are exhaustive and thus represent a valuable resource. Since it can be difficult to ascertain whether a work has fallen into the public domain. The term of copyright has changed many times and the term of protection has been extended several times. If you are working on an important project, and wish to use a work that you believe is now in the public domain, build the cost of a good search into the budget and contact an attorney or someone with good experience with these matters. It is a precaution that is well worth the extra cost and effort.

11.7 Using Type Fonts

Thirty years ago, digital type fonts did not exist. Hot type was difficult to obtain and expensive. Therefore, it was difficult to infringe. Digitization has spawned the almost wholesale trading of unauthorized or pirated fonts. With only minor effort, it is possible to find web sites that contain entire libraries of fonts at little or no charge. Surprisingly, protecting fonts is not difficult. They can be protected by copyright. However unlike many other kinds of design, only the software which comprises a digital font is currently protectable by copyright. However, the actual design of the font, its physical appearance, can only be protected by a design patent. In addition, the title of the font can be protected by a trademark registration.

A visit to any type foundry website quickly reveals that many fonts are not actually sold and that many of their names are subject to trademark registrations. Use of the copyrighted software is licensed to the end user. This license is commonly referred to as an end user license agreement or EULA. Most foundries post a copy of their EULA on their website for your review prior to the purchase of license. Most foundries restrict how you can use a font, and they frequently restrict the embedding of their fonts in the .pdf (page description format) format. Therefore using such software might be prohibited or restricted by the EULA since the improper use of the software could actually "embed" and transfer an unanthorized copy of the font software. Documents that contain improperly embedded fonts are easily hacked depriving the font designer of payment for their hard work. In addition, there may be restrictions as to use of the font in a logo or on how many computers the font can be loaded onto at any one time. Many EULAs restrict the number of printers or other output devices used with a font or the EULA might restrict the use of the font software to a single geographic location. It is important to read and understand the end user license agreement. A designer's use of unauthorized or pirated copies of font software creates liability for themselves and for their clients.

The Internet is a rich source of materials and if properly acquired and properly used can be quire helpful. Prior to using any work acquired from the Internet, know your sources. Ensure that your use is licensed and if not ensure that a license is not required. Furthermore, remember that HTML code can and frequently is copyrighted. Copying and using HTML or photographs directly from another website can lead to problems. In addition, using pirated or hacked software raises the specter of both civil and criminal liability under the Digital Millennium Copyright Act.

11.8 The Internet and Web Sites

Using the Internet and putting up a website poses many challenges for a designer. From a legal perspective the prohibitions under copyright and trademark law are equally applicable to creating a website. Therefore, ensure that any images or software code are properly licensed. It's one thing to be inspired by the page layout of a competitor's website, it's another matter entirely to copy it. If the site that you are creating will be serving or archiving the work of others, ensure that you have permission to both store and distribute the work of others. If the website is commercial in nature, remember that conducting commercial activities in another state will be viewed as submitting yourself to the jurisdiction of the courts in that state. Displaying or using another's trademarks to further your own commercial purpose, could result in liability under the Lanham Act (trademark law).

Anyone involved in a creative endeavor will encounter situations that test their ethics. We are all influenced by the work of other artists and designers, good designers seem to be constantly aware of the work of their peers and studiously avoid copying or infringing even if it creates personal hardship. Original thinking isn't easy. However, we know it when we see it and the capacity for it grows with exercise. A few minutes spent planning a project can save hours, weeks or months of legal heartache. Large design projects require additional planning. The use of freelance help or third-party vendors almost always requires some form of understanding between the parties. Most attorneys will spend a few minutes answering initial inquires with little or no charge and in many cases, simple readily available legal agreements are sufficient. Take the time to investigate a project thoroughly prior to accepting or actually beginning your work. It is time well spent and in the end, your client will be glad that you did.

One of the most common areas of disputes between designers and clients is determining who is permitted to engage third party vendors and who is responsible for payment. When purchasing printing, color separation or other services, this issue can be quite significant since they are so expensive. As a fundamental matter, it's very important that a designer understands whether or not they are permitted to act on behalf of their client. In legal terms, this is referred to as an "agency" relationship which, if the designer is not careful, can create legal liability for the designer who acts outside of the scope of the agency. Stated simply, if the designer acts outside of the authority granted by the client or against the client's interests, the designer could end up responsible for all of those costs.

As a practical matter, the wise designer will clearly understand what, if any, power they have to enter a contract on behalf of their client. Obviously, these terms should be clearly stated in the agreement between the designer and the client. As a corollary issue, a designer who is authorized to purchase printing should also ensure that the printing contract does not contain terms which are outside the authority granted by the client or contrary to the client's interests. Like many other trades, printers frequently include terms regarding the mandatory purchase of printing overages or no requirement that the printer reprint or refund money for a print run that is short. Even if you're authorized to purchase on behalf of your client, it is always prudent to require that a client provide written authorization for third-party services and that the client reviews and approves the terms of any contract related to such matters. If a client wants you to handle everything, make sure that your agreement grants you the right to act on the client's behalf to the extent the project may require.

glossary

This glossary serves as a small dictionary of graphic terms as well as an index to the book. The page references are not stated in numerical order but in order of significance. Some general terms are simply defined without refering to a particular page.

A

.FON   P 212
Bitmap fonts used in Windows program to draw fonts in very small sizes on the screen.

.PFB   6.5.2
Printer Font Binary. Contour fonts in Postscript Type 1 fonts in Windows have the file extension ".pfb".

.PFM   6.5.2
Printer Font Metrics. Screen fonts in Postscript Type 1 fonts in Windows have the file extension ".pfm".

10 BASE 2   2.8.3
An Ethernet version using coaxial cable. It can achieve a transmission speed of up to 10 Mbit/second.

100 BASE T   2.8.3
An Ethernet standard for twisted pair cable that allows a transmission speed of up to 100 Mbit/second.

16-BIT MODE   4.6.4
An RGB image saved in 16-bit mode has 216 = 65 000 gray levels for every channel, which is significantly more than 256 gray levels in images in 8-bit mode. For this reason 16-bit mode is better for images which are to be edited extensively.

24-BIT IMAGE   4.6.8
An RGB image saved in 8-bit mode. The colors for each pixel are therefore indicated as 3×8=24 bits.

2-SET
See Work and tumble.

2-UP
See Many-up.

3D STUDIO MAX   2.5.4
3D illustration program from Autodesk.

4+0
Four-color printing on one side of the sheet and no printing at all on the other side.

4+4
Four-color printing on both sides of a sheet.

48-BIT IMAGE   4.12.7
An RGB image saved in 16-bit mode where each channel is 16-bits. The colors for each pixel are therefore indicated as 3×16=48 bits.

4-UP   7.6.1
See Many-up.

8-BIT MODE   4.6.4
An image saved in 8-bit mode has 256 gray levels for every channel. In an RGB image with three channels each pixel can reproduce one of 256×256×256=16.7 million different colors.

ABSORB   9.5.6
To take in, soak up. During the first drying phase in offset printing, setting, the oil in the ink is absorbed into the paper. If the pigment is also absorbed a lower density is produced.

ACCESS LEVELS   2.8.15
In a network, different access levels can be set, thereby assigning different access to different users in the network.

ACID-FREE PAPER
Paper with low levels of sodium chloride and sulphates. Acid-free paper has a longer lifespan than paper which contains acids.

ACROBAT   7.2.1

Adobe program for creating, reviewing and changing PDF files. Exists in different versions with different advanced functions.

ACROBAT 3D   7.2.1

Adobe program which makes it possible to export and edit PDF files from CAD programs.

ACROBAT DISTILLER   7.2.1

Adobe program to create PDF files from Postscript files.

ACROBAT ELEMENTS   7.2.2

Adobe program which makes it possible to export PDF files directly from Microsoft Office programs. It is only sold as corporate software licenses.

ACROBAT PROFESSIONAL   7.2.3

A developed version of Adobe Acrobat with an array of graphics functions added, e.g. PDF/X and preflight tools.

ACTIVATE TYPEFACE   6.4.6

Where there is a large number of font files, just some of them can be activated, in order to save memory. This is done using special programs, e.g. ATM or Suitcase.

AD

Abbreviation of "Art Director". A person who works with the design of communications in different media such as the web, print, film, etc. in an advertising agency, for example.

ADDITIONAL COPY PRICE

Price charged for the production of additional copies over and above those stated in the order quote request. The additional copy price should be included in the supplier's quote. Often quoted per 1000 extra copies.

ADDITIONAL SERVICES

Changes or additional work which were not part of a job from the start.

ADDITIVE COLOR SYSTEM   3.3

A color system where colors originate by combining (adding) three primary colors of light, e.g. RGB. Different proportions of the three lights produce different colors.

ADJUSTMENT LAYER   5.5.16   5.4.1   5.4.6–10

A tool in Photoshop which enables the color and tone settings in an image to be applied in the form of a layer. This enables adjustments to be made without affecting the original image.

ADOBE (ACE)   3.13

A color management module used in Adobe programs.

ADOBE RGB   3.8

A common color space with a large tonal range which is an established standard within graphic production.

ADSL   2.9.2

Asymmetric Digital Subscriber Links. A means of connecting to the Internet and transferring information digitally through the telephone wire.

ADVERTISING AGENCY   1.1

Company which creates advertising campaigns, e.g. advertisements in newspapers, on TV or internet advertising.

ADVERTISING PROOF

A printed proof of an advertisement which is printed in a printing press.

A-FORMAT   8.6

A standardized paper format range with pages based on the ratio of 1 to the square root of 2. The areas of the sheets in the range relate to each other by a ratio of 2 to 1, with A0 being 1 m², A1 being 0.5 m², and so on.

AFP   7.1

A page description language from IBM.

AGE-RESISTANT PAPER

An international standard for paper which can age for several hundred years without detriment to its quality.

AIR HUMIDITY   8.18.2

The concentration of water vapor in the air. In a printshop it is important that the humidity is carefully controlled, otherwise the paper can absorb or release water, affecting its qualities.

AIRPORT   2.8.5

Apple's name for a wireless network.

AIT   2.6.3

"Advanced Intelligent Tape", a format used for magnetic tapes.

ALIAS MAYA   2.5.4

3D illustration program which is often used to create 3D animation in film and TV production as well as computer games.

ANCHOR POINTS   4.1   7.1.3

The points which make up a curve, for example in a extraction curve for the extraction of an object.

ANILOX ROLLER   9.9.3

A special roller which transfers ink to the image carrier in flexographic printing. The cylinder has a regular grid pattern of small cells.

ANTI-ALIASING   P 213

Technique used to create soft edges on a pixel-based screen using gray levels. Used on text, for example.

APERTURE   4.11.2

An opening for light in a lens. The value of the aperture determines the size of the opening, e.g. in a camera which lets in light during exposure.

APPLE RGB   3.8

RGB standard formerly used in Adobe Photoshop and Illustrator.

APPLETALK

Older Apple network protocol. Used in Macintosh networks.

APPROVAL   7.5.6

A digital proof system from Kodak.

ARCHIVE DURABILITY   8.16

A measure of the lifespan and durability of a paper.

ARCHIVE DURABLE PAPER 8.15

An international standard for paper that can be archived for a long period. It states, for example, that the paper should be able to be folded at least 150 times without the fibers splitting.

ARTIFACT 4.9.6

We often talk about JPEG artifacts. These are visible effects of JPEG compression that should not be in the image. They often appear as checkered patterns.

ARTPRO 7.4.8

A special program for packaging production which has developed functions for, among other things, handling trapping, special separations when using PMS instead of CMYK, overprint and knockout, impositions, etc.

ARTWORKER

Person in an advertizing agency, printshop etc. who handles graphic material, text and images, following specific instructions, i.e. from an AD. Tasks such as layout, typography, text and image mounting, extraction and color adjustment are often carried out by an artworker.

ASCII 6.2.4

Text can be saved in ASCII format. Only the characters are saved, and all the typographical settings – font, row spacing, etc. – disappear. Usually has the file extension ".txt".

ASTERISK

Symbol "*". Is used to refer to a footnote.

AT SIGN

Appears as "@" and is pronounced "at". Used to separate the user name from the domain name in an email address.

ATM, ATM DELUXE 6.4.9

Adobe Type Manager. An extension for managing fonts, improves font management and makes it more effective, e.g. for showing typefaces and for grouping fonts in a project.

B

BACKUP COPYING 2.6.3 2.8.15

Backup of files is often carried out on tape. Ensures that files which have been damaged or lost can be recreated.

BALANCED SCREENING 7.7.1

A screening technique developed by Agfa which combines different halftone dot shapes to avoid distracting patterns.

BAND P 395

A thin strip of paper wrapped around a printed product, for example around a stack of printed products or a poster.

BANDING 5.3.6

Image phenomenon which occurs in fine toning where there are too few gray levels. Instead of soft toning, bands appear with visible boundaries between different shades.

BANDWIDTH 2.8.16

A measure of the theoretical transfer speed in a network, i.e. how fast data can be transported. Measured in bits/second.

BASE LINE P 207

The imaginary line on which all capital letters in a row rest. (An exception is certain cuts of "J" and "Q").

BATCH PROCESSING 5.8.6

A function macro which can be employed automatically on, for example, all images in a folder.

BERLINER 8.6

Newspaper format with six columns. Measures 315×470 mm.

BERNOULLI DISK

An older type of removable, magnetic storage disk, available in different sizes, holds 44 to 105 megabytes.

BEZIER CURVE 4.1

A mathematical description of a curve named after a French Renault engineer, who developed the technique to be able to describe the design of cars. Bezier curves are used in object graphics and to describe typefaces, for example.

BICUBIC INTERPOLATION 5.4.4

See Interpolation.

BILLBOARD

Large advertising poster found at bus-stops, underground train stations or generally outside in an urban environment.

BINARY NUMBER SYSTEM P 41

The number system used by computers, based on the digits 0 and 1. Cf. decimal system, which is commonly used and is based on the digits 0–9.

BINDER 9.5.6 8.19.4

Component of printing ink which encapsulates and binds the pigment.

BINDING 10.1

Joining together of several printed sheets to form a printed product, for example staple binding, glue binding or sewn binding.

BIT 4.6.1

The smallest memory unit used by computers; can have a value of 0 or 1.

BIT-DEPTH 4.12.7 4.6.4

A measurement of the number of colors a pixel in a digital image can display; states how many bits each pixel is stored with. The more bits there are per color, the greater the bit-depth, and the greater the number of colors possible. A regular RGB-image has 3×8 bits = 24 bits.

BITMAP 7.1.1

The digital information which describes a digital image or page using ones and zeros. During ripping the PostScript code is translated into a checkered pattern consisting of ones and zeros – a bitmap.

BLACK EDGE 7.4.8

The darker tone which trapping and choking creates around an object.

BLACK POINT 5.4.7

The darkest tone in an image, controls the contrast in an image along with the white point.

BLACK-PRINTING 9.2.4

Describes a laser printer which designates those areas on the sheet which are to be covered with toner.

BLANKS 9.2.3

Preprinted sheets, e.g. stationery with preprinted logo and footer, on which additional text or images can be printed.

BLEACHING 8.17.2

Treating the paper pulp to increase the brightness of the paper. Common techniques are ECF (Elementary Chlorine Free) using chlorine dioxide, and TCF (Totally Chlorine Free) where oxygen, ozone and hydrogen peroxide may be used.

BLEED [1] 6.11.1–3 5.4.3

Images or objects which are supposed to run all the way to the edge of the paper are printed with bleeds, i.e. are placed so that they run over the edge of the page format, by around 5 mm.

BLEED [2] P 114

Images or objects placed across a two-page spread are called crossover bleeds. Special attention needs to be paid when bleeds cross over false spreads.

BLEEDING 9.3.3

When two colors bleed into each other, i.e. they mix. This problem mainly occurs with ink for ink-jet printers. To avoid bleeding, the ink must dry quickly.

BLEEDING P 394

See Bleed.

BLOCKING P 394

A type of glue binding for note pads.

BLUELINE 7.6.8

Old form of chemical proof used to check imposition. The print result is only displayed in one color, blue. Nowadays the term is sometimes carelessly used to indicate imposition correction.

BLUETOOTH 2.2.4

Wireless transfer technique with a reach of approximately ten meters. Used to transfer files between a computer and a mobile phone, for example.

BMP 4.8.15

Abbreviation of bitmap. A standard format for images in Windows, mainly used for screen graphics and office programs

BOARD 8.7

Paper heavier than 400 g/cm².

BODY TEXT 6.2

The typographic style used for running text. Body text is often preceded by other styles, for example headings, subheadings and an introduction.

BOLD 6.4

A typeface version with bolder or thicker lines on the characters.

BOOK BINDERY 1.1.7

A company which post press treats printed sheets using techniques such as creasing, folding and binding to produce the finished printed product. A book bindery will often provide services such as stamping and foiling.

BOOK BINDING 10.19

A term which describes how a book is bound. The book's cover, made up of the spine and boards, can be whole bound, half bound or quarter bound .

BOOK BLOCK 10.19

Bound insert for a book. Common examples of methods use to create blocks are glue binding, thread stitching, etc.

BOOK PRINTING 9.6

A printing technique where the printing image is transferred to the paper using raised parts, for example lead type, which pick up the printing ink and are pressed against the paper.

BOOLEAN VARIABLES

A way of creating logical combinations by using Boolean variables such as "and," "or" and "not." Often used when combining search criteria, e.g. in archive programs.

BRIDGE 6.15.5

A file management program from Adobe which is included in the program package Creative Suite.

BRIDGE 2.8.10

Network unit which connects different parts of a network.

BRIGHTNESS

The intensity of colors, also called luminance. How light or dark an image is.

BROADSHEET 8.6

The classic daily newspaper format, also known as full format/whole format, measuring 30–43 × 49–60 mm. Twice as large as tabloid format.

BROCHURE

A printed product, often stapled and produced in a format size up to A4 with a limited number of pages, which can contain advertising or other information.

BUCKLE FOLD 10.10

The most common and simplest method for folding in sheet production.

BULK 8.8

Describes how voluminous a paper is, measured in cm³/g.

BULLET

A graphic symbol which is used to mark points in, for example, enumerations and lists.

BUNDLE

A set of books or sheets piled on top of each other.

BYLINE

Name of the journalist/writer who wrote an article, stated next to the text.

BYTE P 41

A measurement of binary memory. One byte consists of 8 bits, which is equivalent to values between 0 and 255 in the decimal system.

C

c P 222

Pantone code from the word "coated", meaning that the ink is printed on a coated paper.

CABLE CONNECTION 2.9.1

Direct connection to the Internet, a high-speed connection, usually with a transfer speed of between 256 and 2 000 kilobits per second.

CABLE MODEM 2.9.2

Used to connect to the Internet and transfer information digitally via a cable TV network's cables.

CACHE MEMORY 2.3

Frequently accessed calculative operations are saved in the computer's cache memory so they can be quickly accessed again.

CAD 4.3.6

Computer-aided design. A program and tools for creating object-based drawings and 3D models. Used by packaging designers, architects and engineers.

CALENDAR FINISH 8.19.4

The paper is pressed to an even thickness and will, as a result, provide good print quality.

CALENDERED 8.19.4

Calendered paper is the same as glossy paper. The gloss is achieved in a calendar and can be a direct part of the manufacturing process on the end of the paper machine (online) or a separate stage afterwards.

CALIBRATION 3.11.2

Setting apparatus to given values so that, for example, 40 percent cyan tone in a computer produces 40 percent in the printer, proof or imagesetter. Often achieved using programs or tools provided with the device.

CAMERA RAW 4.11.6

A module for Adobe Photoshop and Adobe Bridge, used for raw format conversion.

CAPTURE ONE 4.11.7

A Program from Phase One used for raw format conversion.

CARD SLOT

The computer has a number of card slots where you can install different types of circuit boards, for example a network card or a graphics card.

CARDBOARD 8.4

Cardboard is a stiff paper product. Paper manufacturers usually define cardboard as a paper with a weight of over 170 g/m^2. Another definition of cardboard is paper composed of several layers.

CARRIER FILM 7.6

When page films are used for imposition, these are then mounted on a transparent carrier film which is the same size as the image carrier.

CASING-IN 10.19

Joining the insert and the cover of a hardcover book by gluing the endpapers to the cover.

CAT 5 2.8.4

Unshielded twisted pair cables often used in Ethernet solutions.

CATALOGUE FORMAT

Common format in the USA, measuring 170×265 mm and 200×265 mm.

CCD CELL 4.12.4

Charge Coupled Device. Cells which translate light intensity into electronic signals, used in scanners and digital cameras.

CCD MATRIX 4.11.4

A number of CCD cells organized in a grid pattern, a "pixel matrix," in which each CCD cell corresponds to a pixel. Mainly used in digital cameras.

CCITT 4.9.5

Non-distorting compression method used for line art in PDF format and also supported by Postscript.

CD 2.6.4

Compact Disc, a removable optical disc for data storage, can store around 650 megabytes.

CD-DA 2.6.5

Compact Disc-Digital Audio, a CD for storing sound data. A regular music CD.

CD-R 2.6.6

Compact Disc-Recordable. A recordable CD.

CD-ROM 2.6.7

Compact Disc-Read Only Memory, a CD for storing data.

CELLULOSE 8.19.1

Wood fiber is composed mainly of cellulose and lignin. In theory, only cellulose and water are needed to produce paper. Cellulose is extracted chemically from the fiber by removing the lignin.

CENTER ALIGNMENT

Text is adjusted so that every row is placed horizontally in the middle of typeset surface. Fixed spacing is used, which means that neither the right nor left margins will be straight.

CENTER SPREAD 6.11.2

A two-page spread in a printed product which consists of one complete sheet. Makes it easy to print an image across the gutter.

CHANNEL 4.6.6 P 153

The term color channel is often used in image processing. In RGB images there are three channels - red, green and blue.

CHARACTER

A letter, numeral or symbol.

CHARACTER CONTOURS 6.4.11

Characters in a font used in layout can be converted to character contours. This means that they are converted to object graphics and the font does not need to be sent with the document.

CHARACTERIZATION 3.11.3

Measuring the characteristics of a process or machine, e.g. the printing process.

CHEMICAL PROOF

Older technique for producing proofs from film, also known as analogue proof.

CHEMICAL PULP   8.19.1

Chemical pulp is produced by separating out cellulose fibers from wood by heating with chemicals.

CHLORINE BLEACHING   8.17.2

Older form of paper bleaching using chlorine gas to achieve the bleached effect. This technique pollutes the environment and is hardly ever used today.

CHLORINE-FREE   8.17.2

Paper produced using the TCF method (Totally Chlorine Free). See Bleaching.

CHOKING   7.4.8

When the background is shrunk to avoid misregistration. See also Trapping.

CHROMALIN   7.5.5

Analog proof from Dupont.

CIE   3.7

Commission Internationale d'Eclairage (CIE), the International Commission on Illumination, created this color system based on a standard observer. The human perception of color is described with three sensitivity curves called tristimulus values.

CIE RGB   3.8.11

Older RGB standard, hardly ever used any more

CIELAB   3.7

Version of the CIE system.

CIEXYZ   3.7

Version of the CIE system.

CIP3/CIP4   7.3

International Cooperation for the Integration of Prepress, Press and Postpress, the organization which developed PPF, Print Production Format. Now called CIP4 and is responsible for JDF, Job Definition Format, a further development of PPF.

CIRCUMFERENCE SPEED   9.11.9

How quickly the surface of a roller or cylinder in a printing press rotates. Depends on the cylinder's circumference and how fast the axle rotates. It is important that rollers and cylinders which are in contact with each other have the same circumference speed.

CLASSIFIEDS

Newspaper advertisements placed following the main text, usually after the editorial material.

CLEARTYPE   P 213

A technique developed by Microsoft to even out the edges of text on monitors

CLIENT

Term used in network and server contexts. Users contact a server using a client program and ask the server to carry out various services. The internet is based on client-server communications: the server is contacted via the internet using a client program, the web browser, and asks for information about a website. The server sends the information requested, which is then graphically displayed for the user by the client.

CLIPPING PATH   5.5.18 5.3.13

A path which shows how an image is cut out when extracting in an image processing program.

CLOCK RATE   2.3

The processing speed of a processor, measured in megahertz.

CLOSE-UP

A zoomed-in image of a person or object. Close-ups of faces are common.

CLOTH   10.19

Textile covering material for book covers.

CLOTH DENSITY

A measurement of how finely woven the screen cloth is.

CMOS

Complementary Metal Oxide Semiconductor, a technique used in some image sensors. It can be made smaller and more energy-economical than CCD sensors.

CMYK   3.4

Cyan, Magenta, Yellow, Key-color (black), a subtractive color system used in four-color printing and four-color printers.

CMYK MODE   4.6.6

An image saved in CMYK mode technically consists of four separate pixel images in grayscale mode: one representing cyan, one magenta, one yellow and one black. This also means that a CMYK image uses four times as much memory as an image of the same size and resolution in grayscale mode.

CMYK TO CMYK   5.3.3

If an image is print adjusted for one printing situation but then printed under new conditions, a CMYK to CMYK conversion is necessary. The original ICC profile which was used when the image was separated to CMYK and the new ICC profile for the new printing conditions are used to accomplish this.

COATED PAPER   8.1

Paper where the surface has been treated with a special coating in order to maintain high printing quality. The coating consists of binders (starch or latex) and pigment (fine kaolin clay or calcium carbonate).

COAXIAL CABLE   2.8.4

A type of cable commonly used in networks and for antenna cables.

COLDSET   9.5.2

Web offset technique without a drying oven. Used in newspaper printing, for example.

COLLAGE

A composition of graphic elements, e.g. text and images, from different contexts, put together to create a new work.

COLOPHON

A page usually placed at the very front or back of a book and which contains more information than the imprint, e.g. typefaces and paper used. See Imprint.

COLOR   3.1-2

Human perception of light with a mixture of different wavelengths, for example a blue color when looking at a blue surface in a white light.

COLOR BAR   9.11

A special bar added in imposition and printing. The different printing parameters are checked in the different fields of the color bar.

COLOR CAST

Error in the balance between colors in a print or original artwork. Manifested as a generally erroneous color tone in the image.

COLOR COMPOSITION   3.4

What composition of wavelengths a given light has.

COLOR CORRESPONDENCE   P 74 3.6

How well the colors of a print correspond to a proof or color guide.

COLOR FILTER

Light filter which lets through light of a certain color, i.e. of certain wavelengths.

COLOR GUIDE   3.4–5 6.9.1

A printed guide with color samples and color definitions, necessary when selecting colors.

COLOR MANAGEMENT SYSTEM   3.9

Program which takes account of scanners, monitors, printers, proofs and the color characteristics of the print.

COLOR MODE   4.6

Describes color information in a pixel-based image, for example line art, grayscale, index color, RGB or CMYK.

COLOR PIGMENT   9.5.6 9.3.2 9.6.3

See Pigment.

COLOR RANGE   P 76 3.8.1

The size of the color space, how saturated the colors created by a given color standard in a given color system or by a given device (e.g. printer or monitor) can be.

COLOR REPRODUCTION   3.4

The way in which colors are reproduced, for example on a monitor or in print.

COLOR SAMPLE   6.9.1

Samples of color combinations, for example small pieces of paper torn out of color maps such as PMS-guides.

COLOR SETTING   P 281

When some areas of a printed item are printed only with black and others with color, the color setting states which pages will be printed in color. This is particularly important for the planning and placement of images and illustrations which can take advantage of the use of color on those pages.

COLOR SPACE   P 74

The range of color which can theoretically be created by a certain color system. The greater the color space a color system has, the more colors you can create with that particular system.

COLOR STANDARD   P 74 3.8

Standardized and defined primary colors in a given color system, e.g. Adobe RGB, Eurostandard, SWOP.

COLOR SYSTEM   3.3–5 3.7

System for creating, defining, or describing colors, for example RGB, CMYK or CIE.

COLORMATCH RGB   3.8.8

RGB color space based on what a Radius PressView image monitor can display.

COLORSYNC   3.13

Apple's color management system.

COLORTUNE   3.10

A program from Agfa used to produce ICC profiles.

COLOURKIT PROFILES SUITE   3.10

A program from Fuji used to produce ICC profiles.

COLUMN

Text piece which is restricted by the width of the column. Newspapers and periodical are printed in columns to limit the line length where a small print size is used.

COLUMN HEIGHT

The height of a column on a page.

COLUMN MILLIMETERS

Measurement used to decide advertising price. The column system used in newspapers means that width is given in number of columns, and height in millimeters.

COMMENTS   P 232

PDF files can contain comments which can be an effective way to deal with corrections which are detected by different users.

COMMUNICATION PROGRAM

Program which sends or receives digital information in a network.

COMPACT FLASH   2.6.5

A type of memory card using flash technology.

COMPATIBILITY

Statement of whether a given device or system will work with another.

COMPOSITE

Put together. Used to describe PostScript files. In a composite PostScript file, each page contains all of the print colors for that page, in contrast to a pre-separated PostScript file, where each color on the page has its own separate single-color page in the PostScript file. A pre-separated PostScript file would therefore contain 16 single-color pages for a 4-page print product.

COMPRESSION   4.8

Recoding and sometimes reducing the information content of a file so that it takes up less memory. Often used in transporting files.

COMPRESSION LEVEL   P 122

The amount of information which a compression method can remove.

COMPUTER PLATFORM   2.1
Describes the operating system a computer uses, e.g. Mac OS, Windows XP or Linux.

CONDENSING   P 207
Decreasing the character spacing.

CONES   3.2
Small light-sensitive sensory cells on the retina of the eye. Cones are sensitive mainly to color and are not as light-sensitive as rods.

CONING   P 354
The printing phenomenon coning causes the printed image in the first component color to be wider than the last, which means that 100 % registration cannot be achieved. The phenomenon occurs because the paper is compressed in each printing unit. Coning occurs in both sheetfed and web offset.

CONTINUOUS TONES   7.7
Tones with even, soft tonal transitions which do not consist of obvious tonal steps, as in a photograph.CONTRACT proof
The absolutely final proof before starting to print.

CONTRAST   5.4.8
Difference in tone. An image with high contrast has a large tone difference between dark and light areas.

CONTRAST EFFECT   P 54   P 55
A color phenomenon. A color can be perceived in different ways depending on the color it is placed next to. Thus, it can provide two completely separate color impressions if it is placed next to two different colors.

CONTROL PROGRAM   4.12.11
Driver for external units such as printers, scanners, etc.

COOLTYPE   P 213
Built-in font management function in Adobe programs.

COPPERING   9.8.2
Before each etching or engraving in gravure printing, a new copper layer is added to the printing cylinder. The coppering is done using electrolysis with copper sulfate and sulfuric acid.

COPY MACHINE   9.2
A machine used to produce multiple paper originals, using the xerographic method.

COPYDESK   6.3.5
Editing program for opening and writing and changing text in Quark documents. It can, for example, be used by journalists when editing in order to be able to write directly on the layout.

COPYRIGHT   11.6
Right to reproduce copyright-protected material.

COPYRIGHT   11.6
See Copyright law.

COPYRIGHT HOLDER   11.6.1   11.6.3
The person (or persons) who created a work and hold the copyright on it. The copyright holder can allow another party, e.g. an image bureau, to manage the copyright.

COPYRIGHT LAW   11.6
Protects intellectual works, i.e. literature, journalistic texts, manuals, film, music, art etc.

COPYWRITER
A writer in an advertising context.

CORPORATE PRINTING   9.6
Collective name for business cards, correspondence cards, letter paper, invoice pads etc.

CORRECTION MARKS   P 234
Marks used in proof-reading to indicate errors which need to be rectified.

COVER   10.1
The cover of a book.

COVERING   10.18
Gluing the cover of a hardcover book to the spine of the insert.

CREASE   10.11
See creasing.

CREASING   10.11
Creating a fold-mark, or crease, to facilitate folding of stiff and thick papers.

CREATIVE SUITE
A program package from Adobe which includes among other things Photoshop, Acrobat, Illustrator and Indesign.

CREEPING   10.12   7.6.7
A folding phenomenon. As a result of folding the product, the pages are displaced in relation to each other. The problem is greater when using insert imposition. The creep is compensated for during imposition by adjusting the pages in relation to each other.

CRISTALRASTER   7.7.2
AGFA's stochastic screen.

CROP   10.7
See Cropping.

CROP MARKS   7.6.8
Special marks which show where a printed sheet should be cropped. See also Registration mark.

CROPPING MACHINE   10.7
Machine used to crop a printed or unprinted sheet of paper very accurately.

CROPPING 1   5.4.3
Used to remove unwanted and unnecessary parts of an image in order to avoid working with an larger image than necessary.

CROPPING 2   10.7
Paper is cropped to the desired size in order to fit the printing press or post press processing machine. Finished and bound print items are also cropped to achieve the right format and clean, even edges.

CROSS REFERENCES

Cross referencing in databases is a way of providing a file with many different headings so that the same file can be found under different headings/in different places. Basil, for example, could be filed under both "herb" and "plant".

CRT SCREEN   2.4.1

Cathode Ray Tube screens are based on cathode ray technology, whereby the screen is illuminated by a beam of electrons. Monitors and TV sets which are not flatscreens use this technology.

CRW   P 133

Raw format files from Canon brand digital cameras have the file extension .crw.

CS

See Creative Suite.

CSMA/CD   2.8.17

Carrier Sense Multiple Access with Collision Detection. A technology for handling data collision during network transfers.

CTP   9.5.11

Computer To Plate, a technique for setting/outputting printing plates in an imagesetter directly from the computer.

CUMULUS   6.15.6

Client server-based image archiving software from Canto.

CURING   9.5.6

The second drying phase for offset printing ink in which the alkyd reacts with the oxygen in the air through oxidation. The first drying phase is setting.

CURLING   9.5.2

Phenomenon which occurs during heatset printing because of a combination of too much ink on the paper and excessively rapid drying. It is manifest as waviness in the paper of the printed product.

CVC   P 222

Computer Video Coated, a pantone code. A monitor simulation of PMS colors printed on coated paper.

CVM   P 222

Computer Video Matte, a pantone code. A monitor simulation of PMS colors printed on matte coated paper.

CVU   P 222

Computer Video Uncoated, a pantone code. A monitor simulation of PMS colors printed on uncoated paper.

CYLINDER PRINTING   9.6.1

A book printing technique using a flat image carrier against a printing cylinder.

D

DAILY NEWSPAPER

A newspaper which is published at least four days a week, usually every day.

DAMPENING DISTRIBUTION ROLLER   9.5.5

Roller in the dampening system responsible for distributing the dampening solution and ensuring that it forms a thin dampening film.

DAMPENING DROP ROLLER   9.5.5

Roller in the dampening system which transfers the dampening solution from the duct to the distribution rollers.

DAMPENING DUCT ROLLER   9.5.5

Roller in the dampening system of a printing press which takes water from the dampening tub and transfers it to the rollers in the dampening system.

DAMPENING FORM ROLLER   9.5.5

Roller in the dampening system which transfers the dampening solution from the last distribution rollers to the printing plate.

DAMPENING ROLLERS   9.5.5

Collective term for all types of dampening rollers in a dampening system.

DAMPENING SOLUTION   9.5.7

Used in wet offset printing to separate printing from non-printing surfaces.

DAMPENING SYSTEM   9.5.5

Term for the entire system of rollers in an offset printing press which controls the dampening solution supply.

DASH

Appears as "-". Shorter than an em dash but longer than a hyphen. Used to separate an inserted thought from the rest of a sentence.

DAT   2.6.3

Digital Audio Tape, magnetic tape for storing data, can usually hold 2–8 gigabytes.

DATA BUS   2.1.2

A data bus transports information between the processor and the memory in the computer.

DATABASE   6.3.4 6.15.5

Registration program which sorts and tracks digital information, such as images and other digital files.

DCR   P 133

Raw image format from Kodak brand digital cameras have the file extension .dcr.

DCS   4.8.4

See EPS-DCS/EPSF.

DCS2   4.8.4

Development of the DCS format which is often used for printing packaging using a lot of Pantone colors.

DDC   2.4.6

Display Data Channel, a digital connection which allows the computer to communicate with different functions on the monitor. Supported by DVI.

DE FACTO STANDARD   7.1

A standard which has become such because a product has reached a dominant position within an industry without having been endorsed by a major standardization body, e.g. PostScript from Adobe.

DEADLINE

The point in time when a contracted job is to be ready or delivered.

DECAL

A sticker. Often a screen printed product with adhesive on the reverse.

DECIMAL NUMBER SYSTEM　　P 41

The regular number system used on a daily basis, based on the digits 0 to 9.

DECOMPRESS　　4.9

To open up a compressed file.

DEFORMATION　　9.11.9

Dot deformation problems are mechanical or technical errors in the printing press which lead to the halftone dots being distorted. Doubling and slurring are two examples of typical deformation problems.

DELIVERY ADDRESS

The address to which a finished print product is to be sent. May differ from the invoice address.

DELTA E　　3.7

Measurement of the difference between two colors in the CIE system. If delta E between two colors is less than 1, the difference cannot be detected by the human eye.

DENSITOMETER　　9.11.1

An instrument used to measure different printing parameters, for example dot gain and full tone density. Available both for measuring film and reflective surfaces.

DENSITY　　4.13.2 8.8

A measurement of the tonal range in a particular base material, e.g. the tonal range of color print on a certain kind of paper or the tonal range of an original slide.

DEPTH OF FIELD　　4.11.2 4.11.4

In photography, the distance between different motifs at different depths which still appear in focus.

DESCREENING　　5.3.12

A scanning function which replaces an image's halftone screen with gray levels. It is used to avoid moiré effects.

DESKTOP

The work space on the screen where the icons for waste basket, hard disk, etc. are situated.

DEVELOPER　　9.5.11

Machine which develops exposed plate or film using chemical developing fluids.

DEVELOPING　　9.5.11

First stage in the developing process, where the latent image formed from exposure is enhanced using developing solution.

DEVELOPING SOLUTION　　9.5.12

Chemical liquid needed to develop plate or film.

D-FONTS　　P 210

Version of Truetype fonts used as an internal system font in Mac OS X.

DIAMOND SCREENING

Stochastic screen from Heidelberg.

DIE-CUTTING　　10.8

Post press process. Printed products which are to have a shape other than rectangular are die-cut, e.g. dividers used for binders.

DIGITAL ASSET MANAGEMENT SYSTEM6.15.6

See Image bank.

DIGITAL BLUELINES　　7.6.8

Alternative name for imposition proofs.

DIGITAL CAMERA　　4.10

Electronic camera which uses light-sensitive CCD cells instead of film to create a digital image.

DIGITAL IMPOSITION　　7.6

The imposition of digital pages using an imposition program. The entire imposition is then printed directly onto the image carrier.

DIGITAL PRINTING　　9.2-4

Printing press which prints information directly from a computer without printing plates.

DIGITAL PROOF　　7.5.5

Digital proofs are based on the files to be used subsequently for printing. Carried out on high-quality color printers, usually using inkjet or sublimation technology

DIGITAL PUBLISHING

To publish information in a digital format to be read on the screen, for example a reference work on CD or the internet.

DIGITAL ZOOM　　5.3.8

A function of digital cameras. Digital zoom is done mathematically with interpolation rather than optical technology, thereby reducing image quality.

DIMENSIONAL STABILITY　　8.13

A measurement of how resistant a paper is to dimensional changes.

DIRECT ADVERTISING

Printed marketing material which is distributed by mail. Exists in both unaddressed and addressed forms. The latter makes selectivity possible to more effectively reach the desired target group.

DIRECT ENGRAVING　　9.8.2

Technique for producing gravure cylinders where the printing cylinder is engraved directly from digital information.

DIRECT PRINTING PROCEDURE　　P 349

A printing procedure in which the image carrier prints directly onto the material, e.g. flexographic and gravure printing.

DISK MEMORY　　2.1.6

Another name for the computer's hard disk.

DISPERSION VARNISH　　10.3

A kind of varnish which is completely odor-free and can produce greater shine than press varnish.

DISTRIBUTION

The last phase in the graphic production workflow. Indicates the delivery in one or several steps from printshop/bookbindery to the final recipient of the printed product.

DISTRIBUTION ROLLER   9.5.5

Roller in the ink pyramid which ensures that the print ink is distributed evenly and forms a thin film.

DISTRIBUTOR

A person or company who oversees the transportation and delivery of the printed product from printshop/bookbindery to the customer or directly to another recipient.

DLT   9.6.3

Digital Linear Tape. Magnetic tape for data storage, holds up to 80 gigabytes.

DNG   4.8.9

Digital Negative. Standard for how raw image format files can be stored, developed by Adobe. Raw format files can be converted to DNG format without loss.

DOCUMENT TEMPLATE   6.1.4

In layout programs page templates, pagination, columns, etc. can be predefined using a document template.

DOS

An older operating system for PC-based computers.

DOT DEFORMATION   9.11.9

Change in the shape of the halftone dot, often because of mechanical or technical error in the printing press. Doubling and slurring are examples of this.

DOT GAIN   9.11.3

A measurement of the change in size of the halftone dot from film to print. Measured in percent.

DOT GAIN ADJUSTMENT   7.4.5

To adjust an image according to the dot gain it will be subject to in the printing process. Is done during four-color separation. Also see Print adjustment.

DOT GAIN CURVES   7.4.5

Curves which display dot gain over the entire tint area from 0 to 100 %. Is generated by measuring color bars with a densitometer.

DOT REDUCTION   9.11.3

A measurement of the change in size of the halftone dot from film to print when using positive printing plates. Measured in percent.

DOT SIZE   7.7.2 7.7.5 7.7.7

The resolution of stochastic screens is given in dot size instead of screen frequency. Commonly lies between 14 and 41 micrometers.

DOUBLE-HOLE PUNCHING   10.9

The standard hole-punching used for Swedish ring-binders, not an international standard.

DOUBLE-PAGE SPREAD   6.11.2

A two-page spread in a printed product which does not consist of one complete sheet, but of pages made of two different sheets. Double-page spreads complicate the placement of images across the gutter.

DOUBLE-SIDED PAPER

A paper which has the same surface characteristics on both sides. Cf. single-sided paper.

DOUBLING   9.11.9

Print phenomenon which produces dot deformation, a darker print and a double imprint of the halftone dots, one stronger and one weaker. This can be a result of a loose rubber blanket, which causes the halftone dots to land in different places on the paper with each rotation of the cylinder.

DPI   7.7.8

Dots per inch, the number of exposure points per inch, indicates the print resolution of an imagesetter or printer.

DRIVERS   2.5.3

Control programs for external units such as printers, scanners, etc.

DRIVING ROLLER   9.5.5

Roller in the inking pyramid which is placed against the distribution rollers and absorbs and provides ink to them depending on their placement.

DROP ROLLER   P 343

Roller in the inking pyramid which transfers ink from the duct to a distribution roller by "jumping" between them.

DROPLET   5.8.5

An icon created by a droplet on the desktop automatically activates a function in a certain program when you drag a file onto the droplet icon.

DRUM SCANNER   4.12.3

In this type of scanner, the original is attached to a rotating glass drum.

DRY OFFSET

See Water-free offset.

DRY RUN   9.5.18

Occurs in offset printing when there is too little dampening solution in the ink-dampening balance. As a result, non-printing surfaces attract ink and become printing surfaces. Also called tinting.

DRYING POWDER   9.5.6

Powder sprayed between the printed sheets in the stream feeder to prevent the printing ink from smearing onto the sheet above it. Also called spraying powder.

DRYING [1]   9.5.2 9.5.6 9.7.2 9.8.3

The process in which the printing ink dries on the paper.

DRYING [2]   8.19.3 8.13

When the paper dries in the dryer section, the drying level of the paper is decided. This will depend on what the paper will be used for.

DUCT ROLLER   9.5.5

The duct roller in the ink pyramid takes ink from the ink duct and transfers it to the other rollers in the ink pyramid.

DUCTOR BLADE   9.7.1

Tool for spreading ink across a screen frame.

DUCTOR KNIFE   9.5.8

The ductor knife is located in the ink duct and determines the ink supply in the printing press. It is controlled by the ink screws of the printing press.

DUMMY   6.14.1 7.6

A test sample of an imposition, a binding or a complete printed product. It is usually made by hand.

DUOTONES   4.6.3

A grayscale image printed with two printing inks instead of one. Duotones can be used to reproduce fine details in a black and white image, make it softer or tint it a color other than pure black. Usually printing is done using black plus any one spot color.

DVD   2.6.4

Digital Versatile Disc, an optical disc for data storage, holds up to 17 gigabytes.

DWG   4.3.6

Standard format for saving line art files produced by a CAD program.

DVI   2.4.6

Digital Visual Interface, a connection standard between monitors and computers. It exists in the following versions: DVI-D (for digital transfers), DVI-A (analog) and DVI-I (supports both analog and digital transfers).

E

ECI   3.8.5 3.10.4

European Color Initiative. An expert organization which works to develop color and ICC management.

ECI RGB   3.8.5

RGB color standard developed by the European Color Initiative. Has approximately the same color range as Adobe RGB.

EDGE   2.9.4

Transfer technique used in GPRS mobile telephones which allows speeds of up to 400 kbit/s.

EDID   2.4.6

Digital connection which enables a computer to communicate with different functions in the monitor. Supported by DVI.

EDITABLE

Can be changed.

EDITING PROGRAM   6.3.5

Program used to open layout documents and edit limited text sections. Adobe Indesign uses Adobe Incopy and Quark Xpress uses Copydesk.

EDITION[1]

The entire number of copies of a publication issued at one time. Newspapers are often printed in several editions depending on the region in which they are to be distributed.

EDITION[2]   1.3.2

Number of copies produced. Books from the first print run belong to the first edition. New editions can be produced with or without changes.

EDITORIAL SYSTEM   6.3.5

Used by newspapers to effectively maintain the same text and layout production among a large number of users.

ELECTROLYSIS   9.8.2

Electrochemical treatment used to treat the surface of a gravure printing cylinder.

ELLIPTICAL HALFTONE DOT   7.7.1

Halftone dot which is elliptical in shape rather than circular. The shape of the halftone dot changes the characteristics of the screen.

EMAS   9.12.2

Environmental management system. European standard which dictates, among other things, that companies must publish public environmental reports.

EMBOSSING   10.6

Where a relief is required on a print product, embossing is used to raise or lower parts of the paper.

EMF   4.3.4

Enhanced Metafile. Development of the WMF format with larger bit density.

EM-SQUARE   P 207

Typographical spacing system based on a square (hence the name) the sides of which are equal in length to the point size of the text. The space distance is given as a number or proportion of the square, e.g. 1/2 square (wide between most capital numerals) or 4/18 square (normal space between words). The benefit of the em-square system is that it is relative to the point size of the text, such that spacing changes in proportion to changes in point size.

EMULSION

Liquid mixture where an insoluble substance is suspended and scattered through an emulsifying substance. A light-sensitive photographic coating is created by, for example, allowing silver bromide emulsion to dry so that an even light-sensitive film is formed.

EMULSION LAYER   P 350

A layer on a film which consists of photographic emulsion and is exposed in the imagesetter.

EMULSION SIDE   P 350

The side of a graphic film with a light-sensitive emulsion layer.

ENCLOSED FORMAT   6.4.4

A typeface format can be enclosed in a paragraph format so that, for example, the first three words of each paragraph are always in small capital.

ENDPAPERS   10.1

The pages glued to the cover of hardcover books to attach the insert are called endpapers. Sometimes consist of a colored or printed paper which are then called separate endpapers.

ENGRAVING   9.8.2

Technique for producing gravure printing cylinders using physical pressure and a diamond-tipped head to create halftone wells.

ENVIRONMENTAL DECLARATION   8.17.4

European system for declaring environmental facts about a paper quality. Also known as Paper Profile.

ENVIRONMENTALLY FRIENDLY

Literally, a product or process which makes a positive contribution to the environment, meaning that most products and processes cannot be defined as such. We tend instead to talk about products or processes with low environmental impact.

EPS 4.3.2

Encapsulated Postscript. A file format for digital images and illustrations. Manages both object- and pixel based graphics.

EPS-DCS/EPSF 4.8.4

Encapsulated PostScript-Desktop Color Separation. A file format for four-color separated digital images. The image file consists of five component files: a low-resolution image for screen display and a high-resolution file for each of the four component colors.

ETCH 9.6.2 9.8.2

See etching.

ETCHING 9.6.2 9.8.2

Technique for producing gravure printing plates using a chemical treatment.

ETHERNET 2.8.2

One of the most common network solutions.

ETHERTALK

Apple's network protocol used in Ethernet networks for OS 9 or older.

EUROPEAN COLOR SCALE 7.4.1

European standard for defining color characteristics in printing inks. Cf. the American SWOP standard.

EXABYTE 2.6.3

Magnetic tape for data storage, holds around 4 to 8 gigabytes.

EXCEL 6.1.1

Program from Microsoft used for calculations and statistics.

EXIF 4.10

Exchangeable Image File data. Information about, for example, the date, aperture, white balance, exposure time, etc. which can be saved in a digitally photographed image.

EXPANSION 6.4.4

Increasing the spacing between letters.

EXPOSE 7.1.3 9.2.1 9.5.2 9.5.11–13 9.7.2

To illuminate a light-sensitive layer on a film or printing plate with light in order to transfer an image.

EXPOSURE DOT 7.1.3 7.7.6

The dot which is exposed by the laser beam in an imagesetter or printer. Forms the halftone dot.

EXPOSURE FRAME P 350

Equipment needed in exposing a printing plate from film. Comes with vacuum equipment and an timed lamp.

EXPOSURE TIME P 350

The time it takes to expose a printing plate, for example, and achieve the correct result.

EXTENSIONS 2.5.5

Plug-ins which expand the functions of a particular program.

EXTERNAL DRUM 9.5.12

A type of imagesetter where the image carrier is secured and exposed on the outside of a rotating drum.

EXTRACTION 5.3.13 5.5.18

Cutting out part of an image along its contours on a computer. Also called vignette.

EYE-ONE 4.12.13

Equipment from Gretag Macbeth in different versions, used for calibration and color correction in monitors and scanners.

F

FACSIMILE 4.13 P 147 P 219

A small thumbnail image of a printed product. It is used, for example, for displaying earlier printed editions of a periodical.

FALSE DUOTONES 4.6.3

A grayscale image printed on a tinted area is known as a false duotone. The white parts of the grayscale image take on the color of the tinted area.

FDF FILE 6.12.2

Acrobat Forms Data Format. A FDF file contains only commentary on a PDF file. It is used mainly for sending proof comments between several users without the need to send the whole PDF file.

FEATHERING 8.19.2 9.3.4

A phenomenon which occurs with inkjet printers when the ink is absorbed sideways in the paper.

FEEDBOARD 9.5.9

The stream feeder in a sheetfed printing press sets the sheets on the feedboard which transports them to the registration. The feedboard ensures that the stream feeder only feeds one sheet at a time.

FETCH

Internet file transfer program via FTP.

FIBER DIRECTION 8.12

The direction in which the majority of the paper fibers are oriented, the same direction as the paper was produced in.

FIBER-OPTICAL NETWORKS/FDDI

Fiber Distributed Data Interchange. Network based on an optical transfer technology via fiber cables.

FILE EXTENSION P 120

File names often have an extension, for example, .doc for a Word document. In Windows the files always have an extension, but they are not necessary in Mac OS. It can, however, be good to always use file extensions so that the document can be used by both Windows and Mac.

FILE HEAD

The beginning of a digital file where particular information is stored, for example information about which program created the file.

FILE MANAGER   6.15.5

A program which archives and catalogues files which are to be saved digitally, so that they are easy to retrieve.

FILE STRUCTURE   6.15.2

A predetermined order based on which files are organized and sorted.

FILES

Digital blocks of data. A file can be a program, a system file or a driver.

FILL   4.1.2

Curves and enclosed objects can be filled with colors, tones and patterns. Used in object graphics.

FILLERS   P 319

Additives mixed into the pulp stock. The most common fillers are ground marble or limestone ($CaCO_3$) and clay. These ingredients improve the opacity and color of the paper when printed. The fillers also give the paper softness and elasticity. By adding calcium carbonate the paper is better protected from ageing.

FILLING   9.7.2

A technique for filling in undesired holes on the non-printed areas in a screen printing stencil.

FILM   9.8.2

Graphic film is used as the original when producing an image carrier.

FILM DEVELOPMENT   P 350

After exposure, the image on a film is developed and fixed using chemical fluids.

FILM MONTAGE   7.6

Film which is mounted into a complete print assembly and used for producing plates.

FILM SET   P 350

A set of film of the same page, one for each print color, e.g. four films for a four-color page.

FINAL PROOF

A digital print proof system from Fuji.

FINISHING   10.3-6

Collective name for post press techniques such as embossing, foiling, laminating and varnishing.

FIREFOX

A Web browser program from Mozilla.

FIREWALL   2.9.6

A system which protects a local network from external intervention via network connection, for example from the internet.

FIREWIRE   2.7.2

Interface used to connect external units to computers. There are two versions, Firewire 400 and 800, which reach speeds of 400 and 800 Mbit/s respectively.

FIVE-CYLINDER UNIT   9.5.3

A special type of printing unit consisting of two plate cylinders, two rubber blanket cylinders and an impression cylinder.

FIXED SPACE

A special space which connects two words so they cannot end up on different rows in a paragraph. It is used, for example to guarantee that a value and its unit come directly after each other without a row break.

FIXING

A stage in the photographic development process which occurs after development and the halt stage. The fixing bath ensures that the photographic emulsion's sensitivity to light is halted. Helps considerably extend the lifespan of the developed images.

FLASH   4.2

Program from Adobe to create animated object-based images on the web.

FLASH MEMORY   2.6.5

Rewriteable storage medium which is common in USB memories and digital cameras.

FLAT STAPLING   10.13

Form of stapling where the staples are inserted on the edge of the printed product's spine, rather than in the fold.

FLATBED SCANNER   4.12.1

In this type of scanner, the original is placed and scanned on a flat glass plate.

FLATBED SETTER   9.5.12

Type of platesetter where the plate lies flat.

FLEXOGRAPHIC PLATE   9.9.2

The image carrier used in flexographic printing. An elastic plate made of rubber or plastic, with the printing surfaces raised rather like on a stamp.

FLEXOGRAPHIC PRINT EDGE   9.9.6

A print phenomenon in flexography which is manifested as a dark outline around printed areas.

FLEXOGRAPHY   9.9

A direct printing technique. The print areas are elevated compared to the non-print areas. Primarily used in the packaging industry. The image carrier is made of rubber or a plastic material.

FLIGHTCHECK

A Preflight program.

FLOPPY DISK   2.6.8

A removable magnetic storage medium for data, 3.5 inches in diameter. Holds 0.7 or 1.4 megabytes.

FM SCREEN   7.7.2

Frequency modulated screen. Referred to in this book as a stochastic screen.

FOCAL DISTANCE   4.11.1

Indicates the image angle of a camera. Short focal distance means wide angle while long focal distance means telephoto.

FOGRA   3.10.4

A German research institute which provides standard profiles for newspapers.

FOIL EMBOSSING   10.6

Form of embossing whereby gilding or shiny color is applied in the embossing.

FOILING   10.5
Covering selected areas of the print sheet with a metal or plastic foil. Used to create gold and silver lettering, for example.

FOLD MARKS   P 285
Special marks which show where the printed sheet should be folded.

FOLD/FOLDS   10.10
See Folding.

FOLDING   10.10
Putting folds in sheets of paper, usually using folding machines.

FOLDING CYLINDER   10.10
A special kind of folding machine usually used on web offset presses.

FOLDING UNIT   10.10
A simple folding machine.

FONT   6.4
A collection of type in a particular typeface stored in a file. Examples of file types for fonts are Truetype and PostScript Type 1.

FONT BOOK   6.4.3 6.4.6
Mac help program for managing typefaces.

FONT FILE   6.4
See Font.

FONT ID   6.6.3
A unique ID number assigned to all font files.

FONT PROGRAM   6.4.11
Program which can process and edit fonts.

FONT SIZE   P 207
Size of font – stated in points.

FONTDOCTOR
Program for repairing damaged font files.

FONTLAB STUDIO   6.4.11
Fontlab program to convert or modify existing fonts or create new ones.

FONTOGRAPHER   6.4.11
Program to convert or modify existing fonts or create new ones.

FOOT   10.2
The bottom part of a page, or the foot of the page, as opposed to the head of the page.

FOOTNOTE
Piece of text usually placed at the foot of the page (hence the name). Contains information which is superfluous to the main text. The main text refers to the footnote using index numbers. Particularly prevalent in academic circles to establish references to other sources.

FORE EDGE   10.2
The outer margin of a page, as opposed to the inner margin, the gutter.

FORMAT   8.6
States the size of a surface, for example the finished size of a printed product. A common standard format is A4.

FORMAT TEMPLATE   6.4.4
See Typographical template.

FORMATION   8.9
How evenly a paper is built up. If a piece of paper held up to a light source is even, i.e. without "clouds", it has good formation.

FORMER FOLDER   10.10
A special type of folding machine usually used in web-fed offset printing.

FOTOSTATION   2.5.4
Archive program from FotoWare

FOUR-COLOR   3.4
See Four-color printing.

FOUR-COLOR PRINTING   3.4
Printing with the four basic colors CMYK.

FOUR-COLOR SEPARATION   7.4
Converting a digital image from the additive color system RGB to the subtractive color system CMYK. In four-color separation the image is adjusted according to the existing printing characteristics.

FOUR-COLOR SET   9.5.11
A set of four plates, one for each printing ink, which forms the basis of a printed four-color page.

FRAMEMAKER   6.1.1 7.1.2
Layout program from Adobe, particularly suitable for productions with larger formats, such as catalogues or technical documentation.

FREEHAND   4.2
Illustration program from Macromedia, now Adobe.

FREQUENCY
How often something occurs, for example light waves per second, measured in Hz.

FREQUENCY-MODULATED SCREENING   7.7.2
See Stochastic screening.

FRONT SIDE
Cf. back side. The side of a sheet of paper which should be read first.

FTP   2.10.2
File Transfer Protocol. Protocol for transferring files on the internet.

FULL TONE SCREENING
Stochastic screening technique from Scitex

FULL-PAGE
Advertising format which covers a whole page of the given format.

FULL-TONE DENSITY   9.11.1
The density of a full-tone area, used among other things to measure the ink coverage in the printing press, measured with a densitometer. See also Density.

FUNCTION MACRO   5.8.4
A number of pre-defined, linked functions in, for example, Word or Photoshop which are carried out automatically when the function macro is used. Can save considerable time where many or simple repetitive actions are carried out.

G

GAMMA VALUE 3.8.2 4.13.5
A value describing a tone compression curve used to describe how the distribution of different colors differs between different RGB standards. Also used for screen settings.

GB, GBYTE
Gigabyte, i.e. 2^{30} byte = 1,073,741,824 bytes. See Byte.

GCR 7.4.4
A special separating method in digital images whereby the color combinations' common gray components, i.e. combined equal amounts of cyan, magenta and yellow, are replaced with black. This gives a smaller overall volume of color and reduces problems of color cast due to vibrations in the printing press.

GIF 4.8.12
Graphic Interchange Format. A file format in index mode mainly used for the web. Can contain up to 256 colors.

GIGA
10^9 = 1 000 000 000.

GIGABIT ETHERNET
Network technology with theoretical transfer speed of 1 000 Mbit/s.

GIGABYTE
2^{30} bytes = 1 073 741 824 bytes. See Byte.

GILDING 10.6
Post press process whereby a book is decorated with gold leaf. Commonly carried out on the edges of a book, for example.

GLAZING 8.2
A post-treatment in the paper production process which gives the paper a higher gloss. The glazing provides a higher image quality but reduced opacity and stiffness.

GLOSSY
See Glossy paper.

GLOSSY PAPER 8.2
Paper which has been treated to achieve a glossy surface.

GLUE BINDING 10.15
A post press method where sheets are glued together to form a book block. For books, the cover is glued on in the same process.

GPRS, 2.5G 2.9.4
Transfer technology in mobile telephony with speeds of up to 170 kbit/s.

GRAMMAGE SUBSTANCE 8.7 8.4
A measurement of the paper's weight per surface unit, measured in g/m^2.

GRAPHICS CARD 2.1.18
A circuit board installed in the computer which enables the computer to control the monitor.

GRAVURE 9.8.2
Creating sunken impressions (halftone wells) in the image carrier for gravure printing. It is normally done by engraving, etching or laser setting the copper coating on the printing cylinder.

GRAVURE HEAD 9.8.2
Used to engrave the printing cylinders for gravure printing, are supplied with a diamond-tipped head.

GRAVURE PRINTING 9.8
A direct printing technique where the printing surfaces are made up of halftone wells which are sunk into the printing cylinder and filled with ink. Best suited to large runs.

GRAY BALANCE 7.4.2 9.11.7
Describes the point where a certain combination of the primary colors, CMY, gives a neutral, gray tone, for example 40% cyan, 30% magenta and 30% yellow.

GRAY LEVELS
A measurement of the number of gray tones which can be created between black and white in a black-and-white image or tone scale.

GRAY TEST MARKS 9.11.7
Special measurement areas based on a theoretically neutral combination of CMY. If the gray test marks are not neutral gray in print, there is color cast.

GRAY TONES
All tones between black and white.

GRAYSCALE IMAGE 4.6.2
A grayscale image contains pixels which can assume tones from 0 to 100 percent of a color. The tone scale from white (0 percent) to black (100 percent) is divided into a number of stages, often 256, which is standard when working with Postscript.

GRAYSCALE STAGE
Difference between two gray tones.

GRIPPER EDGE 7.6.6 7.6 10.2
The part of the paper which the printing press or post press processing machine grabs when the paper is fed into the machine.

GUMMING
Application of adhesive substance to paper which becomes sticky when wet, e.g. gummed envelopes.

GUTTER 7.6.5
The inner margin of a bound, printed product.

H

HAIRLINE P 207
The thinnest strokes in Roman letters.

HALF BOLD
Type variation with line thickness between normal and bold type.

HALF-PAGE
Advertising format which covers half a page of the given format.

HALF-TITLE
First page of a book's insert which contains only the name of the book in small print.

HALFTONE CELLS   7.7.6

Each halftone dot consists of exposure points within its own halftone cell. The exposure points are placed in the halftone cell such that together they form the halftone dot. The size of the halftone cell is determined by the screen frequency.

HALFTONE DOT   7.7

The smallest unit which a screen consists of. All tones in print, both photographs and illustrations, are based on halftone dots.

HALFTONE MATRIX   7.7.6

See Halftone cells.

HALFTONE SCREEN MATRIX   7.7.6

See Halftone cells.

HALFTONE SCREEN ROSETTES   7.7.10

Halftone screen phenomenon where many halftone dots form a circular pattern in the print which can be perceived as distracting.

HALFTONE SCREENING   7.7

Used to simulate gray tones in print, usually dots of different sizes.

HALFTONE TECHNIQUE   9.3.1 9.4.2

A printing press cannot produce continuous tones. Halftone techniques divide an image into very small parts which the eye blends into continuous tones when image is viewed from a normal distance.

HALFTONE WELLS   9.8.2

Small wells in the image carrier used for gravure printing which form the printing surfaces. Can be generated using etching or engraving.

HALO

Phenomenon which can occur when an image is over-sharpened.

HARD DISK   2.6.2 2.1.6

Magnetic data storage medium. All computers have an internal hard disk where all types of files are stored, e.g. programs, documents, operating systems etc. There are also external hard disks which can be attached to the computer.

HARDEN (CURE)   9.8.2

When etching the image carrier for gravure printing, a light-sensitive gel which is hardened by exposure to light is used.

HARDWARE   2.1 2.8.1

The physical parts of a computer, e.g. hard disc, monitor, network card, etc.

HARDWARE RIP

See Rip.

HD 15   2.4.6

Common VGA contact for connecting a monitor to a computer.

HDTV   2.4.6

High Definition TV, a high quality TV-standard. HDTV is capable of 1920×1080 pixel resolution.

HEADLINE

Very short text in a large size which is placed over a text to present the content of the text and lead the reader in.

HEATSET   9.5.2

Web offset technique using a drying oven to dry the ink before post press processing.

HEIGHT

Vertical measurement which, along with the horizontal width measurement, gives the format of a sheet of paper. Height is always stated last, i.e. 210×297 mm describes a sheet which is 210 mm wide and 297 mm high.

HERTZ

Unit of frequency, abbreviated to Hz. Used, for example, as a measurement of processor speed, based on how quickly it can carry out calculations. Often seen also in the form of MHz (1 000 000 Hz) and GHz (1 000 000 000 Hz).

HEXACHROME-SEPARATION   7.4.1

A version of HiFi color separation based on six print colors.

HIERARCHICAL STRUCTURE

A way of storing and sorting files according to a heading model; files are sorted under main headings and subheadings.

HIERARCHY OF NORMS   11.4

Governs which norm applies where several norms contradict each other, i.e. an individual contract, a standard contract and the Purchase Act.

HIFI COLOR   P 69

Subtractive color system which allows two to four colors to be added in addition to CMYK in order to obtain a wider color range in print.

HIGHLIGHTS   5.5.13

The light parts of an image.

HIGH-RESOLUTION IMAGE   6.7.4 6.8

Image with a sufficiently high resolution to be printed.

HINTED FONTS   6.5.5

A set of suggestions stored in the font about how the printer should print the font. All Postscript Type 1 fonts are hinted.

HINTING   6.5.5

See Hinted fonts.

HISTOGRAM   5.3.1 P 163 P 168

Graphic representation of tone distribution in a digital image. Adobe Photoshop contains a tool to show this.

HKS   3.5

A color system which, like Pantone, is based on combinations of physical base colors. Primarily used in Germany.

HOLE PUNCHING   10.9

Enables the printed product to be placed in binders.

HOUSE PAPER   P 25 P 309

The papers which a printshop usually uses or has in stock. Printshops can usually offer advantageous prices to customers who choose to print on their house paper.

HTML

HyperText Markup Language. Markup language used for the appearance and content of web pages.

HUB   2.8.11

Network unit which connects different parts of a network.

HUFFMAN COMPRESSION   4.9.3
Lossless compression method. Mainly used for line art.

HYBRID SCREENING   7.7.3
Screening technique which combines traditional and stochastic screening.

HYDROPHILIC   9.5.1
Describes a surface which attracts water, for example the printing surfaces on an offset plate which attract the dampening solution.

HYDROPHOBIC   9.5.1
Describes a surface which repels water, for example the printing surfaces on an offset plate which repel the dampening solution.

HYPHEN
A short dash used for linked words and syllabification at line breaks.

HYPHEN
Appears as "-". A short dash which is used, for example, to connect words.

I

ICC   3.9
International Color Consortium, a group of soft- and hardware manufacturers in the graphics industry working to find a common color management standard.

ICC PROFILE   3.10
A standard for describing the color characteristics of scanners, monitors, printers, proofs and prints. Used by most color management systems. Created using a spectrophotometer.

ICON
A symbol used in a computer context, for example the icon for a PDF file.

IEEE 1394   2.7.2
Standard designation for Firewire.

IEEE 802.11   2.8.5
Standard designation for wireless networks.

IEEE 802.3   2.8.2
Standard designation for Ethernet.

ILLUSTRATION SOFTWARE   4.2 2.5.4
Used to make illustrations. Usually object-based.

ILLUSTRATOR   4.2
Illustration program from Adobe.

IMAGE BANK   6.15.6
An archive system for storing images which also tracks the corresponding metadata in order to facilitate effective searching. Image banks can be made accessible to users via the internet.

IMAGE BUREAU   11.6.1
Company which works together with a number of photographers to market and sell images. Many image bureaus also work with royalty-free images.

IMAGE BYLINE
A small photo of a journalist/writer which is placed next to the text written by them. Often used in newspapers and periodicals.

IMAGE CARRIER   9.5.11 9.6.1–2 9.7.2
The material which is printed from, e.g. offset plate, screen frame or gravure cylinder.

IMAGE CARRIER PRODUCTION
To produce the printing plate, e.g. to expose and develop an offset plate.

IMAGE LINK   6.8
See Link.

IMAGE PROCESSING   5.5
Creating, editing, changing or retouching images using a computer.

IMAGE PROCESSING PROGRAM   4.5
Program needed to create, edit, change or retouch images using a computer. The most common image processing program is Adobe Photoshop.

IMAGE RESOLUTION   4.7
Information density of a digital, pixel-based image, measured in ppi (pixels per inch).

IMAGE TEXT   5.6.2
A short text placed next to an image. The image text can give additional information about the image and help the reader to understand the context of the image.

IMAGESETTER   9.5.11–2 P 350
Machine which exposes and prints out image carriers.

IMPORT FILTER   6.2.3 6.3
A layout program sometimes needs import filters in order to import text which has been saved in certain word processing formats.

IMPOSED FILM
Film which is output in the format of the printing sheet, containing a number of pages. Creates a montage.

IMPOSITION   7.6
Arranging the pages in a print product according to a special scheme to make print montages the same size as the print sheets. How the pages are arranged is guided by the post press processing.

IMPOSITION CORRECTIONS   7.6.8
The final corrections made before printing begins. Used primarily to ensure that all the pages in a product are present and correctly oriented. Carried out on sheets the same size as the print sheets.

IMPOSITION PROGRAM   7.6
Program that performs digital impositions from files.

IMPRESSION CYLINDER   9.5.3
Cylinder in the printing press which presses the paper against the cylinder that transfers the ink to the paper.

IMPRINT
Text piece containing the name of the publisher, location and print year. Placed on the imprint page of a book, usually one of the first pages.

INCAMERA   4.11.7
System from PictoColor for designing ICC profiles for digital cameras.

INCOPY   6.3.5

Editing program for opening Indesign documents and simply change the text.

INDENT

Where the first line in a paragraph starts further to the right than other lines in the text. Usually a em-square measurement.

INDESIGN   6.1.1

Well established layout program from Adobe.

INDEX COLOR MODE   4.6.7

An image in index color mode holds up to 256 different colors, defined in a palette in which each box contains a color and is numbered. This means that all the pixels of the image will have a value between 1 and 256 depending on its palette color. The image therefore only contains a pixel image with the same memory size as a grayscale image, plus a palette.

INDEX MODE   4.6.7

See Index color mode.

INDEX NUMBER

A raised numeral in a smaller size type-face often used to refer to a footnote or endnote.

INDIRECT PRINTING PROCEDURES 343 9.5.4

A printing procedure in which the ink from the image carrier is transferred via a rubber blanket cylinder to the paper, e.g. offset.

INFRARED LIGHT   3.1 2.7.4

Heat radiation. The invisible light which is closest to the red hues in the spectrum, i.e. wavelengths around 705 nm.

IN-HOUSE ADVERTISING DEPARTMENT

An internal department in a company, responsible for producing some or all of the company's advertising and information material.

INITIAL   6.4.4

Accentuated initial character at the beginning of a chapter or a paragraph. The character is often considerably larger than the rest of the text, but it can also be distinguished by a contrasting color or typeface.

INK   9.5.6 9.6.3 9.7.3 9.8.3 9.9.3

The physical substance of color, for example printing ink. Also see Color.

INK COVERAGE [1]   9.10.7 6.11.2–3 9.5.8

The amount of ink which is distributed across different areas of the paper. Ink coverage should vary as little as possible across the production.

INK COVERAGE [2] 9.11.2 9.11.4 9.9.7 9.10.4

The amount of ink added in the printing process. Also describes the maximum permissible amount of each component color on a certain paper in a certain printing process.

INK DAMPENING BALANCE   9.10.5 9.10.7

To achieve good print quality in an offset print there must be a balance between the dampening solution and the printing ink.

INK DUCT   9.5.5

The space in the printing press which supplies the ink.

INK FORM ROLLER   9.5.5

Roller in the ink pyramid which transfers printing ink from the last distribution rollers to the printing plate.

INK PYRAMID   9.5.5

Term for the entire system in a printing system which manages four-color supply.

INK ROLLERS   9.5.5

Collective term for all types of rollers in an ink pyramid.

INK SCREWS   9.5.8

Controls the ink doctor and thereby the supply of ink to different parts and areas along the width of the paper. Is controlled digitally, or manually in older printing presses.

INK ZONES   9.5.8

The ink supply is controlled in a number of zones across the printed sheet, which makes it possible to adjust the ink amount within each zone.

INKING   9.8.3

When ink is transferred to the image carrier.

INK-JET PRINTER   9.3

A printer based on a technique which squirts liquid ink onto the paper.

INSERT

An printed product included with another main product, often inside it. A newspaper can, for example, contain a separate sport section which groups all the sports news together.

INSERT

A print item placed inside another, e.g. an advertising leaflet placed inside a news-paper or magazine.

INTEGRATED CIRCUITS   2.1.5

The "chip" of the computer, i.e. processors or memory circuits.

INTELLIHANCE

Extensis program to automatically adjust images.

INTERFERENCE SENSITIVITY   2.8.4

Network cables vary in their sensitivity to electro-magnetic radiation. A sensitive cable can lose signals if there is too much interference.

INTERNAL DRUM   9.5.12

Special construction of imagesetter where the image carrier is stuck to the inside of a drum and exposed with a laser beam guided by a rotating mirror inside the drum.

INTERNAL MEMORY   2.1.3 2.3.1

Also known as RAM, a computer's rapid, temporary memory.

INTERNET EXPLORER

Web browser from Microsoft.

INTERPOLATION   5.3.4 5.3.8 5.4.5

Technique for re-calculating information in a digital image, for example when changing the resolution or rotation of an image.

INTERPOLATION ARTIFACTS   5.3.8

Reduction in quality of an image as a result of increased the resolution "artificially", using interpolation.

IP   **2.8.7–8 2.8.2**
Internet Protocol. A protocol used in data transfer in IP-based networks, i.e. internet.

IPTC   **5.6.2**
International Press Telecommunications Council. Standard for the insertion of metadata into images.

IR   **2.7.4 2.2.4**
Wireless transfer technology using infrared light. Used to transfer files between a computer and a mobile phone, for example.

IRIS PRINTING
Also known as rainbow printing. Several colors are printed next to each other on the same press so that soft tones are created between them. Sometimes used in banknote printing.

ISDN   **2.9.5**
Integrated Services Digital Network. Hardware and software for digital transfers via the telephone network.

ISO 14001   **9.12.2**
Environmental management system. International standard.

ISOPROPYL ALCOHOL   **9.5.7**
Alcohol added to dampening solution in order to reduce surface tensions.

IT8   **3.10.1 9.11.10**
Standard for how test targets should be formed when creating ICC profiles.

ITALICS   **P 207**
Variation of a typeface which slants. "False italics" is when a normal typeface is made to slant. True italics are a new version of the typeface. An italic "a" is drawn in an entirely different way to a non-italic "a".

J

JAZ   **2.6.9**
A removable magnetic disk for data storage. Holds 1 or 2 gigabytes.

JDF   **7.3**
Job Definition Format is a standard for information exchange between different production systems in graphic production. JDF information contains, for example, instructions for how the printed product should be folded and cut so that this can be done automatically.

JMF   **7.3**
Job Messaging Format. Standard for sending status information between different systems in the production chain. Part of the JDF standard.

JOB SPECIFICATION   **7.3**
The digital specification used in the JDF format. Based on XML.

JPEG   **4.9.6 4.8.6**
Joint Photographic Experts Group. A compression method for images which entails some loss. Also operates as an image format in its own right. Compatible with most computer platforms.

JPEG 2000   **4.9.7 4.8.7**
Follow-up to JPEG with increased functionality.

JUSTIFICATION
Spacing between words which is varied to achieve a straight right hand margin. Used to create a justified text.

K

KANJI
A Japanese typeset. Requires more character space than the Latin alphabet.

KBYTE
Kilobyte, i.e. 2^{10} bytes = 1024 bytes. See Byte.

KELVIN   **P 74**
A temperature scale used to describe light sources. Starts at absolute zero and proceeds at the same intervals as the Celsius scale. The freezing point of water, 0 degrees Celsius, is 273.2 degrees Kelvin.

KERNING   **P 207 6.5.4**
Narrowing or widening the spacing between two letters.

KERNING TABLE   **6.5.4**
Table containing kerning values for all pairs of letters in a typeface.

KILO
$10^3 = 1\ 000$

KILOBYTE
2^{10} bytes = 1024 bytes. See Byte.

KNOCKOUT [1]   **7.4.8**
When a graphic object is placed over another, for example a text over a tint area, and the colors of the text and the background are not intended to mix, space is knocked out for the text. A hole the same shape as the text is knocked out in the tint area and the text is printed on an unprinted (paper white) surface.

KNOCKOUT [2]   **4.1.5**
To make a hole in an object-based image so that objects behind it are visible.

L

LAB   **4.6.5**
An image saved in Lab-mode has three channels which combine to describe the color in each pixel. L is for brightness, a for green-red and b for yellow-blue.

LACK OF CONTRAST   **9.11.2**
When a screening tone goes into full tone because of dot gain, i.e. 100 % coverage.

LAMINATING   **10.4**
When a sheet of paper is covered with a protective plastic layer – the laminate. Both shiny and matte laminates are available. These are applied using a special laminating device.

LAN   **2.8 2.8.1**
Local Area Network – a local network, for example in an office.

LASER PRINTER 9.2

A printer which uses laser technology and xerographic methods. Uses toner i.e. ink powder which is heated onto the paper.

LAY-DOWN ORDER 6.9.1 9.11.6

The order in which colors are printed, which varies between different printshops and printing technicians. Is particularly important when printing wet-on-wet, as it affects trapping. In sheetfed offset printing, the lightest colors are usually printed first because they "dirty" least: yellow, magenta, cyan, then black. Some printshops prefer not to print cyan and black in quick succession, and therefore swap magenta and cyan over: yellow, cyan, magenta, then black. Others print black first, as it will be least affected by trapping: black, yellow, magenta, then cyan.

LAYER 5.5.15

A technique in image editing applications for separating different parts of an image until they are finished. Useful when creating manipulations and collage or graphics consisting of several parts, for example an image and a text, or a motif and a shadow.

LAYER MASK 5.5.17

A tool in Photoshop which hides part of a layer so that the masked part is transparent.

LAYOUT

A broad term which describes the design of pages and graphics.

LAYOUT PROGRAM 6.1.1

Used to create layout and finished pages of text and images, e.g. Adobe Indesign and Quark Express.

LCA 9.12.3

See Life cycle analysis.

LCD SCREEN 2.4.2

Liquid Crystal Display, technology used primarily in displays and flat screens.

LEAF 7.6.1

In a bound printed product, e.g. a book or periodical, the insert is composed of a number of pages or leaves. Each page or leaf has two sides, the front and back.

LEAFLET

A printed product which consists solely of a folded sheet, with no binding.

LED

Light Emitting Diode. Commonly used in signal lamps on technical equipment. One variation uses laser light and is used in some types of imagesetters and laser printers.

LED PRINTER 9.2.1

Laser printer which uses a row of laser diodes to "write" the image rather than a laser beam.

LEFT JUSTIFIED

Text setting with a straight left hand edge and fixed spacing. The right hand edge is uneven.

LETRASET

Font publisher.

LETTER

Common paper format for office use, the American equivalent of A4, measuring 216×279 mm.

LETTERPRESS

Printing technique whereby image carriers are composed of raised (printing) and flat (non-printing) surfaces, e.g. book and potato printing.

LETTERPRESS PRINTING 9.6.1

The most common book printing technique where both the image carrier and the surface it is pressed against are flat.

LIBRARY 6.1.5

Common tool in layout programs which enables predefined objects to be saved and subsequently reused.

LIFE CYCLE ANALYSIS 9.12.3

A method for analyzing a product's environmental impact from when it is produced until when it is recycled. The only way to get detailed information on environmental impact.

LIGATURE P 207

Specially created character composed of two separate characters which are made into one. Common examples of ligatures are "ae" and "fi".

LIGHT 6.4.1

Typeface variation using thin lines, the opposite of bold.

LIGHT

Electromagnetic radiation within a certain wavelength range. Visible light has a wavelength of between 385 and 705 nm. Human sight is based on the eye's interpretation of incoming light. As light travels from its source to the eye, it is reflected by objects in the vicinity. This reflected light creates the image we see.

LIGHT INTENSITY

The strength of light, also called brightness or luminance.

LIGNIN 8.17.2

A natural component of wood and paper. Contributes to the paper yellowing, and so is removed from certain qualities of paper.

LINE ARRANGEMENT 7.2.7 7.5.2–3

The way in which the right margin of a text column is broken off. May change when changing RIP or font.

LINE ART

Line art images consist only of surfaces in full color or no color at all. The pixels in the image are either black or white.

LINE REARRANGEMENT 6.6.1

When the line arrangement in a document changes, for example when changing fonts.

LINE SCREEN 7.7.4

A screen based on thin lines of varying thickness, instead of halftone dots.

LINK 6.7.4

Reference, for example from a low-resolution image to the corresponding high-resolution one. When printing a document, the program finds the high-resolution image using the link and replaces the low-resolution one. The link tracks the name and location of the high-resolution image in the computer's file structure.

LINOCOLOR 3.13

Color management module used in Windows.

LINUX

Operating system not usually used in graphic production.

LITHOGRAPHIC PRINCIPLE 9.5.1

Works with printing surfaces which attract grease (ink) and repel water and non-printing surfaces which attract and are covered with water that repels the greasy ink.

LOCALTALK

Apple's network solution for connecting Apple Macintosh computers. Superseded by Ethernet.

LOGO

A graphic symbol for a company, organization, trademark, etc., often made using object graphics. Colours in logos are often required to be reproduced exactly, which is why spot colors are often used.

LOOP STITCH P 390

A version of an ordinary staple, used in staple binding. Used to enable the printed product to be put in a binder, while still being able to flick through pages.

LOOSE LEAF

A sheet, usually with holes punched, which can be put in a folder.

LOUPE

Small magnifying lens used to check print images.

LOWERCASE LETTER 6.4.1

Small letters, as opposed to uppercase letters.

LOWLIGHTS

The darkest parts of an image i.e. shadows.

LOW-RESOLUTION IMAGE 6.7.4

Image with low resolution, often 72 ppi. Requires little storage space. Is usually used as a mounting image and is then exchanged, manually or automatically, for a high-resolution image for printing.

LPI 7.7.5

Lines per inch - a measurement of screen frequency. Describes how close together the halftone dots are.

LUMINANCE

See Brightness.

LZW 4.9.2

Lossless compression method named after the researchers Lempel, Ziv and Welch who developed it. LZW can be used when images are saved in the TIFF format.

M

M P 222

Pantone code indicating that the color is printed on a matte-coated paper.

MAC ADDRESS

A unique identifying address for network cards.

MAC OS 2.5.1

Apple's operating system used in Macintosh-based computers.

MACHINE FINISH

See Calendar finish.

MACHINE POINT 7.7.6

See Exposure point.

MACRO 5.8.4

See Function macro.

MAGAZINE

A periodical, e.g. a monthly magazine, published once a month.

MAGAZINE FORMAT

American format measuring 190–225 × 280–300 mm.

MAGNETIC DIRECTION 2.6.2

Direction in a magnetic field between the magnetic north and south poles. Used in magnetic read and write technology on magnetic data storage media.

MAGNETIC DISK 2.6.7

Data storage medium based on magnetic read and write technology, e.g. hard disks, Zip disks, floppy disks.

MAGNETIC TAPE 2.6.3

Data storage medium based on magnetic read and write technology, e.g. DAT or DLT tape.

MAKEREADY 9.10 1.3.1

Term for all printing press settings and preparations which need to be done before the first approved printed sheet is produced.

MANUAL MOUNTING

Films which are manually mounted into complete film montages.

MANUSCRIPT 6.2

The text document which is the basis for setting.

MANY-UP 7.6.1

A type of imposition in which a page is placed multiple times on the same printing sheet, for example a 2-up which provides two copies of the same page from each sheet.

MANY-UP

Type of imposition. One page is placed multiple times on the same printer sheet, for example two-up gives two copies of the same page from each printed sheet.

MARGIN P 381

Often unprinted area which surrounds a type area. Called gutter (inner margin), fore edge (outer margin), head (upper margin) and tail (lower margin).

MARGIN JUSTIFICATION 6.4.4

The way in which the typography is justified in the right-hand margin. Optical margin justification adjusts the margin to the form of the letters, so that the edge appears as straight as possible.

MARKUP BOX

Grey box used in layout programs to mark the placement of an image. For quick printing the markup boxes can be printed instead of the real images.

MARKUP IMAGE 6.7.4

When undertaking layout work with images which require a lot of memory, low definition markup images can be used, which are then exchanged for the high definition version before printing.

MATRIX 10.6 9.6.2

A sunken relief image which is pressed against a patrix with a corresponding positive, raised image. Used in embossing, for example.

MATTE 8.2

Paper which reflects incoming light unevenly. Makes text easily readable, as it minimizes distracting shine on the paper.

MAXIMUM INK COVERAGE 7.4.3 9.11.4

States the maximum amount of ink of the component colors in percent on a certain paper in a certain printing process. The value is mainly determined by the possibility of smearing and is usually between 240 and 340 % for a four-color print (the theoretical value is 400 %, 100 % for each color). The value is used for print adjustment in four-color separation.

MBYTE

Megabyte, i.e. 2^{20} bytes = 1 048 576 bytes. See Byte.

MECHANICAL PULP 8.19.1

When producing mechanical pulp, cellulose fibers are extracted from the wood by grinding.

MEDIA

Media is another word for communication channels. Examples of media are printing, radio, DVDs or the internet.

MEGA

10^6 = 1 000 000

MEGABYTE

2^{20} bytes = 1 048 576 bytes. See Byte.

MEGAPIXEL 4.10

Unit habitually used to market digital cameras. Describes the maximum number of millions of pixels in the image.

MEMORY CARD 2.6.5

A digital storage device. Used, for example, in digital cameras and computers.

MEMORY STICK P 54

A kind of memory card, usually using flash technology. Common in Sony products. Comes in variations such as Memory Stick PRO and Memory Stick DUO.

METADATA 5.6.2 6.15.4–6

Information in a data file concerning, for example, who created the file and what it contains. Often used to search for and manage images effectively.

METAL BINDING 10.13

See Staple binding.

METAMERISM P 75

When two colors which look identical in a one light look completely different in another.

MIDTONES

Tones in an image between the darkest and lightest.

MINI SD P 54

Smaller form of SD card.

MINIMUM HIGHLIGHT DOT 9.11.5

The smallest halftone dot which can be reproduced in a printer or printing press, or in other words, the lightest tone. Measured in percent.

MIRROR HARD DRIVES

A backup function using double hard drives. A program makes sure that all changes made on one hard disk are also made on the other, ensuring that there are always two identical sets of files.

MISPRINT

Mistake which occurs in a printed product. Can mean both errors carried over from the original material and errors which occur in the printing process.

MISREGISTRATION 9.11.8

Print phenomenon describing when component colors fail to print directly on top of each other, i.e. in register.

MISSING DOT 9.8.6

Undesirable phenomenon which can occur in gravure printing, whereby some wells in the image carrier do not transfer ink to the paper.

MMC P 52

See Multi-media card.

MNG 4.8.14

A variation of the PNG format which can also contain animation.

MO DISKS 2.6.11

Magneto-optical disks, a removable optical data storage disk, available in different sizes. Hold between 128 and 1,300 megabytes.

MODEM 2.9.3 2.9.2

Communication equipment which enables a computer to call up and transfer files to or from another computer via the analog telephone network.

MODEM PORT 2.2.6

A connection in the computer (parallel port) where the modem is connected.

MOIRÉ 7.7.11

A screen phenomenon manifested as distracting interference patterns in images and tint areas. A similar phenomenon occurs on TV, for example when someone wears a checked jacket.

MONITOR RGB/SIMPLIFIED RGB 3.8.10

RGB color space based on the current monitor settings.

MONOTYPE 6.4.10

Typeface publisher.

MONTAGE FILM   P 282

A large film on which individual page films are mounted manually to form a complete imposition.

MRW, THM   P 133

Raw format files from Minolta brand digital cameras, with file extension .mrw or .thm.

MS   P 54

See Memory stick.

MULTIMEDIA CARD   P 54

Less common kind of memory card using flash technology.

MULTIPLE MASTER   P 212

File type for fonts which can assume different widths and boldness, thus simulating a different typeface. Version of PostScript Type 1.

MUNSELL

Color system developed at the beginning of the 20th century by Albert H. Munsell.

N

NANOMETER (NM)

A measurement of length (1 nanometer = 0.000001 millimeters). Used, among other things, to state the wavelength of light.

NARROW   6.4.1

See Light.

NCI LEVEL   9.11.2

Normal Color Intensity, a measure of optimal ink coverage and contrast in the printing press. Measured in terms of the relative print contrast for a given printing process.

NCS   P 77

Natural Color System, a Swedish color system. It is based on the coordinates of brightness, color and saturation and can be visualized as a double-cone. Is mostly used within the textile and painting industries.

NEF   P 133

Raw format files from Nikon brand digital cameras, with file extension .nef.

NEGATIVE FILM   P 350

Graphic film which has black non-printing surfaces and transparent printing surfaces.

NETWORK   2.8

Net connection enabling exchange of information between computers and printers, scanners, servers, etc.

NETWORK CABLE   2.8.4

The physical cable which connects the network.

NETWORK HUB/SWITCH   2.8.11–12

Hubs/switches which ensure that every device coupled to them always has a certain network capacity assigned to it. This means that they can be used simultaneously without overburdening the network.

NETWORK INTERFACE CARD   2.8.9

A circuit board installed in a computer enabling it to communicate on a specific network.

NETWORK PROTOCOL   2.8.7

A collection of rules for how communication on a particular network will be conducted.

NETWORK SERVER   2.8.15

A computer which manages the network, controls and supervises traffic and authorizations.

NETWORK TRAFFIC LOAD   2.8.18

States the level of traffic, i.e. how much information is being sent on a network at a given moment.

NETWORK UNIT   2.8.10

Unit used to build a network, for example switches, bridges and hubs.

NEWS GRAPHICS   4.1

Graphics which complete articles in mass media, i.e. tables or drawings containing information.

NEWSPRINT [1]

Glossy or very thinly coated paper wood-pulp paper, usually used in products with a limited lifespan, i.e. catalogues and newspapers.

NEWSPRINT [2]   8.7

Low weight wood-pulp paper (around 45g/m²), with high opacity and short lifespan.

NEWTON'S RINGS   P 137

Optical interference phenomenon which occurs in repro photography and scanning.

NIP   9.11.3

The point in a printing press where the paper is inserted between the rubber blanket and the impression cylinder.

NOISE   5.3.9

All digital cameras cause a certain amount of noise, especially in dark areas. The level of noise affects image quality in the long run, which can mean, for example, that images with high mega pixel values can still appear to be of low quality.

NTSC   3.8.12

American RGB standard used in video contexts.

O

OBJECT GRAPHICS   4.1

Object graphics consist of mathematically calculated curves and lines which form surfaces and shapes, whereas pixel-based images consist of pixels, i.e. square image elements, in different colors and tones. An image which is object-based can be scaled up or down without any loss of quality. Sometimes incorrectly called vector graphics.

OBJECT MOIRÉ   7.7.11

A kind of distracting interference pattern which occurs when a motif with a repeating pattern, e.g. a lattice, becomes rasterized. See also Moiré.

OBJECT TEMPLATE   6.1.6

Tool in Adobe Indesign used to predefine characteristics of a frame, e.g. line, transparency and shadow. This can then be applied to any frame.

OBJECT-BASED   4.1

See Object graphics.

OCR   P 201

Optical Character Recognition. Computer technology which recognizes letter shapes in image information.

OFF PRESS PROCESSING   10

All the work carried out on printed paper sheets until they are a complete printed product, e.g. cropping, folding and binding.

OFFSET PRINTING   9.5

Printing technique where the image carrier transfers (offsets) the print ink onto a rubber cylinder, which then transfers the ink/print image to paper. Usually indicates lithographic offset printing – a technique where the print surfaces are separated from the non-print surfaces using chemicals, rather than reliefs. See Lithographic principle.

OLEOPHILIC   9.5.1

Describes a surface which attracts grease, for example the printing surfaces on an offset plate which attract the greasy ink.

OLEOPHOBIC   9.5.1

Describes a surface which repels grease, for example the printing surfaces on an offset plate which repel the greasy ink.

OMNIPAGE   P 201

OCR program from Nuance.

ONE SHOT CAMERA

Digital camera technique which exposes all three component colors, RGB, in a single stage. See also Single-pass.

ONE-SIDED PAPER

A paper with different surface characteristics on the front and back sides, for example postcards (which have a coated side with image and an uncoated side to be written on).

ONLINE DEVELOPING   9.5.11

Online developing of printing plates means that the plate setter, any oven used and the developer are joined.

OPACITY   8.11

A measure of the transparency of a paper.

OPAL FILM   9.8.2

Type of graphic film which is white and transparent. Used in gravure as engraving originals.

OPEN DOCUMENTS   6.14

Layout documents from, for example, Adobe Indesign or Quark Xpress, which are sent as graphic originals instead of PDF files. The document is sent together with all its associated files, e.g. image files, typeface and layout instructions.

OPENOFFICE   6.2.1

Program package with equivalent applications to Microsoft Office. Free software, based on open source codes.

OPENTYPE   6.5.1

File type for fonts which can contain a very large number of typefaces. Compatible with both Macs and PCs.

OPERATING SYSTEM   2.5.1

Lowest level of software in a computer, provides its basic functions. All programs which are run on the computer use the operating system, which in turn runs on the hardware.

OPI   6.7.4

Open Prepress Interface, a production and execution program which makes it possible to work with low resolution images in the prepress workflow, with the images subsequently automatically exchanged for high resolution before printing.

OPTICAL DISC   2.6.4

Data storage medium which is read and written using light, e.g. a CD.

OPTICAL KERNING   6.5.4

Kerning which is based on the shape of the letters, rather than a predefined table.

ORDER CONFIRMATION   11.5.1

Document which can be sent physically or digitally to a customer who has placed an order. The order confirmation contains information about the order which has been placed so that the customer can ensure that the order is correct.

ORF   P 133

Raw format image files from Olympus brand digital cameras, with the file extension .orf.

ORIGINAL IMAGE   4.13.1

For example a digital image, slide, paper copy of a photograph or a drawing. Master copy on which reproduction is based.

ORIGINALITY

For a work to be protected by copyright, it must have a degree of independence and originality. This is not a quality requirement; even "bad" works can be protected. However, works which are too simple and banal cannot be protected by copyright. The majority of works written, painted or in any other way created have originality and are protected by copyright.

ORPHAN

Commonly used name for an undesired result. Describes a situation where the first line in a paragraph ends up at the bottom of a column or page with the rest of the paragraph on the following column or page.

OUTLINE CHARACTER

A character composed of outlines which are not filled.

OUTLINE FONT   6.4.2

An object-based font file which can be increased in size without loss of quality. All typefaces have an outline font. Postscript fonts contain two font files, one pixel-based for viewing on a screen, and one outline font which is used for printing.

OUTPUT DEVICE   7.1

For example a printer or imagesetter.

OUTPUT RESOLUTION   7.7.8

The resolution of a given output device, such as a printer or imagesetter. Measured in dpi.

OVERPRINT   7.4.8

When, for example, a text is printed on a tint area and the colors of the two objects mix. The opposite of knockout, where the colors of the objects are not mixed. Black text tends to overprint.

OVERRUN

Excess number of completed copies of a print item, as compared with what was agreed.

OXIDATION [1]

Occurs when an element combines with oxygen. Metals commonly absorb oxygen from the air resulting in build-up of an oxidized layer. Can occur with printing plates, for example.

OXIDATION [2]

The second drying process of the offset printing inks. The alkyd undergoes a chemical reaction with the oxygen in the air, a process called oxidation.

P

PACKBITS   4.9.1

Compression method which uses sequence length coding to compress TIFF files in Adobe ImageReady.

PACKET   2.8.8

Describes an amount of data sent on a network. The information sent on a network is divided into a number of packets.

PACKING   9.5.4

Sheet of paper placed between the rubber blanket and rubber blanket cylinder to ensure that the plate and the rubber blanket rotate with exactly the same circumference speed.

PAGE BREAK

Where one page finishes and another begins.

PAGE DESCRIPTION LANGUAGE   7.1

A code language which describes the design of a page. See PostScript.

PAGE FILM   P 350

Graphic film containing one page of the printed product. Page films are mounted into complete impositions. Cf. imposed film, which corresponds to the format of the printed sheet and contains multiple pages.

PAGE FOOTER   P 381

See Footer.

PAGE HEADER   P 381

Margin above the type area on a page.

PAGE TEMPLATE   6.1.3–4

Page templates for different types of page can be used to enhance efficiency when carrying out layout work. Page templates can contain page numbers, support lines, text blocks, fixed objects, etc.

PAGE-INDEPENDENT

In a document saved in PDF-format, the pages are stored independent of each other. All the information about a page is stored with a description of the page. As a result any page can be printed without having to print the others – the format is "page-independent." The same document saved in the page-dependent PostScript-format would mean having to print out all the pages or none of them because the pages are dependent on each other.

PAGEMAKER   6.1.1

Simple page layout program from Adobe.

PAGE-PROOF

Text set in columns as it is intended to appear in the finished product.

PAGINATION

Page numbering.

PAINTER   4.5

Pixel-based drawing program from Corel.

PAINTSHOP PRO   4.4–5

Medium-level image processing program from Corel.

PAL/SECAM   3.8.13

European RGB standard for TV broadcasting.

PALETTE   4.6.7

A set of colors in a computer. Also see Index color mode.

PALLET

Wooden platform on which paper is usually delivered from a papermill.

PANTONE COLORS   3.5

See PMS colors.

PAPER PULP   8.19.1

A mixture of cellulose, water and fillers which is processed and eventually becomes paper. Pulp is produced in both solid and liquid form. The solid form is used to make export easier.

PARAGRAPH

Continuous text, often separated from other paragraphs by an indent at the beginning and a line break at the end. Titles can also be inserted to further separate paragraphs.

PARAGRAPH FORMAT   6.3.1 6.1.7 6.3.3

Provides the typographic setting for a whole paragraph in a body of text, e.g. typeface, line spacing, indent, etc.

PARALLEL FOLD   10.10

A type of folding in which the folds are parallel to each other, as opposed to right-angle folding.

PARALLEL PORT   2.2.2

A connection in a computer where printers or modems, for example, are connected.

PATHS   5.5.18

See Clipping path.

PATRIX   10.6 9.6.2

A raised relief image used, for example, in embossing. A patrix is often combined with a corresponding negative form called a matrix.

PCL 7.1
Page description language from HP.

PCS 3.9
Profile Connection Space. The device-independent color space (CIELAB) used in the ICC system.

PCX 4.8.16
Image format for pixel-based images in Windows. Less well-suited to graphic production.

PDF/A 7.2.6
PDF files which are created to be archived for long periods are usually created according to the PDF/A standard, which regulates how such files are created and what they must or must not contain.

PDF/X 7.2.6
A PDF file which is produced or controlled from a standardized specification, such that it can be used as a digital print original.

PDF1 7.2
Portable Document Format. A file format from Adobe created with the program Acrobat Distiller.

PEF P 133
Raw format files from Pentax brand digital cameras with the file extension .pef.

PENALTY
A pre-determined punitive charge which can be imposed on a person or company which fails to conform with certain requirements in a contract.

PERFECTOR PRINTING 9.5.3
Printing both sides of a print sheet in one run through the printing press.

PERFECTOR PRINTING UNIT 9.5.3
A type of printing unit which does not have an impression cylinder. Both sides of the sheet are printed simultaneously with two rubber blanket cylinders which use each other as impression cylinders.

PERFORATION 10.8
An indication to tear. Makes it easier to tear off removable parts, e.g. a counterfoil or response card.

PERIODICAL
A publication which comes out on a regular basis.

PERSONALIZED PRINTING P 333
Technique whereby the content of the printed page can be altered at full printing speed for each sheet printed. Also known as variable data printing.

PHOTO MULTIPLIER 4.12.4
Unit which translates light intensity into electric signals in older scanners.

PHOTOCD
CD for image data storage using Kodak's PhotoCD technology.

PHOTOGRAPHIC CONDUCTOR 9.2.1
Material whose electrical charge can be affected by light, used in laser printers. See Xerographic process.

PHOTO-MONTAGE
Combination of several photos, resulting in a new image. Using modern technology, these can appear very realistic and it can be very difficult to see that the image has been artificially produced.

PHOTOPERFECT 4.5
Automatic image adjustment program from Binuscan.

PHOTOPOLYMER 9.5.13
Type of printing plate technique for offset plates where the plate is exposed using light from a laser.

PHOTORETOUCH PRO 4.5
Professional image processing program from Binuscan.

PHOTOSENSITIVE POLYMER 9.5.11
A light-sensitive layer on the surface of a printing plate.

PHOTOSHOP 4.5 5.5
The most common image processing program for professional use, from Adobe.

PHOTOSHOP ELEMENTS 4.5
Image processing program from Adobe which is a simpler version of Photoshop, designed for home use.

PHOTOSHOP FORMAT 4.8.1
Photoshop's own file format. Can contain all information on layers, masks, transparency and other settings.

PHOTOSHOP RAW 4.8.17
Relatively uncommon transport format for digital images. Should not be confused with raw files from digital cameras.

PICKING 9.5.15
When the printing ink tears off paper fibers from the paper.

PICK-OUTS 9.5.15
Paper fragments which are torn off the paper by the ink (in "picking") and which stick to the rubber blanket or the offset plate and cause white dots in the print.

PICT 4.8.11
Picture File. A Macintosh format for images. Used internally in computers for icons and other system graphics. Also used for low definition mounting images in EPS format and OPI systems. PICT images are not suitable for producing printed products.

PICTURE ELEMENT 4.4
Also called a pixel. A digital image or the smallest visual component of a monitor. The number of pixels per inch or centimeter is a measurement of the resolution of an image or monitor.

PIE CHART
A round diagram which shows proportions. The parts are shown as "slices" of a round pie.

PIGMENT 9.5.6 9.3.2 9.6.3
The part of a printing ink or toner which gives it its color.

PITSTOP 7.2.7
Preflight program from Enfocus used to control and adjust PDF files.

PIXEL 4.4 2.4
Abbreviated from "Picture Element". The smallest visual component of a digital image or monitor. The number of pixels per inch can, for example, describe the resolution of an image or monitor.

PIXEL GRAPHICS   4.4

Image based on pixels, as opposed to an object image based on geometric objects and mathematical curves. A pixel-based image should not be enlarged by more than 15–20 %.

PIXEL-BASED   4.4

See Pixel graphics.

PJTF   7.3

Portable Job Ticket Format, part of the JDF standard. Developed by Adobe to manage prepress information in files.

PLACARD

Advertisement for a newspaper or periodical which groups the most important news and articles as headlines.

PLATE   9.5.11–13

See Printing plate.

PLATE CYLINDER   9.5.3

The printing cylinder to which the printing plate is attached. In offset printing, the plate cylinder transfers the ink/image to the rubber blanket cylinder which, in turn, transfers it to the paper.

PLATE DEVELOPMENT   9.5.11 195

After exposure, the printing plate is developed using chemical liquids.

PLATE EXPOSURE   P 351

The process of exposing printing plates using light or heat, sometimes from a laser.

PLATE MAKEREADY   9.10.1

Mounting and adjusting the printing plate in the printing press.

PLATE SCANNER   9.5.8 9.10.4

An older kind of scanner which scans the already exposed printing plates so that the basic ink settings can be adjusted in advance.

PLATE SET   9.5.11

A set of plates for the same print sheet, for example four plates for a four-color sheet.

PLATESETTER   9.5.12

Technique for setting/writing a printing plate in a setter directly from a computer instead of via graphic film, also known as computer to plate

PLOTTER

Inkjet printer for large formats.

PLUG-IN PROGRAM

See Program add-in.

PLUG-INS   2.5.5 6.14.2

Additional programs which enhance the functions of a given program.

PMS COLORS   3.5

Pantone Matching System, based on combinations of nine different colors. Is primarily used for spot colors in printing.

PNG   4.8.13

Portable Network Graphics. Image format which extends the functions of the GIF format.

POINT   P 207

Typographical term for line spacing, measured from base line to base line. Paragraph format can, for example, be stated as "10/12" (10 font size on a 12 point line).

POINT   6.5.2

The smallest unit in typography, measures 0.376 mm.

POLAPROOF

Screening technique for sublimation printers, developed by Polaroid.

POLYCARBONATE   P 53

The plastic material of a CD.

POLYMER LAYER   9.5.13 9.5.11

A light-sensitive layer of plastic (polymer) covering the surface of an offset printing plate.

PORTFOLIO   6.15.5

Archive program from Extensis.

POSITIVE FILM   P 350

Graphic film with transparent non-printing surfaces and black printing surfaces.

POSTAGE AND PACKING   8.16.7

Charge for sending a letter or parcel by post.

POSTER   8.6.2

A classic means of conveying information or advertising in the form of a large printed paper sheet. Typical formats are 50×70 mm and 70×100 cm.

POSTSCRIPT   7.1

A page description language from Adobe, standard for graphic print-outs.

POSTSCRIPT 3   7.1.7

The third version of the page description language PostScript. "Level" has been removed from the name. Cf. PostScript Level 1 and 2.

POSTSCRIPT CODE   7.1

Program code which describes a PostScript file.

POSTSCRIPT EXTREME

A PostScript 3 RIP technique which can RIP several pages of a document at the same time using different processors.

POSTSCRIPT INTERPRETER   7.1.3

Software which interprets PostScript code and transfers it to a bitmap with exposure points or screen points.

POSTSCRIPT LEVEL 1   7.1.5

The first version of the page description language PostScript. Is the basis for PostScript Level 2 and PostScript 3. Level 1 is, in comparison to the other two versions, a relatively simple page description language, e.g. it does not support color management.

POSTSCRIPT LEVEL 2   7.1.6

The second version of the page description language PostScript. Supports, among other things, color management (in contrast to PostScript Level 1).

POSTSCRIPT PRINTER   P 331

A printer based on the page description language PostScript.

POSTSCRIPT RIP   7.1.3

A RIP based on the page description language PostScript. See RIP.

POSTSCRIPT TYPE 1   6.5.2
File type for fonts, based on PostScript.

POSTSCRIPT-HEAD   7.1.1
The information which always comes first in a PostScript file, e.g. information about which program created the file.

POST-TREATMENT   8.19.4
When paper is post-treated in different ways depending on the intended quality and surface.

POWERPOINT   6.1.1
Presentation software from Microsoft. Used for slide and overhead presentations.

PPD   7.1.2
PostScript Printer Description. Contains information about a particular printer unit and is necessary in order to print from it.

PPF   7.3
Print Production Format. System developed by CIP3, makes it possible to exchange information between different production stages.

PPI   4.7   P 290
Pixels per inch. States the resolution of images, monitors and scanners.

PREAMBLE
Introductory piece of text. Often follows the title and is frequently in a different style to that of the main text i.e. bold or italic.

PREFLIGHT   16.13.3
To review, proof and adjust documents and their components using special software before printing on film or printing plate.

PREPRESS AGENCY   P 19
Company which supplies reproductive services, e.g. image scanning, retouching, print adjustment and creation of printable PDF files.

PREPS
An imposition program from Kodak.

PRESS PROOF   7.5.7
A proof run on the printing press before the final edition is printed.

PRESS VARNISH   10.3
Varnish which is put on in a printing press to create a shiny effect, protect the print and avoid ink chalking/powdering.

PRESSWISE
An imposition program from Adobe.

PRIMARY COLORS   3.2–4
Three primary colors from the spectrum: cyan, magenta and yellow in printing and red, green and blue in screens and scanners.

PRIMARY COLORS   P 72
The basic colors in a color system, for example CMY and RGB.

PRINT ADJUSTMENT   7.4
The digital file which is the basis of the print is adjusted according to the conditions and characteristics of the print and the paper.

PRINT BROKER
Originally a foreman at a printshop or typeset shop. The modern meaning is a person with good graphics skills who acts as a middleman between customer and printer.

PRINT CARRIER   3.4 8.5 9.7.1
Material printed on, usually paper, but sometimes plastic, glass, textile or other material.

PRINT CONTRAST   9.11.2
The relative contrast in print is defined as the difference in density between a 100 % tone and an 80 % tone, divided by the density of the 100 % tone. The optimal ink coverage and relative contrast in a printing process is called NCI level.

PRINT CURVES
The various curves characterize the qualities of a printing press on a given paper, e.g. dot gain curves and optimal ink coverage curves.

PRINT CYLINDER   9.8.2
See Plate cylinder.

PRINT MAKEREADY
See Makeready.

PRINTABILITY   8.17.1 8.19.1 8.19.4
A measurement of the printing quality of the paper.

PRINTED IMAGE   9.5.4 9.5.8
Image created by the ink. In offset it is transferred from plate to rubber blanket to paper.

PRINTER DRIVER   P 248
Control program for printers.

PRINTER FONT   6.4.2 6.5.2
Font file used when printing or for monitor display, requires ATM.

PRINTING PLATE   9.5.11
Image carrier used in offset printing.

PRINTING TECHNIQUE
Technique used for printing, e.g. offset, screen or gravure.

PRINTING UNIT   9.5.3
A set of printing cylinders, e.g. plate cylinder, rubber blanket cylinder and impression cylinder in an offset printing press.

PRINTOPEN   3.10
Program from Heidelberg used to create ICC profiles for printers and printing presses.

PRINTSHOP
Company which provides printing services. Receives original material directly from the customer or via a prepress agency. The printshop provides printing and sometimes also post press services and distribution.

PROCESS COLORS   P 296
The colors used for printing, usually CMYK.

PROCESSOR   2.1.1
A computer's "brain." Performs all calculations. The speed of the processor is fundamental in determining the capacity of the computer. It is determined by its clock frequency, the number of possible calculations per second.

PRODUCTION AGENCY   **P 19**

Company employed to carry out layout work from templates and concepts which have already been worked out.

PRODUCTION MATERIAL

Collective name used for the digital and physical foundation needed to produce print products, e.g. digital images, texts and PDF files.

PROFILEMAKER   **3.10**

Program from Gretag Macbeth used to create ICC profiles.

PROFILES   **3.10**

Correction tables which describe the qualities and shortcomings of devices such as monitors, scanners, printers and printing presses, stating how each device's color reproduction deviates from given reference values. ICC profiles are now the most commonly used and standardized type of profile.

PROGRAM ADD-IN   **2.5.5**

Plug-in which expands the functions of a particular program.

PROOF [1]   **7.5**

Short name for proof print

PROOF [2]   **7.5**

General term describing a document used to check that there are no errors in a print item before it is printed. Can be either a physical document (print-out) or a digital one.

PROOF [3]   **7.5.5**

This term comes from "contract proof", the legal contract between customer and printshop.

PROOF PRINT   **7.5.5**

A try-out of how the complete printed product will look using a printer, commonly inkjet or sublimation. Often used in legal agreements and therefore signed.

PROOF SYSTEM

A digital system for producing proofs. See Proof print.

PROOF-READING   **6.12**

Reading through a text to eliminate errors, e.g. spelling mistakes, layout errors, etc.

PROSCRIPT

A preflight program from Cutting Edge Technology which checks PostScript files. Commonly used in newspaper production.

PSB   **4.8.10**

Variation of Photoshop format which supports very large image files.

PSD   **4.8.1**

Image files with the file extension .psd are saved in Adobe Photoshop's own format.

PUBLISHER   **6.1.1**

Simple layout program from Microsoft, not usually used for graphic production.

PULP STOCK   **8.19.2**

The pulp stock is the complete mixture of ingredients for a particular paper quality.

PULP STOCK PREPARATION   **8.19.2**

When preparing the pulp stock the cellulose fibers are beaten; fillers, sizers and, if desired, color are added. See Pulp stock.

PUNCHING **9.5.11** **P 351** **9.10.1**

To make a hole, e.g. holes are punched in offset plates in order to mount them correctly in the printing press using registration pins.

PUNCTUATION MARKS

Examples of punctuation marks are full stops, commas, semi-colons and dashes.

Q

QC   **6.13.3**

Plug-in program for Quark Xpress from Gluon which adds the option of preflight.

QUADTONE IMAGE   **4.6.3**

A grayscale image printed with four printing inks instead of one. Quadtones are used to reproduce fine details in a black and white image, make it softer or tint it a color other than pure black. Usually printed with black plus any three other spot colors.

QUARKXPRESS   **6.1**

Widely used page layout program from Quark.

QUICKSHOT CAMERA

See One shot.

QUOTATION MARKS

Marks which enclose a quotation and appear as follows: "".

QXGA   **2.4.5**

Display standard measuring 2,048×1,536 pixels.

R

RAF

Raw format files from Fuji brand digital cameras with the file extension .raf.

RAG PAPER   **P 301**

Paper which, alongside wood fibers, also contains some cotton fibers.

RAID   **2.6.2**

Redundant Array of Independent Disks. Technology for linking together several hard disks to increase data storage security.

RAM   **2.1.3**

Random Access Memory, a computer's internal working memory.

RANGE   **1.3.2**

Number of pages in a printed product.

RAW   **4.6.8 4.11.6**

See Raw format.

RAW FORMAT   4.6.8 4.11.6

Some digital cameras can store images in raw format. This means that all of the original information from the camera's image sensor is stored in the image file.

RAW FORMAT CONVERSION   4.8.8 4.11.6

Images which are stored in raw format must be converted to RGB before they can be displayed and processed. The image's tones and colors can also be set during raw format conversion.

RCS   3.9

Reference Color Space. The device-independent color space (CIE Lab) used in the ICC system.

READ DEVICE

Device necessary to read certain types of data storage media, e.g. a DVD-reader for DVDs.

READ HEAD   4.12.2-3 2.6.2

Part of a scanner or reader of data storage media, for example a CD-reader, which reads the information in the image or on the disk.

READ SPEED   P 51

The speed with which data can be read and transferred from a data storage medium. Stated in kilobytes per second.

READER   7.2.1

Free program from Adobe used to read PDF files (can be downloaded from www.adobe.se). Formerly called Acrobat Reader.

RECEIVER

Relates to "transmitter". Any person or device which receives information sent from a transmitter is a receiver.

RECTO   7

The front side of the print sheet, i.e. the side printed first.

RECTO-VERSO   7.6.2

Type of imposition for double-sided prints. One imposition is required for recto printing, and one for verso.

RECYCLED PAPER   8.17.1

Paper which contains recycled fibers. The most common qualities contain 50, 75 or 100 % recycled fibers.

REFERENCE AREA

Neutral gray reference areas composed of cyan, magenta and yellow are used to adjust the gray balance. These are compared with gray areas which are composed solely of black.

REFERENCE COLOR   5.1 5.4.6 5.4.9 7.4.2

A well-known color with a natural tone. Common reference colors are skin, grass or sky.

REFERENCE VALUES   3.10

Standard values for different printing parameters, for example dot gain, full-tone density, etc.

REFLECTION   9.5.19

Print phenomenon caused by the ink pyramid's inability to supply enough ink to certain areas of the plate. Is visible as traces of objects in tint areas in the printing direction.

REFLECTIVE IMAGES   4.13.1–2

Photographic images on paper.

REFLECTIVITY   9.11.1

The extent to which in-coming light is reflected by a given material, dependent on its structure, surface treatment and color.

REGISTRATION BOX

Boxes in an archive program where information and descriptions about the object to be archived is entered.

REGISTRATION EDGE   9.5.9

The edges of a sheet which are registered in the printing press.

REGISTRATION MARK   P 365 9.11.8

A special control mark used in printing so that the component colors of a multi-color print on top of each other as accurately as possible.

REGISTRATION PINS   9.5.11 9.10.1

A registration system consisting of small pins, used when mounting films in a printing press to ensure the best possible registration between component colors in a print.

REGISTRATION [1]   9.10.6 9.11.8

Describes a situation where all printing inks are correctly aligned with each other, for example component colors in a four-color print run or the inks on the recto and verso.

REGISTRATION [2]   9.10.3 9.5.9

When the sheets in the sheet transport of a printing press are adjusted in order to ensure that they run through the press in a synchronized manner. If the sheets are not registered, the print may end up in different places on different sheets.

RELATIVE PRINT CONTRAST   9.11.2

A measurement of the relative contrast in print. Defined as the difference in density between a 100 % tone and an 80 % tone divided by the density of the 100 % tone. The optimal ink coverage and relative contrast in a printing process is called the NCI level.

RELIEF PLATE   9.6.2 9.9.2

Image carrier used in high pressure methods such as book printing and flexographic printing.

RELIEF PRINTING   10.6

Relief printing is another surface treatment which creates relief in the print product without the need to emboss the paper. The part where the relief is to be located is printed with a special ink, which is subsequently warmed up and creates the relief. This method is most commonly used on business cards.

REPEATABILITY   9.5.12

Producing the same result all the time. Good repeatability is important in, for example, plate setting, to ensure a good fit between the plate set.

REPEATER   2.8.14

Network unit which connects different parts of a network and improves its signals.

REPRINTING (RERUN)

Printing additional copies of the same printed product without making major changes.

REPRO AGENCY

See Prepress agency.

REPRODUCTION RIGHTS

Right to reproduce material protected by copyright.

RESOLUTION   4.7 4.12.8 4.13.7 5.3.4

Describes the density of information in a digital image. Can also describe the smallest printing or reading point in, for example, setters or scanners. Measured in dpi and ppi.

RESPONSE CARD

A preprinted paper encouraging the recipient to fill in information and return it to the sender.

RETOUCH   5.5

Changing a photographic image, often for the better. Now usually done digitally using an image processing program.

REVERSED FILM   P 350

A film where the printed image is reversed when looking at it with the emulsion side up. Used in offset productions, for example.

REWRITABLE MEDIA   2.6.4

Rewritable data storage media, i.e. information stored on the disk can be erased and rewritten.

RGB   3.3

Red, Green, Blue. Additive color system used in screen displays and scanners, for example.

RGB MODE   4.6.4

An image in RGB mode technically consists of three separate pixel images in grayscale mode representing red, green and blue respectively. This means that an RGB image uses three times as much memory as a grayscale image of the same size and resolution.

RICH BLACK   6.11.4

Adding additional ink/inks to black ink in order to achieve a darker and deeper black color.

RIGHT JUSTIFIED

Text setting with a straight right hand edge and fixed spacing. The left hand edge is uneven.

RIGHT-ANGLED FOLD   10.10

A type of folding in which the folds are placed at a 90-degree angle to each other, as opposed to parallel folding.

RIGHT-READING FILM   P 350

A film where the printed image is the right way round when looking at it emulsion side up, e.g. a film used for screen printing.

RIP   7.1.3

Raster Image Processor. Hard- or software that calculates and rasterizes pages before they are output on an imagesetter or printer.

RIP TIME   7.1.3

The time it takes the RIP to interpret the PostScript code for a page and create the bitmap with exposure points.

RODS   3.2

Small light-sensitive sensory cells on the retina of the eye. Rods are sensitive to differences in light intensity but cannot distinguish colors.

ROLL FOLD   10.10

A type of parallel fold.

ROM   2.1.4

Read Only Memory, pre-programmed memory circuit where a computer's most basic functions are stored.

ROMAN   P 207

A family of fonts with serifs, e.g. Janson and Times.

ROTARY PRINTING [1]   9.6.1

Book printing technique where the image carrier sits on a cylinder and presses against an impression cylinder.

ROTARY PRINTING [2]

Term used for web offset printing.

ROTATION   5.4.2

Changing the angle of objects on a the computer. Images should not be rotated in layout programs.

ROUGHNESS   9.4.3

Describes how uneven or "rough" a paper's surface is. Affects the paper's printability.

ROUND HALFTONE DOT   7.7.1

The normal shape of a halftone dot. The shape of the halftone dot determines the characteristics of the screen.

ROUTER   2.8.13

Network device which connects different parts of a network and divides it into zones. Common used to connect several LANs into a WAN.

ROW

Text pieces are made up of rows of words which follow each other top to bottom. The left and/or right edges are usually lined up with the margins.

ROW BREAK

When one row is finished and a new one started.

ROW COUNT

Number of rows which fit on a page.

ROW LENGTH

Number of characters, including spaces and punctuation marks, per row. An appropriate row length to ensure that the text can be read easily is 55–65 characters per row.

ROYALTY

The proportion of the price of a book or other work which goes to its creator. Stated in percent.

RTF   6.2.5

Rich Text Format. File format for text which can be imported and read by most word processing and layout programs. Can contain typographical information such as typeface and paragraph format.

RUBBER BLANKET   9.5.3-4

Stretched round the rubber blanket cylinder in an offset printing press, transfers ink from the printing plate to paper. Changed frequently due to compression or wear and tear.

RUBBER BLANKET COMPRESSION   9.5.4

Occurs when the rubber blanket loses its elasticity following excessive surface pressure, often when a folded print sheet has gone through the printing press.

RUBBER BLANKET CYLINDER   9.5.3-4

Type of printing cylinder used in offset printing. The plate cylinder transfers ink to the rubber cylinder, which in turn transfers it to the paper.

RUBBERING

Protective rubber layer on an offset plate to combat oxidation. In theory no longer used today, since a new plate can be produced quickly using CTP.

RULER

Tool for measuring the length of a line. Equivalent digital tools are available in layout and illustration programs.

RUNABILITY   8.12

The paper's ability to run through the printing press.

S

SADDLE STAPLING   10.13

Post press treatment whereby folded sheets are joined together in a bundle using staple binding. Requires insert imposition.

SAMPLING FACTOR   4.7.1 P 146

The relationship between the resolution of an image and the screen frequency of the print is called the sampling factor. Tests have shown that the optimal sampling factor is 2, i.e. the resolution of the image should be twice as high as the screen frequency.

SANS SERIF   P 207

Typeface family without serifs, for example DIN and Helvetica.

SATA

SATA, S-ATA or Serial ATA is a computer bus technology for transporting data to and from hard disks.

SATELLITE UNIT   9.5.3

A printing unit with one large impression cylinder around which there are a number of printing units, one for each printing color.

SATURATION

Unit of magnitude for describing color, stating how gray it is compared to the pure color. In the NMI system, colors with a high level of saturation are located furthest from the cylinder model's axle.

SCALING

Changing the size of images and other digital objects.

SCALING FACTOR   4.13.6-8

The size ratio between original image and printed image. An image printed three times the size of the original uses a scaling factor of 3, for example.

SCAN POINT   4.12

The small part of an original image which is read by a scanner and gives the color for the respective pixels that make up the digital image.

SCANNER   4.11

Device used to read image originals into a computer.

SCANNER PROGRAM   4.12.11

Program which controls the scanning of images. The resolution, colors, sharpness, four-color separation, etc. can be adjusted.

SCANNER-CAMERA   P 132

Digital camera which uses scanning technology, i.e. the read head "sweeps" across the motif.

SCANNING RESOLUTION   4.12.8 4.13.6-8

The resolution selected for scanning images. Determined by screen frequency, sampling factor and scaling factor. Determines how many scanning points per inch the scan will have. Measured in ppi.

SCANOPEN   3.10

Program from Heidelberg used to create ICC profiles for scanners.

SCHEDULE

A plan for how a project is to be carried out. Often divided into phases with defined "milestones" for when the phases are to be carried out.

SCORE MARKING   10.11

Mark where cardboard is to be scored.

SCORING   10.11

Scratching into the surface of cardboard to make it easier to fold.

SCRAP

To destroy something which is invalid or unusable.

SCREEN ANGLES   7.7.9

A halftone screen is placed so that the lines formed by the dots are at a certain angle. When printing with four-colors, the screens of the four colors must be placed at certain predetermined angles.

SCREEN CARD

A circuit board mounted in a computer to control a specific screen.

SCREEN CLOTH   9.7.2

A finely woven cloth which lets printing ink through. Is tightened on a screen frame and coated with a photosensitive layer.

SCREEN DUMP   5.3.4

Image which shows how the workspace on a monitor looks at a given moment.

SCREEN FONTS   6.4.2 6.5.2

Font file used for screen display. Consists of small bitmap-images.

SCREEN FRAME   9.7.1

A frame around which the screen cloth is tightened.

SCREEN FREQUENCY [1]   7.7.5

Describes how "fine" a halftone screen is by stating the number of screen lines per inch. Often measured in lines per inch, lpi, although sometimes internationally lpcm, lines per centimeter, is used.

SCREEN FREQUENCY [2]   2.4.3

States how often the image is updated in a monitor display. Measured in Hertz.

SCREEN PERCENT VALUE

Tonal value between 0 and 100 %.

SCREEN PHENOMENA   7.7.10–11

Various screen phenomena that may occur in halftone screening. Often results in undesired patterns, such as moiré.

SCREEN PRINTING   9.7

A printing method used for large formats, such as advertising billboards and hard print carriers, for example metal signs. The image carrier consists of a finely woven cloth which lets printing ink through and is tightened across a frame. The non-printing surfaces are covered so that the ink cannot get through the cloth.

SCREEN RULING METER

Measures screen frequency and screen angles in a halftone screen.

SCREEN STENCIL   9.7.2

Plastic layer which covers the non-printing areas of a screen cloth.

SCRIPT   6.4.8

Family of fonts which are designed to look like handwritten text. Sometimes known as calligraphic fonts.

SCSI   2.2.3 P 57

Small Computer Standard Interface, a standard for transferring information within the computer and between external devices such as hard disks, scanners, printers, etc.

SCSI-CABLE

A special cable for SCSI-transmission between computer and external devices.

SCSI-PORT

Various external units such as hard disks, Jaz-readers and scanners can be connected via a computer's SCSI-port.

SD   2.6.5

See Secure Digital.

SEARCH BOX

The box in which you specify a search in archive software.

SECONDARY COLORS   3.4

If you mix two of the primary colors (CMY) the result is secondary colors: red, green and blue-violet (RGB).

SECOND-LEVEL HEADING

Smaller title used between pieces of text.

SECTOR STORAGE   P 53

Data storage technique based on information being stored in different sectors. Is often used on magnetic disks.

SECURE DIGITAL   2.6.5

A type of memory card using flash technology.

SEGMENTATION   2.8.18

A network can be divided into different network segments in order to reduce network traffic in different parts of the network.

SELF-EXTRACTING

No decompression file is needed for self-extracting, compressed files. They decompress themselves when the file is double-clicked on.

SEMI-COLON

Punctuation mark which appears as ";". Used instead of a comma to separate two clauses, or to separate groups of words in enumerations.

SEPARATION   7.4

See Four-color separation.

SEPARATION SETTINGS   P 270 7.4

The settings which control conversion from RGB to CMYK in four-color separation. See Four-color separation.

SEQUENTIAL CODING   4.9.1

Lossless compression method. Mainly used for line art.

SEQUENTIAL STORAGE   2.6.3

Data storage technique based on information being stored consecutively. Often used on magnetic tape.

SERIAL PORT   2.2.2

Computer connection where, for example, keyboards and mouses can be attached.

SERIFS   P 207

Structural details on the ends of letters found in Roman fonts such as Janson and Times.

SERVER   2.8.15

Powerful computer for special applications, for example file management and outputs in a network.

SETTING [1]   9.5.6 9.6.3

First step in the drying process of offset inks. The oil component is absorbed by the paper and the pigment, alkyd and resin form a gel on the surface of the paper. Curing, or oxidation, is the second phase.

SETTING [2]   P 197 9.6.2

Designing how text is to be placed.

SHARPNESS   7.4.7 5.4.12 5.3.10–11

If an image appears blurred it is generally due to a lack of sharp transitions between the dark and light hues in an outline. Instead of a sharp transition, the outline consists of a soft, tonal transition. To sharpen the image, the soft, tonal transitions which make the image appear blurred must be found and sharpened.

SHEET   8.6

Sheet of paper. A sheet has two sides, the front and back. Printing usually takes place on a sheet of paper, for example in sheetfed offset printing.

SHEET ORDER   7.6.4

Glue and sewn binding require a certain type of imposition whereby the folded sheets are gathered after each other, in "sheet order".

SHEET ORDER IMPOSITION 10.12

When a print item consists of several pages which are to be bound together a right-angle folded sheet is usually used. This term describes how the sheets are placed one after the other instead of inside one another (signature imposition), and this method is used for all types of binding except staple binding. Is either a part of the binding process or is a separate stage immediately before binding.

SHEET TRANSPORT 9.5.9

Describes how a paper sheet is transported through the printing press.

SHEETFED OFFSET PRINTING 9.5.2

Offset printing technique where the printing press is fed with paper sheets, as opposed to web offset, where the printing press is fed with paper on a roll.

SHIELDED P 59

A cable can be protected against noise by shielding. The shield consists of a protective foil which is wrapped around the wire.

SHIPPING NOT INCLUDED

On quotes from printshops this means that delivery is not included in the price.

SHORTCUT COMMAND

A combination of keyboard keys which can be used to activate a tool or function in a program.

SHRINK PLASTIC 8.5

Transparent plastic which is used for labels which cover the whole surface of, for example, a bottle or can.

SHUTTER 4.11.3

The shutter in a camera regulates how long an image is exposed.

SHUTTER SPEED 4.11.3

The time the shutter in the camera is open when exposing an image.

SIDEBAR

A smaller text frame connected to a longer text or article which contains summarized factual information on the content of the article, often in bullet format.

SIGNAL BANDWIDTH

How far a signal maintains its strength. Is affected by the cable type.

SIGNAL STRENGTH P 59

The strength of a given electrical signal.

SIGNATURE

A number of folded sheets arranged together. A book consists of several signatures bound together.

SIGNATURE IMPOSITION 10.12 7.6.4

Type of imposition for binding. The folded sheets are inserted into each other, often used when saddle stitching.

SILHOUETTE 4.2

Program from Freesoft which transforms pixel-based images to object-based graphics.

SILK FINISH 8.2

Coated paper with a matte silk finish, offering good text reproduction and image quality.

SILVER HALIDE 9.5.13

Type of printing plate technique for offset plates where the plate is exposed using laser light.

SIMULATE 3.12.5 3.9 P 86

To try to make something look like something else, for example a print to look like the proof, or on a screen.

SINGLE-PASS 4.12.12

Technique for scanning all three colors (RGB) in an original artwork in one sweep.

SLANTED STYLE

Also known as "false" italics. The existing characters are simply slanted rather than new forms being created.

SLURRING 9.11.9

Print phenomenon which causes dot deformation and a darker print. Slurring means that the halftone dots are smeared, causing elongated oval dots. The phenomenon can occur when the pressure between the rubber blanket cylinder and the impression cylinder is too high or when the plate cylinder and rubber blanket cylinder are not rotating at exactly the same speed.

SMALL CAPITAL P 207

Variation of a typeface where specially formed uppercase letters the same height as the x-height of the lowercase letters are used in their place.

SMART MEDIA 2.6.5

Type of memory card using flash technology.

SMEARING 9.5.16 9.11.2 9.11.4

Sheets smear ink onto each other. Print phenomenon which occurs when too much printing ink is used on the sheet or when the ink does not have time to dry.

SMOOTHING 8.19.4

Rolling paper to create an even thickness and surface, and therefore good printing quality.

SMOOTHNESS 8.9 9.8.4

Describes the quality of a paper's surface. The smoother the paper the finer the surface.

SMPTE-240M 3.8.4

Former name for the color space Adobe RGB.

SMYTH-SEWN 10.17

A technique combining thread stitching with glue binding where each sheet is sewn together and then glued together into a block. Used for soft-bound books.

SNIPPETS 6.1.5

Tool in Adobe Indesign which enables predefined objects to be created with precise page positions. These can then be inserted easily in the right place on other pages in other documents.

SOFT PROOF (SCREEN PROOF) 7.5.2 P 259
A review and evaluation of a printed product on the screen, for example a file in PDF-format.

SOFTENED
Softening of an image or area of an image. Achieved by evening out hard edges.

SOFTWARE 2.5
A term for all types of programs, from operating systems to applications.

SOLID TONE AREA
A printed surface which is 100 % covered with printing ink.

SPECTROPHOTOMETER 3.10.2–3 4.12.13
Instrument used to measure the spectral composition of colors. Also used, among other things, to create ICC-profiles.

SPECTRUM 3.1
The visible part of light, ranges from red tones (705 nm) to blue-violet tones (385 nm).

SPINE WIDTH P 393
The thickness of the inserts in a book affect the spine width. To be able to design the cover it is important to know how wide the spine will be.

SPIRAL-BINDING 10.14
Spiral-binding is an post press process where the sheets are joined with a metal spiral in the spine.

SPOT COLORS 6.9
Printing inks in special colors, e.g. in the PMS system. Generally used as a complement to black or to achieve an precise color which four-color inks cannot provide. Mixed using a recipe.

SPOT VARNISHING 10.3 6.9.6
Varnishing carried out on certain parts of a sheet of paper, e.g. images, for aesthetic effect. The varnished parts have higher gloss than the surrounding areas.

SPRAY POWDER 6.5.6 6.5.16
See Drying powder.

SQUARE HALFTONE DOTS 7.7.1
A screen can consist of square halftone dots instead of the more common round ones. The shape of the halftone dot gives the screen with different characteristics.

SRGB 3.8.6
RGB standard based on the HDTV standard. sRGB has a relatively small color range and is therefore not particularly well suited to graphic production.

STABILIZE 3.11.1
Ensuring that a device or a system of devices consistently provides the same results. Instability can be a result of mechanical or environmental issues, e.g. temperature or humidity.

STANDARD AGREEMENT
Standard agreements are created by a party, an organization to which it belongs or through cooperation and negotiation between different interest groups within an industry to simply dealing with agrements.

STANDARD PROFILE 3.10.4
General ICC profile for, for example, a type of paper, a type of printer or a standardised print form (newspaper, heatset, etc.).

STAPLING 10.13
Stapling or staple-binding is a post press processing method whereby folded sheets are joined together using metal staples in the spine.

START-UP COST 1.3.1
The cost of starting a process, for example the cost for a run through a printing press or an post press processing machine.

STENCIL SETTER 9.7.2
Equipment which exposes and develops stencils for screen printing directly from digital information.

STICKER, LABEL 9.6.4
A small, printed piece of paper, often with adhesive on the back. Stickers or labels with variable print, for example addresses, are very common.

STICKERING P 394
Print product which is sealed with a small adhesive tag, e.g. a roll-folded leaflet or an envelope.

STOCHASTIC SCREENING 7.7.2
A screening method with varying distance between the halftone dots instead of size. Also called FM-screening.

STORAGE CAPACITY
Describes how much memory is available on a particular storage medium, measured in megabytes or gigabytes.

STORAGE DURABILITY
Describes how safe a data storage medium is and for how long it holds its data.

STORAGE MEDIA 2.6
Media used to store digital files, e.g. hard drives, floppy disks, CD's, etc.

STORAGE SPACE
See Storage capacity.

STRAPLINE
Title which is placed over the main title, but in a smaller font size.

STRATA STUDIO
3D illustration program for from Strata.

STREAM FEEDER 9.5.9
The part of the printing press which draws the paper into the press.

STREAM FEEDER EDGE 9.5.9 10.2
The edge of the paper which is drawn into the printing press first.

STREAMER
Long, thin format for posters. Used, for example, above the windows on buses or trains.

STREAMLINE 4.2
Adobe program which converts pixel-based images to object graphics. Sales and development of Streamline have now ceased, as later versions of Adobe Illustrator contain this function.

STUDIO

A room or department in which graphic material is produced. Can also refer to an art school.

STUFFIT

File compression program from Aladdin Systems.

SUBHEADING

Subtitle placed after the main title.

SUBLIMA   7.7.3

Hybrid screening technique from Agfa.

SUBLIMATION PRINTER
(THERMO-TRANSFER PRINTER)   9.4

Printer based on the sublimation technique, i.e. color layers are transferred to the paper by heating an ink ribbon.

SUBSCRIBE

See Subscription.

SUBSCRIPT

Words or symbols of a smaller size than the main text which are placed slightly lower than the baseline. Common in chemical formulae, e.g. H_2O

SUBSCRIPTION

Order of a series of print products, e.g. a newspaper or periodical, which are delivered continuously and periodically.

SUBTRACTIVE COLOR SYSTEM   3.4

Color system which creates colors using primary colors. The print inks are transparent and filter out parts of incoming white light, i.e. some light is let through, whereas other parts are absorbed by the ink and become heat. The inks "subtract" part of the incoming light, which is why it is known as a subtractive color system.

SUFFIX   P 120

Word-ending or file extension. Used for abbreviations at the end of the file name in order to determine different file types, for example xxx.pdf.

SUITCASE   6.4.6 6.4.8

A common utility for typeface management. Allows you to activate fonts which are needed while working, without having to restart programs or keep them in the system folder. Font groups can be created so that all of the fonts belonging to a particular production or customer can be activated in one go.

SUPERSCRIPT

Words or symbols of a smaller size than the main text which are placed above the baseline. Common in measurements, "m²", and index numbers.

SUPPLIER

Person or company which agrees a contract with a customer and undertakes to supply something. Cf. customer.

SURFACE BONDING STRENGTH   8.14

A measurement of the paper surface strength. Important because printing inks can cause the surface of the paper to flake off while printing.

SURFACE TENSION   2.8.18

Physical phenomenon which means that the dampening solution in the offset process does not dampen the plate properly without the addition of alcohol.

SWATCHES   6.1.6

In layout programs, the swatches hold pre-defined color combinations of process or spot colors.

SWF   4.3.7

Shockwave Flash format. Used for object-based animations created in Macromedia Flash.

SVG   4.3.5

Scalable Vector Graphics. File format for object-based images on the web.

SVGA   P 46

A larger version of the VGA standard. SVGA measures 800×600 pixels.

S-VIDEO   2.4.6

Analogue connection which divides the image signal into luminance and color.

SWITCH   2.8.12

Network device which links together different parts of a network.

SWOP   7.4.1

Specifications for Web Offset Publications. Standard for defining printing inks in the USA. Cf. the European standard, the European Color Scale.

SXGA   P 46

Monitor standard measuring 1,280×1,024 pixels.

SYLLABIFICATION   6.4.4

Dividing up a word using a hyphen ("-"). This is done at the end of a row of text when there is insufficient space for the word, but moving the whole word would give the paragraph the wrong appearance.

SYMBOL FONT   6.4.7

A font consisting of different symbols instead of letters, e.g. Zapf Dingbats.

SYQUEST   2.6.10

A removable, magnetic data storage disk which used to be very common in graphic production but is no longer produced.

SYSTEM FOLDER

This folder contains the computer's operating system. Without the operating system the computer cannot start.

SYSTEM PLUG-IN   2.5.2

Plug-in program which increases the functions of a computer.

T

TABLE   6.2.3

Presentation of brief information, often figures.

TABLOID   8.6

Half of broadsheet format. A common newspaper format, formerly associated with the tabloid press and therefore also used to describe newspapers which contain gossip. Nowadays most daily newspapers in Sweden use the tabloid format.

TAGGED TEXT   6.3.2

Text which contains tags (codes) dictating the paragraph and typeface format to be used.

TAGGED TEXT   6.3.2

Marked text is sometimes called "tagged" text because the marking words are surrounded by tags, e.g. <tag>. Habitually used to give typographic instructions in a text.

TAPE BINDING

Simple glue binding method where the insert is secured with a tape in the spine between two separate sheets as a cover. Has limited durability and lifespan.

TARGET GROUP

A generalized picture of target receivers. This could be, for example, people of a certain age, living in a certain area and belonging to a certain professional group.

TCP/IP   2.8.8

Transmission Control Protocol/Internet Protocol, network protocol which is standard on the internet and in local networks.

TEAR RESISTANCE   8.14

Paper with too low a tear resistance risks tearing during printing in a printing press.

TELECOMMUNICATIONS   2.9.3–5

Data communication via the analog telecommunications network.

TEMPERATURE [1]   3.4

The color of light is stated using the term color temperature and is measured in degrees Kelvin (K). Color temperature describes how blue or yellow the light is. Daylight, for example, has a color temperature of around 6 500 K, which is considerably more blue than indoor lighting, which has a color temperature of around 3 000 K.

TEMPERATURE [2]

The air temperature in a printing environment is, just like air humidity, important in ensuring a stable print result.

TENSILE STRENGTH   8.14

If the tensile strength of a paper is too low, it risks splitting during printing in a printing press.

TERA

$10^{12} = 1\ 000\ 000\ 000\ 000$

TERABYTE

1 099 511 627 776 bytes.

TERTIARY COLORS   3.10.1

When secondary colors, derived from primary colors, are mixed together the result is tertiary colors, i.e. colors consisting of all three primary colors.

TEST BAR

See Color bar.

TEST RUN   P 326

A small edition of a printed product printed before the full run.

TEXT ORIGINAL   6.2

An approved text document is known as a text original.

THEORETICAL TRANSMISSION SPEED

A measurement of how fast data can theoretically be transported on a network.

THERMAL PLATE   9.5.13

Type of print plate technology where the plate is exposed using heat in the form of laser exposure.

THERMOTRANSFER PRINTER

See Sublimation printer.

THREAD STITCHING   10.16

The traditional bookbinding method. Folded sheets are placed in sheet order but the backs of the sheets are not glued (as in glue binding) but rather stitched.

THREE-CYLINDER UNIT   9.5.3

The most common printing unit found in sheetfed offset today. Consists of an impression cylinder, a rubber blanket cylinder and a plate cylinder.

THREE-PASS   4.12.12

Scanning technique which scans images originals three times, i.e. once for each of the RGB colors.

THREE-SHOT CAMERA   4.10.5

Digital camera technique for exposing in three rounds, i.e. each component color is read one at a time. See Three-pass.

THREE-UP

See Many-up.

THUMB NOTCH

Notches cut into the outer margins of pages to make it easier for the reader to find the right page. Used in index products of various kinds, e.g. address books.

THUMBNAIL IMAGE

Small, low-resolution images created to facilitate identifying an image.

TIFF   4.8.2

Tagged Image File Format, a common file format for digital images.

TINT AREA   6.11.5

An even color tone across a designated area, e.g. a red rectangle.

TINTING   9.5.18

Print phenomenon in offset printing where non-printing surfaces on the plate pick up ink become printing surfaces. This can occur, for example, when the dampening solution is too hard and the pigments dissolve in the water or when there is too little dampening solution in the ink-humidity balance.

TITLE CASE

Describes when the first letter of a word is uppercase and the letters thereafter are lowercase.

TITLE PAGE

Usually placed on the third page of the insert. Contains the title of the book, name of the author and name of the publisher. The title page is important as this information is used in cataloguing, irrespective of what is on the cover.

TONAL RANGE 4.12.6 7.7.8

The same as density range. The range of tones which can be created in a given color system or by a given device, e.g. a printer or scanner.M875

TONAL SPACE

Part of the tonal range.

TONAL STEP 7.7.8

The difference between two tones.

TONAL TRANSITIONS 4.1.4

Tonal transitions are transitions between a number of colors at certain distances. Tonal transitions can be linear or circular.

TONAL VALUE

Describes the amount of a primary color, given as a percent.

TONE DISTRIBUTION

Describes the distribution of tones in an image across the entire tone scale, from 0 to 100 percent.

TONE SCALE 7.7.7

All tones from 0 to 100 % of a particular color.

TONE TRANSITION 5.3.10

Transition between different tones, change of tone.

TONER 9.2.2

Color toner is used instead of printing ink in the xerographic process. Toner consists of very small color particles which are transferred to the paper using an electrical charge.

TOYO

Japanese printing ink supplier which also has its own spot color system.

TRACKING

Adjustment of character spacing, expanding and condensing in a text piece or line.

TRANS FLASH

Very small memory card based on the miniSD standard.

TRANSFER SPEED 2.7–8

The speed at which data is transferred, for example to or from a storage medium or over a network.

TRANSMIT

Light which passes through a material is transmitted.

TRANSPARENCY

Function in Adobe Indesign which makes objects or images progressively more "see-through", meaning that underlying objects are partially visible through them.

TRANSPARENT

Entirely or partially see-through.

TRAPPING [1] 9.11.6

A print phenomenon. Describes how well printing inks bond to each other. Printing inks printed on top of each other wet-on-wet do not bond 100 %.

TRAPPING [2] 7.4.8

Making one object slightly larger so that it overlaps another is known as trapping. It is a way to avoid misregistration in the printing press.

TRAPPING PROGRAM 7.4.8

Program which carries out trapping in a document, for example Delta Trapper from Heidelberg and Trapwise from Kodak.

TRAPWISE

Program from Imation which performs trapping on documents.

TRIPLEX 4.6.3

A grayscale image printed with three printing inks instead of one. Triplex is used to reproduce finer details in a black and white image, make the image softer, or tone it in a color other than pure black. Printing is usually done with black and any two spot colors.

TRIPTYCH SPAN 10.10

A type of parallel folding for 8-page leaflets.

TRISTIMULUS VALUE

See CIE.

TRUETYPE 6.5.3

File type for fonts, not based on PostScript.

TURNING BARS 9.5.3

Used in some printing presses to turn the printing sheet so that some printing units print on one side and others on the other side.

TV

TV format measures 768×576 pixels.

TWIN WIRE 8.19.3

The main drainage of the pulp stock in the paper machine takes place on the twin wire where the water is absorbed by two straining cloths. It is on this wire that the paper is formed.

TWISTED-PAIR CABLE 2.8.4

A type of network cable.

TYPE AREA P 381

The area inside the margins of a page where the content is usually placed.

TYPE REUNION

A system plug-in from Adobe. Groups all fonts by family.

TYPE WIDTH

The width of the type area. Usually measured in millimeters or typographic points. Unlike row length, type width is an absolute measurement of the length of the rows and does not change depending on the point size of the text.

TYPEBOOK

A program which prints samples of fonts.

TYPEFACE 6.4.1

The distinctive appearance of letters, a set of characters which is distinguished by its unique appearance.

TYPEFACE FAMILY 6.4.8

E.g. Roman, sans serif, script etc.

TYPEFACE FORMAT 6.1.6

Provides typographical adjustments for individual typefaces, e.g. that the typeface will be cursive, or that lowercase numerals will be used.

TYPEFACE SAMPLES   6.4.3
Printed samples of typefaces.

TYPEFACE SET   6.4.1
The number of characters which make up a given typeface.

TYPEFACE SUITCASE   6.5.2
A special folder in which all screen fonts of different versions and sizes for a given typeface are stored.

TYPEFACE VARIATIONS   6.4.1   P 207
Variations of the same typeface, e.g. bold, thin etc.

TYPESTYLE
The weight or posture of a font, distinguished from a font's typeface design and type size.

TYPOGRAPHIC TEMPLATES   6.1.6
Typographic settings in layout programs can be saved as paragraph or typeface format.

TYPOGRAPHY
Setting and designing text.

U

U   P 222
Pantone code which indicates that a color is printed on uncoated paper.

UCA   7.4.4
Under Color Addition. Special separation method whereby extra colored inks are added to black in areas of images which need to be very dark. Mostly used in conjunction with strong UCR.

UCR   7.4.3
Under Color Removal. Method to limit total ink coverage in the dart areas of images. Limits the amount of cyan, magenta and yellow and replaces them with black.

UGRA/FOGRA BAR
A utility consisting of different measuring fields, used to check the quality of the print and printing plate.

ULTRAVIOLET LIGHT   3.1 10.3 9.7.3
Light which is invisible to the human eye and situated closest to the violet colors in the spectrum, with a wavelength of less than 385 nm. Has so much energy that skin protects itself from it by tanning.

UNCOATED PAPER   8.1
Paper which has not been coated. Most uncoated papers have glue applied to the surface to create a good surface strength. Some examples of uncoated paper are notepaper, copy paper and the paper used to produce paperback books.

UNDER COLOR ADDITION   7.4.4
Also known by the acronym UCA. Special separation method used when heavy GCR makes dark tones appear pale in an image. Adds a small amount of color ink to the very darkest tones, i.e. adds cyan, magenta and yellow to black.

UNDERLINING
Text can be marked using a line under the base line. Nowadays often used to mark internet links.

UNICODE   6.5.1
Character code system which contains all of the most common international characters.

UNIX   2.5.1
An operating system mainly used in powerful computers for special applications, e.g. servers.

UNSEPARATED
Image in RGB which has not been prepared for printing, is not separated. See Four-color separation.

UNSHARP MASK   P 176 5.3.10
A blur filter in Adobe Photoshop.

UPPERCASE LETTERS   P 207 6.4.1
Capital letters, as opposed to lowercase letters.

USB   2.2.3
Universal Serial Bus, an interface used to connect devices to computers, e.g. keyboards, external storage devices, mouses. USB 2.0 allows transfer speeds of 480 Mbit/s.

UV VARNISH   10.3
Varnish which hardens under UV light. Can be applied in thick layers.

UWXGA   P 46
Monitor standard in widescreen format, measures 1,920×1,080 pixels.

UXGA   2.4.6   P 46
Monitor standard, measures 1,600×1,200 pixels.

V

VARIABLE DATA
Technique whereby the content of each printed page can be changed at full printing speed. Also called personalized printing.

VARNISHING   10.3
A technique used to add a glossy surface to a printed product. It does not provide noticeable protection against dirt and wear and tear, and is primarily an aesthetic procedure. The varnish is applied by a regular inking unit, or in an offset printing press by a special varnishing unit.

VECTOR GRAPHICS   P 102
Images based on outlines composed of short, straight lines. Formerly used for fonts. The term is sometimes erroneously used for object graphics or Bezier curves.

VECTOR IMAGES
See Vector graphics.

VENTURA   6.1.1
Simple layout program from Corel which is not commonly used for graphic production.

VERSO   7.6.2
The back side of the printed sheet. Cf. Recto.

VGA   2.4.6
Video Graphics Array, a monitor standard measuring 640×480 pixels.

VIDEO CARD   2.2

A circuit board installed in the computer to enable moving images to be displayed on the screen.

VIDEO DATA

Digital information about a moving image.

VIEWING LIGHT   3.4

The light in which, for example, a photograph or printed product is viewed. Affects color perception. Normal, neutral lighting has a color temperature of 5000 K. This corresponds approximately to normal daylight and is therefore used as a reference light for images, proofs and prints.

VIGNETTE [1]

Graphical embellishment.

VIGNETTE [2]

See Extraction.

VISCOSITY   9.5.6 9.5.15

A measurement of how easily a liquid (e.g. printing ink) flows.

VOC

Volatile organic compounds.

VOLATILE INK   9.8.3

Printing ink which dries quickly, used for gravure printing.

VRAM   2.3.2

In order to be able to work with moving or large images, the screen has to have plenty of internal memory, known as VRAM, available.

W

WAN   2.8.1

Wide Area Network. Large network which connects various local networks.

WASTE   P 395

The collected waste paper in post press makeready and production.

WASTE PAPER

Material which goes through a printing press and which is not used in the final product, e.g. setting sheets and areas of paper which are cut off.

WATER-FREE OFFSET   9.5.2

Also called dry offset. A variation of regular offset printing in which ink-repellent silicone is used instead of water for the non-printing surfaces. A special silicone-coated printing plate is used, eliminating the need for water to distinguish non-printing and printing surfaces.

WAVELENGTH   3.1

A physical measurement of the length of the light waves, measured in nanometer (nm). Visible light has wavelengths between 385 and 705 nm.

WEB OFFSET   9.5.2

Offset method which feeds the paper from a roll as opposed to the paper sheets used in sheetfed offset. Both heatset and coldset are web offset techniques.

WEEKLY MAGAZINE

Magazine which comes out once a week. Many popular weekly magazines cover gossip, celebrities and royalty.

WET-ON-WET   9.7.3 9.8.3 9.11.4 9.11.6

Printing inks directly on top of each other before they have had time to dry, used in offset printing, for example.

WHITE POINT   5.4.7

The brightest tone in an image. Together with the black point, the white point controls the contrast of the image.

WHITE-PRINTING PRINTER   9.2.4

A laser printer is white-printing if the laser beam describes the areas of the sheet which should not be coated with toner.

WIDE GAMUT RGB   3.8.9

An RGB color space with a very wide color range. So wide that it contains many colors which the human eye cannot detect.

WIDOW

Commonly used name for an undesired result. Describes a situation where the last line in a paragraph does not fit together with the rest of the paragraph and instead ends up at the top of a new column or page.

WIFI   2.8.5

A wireless network technology.

WINDOWS   2.5.1

An operating system from Microsoft used in PC-based computers.

WIRE-O-BINDING   10.14

A type of spiral binding usually used for manuals and notepads.

WLAN   2.8.5

Wireless Local Area Network. Wireless Ethernet.

WMF   4.3.4

Windows Metafile. An older file format for images in Windows. Based on vectors, but can also contain bitmap information.

WOOD-FREE PAPER   8.3

Paper consisting of less than 10 % mechanical pulp and more than 90 % chemical pulp.

WOOD-PULP PAPER   8.3

Paper consisting of more than 10 % mechanical pulp and less than 90 % chemical pulp.

WORD   6.2.1

A widely used word processing program from Microsoft.

WORD PROCESSING PROGRAM   6.2.1

Program for writing and processing text, e.g. Microsoft Word and Word Perfect.

WORD SPACING

Blank space between the words in a text. When a text is justified, the spacing between the words varies, so that the lines will be of equal length.

WORDPERFECT   6.2.1

Word processing program from Corel.

WORK AND TUMBLE   7.6.3

Imposition technique for double-sided prints with only one makeready. After one side has been printed the sheets are turned and, using the opposite gripper edge, run through the printing press again and printed with the same plate.

WORK AND TURN   7.6.3

Type of imposition for double-sided printing using just one makeready. Once the print sheets have been printed on one side, they are turned and reinserted into the press with the same gripper edge. They are then printed on the other side with the same plate.

WORKS   6.2.1

Word processing program from Apple. Formerly called Claris Works.

WORKSPACE

In some programs the base settings for tools and palettes as well as their placement on the screen is saved as a "workspace".

WQXGA   P 46

Monitor standard in widescreen format, measures 2,560×1,600 pixels.

WRITE HEAD   2.6.2

Writing unit in a reader/printer for data storage media, e.g. CD-burners.

WRITE SPEED   2.6.1

The speed at which data is transferred and written to a data storage medium.

WRITER   6.2.1

Word processing program which is part of Open Office.

WSGA   P 46

Monitor standard in widescreen format, measures 1,024×576 pixels.

WVGA   P 46

Monitor standard in widescreen format, measures 854×480 pixels.

WWW

World Wide Web. A way of publishing pages utilizing multi-media and hypertext links on the Internet.

WXGA   P 46

Monitor standard in widescreen format, measures 1,280×720 pixels.

X

XD PICTURE CARD   P 54

Small and relatively expensive memory card based on flash technology.

XEROGRAPHIC PROCESS   9.2

A process which uses the fact that the electrical charge of a photoconductor can be affected by light. Used in copy machines and laser printers.

XGA   2.4.6

Monitor standard, measures 1,024×768 pixels.

X-HEIGHT   P 207

Typographic measurement of the height of the lowercase letters with no ascenders or descenders, e.g. the height of a lowercase "x".

XML   6.3.3

Extensible Markup Language. System for marking up data content by type.

XMP   5.6.2

Extensible Metadata Platform. A markup language from Adobe which enables files created in, for example, Illustrator, Photoshop and Indesign to contain key words and metainformation.

Z

Z-FOLD

A type of parallel fold.

ZIP [1]   2.6.9

A removable, magnetic disk for data storage, holds 100 megabytes.

ZIP [2]   4.9.4   6.14.3

File compression program.

ZONES/ZONE-DIVIDED NETWORKS   2.8.18

A network can be divided into zones in order to reduce network traffic in various parts of the network.

more guides to graphic print production

A Guide to Graphic Print Production is available in eight languages aside from English. The title and cover vary, but the content remains the same, except for legal and environmental issues which have been adjusted.

SPANISH

Manual de producción gráfica – recetas

PUBLISHER:
Editorial Gustavo Gili, S. L.
www.ggili.com
ISBN: 84-252-1739-3
Based on the first edition

GERMAN

Well done, bitte!

PUBLISHER: Verlag Hermann Schmidt Mainz
www.typografie.de
ISBN: 3-87439-632-0
Based on the first edition

FRENCH

La chaîne graphique

PUBLISHER: Groupe Eyrolles
www.eyrolles.com
ISBN: 2-212-11336-6
Based on the first edition

SWEDISH

Grafisk Kokbok

PUBLISHER: Bokförlaget Arena
www.arenabok.se
ISBN: 91-7843-224-3
Second edition

NORWEIGAN

Grafisk kokebok

PUBLISHER: GAN Forlag AS
www.gan.no
ISBN: 82-492-0206-6
Based on the first edition

DANISH

Grafisk kogebog

PUBLISHER: Medit Publishing
www.meditpublishing.dk
ISBN: 87-91246-02-4
Based on the first edition

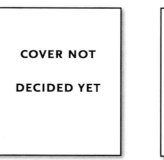

COVER NOT DECIDED YET

FINNISH

Graafinen keittokirja

PUBLISHER: AGI/Arena
www.agi.fi
ISBN: not determined
Based on the second edition

COVER NOT DECIDED YET

ICELANDIC

Grunnbók í grafískri miðlun

PUBLISHER: IÐNÚ bókabúð
www.idnu.is
ISBN: 978-9979-67-175-6
Based on the second edition

thank you

Anders Ekberg

Johanna Ekberg

Roger Johansson

Junior Boys

Eva Kjellström

Paul Lindström

Per Marklund

Alfred Mosskin

Ellinor Sjöqvist

Henrik Svensson
who lent us the drawing
of a tomato landing in water

Sanna Wolk

THE AUTHORS WISH TO PERSONALLY THANK:

Annika

Linda

Milou

Milton

Morris

Nell

...AND THANKS TO ALL OF YOU WHO SENT US COMMENTS AND SUGGESTIONS!